ESSAYS
ANALYTICAL, CRITICAL AND PHILOLOGICAL
ON SUBJECTS CONNECTED WITH
SANSKRIT LITERATURE

ESSAYS
ANALYTICAL, CRITICAL AND PHILOLOGICAL

ON SUBJECTS CONNECTED WITH

SANSKRIT LITERATURE

BY THE LATE

H. H. WILSON, M. A., F.R.S.,

BODEN PROFESSORS OF SANSKRIT IN THE UNIVERSITY OF OXFORD, ETC., ETC.,

COLLECTED AND EDITED BY

DR. REINHOLD ROST

IN THREE VOLUMES

VOL. I

GYAN

Published by

Gyan Publishing House
5, Ansari Road
Daryaganj, New Delhi-110002
Phone: 011-47034999, 9811692060
E-mail: books@gyanbooks.com

Distribution Network
gyanbooks.com
India, USA, Canada, UK, Australia, France

ISBN : 978-81-212-4519-7 (Set)
ISBN : 978-81-212-4731-3 (HB)
First Published, 1864

2nd Impression 2020

Printed at: Gyan Press, Delhi.

Essays Analytical, Critical and Philological Vol. I
Author: H. H. Wilson

ESSAYS

ANALYTICAL, CRITICAL AND PHILOLOGICAL

ON SUBJECTS CONNECTED WITH

SANSKRIT LITERATURE.

BY THE LATE

H. H. WILSON, M.A., F.R.S.,

BODEN PROFESSOR OF SANSKRIT IN THE UNIVERSITY OF OXFORD,

ETC., ETC.

COLLECTED AND EDITED BY

DR. REINHOLD ROST.

IN THREE VOLUMES.

VOL. I.

LONDON:

TRÜBNER & CO., 60, PATERNOSTER ROW.

1864.

PREFACE.

In carrying through the press the various Essays, Analyses, and Translations, which have been selected to form this second division of Professor H. H. Wilson's Works, the editor has rigidly adhered to the principles by which he was guided in the former division: leaving the text almost invariably intact, and adding only such notes and references as would appear to him calculated to supply to the reader the means partly of corroborating, partly of supplementing, and perhaps occasionally also correcting, the statements made in the text. By far the greater number of the articles comprised in these three volumes were written between thirty and forty years ago, several even at a much earlier date, when the study of Sanskrit literature had hardly found more than a few followers yet in Europe. To any one, then, who would compare the present state of research in the field of Indian philology and antiquities with its condition at that early period, in which most of these Essays and Translations originated, it may appear a matter of less surprise that there should be found in them some views and statements at variance with the results of modern science, than that there should be so few of them. In the translations also, made exclusively from MSS. less with a view to literal and philological accuracy than to present to the reader a life-like picture of oriental manners and customs, the author's natural sagacity and his intimate acquaintance with Hindu life and modes of thought have happily unravelled many a knot, from solving which the state of the MSS. would probably have deterred less able scholars. Had Professor Wilson lived to superintend an edition of his works, he would perhaps have made a different selection, inserting some articles now omitted, and excluding others; he would perhaps have amalgamated into one essay several treating of kindred subjects, and certainly he would have reproduced most of them in a new form, with all the additional erudition and experience which a long and uninterrupted course of study and research would have enabled him to bring to bear upon it. But it could, of course, be no business of another editor's to attempt anything of the kind, even if he were either competent or presumptuous enough to do so. All that the present editor could venture to do was, to introduce a few verbal alterations and refer the reader, in the notes, to passages in those modern works from which additional information on the subjects in question may be gleaned. And while he justly claims for the venerable author the thanks of all Sanskrit scholars and students of eastern literature for having opened up new mines and struck out new paths, in which it was comparatively easy to those who came after him to make their way, he cannot refrain from deprecating the ungenerous criticism of some who, while they tacitly own him their master, as indeed must every Sanskrit scholar of the present day, consider it anything but a piece of self-erogation to lose no opportunity of calling him to task.

The *Analysis of the Puráńas* (Art. I.) was intended to have embraced all the eighteen Puráńas, for which purpose Professor Wilson had made the most ample preparations. (See the introductory remarks, Vol. I, p. 5-7, and Journal Asiatique for 1860, Vol. XVI, p. 19.) But after his analysis of the Bráhma and Pádma Puráńas was published, the original plan seems to have been either abandoned or postponed; at any rate, nothing more has appeared, so that, with the analysis of four others previously published in India, the Agni, Brahma Vaivartta, Vishńu, and Váyu, only the third part has actually been analyzed, which is here reprinted. Abstracts of the others, left in MSS., may perhaps ere long follow. In the mean time Professor Aufrecht's "Catalogus Codicum MSS. Sanscriticorum", and Professor Wilson's introduction and notes to his translation of the Vishńu Puráńa, especially with the important additions by Prof. F. E. Hall, will be found rich storehouses of information on the contents of the Puráńas.

The *Introduction to the Mahábhárata* (Art. IV.) was intended to serve merely as a general outline of the leading story of that epic. Since it was printed, Prof. M. Williams' useful and laborious book, entitled "Indian epic poetry", has appeared, to which the reader must be referred for a more detailed account. (See also Prof. M. Williams' remarks, Pref. p. IV f. Note.)

The greater portion of Vols. III and IV is taken up with analyses and translations of works of fiction, the most important of which is the Panchatantra. H. T. Colebrooke was, we believe, the first who, in the introductory remarks to Carey's edition of the Hitopadeśa (Serampore: 1804), drew attention to this ancient collection of fables, which he had "little hesitation in pronouncing to be the original text of the work, which was procured from India by Núshírván more than 1200 years ago," that work being the Pehlevi prototype of the Kalíla wa Damna, or Fables of Pilpay. In the "Mémoire historique" with which the late S. de Sacy accompanied his edition of the Arabic text of the Kalíla wa Damna (Paris: 1816), the question of the sources of that book and its history is discussed in more full and accurate detail than by any of his more immediate predecessors, Weber, Dunlop, and Roebuck: and it was chiefly by the perusal of this "Mémoire" that Professor Wilson's interest was stimulated to investigate the subject by making diligent use of all the means within his reach. After giving an abstract of S. de Sacy's researches, which was printed in Vol. I of the Oriental Magazine (Calcutta: 1823), p. 493-506, he presented to the Royal Asiatic Society in the following year an *analytical Account of the Panchatantra* (Art. VI.), made from three MS. copies of the Sanskrit original, and interspersed with translations, which was the more valuable not only as giving the first authentic and detailed information concerning that work itself, but also as embodying many collateral notices of similar stories in the mediæval literature of western Europe whose origin he traced back to that Indian source. In the history of Comparative Literature, in which Fiction forms one of the most attractive chapters, this treatise will ever deserve to hold a very important place, inasmuch as all subsequent works on the same or kindred subjects have taken their stand upon it. Among these may be mentioned L. Deslongchamps' "Essai sur les Fables Indiennes et sur leur introduction en Europe", an estimate of which is contained in Art. VII; Prof. A. Weber's essay on the connection of Indian with Greek fables ("Indische Studien", Vol. III, p. 327-73); and above all Prof. Th. Benfey's Introduction to the Panchatantra, which forms the first volume of his translation of that work into German, and exhaustively treats of the history and migrations of the fables and stories appertaining to that cycle. Many important contributions to the history of Fiction in Europe and Asia have also been made by the brothers Grimm, F. H. von der Hagen, A. Keller, R. Köhler, A. Kuhn, E. Lancereau, F. Liebrecht, Edéléstand du Méril, A. Schiefner, F. W. V. Schmidt, Th. Wright, and others; but it will suffice here for us to have mentioned their names. The Sanskrit text of the Panchatantra was edited by Kosegarten in the year 1848, and an edition of the more ornate and amplified recension was commenced by the same eleven years later, but interrupted by his death. It is greatly to be hoped that it may not remain a fragment.

The next great work of Hindu fiction which Professor Wilson made accessible to European readers is the *Kathásaritságara,* the largest collection of domestic narrative in India. Out of the eighteen books of which it consists he gave first, partly in a free translation, partly in detailed summary, Books I-V (Art. II.), and subsequently also an abstract of the remaining books (Art. VII.). It was by the former publication that the plan was suggested to Prof. H. Brockhaus of bringing out the Sanskrit text, with a faithful and elegant translation into German. For the latter was substituted from the 6th book onwards a close analysis, which will be continued as the remainder of the text comes out.

The *Daśakumáracharita* is the third work of Hindu fiction, with which Professor Wilson was the first to make us acquainted, in an English translation as well as subsequently in an annotated edition of the Sanskrit original, preceded by an introduction and summary (Art. V. and VIII.). The former—which he termed Extracts from the Daśakumáracharita, but which comprises the whole of the printed text—has hitherto been all but unknown in Europe, and will be read with pleasure, the summary serving as a thread by which to find one's way through the intricacies of the different stories. Since the publication of the text—another edition appeared at Calcutta in the year 1850—Prof. Benfey translated the second chapter, corresponding to pp. 189-210 in Vol. IV, with valuable introductory remarks ("das Ausland", 1859, p. 121 ff.); Prof. A. Weber gave a full analysis of the work, with a literary introduction, in the "Monatsberichte der Königlichen Academie der Wissenschaften zu Berlin" for 1859; and lastly, in the year 1862, Mons. H. Fauche published a French translation of the whole. The same author's Kávyádarśa has recently been edited at Calcutta by Pańḍita Premachandra Tarkabágíśa.

The treatise on the *Medical and Surgical Sciences* of the Hindus (Art. III.) cannot be considered as superseded by later works, such as Royle's and Wise's, on the same subject, though these, especially the latter, enter more into detail; for the opinion and authority of a writer on such difficult and abstruse matters, who had the rare fortune of being able to combine with his knowledge of medicin an unrivalled acquaintance with Sanskrit, is always entitled to the greatest deference.

The lecture *on the art of war as known to the Hindus* (Art. IX.) appears here for the first time in print, having probably been reserved by the author for future publication, that he might extend it and add to it the original text of the passages he translates and comments upon.

On the translation of the *Meghadúta* (Art. X.), which appeared at Calcutta as early as 1813, the author's reputation as a Sanskrit scholar was founded. A second edition came out in London after an interval of thirty years, with various alterations in the translation, and many omissions as well as a few additions in the notes. Excellent critical remarks upon the text will be found in Prof. C. Schütz's annotated German translation of the poem.

The review of Sir F. Macnaghten's *Considerations on Hindu Law* (Art. XI.) is the only treatise in which

Prof. Wilson has touched the province of jurisprudence, but it is no trespass or encroachment. His exposition of difficult points of Hindu law, based on an intimate acquaintance both with the original sources, the Smritis and Commentaries, and the habits and traditions of the people, are of great value even now that the works of Sir W. H. Macnaghten, Sir T. Strange, Mr. Morley and others have become standard authorities on Hindu law.

The review of the first edition, by A. W. von Schlegel, of the *Bhagavadgítá* (Art. XII.) appears to have remained unknown to all subsequent editors and translators of, and writers on, that philosophical poem. In reprinting it we have omitted those few passages that have become needless by the emendations introduced into the second edition (by Lassen. Bonn: 1846).

Though the first edition of the *Sanskrit Dictionary* was published at Calcutta forty five years ago, no work has yet appeared to supersede the *preface* with which it was accompanied (Art. XIII.). Many contributions towards a history of Sanskrit lexicography have, indeed, since incidentally been made by Lassen, Roth, Goldstücker, Weber, Hall, Westergaard, Böhtlingk and others; but they are scattered over various works and periodicals, so that a treatise on this branch of Indian literature, which should reflect the present state of Sanskrit scholarship, still remains a desideratum. The author himself, who was more competent than any other to accomplish such a task, seems to have deferred it from time to time; for not only did he let the second edition (Calcutta: 1832) appear without the Preface, but even long subsequently, when he was asked to allow it to be reprinted for the Journal of the Royal Asiatic Society, he declined to give his permission. That, however, he had an intention of re-writing it, may be inferred from a remark that occurs towards the end of the next Article (XIV.), a *Notice of European grammars and lexicons of the Sanskrit language.* At any rate, no considerations of the kind could prompt us to exclude it from these volumes, in which it will be welcomed by all students of Sanskrit literature who have not the rare first edition of the Dictionary within easy reach.

The last Essay in this division, the review of Prof. M. Müller's *History of ancient Sanskrit Literature*, was the last production of his fruitful pen: it appeared in the Edinburgh Review some months after his death.

Every apology is needed for the long interval of time which has been allowed to elapse since the publication of the first division of Professor Wilson's Works: but for a long illness, which incapacitated the editor for literary occupation for six months, these volumes would in due course have succeeded the two previously published.

St. Augustine's College, Canterbury,
Nov. 20, 1863.

R. R.

CONTENTS OF VOL. I.

I.

ANALYSIS OF THE PURÁŃAS.

From the Journal of the Royal Asiatic Society, Vol. V (1838), p. 61.

INTRODUCTORY REMARKS.

THE earliest inquiries into the religion, chronology, and history of the Hindus, ascertained that there existed a body of writings especially devoted to those subjects, from which it was sanguinely anticipated much valuable and authentic information would be derived. These were the Puráńas of Sanskrit literature, collections which, according to the definition of a Puráńa agreeably to Sanskrit writers, should treat* of the creation and renovation of the universe, the division of time, the institutes of law and religion, the genealogies of the patriarchal families, and the dynasties of kings; and they, therefore, offered a prospect of our penetrating the obscurity in which the origin and progress of the Hindu social system had so long been enveloped. A formidable difficulty, however, presented itself in the outset, arising from the voluminous extent of this branch of the literature of the

* [Vide supra Vol. II, p. 67. Lassen, Ind. Alt. IV, 598.]

Hindus, and the absence of all facilities for acquiring a knowledge of its nature. The Puráńas are eighteen in number, besides several works of a similar class, called *Upa*, or minor, *Puráńas*. The former alone comprehend, it is asserted, and the assertion is not very far from the truth, four hundred thousand ślokas, or sixteen hundred thousand lines, a quantity which any individual European scholar could scarcely expect to peruse with care and attention, unless his whole time were devoted exclusively for very many years to the task. Nor was any plan, short of the perusal of the whole, likely to furnish satisfactory means of judging of their general character: few of them are furnished with anything in the shape of an index, or summary of contents, and none of them conform to any given arrangement; so that to know with accuracy what any one contains, it is necessary to read the entire work. The immensity of the labour seems to have deterred Sanskrit students from effecting even what was feasible, the publication or translation of one or two of the principal Puráńas, and to the present day not one of them is accessible to the European public*.

The plan adopted by Sir William Jones and other Sanskrit scholars, in order to come at the contents of

* [Since this was written, Wilson's translation, with valuable notes, of the Vishńu Pur., and Burnouf's edition and translation of the greater part of the Bhágavata P. have appeared in Europe; and the Márkańdeya P., Vishńu P., part of the Garuḋa P., and at least four editions of the Bhágavata P. have been published in India.]

the Puráńas with the least possible waste of their own time and labour, was the employment of Pandits to extract such passages as, from their report, appeared most likely to illustrate Hindu mythology, chronology, and history: and they themselves then translated the extracts, or drew up a summary of the subjects to which they related. The objections to this process are sufficiently obvious. The Pandits themselves are but imperfectly acquainted with the Puráńas; they rarely read more than one or two, as the Bhágavata and Vishńu, and accordingly the extracts furnished by them are limited mostly to those authorities, especially to the former. As the selection of the extracts was necessarily left to their judgment in a great measure, there was no security that they made the best choice they might have done, even from the few works they consulted. Even if the passages were well chosen they were still unsatisfactory, for it was impossible to know whether they might not be illustrated or modified by what preceded or what followed; and however judiciously and accurately furnished, therefore, they were still but meagre substitutes for the entire composition.

But a still more serious inconvenience attended this mode of procedure. It was not always easy to determine whether the extracts were authentic. Not to describe what was sought for, left the Pandit at a loss what to supply; to indicate a desire to find any particular information was to tempt him to supply it, even if he fabricated it for the purpose. Of this the well-known case of Colonel Wilford is a remarkable instance. The inquirer, under these circumstances, was placed in a very uncomfortable dilemma, as he went to work upon materials which might either say too little or too much—might leave him without the only information that was essential, or might embarrass him with an abundance by which he was afraid to benefit.

Detached portions of the Puráńas were also of little or no value in another important respect. They threw little light upon the literary history of those works, upon their respective date, and consequent weight as authorities. It is true that none of the Puráńas bear any dates, but most of them offer occasionally internal evidence of their relative order to one another, or to other compositions, or to circumstances and events from which some conjecture of their antiquity may be formed. Now if there be much difference in these respects amongst the Puráńas, if some be much more modern than others, if some be of very recent composition, they cannot be of equal weight with regard to the subjects they describe, or with relation to the past social and religious condition of the people of India. How far, however, they are the writings of various and distant periods,—how far they indicate this dissimilarity of date, cannot be guessed at from a few detached passages, constituting a very insignificant portion of a very small part of their number.

Unsatisfactory as to their information, questionable as to their authenticity, and undetermined as to their authority, Extracts from the Puráńas are yet the only sources on which any reliance can be placed for accurate accounts of the notions of the Hindus. The statements which they contain may be of different ages, and relate to different conditions, but as far as they go they are correct pictures of the times to which they belong. Recourse to oral authority, to the conversational information of ignorant and ill-instructed individuals, which constitutes the basis of most of the descriptions of the Hindus, published in Europe, is a very unsafe guide, and has led writers of undoubted talent and learning into the most absurd mistakes and misrepresentations. From these they would be preserved by adhering to the Pauráńik writers; but a full and correct view of the mythology of the Hindus, of their religion as it still exists, and of much of their real history, is only to be expected when the Puráńas shall have been carefully examined and compared, and their character and chronology shall have been as far as possible ascertained.

In order to effect the latter objects, as far as they might be practicable without the actual translation of the entire works, I adopted, several years ago, a plan for the particular examination of the contents of all the Puráńas, which was carried into execution during the latter years of my residence in India. Engaging the services of several able Pandits, I employed them to prepare a minute index of each of the Puráńas. This was not a mere catalogue of chapters, or sections, or heads of subjects, but a recapitulation of the subjects of every page and almost every stanza in each page; being, in fact, a copious abstract in the safer form of an index. It is necessary to call attention to this part of my task, the more particularly that it has been misconceived, and has been supposed to mean nothing more than such a summary as sometimes accompanies a Purāńa in the form of a list of the divisions of the work, and a brief notice of the topic of each. The indices prepared for me were of a very different description, as the inspection of them will at once exhibit[1]. These indices were drawn up in Sanskrit. To convert them into English I employed several native young men, educated in the Hindu college, and well conversant with our language, and to them the Pandits explained the Summary which they had compiled. The original and translation were examined by myself, and corrected wherever necessary. When any particular article appeared to promise interest or information, I had that translated in detail, or translated it myself; in the former case, revising the translation with the original. In this manner I collected a series of indices, abstracts, and translations of all the Purāńas with one or two unimportant exceptions, and of the Mahábhárata and Rámáyana, from which, if I am not much mistaken, a correct notion of the substance and character of these works may now be safely formed.

---

[1] Besides copies in my own possession, one set was deposited in the library of the Asiatic Society of Calcutta, and another is placed in the library of the East India Company. The index of the Mahábhárata occupies four folio volumes.

The shape in which these abstracts exist is, however, too voluminous and unsystematic to admit of their being published, or of being used with advantage, except by persons engaged in the especial study of their subjects. In order to fit them for the perusal of those who wish to learn, conveniently as well as correctly, what the Puráńas have to teach, it is necessary to reduce the summaries of their contents to a connected and accessible form, and to indicate the circumstances which illustrate their purport, authenticity, and date. I have attempted to do this in a few scattered instances; and abstracts of the Vishńu, Váyu, Agni, and Brahma Vaivartta Puráńas have been published in the Journal of the Asiatic Society of Bengal. I propose, however, now to go regularly through the whole series, in the order in which the Puráńas are commonly arranged, and begin accordingly with the Bráhma Puráńa, which stands at the head of all the lists. In this, as in any other abstract which I may offer to the Society, I wish it to be understood that I do not trust solely to the index, or the partial translation which I have described, however satisfied I may be of their general fidelity. They are of great use as auxiliaries and guides, but the original is constantly before me, and nothing is stated except upon reference to the authority of the text. I trust, therefore, that my abstracts may lay claim to as much confidence as anything, except actual translation, can be considered to deserve.

I. BRÁHMA PURÁŃA.

THE Bráhma Puráńa*, or Puráńa of Brahmá, is the first of the eighteen Puráńas, according to all the authorities, except the Pádma Puráńa, which, in the Pátála Khańďa or section, arrogates precedence to itself, and gives the second place to the Bráhma. This rather confirms than invalidates the usual specification, and the Bráhma Puráńa may be regarded as the earliest of the series, at least in the estimation of the Pauráńik writers. According to Bálambhaťťa, in his Commentary on the Mitákshará, it is consequently known by the name of Ádi, or First Puráńa**. It is also sometimes designated as the Saura Puráńa, as in part it treats of the worship of Súrya, the sun. Authorities generally agree in stating the extent of the Bráhma Puráńa to be ten thousand stanzas. The Agni Puráńa makes it twenty-five thousand, but is single in the enumeration. The actual number, in two copies consulted on the present occasion, is about seven thousand five hundred. There is, indeed, a work called the Uttara Khańďa, or last section of the Bráhma Puráńa, which contains about three thousand stanzas more, but it is commonly met with detached; and whether it be properly a part of the Puráńa to which it professes to belong, admits of question.

The first verses of the Bráhma Puráńa, forming an

* [See Aufrecht, Catal. Codd. MSS. Sanscr. Bodl., I, 17-20. Wilson's Vishńu Puráńa, p. XIV, Note 32, and XVI f.]

** [Burnouf, Bhágav. P., Vol. I, p. XVIII.]

address to Vishńu, under the appellations of Hari and Purushottama, sufficiently declare its sectarial bias, and indicate it to be a Vaishńava work. It is not, however, included, in the classification of the Pádma Puráńa, amongst the Vaishńava works, but is referred to the Śákta class, in which the worship of Śakti, the personified female principle, is more particularly inculcated, and in which the Rájasa property, or property of passion, is predominant[1].

After the invocation, it is said that the Ŕishis, seated at Naimishárańya, were visited by Lomaharshańa the Súta, and the disciple of Vyása, to whom in particular the Puráńas were imparted. The sages ask him to repeat to them an account of the origin, existence, and destination of the universe. Accordingly, he narrates to them the Bráhma Puráńa, as it was repeated, he says, by Brahmá, in reply to a similar request which was once made by Daksha, and other patriarchs. In this statement we have a variation, of some importance, perhaps, to the authenticity of the text, for the Mátsya Puráńa asserts, that the Bráhma Puráńa was communicated by Brahmá to Maríchi, who, although a patriarch, is a different person from Daksha, and if accurately designated by the Mátsya, shows, at least, a different reading in the copy consulted by the compiler of that work, and in those which are here followed.

The first chapter of the Puráńa describes the crea-

---

[1] Asiat. Researches, Vol. XVI, p. 10, Note [above Vol. I, p. 12].

tion, which it attributes to Náráyańa or Vishńu, as one with Brahmá or Íśwara. He makes the universe from the indiscrete cause which is one with matter and spirit, and the developement of which then proceeds conformably to the Sánkhya philosophy. The first product from Pradhána, the chief principle or base of all substance, is Mahat, the great or intellectual principle, whence proceeds Ahankára, consciousness, or individuality. From this are produced the rudiments of the elements, and from them are developed the gross or perceptible elements, of which water is the menstruum of the rest, and first sensible ingredient in the formation of the world. The appearance of Brahmá on the waters, and the actual manifestation of the system of the universe, are described in the same manner as in Manu, and partly in the same words. Indeed, in this, and in all the early as well as some of the latter chapters of this Puráńa, the words employed seem to be common to several of the Puráńas, as will be particularly pointed out when we come to the parallel passages of the Vishńu Puráńa; and they appear to have been taken from some older work or works, from which the present Puráńas are, probably, in part at least derived.

The birth of the first Manu Swáyambhuva and his wife Śatarúpá, and their descendants to the origin of Daksha, from the Práchetasas by Márishá, are next described, and are followed by a brief notice of the birth of Daksha's daughters, and the multiplication of beings by the intercourse of the sexes. The next chapter gives detailed accounts of the posterity of Daksha's daughters, especially of those wedded to Kaśyapa, comprising gods, demigods, demons, men, animals, and plants; or, in a word, all creatures, real or fabulous. In the third chapter occurs the history of Príthu; and in the fourth, an account of the fourteen Manwantaras, or reigns of the Manus. We have then a particular account of the origin of Vaivaswata, the reigning Manu, and of his descendants, constituting the solar dynasty, or line of princes descended from the Sun, stopping in one copy with Vajranábha, but in the other proceeding to Vríhadbala, with whom the series usually closes. The princes of the lunar dynasty are then detailed to the period of the great war; and in the account of Kríshńa, the legend of his being accused of purloining a wonderful jewel is narrated at length. In all these details, which occupy fifteen chapters, the Bráhma Puráńa presents the same legends as are found in other Puráńas, except that they are in general more concisely told.

The same may be said of the next chapters, which contain brief descriptions of the divisions of the earth, and of the several Dwípas of which it consists, of Pátála, or the regions under the earth, and of the different hells: of the spheres above the earth, and the size and distances of the planets and constellations, and the influence of the sun and moon in producing rain and fertility. These extend to the twentieth chapter.

Part of the twentieth chapter takes up the subject

of Tírthas, or places to which pilgrimage should be performed, of which a few only are particularised, and the list is interrupted by a short geographical description of Bhárata Varsha, or India Proper, its mountains, rivers, inhabitants, and merits. The portion which may be considered as characteristic* of this Puráńa then commences, and relates particularly to the sanctity of Utkala, or Orissa, arising, in the first instance, from the worship of the Sun, in various forms, in that country, the description of which, including legendary accounts of the origin of the twelve Ádityas, or children of Aditi, the wife of Kaśyapa, and the story of Vaivaswata's birth from the Sun by his wife Sanjná, extends to the twenty-eighth chapter.

The sanctity of Utkala continues, however, to constitute the subject of the book, forming the loosely connecting thread of a variety of legends, the scene of which is laid in the province. Thus we have a description of the forest in Utkala called Ekámra, which is considered most holy from its being the favourite haunt of Śiva; and this suggests the legend of Daksha's sacrifice, the birth of Umá as the daughter of Himálaya, and her marriage with Śiva, the destruction and renovation of the Deity of Love, the disrespect shown by Daksha to Śiva, and the punishment inflicted by the ministers of that deity upon the patriarch and his abettors. The Ekámra wood it appears was the place to which Śiva repaired after these

---

* [Wilson's Vishńu Pur. p. xvi, Note 34.]

transactions, and hence its holiness. It is so called, it is said, from a mango-tree (Amra) which flourished there in a former kalpa or great age. According to the description that follows the legends above mentioned in great detail, its circuit was filled with gardens, and tanks, and palaces, and temples, the latter dedicated to various Lingas; and it comprised many Tírthas, or holy spots, as Viraja, Kapila, and others. Connected with it also was the tract sacred to Vishńu, or Purushottama Kshetra, which is next described; and then follows an account of Indradyumna, king of Avantí, by whom the temple of Vishńu was first erected at this spot; and the image of Jagannátha, made for him by Viśwakarman, originally set up. The proceedings of Indradyumna, on this occasion, are very fully narrated, and the account extends to the forty-sixth chapter.

The text then passes rather abruptly to a conversation between Vishńu and the sage Márkańdeya, at the season of the destruction of the world, in which Vishńu tells the Muni that he is identical with all things, and that Śiva is the same as himself. The especial object of the legend is, however, to account for the sanctity of a pool Purushottama Kshetra, called the lake of Márkańdeya, from its being attached to a temple with a Linga, erected by the Muni with the permission of Vishńu, bathing in which tank is a work of merit. We have then notices of other pools, and of trees and temples, with legends concerning their origin, and directions for bathing, praying and worshipping at various shrines. Copious instructions are given for the adoration of Purushottama or Jagannátha, Balaráma and Subhadrá; and a legend of the image of the former is introduced, in which it is said, that it was originally made for Indra, but carried off from his capital, Amarávatí, by Rávańa; that on the conquest of Lanká by Ráma, he left it with Vibhíshańa, and that it was presented by him to Samudra (Ocean), by whom it was set up on the coast of Orissa.

The advantages of living and dying at Purushottama Kshetra are then expatiated upon, and it is said that many Ŕishis, or sages, resided there at the recommendation of Brahmá. Amongst them was the sage named Kandu, and the mention of his name leads to a story of Pramlochá, the nymph of heaven, who was sent by Indra to interrupt Kandu's austerities, but became enamoured of him, and sojourned with him for many ages upon earth. This story was translated by the late M. Langlès, and the translation forms the first article of the "Journal Asiatique" of the Asiatic Society of Paris.

The praises of Vásudeva, or Kŕishńa, introduce an account of some of the Avatáras of Vishńu, of Brahmá's origin from him, and the production and death of the demons Madhu and Kaitabha. All this, however, is but preliminary to a narrative of the birth and actions of Kŕishńa, including the usual legends of Balaráma, Pradyumna, and Aniruddha, and ending with the death of Kŕishńa and the destruction of Dwáraká. These subjects extend from the sixty-fifth to the eighty-sixth chapter, and are, not only in their purport, but in their very language, the same as those which are found in the fifth book of the Vishńu Puráńa.

A series of chapters then ensues on Śráddhas, or obsequial sacrifices, on ceremonial and moral observances, on the duties of the several castes, and on the merit of worshipping Vishńu, especially at the Ekádaśí, or eleventh day of the moon's increase, which topic is illustrated by several insipid legends. These subjects occupy sixteen chapters. We then have a particular detail of the divisions of time, and the duration and influence of the four Yugas, or ages, introductory to a description of the degeneracy of mankind in the last, or Kali age, and the periodical destruction of the world.

When speaking of destruction, Vyása, to whom the character of narrator has been transferred in the course of the work, Lomaharshańa only repeating what his master had formerly said, describes absolute and final destruction, or the eternal cessation of existent things, by the exemption of an individual himself from all existence; and this leads to a question from the sages as to the nature of Yoga, or the practice of that abstraction by which final liberation is secured. In one copy of this Puráńa the answer is suspended by the abrupt insertion and evident interpolation of several chapters, in which an account of the solar dynasty of princes, from Vaivaswata to Ráma, is repeated; and some notice is taken of the origin of

Soma, or the moon. These chapters are, however, clearly out of place, and in another copy they are wanting, Vyása proceeding correctly to describe the means of obtaining emancipation. With this view he gives a sketch of the Sánkhya system of philosophy, first in his own words, and then in the words of the Muni Vasishťha, as addressed formerly to King Janaka; their conversation also contains a description of the practices of the Yogí, as suppression of breath, and particular postures, intended to withdraw his senses more completely from external objects. After describing the condition of the Sáttwika, or perfect man, attained by these means, and his becoming identified with Vásudeva or Kŕishńa, the work concludes with a panegyric upon itself, and dwells on the vast benefits derived by all classes of men from perusing it, or hearing it read.

That this summary of the Bráhma Puráńa faithfully represents its contents as it is ordinarily met with, may be inferred from the concurrence of the two copies consulted, one belonging to myself, and one to Mr. Colebrooke. In the Catalogue of the Sanskrit Manuscripts in the Royal Library of Paris also, No. V. of the Devanagari MSS., although erroneously denominated Ráma Sahasra Náma, "the thousand names of Ráma", an extract from the Bráhma Puráńa, is a portion of that work, and comprehends the chapters which relate to the worship of the sun, and the sanctity of Purushottama Kshetra, concurring, therefore, as far as it goes, with the copies here analyzed. It is nevertheless obvious, that such a Bráhma Puráńa as has been here described, cannot have any pretension to be considered as an ancient work, as the earliest of the Puráńas, or even as a Puráńa at all. The first few chapters may have belonged to a genuine and an ancient composition, and some of the later sections may be regarded as not incompatible with the character of a Puráńa, but the greater portion of the work belongs to the class of Máhátmyas, legendary and local descriptions of the greatness or holiness of particular temples, or individual divinities. The Bráhma Puráńa as we have it, is, for the most part, the Máhátmya or legend of the sanctity of Utkala or Orissa.

Although the holiness of Utkala is owing especially to its including in its limits Purushottama Kshetra, the country between the Vaitarańí and Rasakoila rivers, within which, on a low range of sand-hills at Purí, stands the celebrated temple of Jagannáth; yet the Bráhma Puráńa also gives due honour to two other forms of Hindu superstition, to the worship of the sun, and that of Mahádeo in the same province, and this may assist us to some conjecture of the date of the work in its present form. The great seat of the worship of Śiva called Ekámra Kánana in our text, is now known as Bhuvaneśwara, a ruined city consisting entirely of deserted and dismantled towers and temples, sacred to the worship of Mahádeo[1]. The great

[1] Stirling. Account of Orissa Proper or Cuttack, Asiatic

temple was erected by Lalita Indra Keśarí, Rájá of Orissa, and was completed A. D. 657. At what period the worship declined, and the temples fell into decay, no where appears, but these events were no doubt connected with the ascendency of the adoration of Vishńu or Jagannáth, which probably began to flourish in its greatest vigour subsequently to the twelfth century.

The worship of the Sun seems to have enjoyed a more modern prosperity, for the remarkable temple at Kanárka, known to navigators as the Black Pagoda, was built by Rájá Langora Narsinh Deo, A. D. 1241. It seems to have disputed for a season preeminence with the homage paid to Jagannáth, for the temple of the latter divinity was constructed only forty-three years prior to the Black Pagoda, or in A. D. 1198. Jagannáth however triumphed over his rivals, and the shrine of the Sun, and the temples of Mahádeo, are now alike in a state of ruin: this could not have been the case when the Bráhma Puráńa celebrated their glories, and they would appear, at the time when the Puráńa was compiled, to have divided the veneration of the Hindus with their more fortunate competitor. The internal evidence which the work offers, therefore, renders it exceedingly probable, that it was composed in the course of the thirteenth or fourteenth century, or after the worship of Jagannátha

---

Researches, Vol. XVI. The local particulars in the text are entirely derived from this admirable document.

predominated, but before Śiva and the Sun had fallen into utter disrepute.

The work which is called the *Uttara Khańďa*, or "Last portion" of the Bráhma Puráńa, is, as has been observed, always met with in a detached form, and as an independent composition. The subjects of which it treats, are also of a character wholly dissimilar from those of the Bráhma Puráńa, and it is very obvious that there is no connexion between the two. If there be any Púrva Khańďa, or prior section of the Bráhma Puráńa, of which the Uttara Khańďa is a continuation, it must be something very different from the work of which the preceding summary has been given.

The Uttara Khańďa of the Bráhma Puráńa consists of thirty-seven chapters, containing about three thousand stanzas. It is repeated by Śaunaka to Śatáníka, as it was formerly narrated by Agastya to Supratíka, a sage. It so far merits the denomination of Bráhma Puráńa, that it has Brahmá for its hero: commencing with his incestuous passion for Saraswatí, and the birth of a son, Sumŕiďíka, in consequence. Sumŕiďíka, being offended with his parent, creates, by arduous penance, the brood of Asuras or Titans, by whom the gods are defeated, and Brahmá is expelled from heaven. Brahmá, however, by propitiating Śiva, is restored to his dignity and power, and employs Viśwakarman to build for him the city Dŕiśyapura, on the banks of the Balajá river, the glory and sanctity of which stream it is the main purport of the work to panegyrize.

The Uttara Khańḍa of the Bráhma Puráńa, then, is nothing more than a Máhátmya of the Balajá river; but where the Balajá river flows, or where the city of Dŕiśyapura is situated, are matters to be decided only by future inquiry. The work itself affords no geographical intimations, except that the scene of Brahmá's penance and sacrifice, in propitiation of Śiva, and of various forms of his goddess, Deví or Umá, is laid in the north Dŕiśyapura means merely the "beautiful city"; and other appellations given to it are derived from legends peculiar to this work, and afford no help in its verification. The Balajá river is called also the Bráhma hrada, "the lake of Brahmá", from his having performed penance on its borders; and Báńanáśá, "the destroyer of arrows", having cured the gods when wounded by the shafts of the demons. As personified, the stream is on one occasion identified with Nandiní or Śákambharí Deví, and the latter goddess is the tutelary divinity of Sambher, and other places in Rajputána[1]. The lake of Brahmá might be thought to refer to the celebrated lake of Pushkara, where is still the only shrine known in India to be dedicated to Brahmá; but the Balajá is always described as a river, a great river, a Mahánadí, not a lake: the name means "Strength-born", the stream being produced by the power of the gods; an appellation that offers no aid in discovering its direction, and no such name occurs in the ancient or

[1] Tod's Rajast'hán, Vol. II, p. 445.

modern geography of India. In Báńanáśá, however, we have in all probability the original of Banás, or Bunass, a river rising in Máŕwáŕ, and flowing into the Chambal; and the Uttara Khańda of the Bráhma Puráńa is therefore most probably the local legend of some temple in Central India, which is now in ruins, and the memory of which has passed away. There is nothing in the record that survives, of interest or importance, as it is made up chiefly of accounts of battles between the gods and demons, and praises of the holiness of the river, intermixed with puerile legends of local invention, and thinly interspersed with others belonging to the general body of Pauráńik fiction.

The Uttara Khańda of the Bráhma Puráńa is not to be confounded with the Brahmottara Khańda, a section of the Skánda Puráńa.

From the Journal of the Royal Asiatic Society, Vol V (1838), p. 280.

II. PÁDMA PURÁŃA.

THE *Pádma Puráńa,* which in the Pauráńik lists occupies the second place, and in its own enumeration the first, is a work of considerable extent; according to the best authorities, and to its own statements, it consists of fifty-five thousand ślokas, and the copies that are current actually contain little less than that number, or about 50,000.

The Pádma Puráńa occurs in various portions—according to its own text in five—the first of which treats of the appearance of Viráṫ or Brahmá, and primary creation; it is termed the Paushkara, or *Sŕishṫi Khańďa*. The second describes the formation and divisions of the earth, and various places of pilgrimage, whence it is called the Bhúmi, or Tírtha Khańďa. The third contains an account of the regions above the earth, and of some celebrated princes, and is called the Swarga Khańďa. The genealogies of princes are comprised in the fourth part; and the fifth, containing the Brahma Gítá, explains the means by which moksha, or final emancipation, may be attained. This is the specification of the divisions of the Puráńa which is given in the first chapter of the Sŕishṫi Khańďa, but it is not very exactly applicable to the work as it occurs. The three first portions are rightly denominated the Sŕishṫi, Bhúmi, and Swarga Khańďas; but the fourth is called the Pátála Khańďa, from its opening with a description of Pátála, the regions under the earth; and the fifth, or Uttara Khańďa, is by no means restricted to philosophical discussion. There is current, however, a sixth division, the Kriyá Yoga Sára, which treats of the practice of devotion, and more nearly corresponds to the definition of the fifth portion given in the text.

The Paushkara, or *Sŕishṫi Khańďa* consists of forty-six chapters and about 8500 stanzas. Lomaharshańa, the disciple of Vyása, sends his son Ugraśravas the Súta to Naimishárańya, to relate the Puráńas to

Śaunaka and other Ŕishis assembled at that place. At Śaunaka's request he communicates to them that Puráńa, which, from its containing an account of the lotus (Padma), whence Brahmá appeared in order to create the world, is termed the Pádma Puráńa. Súta, in replying, proclaims also his right by birth and profession to narrate the Puráńas, which were in the present Kalpa imparted by Vishńu in the Matsya avatára to Brahmá, and by him to the gods in the first instance, and in the second to Lomaharshańa, by Vyása, who was a form of Brahmá. We have here also the assertion that the Puráńas consisted originally of 100 kotís, a thousand million of stanzas, of which 400,000 were thought sufficient for the instruction of man—the rest being preserved by the gods. Súta then recapitulates all that he purposes to narrate to the Ŕishis, the whole of which he says was formerly imparted by Brahmá to his will-begotten son, the patriarch Pulastya, by whom it was related at Gangádwára to Prince Bhíshma; in fact, therefore, Pulastya is the person to whom this portion of the Pádma Puráńa is properly to be ascribed.

Pulastya, at the request of Bhíshma, instructs him how the universe was framed. The process is as usual in the Puráńas that of the Sánkhya philosophy, or from the eternal Pradhána proceed successively Mahat, Ahankára, the senses, the rudimental elements, and the gross elements, to which is superadded the egg of creation, as in Manu. Creation, however, is the will and act of the uncreated supreme Brahma, who takes the form of Purusha, and in that character infuses into Prakŕiti the germ of activity. Brahma is, in his various functions, Brahmá, Vishńu, and Śiva; but there is a peculiarity in this chapter which deserves notice: the different Puráńas commonly identify either Vishńu or Śiva with the Supreme, but in this part of the Pádma, Brahmá and Brahma, the instrument and first cause of creation, are represented as the same; the primeval, excellent, beneficent, and supreme Brahma, in the form of Brahmá and the rest, is the creation and the creator, preserves and is preserved, devours and is devoured, the first immaterial cause being, as is common in the pantheism of the Puráńas, also the material cause and substance of the universe; notwithstanding, however, the character here given to Brahmá, the Pádma Puráńa is, according to its own classification, a Vaishńava Puráńa, and deserves that character by its frequent intimation of the supremacy of Vishńu.

The third chapter contains an account of the divisions of time, from an instant to the life of Brahmá, conformably to the usual Pauráńik chronology, and in words common to different Puráńas. This is introductory to the renewal of creation, after a night of Brahmá, when that deity, in the character of Vishńu, assumed the form of a boar, and having placed the earth upon the waters, created its several divisions, and peopled them with animate and inanimate beings. We have then another detail of the creation, rather of a mystical description, in which the different orders of beings proceed from modified conditions of the body of Brahmá. These not multiplying, Brahmá produces the Prajápatis from his will, then the Rudras, then Swáyambhuva Manu, whose daughters, Ákúti and Prasúti, married to Daksha and Ruchi, give birth to daughters, who are espoused to the Ŕishis, forming the earlier patriarchal families, which are evidently nothing more than an allegorical representation of the institution of moral obligations and ceremonial rites by certain holy personages, the first teachers of the Hindu religion. All these details occur in the same order, and in essentially the same words, in the early chapters of the Vishńu Puráńa*.

The same identity continues with regard to the origin of Lakshmí from the churning of the ocean, but the parallel is then suspended by the introduction of the story of Daksha's sacrifice, which is narrated at some length. We have then an account of the family of the second Daksha, as in the Vishńu and other Puráńas—short notices of the several Manwantaras—the story of Veńa and Ṕithu—the origin of Vaivaswata and the descendants of the sun in the line of Ikshwáku to Śrutáyus, who it is said was killed in the great war. The genealogy of this chapter is little else than a string of names, and agrees with that given in the Kúrma and Matsya Puráńas better than with that of the Vishńu.

Bhíshma then requests to be informed of the origin

* [p. 53 ff.]

and nature of the Pitŕis, or progenitors of mankind; in reply to which, Pulastya describes the Śráddha, or offerings to deceased ancestors, and the merits of its celebration, particularly at Gayá. These subjects, illustrated by the story of Brahmadatta, as it occurs also in the Hari Vanśa*, occupy three chapters, from the ninth to the eleventh inclusive. The two next chapters contain an account of the dynasty of lunar princes to the time of Kŕishńa and his immediate posterity, rather more in detail than the solar genealogy, but the same in substance as in other Puráńas.

We have next a series of legends relating to the wars between the gods and Titans or Asuras, which, although not restricted to the Pádma Puráńa, are in some degree peculiar in their order and details. The Asuras are described as enjoying the ascendency over the Devatás, when Vŕihaspati, taking advantage of their leader Śukra's being enamoured of a nymph of heaven, sent by Indra to interrupt his penance, comes amongst the former as Śukra, and misleads them into irreligion by preaching heretical doctrines; the doctrines and practices he teaches are Jain, and in a preceding passage it is said that the sons of Raji embraced the Jina Dharma — notices which are of some value with regard to the age of the compilation.

An inquiry into the cause of the enmity that prevailed between the two heroes, Karńa and Arjuna, suggests a curious legend of a quarrel between Brahmá

* [c. 21 ff.]

and Śiva, in which a being born from the perspiration of the former puts the latter to flight. Śiva repairs to Vishńu, who offers to put alms into Śiva's dish, when Śiva pierces the hand of Vishńu, and the blood that flows in consequence fills the Kapála, and becomes a Nara, a man—the saint Nara in another birth, and Arjuna in another. Brahmá's progeny becomes in a succeeding existence Karńa, and hence the hostility of the two, the legend considering them evidently as types of the followers of Brahmá and of Śiva in a contest for superiority. The same notion of a struggle between the two sects prevails in what follows. The lustre of Brahmá's fifth head excites the envy of the gods, and Śiva, at their suggestion, tears it off. To expiate the crime of injuring a Brahman, Śiva, by the advice of Vishńu, repairs to various Tírthas, and this leads to the Pushkara Máhátmya, or the description of the holiness of Pushkara or Pokhar Lake near Ajmír, a subject that more or less pervades the rest of the Śrishťi Khańda from the fifteenth chapter to the end.

The praises of Pushkara, instructions for bathing and worshipping there, and the efficacy or gifts and sacrifices performed at this sacred spot, are abundantly interspersed with legends, some peculiar to the work and to the subject, and others belonging to the general body of tradition and mythology, but rather arbitrarily connected in the Pádma Puráńa with the sanctity of Pushkara. Of the former class we have Brahmá's throwing down a lotus (Pushkara) from heaven, whence the name of the place where it fell; his performing a solemn sacrifice there; his marriage with Gáyatrí; the displeasure of his former bride Sávitrí, in consequence of which she denounced imprecations on all the gods and Brahmans; the metamorphosis of King Prabhanjana to a tiger, and his liberation; the fidelity of the cow Nandá, and her elevation to heaven; and similar stories, some of which are curious, but most puerile. Of fictions which are to be found in several other Puráńas, we have the death of Vŕitrásura by Indra's vajra, or thunderbolt, formed of the bones of the sage Dadhíchi, and Agastya's humbling the Vindhya mountain, drinking up the ocean, and destroying the Asuras who had sought refuge beneath its waters. The bed of the ocean was afterwards replenished by King Bhagíratha when he brought the Ganges from heaven.

The subjects that next occur are Vratas, or acts of self-denial and devotion, to be performed on particular occasions, as on the third lunation of each month in the year, when worship is to be addressed to some form or other of Gaurí, either with or without her consort Śiva; also on certain specified days, as the Vibhúta Dwádaśí, Viśoka Dwádaśí, Kalyáńa Saptamí, Bhaimí Ekádaśí, and others, illustrated as usual by legends, amongst which the birth of Vaśishtha and Agastya occurs, and the story of the latter's drinking the ocean is repeated as introductory to the efficacy of worshipping Agastya at Pushkara Tírtha. Márkańdeya Muni's going in pilgrimage to Pushkara gives occasion to some account of him, and of his intercourse with Rámachandra, who passed a month at Pushkara, and performed Śráddha there when on his way to the scene of his exile, circumstances of which the Rámáyańa takes no notice. Kshemankarí Deví, a form of Durgá residing at Pushkara, is wooed by Mahishásura, whose origin is related; he attempts to carry her off by force, but is slain, and an account is then given of some other exploits of the goddess. We have then a eulogium of the merits of giving food and drink, illustrated by the punishment of Śweta, king of Ilávŕita-varsha, condemned to gnaw his own bones after death, as a penance for his omitting to distribute food in charity whilst he lived; and by anecdotes of Rámachandra, including the history of Dańďa, after whom the Dańďakárańya, or great southern forest, was named; Ráma acts as an umpire between a vulture and owl in a dispute for a nest, and the nest being assigned to the owl, the vulture, who was King Brahmadatta, condemned to this transformation, resumes his form and goes to heaven. After returning to Ayodhyá, and celebrating the Rájasúya sacrifice, Ráma again travels to the South, and pays a visit to Vibhíshańa: on his quitting Lanká he broke down the bridge that connected the island with the main land, and on his way home visited Pushkara and shook hands with Brahmá.

After these legends we have an account of the creation in the Pádma Kalpa, prefaced by a second detail of the divisions of time, closing in a periodical dissolution; during which Náráyańa, sleeping upon the waters, is beheld by Márkańdeya Muni, who, by desire of the deity, enters the celestial body, and beholds in it all existent things. This legend occurs in several Puráńas, particularly in that which bears the name of the Muni*. Brahmá, then becoming manifest from a golden lotus, creates the world and its divisions out of the several parts of the lotus, whence this period of creation is called the Pádma Kalpa. After the formation of the world, and the destruction of the demons Madhu and Kaiťabha who sought to destroy Brahmá, by Vishńu, the work proceeds as before, through the intervention of the mind-engered Prajápatis, the daughters of Daksha, and progeny of Kaśyapa. The concluding chapters describe the wars of the gods and demons, the destruction of Máya and Kálanemi by Vishńu, and the birth of Skanda for the destruction of Táraka, the overthrow and death of the demon, and Skanda's marriage with Devasená. "Then," concludes Súta, "Pulastya departed, and Bhíshma having become filled with true knowledge, returned to his government of Hástinapura." A final chapter contains a tolerably copious index of the contents of the Śrishťi Khańda.

Bhúmi Khańda. The second division of the Pádma Puráńa is of much the same extent as the first, containing about 7500 stanzas, which are distributed amongst 133 short chapters. It opens with a question

* [Márk. Pur. 47.]

put by the Ŕishis to Súta, how it happened that Prahráda, or Prahláda, a daitya, and natural enemy of the gods, could have been inspired with the devotion he entertained for Vishńu, and finally united with that deity. Súta replies by stating, that the same question had been formerly asked of Brahmá by Vyása, and he repeats Brahmá's answer as Vyása had communicated it to him, which is a narrative of Prahláda's birth and actions in a preceding kalpa. This allusion to Prahláda, it may be observed, without any preliminary details, implies a knowledge of his history, which can only be derived from some earlier work; what this may have been, it is not very possible to ascertain, as the legend occurs in several Puráńas, and mention is made of Prahláda in the Mahábhárata. For his character, however, of a devout worshipper of Vishńu, the Vishńu Puráńa and Bhágavata are the especial authorities*.

In order to account for Prahláda's eminence as a Vaishńava, Súta repeats a story of Śivaśarman, a Brahman of Dwáraká, who had five sons, equally remarkable for their piety and filial devotion. The latter is put to the test in various ways by their father, and being proof against every trial, the father and the four elder sons are united after death with Vishńu; Somaśarman, the fifth son, was also desirous of the same elevation, and was engaged at Śálagráma Kshetra

* [Vishńu Pur. I, 17–20. Bhâgav. Pur. VII, 4–6. See Burnouf's Pref. ad Vol. III, p. VIII ff. Lassen, Ind. Alt. IV, 582 f.]

in that contemplation on Vishńu which it is the great object of this part of the Pádma Puráńa to inculcate as the most efficacious means of union with the divinity, as it is here said, "The imperishable state is not obtained by sacrifice, by penance, by abstract meditation, by holy knowledge, but by thinking upon Vishńu: the destroyer of Madhu is not beheld through gifts or through pilgrimage, but through the union that is effected by intense contemplation: the Brahman enters the state of Vishńu by the road of profound mental identification." Whilst Somaśarman is endeavouring to effect this coalescence, an alarm spreads through the hermitage that the Daityas are approching, and a loud clamour ensues, which distracts his thoughts, aud fills his mind with fear of the foes of the gods; he dies whilst under these apprehensions, and is consequently born again as a member of that race which engrossed his last thoughts. He is born as Prahláda, the son of Hirańyakaśipu, a daitya, but from the influence of his former life a worshipper of Vishńu. In the war between the gods and demons, however, he takes part with his family, and is killed by the discus of Vishńu. He is again born of the same parents and with the same name, and is then the Prahláda who is the hero of the usual story, the pious son of an impious father, the latter of whom was destroyed by Vishńu in the Nŕisinha, or man-lion avatára, and the former was raised to the rank of Indra for his life, and finally united with Vishńu. The Pádma Puráńa, therefore, in borrowing the subject of this legend from other sources, has added to it circumstances peculiar to itself, evidently of sectarial tenor, and comparatively recent invention.

The elevation of Prahláda to the rank of king of heaven—a dignity which no other Puráńas assign him, although they make him monarch over a division of Pátála—suggests to the Ŕishis an inquiry into the nature of celestial dominion, and upon whom and by whom it is conferred; and this introduces a legend of the birth of a king of the gods, or Indra, as the son of Kaśyapa and Aditi, in consequence of a boon to that effect promised to Aditi by Vishńu. Kaśyapa's other wives, Diti and Danu, the mothers of the Daityas and Dánavas, feeling mortified at the inferiority of their children to those of their sister-wife Aditi, Kaśyapa, in order to console them, enters upon a long philosophical disquisition upon the nature of body and soul. The discussion is conducted in the form of an allegory, in which the Senses endeavour to negotiate a perpetual alliance with Soul, and Soul, after several vain struggles to evade all connexion with the Senses, at last escapes from them altogether by the aid of meditation.

After describing the determination of the chief Daityas to raise themselves to a level with the gods by arduous penance, the Ŕishis rather abruptly ask Súta to tell them the story of a Brahman called Suvrata, the son of Somaśarman and Sumanas, who was a devoted worshipper of Vishńu, and who became, therefore, in a future birth, Indra, the son of Kaśyapa and Aditi. The legend is an insipid sectarial fiction, but contains some curious matter, especially regarding virtue and vice, the reward of the former and punishment of the latter after death, the road to the judgment-seat of Yama, his appearance, and the tortures to which sinners are condemned. The text then reverts to the austerities of the demons, and particularly those of Hirańyakaśipu, which compel Brahmá to grant him a boon that he shall not be slain by any living creature; it therefore becomes necessary for Vishńu to destroy him in the non-descript form of the Nŕisinha; whilst in the Avatára of the boar, he puts to death Hirańyáksha and other demons. These events are briefly referred to, and are but introductory to a longer legend of the birth of Vŕitra, the son of Diti, for the destruction of Indra, and of his being circumvented and slain by the deity. We have then the story of Indra's cutting to pieces another offspring of Diti, destined to be his foe whilst yet in the womb, and thus giving rise to the forty-nine Maruts or winds.

In like manner as Indra was made king of the gods, different persons or things were appointed by Brahmá supreme over their respective orders of beings; and amongst these, the list of which conforms with that which occurs in other Puráńas, Pŕithu, the son of Veńa, was made monarch of the earth. This leads to the story of Veńa and Pŕithu, which is narrated in the usual manner and customary words; but a supplement is added to the legend of Veńa, which is peculiar to this Puráńa. According to this, Tunga, the son of

Atri, having propitiated Náráyańa, by penance, obtained a son equal to Indra; this son was Veńa, who was made by the Ŕishis the first king of the earth: he commenced his reign auspiciously, but lapsing into the Jain heresy, the sages deposed him and pummelled him until the Nisháda, or progenitor of the wild races, was extracted from his left thigh, and Přithu from his right arm. Being freed from sin by the birth of the Nisháda, Veńa retires to the banks of the Narmadá, where he performs penance in honour of Vishńu, who appears to him, and reads him a lecture on the merit of gifts of various kinds, especially at different holy places or Tírthas. But persons are also considered as Tírthas, as a Guru, a father, a wife; and in illustration of this latter, Vishńu tells a story of Sukalá, the wife of a Vaiśya, who, having gone on a pilgrimage, leaves Sukalá in great affliction; her female friends come to console her, and their conversation includes many precepts for the conduct of women, exemplified by narratives. Sukalá continuing to mourn for her absent lord, Kámadeva and Indra attempt to seduce her from her faith, but are foiled, and she remains faithful to her husband, who returns from pilgrimage, and receives blessings from heaven in recompense of the virtues of his wife.

Another series of tales is recited by Vishńu, in illustration of a parent's being a Tírtha, or holy shrine. It commences with an account of the filial piety of Sukarman, the son of Kuńdala, a Brahman of Kurukshetra, but branches off into several other stories: one of the most remarkable of these is a narrative, of which the original is to be found in the Mahábhárata*, that of Yayáti's transferring his infirmities to his son Púru. It is embellished, however, in this place, with much additional matter, and begins with Yayáti's being invited by Indra to heaven, and being conveyed on the way thither by Mátali, Indra's charioteer. A philosophical conversation takes place between the king and Mátali, in which the imperfection of all corporeal existence, and the incomplete felicity of every condition of life are discussed. These attributes belong, it is said, even to the gods themselves, for they are affected with disease, subject to death, disgraced by the passions of lust and anger, and are consequently instances of imperfection and of misery. Various degrees of vice are then described, and their prevention or expiation are declared to be the worship of Śiva or Vishńu, between whom there is no difference; they are but one, as is the case indeed with Brahmá also; for "Brahmá, Vishńu, and Maheśwara, are one form, though three gods: there is no difference between the three: the difference is that of attributes alone." The result of the conversation is, that Yayáti returns to earth, where, by his virtuous administration, he renders all his subjects exempt from passion and decay. Yama complains that men no longer die, and Indra sends Kámadeva and his daughter

* [I, 3157 ff. Bhágav. Pur. IX, 18 f. Vishńu Pur. IV, 10. Cf. Lassen, Ind. Alt. I, Anhang I, XVIII.]

Aśruvindumatí to endeavour to excite passion in the breast of Yayáti; they succeed, and it is in order to become a fit husband for the latter that the aged king applies to his sons to give him their youth in exchange for his decrepitude. As elsewhere related, they all refuse, except Púru, the youngest. After a time, however, Yayáti is prevailed upon by the persuasion of his young bride, at the instigation of Indra, to go to heaven, on which he restores his youth to Púru, and proceeds with his subjects to Indra, who sends them to Śiva, and he directs them to Vishńu, in whose sphere they obtain a final abode.

We then come to a series of narratives in illustration of the assertion that a Guru, or spiritual preceptor, is a Tírtha. Chyavana, the son of Bhŕigu, wandering over the world in pilgrimage, comes to the south bank of the Narmadá, where a Linga, called Oṁkára, is erected; and having worshipped it, he sits under an Indian fig-tree, where he overhears a conversation between Kunjara, an old parrot, and his four sons, in which the latter relate to the former what they have beheld in their flight during the day. Several stories are narrated, the moral of which is the same, the good effects of venerating holy men, and meditating upon Vishńu. In the course of them, the efficacy of various holy places in expiating sin is described, and in one of the stories it appears that the Ganges, the lake Mánasa, Prayága, Pushkara, and Benares, are of less sanctity than the river Revá or Narmadá in various parts of its course, as at the confluence of the Kubjá, Kapilá, Meghanádá, and Chichuká, at Śaivágára, Bhŕigukshetra, Mahishmatí, Śríkańtha, and Mańdaleśwara, places which are little known beyond their immediate vicinity, and of which the specification indicates the local origin of this part at least of the Puráńa. One long narrative is peculiar to the work, and relates to the destruction of the demon Tuńda by Nahusha, the son of Áyus, and the marriage of the latter with Aśokasundarí, the daughter of Párvatí. We have also an account of the destruction of Vituńda, the son of Tuńda, by Bhagavatí herself. Kunjara then relates to Chyavana an account of the preceding births of his sons and himself.

After this, Vishńu desires Veńa to demand a boon, and he solicits to be incorporated with the deity; Vishńu tells him first to celebrate an Aśwamedha, after which the king shall become one with himself, and he then disappears. The conversation between Veńa and Vishńu extends from the fortieth to the end of the one hundred and eighteenth chapter.

Pŕithu enables his father Veńa to consummate the sacrifice, by which he is united to Vishńu, and this incident illustrates the efficacy of a son considered as a Tírtha. The Jangama, or moveable Tírthas, being thus disposed of, Súta proceeds, in the words of Vyása, to describe the Stlávara, the fixed or geographical Tírthas. The principal of those that are named are Pushkara, Mahákála, the Narmadá, the Charmanvatí or Chambal, Arbuda or Abú, Prabhása, the confluence of the Saraswatí with the ocean, Dwáravatí, and the mouths of the Indus, the Vitastá river, the source of the Deviká, Kámákhyá in Ásám, and Kurukshetra. There are many others, most of which are now unknown: one called Rámahrada, the lake of Ráma, introduces the familiar legend of Paraśuráma, and his destruction of the warrior race, which is told in the usual strain, but more concisely than in some other works. The subject of Tírthas continues to the end of the hundred and twenty-seventh chapter.

In the next chapter the compiler seems to have recollected the purport of the appellation of this part of the Pádma Puráńa, and the Ŕishis ask Súta to give them a description of the earth; in reply, he repeats an account attributed to the great serpent Śesha, and related by him to Vátsyáyana and other sages assembled at the coronation of Vásuki as king of the serpent race, in which the seven Dwípas, or insular zones, that form the earth, and the Lokáloka mountain which surrounds the whole, are described in the usual manner. In the account of Jambu-dwípa we have the usual details concerning the several Varshas, and mountains that separate them and Mount Meru and its surrounding elevations. The details, however, are not very particular or full, and are exclusively of a mythological character.

The last chapter of this khańda, as well as that of the Śrishti khańda, contains a tolerably copious index.

Swarga Khańda. The third division of the Pádma Puráńa consists of about 4000 stanzas in forty chapters; it carries on the dialogue between Śesha and the Ŕishis with which the previous portion concluded, and which Súta continues to repeat.

Vátsyáyana having asked Śesha to give him and the other Munis a description of the regions above the earth, the snake-god replies by referring to a conversation on this subject between a messenger of Vishńu and King Bharata. The mention of the latter suggests to Vátsyáyana to inquire into his history; and the first five chapters of the work are appropriated to the narrative of Śakuntalá and Dushyanta, in which the drama of Kálidása is evidently the authority that has been followed. Bharata, the son of Dushyanta, after reigning with glory, becomes a worshipper of Vishńu, in consequence of which Sunanda, a servant of the deity, is sent to convey the king, after his resigning his crown to his son, to Vaikuńt́ha. On the way Bharata asks him to give him an account of the regions which they traverse, and Sunanda accordingly describes to him the situation and extent of the different Lokas or spheres above the earth. The same contrivance occurs in other works, and especially in the Káśí Khańd́a of the Skanda Puráńa, from which possibly the idea has been borrowed.

The atmosphere, planetary regions, heaven, and the four upper worlds, Mahar, Jana, Tapas, and Satya, are noticed briefly in the usual manner, and above these is placed Vaikuńt́ha, the heaven of Vishńu, according to this authority. Recurring to the subject, Sunanda then proceeds to describe in detail the subdivisions of these super-terrene realms, the Lokas or spheres, inhabited by various orders of beings, as the Bhútas, Piśáchas, Gandharbas, Vidyádharas, and Apsarasas, adverting also to the circumstances which people these aërial districts, or obtain for mortals a place in them after death. When describing the Apsaraloka, Sunanda relates the story of Purúravas and Urvaśí after the ordinary Pauráńik fashion, with the addition that Purúravas, by worshipping the Gandharbas, obtained a residence with Urvaśí in the sphere of the nymphs, and that Bharata, by transferring to him the merit of all the sacrifices he had performed in honour of Vishńu, enabled him to proceed to Vaikuńtha.

We have then accounts of the Lokas of the sun, Indra, Agni, Yama, the Dikpálas, Varuńa, Váyu, interspersed with stories. At the Loka of Kuvera an account of the origin of Rávańa, and his expelling Kuvera from Lanká is related. The lunar sphere, or Loka of Soma, affords occasion for the usual legends of the birth of Soma and of Budha, of Daksha's cursing Soma to be afflicted with consumption, as the punishment of his neglecting all his wives except one, Rohińí, and his consequent alternations of increase and wane. In like manner the Loka of Saturn introduces the story of his birth from the wife of the sun, and that of Dhruva suggests the legend of Dhruva's adoration of Vishńu, and his elevation to the dignity of the Polar Star. After rising above this sphere, and passing by the upper Lokas, which are again briefly described, Bharata is carried by Sunanda to Vaikuńtha.

Vátsyáyana then asks Śesha to tell him what princes of the solar and lunar races, who were celebrated when on earth for their religious acts, were raised to heaven. Śesha in reply repeats several narratives, which seem to be preserved in their most ancient and authentic form in the Rámáyańa and Mahábhárata, and to have been thence transferred to the Puráńas with various degrees of detail and modification. In this work they are narrated at length, and embellished occasionally with additions, which are evidence of a corrupt taste and of a comparatively recent date. The narratives are Sagara's exploits and sacrifice, the death of his sons by Kapila's wrath, the birth of Bhagíratha and his bringing Gangá upon earth, the origin of the demon Dhundhu, here called the son of Madhu, and his destruction by Kuvalayáśwa, thence termed Dhundhumára; the generosity of King Śivi in offering his own flesh to rescue a pigeon from the gripe of a hawk, the birds being in fact Indra and Agni, who had assumed their shape to put the benevolence of Śivi to the test; his further trial by Brahmá; the sacrifice of Marutta; Divodása's reign at Káśí; Śiva's regaining possession of that sacred city; and the birth and piety of Mándhátŕi.

At an Aśwamedha performed by Mándhátŕi, the king is visited by Nárada, and a conversation takes place, in which the sage gives a brief description of the course of creation conformably to the Sánkhya tenets. Speaking of the origin of the four castes, Nárada explains their respective obligations, and then proceeds to the duties of the different áśramas or periods of life. Under the last order, he expounds the nature of yoga, practical and speculative, or Karma yoga and Jnána yoga. He then details the Sadáchá-ras, or daily observances, incumbent on all classes of men, ceremonial, purificatory, moral, and devotional. The latter are, of course, to be addressed especially to Vishńu, and to the types of him, the principal of which is the Śálagráma stone, or Ammonite, without which, it is said, worship should not be offered. This fossile is said to be the present Vishńu with his discus, and to drink of the water in which it has been immersed is described as a sure means of obtaining emancipation during life, and being united with Vishńu after death. Great efficacy is also ascribed to sectarial marks, which are to be made after bathing, and before all religious rites, on the top of the arms, the chest, the throat, and the forehead. The merit of fasting on the ekádaśí, or eleventh lunation, and the heinous crime of eating on a day sacred to Vishńu, are then pointed out, and the whole offers a sufficiently decisive indication of the character of the compilation as a purely sectarial work.

Several sections are then devoted to a description of the things that may or may not be eaten; to modes and times of dressing and anointing the person, to postures in which it is proper to sit or lie on different occasions, to the crime of slandering a venerable person, on which it is observed that Śiva is excluded from all share in oblations, on account of his disrespectful conduct towards his father-in-law, Daksha; to lucky and unlucky omens; to actions proper and improper, according to particular seasons; to the favourable characteristics of a wife, and to a variety of injunctions and prohibitions.

Mándhátṙi's asking Nárada if he had ever known any person who had lived a hundred years, a singular question by the way for a monarch to put, who, according to Pauráṅik tradition, lived at a period when a reign of many thousand years was no rarity, Nárada tells him a tale of Brahmaketu, son of Viśwaketu, king of Dráviḋa, who was doomed to die in his sixteenth year, but who, by advice of Angiras, went to Benares, and lay down in the path of Yama, when on a visit to Śiva. Yama, who never deviates from a straight path and even an equal step, and could, therefore, neither walk round Brahmaketu, nor stride over him, at last, to induce him to rise, promised to allow him to live a century, which accordingly happened. There is an underplot of Brahmaketu's marrying the daughter of the king of Kámpilya, in lieu of the hunchbacked son of the king of Kekaya, which has some resemblance to a story in the Arabian nights.

Mándhátṙi next asks Nárada to explain to him what he meant by Śiva's ill-behaviour to his father-in-law, on which Nárada relates the story of Daksha's sacrifice, much in the usual strain, but concisely, and making no mention of Vishṅu amongst the guests. Daksha also is permitted to complete the rite, the head of a goat being substituted for his own, which he had lost in the affray.

In reply to other questions put by Mándhátŕi, Nárada describes the actions by which an individual is sentenced to heaven or hell; the Brahmans who are entitled to gifts and to respect, the necessity of regal government, the consequences of a good or evil administration, the duties of kings, the succession and duration of the four Yugas, and the temporary dissolution of the world. Nárada then takes leave of the king, and goes to the heaven of Indra. A somewhat abrupt introduction of the Muni Saubhari and his marriage with the daughters of Mándhátŕi then occurs, after which the king completes his sacrifice and goes to heaven, with which the series of narratives terminates. The last chapter is an index of the contents of the Bhúmi Khańďa.

The *Pátála Khańďa* of the Pádma Puráńa contains 102 chapters and about 9000 stanzas. It commences with a continuation of the dialogue between Vátsyáyana and Śesha, in which the snake-god describes the different regions of Pátála.

The first, Atala, is subject to Mahámáya. Vitala, the second, to a form of Śiva, called Hátakeśwara, the third, Sutala, to Bali, who, on one occasion, made Rávańa prisoner, which legend is related. Máya reigns over Talátala, the fourth division, he having been raised to that dignity after the destruction of his three cities by Śiva, an account of which exploit is detailed. In Mahátala, the fifth region, reside the great serpents; and in Rasátala, the sixth, the Daityas and Dánavas. The chief Nágas, or snake-gods, under their monarch Vásuki, occupy the lowermost of the subterranean kingdoms, that which is especially called Pátála.

In the account of Rávańa's captivity by Bali, mention was made of his future death by Vishńu, in the form of Ráma, a prince of the solar dynasty, and Vátsyáyana referring to this asks Śesha to give him an account of some of the most celebrated monarchs of this family, and of the descent of Vishńu as Ráma. Śesha accordingly commences with the origin of the Manu Vaivaswata from Áditya, the son of Kaśyapa, the son of Maríchi, the son of Brahmá, previous to whose Manwantara, the Manu was preserved by Vishńu, in the Matsya, or fish Avatára, in a ship during the deluge; the account is in substance the same with that which is given in the Mátsya and other Puráńas. Śesha then continues with the descendants of Ikshwáku, the order and names of whom conform most nearly with the same in the Bhágavata*, although few details are given. Amongst them we have the story of Hariśchandra's sacrifice and elevation to heaven, and Saudása's transformation to a cannibal. The genealogy is then continued to the immediate predecessors of Ráma, and the greater part of the remainder of the work is then devoted to the history of that monarch, and the actions of himself and of the princes of his house.

The story of Dilípa and his service of the cow

* [IX, 6.]

Nandiní, the birth and reign of Raghu, the marriage of Aja, and death of his wife Indumatí, and the birth of Daśaratha, are told exactly in the same manner as in the Raghu Vanśa*, and although in a less poetical style, yet frequently in the same words. In the account of Daśaratha we have a legend of his assailing Śani, or Saturn, who had caused a dearth, the king's car falling from heaven at the angry glances of the planet was upstayed by the bird Jaťáyu, and Daśaratha was thus enabled to accomplish his object, and partly compel and partly propitiate Śani to withdraw his obstruction to the fall of rain. These stories of Ráma's ancestors extend from the fifth to the end of the twelfth chapter, and from thence to the end of the 27th we have in the accounts of the birth of Daśaratha's sons, the actions of Ráma, his exile, his conquest of Lanká, and his return with Sítá to Ayodhyá, nothing more than an epitome of the Rámáyańa.

The compiler of the Puráńa appears, however, to have had again recourse to the Raghu Vanśa**, for the events that occurred after Ráma's return to his capital, the dismissal of Sítá to the hermitage of Válmíki, the death of the demon Lavańa by Śatrughna, and foundation of Mathurá, the birth of Ráma's sons, Kuśa and Lava, Sítá's being swallowed up by the earth, and Ráma's ascending to heaven with his followers and subjects.

---

* [I–III, VII f.] ** [XIV f.]

Vátsyáyana, unwearied of a tale of which Ráma is the hero, solicits further particulars from Śesha, and the snake-god details Ráma's return to Ayodhyá more fully, and dilates upon his meeting with his brother Bharata, and the widows of his father. He then describes the visit of Agastya to Ayodhyá, when the sage relates some of the circumstances of the history of Rávańa, in which the Uttara Khańd'a of the Rámáyańa has been followed, with the addition that, Rávańa being a Brahman by birth, Ráma incurred, in putting him to death, a guilt which can only be expiated by an Aśwamedha. Accordingly the rite is described, and the horse intended for the sacrifice let loose, attended by a body of troops under the command of Śatrughna. The adventures of the steed and his attendants form the subject of a number of chapters, from the thirty-fifth to the ninetieth.

One of the first places of note to which the horse comes, is Ahichchhatrá, a city, which, according to the Mahábhárata*, lies north of the Ganges, and which here seems to be in Ásám, for adjoining to it is the temple of Kámákhyá, a form of Durgá, which has been long especially worshipped in that part of India. The temple it is said was constructed by Sumada, the

* [I, 5511-16. Vishńu Pur. p. 187 and 454. According to Lassen, Ind. Alt. I, 602, Ahichchhatrá (also Ahikshetra) was situated in the Duáb. See also Vivien de St.-Martin in "Mémoires sur les contrées occidentales". Paris: 1858, II, 342. 348, and in his "Étude sur la géographie Grecque et Latine de l'Inde". Paris: 1858, p. 324 f.]

king of Ahichchhatra, at the time of Śatrughna's arrival, in consequence of the goddess having restored him to his dominions, from which he had been driven by his foes. From hence Śatrughna marches to the banks of the Payoshńí*, a river which, according to the Pauráńik lists, rises from the Vindhya mountains, and is rather incongruously, therefore, placed in succession to Ásám. It is noticed, however, for the purpose of introducing the legend of the Muni Chyavana, which is narrated more fully here than in any other Puráńa. The next place described is the Níla mountain and Purushottama Kshetra, or Jagannáth, which involves a legend of Ratnagríva, king of Kánchí (Conjeveram), who, going in pilgrimage to the mouth of the Ganges, makes a very extraordinary detour by the Gańdakí river, all geography being here sacrificed to a determination to eulogize the Śálagráma, which sacred stone is commonly obtained in the Gańdak. Śatrughna ascends the Níla mountain, and worships Purushottama. He next proceeds to Chakránka the capital of Subáhu, where the horse is detained by Damana, the son of Subáhu, and a fierce conflict ensues, which ends in the triumph of Śatrughna, and the recovery of the steed. We have then an account of Satyavat, king of Tejaspura, who was born to his father in reward of his cherishing a cow, the great importance of which is illustrated by a legend of Janaka, who, notwithstanding his being the father-in-law

* [i. e. the Payin Gangá. Lassen, Ind. Alt. I, 175.]

of Ráma, was condemned to hell for having struck a cow. His virtues, however, were such, as not only to make his going there a mere matter of form, but to enable him to redeem all the damned whom he beheld in Tartarus.

The horse is then stolen by the Asura Vidyunmálin, but the theft is detected and the demon slain. He then leads his guards to the hermitage of Áraṅyaka, who questions Śatrughna and his companions concerning Ráma, and in consequence repairs to Ayodhyá, where he is incorporated with the demigod. The steed next falls into the Narmadá, but is followed by the warriors to the caverns of the river-goddesses, and they restore the horse: he then becomes the subject of a still more formidable encounter, being carried off by Rukmángada, the son of Víramaṅi, king of Devapura. The heroes of Śatrughna's host are, in the first instance, victorious, and the king and his son are left for dead, when Śiva, of whom Víramaṅi was a worshipper, comes with Vírabhadra to the aid of his votaries. Pushkala, Śatrughna's chief captain, is beheaded by Vírabhadra, and Śatrughna struck down senseless by Śiva, but Hanumán, after arresting Śiva's progress, brings the drug that reanimates the dead and restores his friends to life; the battle is renewed, but Śiva continuing to have the best of it, Ráma himself is obliged to appear. Śiva then retreats after offering worship to Ráma, and Víramaṅi, who has been also revived, relinquishes the horse and his kingdom.

Several other stories of this kind occur. At last the horse comes to Válmíki's hermitage, where he is detained by Lava, the son of Ráma, yet a youth. The mention of his name leads to a repetition of the story of Sítá's being separated from Ráma, with the addition of its cause, her having, when a girl, caught two parrots, and having let the male go, but kept the female; the latter, after pronouncing an imprecation on Sítá that she should be separated from her husband, died of grief, but repeating the name of Ráma to the last, went to heaven; the male threw himself into the Ganges; and was born again as a washerman in Ayodhyá, in which character he became the main agent in Sítá's exile, for discovering that his wife had spent some time in another man's house, he reviled, and beat her, and when his mother-in-law endeavoured to prevail upon him to forgive her daughter, he replied, "Not I. I am not the king. I am not Ráma, who took back Sítá after she had lost her character in the dwelling of the Rákshas." These words being reported to Ráma by his spies induced the king to send his wife away, and she was taken accordingly to the hermitage of Válmíki, where she bore two sons, Kuśa and Lava. This part of the work agrees in some respects with the Uttara Ráma Charitra, but has several gossiping and legendary additions. Kuśa, coming to Lava's aid, they defeat all Śatrughna's warriors, including Sugríva and Hanumán, but by their mother's injunctions they release the horse, who is then conveyed to Ayodhyá, where Sumati, the counsellor of

Śatrughna, reports to Ráma all that has happened to the party. The account of Kuśa and Lava excites Ráma's curiosity, and he sends for Válmíki to inform him who they are. This leads to his discovery of his sons and his reunion with Sítá. The Aśwamedha takes place, but at the instant when Ráma is about to slay the victim, he becomes a celestial person, being a Brahman, condemned by Durvásas, for hypocrisy, to wear the shape of a horse until released and sanctified by Ráma he goes to heaven. These details succeed an account of the reign of Kuśa, and a summary list of his successors, until the solar line ends with Sumitra in the ninety-seventh chapter. Here also closes the dialogue between Śesha and Vátsyáyana, the latter thanking the former for his narrations, and taking leave of him to wander over the earth.

The Ŕishis then ask Súta to inform them what is the sum and substance of the Puráńas. He is not allowed to answer in his own person, but repeats a dialogue between Śiva and Párvatí on the subject, which at first is a repetition of a discourse between the sage Gautama and the sovereign Ambarísha, in which the former details to the latter, at his request, the names of the eighteen Puráńas, and the number of verses contained in each. There is one important peculiarity in this list; not only is the Bhágavata placed last, but it is said, "Vyása first promulgated the Pádma, then sixteen others, and finally the Bhágavata, as the extracted substance of all the rest, which he taught in twelve Skandhas or books, to his son Śuka." The merits of the Bhágavata as the text-book of the Vaishńava faith are then eulogized, and the particulars alluded to leave no doubt of the work intended, or of the priority of the Bhágavata to the Pátála Khańda of the Pádma Puráńa.

The conversation between Sadáśiva and Párvatí is continued through all the remaining chapters, except the last. In reply to the inquiries of the latter, the former relates to her a description of Vŕindávana and some of the sports of Kŕishńa amongst the Gopís, or milk maids of Gokula, in illustration of the character of the tenth book of the Bhágavata, which is dedicated to the life of that demigod. We have, however, anecdotes not found in that work, relating to Rádhá, the favourite mistress of Kŕishńa, to the origin of the Gopís, and to the temporary transformation of Nárada and Arjuna to females. The distinguishing duties and characteristics of Vaishńavas, or followers of Vishńu, and the efficacy of the Śálagráma stone, of sectarial marks on the person, of chaplets and rosaries, of Tulasí, or sacred Basil, and of worshipping Vishńu on certain days in each month, are then detailed at some length, and this Khańda, like the other, concludes with a tolerably copious chapter of contents.

Uttara Khańda. The last section of the Pádma Puráńa. This portion is more considerable than either of the preceding, consisting of 12,000 stanzas, distributed amongst 174 chapters.

Manuscripts of this portion of the Pádma Puráńa present a variety in their arrangement; some commencing with the legend of Jalandhara, as in the case of the copy of which I possess the index, and in that from which Col. Vans Kennedy has translated that story*: whilst the copy consulted on the present occasion begins with Dilípa's going a-hunting and concludes with the narrative of Jalandhara. This order is confirmed by the Anukrama, or chapter of contents, with which the work concludes.

According to this copy, the Uttara Khańd́a commences, rather abruptly, it must be admitted, with Súta's stating that after king Dilípa had been crowned, he went forth from his capital to the chase. In the wood he met Vŕiddha Hárita, a sage, who commended his having bathed in a pool in the forest, as ablution in the month of Mágha is peculiarly efficacious; he referred Dilípa for further information on this point to the Muni Vaśisht́ha, and the king accordingly repaired to that sage for instruction. Vaśisht́ha's communications to Dilípa on the subject of various observances which are to be held sacred by the worshippers of Vishńu, and the virtue of which is illustrated by a number of legends, mostly of sectarial and comparatively recent origin, constitute the substance of this extensive but uninteresting compilation.

Vaśisht́ha first relates to Dilípa an account of Bhŕigu's residing in the Himálaya mountains, and enjoining a Vidyádhara, who has a tiger's head, to bathe in the

* [Quarterly Oriental Magazine. Calc.: 1825, Vol. IV, 243-65, and Vol. V, 1-20.]

month of Mágha, by which he gets quit of the deformity; he then repeats a story told by Dattátreya to Sahasrárjuna, of Ŕishíká, a Brahman female, who, in consequence of bathing in the month of Mágha, dwelt four thousand ages in Vaikuńt́ha, and was then born as the Apsaras Tilottamá, for the purpose of causing the mutual destruction of Sunda and Upasunda, an incident taken from the Mahábhárata*. Other legends to the same purport are then narrated, of which it will be sufficient to notice the following:—Śríkuńd́ala and Vikuńd́ala were the sons of a Vaiśya, who dissipated their property in profligate pleasures: after death, the former was sentenced to the Raurava hell, the latter to Swarga, much to his own surprise, as he had led the same abandoned life as his elder brother. He had, however, once bathed in the Jamná, in the month of Mágha, and hence proceeded his different destiny. Kánchanamáliní became an Apsaras by bathing in the month of Mágha at Prayága, and by giving the merit of three days' ablutions to a Rákshas, she liberated him from that state, and enabled him to ascend to Swarga. Five Apsarasas endeavouring to compel the son of a Muni to return their affection, were cursed by him to become Piśáchís, they reiterated the imprecation, and the youth was also changed to a Piśácha. They were all redeemed from their metamorphosis by bathing at Prayága, in the month of Mágha, by the advice of Lomaśa Ŕishi. Chitrasena, king of Drávid́a,

* [I, 7619 - 7735.]

was a pious and benevolent monarch, but unluckily, he listened to the persuasion of Śaiva ascetics, here termed Páshańdas, or heretics, who maintained that no deity but Śiva should be worshipped, and Vishńu in particular should be shunned, and the Rájá and his people were not only converted from the adoration of Vishńu to that of Śiva, but demolished the temple of the former, and threw his images into the sea. Chitrasena, on his death, was punished by a sojourn in Tartarus, and by being then born as a Piśácha. Devadyuti, a Brahman, who had gained the especial favour of Vishńu, met with the Piśácha, and recommended him both by precept and illustration, to bathe at Prayága, in the month of Mágha, which he did, and was cleansed from his inquities and transported to Swarga.

Vaśishťha next teaches Dilípa the greatest of all the Mantras, that which was imparted to Brahmá by Vishnú, by the former to Nárada, and by Nárada to the Ŕishis. This consists merely of the two names, Lakshmí and Náráyańa, in the formula 'Om Lakshmínáráyańáya Namaḣ', but it is declared to be the mystery of mysteries, and certain means of salvation. It may be communicated to all classes, to Śúdras and others, and to women, if they have faith in Vishńu. It must, however, be preceded by the ceremony of Díkshá or initiation, the essential part of which is the Tapta Mudrá, or stamping on the skin of the novice, at the part where the arms are set on to the chest, marks, with a heated iron, representing the conch and discus of Vishńu, a practice which is considered by the most respectable authorities to be a highly-reprehensible innovation.

In answer to Dilípa's inquiry in what manner Bhakti, or faith in Vishńu, is best expressed, Vaśishtha repeats, in the beginning of the twenty-sixth chapter, a conversation that occurred on Kailása, between Śiva and Párvatí, on the same topic, in which the former describes to the latter the sixteen modes in which devotion to Vishńu is to be expressed. These are 1. being branded with the conch and discus; 2. wearing the Úrddha puńdra, the perpendicular streak or streaks of white clay and red chalk on the forehead; 3. receiving the initiating Mantra with those streaks; 4. ceremonial worship; 5. silent prayer, or counting a rosary of Tulasí seeds; 6. meditation, in which the figure and symbols of Vishńu are brought to the mental vision; 7. recollecting the names of Vishńu; 8. repeating them; 9. hearing them repeated; 10. hymning Vishńu; 11. adoring his feet, or prostration before his images; 12. drinking water that has washed the feet of his images; 13. eating the remains of food offered to Vishńu; 14. unbounded service of devout Vaishńavas; 15. fasting on the twelfth lunation, and keeping it sacred; 16. wearing necklaces and chaplets of the wood or seeds of the Tulasí. In the course of Śiva's explanation of these characteristic proofs of faith in Vishńu, he relates a number of tales illustrative of their efficacy, and expatiates on the sanctity of various objects and places venerated by the Vaishńava sect.

In describing the frontal marks, Śiva mentions

several places whence the earth should be taken, and the list is remarkable for containing the names of places in the south of India, as Venkaťagiri and Śrírangam. The prayer to be used is called the Eight-syllable Mantra, or 'Om Náráyańáya namaḥ', and he who communicates it is the Achárya, no matter what his caste. The meaning of the prayer, and particularly of the term Om, is here explained in a characteristically mystical strain, and Vishńu is next described as the source and substance of all things. An account is then given of his residence, Vaikuńťha, and of his pastimes, or delusions, which are, in fact, all created beings: Vishńu, at the prayer of Mahámáyá, or Prakŕiti, combining with her as Purusha, or soul, and engendering creation. He then sports with Mahánidrá, or sleeps on the waters, when a lotus springs from his navel, from which Brahmá makes his appearance, and the world is created; a detailed description ensues of the fourfold Vyúha, or disposition of Vishńu's residences, Vaikuńťha, Vaishńava loka, or a mythical Dwáraká, the white island, or Śwetadwípa, and a palace in the sea of milk.

Śiva next relates to Párvatí an account of the Vaibhavas or manifestations, Avatáras, or descents of Vishńu; of the first, or Mátsya, it is said that Vishńu, in the form of a fish, entered the ocean and destroyed Hirańyáksha, who had assumed the shape of the Makara, differing therefore from the usual account of the descent of Vishńu as a fish. In the descent of the Tortoise, an account is given of the churning of the ocean, the chief peculiarity in which is the birth of Jyeshťhá Deví, the elder goddess, or Alakshmí, misfortune. The production of her more amiable sister, Lakshmí, prosperity, occurred on the twelfth lunation, and thence Śiva, at Párvatí's request, explains the sanctity of this and of the eleventh lunation, and the practices proper to be observed on those days. The goddess then inquires who are heretics, and the reply designates especially the followers of Śiva. Párvatí asks naturally enough how this should be, as they imitate her husbańd; and Śiva's explanation is, that he adopted the use of the skull, skin, bones, and ashes, by desire of Vishńu, to beguile Namuchi and other Daityas, who had obtained the mastery over the gods, but lost it by the heresy into which they were seduced by teachers inspired by Śiva, as Kańáda, Gautama, Śaktŕi, Upamanyu, Jaimini, Kapila, Durvásas, Mŕikańdu, Vŕihaspati, and Jamadagni, authors of works in which the quality of darkness predominates. Works of this character are then specified, and are the treatises on the Páśupata worship, or worship of Śiva, as Paśupati; Bauddha works; the Vaiśeshika, Vedánta, and Mímánsá philosophies; the Bráhma and other Puráńas, and the legal institutes of Gautama, Vŕihaspati, Samudra, Yama, Śankha, and Uśanas.

The Varáha and Nŕisinha Avatárs are then related, and in the latter we have the story of Prahláda, much in the same style as in the Vishńu P. The Vámana, or dwarf Avatára is next described at some length, and we have then the Avatára of Paraśuráma in some detail. The story of Ráma next occurs, and forms a complete epitome of the Rámáyańa, and the birth, actions, and death of Kŕishńa, agreeably to the text of the Bhágavata, are last narrated. The Avatáras of Vishńu constitute a considerable portion of the work, extending from the thirty-sixth to the seventy-second chapter.

The construction of the images of Vishńu is next described, and the places are mentioned, where the principal are erected, as Śrírangam, Káśí, Jagannátha, where the image is of wood, Badarikáśrama, Gangáságar, Dwáraká, Venkaťádri, Vŕindávan, &c. Bathing is enjoined in the Ganges, Yamuná, Śarayú, and Gańďakí, in upper India, and in the Káverí, Támraparńí, Godávarí, Kŕishná, and Narmadá, in the Dakhiń; worship is to be offered daily to Lakshmí and Náráyańa, and the mode of so doing is fully detailed. Párvatí then declares her intention of adoring Vishńu, for which Sadáśiva commends her, and repeats to her the hundred and eight names of Ráma. The two deities then devote themselves to the adoration of Vishńu, and the dialogue concludes with the seventy-fifth chapter.

The conversation is then resumed between Dilípa and Vaśishťha, and the king asks the sage how it happened that Śiva attained a form so unattractive and unlike a god. In reply the Muni tells him that at a great sacrifice made by Swáyambhuva Manu, the assembled Ŕishis discussed which of the deities was entitled to the homage of a Brahman; some said Rudra, some Brahmá, some Súrya or the sun, and some Vishńu; but they all agreed that the only being whom they ought to revere was he who was made up of the quality of goodness; and they employed Bhŕigu to visit the deities, and put their characters to the test. Bhŕigu accordingly went to Śiva, but could not obtain access to him, as he was engaged with his wife; finding him, therefore, to consist of the property of darkness, Bhŕigu sentenced him to the form of the Linga, and pronounced that he should have no offerings presented to him, nor receive the worship of the pious and respectable. His next visit was to Brahmá, whom he beheld surrounded by sages, and so much inflated with his own importance as to treat Bhŕigu with great inattention, betraying his being made up of the quality of foulness. The Muni therefore excluded him from the worship of the Brahmans. Repairing next to Vishńu, he found the deity asleep, and, indignant at his seeming sloth, Bhŕigu stamped upon his breast with his left foot and awoke him. Instead of being offended, Vishńu gently pressed the Brahman's foot, and expressed himself honoured and made happy by its contact; and Bhŕigu, highly pleased by his humility, and satisfied of his being impersonated goodness, proclaimed Vishńu as the only deity to be worshipped by men or gods, in which decision the Munis, upon Bhŕigu's report, concurred. This subject extends to the seventy-sixth chapter, and in some copies forms the concluding section. It is not the last of my copy, however, for Vaśishťha having briefly recapitulated the subjects on which he has indoctrinated Dilípa, asks him what more he desires to hear, on which Dilípa expresses a wish to be made acquainted with the Máhátmya of the Bhagavad Gítá. Vaśishtha replies by repeating another dialogue between Śiva and Párvatí, in which Śiva reports a conversation between Vishńu and Lakshmí, the former of whom describes to the latter the holiness of the composition of Vyása, called the Bhagavad Gítá, and exemplifies its sanctity by legends of individuals who were purified from sin, or released from future existence, by hearing or reading one or other of the sections of the Gítá, beginning with the first, and proceeding regularly in succession to the last. There is nothing worthy of note in these stories; they are all purely sectarial, according to Vaishńava notions. The scene of many is laid in the south of India, at Pratishtháña, on the Godávarí; at other places on that river, at Śrí Śailam, at Mahishmatí, on the Narmadá, at Haripur on the Tungabhadrá river, at Sauráshtra (city, or Surat,) in the country of Gurjara, and at other cities, said to be in the Dakhiń, but which are perhaps fabulous, as Amarddaka and Meghankuśa; Kolapur may perhaps admit of verification. The subject extends to the ninety-third chapter.

Sadáśiva then repeats to Párvatí the thousand names of Vishńu, as recited by Nárada to Bhŕigu and other sages, and the reply made by the same holy person to a number of questions put by the Ŕishis, the general purport of which is the transcendent merit of one who constantly recites the names of Vishńu, wears the sectarial marks, and addresses to Vishńu all his thoughts, words, and deeds. This part includes the Kriyá Yoga Sára Máhátmya, or the efficacy of studying a subsequent portion of the Pádma Puráńa, and therefore eulogized here rather out of its place. The whole is nothing more than a reiteration of what has been repeatedly said before, though it proceeds to the end of the one hundred and first chapter.

The subject is still further prosecuted, and the merit of worshipping Vishńu, the certain expiation of all sin thereby, and the faults by which its efficacy is impaired, are communicated to Nárada by Sanatkumára, as he had been taught them by Śiva. We have then two chapters on the unlawfulness of taking away life, consisting chiefly of an account given by Durgá of herself to Śiva, in which she ascribes her sanguinary exploits, as the death of various Asuras, to the Máyá, or illusion of Vishńu, by which those who worship him are not to be beguiled. Śiva then explains to Nárada what Bhakti or faith in Vishńu means, and what practices are incompatible with it; the various modes of worshipping Vishńu; the manner of meditating upon him, or inaudibly repeating his names; the rules of personal purification; the reverence to be shown to a Guru, or spiritual guide; the hundred and eight names of Kŕishńa, which should be repeated every morning; the mystical marks on the soles of Kŕishńa's feet, which should also be called to mind; the duty of morning ablution, and merit of washing with water in which a Śálagráma has been immersed. The subjects continue to the end of the one hundred and thirteenth chapter.

Dilípa then inquires of Vaśishtha what are the most efficacious means of obtaining final emancipation; to which the Muni replies by relating the Máhátmya of the month Kártikeya, as it was imparted to Nárada by Brahmá. In this month whatever gifts are made, whatever observances are practised, if they be in honour of Vishńu, are sure of attaining the end desired, and realizing an imperishable reward. Amongst the especially sacred acts of this month is the gift of lighted lamps. No particular day is enjoined in the section that treats of the Dípa dána Máhátmya, but the eleventh of the moon's wane is alluded to as especially appropriate, and the merit is great even if the lamps be lighted for the purpose of gambling at night in any place dedicated to Vishńu. The fourteenth and fifteenth lunations are also noted as holy days; but the general instruction is, "let a man offer lamps day and night in the month of Kártik." Some legends are narrated in illustration of this general precept, as well as of the efficacy of certain days of the month; thus, the thirteenth dark lunation is specified as the day on which Yama is to be worshipped with offerings of lamps. Bathing is enjoined early in the morning of the fourteenth and fifteenth lunations, and flowers and water are to be then also presented to Yama; lamps are to be offered at night to the deities generally. On the morning of the first light lunation or new moon, bathing is to be performed; libations are to be made to gods, men, and progenitors; the monthly obsequies are to be celebrated; Brahmans entertained; a number of lamps lighted at night in houses, gardens, cow-sheds, meetings of public roads, and holy places; and families are to keep awake through the night, and pass it in diversion, especially in games of chance. As these directions were given by Vaśishtha to a certain female, they suggest to Nárada to inquire by what means women become beautiful, fortunate, fruitful, and faithful. Brahmá tells him a story, in reply, of a lady called Subhará, who was all these, in consequence of duly observing the Sukha-rátri, the happy night which Vishńu passes with Lakshmí, and which occurs on the fifteenth of the dark half of Kártik. The ceremonies on this occasion, consisting chiefly of the worship of Mahálakshmí, and including illuminations, are to be conducted especially by women. On the first of the moon's increase, Bali the Daitya is to be worshipped in commemoration of his gifts to Vishńu, as the dwarf, which took place on that day. Kŕishńa is also to be worshipped as Gopála the cow-herd. On the second lunation, which is thence called Yama dwitíya, Yama is to be adored by those who wish to know not death; and on the eleventh the waking of Vishńu from his periodical slumbers is to be celebrated.

The account of these sacred days in the month of Kártik extends to the one hundred and twenty-sixth chapter.

The Kártika Máhátmya, however, is still considered

to be the appropriate title of this portion of the Puráńa, although most of the chapters treat of topics not exclusively relating to that month. They describe the objects of Vaishńava ceremonies and observances, which are equally sacred at other seasons, as the Dhátrí flower, the Śálagrám stone, the various kinds of Śálagrámas, the conch shell, the Tulasí plant, various perfumes, as sandal, agallochum, and different fragrant flowers, all which are peculiarly dedicated to Vishńu, and are to be worshipped or offered in worship on occasions and in modes which are particularized. A description is then given of the Bhíshma panchaka, or five days from the beginning of the eleventh to the end of the fifteenth lunation of the month of Kártik, dedicated to the worship of Bhíshma; and this properly closes the subject of the holiness of Kártik, or the Kártika Máhátmya, with the one hundred and thirty-second chapter.

In reply, however, to a question of the Ŕishis, Súta relates to them the communication of the legend of Kártika by Nárada, to the wives of Kŕishńa at Dwáraká, and a conversation that ensued between Kŕishńa and Satyabhámá, in which the divinity gives his wife an account of her former existence as the daughter of a Brahman, and her having been exalted to her present dignity in consequence of observing the ceremonies proper to the eleventh lunation of the month of Kártik. Satyabhámá asks how this month obtained its peculiar sanctity; in reply to which, Kŕishńa relates to her the story of the Asura Śankha having stolen the Vedas, and Vishńu's becoming a fish, in order to plunge into the sea and recover them. In this version of the Mátsya Avatára we have the sage Kaśyapa substituted for Satyavrata, and he throws the fish, when it is too large for the pond, into the sea: we have nothing further of a boat or a deluge—the fish kills Śankha, and brings the Vedas back to the gods. This happened in the month of Kártika, and on the eleventh day, whence bathing in that month and on that day is commemorative of this Avatára. Bathing at Prayága and Badarikáśrama are peculiarly enjoined; and then Nárada, who has been the narrator of the previous story, which Kŕishńa has only repeated, describes to Pŕithu the mode of observing the ceremonies, or the fasting, bathing, giving presents, waking, and worshipping, which should be practised in this month. These topics proceed to the one hundred and fortieth chapter. Pŕithu then asks Nárada to explain to him how the Tulasí plant became sacred to Vishńu. Nárada, in illustration, tells him a long legend of the birth, exploits, and death of Jalandhara, a person of whom no mention occurs in any other Puráńa, but whose story has been translated into English by Col. Vans Kennedy. The translation frequently varies from the text of the copy I have consulted, but the variations are not material to the narrative, and it is sufficient to refer to the translation for the details of the story—a story which, whether as it occurs in this place, or in the beginning of the work, appears extremely incongruous with its general tenour, and little, if at all, connected with what precedes or follows: occupies nine chapters: at the close it appears that Vishńu was fascinated with the beauty of Vŕindá, the wife of Jalandhara; to redeem him from which enthralment the gods applied to Lakhsmí, Gaurí, and Swadhá; each gave them seeds to sow where Vishńu was enchanted. Those given by Lakshmí came up as the Dhátrí, Málatí, and Tulasí plants, and appearing in female forms they attracted Vishńu's admiration, and diverted his affections from Vŕindá; hence the estimation in which they are to be held by all devout Vaishńavas. Nárada then relates to Pŕithu a series of stories still in illustration of the merit of acts of devotion in the month Kártik, in which again we have indications of the locality of the origin of this composition in the choice of sacred places in the Dakhiń for the scenes of the wondrous events narrated; as the Sahya mountain; Sauráshtra; the confluence of the Kŕishńa and Veńí rivers; Kánchí; the capital of a prince called Chola, king of Chola, the brother of Anantaśayana. The account winds up with a legend of the origin of the Kŕishńa, Veńí, and Kakudminí rivers, which were formed of portions of Vishńu, Śiva, and Brahmá, whilst the numerous streams of the Sahya mountain proceeded from portions of their several goddesses.

Kŕishńa and Satyabhámá appear again in the one hundred and fifty-seventh chapter, as interlocutors, and the former expatiates to the latter on the three vratas or observances which he most prizes—those of the months Kártik and Mágha, and of the Ekádaśí or eleventh lunation, throughout the year. He then explains to her the manner in which the character of an individual is affected by that of those with whom he associates, and the possibility of interchanging vices and virtues, or of transferring to others the consequences of one's own acts, a doctrine frequently advanced and illustrated in this work. He exemplifies the theory by the narrative of Dhaneśwara, a Brahman of low occupation, who goes to Máhíshmatí, in the month Kártik, to sell skins, and his business leading daily to the banks of the Narmadá, he is thrown into the company of numerous Vaishńavas—hears them constantly recite the name of Vishńu—sees them bathing and offering worship—and joins them, more out of curiosity than devotion, in their rites. Upon his death, and condemnation to Tartarus, it is found that the punishments of hell have no effect upon him, and upon inquiry into the cause, Yama learns his accidental observance of the month of Kártik: he is accordingly dismissed from the lower regions, and becomes one of the inferior divinities called Yakshas. Kŕishńa and Satyabhámá then go to perform the evening Sandhyá, and Súta and the Ŕishis resume their dialogue in chapter one hundred and sixty.

Súta now explains how the Kártika-vrata is to be observed by sick persons, or those who dwell in mountains and forests, which is illustrated by a legend of the metamorphosis of portions of Vishńu, Śiva, and Brahmá, to trees, or severally to the Aśwattha

(Ficus religiosa), Vaťa (F. Indica), and Palásá (Butea frondosa), by the curse of Párvàtí. Another legend of Daridrá, or Poverty, left by Uddálaka, a Muni, to whom she had been espoused under an Aśwattha tree, explains why that tree is to be touched only on a Sunday, for on every other day Poverty or Misfortune abides in it: on Sunday it is the residence of Lakshmí. This concludes the Kártika Máhátmya with chapter one hundred and sixty-one.

The next subject is the history of Rádhá, the favourite mistress of Kŕishńa, who is said to be Mahálakshmí, born as the daughter of the Rájá Vŕishabhánu and Śríkírttidá; she was born on the eighth of the moon's increase in the month Bhádra, and the work therefore describes the Bhádráshťamí vrata, or the ceremonies to be observed on Rádhá's birth-day, with the prayers and worship to be addressed to her and to Kŕishńa, including the catalogue of her hundred and eight appellations: similar injunctions are then given for the observance of Kŕishńa's birth-day on the eighth day of the dark half of the same month, and the three circumstances by which it is modified, as the simple Ashťamí, Rohińí, and Jayantí, or the concurrence of the asterism Rohińí with the eighth lunation and the moon's entering the constellation ad midnight, are described. The holiness of the forest of Vŕindávan, the favourite haunt of Kŕishńa and Rádhá, is the next topic, and we have then the one hundred and eight names of Annapúrńá, a form of Lakshmí. Súta then communicates to the Ŕishis the

the sanctity of another month of bathing, fasting, and worshipping Vishńu, proper to be observed in Vaiśákha, illustrating it by Vaishńava tales, showing how various persons were purified from their sins by the efficacy of acts performed in Vaiśákh. The Vaiśákha Máhátmya ends with the one hundred and seventy-second chapter. The next chapter contains the Anukrama or index, and the one hundred and seventy-fourth or last chapter consists of a panegyric upon the Uttara Khańda of the Pádma Puráńa.

The *Kriyá Yoga Sára* is always considered as a sort of supplement to the Pádma Puráńa, or as a portion of the Uttara Khańda of that Puráńa. It is divided into twenty-five chapters, and contains about 4000 stanzas. It commences with Súta's visit to Naimishárańya, where Śaunaka, on behalf of the Ŕishis, asks him to inform them how, in an age so degenerate as the Kali, religious merit may be attained, mankind being now incapable of those arduous acts of devotion which were commonly practised in more auspicious ages. Súta replies by reciting a dialogue between Vyása and Jaimini, in which Vyása, to satisfy the similar inquiries of his disciple, repeated to him the Kriyá Yoga Sára Puráńa, or Puráńa explanatory of practical devotion, in opposition to the Dhyána Yoga, or devotion of contemplation.

Practical devotion is, according to this authority, the adoration of Vishńu. It was exercised before the creation by Brahmá, upon Vishńu's destroying the demons Madhu and Kaiťabha, and the notice of this circumstance is accompanied by a brief description of the origin of the world, and the birth and destruction of the two demons.

The first act of devotion enjoined is bathing in the Ganges, or celebrating the virtues of the sacred stream, especially at three places—Haridwára, Prayága, and Gangáságara. The holiness of the river is chiefly explained by insipid and extravagant legends, of Swarga, Vaikuńt́ha, and even final liberation, being the reward of different persons, several of whom were most abandoned sinners, who were sprinkled, on their deaths, with Ganges water—who were drowned in the river—or whose bones were cast into it. These stories extend from the third to the end of the eighth section.

A series of precepts and illustrations occupies the next five chapters on the worship of Vishńu in each month of the year, describing how it is to be performed, and what recompense rewards it. The next chapters explain the merits of the simple repetition of the words Hari, Ráma, Kŕishńa, and other names of Vishńu; the efficacy of Bhakti, or faith in Vishńu; the holiness of Purushottama Kshetra, and Jagannátha; the virtue of liberality, and excellence of various kinds of gifts, with the reward that awaits donations to Vaishńavas and to Vishńu; the reverence due to Brahmans; the sanctity of the Ekádaśí, or eleventh lunation. In the story of Kot́iratha and his queen Suprajná, who faithfully observed the Ekádaśí, a description of hell, and the punishments inflicted on the damned, is given. The virtues of the Tulasí and

Dhátrí plants, and merit of planting, and cherishing them, and wearing rosaries and necklaces made of their wood, are the theme of the twenty-third chapter. The next chapter details the duties of hospitality, and the work closes with an account of the decline of virtue in the different ages, and the depravity of mankind in the Kali Yuga. That period has, however, its advantages, for the recompense of years of devotion in the preceding ages is realized by a single repitition of the name of Hari*.

There can be little doubt that the two last portions of the Pádma Puráńa have not much in common, beyond their sectarial tendency, with those by which they are preceded, and it may be questioned if there is any very close connexion even between the four first Khańďas, and whether they can be regarded as constituting one continuous work: at any rate it is clear, that neither individually nor collectively do they correspond with the description of a Puráńa, or embody a representation that can be regarded as ancient or authentic of Hindu tradition and mythology. They are all evidently the compositions of a particular sect, and for a particular purpose — authorities compiled by the Vaishńavas for the promulgation of the worship of Vishńu.

The Srishti Khańďa, or first portion of the work, is the most free from a sectarial character, and con-

---

* [Wollheim's analysis of the Kriyáyogasára in "Jahresbericht der deutschen morgenl. Ges. für 1846", p. 153-59.]

forms best to that of a Puráńa. The earlier and later chapters, indeed, treating of the creation, regal genealogies, and legends which appear to be ancient, mostly employ language used in several of the Puráńas, the original property in which it is difficult to assign to any one of them, and perhaps of right belongs to none, having been borrowed from some common source. In the case of the Pádma Puráńa, however, it is strongly to be suspected that the compiler had before him especially the Váyu, Vishńu, and Bhágavata Puráńas.

A very considerable portion of the Sŕishṫi Khańḋa is, however, as far as can be ascertained, original, although it be not Pauráńik, for it constitutes the Paushkara Máhátmyam, or the golden legend of the lake of Pushkara or Pokhar in Ajmír*, where alone Brahmá is worshipped; and it is a peculiarity of this part of the work, that its sectarianism is the worship of Brahmá rather than of Vishńu. There are some curious legends, as has been observed, of apparent struggles for supremacy between the followers of Brahmá and Śiva, in which, though the latter triumphs, yet it is at the expense of some humiliation.

The advocacy of the adoration of Brahmá, growing out of the legendary sanctity of a place dedicated to that divinity, is a probable clue to the history of the composition, and gives reason to suppose that this part of the Pádma Puráńa owes its origin to the temples at Pokhar, legends intended to enhance the merit

* [Lassen, Ind. Alt. I, 113.]

of acts of devotion at that shrine having been blended not very congruously with others taken from different sources, and embellished according to the taste of the compilers: when this is likely to have been accomplished, is a matter of some uncertainty. Pokhar is still a place of pilgrimage, and a shrine of Brahmá, but it was probably not much resorted to during the Mohammedan supremacy in the vicinity of Ajmír, and the worship of Brahmá has not been popular for some centuries at least. On the other hand, if narratives, legends, and genealogies have been borrowed literally from other Puráńas, including the Vishńu, as appears probable, we cannot go very far back for its composition.

There are also various descriptions and allusions, from which a comparatively modern origin may be inferred. Ráma is said to have recognised Śiva as the guardian of the bridge between Lanká and the peninsula, giving him the name of Rámeśwara, and the temple at that place, which still exists, must therefore have been built when the legend was written. Amongst the wives or favourites of Vishńu Rádhá is named, and her deification there is reason to believe modern. The Brahmans who live to the south of the Vindhya mountains are declared unfit to be invited to a Śráddha, or obsequial feast, an exclusion implying a difference of faith or practice, which is not to be traced in older authorities, and which was probably levelled especially at the Śaiva and Vaishńava sects of the peninsula. The followers of Śiva, who are characterized by carrying a skull, are possibly not of high antiquity; and the specification of the Jain heterodoxy, with the description of a class of their priests carrying a bunch of peacocks' feathers, are indications of no remote date. We have also frequent mention of Mlechchhas, or barbarians, and Sávitrí pronounces, in the seventeenth chapter, an imprecation upon Lakshmí, the goddess of propriety, that she shall take up her abode with them — this looks like an allusion to the presence and predominant authority of the Mohammedans when the passage was written, and there seems reason to believe that this portion of the Puráńa was compiled at some period between the establishment of the Mohammedan kingdom of Delhi in the thirteenth and the fifteenth or sixteenth century.

The Bhúmi Khańđa bears even less of the character of a Puráńa than the preceding, containing very few of those details which belong to the ancient mythological system, and being still more extensively made up of sectarial legends. Its sectarianism is Vaishńava, and is more decided than that of the Sŕishťi Khańđa. Is is less controversial and exclusive, however, and Śiva is more civilly treated, and admitted to share with Vishńu the adoration of mankind.

Brahmá is scarcely noticed at all, and then only to be identified with Vishńu.

The character of the stories which constitute the greater portion of this work, and the additions made to those narratives which are borrowed from older compositions, sufficiently evidence the absence of antiquity. We have also repeated the specification of Jain doctrines, and may therefore infer that these enjoyed some degree of popularity at the time when they were thus assailed. The locality of the Bhúmí Khańda is different from that of the Sŕisht́i, and instead of Pushkara, the places to which the greatest sanctity is attributed are situated along the Narmadá, and in central and western India. Amongst these Mahákála is specified, which may possibly be the shrine of Śiva, at Ujjayiní, that was demolished by Sultan Altmish, in 1231. A shrine of Durgá, under the name of Kámákhya, which lies in Ásám *, is also mentioned, and it may be doubted if that or several of the other Tírthas specified were in possession of celebrity at any remote era. The date of the Bhúmi Khańda then probably differs little from that of the preceding portion: it does not seem, however, to be necessarily connected with it, but to have been the work of different hands in a different part of India, and under circumstances somewhat dissimilar. It may be doubted also if it is the Bhúmi Khańda alluded to in the first chapter of the Sŕisht́i, for although it does contain a description of the earth and of sundry Tírthas, yet, as will have been seen by the abstract of its contents, they occupy but a small part of that of which, according to the specification referred to, they ought to have constituted the substance.

The opening of the Swarga Khańda with the precise

---

* [See note above, p. 48, and Lassen, Ind. Alt. III, 468 ff.]

story of the drama of Śakuntalá, shows that it is posterior to the play. The travels of Bharata appear also to be borrowed from other and probably still later originals, and their boundary, Vaikuńt́ha, the heaven of Vishńu, placed above all the other Lokas, is a later and sectarial addition to the genuine Pauráńik system. The narratives that follow do belong to the old legendary stock, but the long conversation between Mándhátŕi and Nárada, which forms the connecting thread of the latter half of the Swarga Khańd́a, is an original embellishment. The Vaishńava observances, the worship of the Śálagráma stone, the use of frontal marks, the holiness of the eleventh lunation, are not only sectarial, but, as far as has yet been ascertained, are modern, having been adopted by some of the Vaishńava sects, which sprung up after the appearance of Rámánuja in the middle of the twelfth century. We have no reason therefore to assign to this part of the Pádma Puráńa a higher antiquity than to the former, and it seems to be connected with the Bhúmi Khańd́a in order and in subject. It corresponds also well enough with the brief description given of it in the first chapter of the Sŕisht́i Khańd́a.

The Pátála Khańd́a is little else than a history of Ráma, and of his house, the details of which are, to a great extent, taken from the Raghu Vanśa, and, as already observed, in the very same words. The Puráńa is therefore more modern than the poem. The plan of the adventures of the horse turned loose for Ráma's Aśwamedha, which constitute a large portion of the Pátála Khańda, appears to be oríginal, as are most of the stories, although some of them are only embellished versions of legends to be met with elsewhere. Some of the places noticed afford a limit to the antiquity of the work. Kámákhya, as has been stated, is probably no very ancient shrine, and certainly Jagannáth has no pretensions to high antiquity. We have also the Śálagráma, the sectarial marks, and the Tulasí plant, made the subjects of repeated panegyric, and the use of these is characteristic of modern Vaishńava sects. The Bhágavata Puráńa is also named and distinctly particularized, and the Pátála Khańda of the Pádma is therefore more modern than the Bhágavata. Except the ancestors of Ráma, there are no genealogies in this Khańda, and its congruity with the description in the Sŕishńi Khańda is therefore rather questionable.

The Khańdas of the Pádma Puráńa, thus far, are Vaishńava works. The first Khańda, it is true, almost drops that character in the importance attached to Pushkara and the worship of Brahmá, but the three next are obviously written to assert the supremacy of Vishńu. There is a tolerable conformity amongst the three in the tone in which this is enforced, and they also agree in the choice of Ráma rather than of Kŕishńa for the form of Vishńu that is selected as the subject of their panegyric. It seems likely, therefore, that they are nearly cotemporary productions, and that they originated with the followers of Rámánuja, or Madhwácharya, Vaishńava teachers, in the South of India, in the twelfth century.

The moderation that pervades the injunctions of the preceding portions is no longer observed by the Uttara Khańda, and the worship of any divinity, except Vishńu, and of Śiva especially, is positively prohibited. It possesses equally little of the character of a Puráńa, and is a violent sectarial work made up for the most part of legends, invented to inculcate the exclusive worship of Vishńu, the use of distinguishing Vaishńava marks, and the sanctity of particular seasons when Vishńu should especially be propitiated. The latter subjects in the legends, or Máhátmyas, of the months Mágha and Kártik constitute the bulk of the compilation.

The main purport and evident locality of this section sufficiently illustrate the probable period of its composition within certain limits, and show that it was written when a struggle took place between the Śaivas and Vaishńavas of the Peninsula for superiority. One legend, indeed, relates to a king of Drávida, who, listening to the doctrines of heretics (Śaivas), destroyed the temples of Vishńu, and threw his images into the sea. The time at which these contests took place appears to have been about the eleventh and twelfth centuries (*Mackenzie Collection,* Introduction, LXII.)

Amongst the practices especially enjoined is the Tapta Mudrá, stamping the names of Vishńu on the skin with a hot iron, a practice not warranted by ancient texts, and introduced into the Dakhiń apparently some eight or nine centuries ago. (*As. Res.* XVI, 12.)

The principal places at which worship is addressed to Vishńu include Śrírangam and Venkaťádri, or Tripetí. The traditions of the latter acknowledge that it was a Śaiva shrine in the time of Rámánuja, who recovered it for the Vaishńavas, and, consequently, the Uttara Khańďa is posterior to that event and to the twelfth century.

The scenes of many of the legends illustrating the merit of worshipping Vishńu are laid in the South, and amongst them we have Haripur on the Tungabhadrá. In the translated index this is called Hariharapur, and whichever reading be correct, it appears probable, from its situation on the Tungabhadrá, that the capital of Vijayanagara is intended, the city of Bukka and Harihara Ráyas, which was founded in the beginning of the fourteenth century*.

These, as well as the general character of the work and its dwelling upon the sanctity of the Sálagráma stone, Tulasí plant, and other particulars, afford proof sufficiently credible, that it is not entitled to be considered as the composition of a remote period. The fifteenth century will not, in all probability, be very far from the highest antiquity to which it can lay claim.

The Kriyá Yogá Sára seems to have been suggested by the chapters of the Uttara Khańďa, which treat of practical devotion according to Vaishńava tenets. In

* [Lassen, Ind. Alt. IV, 164 ff.]

that case, it is posterior to it, and there is nothing in it inconsistent with a more modern date. Its tone is more moderate, however, and from its dilating more especially upon the holiness of the Ganges, and of Jagannátha Kshetra, and not alluding to other holy places, it differs in the locality of its origin from the other Khańdas, and is most probably the work of a Brahman of Orissa, or Bengal. The work does not appear to be known in the South of India.

From the Journal of the Asiatic Society of Bengal, Vol. I (1832), p. 81—86.

III. AGNI PURÁŃA.

THE *Agni Puráńa*, or more correctly, in a derivative form, the Ágneya Puráńa, is one of the eighteen principal Puráńas. Although, in common with the other compositions so termed, it is attributed to Vyása, it is narrated as usual by his disciple Súta, and was received by him from the Muni Vaśishtha, to whom it was communicated by Agni, whence its denomination.

According to the assertion of its own text the Ágneya Puráńa contains fourteen thousand stanzas; the Bhágavata and other authorities give it 15000 or 16,000. The copy to which this account refers has about the former number.

The text is divided into a number of small sections, according to the subject, but without any enumeration :

the number of them in the present instance amounted to 332. Colonel Wilford speaks of a supplement, and of a chapter, apparently the same, which he calls the 63rd, or last. The supplement, however, from which he derives his account of the modern princes of India up to the Mohammedan invasion, is no part of the work to which the name of Ágneya Puráńa is applied. It is clearly a distinct and subsequent composition.

The Ágneya Puráńa is interesting from the variety of the subjects of which it treats, and in which it deviates very materially from the definition given by its own reputed author of the contents of a Puráńa. These Agni declares to be five: primitive creation; subsequent creations; the genealogies of demigods and kings; the reigns of the Manus, and the histories of royal dynasties*. These, however, occur but imperfectly in the body of this work, and the far greater portion of its contents is of a widely different character.

After the usual opening the *Ágneya Puráńa* describes the ten *Avatáras*, and in the relation of those of Rámachandra and Kŕishńa follows avowedly the Rámáyańa and Mahábhárata, being consequently posterior to those works.

The ensuing chapters relate to the worship of Kŕishńa, as Náráyańa or Vishńu, this Puráńa being of the *Vaishńava* class: at the same time it leans very favourably to the worship of Śiva, as the Linga, and is full of *Tántrika* ceremonies in honor of that form

* [See above p. 1.]

of the deity. It was compiled therefore probably anterior to any wide separation between the Śaiva and Vaishńava sects, and it was undoubtedly prior to that modification of the Vaishńava faith, which pays such infinite veneration to Kŕishńa as Gopála, or Govinda, or Bála Gopála, the cowherd or the infant god; no allusion to whose worship has been found, nor has the name of his favourite mistress Rádhá once been encountered.

The ritual, including the ceremonies of the Homa, or burnt offering; the Mantras, or mystical formulæ; the Mańd́alas, or mystical diagrams; the Pavitra, or purificatory thread; the erection and consecration of temples, images, tanks, gardens, flags, jars, &c. extends through a number of chapters; it is in its general purport Vaishńava, but the Linga and several of the Tántrika forms of Durgá are also especially reverenced; Mantras are abundantly introduced, as are the acts and gesticulations with which they are muttered or recited. The style in which they are narrated is however abrupt and obscure, and the ceremonial so confusedly and indistinctly laid down, that the whole has the appearance of a string of garbled extracts rather than of a systematic detail. There is a general correspondence between these chapters with those of the Śáradá Tilaka and Mantra Mahódadhi, but it does not appear that they are identically the same.

This chapter is followed by the Bhuvana Kosha (the description of the universe,) which corresponds generally with the same in other Puráńas, but is much less explicit than in some of them. This chapter comprises the Tírthas, or places of pilgrimage, of which however it enumerates very few, and those but briefly. It is worthy of notice that the Narmadá and Śrí Śaila are especially noticed, whilst the northern mountains are not mentioned, and also that Benares is called Avimukta * in its religious character; whence it may be inferred, that the chief shrine was that of Śiva, as Avimukteśwara, not Viśweśwara, the form that has been most popular for some centuries at least. The site of Benares was the same as at present, or between the Varańá and the Así rivulets.

The Máhátmyas, or legends of the few Tírthas noticed, are very brief, except that of Gayá, which is so very minute, that it may be suspected to be an interpolation, as it is not in keeping with the rest, nor with the manner in which all such subjects are usually disposed of in a Puráńic miscellany. Such interpolations or rather appendages are not at all uncommon, although the legends are more frequently attached to some of the other Puráńas, as the Brahmáńda and Skánda. We have, however, a case in point with the Agni Puráńa; there being current in the South of India a work called the *Káverí Máhátmyam* of the Agni Puráńa, which is never fouud in the copies of the Puráńa itself, and which indeed is very nearly as extensive as the whole work of which it is called a section **.

---

* [Weber, Ind. Stud. II, 73. Daśakumára charitam, c. 4 init.]

** [Mackenzie Collection I, 67.]

The Tírthas are followed by the description of the Indian continent, and other portions of the world; also the distances and dimensions of the regions below and above it. The whole of this chapter has not been compared with other works, but in some passages, particularly the description of the sun's car, it is word for word the same with the text of the Vishńu Puráńa: being in other respects, however, much less full and satisfactory than that work.

The description of the sun and planets leads to the astronomical or astrological section, and that to magical rites and formulæ; from these the work proceeds rather apruptly to the periods of the Manwantaras, and then to the civil institutes of the Hindu caste, as birth, investiture, marriage, death, &c. the duties of the religious orders, and the contemplation of the deity, conformably to the tenets of the Vedánta: a long string of Vratas or religious obligations, both special and occasional, follows. The next subject discussed is that of gifts as religious duties, and this branch of the work finally closes with the description of corporeal austerities of a meritorious and pious complexion.

The next portion of the Ágneya Puráńa treats at considerable length, and with many interesting particulars, of the duties of princes, beginning with the ceremonies of their coronation, and comprehending their civil and military obligations; it forms what constituted the Níti of Hindu writers, (Polity or the art of government,) and is of a character with which Hindu ideas have long ceased to be familiar. Some of the details correspond accurately enough with those that occur in a passage of the Daśa Kumára*, and both are probably indebted to a common source, possibly the work ascribed to Cháńakya, cited by the author of the Daśa Kumára. As the system is wholly unmixed with foreign notions, and is purely Hindu, it can only relate to a state of things anterior to the Mohammedan invasion; it is not a necessary consequence, it is true, that the Ágneya Puráńa should bear a similar date, but it is an argument rather in favour of such a belief, and contributes with other grounds to authorize such a conclusion, if not for the whole work, for a very extensive portion.

The like genuine Hindu character belongs to the sections that follow on the shape of weapons and on archery, the phraseology and practice of which are no longer known. These sections of the Ágneya Puráńa are indeed particularly valuable, as they preserve almost, if not quite, singly, the memory of former regal and martial usages.

The chapters on the subject of judicature and law are so far curious, that they are literally the same as the text of the Mitákshará, ascribed to the Muni Yájnavalkya. The antiquity of that text is, in the estimation of the Hindus, extravagantly remote; but without reference to their belief, it is certainly not very modern, as passages have been found on inscriptions in every part of India, dated in the tenth and eleventh

* [ed. Wilson, p. 16.]

centuries. To have been so widely diffused, and to have then attained a general character as an authority, a considerable time must have elapsed, and the work must date therefore long prior to those inscriptions; at the same time; this throws little light on the period at which the Puráńa was compiled, the author of which might in any day transcribe the code of Yájnavalkya, although it is possible, that so undisguised a transfer may have preceded the time at which the legislative code was in general and extended circulation.

The chapters on law are followed by a rather miscellaneous series regarding the perusal of the Vedas, the averting of threatened ill fortune, burnt-offerings, and the worship of various deities. We have then a short but curious chapter on the branches of the Vedas; and speaking of the Puráńas, the following remarkable passage occurs: "six persons received the Puráńas from Vyása, and were his pupils; their names are Súta, Lomaharsha, Sumati, Maitreya, Śánśapáyana, and Sávarńi." These, therefore, are probably the real authors of most, if not of all the Puráńas. It is said also, that Śánśapáyana and others compiled a Sanhitá, or epitome of all the Puráńas*.

The next chapter on gifts to be made, when the Puráńas are read, contains the list of the Puráńas and the enumeration of the stanzas they contain. In this respect many differences occur from similar enumera-

* [cf. Vishńu Pur. p. 283.]

tions in other Puráńas, and the Śiva Puráńa is altogether omitted. With regard to the narrators and the chief subjects at least, in some cases, this detail varies from the text of the works as now found; these variations will be best noticed when we come to the respective Puráńas to which they relate.

The list of the Puráńas is followed by the genealogical chapters detailing the families of the Sun and Moon, but more particularly the latter, and especially the houses of Yadu and Puru to the time of Kŕishńa and the Páńdavas. These chapters agree generally with the dynasties usually detailed, but the lists are for the greater part very dry and abrupt, whilst few of the ordinary legends are preserved, and those so concisely as to be very obscure. There are some details relating to Kŕishńa of a rather remarkable character. The time at which these chapters close leaves us no inference regarding the age of the compilation.

The next subject is medicine, taken avowedly from the instruction given by Dhanwantari to Suśruta, or from the medical work attributed to the latter; the extracts are, however, very injudiciously made, with an utter disregard of method; and with a perverse selection of every thing least important: it also alludes to the classification of medicaments as hot and cold, and although it does not attach the same importance to the system as is given to it in Mohammedan medicine, yet its introduction at all is rather in favour of its being derived from such a source, for it is not certain that the ancient writers Charaka and Suśruta laid any greater stress upon these particular properties, than they are entitled to, without reference to a theoretical system. The part of the Puráńa likewise includes much mystic medicine or curing by charms.

Another set of chapters on mystic rites and formulæ follows, and on the worship of different forms of Śiva and Deví. The whole so incompatible with a Vaishńava work that it is difficult not to suppose them additions by other and perhaps later hands.

Poetry and rhetoric form the next subjects, and conform to the systems usually received: the authority of Pingala is specified. The work concludes with a grammar, omitting the verbs: the system is that of Páńini and Kátyáyana: the commentator on Páńini is cited by name. The compilation is therefore posterior to the existence of the great body of Hindu poetical compositions, and to the consummation of the grammatical construction of the Sanskrit language.

From this general sketch of the Ágneya Puráńa it is evident that it is a compilation from various works; that consequently it has no claim in itself to any great antiquity, although from the absence of any exotic materials it might be pronounced earlier, with perhaps a few exceptions, than the Mohammedan invasion. From the absence also of a controversial or sectarial spirit it is probably anterior to the struggles that took place in the 8th and 9th centuries of our era, between the followers of Śiva and Vishńu. As a mere compilation, however, its date is of little importance, except as furnishing a testimony to that of the materials of which it is composed. Many of these may pretend no doubt to considerable antiquity, particularly the legendary accounts of the Avatáras, the section on regal polity and judicature, and the genealogical chapters: how far the rest may be ancient, is perhaps questionable, for there can be little doubt that the Puráńa as it now exists, differing from its own definition of Puráńa, and comprehending such incongruous admixtures, is not the entire work as it at first stood. It is not unlikely that many chapters were arbitrarily supplied about 8 or 9 centuries ago, and a few perhaps even later; to fill up the chasms which time and accident had made in the original Ágneya Puráńa.

From the Journal of the Asiatic Society of Bengal, Vol. I, p. 217–33.

IV. BRAHMA VAIVARTTA PURÁŃA.

The *Brahma Vaivartta Puráńa* is perhaps the most decidedly sectarian work of the whole collection, and has no other object than to recommend faith in Kŕishńa and Rádhá: subservient to this purpose, it records a great variety of legends, of which no traces can be found in any of the other Puráńas, and it deals but sparingly in those which are common to all. It is of little value as a collateral authority, therefore, and most of the stories it contains are too insipid and absurd to deserve investigation. It contains, however, a few remarkable passages that bear an ancient character, and it throws more light than any similar work upon the worship of the female principle or Prakŕiti, as well as of Kŕishńa and Rádhá.

The Brahma Vaivartta is supposed to be communicated by Sauti, the son of Súta, the original narrator of the Puráńas, to Śaunaka, a sage, at an assembly of similar characters, at the forest of Naimisha, whom he happens to visit, and who ask him to relate the work. This commencement opens several of the Puráńas, and more especially the Máhátmyas or chapters descriptive of the virtues of some place or person, said to be taken from some Puráńa. In this case the Ŕishis state, as the motive of their inquiry, their dread of the evil tendency of the present age, and their desire for emancipation; and their hope to be secured in the one, and defended from the other, by being imbued with Bhakti, or faith in Hari, through the medium of the Puráńa, which they style the essence of the Puráńas, the source of faith, felicity, and final liberation, and the dissipator of the errors of the Puráńas, and the Upapuráńas, and even of the Vedas!

Sauti acquired his knowledge of this work from Vyása, by whom it was arranged in its present form, to the extent of eighteen thousand Ślokas. Vyása received the Sútra, the thread or outline of it, from Nárada, who had learnt it from Náráyańa Ŕishi, the son of Dharma, to whom it had been communicated by his father. Dharma had been made acquainted with it by

Brahmá, who had been taught it by Kŕishńa himself, in his peculiar and deathless sphere, the celestial Goloka: —a paradise, it may be observed, of which no trace occurs in any other Puráńa. The Brahma Vaivartta is so named, because it records the manifestations of the Supreme Being in worldly forms, by the interposition of Kŕishńa, who is himself the Supreme Spirit, the Parabrahma or Paramátmá, from whom Prakŕiti, Brahmá, Vishńu, Śiva, and the rest proceeded.

The Brahma Vaivartta Puráńa is divided into four books or Khańđas, the Brahma Khańđa, the Prakŕiti Khańđa, the Gańeśa Khańđa, and the Kŕishńa Janma Khańđa, treating separately of the nature and acts of the supreme; of the female personification of matter; of the birth and adventures of Gańeśa; and of the birth and actions of Kŕishńa. We shall notice the principal subjets of each division.

The *Brahma Khańđa* begins with the creation of the universe, as taking place after an interval of universal destruction. The world is described as waste and void, but the Supreme Kŕishńa, the sole existent and eternal Being, is supposed to be present, in the centre of a luminous sphere of immeasurable extent, and inconceivable splendor. From him the three qualities, crude matter, individuality, and the elements proceed; also Náráyańa or the four-armed Vishńu, in his ordinary garb and decorations, and Śankara, smeared with ashes, and armed with a trident. Náráyańa or Vishńu comes from the right, and Śiva from the left side of the primeval Kŕishńa, and Brahmá springs from his navel: all the gods and goddesses in like manner proceed from his person, and each upon his or her birth utters a short prayer or hymn in honour of him: the following are the salutations of the three principal persons of the Hindu pantheon.

Náráyańa's address to *Kŕishńa.*

"I pay reverence to the cause of causes, to him who is at once the act and the object, the superior boon, the giver and meriter, and source of blessings; who is religious austerity, and its everlasting fruit, and himself the eternal ascetic; who is beautiful, black as a new cloud; delighted in his own spirit; who is void of desire, who assumes forms at will, who annihilates the five desires, and who is the cause of desire; who is all things, the lord of all things, and the unsurpassed form, which is the seed of all things, who is embodied in the Vedas, who is the seed of them, the fruit of the Vedas, and its bestower; who is learned in the Vedas, the ritual they enjoin, and the best of all who are conversant with their doctrines."

Śiva's address.

"I adore him, the invincible, the giver, the lord and cause of victory, the best of the bestowers of victory, and victory itself; who is the lord and cause of all things, lord of the lord of all things, and cause of the cause of all things; who is present in all, who upholds all, who destroys all, generates all, who is the cause of the preservation of all, who is all things; who is the fruit, the giver of the fruit, its seed, and its support; who is identical with light, the irradiator of all, and supreme of all those who shine with divine radiance."

Brahmá's address.

"I adore Kŕishńa, who is free from the three qualities, the one imperishable Govinda, who is invisible and void of form, who is visible and assumed the shape of a cowherd, who seems a youth in years, who is of mild deportment, the beloved of the Gopís, of lovely aspect, black as a new cloud, and beautiful as a myriad of Kandarpas. Inhabiting the place of the Rása in his sojourn in the groves of Vŕindávan, the lord of the mystic dance, and its performer, and the delighter in the graces of its evolutions.

The other divinities continue in the same strain, and the tendency of the hymns furnishes a key to the whole work, the object of which is to identify the cowherd of Vŕindávan with the supreme cause of the world, or to claim for Kŕishńa a rank which the followers of Vishńu and Śiva demand, exclusively, for the object of their respective adoration: with much more reason, it must be confessed; for the actions of Kŕishńa are even still more preposterously incompatible with a divine character than those of his competitors for pre-eminence.

After the several deities are produced from various parts of Kŕishńa's person, he retires into the Rásamańdala, a chamber or stage for the performance of a kind of dance, to which the followers of this divinity attach much importance, although it seems to be no more than a kind of dramatic representation of Kŕishńa's dancing and sporting with the Gopís. There Rádhá, his favourite mistress, proceeds from his heart; from the pores of her skin spring three hundred millions of Gopís, or nymphs of Vŕindávan, and an equal number of Gopas, the swains of the preceding, originate from the pores of Kŕishńa's skin; the herds they are to attend owe their existence to the same inexhaustible source. The Rása and Rádhá, and the origin of the kine, and their keepers, male or female, are amongst the chief characteristic peculiarities of the Brahma Vaivartta Puráńa.

After Kŕishńa's thus evolving the different orders of subordinate deities, the work proceeds to describe the devotion of Śiva towards his creator, and takes this opportunity of expatiating upon the different degrees of Bhakti, or faith, and the various kinds of Mukti, or salvation.

The work of creation is then resumed by Brahmá, who begets by his wife Sávitrí a various and odd progeny, as the science of logic, the modes of music, days, years, and ages, religious rites, diseases, time, and death. He has also an independent offspring of his own, or Viśwakarmá, from his navel; the sage Sánanda, and his three brothers, from his heart; the eleven Rudras from his forehead, and sundry sages from his ears, mouth, &c.

The legends that follow relating to the daughters of

Dharma, and their marriages with various patriarchs, from whom terrestrial objects proceeded, are told in the usual strain. In describing the origin of the mixed classes of mankind, this work contains a peculiar legend, which makes a certain number of them the issue of the divine architect Viśwakarmá by Ghŕitáchí, a nymph of heaven. The chapter often occurs as a separate treatise under the title of Játi Nirńaya, and is considered as an authority of some weight with respect to the descent of the mixed tribes*, although of a purely legendary character.

The succeeding sections contain some legends of little importance, until the 16th, which is occupied with a short, but curious list of medical writers and writings. The first work on medical science entitled the Áyur Veda was, like the other Vedas, the work of Brahmá, but he gave it to Súrya, the sun, who, like the Phœbus of the Greeks, is the fountain of medical knowledge amongst the Hindus. He had sixteen scholars, to each of whom a Sanhitá or compendium is ascribed: none of the works attributed to them are now to be procured.

The chapters that next follow relate a legendary story of the wife of a Gandharva named Málavatí, the efficacy of various Mantras, the story of Nárada, the sage, and rules for the performance of daily purificatory and religious rites. The 28th and 29th chapters, the last of the book, are occupied with the description of

* [See the text in Aufrecht's Catal. Codd. Mss. Sanscrit. I, 21.]

Kŕishńa, of his peculiar heaven or Goloka, of the holy Ŕishi Náráyańa, and of his residence. The style and purport of the whole are peculiar to this Puráńa, and similar to the address of the deities cited above. Goloka is said to be situated 500 millions of Yojanas above the Lokas of Śiva and Vishńu. It is a sphere of light, tenanted by Gopas, Gopís, and cows; the only human persons admissible to its delights are pure Vaishńavas, the faithful votaries of Kŕishńa. It appears, however, that the author of this Puráńa, who in all probability is the inventor of Goloka, had no very precise notions of his own work, as he calls it in one place square, and in another round; and whilst he is content in one passage to give it the moderate diameter of 30 millions of Yojanas, he extends its circumference in another to a thousand millions.

The next section of this Puráńa is also of a peculiar character. It relates to *Prakŕiti,* the passive agent in creation, personified matter, or the goddess nature. The Puráńas in general follow in regard to their cosmogony the Sánkhya school of philosophy, in which Prakŕiti is thus described: Prakŕiti or Múla Prakŕiti is the root or plastic origin of all, termed Pradhána, the chief one, the universal material cause. It is eternal matter, undiscrete, undistinguishable as destitute of parts, inferrible from its effects, being productive, but no production*.

According to the same system, the soul is termed

* [Sánkhya Kár. 3. Colebrooke's Essays, p. 153. Vishńu Pur. p. 10.]

Purusha or Pumán, which means man or male; but the Sánkhya doctrine is twofold, one atheistical, the other theistical. The former defines the soul to be neither produced nor productive, not operating upon matter, but independent and co-existent; the latter identifies soul with Íśwara, or God, who is infinite and eternal, and who rules over the world: and it is to this latter system that the Puráńas appertain, only in this Íśwara they recognise the peculiar object of their devotion, whichever of the Hindu triad that may be, or even, as in the work before us, superadding a fourth in Kŕishńa, who is every where else regarded but as a manifestation of Vishńu, and in a remarkable passage of the Mahábhárata* is said to be no more than an Avatár of a hair plucked from the head of that divinity.

In the true spirit of mythology, which is fully as much poetical as religious, the figure of prosopopeia is carried by the Hindus to its utmost verge; and we need not wonder therefore to find spirit and matter converted by the Pauráńik bards into male and female personifications, with the attributes adapted to either sex, or derived from the original source of either representation. Prakŕiti is consequently held to be not only the productive agent in the creation of the world, but she is regarded as Máyá, the goddess of delusion, the suggester of that mistaken estimate of human existence, which is referable to the gross perceptions of

* [I, 7308.]

our elementary construction. With this character the Pauráńiks have combined another, and confounding the instrument with the action, matter with the impulse by which it was animated, they have chosen to consider Prakŕiti also as the embodied manifestation of the divine will, as the act of creation, or the inherent power of creating, co-existing with the supreme. This seems to be the ruling idea in the Brahma Vaivartta, in which the meaning of the word Prakŕiti, and the origin of this agent in creation, are thus explained:—

"The prefix Pra means pre-eminent, Kŕiti means creating; that goddess who was pre-eminent in creation is termed Prakŕiti: again, Pra means best, or is equivalent to the term Sattwa, the quality of purity, Kŕi implies middling, the quality of passion, and Ti means worse or that of ignorance. She who is invested with all power is identifiable with the three properties, and is the principal in creation, and is therefore termed Prakŕiti. Pra also signifies first or foremost, and Kŕiti creation; she who was the beginning of creation, is called Prakŕiti."

"The supreme spirit in the act of creation became by Yoga twofold, the right side was male, the left was Prakŕiti. She is of one form with Brahma. She is Máyá, eternal and imperishable. Such as the spirit, such is the inherent energy (the Śakti), as the faculty of burning is inherent in fire." *

* [The original is quoted by Aufrecht, in his Catal. Bodl. p. 22, *b* and 23, *a*.]

The idea of personifying the divine agency, being once conceived, was extended by an obvious analogy to similar cases, and the persons of the Hindu triad being equally susceptible of active energies, their energies were embodied as their respective Prakŕitis, Śaktis, or goddesses. From them the like accompaniment was conferred upon the whole pantheon, and finally upon man; women being regarded as portions of the primeval Prakŕiti. The whole being evidently a clumsy attempt to graft the distinction of the sexes as prevailing in earth, hell, and heaven, upon a metaphysical theory of the origin of the universe.

The primeval Prakŕiti, according to our authority, which now becomes wholly mythological, resolved herself, by command of Kŕishńa, into five primitive portions. These were Durgá, the Śakti of Mahádeva; Lakshmí, the Śakti of Vishńu; Saraswatí, the goddess of language; Sávitrí, the mother of the Vedas, and Rádhá, the favourite of Kŕishńa.

In the same manner as the primary creator of the world multiplies his appearances, and without losing any of his individual substance, occupies by various emanations from it different frames, so the radical Prakŕiti exists in different shapes, and in various proportions, distinguished as Anśas, portions, Kalás, divisions, and Kalánśas and Anśánśas, or subdivisions, or portions of portions. Thus Gangá, Tulasí, Manasá, Shashṫhí, and Kálí, are Anśarúpas, or forms having a portion of the original Prakŕiti; Swáhá, Swadhá, Dakshińá, Swasti, a host of virtues and vices, excellences and defects, and all the wives of the inferior deities are Kalárúpas, forms constituted of a minor division of Prakŕiti; whilst all the female race are animated by her minuter portions, or subdivisions, and they are virtuous or vicious, according as the quality of goodness, passion, or ignorance, derived from their great original, predominates in the portion of which they are respectively constituted. Women who go astray, therefore, have by this system a better excuse than the stars.

The compiler of this Puráńa is very little scrupulous as to the consistency of his narrative, and assigns to the principal goddesses other origins than that which he gives in the beginning of the Brahma Khańďa, or in the first chapter of this section. Thus Saraswatí, who came out from the mouth of Kŕishńa in the former, and in the latter is said to be one of the five subdivisions of Prakŕiti, is now described as proceeding from the tongue of Rádhá; and Lakshmí, who in one place is also a portion of Prakŕiti, and in another issues from the mind of Kŕishńa, is described in this part of the work as one of two goddesses, into which the first Saraswatí was divided; the two being Saraswatí proper, and Kamalá or Lakshmí. These incoherencies are quite characteristic of this Puráńa, which from first to last is full of contradictory repetitions, as if the writer was determined to make a large book out of a few ideas, the precise nature of which he forgot as fast as he committed them to paper.

After this account of the origin of the principal

female forms, the third chapter contains a more particular description of the sphere of Kŕishńa or Golaka. It then repeats an account of the creation of the world, through the agency of Brahmá; and the following chapters of the section are devoted to legendary stories of the principal Prakŕitis, or Saraswatí, Gangá, Tulasí, Sávitrí, Lakshmí, Swáhá, Swadhá, Dakshińá, Shashthí, Mangalá, Chańdí*, Manasá, Surabhí, Rádhiká and Durgá. In the course of these narratives various others are introduced, illustrative of the characters of gods, saints, heroes, and heroines, all tending to show the fervour with which they worshipped Kŕishńa. Accounts of Goloka, a description of hell, and an explanation of the chronological system of the Puráńas, are interwoven; besides other subjects of a peculiar and legendary nature, conveying little information or amusement.

The third section of the Brahma Vaivartta Puráńa is the *Gańeśa Khańda,* giving an account of the birth and actions of that deity, in a series of legends, which are not of frequent occurrence, and are in a great degree, if not altogether, peculiar to the work.

Párvatí after her marriage with Śiva, being without a child, and being desirous to obtain one, is desired by her husband to perform the Puńyaka Vrata. This is the worship of Vishńu, to be begun on the thirteenth day of the bright fortnight of Mágha, and con-

* [or M. and Ch. together as Mangalachańdiká, see Aufrecht's Catal. p. 24, b.]

tinued for a year, on every day of which flowers, fruits, cakes, vessels, gems, gold, &c. are to be presented, and a thousand Bráhmańas fed, and the performer of the rite is to observe most carefully a life of outward and inward purity, and to fix his mind on Hari or Vishńu. Párvatí having with the aid of Sanatkumára, as directing priest, accomplished the ceremony on the banks of the Ganges, returns after some interval, in which she sees Kŕishńa, first as a body of light, and afterwards as an old Bráhmańa, come to her dwelling. The reward of her religious zeal being delayed, she is plunged in grief, when a viewless voice tells her to go to her apartment where she will find a son, who is the lord of Goloka, or Kŕishńa, that deity having assumed the semblance of her son, in recompence of her devotions.

In compliment to this occasion, all the gods came to congratulate Śiva and Párvati, and were severally admitted to see the infant: amidst the splendid cohort was Śani, the planet Saturn, who, although anxious to pay his homage to the child, kept his eyes stedfastly fixed on the ground. Párvatí asking him the cause of this, he told her, that being immersed in meditation upon Vishńu, he had disregarded the caresses of his wife, and in resentment of his neglect she had denounced upon him the curse that whomever he gazed upon he should destroy: to obviate the evil consequences of this imprecation he avoided looking any one in the face. Párvatí having heard his story paid no regard to it, but considering, that what must be, must be, gave him permission to look at her son. Śani calling Dharma to witness his having leave, took a peep at Gańeśa, on which the child's head was severed from the body, and flew away to the heaven of Kŕishńa, where it reunited with the substance of him, of whom it was part. Durgá, taking the headless trunk in her arms, cast herself weeping on the ground, and the gods thought it decent to imitate her example, all except Vishńu, who mounted Garuḋa, and flew off to the river Pushpabhadrá, where finding an elephant asleep he took off his head, and flying back with it, clapped it on the body of Gańeśa; hence the body of that deity is crowned with its present uncouth capital. On the restoration of Gańeśa to life, valuable gifts were made to the gods and bráhmańas by the parents, and by Párvatí's father, the personified Himálaya. The unfortunate Śani was again anathematised, and in consequence of the curse of Párvatí has limped ever since.

These legends and others of minor importance, with the various prayers and addresses of the deities, occupy the first 13 chapters. The next five give an account of the birth of Kárttikeya. In the 19th and 21st chapters the reason why Gańeśa's head was lopped off is given. Śiva offended with Áditya, the sun, slew him, and although he restored him to life, incurred the wrath of the sage Kaśyapa, who doomed his (Śiva's) son to lose his head. The elephant was Indra's elephant, and was decapitated because Indra threw over his neck the garland of flowers, which the sage Durvásas gave him, and the disrespect of which, with the consequent degradation of Indra, is noticed in various Puráńas, although in all other respects with different results. Indra was no loser of an elephant by his decapitation, as Vishńu, moved by the prayers of his mate, gave him another head in place of that which he took away. The humiliation of Indra, and his recovery of Lakshmí or glory, are the subjects of the next five chapters, and the remaining half of this section is occupied with the story of Gańeśa's losing one of his tusks. It was broken off by Paraśuráma, and the occurrence therefore involves his history, and that of his ancestor Bhŕigu, the possession of the all-bestowing cow by Jamadagni, the attempt to carry her off by the king Kártavíryárjuna; the conflict that ensued, and the death of the sage; Paraśuráma's avenging his father's loss, by slaying Kártavíryárjuna; his combats with the kings, who came to the aid of that prince; and the destruction of the military race.

After this last exploit, Paraśuráma, who was a favourite disciple of Śiva, went to Kailáśa to visit his master; on arriving at the inner apartments, his entrance was opposed by Gańeśa, as his father was asleep. Paraśuráma nevertheless urged his way, and after a long and absurd dialogue, in which devotion to Kŕishńa is most abruptly and diffusely introduced, the parties came to blows. Gańeśa had at first the advantage, seizing Paraśuráma in his trunk, and giving him a twirl that left him sick and senseless; on recovering, Ráma threw his axe at Gańeśa, who recognizing it as his father's weapon (Śiva having given it to Paraśuráma) received it with all humility upon one of his tusks, which it immediately severed, and hence Gańeśa has but one tusk, and is known by the names Ekadanta and Ekadanshtŕa, (the single-tusked). Párvatí was highly incensed with Paraśuráma, and was about to curse him, when Kŕishńa, of whom he was the worshipper, appeared as a boy and appeased her indignation. This part of the work ends with a recapitulation of the names of Gańeśa, his quarrel with Tulasí, in consequence of an imprecation from whom it was that be lost one of his tusks; Paraśuráma's adoration of him, and retiring to lead an ascetic life.

The last section, the *Kŕishńa Janma Khańda*, is very voluminous, containing 132 chapters. It gives an account of Kŕishńa's birth and adventures, as narrated by Náráyańa to Nárada.

The narrative is introduced by a panegyric of the individual, who is a real Vaishńava, or thoroughly devoted to Kŕishńa: and who consequently becomes endowed with all knowledge and virtue, acquires superhuman faculties on earth, is elevated to the region of Kŕishńa after death, and liberates himself, and seven generations above and below him, from the penalty of regeneration. All crimes avoid him, or are consumed in his purity, like moths in a lamp; and any one meeting him on the road is thereby cleansed of the sins he may have contracted for seven preceding lives; no course of religious practices or devout penances is necessary to the attainment of such miraculous excellence, and the love of Hari or Kŕishńa is the only condition required. He who has received the initiatory mantra, who repeats the name of that divinity constantly, who transfers to him every worldly desire and possession, whose thoughts ever dwell upon him in prosperity or distress, and the hair of whose body stands erect with rapture on his simply hearing any of the appellations of Kŕishńa articulated, has fulfilled every obligation, and merits the designation of a Vaishńava.

According to this Puráńa, and this only, the original cause of Kŕishńa's incarnation was his love of Rádhá. The Rádhá of the Goloka had been compelled to assume a mortal body by the imprecation of a Gopa of that region, Kŕídama, the minister of his master's pleasures, and the object of Rádhá's anger. Him she condemned in a fit of jealous indignation to become the Asura Sankháchúda, and he in retaliation sentenced her to become a nymph of Vŕindávana. To console her in this condition Kŕishńa also came down to this world, as her lover; at the same time, however, granting the prayers of Brahmá and the gods, who solicited his appearance to relieve the earth from the burthen of the iniquities under which she laboured, the legitimate purpose of every descent or Avatára. In order to provide Kŕishńa and Rádhá with suitable associates, all the gods and goddesses also assumed their respective characters as Gopas and Gopís, or members of the family of Yadu, and the heroes of the Mahábhárata. Vasudeva, the father of Kŕishńa, was an incarnation of Kaśyapa, and Devakí, his mother, of Aditi.

Nanda was an incarnation of one of the Vasus, and Yaśodá of his spouse Dhará. Durgá was incarnate as the daughter of the bear Jámbaván. Jámbavatí, one of Kŕishńa's brides, and Lakshmí, multiplied herself into the sixteen thousand princesses, whom Kŕishńa enumerated amongst his wives.

The story of Vasudeva and Devakí, and the birth of Kŕishńa are narrated in the usual manner, which gives occasion to directions for the celebration of the Janmáshthamí, or festival in commemoration of the birth-day of Kŕishńa on the 8th lunation of the month Śrávań, and the Puráńa authorises its observance agreeably to the practice of the Śáktas, which allows it to be independent of the moon's entering into the asterism Rohińí, although should the position of the moon and the lunation occur together, the festival is the more holy, and is termed Jayantí or triumphant. The festival is on no account to commence on that day, in which a part of the 7th lunation may occur. The variety of doctrine and observance on this head is explained in the Asiatic Researches (vol. XVI, page 92, note). To omit the observance altogether is a crime not to be expiated, and is equal in atrocity to the murder of a hundred brahmans.

The infant exploits of Kŕishńa are next related, and require no particular comment. Garga, the Muni, points out Rádhá, the daughter of Vŕishabhánu, as an eligible bride for the youth, and acquaints Nanda, Kŕishńa's foster-father, of the secret of her divinity, in which he thus expounds her name.

"The letter R preserves persons from sin, the vowel A obviates regeneration, Dh shortens the period of mortal existence, and the second long vowel sunders all worldly bonds." The marriage was accordingly celebrated with great rejoicing, and the distribution of viands in large quantities, and the donation of immense treasures. The incompatibility of such profusion with the condition of Nanda, the cowherd, is of no consideration to the author of this work, although it has saved the author of the Bhágavata, the original of the greater part of the story, from any such gross extravagancies.

The hero of the festivities steals the curds in the next chapter, for which he is tied to a tree, and gets a whipping from his foster-mother Yaśodá. After she leaves him, the tree falls, and from it emerges Nalakuvera, the son of Kuvera, condemned to this metamorphosis for indecent behaviour in the presence of Devala[1] Muni.

A long chapter is next occupied with the praises of Rádhá by Kŕishńa and Brahmá, which inculcate her supremacy over all other divinities, male or female, and her being inseparable from and one with Kŕishńa. The sports of the juvenile god are then related, and his destruction of the demons Vaka, Keśi, and Pralamba; the construction of palaces at Gokula, for all its inhabitants, by Viśwakarmá, the divine architect, of whose architectural exploits the village of Gokula

[1] One place has Galava.

now offers no vestiges. This part of the work comprises the history of Vŕishabhánu, and his wife Kalávatí, the parents of Rádhá, and who were rewarded by her birth for the virtues of their former existence, as Suchandra, a king of the family of Manu, and Kalávatí, a will-born daughter of the Pitŕis or progenitors of mankind. This story includes a dissertation upon the virtues of women.

Several chapters follow, partly describing the actions of Kŕishńa, and partly expatiating upon his excellencies and those of Rádhá.

A legend of Sáhasika, the son of the son of Bali, follows, who was turned into an ass by the curse of Durvásas for having disturbed the meditation of that sage, in the prosecution of his amours with Tilottamá, a nymph of heaven. On the penitence of the couple, Durvásas announced to them, that the ass should be destroyed by the discus of Kŕishńa, in consequence of which the spirit of Sáhasika should receive final emancipation, and that Tilottamá should be born the daughter of Báńásura, in which capacity she should become the bride of Aniruddha, the grandson of Kŕishńa.

The marriage of Durvásas with Kadáli, the daughter of Aurva Muni, is the next legend; in this the violent temper of his wife excites the sage's wrath, and he reduces her to ashes. Repenting subsequently of his anger, and soothed by the appearance of Brahmá, he changes the remains of his wife into a plantain tree. The same sage is the subject of another legend of great celebrity amongst the Vaishńavas, as illustrating

Kríshńa's superiority over Śiva. Durvásas, a votary of that deity, being offended with Ambarísha, a devout worshipper of Vishńu, attempted to destroy him, but was repelled, and narrowly escaped destruction himself by the Chakra or discus of Vishńu, which came to the assistance of the king. The merits of fasting on the eleventh day of the fortnight are the subject of the next chapter, and they are followed by an explanation of the eight names of Durgá, which again is relieved by a story of Kríshńa, carrying away and hiding the clothes of the nymphs of Gokula, whilst they were bathing in the Jamná. He gives up his booty upon being prayed to by Rádhá, in the usual strain, eulogising his divine supremacy, and identification with all things known or unknown. Several legends of minor importance follow, to the 32nd chapter; when that, and the two following, are occupied with the advances made by Mohiní, a heavenly nymph, to Brahmá, and his insensibility, in resentment of which she curses him, that he shall not receive any adoration from mankind; the effects of which malediction are said to be evinced in the neglect which Brahmá experienced from the professors of the Hindu faith.

The attention of the work is next directed, through a series of chapters, to the legends of the Śaiva faith, or Brahmá's discomfiture by Śiva, the asceticism of the latter, his marriage with Satí, the daughter of Daksha, her burning herself, and Śiva's second marriage with Párvatí, the daughter of Himálaya. Stories of Vríshaspati, Indra, Vahni, Durvásas, and Dhanwantari then follow. All these legends are supposed to be narrated by Kŕishńa to Rádhá for her entertainment; and their general purport is to shew, that the personages to whom they refer are immeasurably inferior to Kŕishńa and his votaries.

Some cases are then recorded of the humiliation of the leading personages of the Hindu Pantheon, in consequence of their incurring the displeasure of Kŕishńa or some of his followers. Vishńu, whilst boasting himself the god of all, was swallowed by Kŕishńa in the form of a Bhairava, all but his head, and was restored to his form on recovering his senses; Brahmá, whilst making a similar vaunt, was surprised to behold multitudes of Brahmás and Brahmáńd́as, or creations distinct from himself and his works; and Śiva was condemned to pay the penalty of his pride by his marriage with Satí, and distraction for her loss, which were the delusions of Kŕishńa.

The 62nd chapter contains a summary account of Rámachandra, and the next ten proceed with an account of the transactions that immediately preceded Kŕishńa's departure from Vŕindávan for Mathurá, whither he was attracted, with his supposed father Nanda, by a special invitation from Kansa, his uncle, with a view to his destruction, at a sacrifice offered to Śiva. The result of this visit is the death of Kansa, as described in other Puráńas; but there is no detail of the previous wrestling, which occurs in the Bhágavata*.

* [X, 44, 35 ff.]

On taking final leave of his foster father Nanda, Kŕishńa favours him with a code of regulations, for his moral and religious conduct: he is not to look at a single star, nor the setting sun or moon; not to keep company with the wicked, nor to injure or insult Bráhmanas, cows, and Vaishńavas; not to delay payment of the due fees to the priest who officiates at a ceremony; not to eat flesh or fish; not to vilify Śiva, Durgá, or Gańapati; and on no account to omit every possible demonstration of his love for Hari. These injunctions extend to a great length, and are all of as little importance as the above. There are some curious denunciations, however, against acts which are lawful in the institutes of Manu; and no distinction is here made between a Brahman who follows the profession of arms, and one who marries a woman of the Śúdra caste. There is also a singular leaning shown to the Śaiva faith, and the man who forms a single Śiva-linga of clay is said to reside in heaven for 100 Kalpas. The following scale is given of Kŕishńa's affections: "Of all tribes the Bráhmańa is most esteemed by me, Lakshmí is still more beloved than a Brahman, Rádhá is dearer to me than Lakshmí, a faithful worshipper is dearer than Rádhá, and Śankara is the best beloved of all." The instructions to Nanda comprise also a dissertation upon dreams, upon knowledge of the divine nature, and on the duties of the different castes and orders of the Hindus, on the duties of women, and the expiation of offences. This division of the work extends from the 75th to the 85th chapter.

A legend of the birth of Vŕindá, the daughter of Kedára, next follows: from her, Vŕindávana, or as usually termed Bindrában, derives its appellation, she being identified with Rádhá in her birth at that place. This chapter is followed by several others of a very miscellaneous character, in which Brahmá, Śiva, and the Munis eulogise Kŕishńa's power. The next sections are occupied with the mission of Uddhava from Kŕishńa to Gokula, to bear intelligence of the latter to his parents and his mistresses; and we have then a short detail of the usual Pauráńik chronology: Uddhava returns to Kŕishńa, and we have then a narrative of Kŕishńa's being invested with the thread of his tribe; he then prosecutes his studies under Sandípaní Muni, and at their close relinquishes the garb of a cowherd for the robes of a king, presenting to his Guru four lacs of diamonds, an equal number of other sorts of gems, five lacs of pearls, a necklace worn by Durgá, dresses worth all the treasures of the world, and ten crores of Suvarńas, or certain measures of gold:—puerile exaggerations, which, although not unknown to the other Puráńas, are most lavishly multiplied in the work under review.

Although assuming a royal character, this work describes Kŕishńa as resigning the supremacy to Ugrasena, and directing Dwáraká to be built for him by the divine architect Viśwasena—a wide departure from the account every where else given of the circumstances, under which Dwáraká became the capital of Kŕishńa. He having been driven from Mathurá by Jarásandha, the father-in-law of Kansa, whom Kŕishńa had deposed and slain, Kŕishńa and his tribe, on their expulsion from Mathurá, fled to the west coast of the peninsula, and there founded a new city. No notice whatever is taken of these revolutions in this work, although they are told at some length in the Mahábhárata, Vishńu Puráńa, and Bhágavata*. In a subsequent chapter, indeed, this Puráńa refers to the same events, although it does not particularise them, and Rukmí the brother of Rukmińí reproaches Kŕishńa with having fled to Dwáraká through fear of Jarásandha.

Kŕishńa's marriage with Rukmińí is next narrated, bnt he does not carry her off, as in other authorities, Her brother opposes his entrance into the city, but is defeated by Baladeva, and then Kŕishńa enters, and is duly married to the princess in her father's presence. Every where else he runs away with her before the marriage, and Baladeva checks the pursuit.

In the next chapters a conversation between Kádhá and Yaśodá expounds the purport of eleven names of Kŕishńa, and these are succeeded by an account of the birth of Rukmińí's son Pradyumna, his being carried off by a demon, and his recovery, the birth of other sons of Kŕishńa, and marriage of the sage Durvásas to a daughter of Ugrasena. Kŕishńa's share in the war of the Mahábhárata is very briefly dispatched, except a long hymn to him by Śiśupála, whom he slew. The intrigue of Aniruddha, Kŕishńa's grandson,

* [Mahábh. II, c. 13 ff. Vishńu Pur. V. 23. Bhág. Pur. I. 10.]

with Ushá, the daughter of Váńa, is narrated at some length in the usual style, and the unsuccessful contest waged by that prince against Kŕishńa is protracted by the episodical insertion of a variety of stale legends to a disproportionate extent; these stories are related alternately by Aniruddha and Váńa, as they stand prepared to engage in single combat for the purpose of proclaiming the respective might of Kŕishńa and Śiva, Váńa being devoted to the worship of the latter divinity. Śiva however, after vainly attempting to dissuade him from the conflict, is obliged to witness his votary's defeat, with that of Skanda and Bhadrakálí, who had gone to his succour; and Váńa becoming sensible of Kŕishńa's supremacy consents to his daughter's union with Aniruddha.

The next chapters relate to the origin of the Bindusára Tírtha from the tears of Kŕishńa; the reason why it is sinful to look at the moon on the 4th day of Bhádra, and Satrájit's obtaining that gem, whose presence in a country insures its fertility. The adoration of Gańeśa by Rádhá, in the presence of the assembled deities, is the subject of the 122nd and 123rd chapters, and as acknowledged in the text, is one rarely treated of in other Puráńas. Gańeśa, not to be outdone, eulogises Rádhá in his turn, and is followed by Brahmá and Ananta. The worship of Gańeśa by Rádhá marked the termination of the curse, which had sentenced her to a mortal existence; and she was then restored to her celestial nature, in which Durgá is made to declare that there is no difference between

Rádhá and herself, and whoever speaks in a depreciating manner of either, is equally punished in hell.

Kŕishńa, having also offered worship to Gańeśa, returns to Dwáraká, and resumes his lessons to Nanda and his family; he also prophesies the depravity of the world in the succeeding or Kali age, in which men will abstain from venerating Śálagrám stones and Tulasí plants, and attach themselves assiduously to the service of Mlechhas, barbarians and outcastes, who it is said also shall become the rulers of the country:— expressions indicative of the prevalence of the Mohammedan authority, when the Puráńa was compiled.

Rádhá after this returns to Goloka, with all the Gopas and Gopís of divine origin, Kŕishńa creating others to supply their place at Vŕindávan. The circumstances of Kŕishńa's death, by a wound from a hunter, the destruction of his tribe, and the submersion of Dwáraká by the sea, are next alluded to in so brief and obscure a manner, that without a previous knowledge of what is intended the notice would be quite unintelligible; and these events are lost sight of amidst the much more detailed addresses of the gods and goddesses, the ocean, the rivers, and particularly the Ganges, in which the sufferings of the earth, in consequence of Kŕishńa's departure, are most pathetically lamented. After Kŕishńa's death the form that proceeded from his person went to the Śweta Dwípa, where it became two: one-half was Náráyańa, the lord of Vaikuńtha; the other was Kŕishńa, the deity of Goloka, the supreme indescribable source of all, who ascended to his original seat, and was reunited to Rádhá.

The Puráńa properly closes here, at the end of the 128th chapter; but Nárada, who has been its auditor, now hears from the narrator Náráyańa that he, Nárada, was in his former life a Gandharva, the husband of 50 wives, one of whom is reborn, as well as himself, and by the boon of Śiva is to be once more his bride. Nárada submits rather reluctantly, and shortly after his marriage with the daughter of Śŕinjaya, who is declared to be one with Máyá, runs away from his wife to perform penance, through which he is united with Hari.

A supplementary chapter, the 130th, follows, in which Súta, the ordinary narrator or recapitulator of the Puráńas, relates two legends, explaining the birth of Fire from Brahmá, and of gold from Fire. Chapter 131 is a short index to the Puráńas. The last chapter, 132, enumerates the different Paráńas and Upapuráńas, the five works called Páncharátra, and the five Sanhitás or compendia of the Vaishńava faith. It is also remarkable for its definition of the Mahábhárata, and the Rámáyańa, the former of which it terms an Itihása, or history, and the latter a Kávya, or poem: the work terminates with a eulogium on itself; the attentively hearing of one quarter of a verse of which is equal in merit to the gift of the heaven of Kŕishńa.

The preceding sketch of the contents and character of this work will probably have furnished sufficient evidence of its modern origin. It is clearly subsequent to the great body of Hindu literature, not only by the enumeration just noticed, but by reference to the several philosophical systems, the Tarka, Vaiśeshika, Sánkhya, Pátanjala, Mímánsá, and Vedánta, which occurs in a preceding passage. Its being the latest of the Puráńas is also apparent from its own avowal of its being intended to clear up the discrepancies observable in those works, and by the frequent assertion, that the legends it gives, particularly those respecting Gańeśa, are not to be met with in the other Puráńas. That it was compiled subsequent to the Mohammedan invasion, is very probable from the allusions it contains to the supremacy of Mlechha rulers; and the particular branch of the Hindu system which it advocates renders it likely to have emanated from a sect, which there is reason to imagine originated about four centuries ago with Vallabháchárya and the Gosáins of Gokula.

From the Journal of the Asiatic Society of Bengal, Vol. I, p.431—42.

V. VISHŃU PURÁŃA.

THE *Vishńu Puráńa*, as may be inferred from its appellation, is eminently Vaishńava, and considers Vishńu one with the Supreme Being, Parama Brahma, and Paramátmá.

It is supposed to be related by Paráśara, the grandson of Vaśishtha, to his disciple Maitreya, and dispenses with the usual machinery of Súta and the

Ŕishis; it is said in the first chapter, indeed, in the form of a prophetic enunciation by Vaśishtha, that Paráśara is the author of the Sanhitá and the Puráńas.

In other chapters, however, it is again asserted that Dwaipáyana Vyása is the author of all the Puráńas, and to reconcile these two statements recourse is had to a statement in the 3rd chapter of the 3rd section. It is said, that there is a Vyása or Veda Vyása in every Dwápara Yuga of the Vaivaswata Manwantara; of this Manwantara we are now in the 28th Kali: accordingly, 28 Dwápara Yugas have elapsed, and 28 Veda Vyásas have existed; the last is Kŕishńa Dwaipáyana, or the person usually designated as Vyása. Paráśara was the 26th Vyása, and this Puráńa is consequently the work of a preceding Maháyuga, or aggregate of four ages. The Agni Puráńa states Paráśara to be the author of the Vishńu Puráńa. In the classification adopted by itself, (book 3rd, chapter 6,) it is placed the third, after the Bráhma and Pádma.

This Puráńa is divided into six Anśas, books or sections, each being sub-divided into a varying number of Adhyáyas or chapters: it does not follow the order prescribed by the usual definition of a Puráńa, but deviates less widely than most of these compositions: according to the Agni Puráńa it contains 25,000 ślokas. A commentary on this Puráńa exists, but of no great value, except as explanatory of some of the philosophical passages*.

* [More fully described in the Preface to the Vishńu Pur., p. LXXIV.]

The first book opens with the dialogue between Maitreya and Paráśara, as already noticed. Paráśara states himself to be the son of Śakti, the son of Vaśishťha. Buchanan, from the Bhágavata, makes him the son of Upamanyu and grandson of Śakti, but the Mahábhárata* confirms the authority of the Puráńa. "The son of Śakti (Paráśara) next arrived there with his disciples." The passage of the Bhágavata on which Buchanan's statement rests, has not been found; the Bengali manuscripts generally read Śaktri instead of Śakti.

Buchanan has also noticed the incompatibility of Paráśara's genealogy with his being, as it is stated, cotemporary with Śántanu king of Hástinapur, that prince being the 44th in descent from Atri, who is cotemporary with Vaśishťha, who again is but three generations anterior to Paráśara; he supposes, therefore, that many generations in the line of Vaśishťha must have been omitted. It is not necessary, however, to attempt to reconcile these incongruities, for the coetaneous existence of Atri and Vaśishťha is less chronological than mythological, or, perhaps, as they are both enumerated amongst the stars of the great bear, astronomical; it extends throughout the Manwantara; their immediate successors, who hold a sacred character, enjoy a like longevity, and are similarly cotemporary at any period with their ancestry and posterity; if we consider them as mere mortals, we must suppose that Paráśara preceded the great war by three genera-

* [I, 6697 ff.]

tions, Kŕishńa Dwaipáyana, his son, being the father of Dhŕitaráshtra, Pańdu and Vidura by the widow of Vichitravírya. Vyása was however cotemporary with his grandson and their descendants, agreeably to the above system of saintly immortality. Mr. Bentley places Paráśara about 575 B. C. (Hindú astronomy), Buchanan about 1300 B. C. (Genealogies of the Hindús), and Wilford 1391 (A. R. IX. 87).

The first chapters of the first book of the Vishńu Puráńa contain an account of the creation, ascribing it to the association of Vishńu with Pradhána and Purusha, matter and spirit, or the female and male, or passive and active energies. During the intervals of creation, Vishńu exists independant of all connexion or attributes, and is beyond the comprehension of human faculties. When disposed to create the universe, the elements, properties, and senses generated by the two sensible combinations of the deity are collected into an egg floating on the water, in which Vishńu again, as Brahmá, is concealed, and from which he issues to separate, and arrange the constituent portions of the world: the system is therefore perfectly conformable to that anciently entertained as explained in the opening of Manu, substituting Vishńu for Brahmá.

The third chapter contains the usual divisions of time, from the twinkling of an eye to the period of a Kalpa; the fourth, an account of the Varáha Avatára, whence the Varáha Kalpa, or actual great period, derives its appellation. In the 5th chapter we have the series of creations effected by Vishńu, amounting to nine, followed by a more detailed account of the order in which the several classes of beings sprang into existence, extending through the 6th and 7th chapters.

The seventh chapter brings us to the creation of the chief characters of the Swáyambhuva Manwantara, the account of whose family is in part at least obviously an allegory. Swáyambhuva, the son of the self-existent, is married to Śatarúpá, (the hundred or many-formed, the great mother;) their children are two sons, Priyavrata (the lover of devotion), and Uttánapáda (where we are at fault), and two daughters, Prasúti (child-bearing) and Ákúti*, a name not admitting an obvious allegorical etymology. It may be observed, that the Bhágavata adds a third daughter, Devahúti (invocation of the gods), married to Kardama (soil or sin); Ákúti was married to Ruchi (light), a Prajápati, but not included in the usual enumeration of those sons of Brahmá, unless he be the same with Maríchi; their offspring were Yajna (sacrifice), and Dakshińá (donation), who, though brother and sister, were married and begot the twelve divinities called Yámas, a class whose character and office are not known. Prasúti was married to the Prajápati Daksha (ability or power); they had twenty-four daughters, all emblematical, Śraddhá, (faith,) Lakshmí, (prosperity,) Dhŕiti, (fortitude,) Tushṫi, (content,) Pushṫi, (sa-

* However another reading often occurs, usually considered, it is true, an error of the copyist, but possibly the right reading; Áhúti, invocation of the gods, prayer, or sacrifice.

tiety,) Medhá, (apprehension,) Kriyá, (action,) &c.; thirteen were married to Dharma, (equity;) of the other eleven nine were married to the nine Ŕishis, Swáhá (oblation) was wedded to fire, and the collective Pitŕis or progenitors had Śráddha, the funeral sacrifice, for their spouse: their posterity are all of the same significant character, as their appellations satisfactorily indicate. The Puráńas, in general, follow this account of the first race of created beings with some modifications and additions: the Bhágavata, as we shall hereafter see, has supplied the most copious accessions, and has introduced into the series a degree of perplexity and inconsistency that are quite foreign to the simplicity of the Vishńu Puráńa, in which we may therefore conceive the primitive notion is most faithfully represented.

The churning of the ocean for the recovery of Śrí and Amŕita or ambrosia, lost to the gods in consequence of the anger of Durvásas with Indra, is narrated in the ninth chapter, but more concisely than usual. The posterity of the Ŕishis by the daughters of Daksha follow, and we have then a long episode relating to Dhruva, the second son of Uttánapáda, who for his devotion to Vishńu was elevated to the dignity of the polar star.

The descendants of Dhruva are traced in the 13th chapter to the 6th Manu Chákshusha, and from him by Uru, Anga, and Veńa to Pŕithu, from whom the earth was named Pŕithiví: the fourth descent from Pŕithu consisted of the ten Práchetasas, and their son was Daksha the Prajápati in a new birth: this is the father of the 60 daughters, of whom 27 were the constellations, the lunar mansions, or wives of the moon, and thirteen the wives of Kaśyapa, by whom the gods and demons, men and animals, were produced. The remaining chapters of this section contain the accounts in detail of the origin of these races, from the daughters of Daksha married to Kaśyapa. The original refers these in the 21st chapter to the Swárochisha Manwantara, but this is irreconcilable with the descent of Daksha, as before mentioned, from Chákshusha Manu, and as again stated in the third book. This section of the Puráńa terminates with the division of the universe under its respective regents, and praises of Vishńu as the Supreme Being.

The second book contains the usual account of the division of the earth into Dwípas, and the formation of the seven Pátálas, and Naraka, with the situation and course of the planets and the description of their several cars: that of the sun is very fully and curiously detailed: the last chapters give a legendary account of Bharata, the object of which is to inculcate the supremacy of Vishńu, and the unreality of wordly existence, agreably to the doctrines of the Vedánta philosophy.

The third book of the Vishńu Puráńa should have formed, agreeably to the systematic classification of the contents of a Puráńa, its fourth, treating of the reigns of the different Manus and their descendants: the detail however is little more than a bare enumeration of names, the appellation of the Manu, the Indra, or king of the gods, the Gańas or classes of Devas, the seven Ŕishis, and the sons of the Manu, and who are all distinct in each Manwantara. Those of the first, sixth, and seventh periods are of the most note. In the intermediate ones little of interest occurs, and less in those that are to come. We may therefore here insert the names of the persons of these three Manwantaras.

MANU.	Swáyambhuva.	Chákshusha.	Vaivaswat.
INDRA.		Manojava.	Purandhara.
DEVATÁS.		Ádyas.	Ádityas.
		Prastútas.	Vasus.
		Bhavyas.	Rudras, &c.
		Prithugas.	
		Mahánubhavas, &c.	
ŔISHIS.	Maríchi.	Sumedhas.	Vaśishtha.
	Angiras.	Virajas.	Kaśyapa.
	Atri.	Havishmat.	Atri.
	Pulastya.	Uttama.	Jamadagni.
	Pulaha.	Madhu.	Gautama.
	Kratu.	Abhináman.	Viśwamitra.
	Vaśishtha.	Sahishńu.	Bharadhwája.
SONS.	Priyavrata.	Uru.	Ikshwáku.
	Uttánapáda.	Puru.	Nabhága.
		Śatadru.	Dhrishta.
		Tapaswí.	Śaryáti.
		Satyavatí.	Narishyanta.
		Suchi.	Bhágadheya.
		Agnishthoma.	Kárusha.
		Sadyumna.	Prishadhra.
		Abhimanyu.	Vasumat.
		Atirátra.	

In this manner the persons of the remaining seven Manwantaras are prophetically detailed.

In the next chapter of the third section occurs the enumeration of the 28 Veda Vyásas already alluded to. In the Dwápara age of every Maháyuga, or aggregate of four Yugas, a Muni or sage appears, who makes a new arrangement of these works, and is therefore called Vyása or Veda Vyása. The Vyása of the present period is Kŕishńa Dwaipáyana, the son of Paráśara, and the twenty-eighth of the series, and who, according to this authority, and the sectarial notions it advocates, is a minor descent or incarnation of Vishńu himself.

The origin of the Vedas and Puráńas is treated of in the next chapter of this section, with many curious details. The Veda, it is said, was originally a ritual, containing ample instructions for the five great sacrifices, or oblations to fire, at the full and change of the moon, and in every fourth month the offering of animals, and libation with the juice of the acid Asclepias; these five being doubled as Prakŕiti and Vikŕiti, or simple and modified, became ten, and these were the objects of the Vedas.

The mode in which Vyása is described as arranging the Veda implies its prior existence in separate portions, as he called to his assistance four persons severally acquainted with them, or Paila for the Ŕik, Vaiśampáyana for the Yajur, Jaimini for the Sáma, and Sumanta for the Atharvan. The description is not very clear, but it should seem that he made a kind of digest of the whole collectively, which he again separated according to the purport of the different passages; the Ŕik, containing the Ŕichas, or prayers used with oblations by the Hotŕi, or officiating priest; the Yajur, comprising the formulæ of the rite repeated by the Adhwaryu; the Sáma, composed of the hymns chanted by the Udgátá; and the Atharvan comprehending prayers and rites suitable for princes or the military order, repeated or conducted by the Brahmans on their behalf.

The Vishńu Puráńa then describes the different Sanhitás, or collections of the prayers and formulæ of each Veda, and their respective authors. The Ŕig was divided into two Sanhitás by Paila, who taught one to Indrapramati and the other to Váshkala, each of these and their disciples made further subdivisions. The Yajur was divided into 27 Śákhás by Vaiśampáyana, besides the other great portion of it obtained from the sun, by Vájnavalkya, which subsequently branched into fifteen divisions. The Sáma and Atharvan are in a like manner extensively subdivided. The whole of these details are curious, and indicate a period long forgotten, when the Vedas were extensively studied: the names derived from the subdivisions, as Taittirí, Vájí, &c. still designate tribes of Brahmans in some parts of India, but few of any of the separate Sanhitás are procurable. Mr. Colebrooke has made use of these sections of the Vishńu Puráńa in his account of the Vedas. (A. R. Vol. VIII.)

The origin of the Puráńas is here also ascribed indirectly to various individuals. Vyása is said to have compiled the Puráńa Sanhitá, but he gave it to Súta or Lomaharshańa, who had six disciples, Sumati, Agnivarchchá, Maitreya, Śanśapáyana, Kaśyapa, and Sávarńi; and to them Súta delivered six Sanhitás. Three of the disciples, Śanśapáyana, Kaśyapa, and Sávarńi, composed Sanhitás, also called Múla Sanhitá, and Romaharshańa compiled another. The Vishńu Puráńa, again, it may be inferred, is a subsequent compilation, at it is said to contain the substance of these four works. A list of the Puráńas is then given as usual, omitting the Váyu from the series.

The remainder of the section is occupied with the detail of the duties of the different tribes and orders, and terminates with an absurd legend called the Yama Gítá, the scope of which is to shew that the spirits of those who have faith in Vishńu are not to be approached by the messengers of the infernal monarch; it must be admitted, however, that compared with the other Puráńas the Vishńu Puráńa does not very frequently offend with legendary insipidities of this description.

The *fourth section* contains the genealogies of the royal families, commencing with the lines of the sun and moon, and terminating with the kings of the Kali age, until a modern period. This section has furnished the greater part of the materials with which Sir William Jones, Mr. Bentley, and Colonel Wilford, attempted to adjust the historical chronology of the Hindus; the latter (A. R. Vol. IX.) gives the Vishńu Puráńa as one of his authorities; the first cites a list furnished by his Pandit, but it is the same thing with one or two inaccuracies; as an example of these may be stated what he asserts of the four Káńwa princes, that they reigned 345 years, whence Sir William Jones observes, that the generations of men and reigns of kings are extended beyond the course of nature even in the present age. (A. R. II, 143.)

Adverting to the same circumstance, Mr. Bentley refers (vol. V, page 324,) the extravagant elongation of the reigns of these princes to a deliberate attempt to fill up a chasm occasioned by placing the descendants of Janamejaya at too early a period, and cites this as one of the innumerable absurdities of the modern Hindus.

Colonel Wilford again observes, these Káńwas are said to have reigned 345 years, which is still more extravagant. (Vol. IX, page 110.)

It would scarcely be supposed, that these assertions are all founded on error. In the early stage of Sir William Jones's enquiries, his trusting to his Pandit's authority may be excused; but it seems very doubtful whether Mr. Bentley or Colonel Wilford took the pains to verify that statement. At any rate, in four manuscripts of the Vishńu Puráńa, two in the Devanagarí and two in the Bengali character, instead of 345 years, the term of the united reigns of the four Káńwa princes is stated to be 45 years, a period neither extravagant nor absurd, nor beyond the course of nature.

The ancient dynasties of kings anterior to the Kali age, within the bounds of which they should no doubt be brought, can scarcely be adjusted with much consistency or satisfaction; at the same time this is a consideration rather favourable to their authenticity, as had they been the result of a systematic fabrication, they would easily have been adapted to some fixed periods, and to each other. That many inaccuracies and some falsifications have crept into these genealogies may be readily admitted; but there is no good reason to dispute the actual existence of the principal individuals commemorated, nor the general course of their ancestry or descendants. That their memory was preserved by some means anterior to the Puráńas is established by the Vishńu Puráńa. Reference is made in it repeatedly to former traditions, and old verses are cited as illustrative of the history or character of a number of the princes of whom mention is made. (Sections 8, 10, 11, 12, 13, 19, &c.)

The 11th and following chapters of this book, to the 15th, contain a detailed account of the descendants of Yadu. A curious story is interwoven into the portion that relates to Kŕishńa, of his being falsely accused of having stolen a marvellous gem, the possession of which secured wealth and prosperity to its possessor, if virtuous. It was given to Satrájit, the cotemporary, very inconsistently it must be confessed, of Kŕishńa, and his sixth ancestor, and a member of the Yádava family. Apprehending Kŕishńa's requiring the gem, Satrájit gave is to his brother, who was killed in the forest by a lion. Kŕishńa hunting killed the lion and found the jewel; he returned it to Satrájit, who gave him in requital his daughter in marriage: this led to further family dissensions, in which Kŕishńa was accused by his own brother of having underhandedly appropriated the gem to himself: he at last, however, cleared himself in an assembly of the Yádavas, and the jewel became the undisputed property of his relative Akrúra. In these transactions the character of Kŕishńa, although heightened with marvels, is of a very earthly complexion; and as to Balaráma, it is said of him by Kŕishńa that he is unfit to be master of the jewel, because he drinks wine, and is addicted to sensual pleasures. With respect to the gem, its properties of procuring plenty to the country of its possessor, and of bringing down rain when needed, ally it to the marvellous stone, for the acquisition of which the Tartar tribes not unfrequently had recourse to hostilities.

In detailing the lists of Mágadha kings the Vishńu Puráńa states, that from the birth of Paríkshit to the coronation of Nanda 1015 years elapsed. Nanda preceded Chandragupta 100 years, and Chandragupta, as identified with Sandrakoptus, ascended the throne 315 B. C. Paríkshit was the grandson of Arjuna, consequently the war of the Mahábhárata occurred 1430 years before the Christian era. Wilford reduces this by 60 years, and places the conclusion of the great war 1370 B. C.: the difference is not very material, and either date may present an approximation to the truth.

From Chandragupta to the accession of the Andhra princes three dynasties occupy an interval of 294 years: the Andhras therefore commenced their rule about 20 years before Christ, which will agree well enough with the account of the power of the Andræ, as given by Pliny, about the end of the first century of our era. According to the Puráńa, there were 30 princes, who reigned 456 years, which brings them to A. D. 436. Colonel Wilford has endeavoured to extend them, however, to the seventh century, identifying the last or Pulomarchi with the Pouloumíen of the Chinese Annals, who died in 648, according to De Guignes. (As. Res. IX, 87.) If this is correct, the Andhra dynasty must be imperfectly given. The commencement being corroborated by Pliny is apparently accurate, but we want two centuries at the termination. Wilford proposes to supply part of the deficiency, which is less in his statement, by inserting seven princes, whom he calls genuine Andhras, before the Andhrabhŕityas; but there is no warrant for this, and the number is inadequate to the interval required. There is however evident confusion here in our authority, the text and comment state expressly that the dynasty is composed of 30 princes, and yet even with the repetition of the name Śátakarńi five times, although it is probably intended in most cases as a title, we have but 27 names. Wilford's list, indeed, contains but 25 names. It is likely, therefore, that some of the names have been lost; and if we can suppose the dynasty to have comprised nearer 40 than 30 princes, we may extend the time of Pulimán, so as to be the same with that of Pouloumien.

There is another identification in this list with the Chinese history, which may be even more readily adjusted than the preceding. The annals of China record that in 408 ambassadors arrived from Yuegnai, king of Kiapilí in India, the Kapila of the Bauddhas, to which possibly the authority of the Mágadha prince as Lord paramount extended. The name of the prince is clearly Yajna, and we have a Yajna Śrí the 24th of the Andhra kings. Agreeably to the commencement of the race 20 years B. C. and the average of reigns authorised by the text, 15 years and five months, Yajna Śrí reigned about 330, or only 78 years earlier than he appears in the Chinese accounts. If indeed, as is allowable, we consider him to be the 27th prince, being the third before the last, then the agreement is almost precise; as he will have reigned from 375 to 390, and we have only to suppose his reign one of those above the average amount, to bring him to the year 408; these identifications, however, whether made out precisely or not, bear favourable testimony to the accuracy of the Hindu lists, as to the existence of the individuals about the time specified: we can scarcely expect a close concurrence in the annals of different nations, at best imperfectly known to each other*.

* [See Lassen, Ind. Alt. II, 755 f. 933 ff. Beil. II, p. XI ff. and Vishńu Pur. p. 472 ff.]

The succession of races which follows the Andhras is evidently confused and imperfect; seven distinct dynasties are detailed, extending through 1390 years, and two others through a period of 406 years: 47 princes of different tribes succeed them, to whom less than four centuries cannot be ascribed, the whole throwing the last of the Andhras back 2190 years, and computing that 4055 years of the Kali age had elapsed: the last periods, grafted probably, as Colonel Wilford has supposed, on the coetaneous existence of different dynasties at undefined intervals, are in all likelihood calculated to fill up the years expired of the Kali age, and so furnish a clue to the date of this Puráńa: if 4055 years of Kali had passed when the work was compiled, it was written 870 years ago, or in the year 954.

The notices that follow would present an interesting picture of the political distribution of India at the date at which it may be supposed the author wrote, if the passages were less obscure; at it is, considerable uncertainty pervades the description. It appears from it that the Kshatriya rule was very generally abolished, and that individuals of various castes, from Brahmans to Pulindas (mountaineers or foresters) reigned in Magadha or Behar, at Allahabad, at Mathurá, Kántipurí, Káśípurí or Kańyápurí, probably Benares or Kanouj, and in Anugangam or Gangetic Hindoostan. The Guptas, a term indicating a Śúdra family, reigned over part of Magadha, and Devarakshita, an individual so named, over the maritime provinces of Kalinga, &c. the Guhas in another part of Kalinga, the Mańidhanus in the Naimisha, Nishada, and Kálatoya countries, or the districts to the east of Benares and Bengal. Śúdras and cowherds ruled in Surat, in Mewár, along the Narmadá and at Ougein; and Mlechchhas possessed the country along the Indus, along the Chandrabhága, or in the Panjáb, Dárvika, and Kashmír*: this last statement is corroborative of the accuracy of the detail, as well as of the date assigned to the composition, as although in the middle of the tenth century, the Ghaznivide princes had not occupied Kashmír, yet they had extended their influence along the Indus, and into the upper parts of the Panjáb.

The fifth book is appropriated to the history of Kŕishńa, and is possibly a graft of more recent date than the original. Although the story is told in the usual strain, yet there is this peculiarity, that Kŕishńa is never considered as one and the same with Hari; he is only an Anśávatára or an incarnate portion of Vishńu; not a very distinguished one either, being only one of Vishńu's hairs (B. v. chapter 1.) plucked off by himself at the prayers of the gods, to become incarnate in the conception of Devakí, to be born for the purpose of alleviating the distresses of the earth.

The subsequent occurrences are related conformably to the tenor of the Bhágavata, and very differently, therefore, from that of the Bhárata; the war with Ja-

* [Lassen, l. l. II, Beilage II, p. XIX f.]

rásandha particularly, and the adventures of Kála Yavana: it also includes what may be supposed to typify some hostile struggles between the followers of Śiva and Vishńu, in the personal conflict between Kŕishńa, and the former, as taking part respectively with Aniruddha and Bánásura.

From the 34th chapter of this section, we learn that there have been spurious Kŕishńas amongst the Hindus, and Pauńdraka, the king of Benares, is described as usurping the title of Vásudeva: he is encountered by the legitimate possessor of the name, defeated and slain: his son continues the war with the aid of Śankara or the Śaivas, and it should appear at first with some success, so as to endanger Dwáraká, the capital of Kŕishńa: the allies however are repelled, and the holy city Káśí burnt by the relentless discus of the victor; the legend seems to delineate, though darkly, actual occurrences.

This book terminates with the destruction of the Yádavas; Kŕishńa's being shot through mistake by a forester, and his ascent to heaven.

The last book of the Vishńu Puráńa, after describing the divisions of time into Kalpas, &c. expatiates on the various pangs that flesh is heir to, and directs mankind to the only remedy for them, faith in Vishńu as the Supreme.

The general character of the Vishńu Puráńa will be readily conceived from this sketch of its contents: it is a sectarial work, but of a much more sober character than such works generally possess, and appropriates to legend and panegyric a comparatively insignificant portion of its contents: the geographical and astronomical systems to be found in it, are of the usually absurd complexion, but they are more succinctly and perspicuously described than perhaps in any other Puráńas: the same may be said of the genealogies, and the fourth book may be regarded as a valuable epitome of the ancient history of the Hindus.

The date of the compilation, it has already been observed, may be inferred to be as low as the middle of the tenth century: there are no other grounds for specifying the date, but the Puráńa is clearly subsequent to the development of the whole body of Hindu literature: the Vedas and their divisions are particularised, the names of all the Puráńas are given as usual, and reference is repeatedly made to the Itihása and Dharma Śástras. In the fourth section of the third book also Paráśara says: Who but Náráyańa can be the author of the Mahábhárata? It is consequently posterior to that work, in common it is most probable with all the Puráńas. Notwithstanding this recent origin, however, the Vishńu Puráńa is a valuable compilation, particularly in its being obviously and avowedly derived from more ancient materials.

From the Journal of the Asiatic Society of Bengal, Vol. I, p. 535—43.

VI. VÁYU PURÁŃA.

The *Váyu Puráńa* is so named from having been originally, it is said, communicated by Váyu, or the deity of the wind, to the assembled sages. It afterwards descended to Kŕishńa Dwaipáyana Vyása, by whom it was taught to his disciple Lomaharshańa, and at his desire it is repeated by his son Ugraśravas to the holy ascetics at Naimishárańya, agreeably to the form in which these works usually commence.

At starting, however, a peculiarity occurs: the right of Súta to the possession of the Vedas is denied, and he admits that he is entitled to teach only the Itihásas and Puráńas. This distinction is attributed to his equivocal origin which is very obscurely assigned to an error at a sacrifice held by Pŕithu, in which the Ghí appropriated to Vŕihaspati, the teacher, was confounded with that set apart for Indra, the disciple, and from the oblation, termed Sútyá, Súta was produced. He consequently held an intermediate station between the Brahman and Kshatriya, whom these gods, it may be inferred, severally represent; and whilst in one capacity he is a scholar of Vyása and a teacher of the secondary scriptures, he is excluded in the other from instructing in the Vedas, and restricted to such means of acquiring a livelihood as are compatible with the military profession.

The origin of Súta as well as of Mágadha at the sacrifice of Ṕrithu is also related in the Vishńu Puráńa*; they are there said to have sprung from the juice of the acid Asclepias, offered on that occasion. The same story opens the Śrishṫi Khańḋa of the Pádma Puráńa**, and is there more fully, if not more intelligibly detailed: the account being in fact the same as that of the Váyu Puráńa, and in the very same words, with the addition of some stanzas, and the partial alteration of others. The legend of the Váyu Puráńa is quoted in the commentary of Nílakańṫha on the Mahábhárata***.

The mixed character of the Súta is, however, more rationally explained in the works of Law. He is the son of a Kshatriya father and Bráhmańí mother, and is consequently one of the Varńa Sankara, or mixed castes. His occupations are properly of a martial character, as driving chariots and tending horses and elephants †, but as partaking of the Brahmanical order, he is also the encomiast, the herald or bard of chieftains and princes; such duty being assigned to him and the Mágadha, by Ṕrithu, the son of Veńa, and it is in this latter capacity that the Súta is the appropriate narrator of the Puráńas ††.

* [I, 13.]

** [Aufrecht, Catal. Codd. Mss. Bodl. I, 12, *a* and 46, *b*.]

*** [and in a commentary on the Vishńu Pur. I, 23, quoted in the Śabdakalpadruma s. v. sútaḣ p. 6253, b.]

† [Kull. ad Man. X, 47. Uśanaḣsanhitá 3.]

†† [Burnouf, Bhágav. Pur. I, XXV–XLI.]

The origin of the Súta, whether legendary or rational, the duties which are assigned to him, and the right conceded to him of teaching the Puráńas, seem to throw some light on the early history of these works. In all probability, they were at first the traditionary tales of a race of family poets, who corresponded precisely in character with the scalds and bards of the north, and were at once the eulogists of the chief and chroniclers of the family. In this manner some historical traditions were preserved before they were formed into any systematic account, but of course imperfectly and rudely. With the genealogies the poets blended, no doubt, fanciful and mythological fictions, and these were the materials which later writers wove into a connected form, and from which they constructed the primitive Puráńas. The character of the compilers, that of religious men, gave however a new complexion to the competition, and the mythological and marvellous portions came to usurp an undue importance, to the neglect of the historical records. The genealogies were, however, probably preserved with some more care, as they were connected with the worship of certain deities or deified princes, particularly Ráma and Kŕishńa. To the mythology also systems of cosmogony, geography, and astronomy were added, and the five divisions of the Puráńas were then complete. They were not long however suffered to continue in this condition. Contending sects arose, and each, desirous of enlisting the Puráńas on his side, foisted into them absurd and tasteless fictions, or metaphysical subtleties calculated to inculcate the worship of some individual manifestation of the Supreme. This began, there is reason to think, about the 7th and 8th centuries with the Yogís. The followers of Śaiva doctrines carried it to a great extent between the 8th and 10th centuries, and in the 11th and 12th, or after the date of Rámánuja and Madhwácharya the Vaishńava Puráńas were, there is little doubt, re-made or remodelled to a very considerable extent. By all classes, however, the historical traditions of the Sútas, or bards, were treated with neglect. They disappeared altogether from most of the Puráńas, and were in all much mutilated and compressed. Such fragments as remain are, however, probably genuine, and when separated from what is marvellous and unnatural, furnish some insight into the actual history of India in periods remotely past.

To return from this digression, however, to the Váyu Puráńa, it may be observed, that as far as can be judged from the portion analysed, it is a work perhaps of the earliest date, amongst the existing Puráńas, and clearly emanates from the Yoga school; it inculcates upon the whole the preferable worship of the forms of Śiva, but its sectarial bias is less violently displayed than is usual in these works, the legends are fewer, the cosmological parts are much more detailed, and there is altogether a copiousness and consistency of system which is not common in the Puráńas. It is impossible in going through this work not to feel an air of originality and antiquity about it, which is not perceptible in any of the others hitherto examined. As far as appears to be the case also, from the translated chapters, there is no allusion to works or systems of an indisputably modern date.

The opening chapters profess to give a summary of the contents of the work, but upon the first glance the detail is far from being applicable to the sections that follow, either in subject or arrangement; on a further examination, however, it appears that the summary is more than once repeated, with different degrees of precision, and without any sufficient mark of distinction between the end of one series and the beginning of another: this want of method is not unfrequent in Hindu works, and the first books of the Mahábhárata and Rámáyańa furnish specimens of the same defective mode of indexing. There appear to be three indexes in the first chapters of the Váyu Puráńa, of which the two first are partial and inappropriate; the third is more regular and entire, and corresponds with tolerable accuracy with the contents of the Puráńa, as far as they extend in our copy, or to the description of the Manwantaras. The index then proceeds to the families of the sages and kings, observing apparently very little order in the details, but comprising some curious particulars: as in the Vishńu Puráńa, the account is carried forward into futurity, and the kings of the present age are noticed. These historical sections are followed by cosmology, terminating with the destruction of the world at the end of a Kalpa; the Puráńa then gives the history of Vyása, and of the divisions of the Vedas; it comprises the legendary origin of Naimishárańya, and the occasion of the assemblage of the Ŕishis at that place, and concludes with an account of the incarnations of Śiva, which, if we may judge from the way in which that subject is treated in the Kúrma Puráńa*, is the succession of teachers of the Yoga doctrines. All these chapters are wanting in the only copy of the Váyu Puráńa we have been yet able to meet with. They should form the latter half of the Puráńa.

In *the fourth chapter*, the deity who existed before creation is represented as eternal, without beginning or end, and the origin of all things, comprehending within himself the two substances or attributes by whose joint operation perceptible objects were formed, or Átmá, Spirit, and Pradhána or Prakŕiti, Matter: the mode in which elementary or primitive creation was evolved from the action of these two is then described in technical language, conformable to the Sánkhya cosmogony. The seven principal elements are the Mahátattwa, Ahankára, Ákáśa, Váyu, Tejas, Ap, and Pŕithiví. The first may perhaps be termed the principle of collective animated elementary existence, and the second the principle of individual animated elementary existence, although it must be confessed, that no very distinct and definite idea appears to be any where attached to them; they may be sometimes distinguished

* [Uttarakhańda, c. 1-11. See Aufrecht, l. l. p. 8, *a*. Weber, Verzeichniss der Sanskrit-Handschriften, p. 128.]

as mind, generally and individually, or elementary intellect free from passion or emotion in the first case, and joined with it in the second. The Mahátattwa again might occasionally be rendered the Divine Spirit connected with substance, but exempt from passion, and which upon addition of the Gunas, or qualities, becomes Ahankára: the difficulty of explaining these terms satisfactorily is however inseparable from the visionary character of the existence of the things which they denominate. The other five elements, if not more intelligible, are at least more familiar to us, and though as little susceptible of definition are, with one exception, cognisable by our senses, and therefore suggest positive notions. Ákáśa is ether, a subtile element thinner than air. The other four are air, fire, water, and earth. These partially combined into an egg which lay in water, the water was invested by fire, the fire by air, the air by Ákáśa, the Ákáśa by Ahankára, the Ahankára by the Mahátattwa, and the whole by the Avyakta or imperceptible, identified with Prakŕiti or Nature; from the egg, Hirańyagarbha, the fourheaded Brahmá was produced, the immediate agent of creation, the materials of which, as far as this universe consisting of fourteen Lokas or worlds is concerned, lay concealed within the same recess from which he issued.

Brahmá, the Creator, is in fact only an embodied portion of the Rajo Guńa, the quality of passion or desire, by which the world was called into being. Rudra is the embodied Tamo Guńa, the attribute of darkness or wrath, and the destructive fire by which the universe is annihilated, and Vishńu is the embodied Sattwa Guńa, or property of mercy and goodness, by which the world is preserved; the three exist in one, and one in three; as the Veda is divided into three and is yet but one, and they are all Áśrita, or comprehended within that one being who is Parama or supreme, Guhya or secret, and Sarvátmá the soul of all things.

So far the theology of the Váyu Puráńa agrees with the deism of the Vedánta, but it presently deviates from this doctrine in the manner common to all the Puráńas, and to a purport which may be supposed to have mainly influenced the present form of these compositions. Agreeably to the Vedánta school, the Supreme Being, though of one nature with his emanations, possesses a sort of separate existence, and is always Nirguńa or void of attributes. According to the Pauráńik doctrines however, he is not merely Nirguńa, but is occasionally Saguńa or Sakalyáńa guńa, possessed of attributes, or at least of all excellent attributes. In this latter case he becomes perceptible, and appears in the form either of Vishńu or Śiva, according to the sect to which the work that so describes him appertains: his appearances are regarded as his Lílá or pastime, and in this sense, the Váyu Puráńa observes, the Paramátmá, or Yogeśwara, has engaged in various sports and consequently assumed a variety of incarnations, and is known by different names.

The successive stages of the creation of the world are enumerated as in the Kúrma Puráńa, and amount to nine. They are somewhat differently named in one or two instances, but the meaning is probably alike. The nine Sargas are the Mahat, Bhúta, Aindreyaka, Maukhya, Tairyaksrotas, Úrddhasrotas, Arváksrotas, Anugraha, and Kaumára*, or matter, the elements, the senses, the earth, animals, gods, men, goblins, and Brahmá's sons, a list agreeing with that of the Kúrma Puráńa, except in the third, which is there called the Tejassarga, or creation of light or lustre. The two works also agree in calling the three first creations Prákŕita, or elementary, and the six last Vaikŕita or secondary, the elements being only made to assume Vikŕiti or change of form.

The subject of creation is continued through the 7th and 8th chapters, and the next sections are occupied with directions to practise abstract devotion, and obtain a knowledge of the Supreme Being, interspersed with an account of the origin and duties of various sages, and the attributes and power of some of the forms of Śiva. In the eighteenth chapter commences an enumeration of the Kalpas which is continued through the 19th and 20th. Thirty-three Kalpas are mentioned, the last of which is called the Viśwarúpa or Śweta, from the prevailing form of Śiva being of a white complexion. From this circumstance it appears to be the same with the Vaishńava Váráha

* [Vishńu Pur. I, 5. Bhágav. Pur. III, 10. Márkańd. Pur. 47.]

kalpa, in which Śiva is incarnate on the mountain Chhagala as the Muni Śweta; having for his disciples Śwaita, Śwetaśikha, Śwetásya and Śwetalohita*, the same who are mentioned in the Kúrma Puráńa; the list of the Kalpas is followed by that of the Maháyugas in the present Manwantara, in each Dwápara of which, as well as a Vedavyása, there is an incarnation of Śiva, who has four sons or disciples, all Mahá-yogís and portions of the divinity. Those of the present period are Lakulí, and his sons Kuśika, Gárgya, Mitraka, and Rushťa; the scene of their Yoga is called the Káyárohańa Kshetra on mount Meru**.

The subject of creation is not yet dismissed, and blended with illustrations of Śiva's supremacy continues through several other chapters. In the 23rd chapter Brahmá and Vishńu are introduced as propitiating Mahádeva and receiving boons from his favour. To Brahmá he grants progeny; to Vishńu praise; admitting him to be along with himself the source of all things, though in an inferior degree, thus he says to Vishńu "I am Agni or fire, thou art Soma the moon; thou art the night, I the day, thou art falsehood, I am truth: thou art sacrifice, I am the fruit of it; thou art knowledge, I am that that is to be known," &c.

The origin of Rudra from Brahmá by virtue of the boon given to him, and the various appellations assigned by Brahmá to that form of Śiva are next de-

---

* [Weber, Ind. Stud. I, 421.]

** [Aufrecht, l. l., p. 53, *b*.]

tailed, and this is followed by an account of the families of the seven Ŕishis, Bhŕigu, Maríchi, Angiras, Kardama or Pulaha, Pulastya, Kratu, and Vaśishťha. Atri is not mentioned here, but his wife Anasúyá is named as the mother of Śruti, the wife of the son of Kardama or Pulaha, named also Kardama, from which alliance the patronymic Átreya is applied in the text to the descendants of that sage. The place left by Atri's exclusion is occupied by Bhŕigu, who it appears is considered as a form of Mahádeva. The descendants of Bhŕigu are called Bhárgavas, and a branch of them sprung from the grandson of Bhŕigu named Mŕikańďa are termed Márkańďeyas; the descendants of Maríchi are the Káśyapas from Kaśyapa his grand-son, the posterity of Angiras are the Ángirasas; of Pulastya the Paulastyas, of Vaśishťha the Váśishťhas, and of Kratu the pigmy sages called Bálakhilyas. These denominations and genealogical classifications, as well as several other details to be found in the same chapter, differ materially from the notions more generally received. We are not yet prepared to say how far they are peculiar to this Puráńa.

Some curious, and as far as yet known, peculiar mythology follows, describing the different kinds of Agni or fire, and particularising the Pitŕis as the same with the Ŕitus or seasons of the year. A mythological description of the divisions of time then ensues; it is clearly an attempt to allegorise the year and its divisions, in common with the worship of collective ancestors by fire; hence the year is called Agni, the seasons the Pitŕis, and the five portions of animate and inanimate creation of men, birds, beasts, reptiles, and trees, &c. are the five Ártavas, the sons of the seasons or progeny of time: the allegory however is rather perplexed, and the whole description mystified and obscure. The names given to the months and seasons here are double. One set being the usual terms, and the other being peculiar: the names of the months are the same as those cited by Sir William Jones from the Vedas, as the names of the solar months (A. R. III. 258.) The seasons as the Pitŕis are called Káśa, Agni, Jíva, Sudháván, Manyamána and Ghora.

The Pitŕis are distinguished into two classes, the Várhishadas and Agnishwáttas; these are said to have had two daughters, Mená and Dhárińí; the former became the wife of Himávat, the latter wedded Meru, and from her was descended Daksha, the mention of whom gives occasion for the narration of his celebrated sacrifice, and for a number of stanzas in praise of Śiva's supremacy.

The 30th chapter contains a very summary account of some royal dynasties, and then particularises the duration of the four ages as 12,000 years. This calculation implies that the years are years of the gods, such being the period of a Maháyuga, agreeably to Pauráńik chronology, at the same time the text does not specify what years are intended*. As analogous

---

[1] The proportion in which the years are divided are,

to the divisions of time, the Puráńa itself is here stated to consist of 12,000 stanzas; a number different from that stated in the Matsya which assigns twice that amount or 24,000 Ślokas to the Váyu Puráńa.

A number of chapters then follow, appropriated to Pauráńik geography, the description of mount Meru and the residence of the gods, the seven continents and the divisions of the universe above and below the earth; considerable portions of these chapters have been translated by the late Colonel Wilford. The Pauráńik system is here very fully and, upon the whole, distinctly detailed. The chief difficulties that occur being perhaps rather the fault of the transcript than of the original work.

The same remark applies to the chapters that follow, in which the astronomy of the Puráńas is detailed with the same minuteness as the geography: on these two topics, therefore, the Váyu Puráńa is a valuable authority.

Some of this astronomy is rather unusual, the relative sizes and situations of the planets, their cars, their steeds, and other appurtenances, and their revolving round Dhruva or the pole, to which they are attached

---

Kŕita	4800
Treta	3600
Dwápara	2400
Kali	1200
	12,000

the same is given in the Pauliśa Siddhánta, as cited by Bhaťťotpala. (A. R. XII. 249.)

by cords of air, as the potter's wheel turns on its pivot, are in all the ordinary strain; but we have a statement regarding the length of a Yuga, and the commencement of the solar year, which are not conformable to received notions, or the actual state of things. It is said, for instance, that a Yuga consists of five years; what kind of Yuga is intended is not specified. Bentley (A. R. VIII. 227) cites the Graha Manjari for a Mahá Yuga of five years, and in his last work on the ancient astronomy of the Hindus he refers the construction of a cycle of five years to what he considers the first period of Hindu astronomy, or from B. C. 1181 to 961.

This cycle it is said begins when the sun is in Śravańa, and it is again stated that Śravańa is the first of the Nakshatras, and Mágha the first of the months; according to the authority just cited, such could have been the case only beetwen the years 204 B. C. and A. D. 44. when the year began with the month Mágha. If Mr. Bentley is correct, this portion of the Puráńa at least is of considerable antiquity, whatever may be the date of the rest (Ancient Hindu Astronomy, p. 271). Mr. Bentley also adds that the mode of computation by which the commencement of the year was made to begin with a different month and asterism was entirely laid aside by the Hindu astronomers subsequent to A. D. 538.

The same chapter contains a description of the Śiśumára, which is interpreted by Mr. Davis to typify the celestial sphere (A. R. II. 402). The description is to a similar effect with that which he has translated from the Bhágavata*, but is shorter and less particular. There is also this rather unintelligible addition, that the stars of the sphere never set; but the passage may signify, that they are not annihilated at the usual periods of destruction. The text is in this place evidently incorrect, and the translation being made from a single copy, it is not safe to venture any emendation.

A legendary account of Nílakańt́ha or the blue-necked Śiva follows, and the description of the classes of the Pitŕis, and their feeding upon the lunar nectar ensues. The introduction of obsequial ceremonies and the worship of the manes appears to have originated with Pururavas, a not unlikely circumstance, and one which explains the legend of his being descended both from the sun and moon; the worship of the manes being connected with the conjunction of the luminaries. The list of Pitŕis differs in some respect from that of Manu, and from that given in a manual used by the Brahmans of Bengal, in which a verse cited from the Váyu Puráńa enumerates the following as the seven classes, Saumyas, Agnishwáttas, Varhishadas, Havishmantas, Ushmapás, and Ájyapás. In the chapter now under consideration there are but four particularised: the Saumyas or Somapás; the Kavyas or Ájyapás; the Varhishadas, and Agnishwáttas. Three others are merely named, the Ushmapás, Devakírttyas, and apparently the Lekhas and Bahwikásyas**;

* [V, 23. Vishńu Pur. II, 12.] ** [Vishńu Pur. p. 321.]

but these are unusual and probably inaccurate appellations. The whole of the section is obscure, incorrect, and often unintelligible. The same may be said of the two remaining chapters, which treat of the divisions of time and the influence of the four ages.

Without being in possession of the contents of the remaining portion, at least one-half of the Váyu Puráńa, it is impossible to offer any opinion on the date as derivable from internal testimony. As far as the portion analysed extends, it may be considered perhaps as the oldest of the actually existing Puráńas, and it has every appearance of being a genuine work, conforming more closely than any yet examined to the definition of a Puráńa, and admitting few of the unconnected digressions and legendary absurdities by which the course of these compilations is so commonly interrupted, and the established order widely disarranged or wholly obliterated.

The Váyu Puráńa is not unfrequently omitted in lists of the eighteen Puráńas, but in that case it is considered to be the same with the Śaiva Puráńa, which takes its place. As now met with, however, the two works are not identical.

II.

HINDU FICTION.

From the Oriental Quarterly Magazine. Calc., March 1824, p. 63—77.

It was intimated on a former occasion[1] that Hindu Literature included collections of domestic narrative, of an extent surpassing that of any other people, anterior to the two last centuries, and of an antiquity at the least exceeding similar compilations in any Oriental tongue; and that it was consequently probable that much of the invention displayed on the revival of letters in Europe was referable to an Indian origin. In confirmation of these opinions, the learned labours of the Baron de Sacy were then cited, and his history of the migrations of Pilpay's Fables presented to our readers. Those fables, in their former, and in their modern and more authenthic shape, are well known, and need not be here adverted to; and it will be easy to adduce other proofs of the accuracy of our sentiments.

The study of the Hindi and Bengali languages has rendered a number of persons familiar with the Sin-

---

[1] Number for April 1823.

hásan Battísí and Beitál Pachísí, or the narratives related to Bhoja by the statues which supported his throne, and the tales told to Vikramáditya by the spirit he endeavoured to make captive for the magician. Both these are originally Sanskrit, and exist in detached forms, as well as embodied with other compilations. There is also another collection of tales in which Vikrama plays a prominent part, the Vikrama Charitra; and another compilation, the Víra Charitra, has Saliváhana for its hero. The Túti Náma, or Tales of a Parrot, has a Sanskrit prototype in the Śuka Saptatí. The Kádambarí of Báńa Bhaťťa, and the Daśa Kumára of Dańďí, are collections of entertaining narratives growing out of one entire plan. A more miscellaneous compilation is the Kathárńava, or Sea of Narratives, a work in four books, of which the two first are the Beitál Pachísí and Sinhásan Battísí; and the two last contain miscellaneous stories, probably from some original no longer known. The largest and most interesting collection, however, yet met with is the Kathá Sarit Ságara, the Ocean of the Streams of Narrative, or, as more generally, though less correctly denominated, the Great Narrative, or Vŕihat Kathá. This collection is not only more important than either of the preceding, from its copiousness and variety, but because its history is well authenticated, whilst considerable uncertainty obscures their date and origin.

Somadeva, the compiler of the Vŕihat Kathá, states, at the conclusion of his work, that it was composed for the recreation of the grandmother of Harsha Deva, a pious old lady, a great patroness of the Brahmans, and a zealous worshipper of Śiva and his spouse. Harsha Deva, king of Kashmir, was the son of Kalaśa, the son of Ananta, the son of Sangráma Rájá, all in succession sovereigns of the same country. The genealogy thus given we can verify. The eighth table of the dynasties of Kashmir kings in Gladwin's Áyíni Akbarí, runs thus: Sangrama, who reigned two months; Hurray, twenty two days; Ananta, five years and five months; Kulussder, twenty six years; Ungruss, twenty two days; and Hurruss*. These names are corrupted by their twofold transfiguration, first in Persian, and then in Roman characters; but they still retain their primitive form sufficiently to be at once identifiable with the Sanskrit denominatives. Abúlfazl gives us two more princes, it is true, than Somadeva; but their joint reigns amount to but forty-four days, and they are chronologically nonentities. There was, probably, also very good reason for Somadeva's omitting them, as, if they were either infants or individuals of mature years, the shortness of the reigns indicates violence or usurpation. Taking the total period, as stated in the Áyíni Akbarí, all these princes reigned less than thirty-two years. We know from good authority, that Sangráma ascended the throne of Kashmir about 1027; and Hurruss, or Harsha, therefore, came to the crown in 1059. He reigned, according to Abúlfazl, but twelve

* [i. e. Sángráma, Hari, Ananta, Kalaśa, Utkarsha, Harsha. See Lassen, Ind. Alt. III, 1046–85. 1178.]

years, and consequently Somadeva wrote between 1059 and 1071*, if not, indeed, a few years earlier. The latter seems most probable, by the dedication to the grandmother of this prince, who, as the patron of religion, the endower of temples, and embellisher of the kingdom, must have possessed considerable authority, and was possibly regent during Harsha's minority. At any rate, however, these dates are quite sufficient to establish the priority of the compilation; and as it is also to be observed, that Somadeva takes care to call his work by that name, or a Sangraha, the materials are still older than the frame in which he has set them.

Besides the positive assertion, that he has only collected various stories, and arranged them in his own manner, Somadeva assigns a fictitious original to the whole, and represents the Vŕihat Kathá as proceeding from Śiva himself. To the original, or such part of it as was handed down, he professes to adhere, in terms which would seem to imply that there was actually a prior Sanskrit compilation known as the Vŕihat Kathá; but it may be doubted whether they are intended to assert any such fact, the fiction being part of his plan, and well enough in keeping with the character of his work. Some writers, however, amongst the Hindus, have maintained the reality of the original, and attributed it to Guńáďhya, as to an actually existing au-

* [or, according to Lassen, l. l., p. 1083, between 1090 and 1103. Troyer, Rájatarangińí III, p. 655.]

thor*. Guńáḋhya, as we shall see, is one of Somadeva's personages, and, like many of his characters, may have been derived from a substantial prototype of the author of a collection of tales: however, they must have been written in some dialect, agreeably to our guide, or what he calls the Paiśáchí Bháshá, a conclusion still hostile to the prior existence of the Vŕihat Kathá spoken of, as that is a Sanskrit composition. The fabulous origin of the stories, whatever portion of truth it may comprehend, suggests the introductory chapters of the compilation; and we shall therefore give the substance of them. We shall then proceed to the other chapters of the collection, compressing, of course, the narrative as much as possible, and omitting such anecdotes and tales as are least amusing or characteristic.

Introduction.

On the summit of Kailása, a lofty peak of the Himalaya range, resided the mighty deity Maheśwara, attended by innumerable spirits and genii, and worshipped even by the superior divinities. The daughter of the mountain monarch, and the spouse of Mahádeva, propitiated her lord by her celestial strains; and, being pleased by her adulations, he proffered her whatever boon she might request. Her only demand

* [See Prof. F. E. Hall's introduction to his edition of the Vásavadattá, Calc. 1859, p. 22 f.]

was to receive instruction from his lips, and to hear from him such narrations as were yet unknown to the immortals or herself.

In compliance with the desire of Bhavání, Śiva repeated to her the history of the worship offered him by Brahmá and Vishńu in former ages, and the favour found by the latter, on account of his wish to be accepted as a servant of Maheśwara. He also related to her the events of Daksha's sacrifice, the death of Satí, and her being born again as the daughter of the king of the snowy mountains, and once more his bride. Deví, offended, here interrupted his narration, and told him these things she was not desirous to hear: on which Śiva, giving orders that no person should be admitted, proceeded to reveal to the goddess those narratives which illustrate the felicity of the gods, the troubles of mankind, and the intermediate and varying conditions of the spirits of earth and heaven.

It happened that Pushpadanta, one of the god's principal attendants, came to the palace gate, and was refused admission by the warder. As he was a great favourite with his master, and had always ready access to his person, the refusal excited his astonishment and curiosity; and, rendering himself invisible, he passed in, determined to ascertain why entrance was so rigorously barred. In this manner having come to where Śiva and Bhavání were seated, he overheard all the marvellous stories repeated by the deity. When these were concluded, he retired as he had entered, unobserved, and going home communicated the narratives to his wife Jayá, it being impossible to keep wealth or secrets from a woman. Jayá, equally unable to preserve silence, communicated what she had heard to her fellow attendants on Párvatí; and the affair soon became known to the goddess and her lord. As the punishment of impertinence, Pushpadanta was condemned to a human birth, and his friend Málayaván, who presumed to intercede for him, was sentenced to a like fate. Being, however, subdued by the distress of Jayá, the offended goddess fixed a term to their degradation, and thus spake: When Pushpadanta, encountering a Yaksha, who has been doomed by Kuvera to haunt the Vindhya mountains as a goblin, shall recollect his original condition, and shall repeat the tales he has rashly overheard, the curse shall no more prevail. So saying, she ceased, and the two culprits instantly, like a flash of lightning, blazed and disappeared.

After a due interval, Málayaván was born at Pratishṫha[1], under the name Guńáḋhya, and Pushpadanta at Kauśámbí[2], as Vararuchi. The latter, when ar-

---

[1] [or Pratishṫhána] the capital of Śáliváhana, supposed to be the same with Pattan, or Pyetan, on the Godávarí. [Lassen, Ind. Alt. II, 884 ff.]

[2] Kauśámbí succeeded Hástinapur as the capital of the emperors of India. Its precise site has not been ascertained, but it was probably somewhere in the Doáb, or at any rate not far from the west bank of the Jamná, as it bordered upon Magadha, and was not far from the Vindh hills. Hamilton thinks it probable, that the ruins which have been called those of Hástinapur are

rived at years of discretion, found the goblin follower of Kuvera at Vindhya Vásiní[1], and recollecting his origin, repeated to him the seven great narratives of Śiva, each comprehending a hundred thousand verses: he also gave him the history of his mortal adventures.

Story of Vararuchi.

I was born at Kauśámbí, the son of a Brahman, named Somadatta, who died whilst I was a child, and left my mother, Vasudattá, in indigence with the charge of my education. Whilst struggling with distress, it chanced that two Brahmans, named Indradatta and Vyáďi, stopped at our dwelling, and solicited hospitality for the night, as they were strangers, and

---

those of Kauśámbí, as the former city was carried away by the Ganges before the latter was built. The concluding assertion, however, wants authority, as the Vishńu Puráńa and the Vŕihat Kathá merely notice the removal of the capital, without stating any cause. It is said, that there are ruins at Karári, or Karáli, about 14 miles from Alláhábád, on the west road, which may indicate the site of Kauśámbí; and in Cooseah, another stage on the road, we may trace an affinity to the name. It is not impossible, also, that the mounds of rubbish about Kurrah may conceal some vestiges of the ancient capital — a circumstance rendered the more probable by the inscription found there, which specificies Kaťa, as comprised within Kauśámba mańďala, or district of Kauśámbí. — As. Res. IX, 433. [Lassen, Ind. Alt. III, 201. Vivien de Saint-Martin in "Mémoires sur les contrées occidentales". Paris: 1858, II, 352.]

[1] Still a celebrated shrine of Durgá, a short distance from Mirzapur.

weary with long travel. They were received. Whilst sitting together, we heard a drum, and my mother exclaimed, in a tone of regret, Your father's friend, boy, the actor Navananda, holds some representation. I replied, Do not be vexed, mother, I will go to see what is exhibited, and will bring every word to you. This vaunt astonished our guests, who, to try my memory, recited the Prátiśákhya[1], which I immediately after repeated to them. They then accompanied me to the play, of which I repeated every speech to my mother, on our return home. One of the Brahmans, Vyáḍi*, then addressed my mother, and told her I was the person of whom he was in search.

It appeared that he and Indradatta were born at Vetasa, cousins, and were both left orphans at an early age. They were after a time commanded in a dream to seek for a preceptor at Páṭaliputra, in a Brahman, named Varsha; and the youths repairing thither discovered him, but found him an idiot. They ascertained, however, that in consequence of a special boon conferred upon him by Kumáraswámí[2], he was endowed with every science, under a condition to impart it only to a Brahman, who should retain the whole upon once hearing the lesson. As neither of these

---

[1] A short section of the Vedas [or, more strictly, "a collection of phonetic rules peculiar to one of the different branches of the four Vedas." Müller, Anc. Sanskrit Lit., p. 119.]

* [On *Vyáḍi* comp. Goldstücker, Páṇini. London: 1861, p. 210 ff. and Weber, Ind. Stud., V, 127 ff.]

[2] The deity Kártikeya.

Brahmans were gifted with such retentive faculties, they were accordingly in search of one so qualified, through whose intermediation they might be instructed in all that Varsha was competent to teach.

Having obtained my mother's assent, Vyádi and Indradatta conducted me with them to the dwelling of Varsha. There the gifted Brahman repeated to us the whole of the Vedas, and their dependent sciences. This repetition sufficed for me, and when I had once more gone over the subject, Vyádi acquired his lesson. His communication of it again to Indradatta fixed it in the recollection of the latter. The circumstances were speedily noised abroad; and Nanda[1], who then reigned at Pátaliputra, hearing of them, adopted Varsha as the object of his munificence, and enabled him to spend the remainder of his days in affluence and ease. The defects of his understanding were also dissipated, and he became a teacher of great repute.

Origin of Pátaliputra.

The capital of Nanda, Pátaliputra, was a place of great sanctity, being the favoured shrine of Lakshmí and Saraswatí. Its origin is thus narrated. A Brah-

---

[1] The contemporary existence of Nanda with Vararuchi and Vyádi is a circumstance of considerable interest in the literary history of the Hindus, as the two latter are writers of note on philological topics. Vararuchi is also called in this work Kátyáyana, who is one of the earliest commentators on Pánini. Nanda is the predecessor, or one of the predecessors of Chandra-

man from the south, whilst engaged on a pilgrimage to Kanakhala, near Gangádwára[1], died, and left three sons. They subsequently repaired to Rájagŕiha[2] for instruction, and thence removed to Chinchiní, a city on the sea shore, south from the shrine of Kumára Swámí. They were kindly entertained by Bhojika, a Brahman, who gave them his three daughters in marriage. After a time, the country was afflicted by famine; and the three husbands, deserting their wives, set off to seek their fortunes elsewhere. Talents and relationship touch not the hearts of the wicked. The wife of the second brother proved pregnant, and was delivered of a son, whose helpless situation attracted the pity, and propitiated the guardian care of Deví and Śiva. The first effect of this powerful patronage was the discovery, by the women, of an immense treasure, which being judiciously expended, elevated the boy to princely possessions. By the advice of his grandfather's friend, and his own guardian Yajnadatta, Putraka, as the lad had been named, distributed publicly

---

gupta, or Sandrocoptos; and consequently the chief institutes of Sanskrit grammar are thus dated from the fourth century before the Christian era. We need not suppose that Somadeva took the pains to be exact here; but it is satisfactory to be made acquainted with the general impression of a writer, who has not been biassed in any of his views by Pauráńik legends and preposterous chronology. [Weber, l. l., V, 143. Müller, l. l., 240-43.]

[1] The modern Haridwár, and village of Kankhal near it. [Saint-Martin, l. l., III, 347.]

[2] The ancient capital of Magadha, or Behár, the ruins of which were described in our number for July.

splendid gifts, at various seasons, to the Brahmans, in the hope of attracting and discovering his father. The scheme succeeded, and the three brothers returned to claim their wives, and interest in the young Rájá. The claim was joyfully recognized; but the evil propensities of the fraternity prevailing over natural affection, they conspired the death of the prince, and his own father led him into a temple, where he left him to be murdered by assassins, covertly stationed for the purpose. The murderers were, however, induced, by the intreaties and presents of Putraka, to let him escape, and he fled into the forests. His father and uncles met the fate that ever attends the ungrateful[1]: the officers of the young Rájá accused them of having killed him, and falling upon the culprits, sacrificed them to his memory.

In the mean time, Putraka, whilst wandering in the woods, beheld two men struggling with each other. He enquired who they were. They replied, that they were the sons of Mayásur, and were contending for a magic cup, staff, and pair of slippers: the first of which yielded inexhaustible viands, the second generated any object which it delineated, and the third transported a person through the air. The strongest of the two was to possess these articles. Putraka then observed

---

[1] We may here observe, once for all, that the stories of the Kathá Sarit Ságara are constantly interspersed with pithy maxims of sound morality. The expression here is Kŕitaghnánám Śivam kutaḿ, "whence (should be) the prosperity of the ungrateful?"

to them, that violence was a very improper mode of settling their pretensions, and that it would be better they should adjust the dispute by less objectionable means. He therefore proposed, that they should run a race for the contested articles, and the fleetest win them. They agreed, and set off. They were no sooner at a little distance, than Putraka, putting his feet into the slippers, and seizing the cup and staff, mounted into the air, and left the racers to lament in vain their being outwitted.

Putraka alighted at a city called Ákarshiká, and took up his residence with an old woman, from whom he received accounts of the beauty of the king's daughter, whose name was Pátali. Having in consequence formed an intimacy with the princess, he carried her off, and alighted on the bank of the Ganges, where tracing the walls and buildings of a city with his staff, a stately town immediately arose. The people attracted to this place he maintened by the stores of his cup; and the place, named after his bride and himself Pátaliputraka, became the capital of a mighty empire[1].

Story of Vararuchi continued.

Whilst residing with my preceptor, I became acquainted with his niece Upakośá, at the festival of In-

---

[1] The famous and much disputed city of Palibothra. [V. de Saint-Martin, étude sur la géographie Grecque et Latine de l'Inde. Paris: 1858. p. 489–47.] We may attach what credit we please to this account of its origin. The marvellous properties of the cup

dra; and as we were inspired by mutual affection, we were soon married, with the consent of our relations. After having enjoyed the felicity of a wedded life some short time, I was induced to relinquish it, and repair to the Himálaya Mountains.

Amongst the pupils of Varsha was a Brahman, named Pánini, a fellow of remarkable dullness, and so incapable of learning, that he was at last expelled from the classes. Deeply sensible of this disgrace, he had recourse to devotion; and setting off to the snowy mountains, propitiated Śiva by a course of severe austerities, in consequence of which the god communicated to him the system of grammar which bears his name. Returning in triumph, he challenged me to a public disputation, and we argued on an equality for seven days: on the eighth the discussion was interrupted by a hideous noise, which disconcerted me and my abettors, and left Pánini without a competitor. From this time his grammar supplanted mine, and In-

---

and slippers will have, no doubt, struck our readers as fictions with which they have long been familiar. The story is told almost in the same words in the Behár Dánish, a purse being substituted for the rod; and Jehándár obtains possession of them in a very similar manner. Weber (Eastern Romances, Introd. 39,) has noticed the analogy which the slippers bear to the cap of Fortunatus. The inexhaustible purse, although not mentioned here, is of Hindu origin also; and a fraudulent representative of it makes a great figure in one of the stories of the Daśa Kumára [ch. 2. See also L. Deslongchamps, Essay sur les Fables Indiennes. Paris: 1838, p. 35 f. and Grässe, Sagenkreise des Mittelalters. Leipzig: 1842, p. 191 f.]

dra's and all others, and we were compelled to acknowledge his superiority.

The degradation I thus experienced poisoned all my enjoyments. I determined therefore to have recourse to the origin of my humiliation, and by acquiring the favour of Mahádeva, regain my lost distinction. I therefore departed to the mountains, leaving to Upakośá the management of our affairs.

Story of Upakośá, the Wife of Vararuchi.

Whilst I was thus absent, my wife, who performed with pious exactitude her ablutions in the Ganges, attracted the notice and desires of several suitors, especially of the king's domestic priest, the commander of the guard, and the young prince's preceptor, who annoyed her by their importunities, and terrified her by their threats, till at last she determined to expose and punish their depravity.

Having fixed upon the plan, she made an appointment for the same evening with her three lovers, each being to come to her house an hour later than the other. Being desirous of propitiating the gods, she sent for our banker the obtain money to distribute in alms; and when he arrived, he expressed the same passion, as the rest, on her compliance with which he promised to make over to her the money that I had placed in his hands; or on her refusal he would retain it to his own use. Apprehending the loss of our property, therefore, she made a similar assignation with him; and desired him to come to her house that evening, at an hour when she calculated on having disposed of the first comers, for whose reception, as well as his, she arranged with her attendants the necessary preparations.

At the expiration of the first watch of the night, the Preceptor of the prince arrived. Upakośá affected to receive him with great delight; and after some conversation, desired him to take a bath which her handmaids had prepared for him, as a preliminary condition to any further intimacy. The Preceptor made not the least objection, on which he was conducted into a retired and dark chamber, where his bath was ready. On undressing, his own clothes and ornaments were removed, and in their place a small wrapper given to him, which was a piece of cloth smeared with a mixture of oil, lamp black, and perfumes, Similar cloths were employed to rub him with after bathing, so that he was of a perfectly ebon colour from top to toe. The rubbing occupied the time till the second lover, (the Priest,) arrived, on which the women exclaimed, "Here is our master's particular friend—in, in here, or all will be discovered;" and hurrying their victim away, they thrust him into a long and stout wicker basket, fastened well by a bolt outside, in which they left him to meditate upon his mistress.

The Priest and the Commander of the guard were secured, as they arrived, in a similar manner; and it only remained to dispose of the Banker. When he made his appearance, Upakośá, leading him near the baskets, said aloud, You promise to deliver to me my husband's property; and he replied: The wealth your husband entrusted to me shall be yours. On which she turned towards the baskets, and said, Let the gods hear the promise of Hirańyagupta. The bath was then proposed to the banker. Before the ceremony was completed, the day began to dawn, on which the servants desired him to make the best of his way home, lest the neighbours should notice his departure; and with this recommendation they forced him, naked as he was, into the street. Having no alternative, the banker hastened to conceal himself in his own house, being chased all the way by the dogs of the town.

As soon as it was day, Upakośá repaired to the palace of Nanda, and presented a petition to the king against the banker for seeking to appropriate the property entrusted to him by her husband. The banker was summoned. He denied having ever received any money from me. Upakośá then said: When my husband went away, he placed our household gods in three baskets; they have heard this man acknowledge his holding a deposit of my husband's, and let them bear witness for me. The king, with some feeling of surprise and incredulity, ordered the baskets to be sent for; and they were accordingly produced in the open court. Upakośá then addressed them: Speak, gods, and declare what you overheard this banker say in our dwelling. If you are silent, I will unhouse you in this presence. Afraid of this menaced exposure, the tenants of the baskets immediately exclaimed,

"Verily, in our presence, the banker acknowledged possession of your wealth." On hearing these words, the whole court was filled with surprise; and the banker, terrified out of his senses, acknowledged the debt, and promised restitution.

The business being adjusted, the king expressed his curiosity to see the household divinities of Upakośá, and she very readily complied with his wish. The baskets being opened, the culprits were dragged forth by the attendants, like so many lumps of darkness. Being presently recognized, they were overwhelmed with the laughter and derision of all the assembly. As soon as the merriment had subsided, Nanda begged Upakośá to explain what it all meant, and she acquainted him with what had occurred. Nanda was highly incensed, and, as the punishment of their offence, banished the criminals from the kingdom. He was equally pleased with the virtue and ingenuity of my wife, and loaded her with wealth and honours. Her family were likewise highly gratified by her conduct, and she obtained the admiration and esteem of the whole city [1].

---

[1] This story occurs in Scott's additional Arabian Nights, as the Lady of Cairo, and her four Gallants [and in his "Tales and Anecdotes." Shrewsbury: 1800, p. 136, as the Story of the Merchant's wife and her suitors.] It is also one of the Persian Tales, that of Arouya [day 146 ff.] It is a story of ancient celebrity in Europe, as Constant du Hamel, or La Dame qui attrapa un Prêtre, un Prevot et un Forestier. [Legrand d'Aussy, Fabliaux et Contes. Paris: 1829, Vol. IV, 246–56.] It is curious that the Fabliau alone

Story of Vararuchi—continued.

I now returned from my sojourn in the Snowy Mountains, where by the favour of Śiva I had acquired the Páńiníya grammar. This I communicated to my preceptor Varsha, as the fruit of my penance; and as he wished to learn a new system, I instructed him in that revealed by Swámí Kumára. Vyáḋi and Indradatta then applied to Varsha for like instruction; but he desired them first to bring him a very considerable present. As they were wholly unable to raise the sum, they proposed applying for it to the king, and requested me to accompany them to his camp, which was at that time at Ayodhyá. I consented, and we set off.

When we arrived at the encampment, we found everybody in distress, Nanda being just dead. Indradatta, who was skilled in magic, said: This event need not disconcert us; I will transfuse my vitality into the lifeless body of the king. Do you, Vararuchi, then solicit the money: I will grant it, and then resume my own person, of which do you, Vyáḋi, take charge till the spirit returns[1]. This was assented to, and our companion accordingly entered the carcase of the king.

---

agrees with the Hindu original, in putting the lovers out of the way, and disrobing them by the plea of the bath.

[1] This forms the leading event of the story of Fadlallah, in the Persian Tales. The dervish there avows his having acquired the faculty of animating a dead body from an aged Brahman in the Indies.

Story of Yogananda.

The revival of Nanda caused universal rejoicing. The minister Śakaťála alone suspected something extraordinary in the resuscitation. As the heir to the throne, however, was yet a child, he was well content, that no change should take place, and determined to keep his new master in the royal station. He immediately, therefore, issued orders that search should be made for all the dead bodies in the vicinage, and that they should forthwith be committed to the flames. In pursuance of this edict, the guards came upon the deserted carcase of Indradatta, and burning it as directed, our old associate was compelled to take up his abode permanently in the tenement, which he had purposed to occupy but for a season. He was by no means pleased with the change, and in private lamented it with us, being in fact degraded by his elevation, as having relinquished the exalted rank of a Brahman for the inferior condition of a Śúdra.

Vyáďi having received the sum destined for our master, took leave of his companion Indradatta, whom we shall henceforth call Yogananda*. Before his departure, however, he recommended to the latter to get rid of Śakaťála, the minister, who had penetrated his secret, and who would, no doubt, raise the prince Chandragupta to the throne, as soon as he had attained to years of discretion. It would be better, there-

* [i. e. Nanda through Sorcery.]

fore, to anticipate him, and, as preparatory to that measure, to make me, Vararuchi, his minister. Vyáḋi then left us, and in compliance with his counsel, I became the confidential minister of Yogananda.

A charge was now made against Śakaťála of having, under pretence of getting rid of dead carcases, burnt a Brahman alive; and on this plea, he was cast into a dry well with all his sons. A plate of parched pulse and a pitcher of water were let down daily for their sustenance, just sufficient for one person. The father, therefore, recommended to the brothers to agree amongst themselves, which should survive to revenge them all, and relinquishing the food to him, resign themselves to die. They instantly acknowledged their avenger in him, and with stern fortitude, refusing to share in the daily pittance, one by one expired.

After some time, Yogananda, intoxicated, like other mortals, with prosperity, became despotic and unjust. I found my situation, therefore, most irksome, as it exposed me to a tyrant's caprice, and rendered me responsible for acts, which I condemned. I therefore sought to secure myself a participator in the burthen, and prevailed upon Yogananda, to release Śakaťála from his captivity, and reinstate him in his authority. He therefore once again became the minister of the king.

It was not long before I incurred the displeasure of Yogananda, so that he resolved to put me to death. Śakaťála, who was rejoiced to have this opportunity of winning me over to his cause, apprised me of my danger, and helped me to evade it, by keeping me concealed in his palace. Whilst thus retired, the son of the king, Hirańyagupta, lost his senses, and Yogananda now lamented my absence. His regret moved Śakaťála to acknowledge that I was living, and I was once more received into favour. I effected the cure of the prince, but received news, that disgusted me with the world, and induced me to resign my station, and retire into the forests. My disgrace and disappearance had led to a general belief, that I had been privately put to death. This report reached my family. Upakośá burnt herself, and my mother died broken-hearted.

Inspired with the profoundest grief, and more than ever sensible of the transitory duration of human happiness, I repaired to the shades of solitude, and the silence of meditation. After living for a considerable period in my hermitage, the death of Yogananda was related to me by a Brahman, who was travelling from Ayodhyá, and had rested at my cell.

Śakaťála, brooding on his plan of revenge, observed one day a Brahman of mean appearance digging in a meadow, and asked him what he was doing there. Cháńakya, the Brahman, replied: I am rooting out this grass, which has hurt my foot. The reply struck the minister as indicative of a character, which would contribute to his designs, and he engaged him, by the promise of a large reward and high honours, to come and preside at the Śráddha, which was to be celebrated next new moon at the palace. Cháńakya arrived, anticipating the most respectful treatment; but Yogananda had been previously persuaded by Śakaťála to assign precedence to another Brahman, Subandhu, so that when Cháńakya came to take his place, he was thrust from it with contumely. Burning with rage, he threatened the king before all the court, and denounced his death within seven days. Nanda ordered him to be turned out of the palace. Śakaťála received him into his house; and persuading Cháńakya that he was wholly innocent of being instrumental to his ignominious treatment, contributed to encourage and inflame his indignation. Cháńakya thus protected, practised a magical rite, in which he was a proficient, and by which, on the seventh day, Nanda was deprived of life. Śakaťála, on the father's death, effected the destruction of Hirańyagupta, his son, and raised Chandragupta[1], the son of the genuine Nanda, to the throne. Cháńakya became the prince's minister; and Śakaťála, having attained the only object of his existence, retired to end his days in the woods.

End of the Story of Vararuchi.

All these things confirmed my satisfaction with the life I had adopted, and inspired me with the more anxious desire of being quickly liberated from such a fickle and feverish world. I therefore came to offer

[1] This is the Sandrocottus, or Sandracoptos of the Greek writers. The story is told rather differently in the Puráńas, and with still greater variation in the Mudrá Rákshasa. [Wilson, Hindu Theatre, Calc. 1827. III, 14 ff. Lassen, Ind. Alt. II, 196–204.]

my prayers for final emancipation to Vindhya Vásiní, when I encountered you, and was reminded of my former state. I have related to you the wonderful narratives I learnt unbidden from the mighty Mahádeva. The period of my transformation and punishment has expired. I therefore depart to the holy asylum of Vadariká. Do you yet tarry here awhile, until a Brahman, Guńáďhya, arrive. Impart to him what you have learnt from me, and your task will then be accomplished. So saying, Vararuchi took his leave of Kánabhúti, and departed to Vadarikáśrama, where, throwing off this mortal coil, he resumed, as Pushpadanta, his seat amongst the brilliant spirits of heaven.

Ib. June 1824, p. 266—87.

Story of MálYaván, or Guńáďhya.

After Vararuchi had departed, it happened that his friend Mályaván, who had been born as Guńáďhya, came to Vindhya Vásiní, and encountered Káńabhúti. Upon beholding him, he recollected his original condition, and requested him to communicate the stories he had heard from Vararuchi, as the means of their being mutually restored to their state in heaven. Having complied with his request, Káńabhúti begged him to relate his adventures on earth, to which Guńáďhya readily acceded.

Story of Guńáďhya.

Somadatta, a Brahman of Pratishťhána[1], died, and left two sons and an unmarried daughter. The latter, named Śrutárthá, became a mother before she was a bride; and when questioned by her brothers, she asserted that she had been espoused privately by Kírtisena, the nephew of the serpent monarch Vásuki, who upon the brethren continuing incredulous appeared to them and acknowledged the marriage. I was born his son. After a short time, my mother and my uncles died, and left me friendless. I repaired to the south, and having acquired the knowledge becoming my caste, returned to my native city. As I wandered through Pratishťhána, I mingled with various orders of men, and overheard their conservation[2], until I

[1] Pratishťhána, in the south, is celebrated as the capital of Śáliváhana. It is identifiable with Peytan on the Godávarí—the Bathana, or Paithana of Ptolemy—the capital of Siripolemaios—a name in which, although much distorted, some affinity to Śáliváhana may be conjectured. [Lassen, l. l., II, 935. III, 171., more correctly, identifies this name with that of Śrí Pulimán, of the Andhra dynasty, who reigned at Pratishťhána, after the overthrow of the house of Śáliváhana, about 130 A. D.]

[2] Some stories of no particular interest are here related; amongst others, one of a young merchant, who begins the world with an empty crucible, exchanging it for a frying pan and a handful of pulse, with which he procures a few bundles of sticks from the wood-cutters, which he again sells, and in this manner gradually acquires a large fortune, presents some affinity to the first incident in the story of the king's son and his companions in the Kalíla wa Dimna. [ch. 14.]

found my way to the royal palace. Having attracted the notice and approbation of one of the ministers, I was introduced by him to the king Sátaváhana; and the prince, being pleased with my address, retained me in his service.

Káńabhúti now interrupted Guńáďhya, and asked him to explain how Sátaváhana had acquired that appellation. Guńáďhya then related the story.

Legend of Sátaváhana[1].

There was a monarch, called Dípakarńi, whose wife, named Śaktimatí, more dear to him than his existence, whilst reposing in a bower in the garden, was bitten by a snake, and died. The king, overcome with grief for her loss, made a vow to observe perpetual continence—a vow to which he rigidly adhered, although the want of a son to succeed him in the kingdom was a subject of profound affliction to him. Whilst thus

---

[1] Sátaváhana is usually considered synonymous with Śáliváhana, the enemy of Vikramáditya, and the prince of whose juvenile career those marvels are narrated, which appear to be derived from the Evangelium Infantiæ, and other spurious gospels. (As. Res. Vol. X, p. 42.) At the same time, it is to be observed, that these stories are not to be found in the Puráńas. The chief authority cited by the late Colonel Wilford is the Vikrama Charitra, a compilation of fables of uncertain date, and no consideration. He quotes also the Kumárika Khańda of the Skanda Puráńa, for some circumstances of a less miraculous character; but even here the authority is very disputable, as the Khańdas, or detached sections of the Puráńas, have been multiplied at pleas-

distressed, he was directed by Śiva, in a dream, in what manner to obtain a son and successor, without violating his faith to his departed wife. In obedience to the god's commands, he repaired to a certain forest to hunt; and whilst thus employed, met, as he had been forewarned, a lovely boy, riding upon a monstrous lion. Still acting as he had been enjoined, the king aimed an arrow at the beast, and he fell as dead. Immediately, however, uprose from the carcase a celestial form, who thus addressed the astonished monarch. "Dismiss your apprehension. I am a Yaksha, Sáta by name. It was my chance to see and love the beautiful daughter of a holy sage: my passion was returned; and this boy whom you behold is our son. When the secret of our union was discovered, the angry sire condemned us both to wear the forms of brutes, during the remainder of our earthly career. My bride was liberated from the effects of the curse in giv-

---

ure, and are in many instances decidedly modern. The last work noticed is the Appendix to the Agni Puráńa, which is no part of that Puráńa, and is a modern composition. The legends relating to Śáliváhana may therefore, as is most likely, have been borrowed from the spurious gospels; but they do not, therefore, bear unfavourably upon the antiquity of the Puráńas, as they are not found in the body of those works: how far they may be traced, even in the books cited, is a little doubtful, at least, as applicable to Śáliváhana; for in the legend said to be extracted in the same essay from the Rája Tarangińí, it is true, that the story is correctly given; but the person is not, as is said, Śáliváhana, nor in any way connected with his character. [The errors into which Wilford had fallen are fully exposed by Lassen, Ind. Alt., II, 881 ff. See also Append. VI, p. XXVII.]

ing birth to her son, and your shaft has rendered me the same kind office. I am now at liberty; but ere I depart to the region of the gods, I bequeath to you this child, to be cherished by you as your own." So saying, he vanished, leaving the boy with the king, who gladly received him, and gave him the name Sátaváhana, in reference to the appellation of his father, and the Váhana, or vehicle, on which the king had first beheld the infant mounted. Upon the death of his adoptive father, Sátaváhana succeeded to the throne, and became a mighty monarch.

Amongst the remarkable transactions of his reign was the introduction of a new grammar[1], the Kálápa, or Kátantra. This was communicated to the king for his special use by the god Kártikeya, who had been propitiated by the worship of Sarvavarmá, the king's minister. It was termed Kátantra, from its small extent, and Kálápa, from the peacock (Kalápa) on which Kumára Swámí rides.

---

[1] This grammar is extensively in use in the eastern parts of Bengal. The rules are attributed to Sarvavarmá, by the inspiration of Kártikeya, as narrated in the text. The vŕitti, or gloss, is the work of Durga Singh; and that again is commented on by Trilochana Dása and Kavirája. Vararuchi is the supposed author of an illustration of the Conjugations, and Śrípati Varmá of a Supplement. Other commentaries are attributed to Gopínátha, Kula Chandra, and Viśweśwara. [Aufrecht, Cat. Bodl. I, 168–70. Çolebrooke, Miss. Essays, II, 44 f.]

Story of Guńáđhya—resumed.

The proficiency of the king in the new science being attained without my interference, I felt myself an unnecessary addition to his attendants, and accordingly took leave of him. Accompanied by two of my disciples, I set off for Vindhyavásiní to worship the goddess, having been so enjoined by a dream. On my way hither, I fell in with a variety of goblins, and acquired their language, which makes the fourth I have now mastered[1]. When I first arrived, you were absent; but your return recalls to my recollection all the past, and I now anticipate a speedy restoration to the height from which I fell.

Káńabhúti, having heard the account from Guńáđhya, professed himself ready to communicate the great narrative he had heard from Vararuchi; but intimated his wish first to learn how Pushpadanta and Mályaván had attained a place amongst the bands of heaven. Guńáđhya in consequence related to him the following

Story of Pushpadanta.

In a village on the banks of the Ganges lived Govindadatta, a Brahman. He had five sons, of goodly persons, but rude manners, and uncultivated minds.

---

[1] These are in another place said to be Sanskrit, Prakrit, Deśya, and Paiśáchí.

A Brahman of great learning, having on one occasion, whilst the father was abroad, demanded the rites of hospitality at the house of Govindadatta, was treated with disrespect and derision by the youths, and was about to depart in wrath, when the father arrived. The severity with which both he and his wife rebuked the lads, pacified the Brahman, and induced him to accept their invitation to remain. The anger of his parents produced a favourable impression on one of the sons, Devadatta, who, repenting of his idle habits and unprofitable life, set off to Badarikáśrama[1] to propitiate Śiva. The rigour of his austerities engaged the approbation of the god. Śiva appeared to him, and promised him that he should become possessed of learning, for which purpose he directed him to go to Pátaliputra, and study under Vedakumbha. Devadatta remained some time with this teacher, until his master's wife cast the eyes of illicit affection upon him, and endeavoured to win him to her desires. Devadatta, however, was not to be corrupted; and when he found he could in no other way avoid her importunities, he fled. He repaired to Pratishthána, where he studied with great diligence and success under another teacher of repute.

Whilst studying at Pratishthána, it chanced that Devadatta beheld the daughter of the king Suśarmá at a balcony of the palace. She also noticed him, and

---

[1] The part of the Himálaya known as Badarínáth. It is a shrine of ancient celebrity.

they were instantly fast bound in the indissoluble chains of love. After they had interchanged glances, she beckoned to him to approach. He obeyed: on which she took a flower, and having touched her teeth with it, threw it to him, and then disappeared. Devadatta, taking the flower, returned home. The flame that preyed upon his heart soon betrayed itself to the experience of his preceptor, and he quickly drew from him the secret of his passion. When he heard of the flower, and the manner in which it was presented, he immediately concluded that some mystery was concealed in the act, and at last explained it to signify an assignation, on the part of the princess, to meet Devadatta at a temple called Pushpa, (a flower.) The youth was charmed with this explanation, and set off to the temple to await the coming of the princess. On the 8th day of the fortnight, she repaired thither to offer her adorations, and entering within the chamber where her lover lay concealed, was immediately pressed to his bosom. She enquired how he had so readily apprehended her meaning: but when he confessed he was indebted to his preceptor's sagacity, rather than to his own, she was highly offended with his lack of discernment, and left him in displeasure.

Devadatta was now more wretched than ever, and his life was fast dissolving in the fire of separation; when Śambhu, commiserating his condition, sent one of his attendants, Panchaśikha, to console and assist him. Panchaśikha made the youth put on a female garb, whilst he assumed the appearance of an aged

Brahman. Thus changed, they repaired to the palace, where the supposed Brahman addressed the monarch thus:—"King, I am an old man without connexions in your capital. I sent my only son on family affairs some time ago to a distant country, and he does not return. I am weary of expecting him, and fear some evil may have befallen him. I will therefore go forth in quest of him; but how can I dispose of my daughter-in-law in the mean time? I leave her, king, as a sacred deposit in your charge." The monarch, afraid of the Brahman's malediction, reluctantly accepted the trust, and the supposed Brahman departed. The daughter was transferred to the interior of the palace, where, revealing himself to the princess, Devadatta succeeded in pacifying her indignation, and recovering her regard. She listened to his suit with complacency, and they pledged their troth to each other by the ritual that unites in wedlock the inferior spirits of heaven[1].

When it became no longer possible to conceal their secret intercourse, the friendly sprite was summoned by a wish to their assistance — he appeared, and conveyed Devadatta out of the palace by night. The next morning he made the youth discard his female habiliments, and accompany him, again metamor-

[1] The form of marriage called Gándharva, in which the parties exchange garlands of flowers. [Man. 3, 32. Yájnav.1, 61. In the laws of Vishńu ch. 24 it is called "the union of two parties by mutual consent and in the absence of their parents", dwayoh́ sakámayor mátápitŕirahito yogah́.] The subject of this story is imitated in the Daśakumára, fifth section.

phosed to a venerable Brahman, to the palace in the character of the son of whom he had been in search. He came, he said, to claim his daughter-in-law, and the king ordered her to be sent for; but all parties were struck with real, or seeming consternation, when it was announced that she was no where to be found. The king, at a loss to comprehend the possibility of her evasion, and recollecting old legends, suspected that the Brahman was not what he seemed to be, and, apprehensive of incurring his displeasure, professed himself willing to submit to any conditions he should impose. These were readily arranged, and the princess was given to the Brahman's supposed son, in exchange for the bride that he pretended to have lost. The princess bore a son, who was named Mahídhara. When the king was advanced in years, he retired to the forests, resigning his sovereignty to his grandson; and after witnessing the glory of Mahídhara, his parents also withdrew from the world to the silence of the hermitage: devoting all their thoughts to Śambhu, they obtained his favour; and when released from this mortal coil, they were elevated to the rank of spirits, attendant on the god and his celestial consort, as Pushpadanta and his wife Jayá, the same whose indiscreet curiosity had lately been punished by their temporary return to the infirmities of human nature.

Story of Guńádhya, or Málýaván—continued.

Guńádhya then proceeded. Having thus related to you the history of my friend and fellow spirit, I will now resume my own. In my former existence, Govindadatta, the father of Devadatta, was also mine: my name was Somadatta; and in imitation of the example of my brother I set off to the Himálaya mountains, to propitiate the crescent-crested deity. I performed austere penances in honour of him, and offered constant garlands to him, until, at last, he manifested himself, and proffered me a boon. I prayed to be admitted into the train of his attendants, and he granted my prayer, naming me, with reference to my offerings, Mályaván, (from Málá, a garland.) The community of our original has influenced the friendly connexion, which has ever subsisted between me and Pushpadanta, and rendered me a sharer in his recent humiliation.

Having thus communicated his adventures to Káńabhúti, Guńáďhya received from him the seven great tales, the cause of his and Pushpadanta's fall. Káńabhúti imparted them in the Paiśáchí language, in which Guńáďhya wrote them with his own blood, as there was no procuring ink in the wilderness. The tales were comprised in seven lacks of stanzas: the communication of them was the work of seven years[1],

---

[1] The number is a favouirite one with the Hindus; so in the Mahánáťaka, when Ráma pierces the seven palm trees with his arrow:

अश्वाः सप्त जगन्ति सप्त मुनयः सप्ताब्धयः सप्त गाः ।
सत्यं सप्त च मातरो भयभृतः संख्यानसाम्यादिह ॥

"The seven steeds, seven worlds, seven sages, seven oceans, seven and all the subordinate spirits of earth and air attended the daily recitation. At the close, Káńabhúti was liberated from the effects of his curse, and returned to his station, an attendant on the god of wealth.

Guńáďhya was now the only one who had a duty to fulfil before he was restored to his heavenly honours: this was the communication of the Great Tales to Sátaváhana, to secure their perpetuation upon earth; accordingly he repaired to the vicinity of Pratishťhána, and sent the books by two of his disciples to the king. Sátaváhana treated the present with contempt, and desired the scholars to carry it back to their master; for a work, he observed, in the language of fiends could not be worth human perusal, and characters traced with blood were only suitable to their infernal origin. The disrespect shewn to such holy volumes affected Guńáďhya profoundly. Retiring to a neighbouring mountain, he read to his pupils, and the beasts of the field, and birds of the air, who flocked round him to listen, all the stories, except the history of Naraváhanadatta, throwing each of the series as he completed it, into a fire kindled for the purpose. The extraordinary character of Guńáďhya's auditory at last came to the king's ears, and he was induced to visit the spot, and verify the report in person. Upon finding that it was true, Sátaváhana humbled himself be-

---

continents, and seven Mátŕis, were filled with fear, as being of the like enumeration."

fore the sage, and learned from him his story. He was then anxious to have possession of the tales; and the one lack out of the seven which had escaped the flames was presented to him by Guńáďhya, who presently, resuming his celestial character, returned to the service of Śiva. The stories were expounded to Sátaváhana by Guńáďhya's two disciples, Guńadeva and Nandideva, and they were rewarded liberally with wealth and honours. Sátaváhana also had the tales translated into the Sanskrit language, and this preparatory account of their origin composed[1].

End of the Introduction.

THE FIRST, OR INTRODUCTORY CHAPTER OF THE HISTORY OF NARAVÁHANADATTA.

Birth of Udayana, or the king of Vatsa[2].

In the central district of the delightful country call-

---

[1] The date of the first compilation should therefore be about A. D. 78; but we must not forget that this is fable—whether founded on fact is doubtful. [See Prof. F. F. Hall's edition of the "Tale of Vásavadattá", Introd. p. 22 ff.]

[2] Udayana is a celebrated character in Hindu fable: so Kálidása calls Oujein the populous resort of the bards who have celebrated the story of Udayana:

प्राप्यावन्तीमुदयनकथाकोविदग्रामवृद्धाम् ।

Megha Dúta [32. Comp. Hall's edition of Subandhu's Vásavadattá, Introd. p. 2–6. Vatsa being the name of the region in which Kauśámbí lay, we have throughout this story to under-ed Varsha[1], is the extensive city Kauśámbí, the first monarch of which was Śatáníka, the son of Janamejaya, whose father was Paríkshit, the son of Abhimanyu, the son of Arjuna. Śatáníka was killed in battle with the Titans, having gone to the assistance of Indra, and was succeeded in his throne by Sahasráníka.

The fate of his father naturally interested Indra for the young prince, and he not unfrequently conveyed him to visit the regions of the skies. On one of these occasions he incurred the displeasure of Tilottamá, a nymph of paradise, and she denounced an imprecation on his future fortune, sentencing him to the pangs of separation from his beloved. Sahasráníka was married to Mŕigávatí, daughter of Kŕipavarmá, King of Oude. During her pregnancy she was seized with a strange fancy, inspired, in fact, by the influence of the imprecation, to bathe in human blood. When the king found compliance with her longing was unavoidable, he deceived her by substituting an infusion of the lac-dye, in which the queen contentedly performed her ablutions. The crimson tint left upon her person by the effect of the immersion, deceived one of the gigantic brood of Garuda[2], as he pursued his flight through

stand by "Vatsa" the king of that country, Vatsarája in the original. Hall, l. l., Introd. p. 2 ff.]

[1] Bharata Varsha, or India, is probably intended. Of Kauśámbí we spoke above, (note, p. 162.) The foundation of this city is here placed in the 5th generation, about a century and a half subsequent to the war of the Mahábhárata.

[2] This is the Roc, or Rokh, of Arabian romance, agreeing in the multiplicity of the individuals, as well as their propensity for

the air. Thinking her to be a lump of flesh, he pounced upon the queen, and carried her off to the mountain Udaya, where, finding her alive, he abandoned her to her destiny, having thus been the unconscious instrument of separating Sahasráníka from his bride.

In this helpless condition the queen, overcome with terror and affliction, sought alone for death to terminate her distress. With this view she threw herself in the way of the wild elephants and the vast serpents, with which the thickets were peopled; but in vain—an unseen spirit of the air protected her, and guided her unharmed amidst the ferocious monsters of the forest, until she was encountered by a holy hermit, Jamadagni, who resided on the mountain, and who led her to his cell, where he consoled her with assurances, that she would in time be re-united to her lord. Mrigávatí was here delivered of a son, whom, in allusion to the place of his nativity, she named

raw meat. (See Sindbad's Voyages [ed. Langlès, p. 149.]) The latter characteristic, to the utter subversion of all poetical fancies, has acquired, it may be supposed, for the Adjutant (Ardea Argila) the name of Garuda. A wundervogel, or wonderful bird, is the property of all people; and the Garuda of the Hindus is represented by the Eorosh of the Zend, Simoorgh of the Persians, the Anka of the Arabs, the Kerkes of the Turks, the Kirni of the Japanese, the sacred dragon of the Chinese, the Griffin of Chivalry, the Phœnix of classical fable, the wise and ancient bird that sits upon the ash Yggdrasil of the Edda, and, according to Faber, in common with all the rest, is a misrepresentation of the holy cherubim that guarded the gate of paradise. Some writers have even traced the twelve knights of the round Table to the twelve Rocs of Persian story.

Udayana, and who was trained in letters and arms, and in the duties of his regal birth, by his venerable guardian.

When Udayana grew up, he rambled fearlessly through the forest, and on one occasion beheld a mountaineer catch a snake. The boy, in pity for the captive animal, requested the barbarian to liberate him; but the man stated, that he subsisted by snaring and exhibiting serpents, and that to part with his prize would injure himself. Udayana then offered him a golden bracelet for his expectations, for which equivalent the mountaineer relinquished the snake, and departed, well pleased with his bargain. As soon

---

[1] The regions below the earth, inhabited by the Nágas, or serpents, who seem, however, to assume at will the human shape. Their subterrene domiciles are remarkable for their splendour, particularly in gold and gems.

——"Let none admire
That riches grow in hell—that soil may best
Deserve the precious bane."

Connected with this notion is the popular superstition of the Hindus, that hidden treasures are often indicated by the haunts of particular serpents. [Grimm, deutsche Mythologie. 1844, p. 648 ff. Mannhardt, german. Mythen. Berlin: 1858, p. 148 ff. Schwarz, Ursprung der Mythologie. Berlin: 1860, p. 42 ff. Wolf, Beiträge zur d. Myth. II, 440 ff.] In fable, the Nágas have supplied the Arabian Nights, and chivalric romance, very liberally. Their mythological character is very important and curious. Faber has noticed some of the circumstances. The Nágas of the Hindus, however, appear an inoffensive race. [Troyer ad Rájataranginí, Vol. II, p. 457-64.] They took refuge in Pátála, to escape from the destructive hostility of Garuḍa. They often mix with mortals, but rarely, if ever, for malignant purposes. We shall have occasion to recur to their history.

as he was gone, the snake, assuming a human shape, addressed Udayana, and told him he was the Vasunemi, the elder brother of Vásuki, the sovereign of the serpent tribes of Pátála[1]. He begged the young prince to accompany him to his palace, and Udayana readily assented; when, in requital of the service rendered to Vasunemi, both he and his brother loaded Udayana with the most precious and curious gems, presenting him, amongst other valuable gifts, with a lute of celestial manufacture—after which they reconveyed Udayana to the abode of his preceptor. In the mean time the mountaineer descended to the plains to dispose of the bracelet, and speedily met with the tents of Sahasráníka, who was traversing the world in search of his queen. The bracelet had been given to Udayana by his mother, who, to amuse her sorrows, had engraved the name of her husband on its inner surface. The inscription caught the eye of the persons to whom it was offered, and they conducted the barbarian to the king, to account for its possession. When Sahasráníka heard his story, he was transported with the hope of beholding his queen and son, and commanded the forester to conduct him and his train to the mountain without delay. The man obeyed, and they found themselves shortly at the hermitage of Jamadagni, where Mŕigávatí and her son were restored to the embraces of the delighted king. They returned together to Kauśámbí. When Udayana had reached adolescence, his father resigned the sovereign authority into his hands, and returned with his consort to the Himála mountains, to terminate their days in solitude and devotion.

Story of Vatsa—continued.

The young prince of Kauśámbí, ascending the throne in a period of peace and prosperity, had little other occupation than his pleasures. Reposing the cares of state upon his trusty minister Yogandharáyańa, he spent much of his time in the forest engaged in the chase, which he followed, armed with the lute presented him by the serpent monarch, whose dulcet notes attracted and tamed the most ferocious elephants. At this period Chańďasena was king of Ujjayiní. He had a daughter named Vásavadattá, of such singular beauty and accomplishments, that her father held all the princes of the earth unworthy of her hand, except the young monarch of Kauśámbí: at the same time their union was not easily to be effected, as the two kings were politically enemies of each other, and the sovereign of Ujjayiní determined therefore to have recourse to stratagem.

With this view he sent an embassador to Vatsa, to say, that having heard of his musical proficiency, he was desirous of securing him as his daughter's preceptor, and would be happy to see that monarch accordingly at Ujjayiní. Vatsa heard this affronting message with great indignation, but suppressed his resentment till he had consulted his minister. Yogandharáyańa availed himself of the opportunity to give some salutary admonition to the young prince. He observed that he had drawn this affront upon himself,—that his addiction to frivolous pursuits was evidently noised abroad, and that indignity was the bitter fruit of an indifferent reputation—that it was clear the king of Ujjayiní, trusting to the attractions of his daughter, purposed merely to get him into his power, when he would hold him captive, and seize his dominions—and that dissipation was a snare, by which princes were entangled, as elephants were caught in pits, covered over with seeming verdure. After receiving these lessons, Vatsa returned to the hall of audience, and calling the envoy from Ujjayiní before him, desired him to return to his master, and inform him, that if he were anxious his daughter should receive any instructions from Vatsa, he must send her to Kauśámbí. With this retort the ambassador was dismissed.

Upon the departure of the messenger, Vatsa called a council of his ministers, and announced to them his intention of marching against Ujjayiní, and seizing the person of its king. From this his counsellors dissuaded him, and none more earnestly than Yogandharáyańa. Chańdasena, he urged, was a prince of great prowess and prudence, and one not easily overcome; in proof of which he related his adventures.

Story of Chańdasena, King of Ujjayiní.

The city of Ujjayiní is the ornament of the earth, and with its white palaces derides the capital of Indra: for the agreeableness of whose site the Lord of the universe, in his actual presence as Mahákála[1], disdains the summits of Kailása[2]. Mahendravarmá was king of this city: his son was Jayasena, and his son was Mahásena. This last prince obtained in his youth a sword of celestial temper, through his propitiation of the goddess Chańd́í; from which circumstance, and his own fiery disposition, he derived the appellation of Chańd́amahásena, or Chańd́asena.

By direction of his tutelary goddess, Chańd́asena set off in quest of a suitable bride, none of the daughters of his brother kings being worthy, in his own estimation, of the honour of his alliance. Having pursued his way for a considerable distance through the shades of an extensive forest, he encountered a wild boar of gigantic stature, and as black as night. The king drew his bow, and struck him repeatededly with his shafts, but in vain. The animal was invulnerable. Leaping from his car, the prince prepared to assault him with his scymitar; but the monster fled from before him, and plunged into a yawning cavern. The king pursued him. After penetrating some distance, a blaze of light burst suddenly upon him, and he found himself in front of a splendid palace, on the lawn before which was a spacious reservoir of water.

Whilst Chańd́asena was meditating on this strange

---

[1] A famous Linga, so termed, existed at Ougein when the Mohamedans invaded India. It was broken to pieces by Altamsh, in A. D. 1231.

[2] A part of the Himálaya mountains, the supposed favourite residence of Śiva. A lofty portion of the range is still so named.

discovery, a bevy of beauteous damsels approached him, conducted by a nymph of exquisite loveliness, who courteously enquired the purpose of his coming. He related to her the occurrences of the forest, and in return begged her to gratify his curiosity by informing him whither accident had led him. Whilst the tear-drop started from her large and lucid eye, the nymph replied:—

"You have been conducted, prince, by your evil destiny to the residence of my father. My name is Angáravatí: my sire is Angáraka, a Daitya, formidable to the gods, and endowed with a frame of adamant, impervious to hostile weapons. The effect of an imprecation denounced upon him compels him to assume at times the condition of a fiend who preys upon mankind, when, in the form of a beast of the forest, he roams the thickets, and overpowers or ensnares the traveller. Fatigued with to-day's encounter, and secure in imagination of his victim, he now reposes: when he wakes, your destruction is unavoidable." Saying which, the damsed expressed the interest she took in the fate of the king.

Chańd́asena having thanked the nymph for the sympathy she displayed, and declared the impression she had made upon his heart, told her to endeavour to ascertain whether her sire was every where alike impenetrable, and directed her how to obtain the secret. Going to Angáraka, therefore, she was found by him, when he woke, seemingly immersed in deep affliction. He asked the cause; to which she answered, she feared for his life; and should any mischance occur—should he fall by any hostile hand, what was to become of her? He told her to dismiss her apprehensions, as he incurred no peril. The whole of his skin was of adamant, the only vulnerable part being the palm of his left hand:—a wound there indeed would be fatal; but as it was employed in grasping the bow, it was consequently never exposed." This was overheard by Chańdasena, who had been covertly stationed by Angáravatí, where he might listen to what passed between her sire and her.

Having risen from his couch, the Titan went forth to bathe, and address his prayers to Hara. Whilst engaged in their silent repetition, the king appeared, and challenged him to combat. Angáraka, unwilling to break off his devotion, or to interrupt his inaudible prayer, waved to the king with his left hand to wait for a short period. Chańdasena seized the opportunity, and, whilst the palm of the hand was turned towards him, let fly a shaft, which pierced the vital spot, and the Daitya instantly fell to the ground. As he breathed his last, he murmured, "Let my conqueror offer daily libations to my spirit, if he hope to retain imperial sway."

After the fall of Angáraka, Chańdasena married Angáravatí, and returned to Ujjayiní, where he continued to reign with uninterrupted prosperity. He had two sons by his queen, Bhúpálaka and Pálaka, and one daughter, Vásavadattá, so named because she was the gift of Indra, (or Vásava,) the deity having appeared in a dream to the prince, and announced her birth as the recompence of the magnificence with which the king had celebrated his festival. Thus favoured by the gods, and formidable in his own prowess and political resources, the monarchs of the earth must be careful how they provoke the resentment of Chańdasena.

Story of Vatsa—resumed.

When the messenger of Chańdasena returned to his master with Vatsa's reply, the king of Ujjayiní secretly pleased with the young prince's spirit, was only the more bent upon securing him for a son-in-law. With this purpose he had recourse to stratagem, and caused an elephant, the exact similitude of a celebrated animal in his possession, to be constructed by able artists. This he privately sent into the forests, where he knew Vatsa was accustomed to hunt, and left it there, filling the interior cavity with a party of armed men[1].

---

[1] "Huc delecta virûm sortiti corpora furtim
Includunt cœco lateri penitusque cavernas
Ingentes uterumque armato milite complent."

Virgil [Aen. II, 18.]

——"In the hollow side
Selected numbers of their chiefs they hide;
With inward arms the dire machine they load,
And iron bowels stuff the dark abode."

Dryden.

The conception was, however, as old as Homer at least.

Ἵππῳ ἔνι ξεστῷ ἵν᾽ ἐνήμεθα πάντες ἄριστοι
Ἀργείων, Τρώεσσι φόνον καὶ κῆρα φέροντες.

Od. 4. 273.

In a few days the prince of Kauśámbí, resuming his usual habits, repaired to the Vindhya woods. His scouts, observing the artificial elephant at a distance, mistook it for a living animal, and carried the news to their master. Eager to seize so stately a captive, Vatsa advanced towards the elephant, in no degree surprised by its tranquillity, which he attributed to the effects of his magical lute, whose cords he struck as he approached slowly and alone, accompanying the sound with the sweetness of his voice. When he was close to the figure, the armed men sprang from their concealment. Vatsa struck the foremost to the ground; but he was presently surrounded, and resistance rendered vain. They hurried him off; and, being protected by strong parties stationed along the road, conveyed their prisoner in triumph to Ujjayiní.

On Vatsa's entering Ujjayiní, the people who had collected in crowds to see him were so much prepossessed by his blooming countenance and graceful deportment, that they exclaimed with one voice: "Vatsa must not be put to death; keep him, but kill him not:" and Chańdasena, in order to allay the tumult, was

---

"When in the finished horse, the best of Greece
Sat breathing fate and misery to Troy."

And again, in the 8th Book. The story was told over and over again, before it got to Virgil; and therefore Heyne concludes: "Habebat poeta fabulam a multis tractatam et vulgarem ante se positam." Whether any of these earlier tales came from, or wandered to the east, can scarcely receive any illustration from what is here probably only an accidental coincidence.

obliged to promise them his prisoner's personal security.

The king of Ujjayiní next delivered Vatsa to his daughter, as her preceptor in musical science. He told the prince, that if he would render Vásavadattá a proficient, he had nothing to apprehend, but might expect an equivalent reward. And Vatsa, as soon as he beheld the beauty of the princess, felt not a whit reluctant to undertake her tuition. She was equally well contented with her master, and gave up all her thoughts to him; for though modesty may check the eye, the heart is beyond control. Thence many delightful hours were passed by both in the musical saloon, as Vatsa, with his lute suspended from his neck, gave utterance to the impassioned notes, that were re-echoed by his fair pupil, as she stood in all her loveliness before him.

When the news of Vatsa's capture reached Kauśámbí, the people, inflamed with resentment, urged an immediate invasion of the territories of Ujjayiní. The wisdom of the ministers, however, afraid to contend openly with the power of Chańdásena, allayed the ferment, and they engaged to rescue their prince by less hazardous means. Yogandharáyańa undertook to effect his liberation in person, and set out, accompanied by Vasantaka, for Ujjayiní, leaving to Rumańwán [1] the charge of Kauśámbí.

---

[1] Wherever the king of Vatsa is the hero of the history, these three are part of the dramatis personæ. Yogandharáyańa, as chief minister, possessing also magical power, unites the character of Turpin and Merlin. Vasantaka is a sort of buffo, as well as a

On his way through the Vindhyan thickets, vast as his experience, and intricate as his policy, Yogandharáyańa paid a visit to the chief of the forest tribes. The king of the Pulindas[1] was an ancient ally of Kauśámbí; and, by desire of the minister, he prepared his bands to cover the escape of Vatsa, as he should return through the woods. This arrangement being effected, the minister resumed his route to Ujjayiní. He halted on the funereal ground without the city, where, employing his magic skill, he transformed himself to the semblance of a decrepid and crazed old man, and

---

minister, and the personal friend of the prince; and Rumańwán is the general, or commander in chief.

[1] In vocabularies, the term Pulinda is applied to any forest or barbarous tribe. In these stories it is especially assigned to the foresters of the Vindhya mountains, extending across India, from Vindhyavásiní, or Mirzapur, and even as high up as near Mathurá, along the line of the Narmadá, to Guzerat. The author of the Vŕihat Kathá here probably describes this part of India, as it was delineated in works prior to his day, when the tract of central forest must have been vastly more extensive than in modern times, and the greater part of Málwa and Ajmír were occupied by barbarians, the ancestors of the Bhils and Gońds, who are now confined to the hills, and who do entertain some traditionary notions of having once occupied less ungenial sites. The Pulindas were known to the ancients by the same appellation, and, according to their information, tenanted similar tracts. The Pulindas of Ptolemy extend along the banks of the Narmadá to the frontiers of Larice, which corresponds generally with Guzerat. Both they and the river are north of Ozene, or Oujein, and between it and Modura Deorum, or Mathurá, on the north—a strange dislocation of positions, it must be confessed, in some respects, but corresponding, as far as the Pulindas are concerned, very faithfully with our text, and with the probable truth.

his companion Vasantaka to a figure of singular and ridiculous deformity. Thus disguised, they entered the city severally by different gates. Yogandharáyańa made direct for the palace, attracting and diverting the mob by his songs and gesticulations. The servants of the princess joining the throng, and amused by the antics of the supposed idiot, reported his entertaining gambols to their mistress, and excited her curiosity to witness them. Accordingly, by her command, the disguised Yogandharáyańa was introduced into the presence of Vásavadattá, and there beheld his master in bonds. Having contrived, by a private signal, to let Vatsa know him, he suddenly became invisible to the court, and the attendants questioned each other with astonishment what had become of the antic. The princess was no less surprised; and Vatsa, availing himself of the general feeling to get rid of all spectators, recommended to Vásavadattá to go and offer propitiatory devotions at the shrine of Saraswatí. The princess and her train departed for that purpose, and left Vatsa alone with his friend.

Having thus obtained an opportunity of communicating with the prince, Yogandharáyańa imparted to him the plan he had devised for his escape; and finding that his master was resolved not to leave Ujjayiní without the princess, now comprised her in the plot. Having imparted to Vatsa the means of extricating himself from his chains, and desired him to admit Vasantaka, when he arrived, to his councils, he departed to superintend the arrangements of the retreat.

When the princess returned from the temple, Vasantaka presented himself at the palace gate, and at the instance of Vatsa was invited to enter. His deformities excited the mirth and compassion of Vásavadattá, and she desired him to remain in the palace, promising that he should be taken care of. On her further asking him whether he possessed any learning, he said, he was deeply read in story-telling, and gave her the following proof of his talent.

Story of Lohajangha.

In Mathurá dwelt a public dancer, named Rúpańiká, of great beauty and accomplishments. Her charms attracted universal admiration; and many advantageous proposals were made to her. To the great vexation of her mother, however, she treated all her suitors with disdain, and fixed her undivided affections upon a young and indigent Brahman, named Lohajangha, whom she had met at a public festival in one of the many temples, which decorate the birthplace of Kŕishńa.

Finding that remonstrances were unavailing, the old woman determined to have recourse to other means, and to get rid of the obnoxious lover by violence. For this object she had Lohajangha waylaid by bravoes, and so unmercifully beaten, that he scarce escaped with life. He got away, however, from his assailants, and fled to the neighbouring forests, where, still doubtful of his security, he was rejoiced to creep into an elephant's hide, which had been completely hollowed out by jackals, so that the skin alone remained. The effect of his bruises, and the cold breeze, lulled him to sleep; but he was speedily awakened by fresh misadventures. A tremendous fall of rain came on, and the river, overpassing its boundaries, swept through the forest, and carried the hide and its inhabitant along with it in its course. Whilst floating down the stream, a bird of Garuḋa's breed, perceiving it, darted on the skin, and bore it in his beak across the main to Lanká. Here alighting, he prepared to gorge upon his prize, when Lohajangha making his appearance, frightened the animal, and put him to flight.

Lohajangha looking round him, and observing the ocean, rubbed his eyes, and fancied he was in a dream. To add to his apprehensions, two Rákhasas of hideous aspect presented themselves at some distance; but, luckily for him, they were no less alarmed than himself. They still recollected the humiliation their race had sustained from mortal prowess, and dreaded another Ráma in the individual they beheld. One of them set off forthwith to Vibhíshańa, to announce the event to the prince[1], who, partaking the sentiments of

---

[1] Vibhíshańa, the brother of Rávańa, endeavoured to persuade him to avoid hostilities with Ráma, by resigning Sítá to her husband. On Rávańa's persisting to retain her, Vibhíshańa deserted him, and joined Ráma, in reward of which he was appointed, after his brother's overthrow, monarch of Lanká. This Rákshasa chief is supposed by the Hindus still to exercise the sovereignty of the island; and they will not admit, therefore, the identity of

his followers, desired the Rákshasa to go immediately, and with all possible respect invite the man to his palace.

When the Rákshasa returned to Lohajangha, and conveyed to him his monarch's message, apprising him at the same time into whose hands he had fallen, the courage of Lohajangha revived, and he determined to turn his visit to good account. Repairing, therefore, to Vibhíshańa, he told the Rákshasa chief that he was a Brahman of Mathurá; that, being in extreme indigence, he had applied for succour to Vishńu; and that the deity had instructed him to go to Lanká, where Vibhíshańa, his faithful votary, would gladly relieve the distress of one who was equally attached to his worship. Lohajangha added, that he had enquired who Vibhíshańa was, and where he was to be found; on which he was told not to take any trouble upon the subject; and accordingly, having gone to sleep as usual, he found himself, when he awoke, on the sea coast of Lanká.

Vibhíshańa, knowing that Lanká was accessible by

Lanká and Ceylon, conceiving the former invisible, or inaccessible to mortals. It is rather singular that the traditions of Rávańa and Ráma seem unknown on the island, or at least that they are not locally applied. The only mention, indeed, of Rávańa that occurs, is in the history of Ceylon, published in the Annals of Oriental Literature; and he is there made a prince of the mainland. "The demon Rávańa governed the country between Tutacoreen and Ceylon." The traditions of the south also extend the dominion of Rávańa to the Terra Firma, and make Trichinapali one of his frontier fortresses.

no ordinary means, was induced, by the mere fact of Lohajangha's presence, to credit his story, and accordingly sent his emissaries to bring treasure from the mountain with the golden base. He gave him also a young bird of the Garuḋa breed to convey him back to Mathurá, instructing him how to manage the animal. Lohajangha, in the mean while, spent his time agreeably in conversation with Vibhíshańa, who related to him this legend, explaining how it chanced that Lanká was made of wood.

Origin of Lanká.

Desirous of liberating his mother from the state of servitude to the parent of the Nágas, and to pay the fixed price of her liberation, the ambrosia of the immortals, Garuḋa prepared to carry off the celestial beverage by fraud or force[1]. To collect sufficient strength for his enterprize, he applied to his father Kaśyapa for invigorating food. The seer directed him to go to the ocean, where he would find a large elephant and tor-

[1] Kadrú, the mother of the serpents, and Vinatá, the mother of Garuḋa, both wives of Kaśyapa, disputed about the colour of the horses of the sun. They agreed to decide by a bet—an ancient custom, it should seem; and the loser was to become the bondswoman of the winner. Vinatá, the mother of Garuḋa, lost the wager, and her liberty: but Kadrú agreed to give her her manumission, if her son would procure the amrita, the beverage of immortality, for the benefit of her own ophitic progeny. This is the legend alluded to in the text. [Mahábh. I, ch. 16 ff. Weber, Ind. Studien, I, 224, Note.]

toise, whom he might seize and devour. Garuḋa did as he was instructed, and after his meal rested on a branch of the Kalpa tree, or tree of heaven. The branch gave way with his weight. In fear of its falling upon the holy Bálakhilyas[1], who prosecuted their devotions at the foot of the tree, he laid hold of it, and bore it away with his beak. Kaśyapa, out of regard to the security of mankind, commanded Garuḋa to carry it to some lonely spot, where he might let it fall without doing mischief. He accordingly deposited it on the ocean, and it served as a base, on which the wooden fabric of the island was subsequently reared[2].

Story of Lohajangha—concluded.

After this, Lohajangha, being well laden with gold and gems, mounted his now docile bird, and returned with the speed of thought to Mathurá, carrying also a golden club, shell, and discus, as presents from Vi-

---

[1] Pigmy saints, the size of the thumb, the probable original of
——"That small brood
Warred on by cranes;"
and not improbably connected, as supposed by the writer in the Quarterly Review No. XLI, with the character of Däumling, Thaumlin, Tamlane, Tom-a-lyn, or Tom Thumb. [Vishńu Pur. p. 83.]

[2] This legend, absurd as it is, is rather of a curious character, especially as it differs from the Pauráńik story. According to a supplement to the Rámáyańa, Lanká was made of gold by Viśwakarmá, for the especial residence of Kuvera, from whom it was taken by Rávańa.

bhíshańa to the shrine of Vishńu. He alighted in a deserted temple without the city, and there concealed his treasures, and fastened his bird: taking one of the jewels, he sold it in the market, and with the price bought food, clothes, and ornaments. He then returned to his hiding-place, and at night, mounting his winged steed, he repaired to the dwelling of his mistress. Having been received by her with joyful recognition, he taught her how to play her part to be revenged on the cause of their separation, and then returned to his concealment.

In the morning, Rúpańiká kept herself in her apartment, and assumed a mysterious silence. She would only speak with her mother*, after causing a screen to be drawn between them; and then condescended to tell her, that she was the bride of Vishńu, and could not commune any more with mere mortals. To remove the old woman's doubts, she told her to keep watch at night, in consequence of which she beheld the pretended Vishńu arrive with the emblems, and mounted on the vehicle of the god. Entertaining no further doubt, she requested her daughter to impart to her some of the benefits of such exalted visitation.

The reply to the request of Makaradanshtrá was to this effect. She was told she was too wicked to be admissible into Swarga in her own person; but that on the early morning of every eleventh day of the fortnight, the gates of Indra's heaven were set open to

* [Makaradanshtrá.]

all comers. At this time the followers of Śambhu passed in and out in bands, and if she could get amongst the crowd, she might perhaps pass in unobserved. For this purpose it would be necessary for her to disguise herself like them, by tying her hair in five tresses, hanging a string of bones round her neck, throwing off all her attire, and smearing one side with lamp black, and the other with vermilion[1]. The old woman assented to these conditions, and at the appointed time Lohajangha carried her off on his bird. He had observed in the front of a temple a tall pillar, surmounted by a stone ring, or wheel; and here he lodged her as the banner of his retaliation: here she remained throughout the night, suspecting she was tricked, dreading discovery, and with difficulty maintaining her station[2]. The morning had scarcely dawned, when she was recognised by the people, and young and old assembled in crowds, enjoying her mishap, and laughing heartily at her ridiculous appearance: at length Rúpaṅiká came to her aid, and had her carried home. The prince of Mathurá offered a reward to the individual whose ingenuity had devised the frolic; and Lohajangha, coming forward, related his story, to the

---

[1] Thus she represented the Ardhanáríśwara, or Śiva, half male, and half female, which compound figure is to be painted in this manner.

[2] This presents some analogy to the story in the Decamerone (Nov. 7, Gior. 8,) of the scholar and the widow, "la quale egli con un suo consiglio, di mezzo luglio, ignuda, tutto un dì fa stare in su una torre."

entertainment and astonishment of the people and their lord. With the approbation of the latter, Lohajangha was married to Rúpańiká, and they passed their days in affluence and pleasure[1].

Story of Vatsa—resumed.

In the course of a short time, the affections of Vásavadattá were so firmly fixed on Vatsa, that country and parents were light in the comparison. Yogandharáyańa now reappeared, to announce that every thing was prepared for their flight, and the keeper of Vá-

---

[1] The bold assumption of a masquerade character of divinity is probably borrowed from practices not unknown to the Hindus, although more rare than with the Babylonians, Lycians, and Egyptians, when the priest pretended

> "That sometimes did the mightiest not disdain
> To veil his glories in a mortal shape;
> And that he trod
> This earth so conscious, that the best of deity,
> The power and majesty resided in him,
> That be but stooped to win himself a bride,
> Beneath another name."
>
> *Milman's Belshazzar.*

As a fable, the mortal personation of Vishńu is similarly related in the Pancha Tantra [I, 5]; only instead of a real bird, the lover rides an artificial one, the prototype of the "wondrous horse of brass", the flying steed of Rugiero, and other marvellous fabrications familiar to romance, more closely imitated, in object as well as structure, however, in the Labourer and Flying Car of the additional tales of the Arabian Nights, and in Málek and Shirín, in the Persian Tales. [Benfey, Pantschatantra. Leipzig: 1859. I, 148. 159-62. Boccaccio, Decam. IV, 2.]

savadattá's elephant, a beast of unequalled velocity, bribed to lend them aid. He therefore desired Vatsa to prevail on the princess to accompany him, and thus retaliate on Chańdasena the trick he had practised, not doubting that he would subsequently assent with joy to their espousal. The minister then departed to give notice to the forest monarch. Vatsa repaired to the princess. It needed little eloquence to persuade her to a measure to which she was so well inclined, and her concurrence was readily obtained. Accordingly, when night came, Vásavadattá, with a confidential attendant, and Vatsa, with his friend Vasantaka, mounted the elephant, and set forth on their flight. They took their way out of the city by a part of the wall that was broken down, Vatsa having been compelled to engage and slay the two soldiers who were stationed at the post. They then got clear of Ujjayiní, and plunged into the adjacent woods.

Ib. Sept 1824, p. 101—109.

Flight of Vatsa.

Vatsa continued his journey with unrelaxed speed, and by noon the following day reached the Vindhya forests, a distance of sixty-three yojanas[1]. Here his

[1] A yojana, as a measure of distance, is four cos; but as the

elephant was so overcome with fatigue and thirst, that the prince and his campanions alighted to relieve her. Seeing a pool, she hastened to drink; and the effect of the draught, whilst thus heated, was presently fatal. She fell, and expired. Vatsa was thus compelled to pursue his journey on foot. On entering the forest, he was attacked by a party of robbers; but maintained a conflict with them, until fortunately the chief of the Pulindas, on the watch for his return, came to his rescue, and conducted him and his attendants in safety to his village. On the following morning Rumańwán, the general, arrived with a strong force; and Vatsa, now in security, continued to occupy the forest, until he received intelligence from Ujjayiní of the events

---

cos is variously computed, it will be equal to $4^1/_2$, 5, or 9 miles. We need not estimate it in either case by the powers of the elephant, for they were supernatural; but it may furnish some clue to the actual situation of Kauśámbí. Kauśámbí was on the Ganges. Its dependencies bordered on Magadha, the northernmost boundaries of which extended to Chúnar. At five miles to the yojana, its frontier began 315 miles from Ougein. This was some short distance, say five miles, from the Palli, or station of the forest chief; and it will hereafter appear, that the latter was at a distance of a day's march from the capital for cavalry. Allowing, therefore, 30 miles for this, Kauśámbí was on the Ganges, not far from Chúnar, about 350 miles from Ougein. There can be no doubt, therefore, that it was in, or about, the lower part of the Doáb, which is not above 380 miles from Ougein, and sufficiently near to Magadha. These circumstances confirm the opinions stated in a former note, that the site of Kauśámbí is to be sought in the vicinity of Kurrah; though it is rather singular, in that case, that no mention is made of the Jamná, which Vatsa should have crossed in his return to his capital.

which had followed his departure. To amuse the princess during their halt, Vasantaka, at her request, related to her the following story.

Story of Guhasena and his Wife Devasmitá.

In the city of Támraliptí[1] dwelt a wealthy banker, named Dharmadatta. He was unhappy in the midst of his riches that he had no child to inherit them, and he applied to the Brahmans to obtain a son. To propitiate their favour, he celebrated the Homa, or sacrifice to fire, and distributed amongst them presents of great value. The consequence of his devotion was the birth of an heir, whom he named Guhasena.

When Guhasena approached manhood, his father carried him along with him in his mercantile expeditions, both to initiate him into the mysteries of trade, and procure him a suitable bride. With this last intention he applied to Dharmagupta, an opulent merchant of the island Kaṫáha; but he was unwilling to give his daughter to one, who resided so far away as in Támraliptí, and on this account declined the alliance. His daughter, however, was of a different opinion. Having seen Guhasena, she was disposed to relinquish home and friends for his sake, and contrived, with the intermediation of a friend, to apprise

[1] Támraliptáḣ is considered to be the same with Tumlook. Támraliptí is the capital. [V. de S. Martin in "Mémoires sur les contrées occidentales", Paris: 1858. II, 392; and in his "Étude sur la géographie Grecque et Latine de l'Inde", p. 303 f.]

him of her sentiments. He was equally ready to avail himself of her good wishes, and accordingly carried her off privately to Támralipti, where they were married, and continued to reside happy in the unvarying attachment of each other.

After a time the father of Guhasena died, and it was necessary that he should visit foreign countries, in order to look after the mercantile concerns, that had now devolved on his sole care. His wife, however, would not hear of his leaving her, apprehending not only the perils of travel, but her husband's becoming attached to some other woman in her absence. It was in vain that he vowed the most unalterable fidelity, and undeviating affection. She was not to be persuaded; and between the violence of her opposition and the urgency of his affairs Guhasena was utterly at a loss what conduct to adopt.

In this dilemma he had recourse to the gods; and having fasted and prayed in the temple of Śiva, returned sorrowfully home. His appeal, however, was not in vain, and at night the deity appeared to Guhasena and his wife, presenting either with a red lotus, which would lose its colour and freshness, he said, only, if one of them in absence should prove inconstant[1]. On their waking they found the flowers; and

[1] Some marvellous test of the fidelity of absent lovers is well known to western fable, although, with a want of gallantry very irreconcileable with chivalric feelings, the application of it is usually directed to the exposure of female inconstancy alone. The test is, however, of very various complexion, though flowers are

with this indication of her husband's fidelity Devasmitá was contented to permit his departure.

---

not omitted. Thus in Perce Forest, it is a rose which, borne by a wife or maid of irreproachable virtue, preserves its freshness, and fades if the wearer is unchaste. In Amadis de Gaul, it is a garland, which blooms on the head of her that is faithful, and fades on the brow of the inconstant. In Les Contes à rire, it is also a flower. In Ariosto, the test applied to both male and female is a cup, the wine of which is spilled by the unfaithful lover. This fiction also occurs in the romances of Tristan, Perceval, and La Morte d'Arthur, and is well known by La Fontaine's version, La Coupe Enchantée. In La Lai du Corn, it is a drinking-horn. Spencer has derived his girdle of Florimel from these sources, or more immediately from the Fabliau, Le Manteau mal Taillé [Legrand I, 126], or Le Court Mantel, an English version of which is published in Percy's Reliques, the Boy and the Mantel, (Vol. III.) In the Gesta Romanorum [c. 69.], the test is the whimsical one of a shirt, which will neither require washing nor mending, as long as the wearer is constant. [See the literature ap. Grässe, Sagenkreise des Mittelalters, p. 185 ff.] Davenant has substituted an emerald for a flower.

——"The bridal stone,
And much renowned, because it chasteness loves,
And will, when worn by the neglected wife,
Shew when her absent lord disloyal proves,
By faintness, and a pale decay of life."

Gondibert, Canto IV.

The miraculous properties of stones are of eastern origin, although we do not find in the Sanskrit or Arabic account of the emerald the property which Davenant has assigned it, unless he has fabricated a poetical notion from that which the Arabs derived from the Greeks, that this stone and jasper facilitated parturition.

"*Λέγονται δὲ πάντες εἶναι φυλακτήρια περίαπτα καὶ ὠκυτόκια μηρῷ περιαπτόμενα.*"—Dioscor.

Wieland has employed the flower and its change of colour, al-

Guhasena, having arrived at the island of Katáha, proceeded to dispatch his affairs, and to traffic in the sale of jewels. Having, in the course of these transactions, formed an intimacy with four young merchants, they noticed the lotus, which was frequently in his hand, and yet never faded, and were curious to learn its history. As he appeared reluctant to gratify their curiosity, they had recourse to stratagem, and invited him to an entertainment, at which they plied him with wine till he became intoxicated, and then acquainted them in his cups with the properties of the flower. The story only tended to make them anxious to know the object of Guhasena's affections; and relying upon his being detained some time at Katáha, they shortly afterwards embarked for Támraliptí, with a determination to subvert the fidelity of his wife.

On arriving at Támraliptí, they looked out for a proper agent of their iniquitous design, and soon found one in the person of an old Bauddha priestess,

---

though for a different purpose. Titania gives her three attendants a rose each from her garland; and when they lose their colour, it is to indicate her reconciliation with Oberon.

> "Thut wie ich euch gesagt, und alle Tag' und Stunden
> Schaut eure Rosen an, und wenn ihr alle drey
> Zu Lilien werden seht, so merket dran ich sey
> Mit Oberon versöhnt und wieder neu verbunden."

> "Observe then my commands, and every day and hour,
> With care behold each rose, and when it changes hue,
> And like a lily pines, be sure that with the power
> Of Elfinland appeased, my union I renew."

Canto IX, 35.

named Yogakarańdiká, with whom they formed an intimacy. Being secure of her friendly disposition, they communicated their purpose, and promised to reward her liberally, if she would assist them in their views on Devasmitá. She very readily promised to aid them, but declined their reward, as, thanks to her pupils, she was, she said, sufficiently wealthy; and her services were at their command, in requital of the civility with which they had treated her.

Accordingly the old priestess set about forming an acquaintance with Devasmitá, and, leading with her a bitch in a chain, repaired to her house. The wife of Guhasena, although mistrustful of her mission, desired her to be admitted, and enquired what she wanted. The old priestess replied, that she had been long desirous of beholding so much excellence; but that she had now been directed in a dream to visit Devasmitá, and to advise her not to lose in joyless widowhood the precious moments of her youth. Devasmitá pretended to listen favourably to these and similar suggestions, and the old woman departed, well satisfied with the impression she had made.

On the day following, she repeated her visit to the wife of Guhasena, taking with her the bitch as before, and some morsels of meat highly seasoned. These she contrived to give the animal, till from the effects of the pepper the tears trickled in large quantities from her eyes, so as to attract the notice of Devasmitá. She bewails, said the woman, in answer to her remarks, the errors of her former life; and then told her that the bitch and she were, in their former existence, the joint wives of a Brahman, who was frequently employed on foreign missions by the king of the country. That during his absence she had never imposed any restraint upon her inclinations; but her companion had been more rigid, and had severely repressed the natural sentiments of her age and sex. The consequence of their different line of conduct was their respective births in the characters in which they now appeared, together with the recollection of their former existence. The old woman concluded by recommending Devasmitá to take warning from the story, and to learn that nature was not to be outraged with impunity[1].

[1] This incident, with a very different, and much less moral denouement, is one of the stories of the Disciplina Clericalis [XIV, see the notes in F. W. V. Schmidt's edition, p. 129–34.], a collection of stories professedly derived from the Arabian fabulists, and compiled by Petrus Alfonsus, a converted Jew, who flourished about 1106, and was godson to Alfonso I. king of Arragon. In the analysis prepared by Mr. Douce, this story is the 12th, and is entitled, "Stratagem of an old woman in favour of a young gallant." She persuades his mistress, who had rejected his addresses, that her little dog was formerly a woman, and so transformed in consequence of her cruelty to her lover. (Ellis's Metrical Romances, I, 130.) This story was introduced into Europe, therefore, much about the period at which it was enrolled amongst the contents of the Vrihat Kathá in Cashmir. The metempsychosis is so much more obvious an explanation of the change of forms, that it renders it probable the story was originally Hindu. It was soon copied in Europe, and occurs in Le Grand as La vieille qui seduisit la jeune fille, III, 148. [ed. III, Vol. IV, 50.] The parallel is very close, and the old woman gives "une chienne à manger des

Devasmitá, who well knew the drift of the old woman's narration, pretended to give it implicit belief, and encouraged her to propose the introduction of the lovers. A ready assent was given to the proposal; and whilst the priestess departed to announce her success to them, Devasmitá prepared for their reception. The first who arrived was welcomed with great seeming cordiality, and invited to partake of a banquet, in which he was liberally plied with wine, into which some Datura powder had been infused. The drug quickly deprived him of consciousness, on which the servants of Devasmitá stripped him, branded his forehead with the mark of a dog's foot, and turned him

---

choses fortement saupoudrées de senève qui lui picotait le palais et les narines, et l'animal larmoyait beaucoup." She then shews her to theyoung woman, and tells her the bitch was her daughter, "Son malheur fut d'avoir le cœur dur; un jeune homme l'aimait, elle le rebuta. Le malheureux après avoir tout tenté pour l'attendrir, désespéré de sa dureté, en prit tant de chagrin qu'il tomba malade et mourut. Dieu l'a bien vengé; voyes en quel état pour la punir il a reduit ma pauvre fille, et comment elle pleure sa faute." The lesson is not thrown away. The story occours also in the Gesta Romanorum [c. 28, ed. Swan, I, 120 & 347; ed. Grässe, I, 54. II, 259], as "The old Woman and her little Dog;" and it also holds a place where we should scarcely have expected to find it, in the Promptuarium of John Herolt of Basil, an ample repository of examples for composing sermons: the compiler, a Dominican friar, professing to imitate his patron saint, who always abundabat exemplis in his discourses. [Comp. on the literature and history of this story: Th. Wright, Latin Stories. London: 1842, p. 218. Loiseleur Deslongchamps, Essai sur les Fables Indiennes. Paris: 1838, p. 106 ff. F. H. von der Hagen, Gesammtabenteuer. 1850, I, CXII ff. and III, LCCCIII–CXII, and Grässe, l. l., 374 ff.]

into a foul drain, where he lay till morning. Waking before dawn, and finding himself in a miserable plight, he hastened to conceal his disgrace in his dwelling; and being ashamed to acknowledge what had befallen him, and determined that his companions should have no reason to laugh at him, he said not a word about his treatment, but pretended he had been robbed and beaten by a set of thieves. Accordingly, his fellow travellers in succession were introduced to Devasmitá, and shared a like reception, losing their clothes and ornaments, and bearing away nothing but the indelible mark of their ignominy. They were sensible, however, that they had only met with their deserts, and could expect no redress; and they accordingly determined to set off quietly, and return at once to their country, without acquainting their ancient counsellor with their mishap, or remunerating her for her share in their discomfiture and disgrace.

After she was thus rid of her suitors, Devasmitá communicated the story to her mother-in-law, who highly approved of her conduct, but expressed some apprehension that Guhasena might suffer from the resentment of the traders, when they had returned home. Devasmitá, however, bid her be of good cheer; for she was determined to anticipate their devices, and to display as much devotion to her husband as was shewn by their countrywoman Śaktimatí.

Story of Śaktimatí.

In the island of Katáha was a temple dedicated to

the great Yaksha, named Mańibhadra, whose shrine was much frequented by the people, as he was supposed to grant whatever his worshippers requested. Offenders against law or decorum, taken by the police during the night, were locked up in this temple. In the morning they were brought before the king; and if proved guilty, the offence was made public, and they were taken away by the ministers of justice.

It so happened, that the husband of Śaktimatí, being detected in an improper intercourse with the wife of another merchant, was carried off with the adultress, and imprisoned in the temple as usual. When Śaktimatí heard the news, she forgot every thing but her husband's danger, and determined to attempt his release. With this purpose she proceeded at night to the temple with her attendants, and pretended extreme urgency to offer her homage to Mańibhadra. The priests, afraid of losing a valuable contribution, were prevailed upon to give her admittance, and she was allowed to enter the temple alone. Having discovered herself to the culprits, she exchanged clothes with the partner of her husband's offence, and took her place in the prison[1]. In the morning, when the parties were brought before the king, and the merchant and Śaktimatí were recognised as man and wife,

[1] A precisely similar story occurs in the Bahár Dánish. The turn of the chief incident, although not the same, is similar to that of Nov. VII. Part 4, of Bandello's Novelle, or the Accorto Avvedimento di una Fantesca à liberare la padrona e l'innamorato di quella de la morte.

they were dismissed with credit, whilst the superintendant of police was reprimanded and punished for the mistake.

Story of Devasmitá—concluded.

Being equally determined to extricate her husband from all possible peril, Devasmitá disguised herself and some of her servants in man's attire, and embarked as a merchant for Kaťáha. Soon after her arrival, she found out her husband, and as he was unconsciously influenced by his secret affections, had no difficulty in forming acquaintance and friendship with him. Having also ascertained the presence of her suitors, Desvamitá repaired to the king, and demanded justice. He enquired on what account; to which she replied, that she was in pursuit of four runaway slaves, whom she demanded the king's assistance to recover. The king told her to look round her, as all the people of the city were assembled, and point out the persons she claimed. She immediately designated the four merchants. They were filled with fury at the charge, and appealed to all about them, if they were not known as freemen, and the sons of respectable traders. Devasmitá paid no heed to their vehemence, but coolly desired the Rájá, if he doubted her words, to direct their turbans to be taken off. This was accordingly done, when the branded badge of slavery was manifest upon their foreheads, to the great astonishment of the Rájá and the assembly. To satisfy their curiosity, Devasmitá related her story. All parties present applauded her spirit, and pronounced the culprits to be in justice her slaves. But in respect to their origin and station, they proposed to give her a large sum for their ransom. With the consent of her husband, this was accepted by Devasmitá, and she and Guhasena returned together to Támraliptí, where they continued to reside, possessed of abundance, and happy in each other.

Story of Vatsa—resumed.

Whilst Vatsa and the princess yet remained with the friendly forest chief, an envoy arrived from Chańďasena, to tell them that he was far from displeased with what had occurred, and was about to send his son Gopálaka to represent him at his daughter's marriage. Vatsa was well contented with this intelligence; and, leaving a considerable portion of his attendants to await the arrival of Gopálaka, he and Vásavadattá set off to Kauśámbí.

A mighty train of elephants followed in the prince's march, as if the forest had yielded its stateliest tribes to do him honour. The earth, echoing to the hoofs of numerous steeds, heralded his advance; and the clouds of dust that canopied the host appeared like the flying mountains before Indra had clipped their wings[1]. Having set off at dawn, Vatsa came in sight

[1] This alludes to an absurd Pauráńik legend stating that the mountains formerly had wings—an addition which rendered them so very troublesome and refractory to Indra, the deity of the at-

of his capital on the following day, and halted for the night at the residence of Rumańwán. On the third day he made his public entry into the city, which assumed all her ornaments, and looked like a bride that welcomed her long absent lord. The roads and streets were lined with the citizens, delighted to behold their monarch again; and the windows and houses were crowded with their wives and daughters, eager to behold their master's choice. The air was rent with their acclamations, when Vatsa and the princess[1] passed, mounted on the same elephant, and resembling a dark cloud girt with lightning; as if the prince had brought back in person the tutelary goddess of his fame.

In a short time Gopálaka arrived. Vatsa went out to meet him, and conducted him to his sister, who welcomed him with tears. The marriage ceremony was immediately solemnized. As Vatsa took her hand, the whole frame of Vásavadattá shook with agitation, a thick film overspread her eyes, and existence seemed to be on the point of yielding to the shafts of Kámadeva[2]. The prompt support of her lord sustained her steps, and led her in due repetition round the holy fire[3]. When the ceremony was completed, Gopálaka

mosphere, that he was obliged to cut them off with his thunderbolts.

[1] The public appearance of the princess, as well as that of the women of the city, indicates a state of manners long unknown in Hindústán.

[2] The deity of love.

[3] The bride's taking seven steps round the consecrated fire is

presented the prince with splendid gifts on the part of Chańdasena. Vatsa and his new bride shewed themselves to the people, and received their loud and delighted acclamations. They then repaired to the palace, where Vatsa conferred the honour of the fillet[1] on Gopálaka and the Pulinda prince; and then, deputing Yogandharáyańa and Rumańwán to superintend the festivities, both of the court and the people, retired with his bride.

Ib., Dec. 1824, p. 194—208.

Vatsa's Second Marriage.

After some period had elapsed, Yogandharáyańa, the minister, anxious to excite the prince to exploits worthy of his character and descent, held this discourse with Rumańwán.—"Our sovereign Vatsa, as descended from the illustrious house of Pańdu, is undoubtedly entitled to the capital Hástinapura, and dominion over the world. Neglecting these lofty claims,

part of the Hindu marriage ritual, according to the Vedas [or, more strictly, according to the Gŕihyasútras. See A. Weber's Indische Studien, Vol. V, 320 ff. Colebrooke's Essays, p. 138.]

[1] Pat́t́á bandha, binding of a fillet or tiara on the brow. It was part of the ceremonial of coronation with the ancient Hindu princes; but was perhaps sometimes, as in this case, only an acknowledgment of princely rank conferred by a superior on his inferior or feudatory.

he is contented to rule over a limited territory, and wasting his time upon women, wine, and the chace, leaves to our charge the conduct of the state. But this is highly unbecoming his family and his talents, and we must endeavour to animate him to such efforts as shall retrieve his character, and extend his power. There is no occasion to despair. The worst cases are susceptible of cure, and ingenuity can effect any thing. In proof of what I say, listen to this anecdote.—There was a king, named Mahásena, who was attacked by another sovereign, defeated, and compelled to pay tribute. He was a prince of high spirit, and his humiliation preyed upon his mind, so that he fell ill of the spleen, and was brought by fretting and the disease to the verge of the grave. Medicines were administered in vain; and his physician, as a last hope, entered suddenly into his chamber, apparently in great distress, and abruptly announced to him that the queen was dead. The news agitated the king violently, and he cast himself on the ground in a paroxysm of sorrow. The abscess in the spleen was burst by the effort, and his health immediately improved. The physician, satisfied with the manifest change, confessed the falsehood by which it was occasioned. This giving a fresh impetus to the king's spirits, he speedily resumed his former energies, and was soon able to levy an army, with which he attacked, and triumphed over his former conqueror[1].—In this manner let us serve our prince

[1] The circumstances here narrated are not without analogies

in his own despite;—and in the first place, we must gain over the only monarch that stands in our way, Pradyota, king of Magadha[1].

The two counsellors accordingly debated how Pradyota was to be made their master's friend, and determined that it could only be contrived by Vatsa's marrying his daughter. At the same time they knew that he never would permit the princess to be the second wife of any monarch; and Yogandharáyańa proposed that they should secure the aid of Vásavadattá, and with her concurrence disseminate a belief of her death. To this Rumańwán objected the discredit they should sustain if their scheme were detected, as happened to the ascetic at Sákarmiká on the Ganges.

Story of an Ascetic.

An ascetic, who professed to have imposed upon himself a vow of perpetual silence, lived in great repute at that city. He subsisted on charity, had many mendicant disciples, and occupied with them a conventual dwelling, with a temple attached. At the house of a pious banker, who held the holy man in great

---

in fact. It is not marvellous, therefore, that we may trace them in fiction. The point of the story is the same as that of the "Deux Anglais à Paris", a Fabliau, and of "Une femme à l'extremité qui se mit en si grosse colère voyant son mari qui baisoit sa servante qu'elle recouvra la santé", of Marguerite of Navarre. [Heptameron, Nouvelle 71.]

[1] Magadha was the kingdom of Behár, extending along the Ganges from Patna to Mirzapore.

reverence, the ascetic was accustomed to receive alms, and in so doing had frequent opportunities of seeing the banker's daughter, a girl of extraordinary beauty. Her charms made an impression upon the mendicant; and allowing his passions to master his penance, he long meditated upon the means by which, without betraying his hypocrisy, he might get her into his power.

Having at last devised what he thought a likely scheme, he repaired to the banker's house, and received his usual donation from the fair hands of the damsel. As he departed, he exclaimed, loud enough to be overheard by the father, "Alas! alas! that such things should be!" Exclamations that in themselves, as well as their violation of the mendicant's supposed vow, could not fail to excite the banker's curiosity. He therefore followed the ascetic to his cell, and when there, asked him earnestly what had induced him to break his silence. The mendicant replied, with some hesitation, and affected distress: "Regard for you, my good friend, overcame my solemn obligations. I read in your daughter's countenance a sad reverse for you: and whenever she marries, you, your wife, and sons, will inevitably perish. This conviction forced from me the exclamations you heard. It cannot now be remedied; but if you have any affection for the rest of your family, you will rid yourself of your daughter. Put her by night into a basket covered with leather[1], place

[1] This rude contrivance is still in use in the south of India

a lamp upon it, and thus offer her to the holy Ganges." The banker, who implicitly trusted in the words of this villainous hypocrite, went home in an agony of fear and affliction, and, when night came, did as he had been enjoined.

The ascetic, at the same hour, directed his disciples to repair to the river; and if they saw a basket with a lamp upon it, bring it ashore, and privately convey it to him, prohibiting them rigidly from any attempt to inspect its contents. They obeyed his commands, and kept a look out for the object to which their attention had been directed by their master.

In the mean time, however, a Rajput, walking upon the bank, was struck by the appearance of the floating light, and with the assistance of his servants, brought the basket ashore, before the current had conveyed it where the mendicant's followers were stationed. Having opened it, and found the maiden, to his great surprise and delight, the Rajput conveyed her to his house, which was near at hand; and learning her story, determined to expose and punish the ascetic. He therefore substituted a fierce baboon for the damsel; and fastening the basket again, committed it to the current as before. It was now taken possession of by the mendicants, and agreeably to the orders of their chief, carried unopened to the convent. He commanded them to place it in his chamber, and then desired them to

---

for crossing rivers: it is also still employed upon the Euphrates, as it was in the time of Strabo.

go to rest, and on no occount to approach his cell, whatever noises they might hear, at it was his design to pass the night in some very solemn and momentous mysteries. They obeyed, and repaired to their repose.

The ascetic, being thus at liberty to accomplish his purposes, secured the door of his cell, and eagerly opened the basket. He had scarcely done so, when the baboon sprang upon him, and bit and scratched him unmercifully. It was in vain he called for assistance; his disciples were too mindful of his previous injunctions to venture near him. At last, with much difficulty, and after the loss of his nose and ears, he contrived to get out of his cell, and alarm the other inhabitants of the domicile, by whose aid he was extricated from the clutches of his savage assailant. His secret, however, was divulged, and in the morning the story was spread throughout the town. The banker gave his daughter to her deliverer, and the ascetic was glad to make his escape in a whole skin from a place where his iniquitous schemes had exposed him to universal derision and contempt*.

This story was insufficient to deter Yogandharáyańa from the prosecution of his scheme; and Rumańwán, therefore, shifting his ground, argued the danger of

* [Two other versions of the same story occur, one in the Katharńava, chapt. 2, and the other in the Bharaťakadwátrinśiká, c. 3. See the Sanskrit text, with a German translation by Prof. A. Aufrecht, in "Zeitschrift der deutschen morgenl. Gesellschaft", XIV, 569-81.]

Vatsa's dying through grief for the supposed loss of his queen: separation from the object of our affections being often, he said, attended with serious results, as was the case with Devasena.

Story of Devasena.

In Śravastí dwelt a merchant of great opulence; but his richest treasure was a daughter of such surpassing loveliness, that all who beheld her became her slaves, and sacrificed their understandings to their passion. The father, conscious of her extraordinary beauty, resolved to offer her to the king, Devasena, as, should he wed her to any other person, he apprehended he might afterwards incur the resentment of the Rájá. Accordingly, he requested Devasena's acceptance of the damsel, and the Rájá sent some trustworthy Brahmans to visit the maiden, and report upon her qualifications. When they beheld her, and found her so singularly beautiful, it occurred to them that if the Rájá married her he was likely to be fascinated with her charms, and to neglect on her account the duties of his station. They therefore reported, that, although a girl of good appearance, yet the marks upon her face and hands[1] were indicative of misfortune, and she was consequently unfit to become the bride of the king.

---

[1] The Sámudriká Vidyá, or science of palmistry, as intimately connected with astrology, was once carried to as extravagant a height in India as in Europe. It is not much cultivated at present, but is not perhaps the less believed. [Comp. the Śabdakalpadruma, s. v. Sámudrakam.]

This negotiation being closed, the merchant soon afterwards married his daughter to the commander of the army, and nothing more was thought of the matter. It happened, however, some time afterwards that the Rájá beheld the bride at the window of her husband's palace, and was instantly the victim of a violent passion, blended with the mortifying recollection that he was the cause of his own disappointment. These thoughts preyed upon his mind, and induced a severe fever, which put an end to his existence[1].

Yogandharáyańa, being unmoved by these examples, proposed to refer the point to the queen's brother, and he concurring heartily in the project, Rumańwán was compelled to wave his objections. With a view, therefore, to effect their purpose, they persuaded Vatsa to set out on a hunting expedition to the district of Láváńaka[2], which bordered on Magadha.

When Vatsa was about to quit his capital, he was surprised by no ordinary visitor. The sage Nárada descended from mid heaven, and was received by the prince and princess with every mark of veneration.

---

[1] The first part of the story may remind the reader of the events which we have elevated to the dignity of history in the persons of Edgar and Elfrida. Lingard, however, has shewn that the whole is a mere fiction, first told by William of Malmesbury, and borrowed by him from an old ballad.

[2] This name is not now to be traced in any maps of that part of the country. [It is probably the same as Lavańanagara, a place mentioned in an inscription from Chedi. See Journ. As. Soc. Bengal, Vol. XXX, p. 321.]

The object of his visit was in fact to prepare the minds of both for the events about to take place; and he announced to Vatsa the approach of temporary affliction, which would end in increased happiness, whilst he foretold to Vásavadattá, that she would be the mother of a prince, who should obtain the sovereignty over the Vidyádharas, or spirits of air. Having made these communications to them, he again disappeared.

Vatsa now set off upon his hunting excursion, leaving his minister, as usual, to conduct public affairs. Yogandharáyańa lost no time in imparting the scheme to Vásavadattá, who, foregoing, in the prospect of her husband's aggrandizement, all selfish considerations, cheerfully consented to contribute to its success. Accordingly the old minister assumed the dress of a Brahman, and Vásavadattá the character of his daughter. Vasantaka, fantastically disguised, was the supposed Brahman's disciple; and in this capacity they proceeded to Magadha. Rumańwán, left behind, shortly after their departure set fire to the palace, so effectually, that it was half consumed before any assistance could be procured; and he circulated a report, which was generally credited, that the queen had perished in the flames.

The party who had proceeded to the capital of Magadha soon contrived to throw themselves in the way of Padmávatí, the young princess. She was interested by the appearance of Vásavadattá, and summoned the trio to her presence to ascertain who they were. Yogandharáyańa's story was, that Vásavadattá was his daughter, and had been deserted by a husband of whom they were now in search; and at his request the princess gladly undertook to take care of the supposed daughter, whilst he was engaged in the pursuit more actively by having safely disposed of her. Vásavadattá being thus provided for, the two ministers, relinquishing their disguises, repaired to Láváńaka to seek Vatsa, and condole with him for his loss.

Upon the first communication of the afflicting news, Vatsa was overcome with grief, and was with some difficulty prevented from laying violent hands upon himself. After his first emotions had subsided, however, he recollected the prophesy of Nárada; and observing something rather suspicious in the pretended sorrow of his friends, he felt inclined to conjecture that Vásavadattá was still alive, and in expectation of her re-appearance, determined quietly to await the result.

When the news of Vásavadattá's death reached the king of Magadha, he readily availed himself of the opportunity to secure a suitable bridegroom for his daughter, and sent his ambassadors to propose the alliance. Vatsa, conformably to the plan he had laid down for himself, made no difficulty upon Yogandharáyańa's urging the match, and the young princess had been prepared by Vásavadattá to think of Vatsa with interest and affection. All parties being thus agreed, there was no plea for delay; and Vatsa going from Láváńaka to the capital of Magadha, the marriage was celebrated with due solemnity and pomp.

In a short time Vatsa, having taken leave of his father-in-law, returned to his own kingdom, his heart still pining for Vásavadattá, and impatient at her protracted disappearance. She in the mean while had been secretly conducted back to Láváńaka, where Vatsa continued to reside, and was concealed in her brother's palace. There at last Vatsa was allowed, as if by chance, to see her. He hastened towards her, but before he could clasp her to his breast, his agitation overcame his faculties, and he fell senseless on the ground. He was recovered by the endearments of his beloved wife, and awoke to be conscious that Vásavadattá was once more his. It is unnecessary to describe his happiness. The affection that had before united the two princesses was increased by their affinity; and although the king of Magadha was at first displeased by the trick that had reduced his daughter to the station of a younger wife, yet when he learnt the perfect union which prevailed between her and Vásavadattá, he suppressed his indignation, and cordially rejoiced in the success of the scheme that had given Padmávatí to Vatsa.

History of Vatsa—continued.

When a sufficient period had been devoted to domestic enjoyments, the minister Yogandharáyańa urged his master to undertake the subjugation of the surrounding regions especially those to the east, assigning as reasons for such a preference, that the north was occupied by barbarians; in the west, the sun and planets were obscured; the south bordered on the domains of the Rákshasas; whilst the east was under the regency of Indra, and was the quarter in which the sun rose, and to which the Ganges flowed. The country between the Vindhya and Himála mountains, and that watered by the Jáhnaví, was the more excellent; and the progenitors of Vatsa had established themselves along the course of the sacred stream, having held their court at Hástinapura, until Śatáníka transferred it to Kauśámbí.

The advice of the minister was highly agreeable to the ambition of the monarch, and Vatsa therefore immediately prepared for his expedition. His fathers-in-law, the kings of Ujjayiní and Magadha, furnished powerful accessions to his force; and Gopálaka, the brother of Vásavadattá, whom Vatsa had made king of Vaideha, and Sinhavarmá, the brother of the queen Padmávatí, who held the sovereignty of Chedi*, both accompanied Vatsa with all their troops. The friendly chief of the forest tribes likewise joined the army, and the host spread over the country like the mighty clouds that precede the rains: the steeds glittered with golden trappings, and the war elephants were decorated with vermilion and flowers. The sun was concealed by the dust that canopied the multitude, until scattered by

* [On the site of Chedi, near Jubulpore, see F.-E. Hall in "Journal of the Amer. Or. Soc.", VI, 520 ff. and in Journ. As. Soc. Bengal, XXX, 317. 334.]

the countless banners that agitated the labouring air. Vatsa rode a stately elephant, whilst the imperial umbrella waved over his head, like a fierce lion recumbent beneath a tree that spreads its solitary shade upon the summit of a mountain. The two queens followed his march, like the personified divinities Victory and Fame.

The arms of Vatsa were first directed against Brahmadatta, king of Benares, who finding resistance hopeless hastened to acknowledge submission. Hence the conqueror proceeded to the shores of the eastern Sea, where he erected columns commemorative of his triumph[1]. He then exacted tribute from Kalinga[2] and Anga, and proceeded westwards to the Mahendra mountains. The terrified inhabitants fled to the Vindhyan caves[3], and the forest monarchs promptly prof-

---

[1] Jaya stambhas, pillars of victory, the erection of which by Indian conquerors is often alluded to by Hindu writers, and explains the character of the solitary columns, which are occasionally met with, as the Lát at Delhi, the pillars at Alláhábád, Buddal, &c.

[2] Kalinga is usually described as extending from Orissa to Drávida, or below Madras, the coast of the northern Sircars. It appears, however, sometimes to be the Delta of the Ganges. It is familiar to the natives of the eastern Archipelago by the name of Kling, and was known to the ancients as the Regio Calingarum. Anga is the country along the west bank of the Ganges, including Rájamahal and Bhagalpur. [Lassen, Ind. Alt., I, 143, 180.]

[3] The Vindhya mountains are divided into three parts, of which the first, or eastern part, extends from the Bay of Bengal to the source of the Narmadá and Śoṅe. The western portion extends

fered their submission. Thence Vatsa marched to the south, where he crossed the Káverí, and humbled the pride of the Chola[1] monarch. He then subdued the Muralas[2]; and fording the sevenfold channel of the Godávarí he reduced the Málavas to obedience. Having then crossed the Revá, he arrived at Ujjayiní, where he remained some time with his father-in-law, the delighted sire of Vásavadattá.

After a short interval of repose, Vatsa proceeded to the west, where he overran the province of Láṫa[3],

---

from thence to the Gulph of Cambay. The third, or southern, lies on the south of the Narmadá and Śońe, and gives rise to the Taptí, and the Vaitarańí, or Cuttack river. The first portion, it appears, is designated in the text by the term Mahendra. Ptolemy has a range called Maiandrus, but it lies east of Bengal. Wilford supposes the Maiandrus mountains, to derive their name from Mayanádri, the mountains of the Mayun, a people between Chittagong and Aracan. It is not impossible, however, that they bore the appellation of Mahendra, and that either Ptolemy or our text, or both, have mistaken their precise situation.

[1] Chola was the sovereignty of the western part of the Peninsula on the Carnatic, extending southwards to Tanjore, where it was bounded by the Pańdyan kingdom. It appears to have been the Regio Soretanum of Ptolemy; and the Chola Mańḋala, or district, furnishes the modern appellation of the Coast Coromandel. [Lassen, l. l. I, 166. III, 205 ff.]

[2] The Muralas are not traceable in classical geography, unless we are allowed to conjecture, that they are the same with the Curula of Ptolemy, a town lying in the direction, where we might expect to meet with the Muralas of the text. ["Murala is another name for Kerala, now Malabar". F.-E. Hall in Journ. Amer. Or. Soc., VI., 527.]

[3] The position of Láṫa, and its name, which, as written with

as far as to the ocean. He next marched towards the north, and compelled the Sindhu[1] prince to acknowledge a superior, triumphing over the Mlechhas and Turushkas, like Ráma over the Rákshasas. He then proceeded along the frontiers of Persia, after decapitating its king; and turning eastwards, skirted the Himálaya, as far as Kámarúpa[2], where he received the submission of the sovereign. He then visited the father of his queen Padmávatí at Magadha, and after enjoying the pleasures of his court for a short interval, returned in triumph to Lávánaka.

After his return to his capital, Vatsa continued to spend his time in the society of his queens and friends with uninterrupted felicity. His only anxiety was now to possess offspring to perpetuate his race; and his wish was soon gratified, the queen Vásavadattá being delivered of a son, who was an incarnation of the god of love, and who, as was announced by Nárada, was destined to exercise sovereignty over the spirits of heaven. He was named Naraváhanadatta. At the same period, the king's three ministers and the chamberlain had sons; and these four, with two other youths, the offspring of a Brahman female, a favourite of the

---

the ṭ, is convertible in the spoken dialects to Lár, identify it with the Larice of Ptolemy. [Lassen, Ind. Alt., I, 108. III, 170.]

[1] Sind, or the country along the Indus, occupied by tribes, that came originally perhaps from central Asia, and correctly, therefore, termed Turushkas, or Turks. They were the Indo-Scythi of the ancients.

[2] The western portion of Ásám.

queen, were attached to the young prince, to be educated along with him, that they might he his companions in youth, and counsellors in maturity[1].

Story of Naraváhanadatta, the Son of Vatsa.

Vatsa now devoted his whole attention to the care and education of his only son, in such a manner as to occasion inattention to his public duties. His minister Yogandharáyańa expostulated with him on this account, and told him, that there was no need of anxiety for one, whom Śiva had announced should become the supreme monarch of the Vidyádharas[2], and who was attended unremittingly by an invisible guard. As he said this, a celestial being, wearing a gorgeous diadem, and armed with a scymitar, stood before them. To Vatsa's demands who he was, and what was his purpose, he replied, that he was the king of the Vidyádharas, obliged by the superior power of his enemies to withdraw from his dominions: that he knew the son of Vatsa was destined to be his paramount

---

[1] We soon after this take leave of Vatsa and his train, and his son and the young men his companions form the leading personages in the narrative.

[2] The Vidyádharas, in Hindu mythology, are the spirits of air. They have a monarch of their own, are of both sexes, travel wherever they list, possess superhuman power, and are of kindly disposition. They are the servants chiefly of Kuvera and Indra, but form part of the state of all the gods, being a sociable race, and excelling in music, the dance, and other lighter accomplishments. They resemble the good genii of the Arabian Nights.

lord, and he was desirous of being the first to do him homage. Vatsa felt highly gratified by his confirmation of his son's future elevation, and received Śaktivega, (so the king of the Vidyádharas was named,) with every mark of respect. In their conversation he enquired how the station of Vidyádhara was to be obtained; to which Śaktivega replied, it was the recompense of propitiating the deity Śankara; and in evidence of this assertion narrated his story to Vatsa, and the queen Vásavadattá.

Story of Śaktivega.

In the city of Varddhamána, the ornament of the earth, reigned Paropakárí, a pious and benevolent prince. He had an only daughter, named Kanakarekhá, a princess of surpassing charms, created by Brahmá to humble the conceit of Lakshmí in her beauty. As she grew in years, the king became desirous to see her married, but was much at a loss to find a suitor worthy of her hand. Nor was this the only cause of perplexity: the princess could not endure the idea of becoming a wife, and professed she would rather die than be separated from her parents. As they, however, continued to urge the propriety and necessity of her marriage, she at last consented to take for her husband any one of Brahmanical or Kshatriya origin, who should have beheld "The Golden City;" and with this the king her father was of necessity contented.

The object of Paropakárí was now to find some man of exalted rank who had seen this city; but all the princes and nobles of his court declared, they not only had never seen, but had never heard of such a place. The king's only resource, therefore, was to appeal to the people; and public proclamation was repeatedly made, that any man of the priestly or military tribe who had beheld "The Golden City" should have the princess for his bride, and be installed in the joint administration of regal authority. The proclamations were unavailing: no one knew any thing about the "Golden City".

At last a young Brahman, named Śaktideva, who for his idle habits had been expelled his father's house, and who had lost all his money in gambling, considering his situation desperate, and indifferent to the consequences, falsely pretended having sojourned in the "Golden City". As the king was unable to judge of his veracity, he referred the pretender to his daughter. The princess having heard his story, was at no loss to detect the fraud, and ordered Śaktideva to be turned out of her presence without any ceremony. She then reproved her father for being so credulous, and told him it was his duty, both as a father and a king, to be upon his guard against impostors. They were sufficiently numerous, she said, and many were their contrivances; and she related to the king the following story in confirmation of her remarks.

Story of Śiva and Mádhava.

In the city of Ratnapura, two rogues, one named Śiva, and the other named Mádhava, had resided for some time, and had fleeced every inhabitant of the place. They thought it high time, therefore, to change the scene of their operations, and selected Ujjayiní as the object of their next visitation; particularly as they heard that the king's Brahman, Śankara Swámí, was a weak, credulous old man, and immensely rich, with an only daughter exceedingly beautiful. Having concerted their scheme, they set out to Ujjayiní.

Mádhava having collected a respectable train, assumed the character of a Rajput nobleman, and halted with his attendants at a village without the city. Śiva entered Ujjayiní alone, and having found a deserted temple on the banks of the Siprá, he took up his abode in it in the character of a religious ascetic. In this capacity he soon attracted notice by the seeming severity of his penance. Having well smeared himself with mud, he plunged every day at dawn head foremost into the stream, and remained for a long period under water. Rising with the sun, he faced the luminary, as if lost in prayer and meditation. Repairing to the temple, he worshipped the deity with flowers, and seated in the positions practised by the tribe of Yogís, appeared wholly occupied with abstract devotion, whilst in fact he was only devising fraudulent projects. In the afternoon, clad in the skin of the black deer, and taking his staff and hollow cocoanut, he traversed the city to gather food in alms. Of the rice so collected he made an ostentatious distribution, dividing it into three parts, giving one to the crows, one to any person who chose to take it, and reserving the third for himself. At night he remained alone in the temple; for he made light of those places, which people in general avoid. The inhabitants of the city, beholding these daily observances, and the life of austerity that Śiva led, very soon formed a high opinion of his sanctity, and numbers flocked about the holy man, eager to prostrate themselves at his feet.

When Mádhava had ascertained by his emissaries the success, that had attended his comrade's imposture, he judged it time to play his part. He therefore entered the city, and engaged a spacious mansion at some distance from the palace. Performing his ablutions in the Siprá, he took the opportunity of renewing his intercourse with his associate by professing to recognize him as a religious man of singular sanctity, whom he had before encountered on his travels, and shewing him accordingly extreme veneration. Śiva at night repaid his visit; and they ate and drank, and made merry together, and concerted their future measures.

On the following morning, Mádhava sent a messenger with a present to Śankara Swámí, the king's priest, to announce himself as a Rájput of rank, who had just arrived from the Dakhiń, and would gladly take service along with his followers with the monarch of Ujjayiní. He hinted also, that he did not want either the means or inclination to be liberal; in proof of which he sent two pieces of fine cloth for his acceptance. The old man fell into the snare, and, blinded by cupidity, promised the stranger his influence with the king. This promise, his zeal being stimulated by fresh presents, he speedily performed; and at his recommendation Mádhava and his followers were enrolled amongst the prince's retainers. The priest carried his attention still further, and in the hope of ultimate advantage, gave the pretended Rájputs accommodation within the precincts of his own stately residence.

When Mádhava took up his abode in the dwelling of Śankara Swámí, he requested permission to deposit his jewels in the old man's private treasury—a permission readily granted. The jewels, which were numerous, and seemed costly, were all artificial; but they were fabricated with great skill, and impressed the old priest with the conviction of their being genuine, and of immense value. Mádhava then, by a course of extreme abstinence, reduced himself to a most meagre condition; and pretending to be dangerously ill, requested Śankara Swámí to bring him some pious Brahman, to whom he might present his property, as he was certain he could not long survive. The old man consented; but whilst he hesitated about a choice, one of the attendants, previously prepared, suggested, that they should send for the holy man, who occupied the temple on the banks of the Siprá, and who was held in high repute throughout the city. This was Mádhava's confederate, Śiva, who was now to be brought into action. Śankara Swámí readily assented; and having his own views in the arrangement, undertook to summon the ascetic himself. He accordingly repaired to Śiva, and with profound reverence opened the business to him. A Rájput of rank, he said, was on the point of death, and was anxious to present him with all his wealth, which in jewels was most valuable, if he would condescend to accept it. To this Śiva replied, that he pardoned him for making such a proposal; but it was very absurd, to offer transitory and perishable treasures to one, whose whole delights were penance and mortification, and whose sole object was divine knowledge: he therefore declined accompanying him to the sick man. This affected indifference only served to whet Śankara's zeal, and he expatiated eloquently on the enjoyments of social life, as contrasted with ascetic privation; the superiority of the householder in the discharge of his obligations to the gods and to mankind, and the happiness conferred upon the human condition by the possession of wife and children. By arguments of this nature Śiva suffered himself to be softened; and at last he acknowledged, that he might be induced possibly to resume his connexion with society, if he could meet with a wife in any family sufficiently pure to be affianced with his own. Śankara Swámí availed himself instantly of this opening, and proposed his own daughter, if Śiva would relinquish to him the wealth he should receive from the Rájput, engaging at the same time to provide handsomely for his maintenance. With much affected reluctance, Śiva at last consented to wed the daughter of the priest; and as to the property, he left that entirely to his father-in-law's disposal. Śankara Swámí, internally setting down the ascetic for a fool, and congratulating himself on his own cunning, lost no time in executing the conditions. He took Śiva with him to his house, and married him to his daughter, and on the third day conducted him to Mádhava. Mádhava received them with every mark of reverence, and requesting the prayers of the pretended saint, presented him with the casket of false jewels. Śiva having received them, handed them over to his father-in-law, professing to be utterly ignorant of their quality or value. He then bestowed his benediction on the invalid, and withdrew with the delighted Śankara Swámí, now in possession of the prize he had been so anxious to secure.

After a short interval Mádhava pretended to recover his health, being restored, he asserted, by the benediction of the Brahman. Śiva also by degress shewed himself dissatisfied with his situation; and at last expressed his determination to dwell apart from his father-in-law, claiming at least half the jewels, which had been presented to him. Śankara, to appease his clamours, and unwilling to part with any of the jewels, transferred to him all his own personal property; and with this Śiva maintained a house and establishment of his own. In order to raise money, the priest was now induced to dispose of one of the supposed inestimable ornaments. When the jewellers examined it, they admired the skill with which it was fabricated, but pronounced it made of crystal and coloured glass, set in brass, and of no value. Bewildered with apprehension, Śankara produced the casket, and all its contents proved to be counterfeits like the first. He was struck, as if with a thunderbolt, and was some time before he knew where he was, or what had become of him. His dream of wealth was at an end, and he found too late that he had been grossly imposed upon.

The priest's first thought was to get back his own money from Śiva, to whom he repaired, and proposed to give him up the jewels, saying not a syllable of his discovery. To this offer, however, Śiva replied, that he should have no objection, but that in truth all the money was expended. Śankara then applied to the king for redress, and at his suit the confederates were brought up for enquiry. When called upon for his defence, Śiva averred, that he had not sought the bargain, and that he had all along professed his entire ignorance of the nature, and cost of the ornaments. If they were false, therefore, Śankara could not blame him on that account, as he had taken them entirely on his own proposal and valuation. In like manner, Mádhava protested his innocence of any intention to defraud. Such as the ornaments were, he said, he had inherited them from his father, and he was wholly unacquainted with their real worth. In giving them as a free-will offering to a holy man, he could have had no object in passing off artificial gems as genuine, as he had nothing to gain by the imposition; and that he was free from all dishonest purposes, was manifest by his recovering, in consequence of his donation, from a malady which threatened to put a period to his existence. The defence set up by the two rogues was so plausible, that they were immediately acquitted of all fraudulent intention, and Śankara Swámí was judged to have deserved the consequences of his own avarice. He was therefore dismissed with the ridicule of the court, and lost his credit, as well as his daughter and his money. Śiva and Mádhava, on the contrary, were held as innocent and fortunate men, and their knavery was rewarded with the countenance of the king, and the enjoyment of the prosperity they so ill deserved[1].

---

[1] Part of the fraud, or the substitution of false for real ornaments, is similar to the incident in "Rule a Wife and have a Wife", which procures Perez the title of the Copper Captain; as Estifania says:

> "Sir, there's your treasure, sell it to a tinker,
> To mend old kettles.
> Your clothes are parallel to these, all counterfeit;
> Put these and them on, you're a man of copper."

Ib., June 1825, p. 302—14.

Story of Śaktivega, continued.

Having finished her story the Princess recommended to her father to benefit by the lesson, and to be cautious to whom he gave credit, and she repeated her wish, that he would not be anxious with respect to her marriage, as she was contented to remain unespoused. To this the king replied, that it was not good for a young woman to grow up unmarried. The world was censorious, and very ready to attach blame undeserved, and the more amiable the character, the more was it the mark of malice. In proof of which he cited the adventure of Haraswámí.

Story of Haraswámí.

On the banks of the Ganges in the city of Kusumapura resided a holy man named Haraswámí, the simplicity of whose manners, and whose uninterrupted course of devotion, had won the regard and esteem of all the citizens: there was one man however on whom they produced an opposite effect, and who unable to bear the sight of so much piety resolved to attempt the ruin of the Ascetic.

With this intent he contrived to disseminate a report, that Haraswámí was very far from being the character he appeared, that his sanctity was assumed, and that in secret he was the worshipper of some of the terrific divinities, to whom he made a practice of sacrificing children. The rumour soon gained ground, and it was asserted and generally believed, that a great number of children had recently been lost to their parents, whose disappearance was thus accounted for.

The people of the city now flocking together would have proceeded to the hermitage of Haraswámí to put him to death; but the chief Brahmans, standing in some awe of his character, prevailed upon them to be satisfied with his exile. Messengers were sent to him, therefore, to desire him to leave the neighbourhood without delay. Highly surprised by this command, Haraswámí begged to know how he had incurred such a sentence, and on being informed determined with the courage of conscious innocence to face his accusers. He therefore repaired to the city, and, addressing the people collected on the walls, begged them to listen but for a moment, before they condemned him for ever. Has any one amongst you, continued he, lost his child? The question startled them. Each looked at his fellow and saw himself reproached for precipitation. Many had their children by their sides—others went off to their different homes to ascertain if their children were safe, and in a short time all were obliged to confess that the accusation was wholly unfounded, and that they had unjustly banished the pious man! So easy is it, said the Prince, to affix a stigma on the most spotless characters. You must not expect my child, added Paropakárí, to escape, and should this happen, should calumny blight your youth, you will be the means of plunging a shaft in your father's heart.

When Kanakarekhá observed her father thus earnest, she forbore to press the subject, contenting herself with repeating her readiness to marry any one of the priestly or martial tribe, who should behold the Golden city, and with this the king was compelled to be satisfied.

Story of Śaktivega, continued.

In the mean time Śaktideva, ashamed of the exposure he had suffered, and deeply enamoured of the princess, determined to discover this unknown city, or perish in the undertaking. If he succeeded, he should win the only object for which he now felt life desirable, and if he failed, existence was well sacrificed in such a cause.—Resolved therefore to return successful or return no more, Śaktideva quitted Varddhamána, and directed his course to the South[1].

After winding his way for some time through the intricacies of the Vindhya forest, he came to a hermitage by the side of a pellucid pool, the residence of a pious ascetic and his disciples: having been received with kindness and hospitably entertained by the venerable Sage who had counted a hundred years, Śakti-

---

[1] The incidents that follow, are precisely in the style of the marvellous in the Arabian Nights, and many of them will be recognised as occurring in that collection.

deva informed him of the object of his journey, and enquired of him, if he knew where the Golden city was to be found. The Sage replied, he had never heard of the name, but recommended Śaktideva to seek the hermitage of his elder brother[1], who might possibly give him some information, and directed him to the place, three hundred Yojanas remote in the country of Kámpilya: with this direction Śaktideva cheerfully resumed his route.

Upon his arrival at the habitation of the elder ascetic, he speedily announced the purport of his visit, with no better success, however, than before. The Sage had never heard of the Golden city. He recommended Śaktideva to visit an Island in the ocean named Utsthala, the Nisháda Prince of which would probably know something of the city, if any such place existed, and he directed his visitor how to shape his course for that Island. In conformity to the instructions of the Sage, Śaktideva, after a wearisome journey, arrived at Viťankapura, a flourishing city on the sea shore. Here he found a vessel bound for Utsthala, and took his passage on board.

After they had been at sea a few days they encountered a furious storm. The lightning shot along the heavens like the forky tongue of fate, and the thunder growled as if a demon roared: the wrathful breeze

[1] Thus in the story of Mazin of Khorasan, Mazin in his search after the Islands Wak al Wak, is directed by the seven good Genii to one of their Uncles 'Abd al Kuddary, a venerable old man, who refers him to 'Abd as Sullíb his elder brother.

bowing the light, and uprooting the resisting objects, lashed the ocean, and mighty waves as vast as mountains angrily heaved upon the deep. The vessel, now tossed to the clouds, and now precipitated into the abyss, was unable to resist the fury of the elements and was rent asunder: some of the crew clinging to the broken spars were taken up by other vessels, which were scattered by the gale, but Śaktideva who had clung to a plank was cast ashore upon a distant Island. It happened, that this was the Island he was bound to, and one of the first persons he encountered on the head, was Satyavrata the king. Satyavrata having heard his story expressed great interest in Śaktideva's adventure, and, although unable to direct him to the Golden city, undertook to assist him in his search.

After a short time, Satyavrata proposed to Śaktideva to go to an island at some short distance, where at a particular season of the year, now at hand, a solemn festival in honour of an image of Hari was observed: on this occasion people from all quarters resorted to the place, and some of them might probably afford information of the Golden city. Śaktideva readily consented, and they embarked on board a sloop, and set off for the island named Ratnakúťa: on their way Śaktideva observed an object in the middle of the sea, the nature of which he was at a loss to comprehend. It looked like a Beŕ tree, but in size equalled a mountain: he called Satyavrata to look at it, who immediately exclaimed, they were lost: the object they beheld was a vast tree of miraculous growth, rising from the centre of a whirlpool: every thing caught within the gulph inevitably perished, and they had been carried by the current so near it that there was now no chance of escape. As he spoke this the ship was whirled within the circling tide, and in an instant was submerged. Śaktideva, however, exerting all his activity sprang from the deck as they were sinking, and clung to one of the pendulous branches of the tree, from which he ascended, and perched himself securely on a more substantial bough[1]. The rest of

---

[1] These incidents offer coincidences of exceeding interest, for they are neither more nor less than Homeric: in the same manner as the Beŕ or Indian Fig rises from the whirlpool, so an immense Wild Fig tree hangs over Charybdis, and Ulysses like Śaktideva makes his escape by jumping upon the tree. The course of this fable eastward or westward connot now be conjectured, but the specification of the Tree seems to make it of Indian origin. The character of the Beŕ and its spreading and pendulous branches render it appropriate enough in our story, whilst there is no obvious reason why Homer should have availed himself of the Fig, any more than of any other tree: the following are the passages referred to;

Τὸν δ᾽ἕτερον σκόπελον χθαμαλώτερον ὄψει, Ὀδυσσεῦ,
Πλήσιον ἀλλήλων· καί κεν διοϊστεύσειας.
Τῷ δ᾽ ἐν ἐρινεός ἐστι μέγας, φύλλοισι τεθηλώς.
Τῷ δ᾽ ὑπὸ δῖα Χάρυβδις ἀναῤῥοιβδεῖ μέλαν ὕδωρ.

Close by a rock of less enormous height
Breaks the wild wave and forms a dangerous streight;
Full on ifs crown a fig's green branches rise,
And shoot a leafy forest to the Skies,
Beneath Charybdis holds her boisterous reign
Midst roaring whirlpools, and absorbs the main.

Pope, Odyssey XII, 125-130 (101-4).

the day was spent in this position, and Śaktideva despairing of any chance of being extricated from it, was about to precipitate himself into the gulph below, when a sudden noise interrupted his design. This

---

* Παννύχιος φερόμην· ἅμα δ' ἠελίῳ ἀνιόντι
Ἦλθον ἐπὶ Σκύλλης σκόπελον, δεινήν τε Χάρυβδιν.
Ἡ μὲν ἀνεῤῥοίβδησε θαλάσσης ἁλμυρὸν ὕδωρ·
Αὐτὰρ ἐγὼ ποτὶ μακρὸν ἐρινεὸν ὑψόσ' ἀερθείς,
Τῷ προςφὺς ἐχόμην, ὡς νυκτερίς· οὐδέ πῃ εἶχον
Οὔτε στηρίξαι ποσὶν ἔμπεδον, οὔτ' ἐπιβῆναι.
Ῥίζαι γὰρ ἑκὰς ἦσαν, ἀπήωροι δ' ἔσαν ὄζοι,
Μακροί τε, μεγάλοι τε, κατεσκίαον δὲ Χάρυβδιν.

All night I drove and at the dawn of day
Fast by the rocks beheld the desperate way:
Just when the Sea within her gulfs subsides,
And in the roaring whirlpools rush the tides,
Swift from the float I vaulted with a bound,
The lofty fig-tree seized, and clung around;
So to the beam the bat tenacious clings,
And pendant round it clasps his leathern wings:
High in the air the tree its boughs displayed,
And on the dungeon cast a dreadful shade.

Pope, Odyssey XII, 517-526 (429-36).

The translation is however exceedingly loose here, and the description of the tree in the original is in fact exceedingly applicable to the Banyan tree. Ulysses says he could neither find a place to fix his foot nor could he climb upwards, for the roots were far off, and the branches were lofty and long, and large, and hung ever the gulph: but to what then did he cling? if he had got hold of a branch at all it might be supposed possible for him to have ascended it. If however it was a pendulous or radicating branch, the passage is clear enough. Cowper says:

"I seized the branches fast of the wild fig."

But the original is merely,

"Sprung upon the tall fig tree."

was occasioned by the approach of a flight of birds of enormous size, the progeny of Garuda, the wind of whose wings fanned the ocean into foam. They perched for the night upon the tree, and their presence inspired Śaktideva with the hope of deliverance. As morning was about to dawn he gently approached the stoutest of the flock, and threw himself upon the back of the bird. The bird startled from his repose immediately took to his wings, and carried his load rapidly through the air*: at last he made for an island, and nearing the ground allowed Śaktideva to cast himself on the grass. Thus the hand of destiny rescued him from death and, being exerted still more wonderfully in his behalf, Fate brought him to the very place he was in search of, the site of the Goldencity.

The bird alighting in a garden, Śaktideva took the opportunity of sliding from off his back, and safely lodged upon the rich and downy turf. He then rose to survey the place, and observing two damsels gathering flowers, he approached and enquired where he was. To his great joy they replied, the place was named the Golden city, and that it was the residence of Chandraprabhá their mistress, who as well as themselves were of the race of Vidyádharas, and that none but females resided on the island. Śaktideva then desired them to lead him to their queen, with which they readily complied. They conducted him to a stately palace, the columns of which were radiant with prec-

* [Arabian Nights, Night 77.]

ious gems, and the walks were of beaten gold,—a numerous train of beautiful damsels thronged wondering about the new comer, and having learnt his errand, flew to apprise Chandraprabhá of the arrival of a mortal Brahman at their residence. She desired him to be admitted, and rising from her gorgeous throne, upon his entrance, welcomed him with every mark of attention and respect to her court.

Having heard the circumstances, which occasioned his visit, she proceeded to communicate her own story to him. We are four sisters, she observed; the daughters of the king of the Vidyádharas: my three sisters went one day to bathe in the Mandákiní and observing a holy Muni immersed in meditation near the bank, they, giddy with youth, and mirth, disturbed his devotion by sprinkling water upon his holy person. Immodest girls, exclaimed the sage, be born of mortal wombs. Afterwards, in consideration of my father, he announced the termination of the curse to each, and gave them the power of recalling the events of their prior birth: they quitted their celestial forms and were born the daughters of men. My father, overwhelmed with sorrow for their fate, abandoned his condition, and retired to the forests, leaving to me the uncontrolled sovereignty over this residence and the female train. I have expected you, she continued, some time, and on your account have refused the proffered suit of many a Vidyádhara, for the goddess Ambiká appeared to me in my sleep, and announced my espousal with a mortal bridegroom. She now fulfills her prophecy, and brings you hither, where no human means could possibly have procured your access. If you will accept my hand, it only remains that I give my father notice of the event, and ask his approbation. On the approaching fourteenth of the month, he holds the anniversary of a meeting of the Vidyádhara chiefs on mount Ŕishabha to offer worship to the God of gods: it will be but an absence of two days, and on my return, with his assent, of which there is no doubt, you may receive me as your bride. The charms of Chandraprabhá were more than sufficient to secure her from Śaktideva's rejection, and he awaited in joyful impatience the season that should so richly recompense his toils.

When the day of her departure arrived, Chandraprabhá desired Śaktideva to consider himself master of the palace, but she recommended to him not to ascend the central terrace, as nothing but evil would be the consequence, and with this caution she quitted him: the prohibition only served to whet his curiosity, and he very shortly found himself in the vicinity of the forbidden ground: he ascended the terrace, and beheld three doors richly decorated, leading to separate chambers. One of these he opened, and entered. In the chamber was a bed of gold, and gems, and on it something like a body covered by a sheet of fine cotton: having lifted this up, he was struck with horror to behold his first love, the princess Kanakarekhá, a corpse, as he thought, before him; he could scarcely believe that it was not a dream, and although he could not but be conscious of his possessing his waking faculties, yet as he was satisfied of the impossibility of the princess having been conveyed to the place where he was, he concluded it was some magic device, intended for his perplexity and destruction: he therefore hastily quitted the chamber to explore the others, in each of which he found a similar spectacle, and the apparently lifeless hody of a lovely damsel lay extended on a splendid couch. Quitting the last apartment, he looked more deliberately round him, and beheld on a lower level a spacious reservoir of water: descending to this he observed grazing on the borders a handsome horse ready saddled: the animal allowed him to approach, and appeared so perfectly gentle that Śaktideva proceeded to mount. On this, however, the horse started away, and at the same time throwing out his hinder leg, kicked Śaktideva with such violence, that he fell backward into the reservoir: the violence of his fall plunged him considerably below the surface; and upon his rising again above the water, what was his surprise to find himself in the midst of a well known pond in his native city Varddhamána[1]!

It was with much difficulty that Śaktideva on making his way out of the water could believe the evidence of his senses, and when he could no longer doubt, he repaired to his home, sorrowfully pondering

[1] There is more humour, though less poetry, in this version of the adventure with the horse, than in the story of the second Calendar, in the Arabian Nights, the conception is however clearly the same in both, as is that of the forbidden chambers.

on the marvellous event that had befallen him. His father who had long considered him as lost, welcomed his return with rapture, and called his kinsmen to a festival, to celebrate his son's recovery. On the day following, the first thing that saluted Śaktideva's ears, was the old proclamation, that whoever had seen the Golden city, should be rewarded with the Princess. Consoling himself with the idea, that if he had lost Chandraprabhá he had made sure of the Princess, he hastened to the palace, and announced that he was come to claim her hand. The king referred him to her as before. She recognised him, and said ne was again come with some tale of his own invention, and should be punished as an impostor. Whether I am an impostor or not, replied Śaktideva, I hope, Princess, you will satisfy my curiosity. I have just seen you in the Golden city, lifeless on a couch. I find you living here. How can this be? He speaks the truth, exclaimed the Princess—he has visited the Golden city, and fate reserves him for still greater wonders. For me, I resume my own body and my own abode: a curse denounced upon me by a holy Sage made me, Gracious king, thy daughter, but in me behold a female of celestial origin, and not of mortal mould. The knowledge of my former state accompanied my present being, and hence my reluctance to wed with one of human kind. Hence also the condition to which my hand was attached; for the discovery of the Golden city by a man was the period assigned by the Sage to my humiliation. It is now terminated and I return to my former rank." So saying she vanished. The sorrow of the king was excessive for her loss, nor was Śaktideva less affected by this, his second disappointment—collecting his fortitude, however, he determined to follow the Princess, and endeavour to find his way to the Golden city once more.

With much fatigue, but little danger, Śaktideva effected his return to the Island of Utsthala, the Princely chief of which had lost his life in endeavouring to promote his success: as the whole of the crew perished, the Islanders had never learned his fate, and upon Śaktideva's re-appearance amongst them, without his companion, the sons of the chief accused him of having murdered their father. Had the latter been engulphed as Śaktideva asserted, how happened it, they urged, that he who was in the same vessel could have escaped? They therefore commanded him to be secured, and confined in a temple of Chańdí, to whom they determined to sacrifice him a victim on the following morning.

Being left thus secured, he addressed himself to the Goddess, and entreated her protection, and his prayers were not in vain. The Goddess appeared in his dreams, and told him not to fear, and cheered by her assurances he rose in the morning with all his apprehensions removed. At day-break the sister of his persecutors came to the temple to offer her devotion, and was instantly struck by the personal graces of the prisoner. She enquired his story, and being satisfied of his innocence promised, if he would become her husband, she would intercede with her brothers in his behalf. Śaktideva was nothing loth, and Vindumatí accordingly prevailed on the brethren, influenced also by the power of Chańd́í, to give trust to their prisoner's protestations of his innocence, and assent not only to his release, but to his marriage with their sister.

Some time after their nuptials Vindumatí, having excited his curiosity with respect to her origin, consented only to gratify it upon his taking a vow to do what she should desire him: to this with some hesitation he agreed, and she then told him that she was a native of the skies, a Vidyádharí, condemned to assume a mortal form for touching her face with the dry tendon of a cow. While thus engaged in conversation, her brothers entered in violent apprehension, and called upon Śaktideva to arm, and go forth, for a wild boar was laying waste the lands, and had destroyed a number of persons. Śaktideva immediately mounted his horse, and went in pursuit of the animal whom he attacked, and wounded; the Boar fled, and plunged into a cave into which Śaktideva followed him. He had gone but a few yards, when the whole scene was changed, and he found himself in a garden adjoining to a palace in the presence of a damsel of exceeding loveliness: as soon as he recovered a little from his surprise, he addressed the damsel, and enquired who she was. She replied that she was a princess, daughter of a King of the south, termed Chańd́avikrama, that her name was Vindulekhá, and she had been carried off from her father's house by a

Daitya, the owner of the garden, and who, being accustomed to ravage the country in the form of a boar, had that day received a mortal wound from the hand of some gallant chief. The princess having communicated her story to Śaktideva put similar questions to him, and on his complying with her request, she claimed him as her fated husband, and returned with him to his dwelling, where they were married.

Vindumatí became pregnant, and when the eighth month had arrived, the first wife of Śaktideva reminded him of his vow: her demand was that he should put Vindulekhá to death, and strangle the babe with his own hands. Śaktideva stood aghast at this horrible proposal, but his wife insisted on the fulfillment of his vow, nay she appealed to the Princess, who to the surprise of her husband was equally urgent with him to accomplish the barbarous act. These importunities and the weight of his obligation at last prevailed, and he perpetrated the act: in the same instant the Princess vanished, and instead of an unborn babe Śaktideva held a Scymitar of more than earthly splendour in his grasp. He turned to Vindumatí, and she explained the mystery. We are all of the Vidyádhara race, four sisters, the daughters of their ancient King, condemned to mortal shapes for the offences of our former being; our deliverance was only to be effected by the achievements you have performed: one sister you saw at the Golden city, another was the Princess of Varddhamána, I am the third, and the fourth has just disappeared. Come; let us to the Golden city:

the sword you hold commands a free passage through the air, and you are yourself changed to the condition of a Vidyádhara. So saying she also vanished. Śaktideva followed them and, arriving at the Golden city, found the four Vidyádharís assembled awaiting his arrival; they then repaired together to the old king, who welcomed Śaktideva as his son-in-law, and consigned to him the sovereignty over the Golden city, changing his name from Śaktideva to Śaktivega.

Your Majesty is now made acquainted with my story, continued the king of the Vidyádharas, for I was the Brahman in my former existence, and was elevated to the rank I hold by the favour of Śankara. At the time I succeeded to this dignity my father-in-law announced to me that I must be prepared to resign it, upon the birth of the Son of Vatsa, who in due season should obtain the sovereignty over the spirits of air. Our master is now born, and I was anxious to be the first to offer my homage. I have been highly honoured by the permission to behold him, and I now take my departure.

So saying Śaktivega bowed to the young Prince, to Vatsa, and the queens, and vanished from their sight.

III.

ON THE MEDICAL AND SURGICAL SCIENCES OF THE HINDUS.

From the Oriental Magazine, Vol. I (Calcutta: Febr. 1823), p. 207—12.

The successful cultivation of the healing art by European skill and learning has left us nothing to learn from the Hindus. In the present state of their knowledge, indeed, we have every thing to teach them; but we are not to infer from what we now behold, that they were never better instructed: there is reason to suspect the contrary, and to conclude, from the imperfect opportunities of investigation we possess, that in medicine, as in astronomy, and metaphysics, the Hindus once kept pace with the most enlightened nations of the world; and that they attained as thorough a proficiency in medicine and surgery, as any people whose acquisitions are recorded, and as indeed was practicable, before anatomy was made known to us by the discoveries of modern enquirers.

It might easily be supposed, that their patient attention, and natural shrewdness, would render the Hindus excellent observers; whilst the extent, and fertility of their native country would furnish them with many valuable drugs and medicaments.—Their Nidána or Diagnosis, accordingly, appears to define and distinguish symptoms with great accuracy, and their Dravyábhidhána, or Materia Medica, is sufficiently voluminous.—They have also paid great attention to regimen and diet, and have a number of works on the food and general treatment, suited to the complaint, or favourable to the operation of the medicine administered. This branch they entitle Pathyápathya. To these subjects are to be added the Chikitsá, or medical treatment of diseases—on which subject they have a variety of compositions, containing much absurdity, with much that is of value; and the Rasavidyá, or Pharmacy, in which they are most deficient. All these works, however, are of little avail to the present generation, as they are very rarely studied, and still more rarely understood, by any of the practising empirics.

The divisions of the science thus noticed, as existing in books, exclude two important branches, without which the whole system must be defective—Anatomy and Surgery. We can easily imagine, that these were not likely to have been much cultivated in Hindustan, and that local disadvantages, and religious prejudices, might have formed very serious impediments to their acquirement.—Something of the former might be accidentally picked up by the occasional inspection of bodies, either brutal or human, which happened to be exposed; but we can scarcely expect dissections of the latter, amongst the Hindus, when we find that the Greeks themselves did not venture beyond animal subjects, even in the time of Aristotle.—In the absence of anatomy, of course, little was to be looked for in surgery; and it has been taken for granted that, whatever might have been the character of medical science, amongst the Hindus in former days, an almost utter ignorance has always prevailed on the subjects most essential to its perfect possession and practical application.—These ideas, however, are perhaps partially erroneous, and rest on our own imperfect knowledge of the medical literature of the Hindus.

The Hindu compositions on medical subjects, and even their own accounts of them, whether fables or facts, have hitherto scarcely been adverted to by Sanskrit scholars. The subject is not of general interest; and requires a twofold qualification, not likely to be often combined, in the individual who embarks in it: —as it is also a matter more of curiosity than utility, there is little inducement to its prosecution. At the same time, vulgar errors are always mischievous, and their correction would in some sort repay the labour that should effect so salutary a purpose. There are no doubt, amongst the members of the medical profession in India, many competent to the task of giving to the world an accurate view of the Hindu systems; and it is not intended here to anticipate any part of their labours, in the few desultory notices we propose to offer, on the existence and history of Hindu Surgery.

The Áyur Veda, as the medical writings of highest

antiquity and authority are collectively called, is considered to be a portion of the fourth or Atharva Veda, and is consequently the work of Brahmá—by him it was communicated to Daksha, the Prajápati, and by him the two Aświns*, or sons of Súrya, the Sun, were instructed in it, and they then became the medical attendants of the gods—a genealogy, that cannot fail recalling to us the two sons of Esculapius, and their descent from Apollo. Now what were the duties of the Aświns, according to Hindu authorities?—the gods, enjoying eternal youth and health, stood in no need of physicians, and consequently they held no such sinecure station. The wars between the gods and demons, however, and the conflicts amongst the gods themselves, in which wounds might be suffered, although death was not inflicted, required chirurgical aid—and it was this, accordingly, which the two Aświns rendered. They performed many extraordinary cures, as might have been expected from their superhuman character. When Brahmá's fifth head was cut off by Rudra, they replaced it—a feat worthy of their exalted rank in the profession to which they belong, and little capable of imitation by their unworthy successors.

The meaning of these legendary absurdities is clear enough, and is conformable to the tenor of all history. Man, in the semi-barbarous state, if not more subject to external injuries than internal disease, was at least more likely to seek remedies for the former, which

* [Lassen, Ind. Alt., I. 763. Anhang. p. xxx. II, 512.]

were obvious to his senses, than to imagine the means of relieving the latter, whose nature he could so little comprehend.

Surgical, therefore, preceded medicinal skill; as Celsus has asserted, when commenting on Homer's account of Podalirius and Machaon, who were not consulted, he says, during the plague in the Grecian camp, although regularly employed to extract darts and heal wounds. The same position is maintened, as we shall hereafter see, by the Hindu writers, in plain, as well as in legendary language.

According to some authorities, the Aświns instructed Indra, and Indra was the preceptor of Dhanwantari; but others make Átreya, Bharadwája, and Charaka prior to the latter.—Charaka's work, which goes by his name, is extant.—Dhanwantari is also styled Káśírája, prince of Káśí or Benares. His disciple was Suśruta, the son of Viśwamitra, and consequently a contemporary of Ráma: his work also exists, and is our chief guide at present. It is unquestionably of some antiquity, but it is not easy to form any conjecture of its real date, except that it cannot have the prodigious age, which Hindu fable assigns it—it is sufficient to know, that it is perhaps the oldest work on the subject, excepting that of Charaka, which the Hindus possess. One commentary on the text, made by Vágbhat́t́a a Cashmirian, is probably as old as the twelfth or thirteenth century, and his comment, it is believed, was preceded by others. The work is divided into six portions—the Sútra Sthána, or Chirurgical Definitions; the Nidána Sthána, or section on Symptoms, or Diagnosis; Śaríra Sthána, anatomy; Chikitsá Sthána, the internal application of Medicines; Kalpa Sthána, Antidotes; Uttara Sthána, or a supplementary section on various local diseases, or affections of the eye, ear, &c.—In all these divisions, however, surgery, and not general medicine, is the object of the Sauśruta.

The Áyur Veda, which originally consisted of one hundred sections, of a thousand stanzas each, was adapted to the limited faculties and life of man, by its distribution into eight subdivisions, the enumeration of which conveys to us an accurate idea of the objects of the Ars medendi amongst the Hindus. The divisions are thus enumerated—1 Śalya. 2 Śálákya. 3 Káya chikitsá. 4 Bhútavidyá. 5 Kaumárabhṙitya. 6 Agada. 7 Rásáyana, and 8 Vájíkaraṅa—They are explained as follows:

1. Śalya is the art of extracting extraneous substances, whether of grass, wood, earth, metal, bone, &c. violently or accidentally introduced into the human body, with the treatment of the inflammation and suppuration thereby induced; and by analogy, the cure of all phlegmonoid tumours and abscesses. The word Śalya means a dart or arrow, and points clearly to the origin of this branch of Hindu science. In like manner the Ἰατρὸς, or physician of the Greeks, was derived, according to Sextus Empiricus, from Ἰὸς, an arrow or dart.

2. Śálákya is the treatment of external organic af-

fections, or diseases of the eyes, ears, nose, &c.—it is derived from Śaláká, which means any thin and sharp instrument; and is either applicable in the same manner as Śalya to the active causes of the morbid state, or it is borrowed from the generic name of the slender probes and needles used in operations on the parts affected.

3. Káya Chikitsá is, as the name implies, the application of the Ars medendi (Chikitsá) to the body in general (Káya), and forms what we mean by the Science of Medicine—the two preceding divisions constitute the Surgery of modern schools.

4. Bhútavidyá is the restoration of the faculties from a disorganised state induced by Demoniacal possession. This art has vanished before the diffusion of knowledge, but it formed a very important branch of medical practice, through all the schools, Greek, Arabic, or European, and descended to days very near our own, as a reference to Burton's Anatomy of Melancholy may prove to general readers.

5. Kaumára bhṛitya means the care of infancy, comprehending not only the management of children from their birth, but the treatment of irregular lactic secretion, and puerperal disorders in mothers and nurses—this holds with us also the place that its importance claims.

6. Agada is the administration of antidotes—a subject which, as far as it rests upon scientific principles, is blended with our medicine and surgery.

7. Rásáyana is chemistry, or more correctly alche-

my, as the chief end of the chemical combinations it describes, and which are mostly metallurgic, is the discovery of the universal medicine—the elixir that was to render health permanent, and life perpetual.

8. The last branch, Vájíkaraña, professes to promote the increase of the human race—an illusory research, which, as well as the preceding, is not without its parallel in ancient, and modern times.

We have, therefore, included in these branches, all the real and fanciful pursuits of physicians of every time and place. Suśruta, however, confines his own work to the classes Śalya and Śálákya, or Surgery; although, by an arrangement not uncommon with our own writers, he introduces occasionally the treatment of general diseases, and the management of women and children, when discussing those topics to which they bear relation. Pure Surgery, however, is his aim, and it is the particular recommendation of Dhanwantari —Śalya being, he declares expressly, "the first and best of the medical sciences; less liable, than any other, to the fallacies of conjectural and inferential practice; pure in itself; perpetual in its applicability; the worthy produce of heaven, and certain source of fame."

From these premises we may be satisfied, that Surgery was once extensively cultivated, and highly esteemed by the Hindus. Its rational principles and scientific practice are, however, now, it may be admitted, wholly unknown to them—what they formerly were, we may perhaps take some future opportunity of specifying.

IV.

INTRODUCTION TO THE MAHÁBHÁRATA,

prefixed to Prof. F. JOHNSON'S "Selections from the Mahábhárata". London: 1842,

and

TRANSLATION OF THREE EXTRACTS,

originally published in the Quarterly Oriental Magazine.

THE Mahábhárata and Rámáyaňa were designated by Sir William Jones the two epic poems of the Hindus. The appropriateness of the epithet has been denied by some of those ultra-admirers of Virgil and Homer, who will allow the dignity of the Epos to be claimed by none but the objects of their idolatry: and, in the restricted sense in which a poem is entitled epic, agreeably to the definition of Aristotle, it may indeed be matter of question, if the term be strictly applicable to the Hindu Poems. Although, however, it might not be impossible to vindicate their pretensions to such a title, yet it is not worth while to defend them. It matters little what they are called; and they will not lose their value, as interesting narratives of important events, as storehouses of historical traditions and mythological legends, as records of the ancient social and political condition of India, and as pictures of national manners, if, instead of epic, they be denominated heroic poems.

The Mahábhárata, then, is a heroic poem in eighteen "Parvas", Cantos or Books; which are said to contain 100,000 "ślokas" or stanzas. The printed edition contains 107,389 ślokas; but this comprises the supplement called Hari-vanśa, the stanzas of which are 16,374, and which is certainly not a part of the original Mahábhárata. There is reason to believe that the primary authentic poem was of a still more limited extent than it would reach even after the deduction; for it is said, in the first book, that, exclusive of its episodes, the poem consisted of 24,000 ślokas. Some of the episodes are equivocal additions; others spring naturally out of the business of the story; and many of them are, no doubt, of considerable antiquity.

The author of the poem is said to be Kṙishṅa Dwaipáyana, the "Vyása" or arranger of the Vedas, and the actual father of the two princes Páńḋu and Dhṙitaráshṫra, whose progeny are the principal characters of the fable. He taught the work to his pupil Vaiśampáyana, who recited it at a great sacrifice celebrated by Janamejaya, the great-grandson of Arjuna, one of the heroes of the poem. As we have it, it is said to have been repeated by Sauti the son of Lomaharshańa to the Ṙishis, or sages, assembled on occasion of a religious solemnity in the Naimisha Forest.

The subject of the Mahábhárata is a war for regal supremacy in India, between the sons of two brothers, Páńďu and Dhŕitaráshtra. The sons of the former were five in number; Yudhishthira, Bhíma, and Arjuna, by one of his wives, Pŕithá; and Nakula and Sahadeva by his other wife, Mádrí. Dhŕitaráshtra had as numerous a family as King Priam: but they were all sons, with the addition of a single daughter. Of the hundred sons, Duryodhana was the eldest, and the foremost in hate and hostility to his cousins.

Although the elder of the two princes, Páńďu, "the Pale" (as the name denotes), was rendered by his pallor (which may be suspected of intimating a leprous taint) incapable of succession. He was obliged therefore, to relinquish his claim to his brother; and retired to the Himálaya mountains, where his sons were born, and where he died. Upon his death, his sons, yet in their boyhood, were brought to Hástinapura by the religious associates of Páńďu's exile, and were introduced to Dhŕitaráshtra as his nephews. Some doubts were at first expressed of the genuineness of their birth; and, in truth, they were the sons of Páńďu only by courtesy, being the children of his wives by sundry divinities. Thus Yudhishthira was the son of Dharma, the god of justice, the Hindu Pluto: Bhíma, of Váyu, or god of the wind, the Indian Aeolus: Arjuna was the son of Indra, the god of the firmament, Jupiter Tonans: and Nakula and Sahadeva were the sons of two personages peculiar to Hindu mythology, their Dioscuri, twin-sons of the Sun, the Aświní-Kumáras.

As, however, Páńdu had acknowledged these princes as his own, the objection to their birth was overruled by his example: and the boys were taken under the guardianship of their uncle, and educated along with his sons.

The principal performers in the Mahábhárata are distinctively and consistently characterized. The sons of Páńdu, with the exception of Bhíma, are represented as moderate, generous, and just: and Bhíma is not ungenerous, although somewhat of a choleric temperament, and of overweening confidence in his herculean strength. The sons of Dhŕitaráshtra are described as envious, arrogant, and malignant: and this contrast of character enhances, even in boyhood, the feelings of animosity which the consciousness of incompatible inheritance has inspired.

The genealogial descent of the two families, the circumstances of the birth and education of the princes, their juvenile emulation and enmity, and the adventures of the Páńdavas when they attain adolescence, are narrated in the "Ádi Parva" or First Book. From this book, the first of the following selections, the Passage of Arms at Hástinapura, is extracted as illustrative of the spirit of rivalry which animated the young princes, and of some of the ancient usages of the Hindus. Subsequently to the transactions there described, the practices of the sons of Dhŕitaráshtra against the lives of the Páńdavas become still more malevolent; and they privily set fire to the house in which Ṕrithá and her sons reside. As the Páńďavas had been warned of the intention of their enemies, they eluded it, and escaped by a subterranean passage, leaving it to be reported and believed that they had perished in the flames of their dwelling. They secrete themselves in the forests, and adopt the garb and mode of life of Brahmans. It is during this period that they hear of the "Swayamvara", a rite familiar to the readers of Nala, the choice of a husband by a princess from the midst of congregated suitors, of Draupadí, daughter of Drupada, King of the upper part of the Doáb; and they repair to his court, and win the lady. The circumstances of this exploit, and its immediate consequences, form the subject of the second of the following Selections.

The existence of the sons of Páńďu having become generally known by the occurrences at the Swayamvara of Draupadí, King Dhŕitaráshťra was prevailed upon by his ministers to send for them, and to divide his sovereignty equally between them and his sons. The partition was accordingly made. Yudhishťhira and his brethren reigned over a district on the Jamná, at their capital Indraprastha; and Duryodhana, with his brethren, were the Rájas of Hástinapura on the Ganges. The ruins of the latter city, it is said, are still to be traced on the banks of the Ganges *; whilst a part of the city of Delhi is still known by the name of Indraprastha**. The contiguity of these two cities, and

---

* [Lassen, Ind. Alt., I, 126.]

** [Journal Asiatique, Vol. XV (1860), 511 ff.]

consequently of the principalities of which they were respectively the capitals, necessarily suggests the inference, that in the days of the Mahábhárata, as well as in later times, India was parcelled out amongst a number of petty independent sovereigns. This inference becomes certainty from the valuable specification which the poem contains of the very many Rájas who took part in the struggle in favour of one or other of the contending houses. This state of things, however, was not irreconcilable with the nominal supremacy of some one paramount lord: and after the partition of the kingdom of Hástinapura, a fresh source of envy and hatred springs up in the minds of the sons of Dhŕitaráshtra, from the pretensions of Yudhishthira to celebrate the "Rájasúya" solemnity—a sacrifice, at which princes officiate in menial capacities, and make presents in acknowledgment of submission. This forms the topic of the "Sabhá Parva", the Second Book of the Poem.

The claims of Yudhishthira to universal homage are preceded by the subjugation of the Powers of India by himself and his brothers. These conquests are merely predatory incursions, and are characteristic of the mode of warfare practised in India even in our own days in which the object of the Mahrattas, as of the Moguls before them, was commonly nominal submission, and the payment of tribute, varying in amount, according to the power of the superior to exact it, rather than the actual annexation of territory to their dominions. Sháh Álem was titular sovereign of India; and the coins were everywhere struck in his name, even after he was a captive in the hands of Sindhia, and a pensioner in those of the British Government. It does not follow, therefore, from the existence of a number of petty cotemporary princes, that there never was one, nominally at least, supreme monarch; nor is there the least incompatibility, in Indian history, between a sovereign ostensibly paramount, and numerous princes virtually independent. The notices of the countries subdued by the Páńd́ava princes, and the articles brought as tribute by the subjugated nations, furnish in this chapter much valuable and curious elucidation of the ancient civil and political circumstances and divisions of India.

Amongst the gaieties of the occasion, the sight of which embitters the animosity of the sons of Dhŕitaráshṫra, a diversion is insidiously proposed by them, which is the mainspring of all the subsequent mischief. The inveterate passion for play by which the early Hindus were inspired, as we learn from various parts of the Mahábhárata, as well as from other authorities, is a remarkable feature in the old national character. It is far from entirely obliterated, and it is as strong as ever amongst some others of the Eastern people: as the Malays, for instance, who, when they have lost every thing they possess, stake their families and themselves. So, in the gambling which ensues in the Mahábhárata, at what appears to be a kind of backgammon, where pieces are moved according to the cast of the dice, Yudhishṫhira loses to Duryodhana his palace, his wealth, his kingdom, his wife, his brothers, and himself. Their liberty and possessions are restored by the interference of the old king Dhṙitaráshṫra: but Yudhishṫhira is again tempted to play; conditioning, that if he loses, he and his brothers shall pass twelve years in the forests, and shall spend the thirteenth year incognito. If discovered before the expiration of the year, they are to renew the whole term of their exile. He loses: and, with Draupadí and his brethren, goes into banishment, and lives the life of a forester. A description of the forest life of the Páńd́avas constitutes the topic of the Third Book, the "Vana Parva". Many episodes occur in this book: one of which is the story of Nala, which is recited to teach Yudhishṫhira and his brethren resignation and hope. Another is the attempt of Jayadratha to carry off Draupadí by force which is the third of the following Selections.

At the expiration of the twelfth year, the Páńd́avas enter the service of King Viráṫa in different disguises. Their adventures are described in the "Viráṫa Parva", the Fourth Book. They acquire the esteem of the King; and when they make themselves known to him at the end of the thirteenth year, obtain his alliance to avenge their wrongs and vindicate their right of sovereignty.

The Fifth Book, the "Udyoga Parva", represents the preparations of the two parties for war, and enumerates the princes who enter into alliance with them. Amongst these is Kṙishńa, the ruler of Dwáraká, and an incarnation of Vishńu. He is related by birth to both families, and professes a reluctance to join either; but prescient of what is to happen, he proposes to Duryodhana the choice between his individual aid and the co-operation of an immense army. Duryodhana unwisely prefers the latter; and Kŕishńa, himself more than a host, becomes the ally of the Páńďavas, the charioteer of his especial friend and favourite Arjuna, and the principal instrument of the triumph of his allies.

The four following Books are devoted to descriptive details of the battles which take place. Some of these are very Homeric; but, in general, the interest of the narrative is injured by repetition, and the battles are spoiled by the introduction of supernatural weapons, which leave little credit to the hero who vanquishes by their employment. The armies of Duryodhana are commanded in succession by Bhíshma his great-uncle, Drońa his military preceptor, Karńa the King of Anga, his friend, and Śalya the King of Madra, his ally: and the description of their operations is contained in as many Parvas, named after them "Drońa-Parva" &c. These chiefs, and many others, are slain at the close of their commands; and in the Ninth or "Śalya-Parva", Duryodhana himself is killed by Bhíma in single combat with maces, in the use of which weapon they are both represented as excelling. A few of the surviving chiefs on the side of Duryodhana attempt to avenge the destruction of their friends by a night attack on the camp of the Páńďavas, as narrated in the Tenth, or "Sauptika Parva". The attack is repelled chiefly by the metily assistance of Kŕishńa.

A short Book, "the Strí Parva", describes the grief and lamentations of the women of either party over the slain, and the sorrow and anger of the old king Dhŕitaráshŕra. Yudhishŕhira himself gives way to poignant regret for what has passed: and the next Book, the "Śánti Parva" or "Chapter of Consolation", details, with more than sufficient diffuseness, the duties of Kings, the efficacy of liberality, and the means of obtaining final emancipation from existence. Hence the sections of this Parva are entitled "Rája-dharma", "Dána-dharma", and "Moksha-dharma" Parvas, or more properly "Upaparvas", minor cantos. The Thirteenth Book, the "Anuśásana Parva", is a long and prolix series of discourses upon the duties of society, as communicated by Bhíshma, whilst about to die, to Yudhishŕhira. In this, as well as in the sections of the "Śánti Parva", the didactic portions are enlivened by appropriate tales and fables: each of the Books contains many sound doctrines and interesting illustrations, although both are somewhat misplaced in a narrative heroic poem.

The remaining Books of the Mahábhárata, although more or less episodical, are in better keeping with the story. They are also short, and hasten to the catastrophe. The Fourteenth or "Áśwamedhika Parva" describes the celebration of the "Aśwamedha" rite—the sacrifice of a horse, by Yudhishŕhira, in proof of his supremacy. In the Fifteenth Book, the "Áśrama

Parva", King Dhŕitaráshtra, with his queen Gándhárí and his ministers, retires to a hermitage, and obtains felicity or dies. The Sixteenth or "Mausala Parva" narrates the destruction of the whole Yádava race, the death of Kŕishńa, who was one of the tribe, and the submersion of his capital Dwáraká by the ocean. The Seventeenth Book, called the "Mahápraśthánika" or "Great journey", witnesses the abdication of his hardly-won throne by Yudhishṫhira, and the departure of himself, his brothers, and Draupadí, to the Himálaya, on their way to the holy mountain Meru. As they proceed, the influence of former evil deeds proves fatal, and each in succession drops dead by the way-side: until Yudhishṫhira, and a dog that had followed them from Hástinapura, are the only survivors. Indra comes to convey the prince to Swarga, or Indra's heaven: but Yudhishṫhira refuses to go thither, unless

> admitted to that equal sky,
> His faithful dog shall bear him company;

and Indra is obliged to comply.

The Eighteenth Book, the "Swargárohańa", introduces Yudhishṫhira in his bodily form to heaven. To his great dismay, he finds there Duryodhana and the other sons of Dhŕitaráshtra; but sees none of his own friends, his brothers, or Draupadí. He demands to know where they are, and refuses to stay in Swarga without them. A messenger of the gods is sent to shew him where his friends are, and leads him to the "fauces graveolentis Averni", where he encounters all sorts of disgusting and terrific objects. His first impression is, to turn back; but he is arrested by the wailings of well-remembered voices, imploring him to remain, as his presence has already alleviated their tortures. He overcomes his repugnance, and resolves to share the fate of his friends in hell, rather than abide with their enemies in heaven. This is his crowning trial. The gods come, and applaud his disinterested virtue. All the horrors that had formerly beset his path vanish; and his friends and kindred are raised along with him to Swarga where they become again the celestial personages that they originally were, and which they had ceased to be for a season, in order to descend along with Kŕishńa in human forms amongst mankind, and co-operate with him in relieving the world from the tyranny of those evil beings, who were oppressing the virtuous and propagating impiety, in the characters of Duryodhana, his brothers, and their allies.

The Hari-vanśa is a sort of Supplement to the Mahábhárata. It professes to give an account of the genealogy of Hari or Vishńu, in the character of Kŕishńa; but adds to it genealogical details, the narrative of Kŕishńa's exploits, and a variety of legends and tales tending to recommend the worship of the demi-god. The internal evidence is strongly indicative of a date considerably subsequent to that of the major portion of the Mahábhárata. It has been translated into French by M. Langlois, and the translation has been published by the Oriental Translation Committee.

The text of the Mahábhárata has been printed at Calcutta, in four quarto volumes. The work was commenced by the Committee of Public Instruction, and completed by the Asiatic Society of Bengal.

The great extent of the work, and the tediousness of much of its contents, preclude the prospect of its ever being translated throughout; though, as a monument of Hindu antiquity, it merits entire translation. Although, however, we can scarcely expect a translation of the whole, yet very many portions of it well deserve to be rendered into some of the languages of Europe. Something of translation in detail has already been effected. The late Sir Charles Wilkins led the way, by his translation of the "Bhagavad Gítá", which is an episode of the "Bhíshma Parva". Part of the opening of the first "Parva", rendered into English, it is believed, by Sir C. Wilkins, is published in the "Annals of Oriental Literature". Professor Bopp has also published the "Nalus", the "Diluvium", the Journey of Arjuna, the "Story of Sávitrí", and the "Rape of Draupadí", with translations in Latin and German; and the first of these has assumed an English garb, from the distinguished pen of the Rev. H. Milman, in which surpassing grace of style is combined with extraordinary faithfulness, both to the letter, and the spirit of the original poem. As contributing to elucidate the ancient geography of India, a portion containing the enumeration of a variety of countries has been translated and illustrated by the writer, and incorporated in the pages of the Vishńu Puráńa: and the illustration of ancient India, derivable from the Mahábhárata, is in course of very careful and learned prosecution by Professor Lassen of Bonn, in a series of valuable dissertations published in the Zeitschrift für die Kunde des Morgenlandes. By these means, the merits, both poetical and historical, of the Mahábhárata are becoming more extensively known: but in the amplitude of its extent, in the numerous traditions, legends and tales which it contains, and in its many didactic and philosophical passages, it offers an accumulation of materials adapted to different tastes, and auxiliary to diverging researches, which must long advantageously engage the attention, and reward the industry, of Sanskrit scholars.

From the Quarterly Oriental Magazine, Vol. II (Dec. 1824), p. 249–57.

FIRST DAY'S BATTLE.

[Book VII, c. 14-16.]

The Kuru[1] host entrusted to his care,

---

[1] Kuru, it is usually supposed, is the prince who gives the designation to Duryodhana and his brothers, thence called Kauravas, in opposition to their cousins, the sons of Páńdu, termed Páńdavas, Kuru being a remote ancestor of both. The Mahábhárata, however, gives a different account, and derives the term Kaurava from the country, Kuru-jángala, or Kurukshetra [Lassen, Ind. Alt. I, 593.], which was subject to the family of Duryodhana, the upper part of the Panjáb beyond Dehli, or Panniput, which is still commonly called by the Hindus Kurukhetr. — Kuru, the prince, was descended from Nahusha, the great grandson of Soma,

The son of Bharadwája[1] marshals; first
The chiefs[2] of Sindhu, and Kalinga's[3] king,
With the young prince Vikarńa[4] on the right
He stations, by Gándhára's[5] martial chivalry,

---

or the moon, by his grandson Puru. The thirteenth descendant of Kuru was Śántanu, who had four sons, Bhíshma, Chitrángada, Vichitravírya, and Vyása. Of these, Bhíshma and Vyása lived unmarried, and Chitrángada and Vichitravírya both died without offspring; on which, to prevent the extinction of the family, and conformably to the ancient Hindu law, Vyása begot offspring on his brother's widows. The sons were Dhŕitaráshťra and Páńdu. Dhŕitaráshťra had a hundred sons by Gándhárí, the princess of Gandhára, of whom Duryodhana was the eldest. Páńdu had five sons, the celebrated princes Yudhishťhira, Bhíma or Bhímasena, Arjuna, and the twin brothers Nakula and Sahadeva. Of these the first was remarkable for his piety and integrity; the second for his gigantic bulk and strength. Arjuna was eminent for his valour, and was the particular friend of Kŕishńa.

[1] Drońa was the son of Bharadwája, the son of Vŕihaspati, or Jupiter. He learnt the use of arms from Paraśu Ráma, and taught both the Kaurava and Páńdava princes. With the aid of his pupils, he made war upon his ancient friend Drupada, king of Pancháala, carried his capital, and compelled him to give up part of his kingdom, including the city of Ahichhatrá, possibly the same as the Oxydracæ of Arrian. [Ahichhatrá is, more correctly, identified by V. de S. Martin (Étude sur la géographie grecque et latine de l'Inde p. 324 f.) with the Adisdara of Ptolemy, whereas the Kshudrakas correspond to the Oxydracæ of Arrian.] The alliance that was subsequently formed between Drupada and the Páńdavas sufficiently accounts for Drońa's being found in the Kuru ranks.

[2] The Indus, or country along the river Sind.

[3] Kling, the northern portion of the Coromandel coast.

[4] One of the youngest of the Kaurava princes.

[5] The Gándháras are the Gandari of the ancients, the people

With glittering lances armed, and led by Śakuni,
Their sovereign's son, supported. On his left
Duńśásana[1] and other chiefs of fame
Commanded the array: around them rode
Kámboja's[2] horse, Śakas[3] and Yavanas[4],
On rapid coursers, mighty in the field.
The nations of the north, and east, and south[5],
Composed his main battalia: in the rear
Secure the monarch[6] marched; whilst in the van
The gallant Karńa[7] led his faithful bands,

---

of part of Afghanistan and Kandahar of modern times. Their leader Śakuni was the brother of Gándhárí, the mother of Duryodhana. [Vivien de St. Martin, l. l., p. 364–96. Lassen, II, 142.]

[1] Another of Duryodhana's brothers. He was the object of the particular hatred of the Páńdavas, having offered an insult to their common bride Draupadí, dragging her by the hair of her head into the public assembly. To avenge this wrong, Bhíma vowed the death of Duńśásana, and that he would drink his blood —a vow he at last accomplished.

[2] The horse of Kamboja are the troops of Khorasan, Balkh, and Bokhara. [Vishńu Pur., p. 194. Lassen, I, 439.]

[3] The Śakas are the Sakai, or Sacæ of the ancients, some of the Scythian, that is, the Nomadic races of Turkestan and Tartary.

[4] The Yavanas, it is generally supposed, must mean the Greeks of Bactria. It is usually applied now to the Mohammedans; but no satisfactory account can be given of its meaning in such application, and there is no great reason to question its derivation from Ionia, as proposed by Sir William Jones. The Hindus have a distinct name for the Persians. [Vishńu Pur., p. 194. Lassen, I, 861 f.]

[5] These are named in the original the people of Trigartta, the Ambashťhas, Málavas, Śivis, Sauvíras, Śúrasenas, Śúdras, &c. Several of them are traceable in classical geography.

[6] Duryodhana, the eldest son of Dhŕitaráshťra.

[7] Karńa was the half brother of the Páńdavas, being the son

Exulting in their sovereign's stately stature,
High raised upon his elephant of war,
And gorgeous shining as the rising sun.
His warriors deemed the gods themselves were weak,
With Indra at their head, to stem his prowess,
And each to each their thoughts revealed, they moved,
Secure of victory, to meet the foe.

The sons of Páńdu marked the coming storm,
And swift arrayed their force. The chief divine[1]
And Dhananjaya[2], at the king's request,
Raised in the van the ape-emblazoned banner[3],

---

of Príthá, the princess of Śúrasena, before her marriage to Páńdu, by the Sun; this lady being presented by the saint Durvásas with a charm, by which she could compel any god she pleased to her embraces—a power she did not suffer to lie idle. Afraid of discovery, Príthá cast the infant into the Jamná, where he was found by Rádhá, the wife of Śatánanda, the charioteer of Dhŕitaráshtra. The king adopted the boy, and brought him up with his own sons; and subsequently Duryodhana gave him the kingdom of Anga, and after Kansa's death that of Mathurá. Karńa, therefore, adheres to his adoptive, in preference to his natural brothers. He is one of the most distinguished amongst the Kuru champions. Although placed in the van, no particular mention is here made of his exploits, probably because the poet has dedicated to them an entire canto, the next, called the Karńa Parva. Karńa is killed by Arjuna.

[1] Kŕishńa, who acted as the companion and charioteer of Arjuna.

[2] A name of Arjuna, the third of the Páńdava princes, "the conqueror of wealth".

[3] Arjuna's banner bore a figure of Hanumán. Having propitiated that monkey demigod, he was desired to ask a boon, on which he solicited Hanumán's personal aid in battle. He was told

The host's conducting star, the guiding light
That cheered the bravest heart, and as it swept
The air, it warmed each breast with martial fires.
Before the ranks the prince impelled his car,
By Vásudeva, of created things[1]
Supremest, driven; and as he sternly grasped
His massy bow Gáńdíva[2], he appeared,
The formidable minister of fate.

Now as on either hand the hosts advanced,
A sudden tumult filled the sky: earth shook:
Chafed by wild winds, the sands upcurled to heaven,
And spread a veil before the sun. Blood fell
In showers, shrill screaming kites and vultures winged
The darkling air, whilst howling jackals hung
Around the march, impatient for their meal;
And ever and anon the thunder roared,
And angry lightnings flashed across the gloom,
Or blazing meteors fearful shot to earth.

Regardless of these awful signs, the chiefs
Pressed on to mutual slaughter, and the peal
Of shouting hosts commingling shook the world.

---

to mount the monkey's figure on his banner, which would answer as well.

[1] The best of all things that have been, Śresht́ha Bhútánám, or the best of all elementary things. In either case, however, the expression is not equivalent to the assertion of a divine nature. Vásudeva is the patronymic of Kŕishńa.

[2] Gáńdíva is the name of Arjuna's bow; the Hindu writers, like our bards of chivalry, giving appellations to the favourite weapons of their chief heroes.

Contending warriors, emulous for victory,
And great in arms, wielded the sharp-edged sword,
And hurled the javelin; frequent flew the dart,
And countless arrows canopied the combat.
Against the leader of the Kuru force
The Páńdu chiefs their clustering cohorts urged;
But soon the bands were broken by his prowess,
Like clouds that scattering fly before the gale.
Next felt the force of Srinjaya his might,
And shrunk from his encounter, like the Titans
From Indra's valour. To their succour came
Panchála's sons, by Dhŕishtadyumna[1] led.
A momentary check the veteran troops
That followed Drońa from the shock sustained;
But soon his skill the cohorts re-arrayed,
Revived their hopes, and roused them to redeem
Their fame. The foe in turn arrested paused,
And fled in fear, like deer before the lion.
The victors chased, and circling in pursuit,
As in a fiery circle, hemmed them round.
Before the rest rode Drońa on his car,
By art immortal framed—the banners stood
Unwaving as they rapid met the breeze;

---

[1] Dhŕishtadyumna is the brother of Draupadí, the son of Drupada, king of Panchála, which appears to designate a country between Dehli and the Panjáb, but descending to the south as low as to Márwár, or Ajmír, being bounded in that direction, if the author of the Mahábhárata is not mistaken, by the Charmanvatí, or Chumbul. [Lassen, I, 601.]

Swift plunged the bounding steeds amidst the throng,
And terror hovered o'er the warrior's course.

When Yudhishthira[1] marked the fearful rout,
And broken cars, and elephants, and steeds,
And men, that strewed the sanguinary plain,
He called his brother Arjuna to lead
His choicest squadrons to restore the day.
The generous youth obeyed him: followed fast
The five brave brothers of Kaikeya's realm,
Śikhańdí[2], Dhŕishtadyumna, and the son
Of fair Subhadrá[3]: next came mighty Bhíma[4],
Ghatotkacha[5] his son, half fiendish born;

---

[1] Yudhishthira, the firm in war, the eldest of the Páńdava princes: he is also called Dharmarája, the pious prince, Dharmaputra, the son of Dharma.

[2] Kaikeya, a country and a prince so named. The monarch's five sons assisted the Páńdavas, as he was also the father-in-law of Kŕishńa. His name in the Bhágavata [IX, 24, 37.] occurs, Dhŕishtaketu.

[3] Abhimanyu, the son of Arjuna by Subhadrá, the sister of Kŕishńa.

[4] Bhíma, or Bhímasena, the third of the Páńdava princes. In his youth he was carried to Pátála, the subterrene habitation of the serpent demigods, and was given a beverage which conferred upon him enormous and gigantic strength.

[5] Ghatotkacha was the son of Bhíma by a Rákshasí, or female fiend, Hidimbá, whose brother he slew. The scene of these transactions was on the east of the Ganges, and the Rákshasi may therefore mean a princess of some of the bordering tribes east of Hindustan, or between Bhote and Ava; all of whom, eating meat and following other impure practices, might well be considered Rákshasas, or "cannibals", by the Hindus. Heramba is in

The sons of Drupada, and Dhŕishtaketu[1],
And Chekitána[2], and the martial[3] twins,
And the brave monarch[4] of the Páńdu race.
These all, and more, came flocking to the fight.
Such were their deeds, as their high birth became,
And name in arms, and Bharadhwája's son
Was stopped in his career. Awhile he paused—
Rose in his car—he cast his eyes around,
Glowing with rage, then furious rushed amidst
The adverse host, as bursts the roaring gale
Amongst the vollied clouds, and over men,
And steeds, and cars he forced his headlong way,
Borne by his coursers, rapid as the breeze,
And stained a red still ruddier than their own,
As wading onwards midst the plashy gore.
Forgot his years, the veteran chieftain, fired
With rage, the energy of youth resumed;
Amidst the Páńdu ranks he smote resistless,
And many a headless corse, and mangled limb,

---

fact applied geographically to designate the western portion of Asam. Ghatotkacha was slain by Karńa. See the passage descriptive of his death. As. Res. Vol. XIII, p. 170. [Lassen, I, 663. III, 471.]

[1] Dhŕishtaketu here is probably the son of Dhŕishtadyumna, and a prince of Panchála. He commanded, however, the troops of Chedi, or Chandail, and Málwá.

[2] Chekitána was a king, but of what part of India we are not apprized.

[3] Nakula and Sahadeva, the two youngest of the Páńdavas, the sons of Páńdu's second wife, Mádrí, by the Aświní Kumáras.

[4] Yudhishthira.

And car deserted, marked the warrior's path.
Fast flew his arrows with unerring aim,
And heaven loud echoed to his rattling bow.
The soil was soddened with the crimson stream
Of the vast numbers, men, and steeds, and elephants,
Whom Drońa's shafts to Yama's halls consigned.

And Yudhishṫhira feared. His fears observed
His noble brother Arjuna: he soothed
The monarch's terror, and with solemn vow
Plighted his faith to brave the arm of Drońa,
And fall or triumph—to his vow the drums,
And trumpets, and hoarse sounding shells replied.
The animating notes recalled the chiefs
Who shrunk from conflict, and the shouting throng,
Rending heaven's concave with their clamours, rushed
Again to face the perils of the war.

Collected thus the Pánd́avas opposed
The veteran chief, whilst to his aid there came
The noblest of the Kuru bands: first Śakuni
Against the youthful Sahadeva aimed
His shafts, and levelled prostrate on the plain
His charioteer and banner—nor unscathed
Launched he his arrows; in the shock his steeds
And car were crushed, and from his hand the bow
Was wrested. On the ground he foaming sprang,
And whirled on high his ponderous mace—on foot
The warriors, like two towering mountains, met.
The shafts of Drońa fierce Panchála's king
Struck from his chariot. Bhíma hurled his darts

Impetuous on Vivimśatí[1]: unbowed
The hero stood, and all the warriors praised
The strength that foiled the giant. Furious, Bhíma
Dashed with his club the coursers to the earth;
Composed the prince leapt forth, and either chief,
Like a wild elephant, defied his foe.
Then Śalya[2], as in sportive mood, transfixed
The banner and the charioteer of Nakula.
An iron dart, by Sátyaki[3] propelled,
Gored Kŕitavarmá's[4] breast—he of the wound
Regardless, on the son of Śini hurled
His frequent shafts. High on a stately car
Swift borne by generous coursers to the fight,
The vaunting son of Púru[5] proudly drove,

---

[1] One of the sons of Dhŕitaráshtra, brother of Duryodhana.

[2] Śalya was king of Madra, a country on the north-west confines of India, apparently about Ghizni and Gor, and the site of the ancient Mardi, who were well known to classical writers as a warlike and savage race. Buchanan apparently has strangely erred in placing this country in Bhotan.

[3] The son of Satyaka, a prince of the lunar line, and of the house of Yadu, apparently the same with Yuyudhána. He is properly the grandson of Śini.

[4] A son of Hŕidíka, a chief of the house of Yadu, and kindsman of Kŕishńa. He brought to the field the adherents of the Bhoja, Andhaka and Kukkura, branches of the same family, who with Kŕitavarmá, being nearly connected with the Mathurá branch of the Yádavas, of whom Kansa, the head, was murdered by Kŕishńa, are very consistently opposed to that prince's allies.

[5] Paurava, or son of Púru; but a more particular definition of this person is wanting. He is called in another section a powerful prince.

Secure of conquest, on Subhadrá's son.
The youthful champion shrunk not from the contest:
As bounds the lion's cub upon the elephant,
The gallant boy sprang fierce upon the chief.
The royal shade and flaunting banner fell;
And now himself had perished, but his dart
With timely aim the bow of Abhimanyu
Struck into pieces—from his tingling hand
The youthful warrior cast the fragments off,
And drew his sword, and grasped his iron-bound shield.
Upon the car of Paurava he leapt,
And seized the chief—his charioteer he slew,
And dragged the monarch senseless o'er the field.
Above the prostrate prince he stood triumphant,
As o'er the slaughtered bull the lion strides.
The Kuru princes marked their friend's disgrace,
And Jayadratha[1], burning for revenge,
Alighted from his chariot, and defied
The son of Arjuna to nobler combat.
The youth obeyed the call; he left his prize,
Sprang from his car, and stood awhile exposed
Unsheltered to a shower of darts and spears
From circling foes, but by his active sword,
Asunder cloven, or his shield repelled.

[1] Jayadratha brought to the field the troops of Sindhu, or Sind, and the Sauvíras. His father Vŕiddhakshetra had been killed by Arjuna, the father of Abhimanyu, with whom, therefore, he had a debt of vengeance to settle. He had also been an unsuccessful suitor for the hand of Draupadí.

The warriors met—revenge and glory fired
Their hearts, and old hereditary hate:
Such was the strife, as when the tiger braves
The lion's prowess. Blows incessant rained
From either arm, nor pause nor rest they knew,
Nor vantage gained, nor bated of their fury.
At length Saubhadra's side exposed, his foe
With deadly aim assailed—assailed in vain;
The heavenly tempered arms repelled the stroke,
And into fragments flew the brittle steel.
Reft of his sword, the king of Sindhu sprang
Back from the field, and instant on his car
Securely stood—his chieftains closed around,
And in firm phalanx saved their recreant lord.
In vain the son of Arjuna defied
The monarch to the fight, or strove to pierce
The serried bands—in wrath he turned away,
And carried death and terror o'er the plain.

As on he passed, the king of Madra marked
His course, and at the prince infuriate launched
His javelin, chased with gold;—but as the son
Of Vinatá upon the flying snake
Unfailing darts, so Abhimanyu seized
The lance, and hurled it at its lord again;
With happier aim—the luckless charioteer
Received its weighty barb, and gasped in death.
Loud Śalya raved, and armed with iron mace,
Swift left his car—nor feared the youth his prowess;
But Bhíma stepped between, nor deemed his years

Fit match for Śalya's might, the worthy peer
Of his own giant strength. Onward he moved
To meet the king, and pleased the monarch marked
A coming foe that would not shame his valour.
On either side the anxious hosts beheld
The warrior pair, and loud the trumpets blew,
And echoing clamours heralded the conflict.
For who of all the Kuru bands but Śalya
The force of Bhímasena could encounter?
And who amongst the Páńd́us could oppose,
Save Bhímasen, the might of Madra's king?
Each chieftain raised a ponderous iron mace,
Studded with spikes, and gorgeous set with gold;
And as they circled rapid through the air,
Like flashing lightning gleamed the whirling weapons.
Fierce as two savage bulls the chieftains stood
Opposed, nor long delayed the interchange
Of deadly blows. As met the clashing iron,
Fast from the stroke the fiery flashes flew,
And radiant splinters sparkled round the head
Of each tall champion, like a glittering swarm
Of fire-flies round some venerable tree.
From the deep gashes trickling torrents ran;
And like the Kinśuka[1], when thickly set
With vermil blossoms, glowed each warrior form.
Unshaken as a mountain, Bhíma bore
The rain of blows: with like unyielding strength
The Madra king sustained the mace of Bhíma;

[1] A tree that bears blood-red flowers, (Butea frondosa).

Like a tall rock, whose base is rooted firm,
Though frequent thunder-strokes have scarred its summit.
To gain the vantage of the fight intent,
Their practised skill the combatants display;
Alternate they advance, retire, or move,
In circling round—ten paces they retreat,
Then rush like butting elephants together.
At last, concentring all their strength, they struck;
And both, like Indra's banners by the storm
Uprooted, fell. When Kŕitavarmá saw
The king of Madra senseless on the earth,
He urged his troops to aid, and in the instant
The fainting warrior to his car they bore.
Reeled though his brain, as he had deeply quaffed
The wine cup, Bhíma in a moment rose.
With rage he maddened, when he saw the foe
Escaped his vengeance, and in vain he called
The king of Madra to renew the war.
The sons of Páńdu with redoubling shouts,
And mingled clang of horn, and drum, and shell,
Proclaimed their joy, and hailed their champion's triumph.

The Kuru host disheartened when he saw,
The son of Karńa, valiant Vŕishasena,
Foremost to rally strove, and with his shafts,
Thick darting as the solar rays, he hurled
The Páńdu warriors to the shades of hell.
Like trees uprooted by the gale, they strewed
The field. The Kuru bands their hopes resumed,

And ardent sought the war—their kindling fires
Their veteran leader fanned, and led them on
Against the monarch of the adverse host.
Fierce in their van his chariot Droṅa urged
Full on Yudhishṫhira, and with a shaft
Struck from his grasp his bow. The noble Arjuna,
Encouraging his brave Panchála guard,
Stood fearless by his brother, and repelled
Unmoved the shock, as breasts some ample stream,
And reflux drives, the waters of the main.
Still Droṅa strove—across his threatening course
The valiant Yugandhara[1] daring rushed,
As blows a gale athwart the angry deep.
A spear dislodged him from his car, and doomed
His soul to Yama's dwelling. Droṅa next
With fatal shaft the head of Sinhasena
Lopped from the trunk—then flew his weighty lance
At Vyághradatta[2]—in the breast infixed
The weapon quivered, and the hero fell.
Such deeds appalled the Páṅḋavas; they cried,
This day to Dhṙitaráshṫra's sons gives victory:
A moment more, and their resistless chief
Shall captive lead our king. Yet not the less
They closed around; and Arjuna exclaimed,
Fear not, my friends, still, still your fame maintain.

So speaking, on he dashed with whirring wheel

---

[1] A prince of the Yadu family, of the branch of Śini.

[2] We cannot pretend to give any satisfactory account of this person, or the preceding victim of Droṅa's exploits.

Through the deep streams of blood, with carcases
And shattered weapons choaked, and thundering
drove
Against the Kuru ranks. Around his course
In clouds the arrows flew, and darkened earth
And heaven, and hid the combatants from sight.
Precursor of nocturnal shades; for now
The sun behind the western mountains sunk,
And gloom profound ensued, nor friend nor foe
Could longer be distinguished. Dróńa then
Commanded conflict cease, and Arjuna
Restrained his now re-animated troops.
Each to their tents withdrew. Amidst his peers
The glorious Arjuna unrivalled shone,
As gleams the moon amongst the stars of heaven.

End of the first day's Battle.

From the Oriental Quarterly Magazine, Vol. III (March 1825), p. 134–44.

THE PASSAGE OF ARMS AT HÁSTINAPURA.

From the first book of the Mahábhárata [c. 130–136].

Now prudent[1] Bhíshma deemed the time arrived,
When the brave scions of each royal house,

---

[1] Bhíshma was the son of Śántanu by Gangá, he was the paternal uncle of Dhŕitaráshŕra, and as the Prince was blind, he acted as Regent during the minority of his grand nephews: he

Of Kuru and of Páńdu, should improve
Their growing years in exercise of arms.
With sage deliberation long he scanned
A suitable preceptor for their youth,
Who to meet skill in war and arms should join
Intelligence and learning, lofty aims,
Religious earnestness and love of truth.
And such in Drońa Bharadwája's son,
Wise, brave and pious did Gángeya[1] find.
Revered as his high fame and rank demanded,
Well pleased assented Drońa to the charge,
And by his cares the gallant sons of Páńdu
And Kuru's princely heirs were quickly trained
In arms and warlike practice, as became
Their martial origin and regal birth.

Where Gangá[2] from her mountain portal issues,
Dwelt Bharadwája, a most holy sage;
Who penance plied through many a painful year:
Nor did he softer sentiments disdain.
For, viewing sportive in the cooling stream
A beauteous nymph of heaven, he owned the force
Of charms celestial, and confessed desire.

---

disapproved of the conduct of Duryodhana towards his cousins, but when the war broke out, sided as a matter of duty with the Kuru Princes; he was killed early in the conflict: at the period in the text both they and the Páńdava youths were equally under his care.

[1] Gángeya a name of Bhíshma, the son of Gangá.

[2] Gangádwára or Haridwára, the gate of Gangá or of Vishńu.

Hence Droń a sprang—his tenderest youth was
taught
Lessons of wisdom from his saintly sire,
Nor less in arms instructed by the son
Of Fire[1], his father's faithful friend, directed
To wield the blazing[2] shafts with fatal aim—
His lessons and his sports the royal heir
Of Prishat shared—alike the sage's charge
In friendship for the father, and in hope
That like regard should mutual bind the sons.

When unto man's estate the youthful pair
Arrived, their fortunes sundered them. The king
Relinquished life and throne, and Drupada
The powerful sceptre of Panchála[3] swayed:
Next Droń a wept his holy sire exalted

---

[1] Agniveśa is the name of this individual, who is known by few other circumstances; a work on medicine is ascribed to him. [Weber, Catal. der Sanskrithandschriften, No. 940. 41. 47.]

[2] The Ágneya Astra, the weapon of fire, a musket or match-lock if our readers will, although we are afraid, our text intends something more visionary. [Sir H. Elliot's Bibliogr. Index to the Historians of Muhammedan Indian. Calc. 1849, p. 359-64. 373f.]

[3] The kingdom of Panchála seems to have occupied part of Oude, the lower Doáb and Agra; it could not have extended far in the latter direction, as Mathurá was the seat of an independent principality, whilst the states of Benares and Magadha must have pressed closely on its southern limits. [Lassen, Ind. Alt. I, 602. St. Julien, Mémoires sur les contrées occidentales, II, 348 f.] It may be doubted whether Kanoj was a distinct state at the period of the Mahábhárata. Panchála is said to derive its name from the five (Pancha) sons of Haryáśwa; Mudgala, Sŕinjaya,

To heavenly regions from a transient world.
He wedded, so his father had ordained,
The virtuous Kŕipá[1], from whose bosom sprang
The mighty Aśwatthámá[2]—him to rear
To virtue and to glory strove the sage,
The pleasing task absorbing all the thoughts,
That holy rites and pious duties spared.

The wrathful son of Jamadagni[3] closed

Vŕihadishu, Pravíra and Kámpilya, whom their father declared able (alam) to rule the kingdom. Vishńu Puráńa [p. 454]. The Panchálas as well as the Kauravas were of the family of Púru—descending immediately from Ajámíd́ha. Ajámíd́ha had several sons of whom the elder was Ŕiksha the father of Samvarańa, the father of Kuru; the younger was Níla, according to the Vishńu Puráńa [p. 453. 5]. The Mahábhárata differs in the name, but adds that the Panchála branch expelled the elder branch from Hástinapura, and obliged Samvarańa to retire to the Indus; his son Kuru, however, returned to a more westerly direction, and having established himself in the woods above Delhi, thence called from him Kurukshetra or Kurujángala, finally recovered his ancient patrimony.

[1] Kŕipa and his sister Kŕipá were the children of Śatadhŕiti, a descendant of the Panchála branch of the Kuru family [but, according to the Mahábh. I, 5074 ff., of Śaradwat. Lassen, II, 598 f.]: they were exposed in their infancy in a thicket of Śara grass, where they were found by Śántanu, who took them home and reared them as his own.

[2] So named it is said from his making a noise at his birth as sturdily as a horse, (aśwa, a horse and stháma, sound,) a better etymology however is aśwa a horse, and sthámá strength. [Mahábhárata I, 5115. 16.]

[3] Jamadagni was a pious ascetic descended from Bhŕigu: amongst the fruits of his penance was the possession of the divine cow from whom all that was desired was obtained: by her aid

His dread career, now satiate with revenge,
And bounteous on the priestly tribe bestowed
The boundless treasures of the Kshatriya slain—
Nought for himself reserved, as all he sought
Was heavenly knowledge and the hermit's cell.
Drońa amongst the Brahman race preferred
His suit and followed by a numerous train
Of pious scholars travelled from his home
To mount Mahendra, where the hero sage,
The son of Bhŕigu, eminent in wisdom

---

he entertained the monarch Kártavírya and his train: the King was desirous of obtaining so valuable an animal, and as the Muni refused to part with her, he attempted to carry her off by force: in this he failed, as the cow who had a voice of her own in the business flew to heaven, but her pious master lost his life; his son Paraśuráma vowed in revenge to exterminate the Kshatriya race, and this he effected in twenty-one successful attacks upon them: he then gave the earth to the Bráhmańas. The story is apparently an allegorical account of a struggle for the sovereignty of India between the military and priestly castes. Paraśuráma is the seventh descent of Vishńu. In consequence of sparing some of the Kshatriya women who became wives of the Bráhmańas, the military tribe was suffered to revive: we may suppose

——in Ráma's reign,
Such mixture was not held a stain,

as otherwise the great Rámachandra, Kŕishńa, and all the heroes of the Mahábhárata would be no better than of the Varńa Sankara, mixed and degraded castes. The Brahmans treated their benefactor with great ingratitude and allowed him to call no part of all the earth his own, upon which he repaired to the Malabar coast and commanded the sea to withdraw as far as he could fling his hatchet: this was done and he obtained a domicile in the present land of the Nairs—whence for a long time the legend says the Brahmans were utterly excluded.

As irresistible in war, sojourned.
His name and lineage known, the warrior gave
Kind greeting to his guest, and bade him speak
His wish, secure he could not speak in vain.
Exhaustless wealth was Drońa's seeming suit,
Though different purpose lurked beneath his prayer—
Ráma replied, whate'er of costly gems
Or gold was made my spoil, I have bestowed
On Brahma's sons; and upon Kaśyapa
The sea girt earth and all her smiling towns
Have I conferred: there but remain myself
And heavenly arms, chuse between them and me;
I chuse the weapons, Drońa cried, but scant
My skill to wield them, give me that, and all
I seek is granted; Ráma smiled assent,
And from his lessons quickly Drońa caught
The needful art. Contented then the sage
Departed from Mahendra and repaired
To share the boon with Pŕishat's regal son,
The friend and fellow of his earliest years.

Soon in the presence of Panchála's King
Heedless of ceremony, Drońa hailed
The haughty Drupada, "Behold in me
Your friend" he cried, the monarch sternly viewed
The sage and bent his brows, and with disdain
His eyeballs reddened: silent awhile he sat,
Then arrogantly spoke: Brahman, methinks
Thou shewest little wisdom or the sense
Of what is fitting when thou call'st me friend.

What friendship, weak of judgment, can subsist
Between a luckless pauper and a king—
Grant that such bond did formerly unite us,
What then: with age it wanes and feels decay—
Think not that everlasting friendship dwells
In human hearts, the hand of time impairs
Its strength, and passion plucks it from the bosom.
And whom does Friendship but as equals join
Such as we once might be, but are no more?
The poor and rich, the ignorant and wise,
The brave and recreant never can be friends.
Those who in wealth compete or in like rank
Exalted move acknowledge mutual worth:
The learned Brahman cannot know esteem
For him to whom the Vedas are a mystery:
The warrior scorns the man who cannot guide
The rattling chariot through the ranks of war;
And he to whose high mandate nations bow
Disdains to stoop to friends beneath the throne.
Hence then with idle dreams, dismiss the memory
Of other days and thoughts—I know thee not."[1]
Struck with amaze, a moment Droṅa paused,
Then turned away nor vouchsafed a reply—
He left the city and indignant sought
The stately capital that from the elephant,
Derives its name[2], the seat of Kuru's sons.

---

[1] Drupada had cause to repent this, Droṅa with his scholars invading Panchála and completely subduing it. Drupada's daughter, thence named Draupadí, became the wife of the five Páṅḍavas.

[2] Nágákhya, also Gajákhya meaning the same. Hástinapura

Not long unknown the mighty master dwelt
Within the capital, when Bhíshma heard
The tale, and for his nephews sought his aid.
The palace was his home, and all, the realm
Of cost produced, was placed at his command:
Thus honoured, pleased he trained the princely cohort
To martial excellence: quick spread his fame
To other climes and from all regions gathered
Illustrious youth, and with the heirs of Kuru
And Páńd́u's sons the hopes of Vŕishńi's line
And sons of Andhaka[1] partook his lessons.

But all the blooming troop in warrior skill,
And gallant bearing, Arjuna[2] surpassed:
Like him none reined the steed, guided the elephant,
Or drove the chariot; none unyielding stood,
The battle onset on the level plain:
And none, with like dexterity or vigour
Opposed in single fight his practised arm,
Whether he launched the javelin, hurled the dart,

---

means probably the same, though it is explained the city of King Hastí having been founded by a Prince of that name, the son of Suhotra and father of Ajamíd́ha: the ruins of Hástinapura, long the capital of Gangetic India, are now covered with ant-hills, and only a place of worship remains, about 20 miles S. W. from Dáránagar, on a branch of the Ganges, formerly the bed of the river. [Lassen, I, 597. Beilage I, p. XXIII.]

[1] The families of Vŕishńi and Andhaka were divisions of the line of Yadu, of which Kŕishńa was a descendant.

[2] Arjuna the third of the Páńd́avas, the youngest son of Pŕithá by Indra. [Lassen, I, 634. 41.]

Wielded the battleaxe or whirled the mace
Or rapid with the trenchant falchion smote.
Nor less in peaceful virtues shone the Prince:
Submissive ever to his teacher's will
Contented, modest, affable and mild—
Him Drońa favoured, and prophetic hailed
Unequalled archer 'mongst the sons of men.

And now expert in arms the youthful band,
Their great preceptor thus addressed the king
Amidst his peers assembled, holy Kŕipa
And wise Bahlíka, valiant Somadatta,
Sagacious Bhíshma, the immortal bard
Vyása and the prudent Vidura[1]: Great King,
Thy princes have acquired due skill in arms;
Command and let their prowess be approved
By public trial. Pleased the monarch cried:
Thy task, illustrious son of Bharadwája,
Is worthily accomplished; speak the time,
The place, and all thy judgement shall esteem
Essential to the honourable proof:

---

[1] Kŕipa and Bhíshma have been already introduced to our readers. Bahlíka, whence the country of Báhlíka or Balkh is supposed to be named [Lassen, I, 597. Weber, Ind. Śtud., I, 205.] was the brother of Śántanu, uncle of Bhíshma and great uncle of Dhŕitaráshtra, Somadatta is his son. Vyása is the author of the Mahábhárata, the arranger of the Vedas and the supposed author of the Puráńas, he was the son of the sage Parásara by Satyavatí, the adopted daughter of a fisherman, afterwards married to Śántanu, and the appointed father of Dhŕitaráshtra and Páńdu. Vidura is also the son of Vyása by a female slave, and consequently the half brother of Dhŕitaráshtra. [Lassen, I, 629. 34,]

Do thou command, we shall obey thy will:
And deeper now our grief that light no more
Revisits these sad eyes, and much we envy
Our happier peers who may behold with joy
The martial promise of our princely sons.
Go, Vidura, and what the sage ordains
Attentively fulfill, no dearer thought
Our bosom cherishes than his content.

Attended by the brother of the king,
The sage went forth and chose the field of arms:
A level plain, where tree and bush was none
To break the smoothness of the turfy ground.
Wide was the champain spread and round the marge
A cool pellucid stream meandering flowed—
Within the circle pious Droṅa reared
An altar for an offering to the Gods.
Next on the borders of the plain arose
A tall pavilion rich with gold and pearl,
And hung with trophies and the spoils of war—
With gorgeous seats provided for the King,
The peers, the Queens and beauty of the palace.
Then soon around, the busy artists reared
Innumerous galleries, and tents and booths,
To shade the throngs that from the city poured
In countless concourse to behold the scene.

Now all the lofty instruments of war
Proclaimed the festival; the King went forth
In long procession, by his peers attended.

Then came the royal matron, great Gándhárí[1]—
The widowed mother of the sons of Páńdu
Walked at her side; a lengthening line of dames,
And maidens eminent in rank as beauty,
Followed their steps, like a bright train they moved
Of heavenly nymphs ascending the steep mount
Of Meru, with the brides of the immortals:
Fast from the city rushed a mingled swarm,
Of every age and tribe, and wide around
A tossing multitude enclosed the field,
Like ocean heaving with unresting waves.

Arrayed in white, and white with hoary age,
The venerable Drońa in the midst
Of the vast circle stood: his valiant Son
Upstayed his steps, as moves the stately moon,
With fiery Mars attendant, through the skies;
Attentive to his beck the priestly choir
Advanced, and on the altar sacrificed
The offering to the gods, with holy texts
Made sacred, and from fear of evil guarded:
The ceremony closed, the heralds cried
The hour propitious, and the gallant band
Of youthful rivals marched into the field.

Their loins were girt, their left arms bound with horn[2],
The breast with corselet mailed; the quiver graced

---

[1] The wife of Dhŕitaráshtra, princess of Gandhára, the Gandarii of the ancient, and Candahar of modern geography.

[2] Or leather, to protect them from the bowstring.

The shoulder, and the better hand sustained
The sturdy bow; a martial host preceded,
Who various implements of war conveyed:
In decent file according to their years
Arrayed, the Princes graceful trod the field,
And Yudhishṫhira eldest led the van:
The sports commenced and at the destined aim
The arrows flew, the multitude beheld
With wonder their unerring flight, and many
Declined their looks, unable to sustain
The dazzling aspect of the fearful shower;
Now standing on the ground they drew the bow
And struck the distant mark with glittering shaft,
Nor with less truth the feathered arrows plied,
On generous steeds in rapid circles borne;
The crowds delighted marked their youthful prowess,
And long continued plaudits shook the field[1].

Next on the thundering car the heroes stood,
And dexterous guided in its swift career.
Then on the giant elephant ascended
Or strode the steed, and in the mimic fight
With sword and shield the shock of war pourtrayed:
Then mingling in tumultuous mellay waved
The falchion and here singly one sustained
The blows of numbers, or there numbers mixed
Opposed, and all in strength and speed and grace,

---

[1] Many passages in this and other works prove the Hindus to have cultivated archery most assiduously, and to have been very Parthians in the use of the bow on horseback.

Alacrity of limb, unyielding grasp,
Firmness of foot and steadiness of soul,
Displayed their master's merits and their own.

With more than seeming enmity inspired,
The proud Duryodhana and gallant Bhíma
Apart from all, upon the plain alighting,
Each other to the proof of arms defied:
With ponderous mace they waged the daring fight:
As for a tender mate two rival elephants
Engage with frantic fury, so the youths
Encountered, and amidst the rapid sphere
Of fire their whirling weapons clashing wove:
Their persons vanished from the anxious eye—
Still more and more incensed their combat grew,
And life hung doubtful on the desperate conflict:
With awe the crowd beheld the fierce encounter
And amidst hope and fear suspended tossed
Like ocean shaken by conflicting winds.
Then Drońa interposed: he bade his son
Intrepid Aśwatthámá part the combat,
Swelling like ocean waves when gales uplift
The mighty main: the daring youths obeyed
Their teacher's mandate, and surceased the strife.

Then Drońa summoned from his princely peers
His favorite pupil: "Dearer than a son,
Come hither, Arjuna," the youth advanced,
Begirt with radiant arms and mailed in gold,
As glorious as a cloud at set of sun
Upon whose edge the parting day yet lingers,

While lightning streams along its glittering sides,
And Indra's bow shoots gorgeous o'er its breast[1]:
As modest moved the youthful hero, rose
The clang of shells and trumpets, and loud shouts
Of admiration from the gazing crowd:
They hailed him Arjuna, the first in arms,
And worth; the flower of modesty and valour;
The cries ascended where his mother sat,
And o'er her bosom, swelling with delight,
And pride, fast fell the fond maternal tear.

Commanded by his teacher, Arjun drove[2]
His chariot bounding o'er the spacious field,
With dexterous rein, and as it rolled he rose,
Erect or cowering shrunk, now in the midst
He stood, then forward on the pole, then leaped
To earth, then vaulted on the whirling car,
And still with shaft undeviating pierced
The subtlest mark, the softest and most flexile
And most refractory, with equal aim:
At once five arrows in the iron jaws
Of a vast boar who formidable scoured
The plain[3] he lodged: then twenty shafts he shot

---

[1] This is the genuine offspring of a tropical climate and no less just than splendid.

[2] We omit Arjuna's exploits with the mystical weapons of fire, water, &c. as they are implements of which we cannot form, much less convey any exact idea.

[3] We believe the author means an iron effigy and therefore plead guilty to a gratuitous innovation: in this and still more in the following feat it will be thought that our author draws a

Together in the hollow of a horn
Suspended by a lithe loose waving string.
Applauding shouts repaid the archer's skill,
And heaven and earth loud echoed with his praise.

And now in troops the youthful bands divided
Awhile reposed, the five brave brethren here
With Drońa in their centre, like the moon
When through the five-starred house of Hasta[1] moving:
The hundred Sons of Dhŕitaráshŕra there
Round Aśwatthámá gathered like the Gods,
Around their monarch when the giant race
Of Daityas threat with impious war the skies.
When on the sudden from the barrier rose
A clamour rending heaven: all eyes were turned
Towards the place, and from the gate approached
Through wondering crowds the Sun's bright progeny,
The valiant Karńa[2]: on his breast he wore

---

reasonably long bow: to shoot a number of arrows at once in a firm compact manner was however no doubt the ambition of Hindu archery in ancient days.

[1] The thirteenth of the lunar mansions or asterisms which mark the moon's path: it contains five stars of which the brightest is supposed to be γ or δ corvi. [Journal of the Amer. Or. Soc. VI, 334.]

[2] Karńa was the son of Pŕithá by the Phœbus of Hindu mythology: as he was born before the lady was married she exposed him in the Jamná, where he was found and preserved by Dhŕitaráshŕra's charioteer: the protection of his real father was also extended to him, and consequently in his youth he became a hero of the first order: the circumstances of this encounter, and other oc-

The mail that to his birth was given[1]: his ears
With gorgeous pendants shone: with bow in hand
And mighty falchion girt, he proud advanced
And like a moving mountain strode the field.
The virgin-born, the offspring of the sun,
The tamer of his foes, the chief of fame,
Tall as a palm, and as a lion strong.

Erect amidst the plain he paused, and viewed
With looks of pride the multitude around;
To Droṅa homage paid, then turned to Arjuna,
And thus defied the prince, "whate'er thine arm
This day has wrought I pledge me to surpass,
The holy sage permitting": at his words,
As by a vast machine at once upraised
All rose, and most Duryodhana rejoiced
To hear his vaunt, for shame and indignation,
Surprise and envy of his kinsman's glory
And ancient hatred rankled at his heart.

Then Droṅa gave assent, and every feat
By Arjuna achieved was wrought by Karṅa.
Duryodhana his joy proclaimed aloud, he clasped
The hero to his heart: whate'er the realm
Affords, demand, I plight my princely vow,
'Tis thine my friend: and Karṅa made reply,

---

casions on which he experienced the disregard of his brethren threw him into the arms of their enemies and he proved one of the chief supports of Duryodhana and the Kurus.

[1] Karṅa like Minerva was born ready equipped for the field; armed with a miraculous cuirass and lance.

The name of friend contents my proudest hopes.
Again to Arjuna he turned and said,
Thus far our skill is equal, let it now
Be seen in single fight where vantage lies.
The Prince replied: Quick be it mine to send thee
To learn what regions tenant those who come
Unbidden guests or vaunt uncalled their prowess:
The field of conflict, Karńa cried, is free
To all the brave, and to the princely mind
The proof of valour is the proof of virtue:
Why should these idle pastimes swell your pride
To strike with shafts innocuous, toys like these:
Mine seek a nobler mark. My arrows fly
Here in thy teacher's presence at thy head.

Thus vaunting he, and either stood prepared,
To wage no sportive war, when from the seat
Where sat the royal dames a cry of grief
Broke wild upon their purpose. By his arms,
And voice and bold demeanour Přithá knew
Her first-born Son in Karńa, and appalled
To see the Brothers, mutually unknown,
On hostile thought intent, she strove to stay
The horrid strife: in vain: oblivion sealed
Her every sense and Vidura conveyed
The dame unconscious to the regal dome.

To grace his martial Son the valiant Arjuna,
The monarch of the elements[1] descended—

[1] Indra the father of Arjuna: all the sons of Přithá were be-

Upon his path the muttering thunder followed;
The brilliant lightning waved; his own bright bow
Its many-coloured banner spread, and high
A pearly line of wild fowl winged the air.
This when the sovereign of the day, the sire
Of gallant Karńa, saw, he quick repaired
To grace his darling son with rival glory.
So stood the youths opposed, protecting shade
O'er Arjuna impending hung, his foe
Stood radiant glittering in the solar ray.
Conflicting feelings filled the anxious crowd
And equal shared the interest of the fight.

And now stood either on the verge of fate
When sapient Kŕipa Karńa thus addressed:
Undaunted stranger,—this the youngest son
Of Ṕithá and of Páńd́u will not shrink
From thine encounter, but do thou declare
Thy name and lineage; of what royal house
Art thou the ornament: this known, the fight
Proceeds, if thou an equal champion prove
With princes to contend: the sons of kings
Strive not with rivals of inferior birth.
He said and ceased, and Karńa silent stood
And hung his head, as when surcharged with dew
The drooping Lotus bows its fragrant blossom.

Him thus abashed Duryodhanabeheld

gotten by divinities; it being death to her own husband Páńd́u to approach her.

And instant cried: awhile the sports suspend,
And then no plea be wanting to the trial;
The state of Anga[1] of its lord bereft
Upon our will depends, this valiant chief
Be crowned its sovereign; then with equal pride
He calls thee Arjuna to equal arms.
Away,—this instant sees the hero king.

Impetuous thus the Prince, and none presumed
To question his resolve; so ceased the sports,
And Karńa was installed as Anga's king[2].

Ib. Vol. IV (Septbr. 1825), p. 141—150.

(The Swayamvara, the free, or self election of a husband, was a not uncommon practice amongst the Hindus, and forms the subject of frequent description both in ancient and modern poetry: the Princes being assembled in a public place, with appropriate ceremonies, the Princess performed the tour of the circle, and signified her preference by throwing a garland of flowers

---

[1] Anga lay upon the Ganges including part of Behar and Bhagulpur and Rájmahal.

[2] In the original some further squabbling takes place after Karńa's installation before the party breaks up, and Karńa's adoptive father, Dhŕitaráshŕra's charioteer, makes his appearance, and claims him as his son, to the great triumph of the Páńdavas. Duryodhana continues to advocate his cause, but no strife ensues, and embittered hostility is the only result of the sports.

upon the neck of the successful competitor: the marriage rite was subsequently performed as usual. It may be easily supposed that the preference was not always the suggestion of the moment and grew out of previous acquaintance: thus Damayantí adopted this mode of chusing Nala in concert with her lover: Táràvatí chose Chandraśekhara by the guidance of her nurse, and the Princess of Canoj invited Ṕrithu Rai to her Swayamvara. The consequences may also be easily conjectured, and mortified vanity or disappointed expectation must often have engendered personal hostility: the result may not unfrequently have been long and widely felt, and though neither the Swayamvaras of Draupadí or Damayantí may have been attended with any remarkable events, the choice of the Princess of Canoj was less innoxious; for the animosity which it excited between her father and her lord, laid India bare to Mohammedan aggression, and paved the way for European ascendancy.)

THE CHOICE OF DRAUPADÍ.

[Mahábh. I, ch. 184–192.]

From Bhágírathí's[1] pleasant borders went
The five brave brothers[2], and towards the north

[1] The Ganges, named Bhágírathí from Bhagíratha, the fourth in descent from Sagara, by whose devotions she was induced to come down upon the earth for the purification of the bones of his ancestors.

[2] Yudhishthira, Bhíma, Arjuna, Nakula and Sahadeva, the

Their wandering steps directed: on the road
They past assembled throngs, travelling alike
A northward journey. From a pious troop
Of Brahmans Yudhishṫhira asked the cause
Of this advancing host, and whither bound.
They answered:—In Panchála's[1] spacious realm
The powerful monarch Drupada observes
A solemn feast: attending princes wait
With throbbing hearts his beauteous daughter's choice;
The royal Draupadí[2], whose charms surpass
All praise, as far as her mild excellence
And mind transcend the beauties of her person.
She from the sacrificial hearth was born
When her imperial Sire performed the rite
To win him sons, whose prowess might avenge
The wrongs he had sustained from Dróńa's pride.
Then too her gallant brother Dhŕishṫadyumna,
Arrayed in shining mail, and armed with bow
And falchion, like the flashing gleam of flame[3]

---

two last were the twin sons of Mádrí, the second wife of Páńdu, the three first are the sons of Pŕithá.

[1] Panchála. In addition to the observations on this country made on a former occasion (see above), we may add that we have since met with a tract in which Nepal is said to be comprised within Northern Panchála.

[2] Draupadí, a patronymic, the daughter of Drupada.

[3] The birth of Draupadí and Dhŕishṫadyumna is thus related in the Mahábhárata [I, ch. 167]. Although Drupada was compelled to acquiesce in the arrangement made by Dróńa, by which his rule was confined to the country south of the Bhágírathí, the partition

Sprang radiant from the consecrated fire.
Now ripe the nymph in years and charms, the king
Commands her wed some prince of her election.
Fast to his court from every clime repair
Kings and the sons of kings, and chiefs of fame
Exulting emulous in youth and valour.
And aged priests and venerable Brahmans
Well skilled to solemnize each sacred rite.

---

was the cause of deep mortification, and he long meditated on the means by which he might recover his former power and be revenged upon his enemy. He especially regretted the want of a son whose youth and valour might compete with Drońa's disciples, and he visited the chief resorts of the Brahmans, in hope to meet with some holy sage, whose more than human faculties might secure him progeny. He found two Brahmans of eminent learning and sanctity named Yája and Upayája, and addressed himself to the latter, promising him a million of cows if he enabled him to obtain the son he desired. Upayája, however, declined the task and referred him to his elder brother Yája, to whom the King repaired and promised ten million of kine: with much reluctance he undertook to direct a sacrificial ceremony by which the King should obtain offspring, and called his younger brother to his assistance. When the rite had reached the proper period the queen was invited to partake of it, but she had not completed her toilet and begged the Brahmans to delay the ceremony. It was too late, and the sacrifice proceeding without her, the children were born independent of her participation. The son Dhŕishťadyumna appeared with a diadem on his head, in full mail and armed with a bow and falchion from the middle of the sacrificial fire. Draupadí the daughter from the middle of the vedi, or altar, on which the fire had been kindled! she was of very black colour although exceeding loveliness, and was thence named Kŕishńá; the name of the son is derived from the pride and power with which he was endowed from his birth.

Thither we go and willingly shall guide
Your steps to share with us the liberal gifts
That princely bounty on our tribe bestows;
Or to behold, if so your youth prefer,
The joyous revelry that gilds the scene;
For thither mummers, mimes and gleemen throng,
Athletics, who the prize of strength or skill
Contend in wrestling or the gauntlet's strife:
Minstrels with sounding lutes and Bards[1] who chant
Their lord's high lineage and heroic deeds—
These merry sports beheld, you may return
With us or where you list, unless it chance
The Princess toss the wreath to one of you—
For you are goodly and of God-like bearing.
Thus he, and blithe Yudhishthira replied—
Have with you to the wedding. So they went
To South Panchála with the Brahman band.

---

[1] The persons named in the text are Natas, Vaitálikas, Narttakas, Sútas, Mágadhas, and Niyodhakas. The Nata is properly an actor, but in popular acceptation it comprehends jugglers, buffoons, and persons practising slight of hand and exhibiting feats of agility; in this last also the Narttaka partakes, although properly speaking a dancer. The Vaitálika in his official character is a poetical watchman or a bellman—one who announces in verse the change of the seasons and the hours of the day—when not retained for the purpose he is a public singer. The Sútas and Mágadhas are both considered to discharge the same kind of duty, and are the bards and heralds of the Hindus, being attached to the state of all men of rank to chaunt their praises, celebrate their actions, and commemorate their ancestry. The Niyodhaka is a prize-fighter either as a wrestler or boxer or a swordsman—in some parts of India also he fights with gauntlets, armed with steel spikes.

Through many a smiling grove their journey lay
And by the marge of many a limpid lake.
And oft they loitering paused upon their route
To mark the beauties of each grateful scene.
At length arrived, they made their humble dwelling
A Potter's lowly roof—and daily forth
They fared as mendicants to gather alms.
And now the day of festival drew nigh;
When Drupada, whose anxious hopes desired
A son of Páńd́u for his daughter's lord,
And who had sent his messengers to search
The banished chiefs, still sought by them in vain,
Devised a test—no other force but theirs
He deemed could undergo, to win the bride.
A ponderous bow with magic skill he framed[1],
Unyielding but to more than mortal strength.
And for a mark he hung a metal plate
Suspended on its axle, swift revolving
Struck by a shaft that from the centre strayed.
This done he bade proclaim—that he whose hand
Should wing the arrow to its destined aim,
Should win the Princess by his archery.

---

[1] Trial of strength by the drawing of a bow is a favourite subject in Hindu poetry, and the heroes of two of the most celebrated and most ancient works in Sanskrit, the Mahábhárata and the Rámáyańa, both win their wives in a similar manner. Arjuna gains Draupadí as in the text, and Ráma obtains Sítá by breaking the bow of Śiva, which other princes were unable to bend. We need not remind our readers of the bow of Ulysses here—we lately pointed out one coincidence between Hindu and Homeric fiction (above p. 259) and this seems to furnish a second.

Before the day appointed, trooping came
Princes and chiefs innumerous: 'midst the throng
Duryodhana and all the hundred sons
Of Dhŕitarásh́tra with the gallant Karńa
In haughty cohort at the court appeared.
With hospitable act the king received
His royal guests and fitting welcome gave.

Between the North and East without the gates
There lay a spacious plain: a fosse profound
And lofty walls enclosed its ample circuit,
And towering gates and trophied arches rose,
And tall pavilions glittered round its borders:
Here ere the day of trial came, the sports
Were held: and loud as ocean's boisterous waves,
And thick as stars that gem the Dolphin's brow[1],
The mighty city here her myriads poured.
Around the monarch's throne on lofty seats
Of gold with gems emblazoned sat the kings,
Each lowering stern defiance on the rest.
Without the barriers pressed the countless crowd

---

[1] In the head of the Śiśumára.—The Śiśumára is properly the Gangetic porpoise (Delphinus gangeticus), but the astronomical Śiśumára [Vishńu Pur. II, 12. Bhágav. Pur. V, 23.] to which the allusion is made is as much a non-descript as any of the pictured monstrosities on our celestial globe—(see Sir Wm. Jones' supplement to the Essay on Hindu chronology A. Res. II, 402). The commentator says the expression is a parenthetical equivalent for the North-east quarter, that being the situation of the asterism—and implies, that the people assembled in that direction. He is probably right; but we prefer being wrong.

Or clambering upon scaffolds clustering hung.
Skirting the distance multitudes beheld
The field from golden lattices, or thronged
The high house-tops, whose towering summits touched
The clouds, and like the mountain of the gods[1]
With sparkling peaks streamed radiant through the air.
A thousand trumpets brayed, and slow the breeze
With incense laden wafted perfume round.
Whilst games of strength and skill—the graceful dance,
The strains of music, or dramatic art,
Awoke the gazer's wonder and applause.

Thus sixteen days were passed, and every chief
Of note was present—and the king no more
Could with fair plea his daughter's choice delay.
Then came the Princess forth in royal garb
Arrayed and costly ornaments adorned:
A garland interwove with gems and gold
Her delicate hands sustained—from the pure bath
With heightened loveliness she tardy came,
And blushing in the princely presence stood.
Next in the ring the reverend Priest appeared
And strewed the holy grass and poured the oil,
An offering to the God of Fire, with prayer

---

[1] Kailása—the favourite residence of Śiva; a very conspicuous part of the Himálaya bears this appellation.

Appropriate, and with pious blessings crowned.
Then bade the king the trumpets' clangor cease
And hush the buzzing crowd—while his brave son
The gallant Dhŕishtadyumna on the plain
Descended and his father's will proclaimed.
"Princes, this bow behold—yon mark—these shafts—
Whoe'er with dexterous hand at once directs
Five arrows to their aim, and be his race,
His person and his deeds equivalent
To such exalted union, He obtains
My sister for his bride—my words are truth."
Thus said, he to the Princess next described
Each royal suitor by his name and lineage[1]

[1] The author favours us with their names—and as a catalogue of the chief dramatis personæ of the Mahábhárata it may be admissible in a note, although a hopeless recapitulation for the text. The principal sons of Dhŕitaráshtra are Duryodhana, Durvishaha—Durmukha—Dushpradarshańa, Vivinśati, Vikarńa, Duhśásana, Yuyutsu, Váyuvega—Bhímavegarava, Ugráyudha, Valákí, Karakáyu, Virochana, Kuńdaka, Chitrasena, Kanakadhwaja, Nandaka, Báhnśálí, Tuhuńda, and Vikaṫa—the other princes are Karńa, the half brother of the Páńdus; Aśwatthámá, the son of Drońa; Bhoja, whose rame is traceable in many parts of India and at different periods; Vŕihanta, Mańimán, Dańdadhára, Sahadeva, Jayasena—Meshasandhi, Viráṫa, his two sons Śankha and Uttara, Várddhakshemi, Suśarmá, Senávindu, Suketu, and his son Suvarchas, Suchitra, Sukumára; Vŕika, Satyadhŕiti, Súryadhwaja, Rochamána, Níla, Chitráyudha, Anśumán, Chekitána, Śreńimán, Chandrasena, the son of Samudrasena, Jalasandha, and his sons Dańda and Vidańda, Vásudeva, king of Pauńdra, Bhagadatta, Kalinga and Támralipta or the kings of those countries.—The king of Madra, Śalya with his sons Rukmangada and Rukmaratha.—Kauravya, Somadatta, Bhúri, Bhúriśrava, Śala, Sudakshińa, the king of Kamboja,

And martial deeds, and bade her give the wreath
To him whose prowess best deserved the boon.
Quick from their gorgeous thrones the kings uprose,
Descending to the conflict, and around
The lovely Draupadí contending pressed;
Like the bright gods round Śiva's mountain bride[1].
Love lodged his viewless arrows in their hearts,
And jealous hatred swelled their haughty minds;
Each on his rivals bent a lowering glance,
And friends till now, they met as deadliest foes.
Alone the kindred bands remained aloof
Who owned[2] Janárdana their glorious chief.
He and the mighty[3] Haláyudha curbed
Their emulous zeal,—and tranquil they beheld
Like furious elephants the monarchs meet;

Dhŕidhadhanwá, Paurava, Vŕihadbala, Sushena, Śivi, Ausínara— The destroyer of Paṫachchara — The sovereign of the Kárushas. The chiefs of the house of Yadu are Balaráma, Kŕishńa, the son of Vasudeva; the son of Rukmińí, Śámba Chárudeshńa, and the son of Pradyumna, Akrúra, Sátyaki, Uddhava, Kŕitavarmá, Hárdikya, Pŕithu and Vipŕithu, Vidúratha, Kanka, Śanku, Gaveshańa, Áśávaha, Niruddha, Samíka, Sárimejaya, Vátapati, Kshillí, Pińḋáraka, and the valiant Usínara. Other Kings are Bhagíratha. Vŕihatkshatra, Jayadratha the Prince of Sindhu, Vŕihadratha, Báhlika, Śrutáyu, Ulúka, Kaitava, Chitrángada, Śubhángada, Vatsarája the King of Kośalá, Śiśupála, the king of Chédi, and Jarásandha, the sovereign of Magadha. All these perform parts more or less prominent in the subsequent conflict.

[1] Párvatí, the daughter of Himálaya.

[2] A name of Kŕishńa, the object of human adoration.

[3] A name of Balaráma, the elder brother of Kŕishńa, from his being armed with a plough. [Lassen, Ind. Alt., I, 620 ff.]

Their rage by courteous seeming ill represt
Like fire amidst the smouldering embers glowing.

And now in turn the Princes to the trial
Succeeding past, in turn to be disgraced—
No hand the stubborn bow could bend—they strained
Fruitless each nerve, and many on the field
Recumbent fell, whilst laughter pealed around.
In vain they cast aside their royal robes
And diamond chains and glittering diadems,
And with unfettered arm and ample chest
Put forth their fullest strength—the bow defied.
Each chief nor left the hope he might succeed.
Karńa alone the yielding bowstring drew
And ponderous shafts applied, and all admired.
The timid Draupadí in terror cried,
I wed not with the base-born[1]—Karńa smiled

[1] As previously intimated, the birth of Karńa was secret, and he was reputed to be the son of Nandana the charioteer of Dhŕitaráshtra, having been found floating in the river Yamuná although the son of Príthá, the mother of the three elder Páńdava princes by the Sun—he was born in celestial panoply, and with splendid ear-rings, whence his first appellation was Vasusheńa, or abounding in wealth. Indra disguised as a Brahman begged of him his divine coat of mail, in order to obtain it for his own son Arjuna, aud from the act of cutting or detaching it from his body the prince was named Karńa; he is also entitled Vaikarttana from Vikarttana, the sun. Indra, in return for the armour, presented Karńa with a Javelin freighted with the certain death of one individual whether god, man, or demon. Karńa launched it at Ghatotkacha, the Rákshasa son of Bhíma, and it destroyed him, but left its possessor helpless against the charmed weapous offensive and defensive of Arjuna, by whose hand Karńa ultimately fell.

In bitterness and upwards turned his eyes
To his great Sire the Sun—then cast to earth
The bow and shafts and sternly stalked away.—

Thus foiled the Princes, through the murmuring crowd
Amazement spread—then Arjuna from where
He and his brethren with the Brahmans placed
Had viewed the scene advanced to prove his skill—
The priestly bands with wonder struck beheld
Who seemed a student of their tribe aspire
To triumph where the mightiest chiefs had failed—
They deemed the like disgrace would shame the attempt,
And ridicule their race and name assail,
And many a venerable elder strove
To turn the stripling from the hopeless task:
They strove in vain—nor did they all despair—
For many marked his elephantine strength,
His lion port and self-collected soul;
And fancied that they saw revived in him
The son of Jamadagni[1]: to o'erthrow
Once more the haughty Kshatriya's[2] power and pride.

---

[1] Paraśuráma, by whom the Kshatriya or military race was exterminated. [Mahábh. III, c. 117.]

[2] Walking round a temple, an image, a venerable personage, or any object of veneration is an act of worship, amongst the Hindus. The rite was not unknown as a purificatory one to the ancients; as Virgil: Idem ter socios pura circumtulit unda. The circumambulation of holy shrines is also an act of frequent practice in Roman Catholic countries.

Unheeding praise or censure, Arjuna
Passed to the field: with reverential steps
He round the weapon circled, next addressed
A silent prayer to Mahádeo and last
With faith inflexible on Kŕishńa dwelt.
One hand the bow upbore, the other drew
The sturdy cord, and placed the pointed shafts—
They flew—the mark was hit—and sudden shouts
Burst from the crowd long silent: fluttering waved
The Brahman scarfs, and drum and trumpet brayed,
And Bard and Herald sung the hero's triumph.

Well pleased the monarch marked the youthful might
That had succeeded where so many chiefs
Of high renown were foiled, and deemed secure
His state by such alliance—nor was Draupadí
The less content, her beauties were the prize
Of youth and grace as well as skill in arms.
But in the bosoms of the Princes burned
Indignant wrath, and each to other spake
Congenial rage. Behold, they cried, the king
Regards us light as straws, and deigns to wed
His daughter to this Brahman boy whose craft
Has humbled royalty: but shall this be?
Destroy the parent tree, and with it falls
The fruit distasteful: haughty and unjust
This heedless monarch from our rank withholds
The reverence due to kings. Then let him die—
Him and his son together. He invites us

Here to his palace, and with outward seeming
Of hospitable rite receives us, soon
In scorn to end: what makes a Brahman here
In scenes like these? The Vedas have ordained,
A royal maid's election of her lord
Alone is fitting to the martial race.
Though Brahman arrogance or avarice urge
This trespass on our birthright, yet on them
We may not as we should avenge our wrongs;
The Brahman's life is sacred: then descend
Our fury on the guilty race of Drupada.
He and his son shall feel our swords: the maid,
Unless she chuse a royal lord, be tossed
Into the flame: then part we to our homes.

Thus they, and soon their gleaming weapons menaced
The life of Drupada: the king in terror
Turned to the Brahmans: Arjuna at once
Rushed to his succour and defied his foes.
Quick to his side came Bhíma[1]: like the judge

---

[1] Bhíma [Mahábh. I, c. 123.] is the Hercules or Orlando of the mythological poetry of the Hindus; his uncommon strength was a supernatural endowment. In his youth, he was the great plague of the Kuru princes, beating them in every sport and contest. They therefore plotted to get rid of him, and at a juvenile party, at one of the water palaces of the king, administered a poisonous drug to him, and took advantage of his slumber to push him into the Ganges. He fell into the region of the subterrene snakes, by whom he was bitten; one poison was the antidote of the other, and Bhíma recovering from his sleep, soon beat off his antagonists: they fled

Of hell with ponderous mace, for as he passed
A stately tree he by the roots uptore
And wielded for the fight: nor long delayed
The great Yudhishthira, nor the brave twins,
And all in firm fraternal phalanx stood.
The Brahmans round the princely cohort gathered,
In vain by Arjuna advised to shun
A strife ill suited to their gentler studies.—
Awhile the kings their course restrained, admiring

---

to their king Vásuki, who was induced by their report to see the wonderful boy, and went to meet him. In his train was Aryaka the maternal great great grandfather of Bhíma, who recognised and welcomed his descendant. Aryaka being a great favourite with the King of the Nágas, Vásuki offered to give his relation any treasure or gems he could desire, but Aryaka asked permission for him to quaff the invigorating beverage, of which one bowl full contained the strength of a thousand Nágas: permission being granted, Bhíma drained this bowl eight times at as many draughts and then went quietly to sleep for eight days: on his waking he was feasted by the Nágas and then restored to his sorrowing mother and brethren. From this period dates his miraculous strength.—Many of these incidents find parallels in western Romance. The Lady of the lake inhabits the depths of the water and is called by Merlin the "white serpent"; the Fata Morgana resided beneath a lake while caressing one of her lovers as a serpent. She is also styled the Fairy of Riches: her treasures were spread over a plain to which Orlando arrived by falling in a conflict with Arridano to the bottom of an enchanted lake: Manto, the protecting fairy of Mantua, [Orl. Fur. 43, 74.] being saved by Adonio when pursued in the form of a snake, proffers him any thing he may desire. The account she gives of herself makes her to be a regular Nága Kanyá or Ophite Maiden. The feat of Bhíma may be paralleled by a similar one of Orlando, and many others of the preux chevaliers of Chivalry.

The novel daring of the priestly tribe,
Then more indignant hastened to chastise them.
By Karńa and by Śalya led, opposed
To Arjuna and Bhíma as to those
Who best deserved their force, like Elephants
With passion maddening, headlong on they rushed:
Like Elephants the brothers met their might.
Against the Brahman band Duryodhana
The royal squadron led, buth with disdain
For foes unwarlike filled, they curbed their prowess—
And waged contemptuously sportive strife.
When Karńa felt the vigour of that arm
Unequalled, he, astounded, paused and spake.
Brahman, thy prowess should not want my praise,
But that it wakes my wonder: what? art thou
Some deity disguised in mortal form?
No Brahman could display such martial skill,
Nor breathes the man who could defy my strength,
Save Arjuna. To Karńa then the Prince:
No God am I—nor hero—to the use
Of arms my holy teachers trained my youth.
And here I stand to tame thy haughty pride
And triumph o'er thy fame: then, chief, be firm!
But Karńa from the field withdrew: for vain
He deemed it to contend with Brahman might.

Elsewhere the furious king of Madra fought
With powerful Bhíma: both alike in arms
Expert, and with gigantic force endued.

Long they contended, nor could either boast
Of vantage gained: their shattered arms they threw
Aside, and grappling to each other clung:
With hand and knee and chest to chest opposed,
They struggled long; at length the sudden grasp
Of Bhíma from the ground the king upbore
And dashed him with resistless sweep to earth.
Stunned by the fall the haughty monarch lay
Senseless and bleeding at his victor's feet.

Appalled by Śalya's fate and Karńa's flight,
The princes changed their anger for surprise,
And humbled to the seeming Brahmans spake.
'Tis bravely done, and we confess your prowess.
But what your birth, or where your country, tell,
Whose is the valour that has equal stood
The son of Rádhá[1]: whose the strength that felled
The king of Madra? they are champions both
That few of their compeers would dare encounter.
Suspend the strife: although we stand as foes,
We own due reverence for your sacred race.
Comply with our request: then if ye list
The conflict be resumed. Thus humbly they.
The sons of Páńdu stern surveyed the kings
Nor deigned reply: but Vásudeva's[2] glance
Had penetrated their disguise, not yet
To be unveiled to hostile eyes: and soothed

---

[1] Rádhá was the adoptive mother of Karńa.
[2] The patronymic of Kŕishńa.

The wounded indignation of the Princes.
His gentle intercession lulled their rage,
And sullen from the field the Kings retired,
Midst shouts of triumph from the Brahman train.
Then round the hero's neck the trembling hand
Of Draupadí the marriage chaplet flung,
And with his lovely bride, the prize of valour[1],

---

[1] Although won by Arjuna, Draupadí became, as is well known, the wife of all the brothers—or as Sir Wm. Jones calls her— "a five male single female flower." This plurality of husbands is unauthorized by any provision in the Hindu law, although prevalent throughout the Himálaya mountains, and in Malabar. The author of the Mahábhárata, in preserving a circumstance, that must have been repulsive to his own feelings, must have been influenced by the general belief in a tradition, which he could not have invented. Its insertion is a proof, that he drew the materials of his poem from other sources than his own imagination—he is clearly very much embarrassed with it, and endeavours to make sundry apologies for it. On the brothers returning to their college with Draupadí, they tell their mothers they have brought alms (Bhikshá) to which she replies without looking at them—being engaged in household matters—"Share it among ye all." When she finds the article to be so divided is a daughter-in-law, she is much shocked, but her words cannot be recalled, and Draupadí consequently becomes the bride of all her sons. As if conscious, however, that this excuse is not quite sufficient, the author of the Mahábhárata puts strong objections to it in the mouth of Drupada, who states that he had heard of one husband having many wives, but never of one wife's having many husbands, and declares it to be forbidden by usage, and the Vedas. [M. Müller, History of ancient Sanskrit Literature, p. 44 ff.] Yudhishṫhira replies that the practice may plead precedent, and instances the case of the ten sages called Práchetasas who had one wife, Gautamí, in common. Drupada, however, continuing to refuse his assent, Vyása

The victor from the scene of strife withdrew.

---

is obliged to appear, the dilemma requiring such an arbitrator; and he overrules the objections of the king by relating to him a legend, by which it appears, that the five Pańdus are five forms of Indras four of whom were exhibited to the fifth by Mahádeva, to humble the pride of the king of Swarga, and all five are with the same view condemned to a mortal birth, their Śrí also, or the personified glory of their royal condition, is sentenced to be born as their wife. She is Draupadí. At the same time Vishńu, on being made acquainted with the story by Indra, takes two hairs, a white and a black one, and these become the children of Devakí, Balaráma and Kŕishńa. The worshippers of the latter who maintain, that he is Vishńu's whole self, are not well pleased with this account of his origin.

V.

INTRODUCTION TO THE DAŚA KUMÁRA CHARITA.

Oriental Text Society. London: MDCCCXLVI.

The Daśa Kumára Charita, or "Adventures of the Ten Princes", has been selected for publication on account of its manifold claims on the attention of the cultivators of Sanskrit literature.

It is scarcely necessary to remind Sanskrit students, that the works hithertho published, conformably to the general character of Sanskrit composition, have been almost exclusively written in metre; and that the only specimens of prose which have been placed within their reach are the narratives of the Hitopadeśa, the occasional dialogue of the dramas, technical works on law or grammar, or Scholia on metrical texts. A continuous and standard prose composition is still wanting in printed Sanskrit literature, and the want is now supplied by a work written in a highly cultivated style, but entirely in prose; a work of deservedly high reputation among the learned of India, and one presenting various objects of interest to the scholars of Europe.

The style of the Daśa Kumára Charita is of that elaborate description which has induced native scholars to ascribe to the work the denomination of a Kávya, or Poem. It is not uniformly, however, of a poetical elevation; and although passages occur in which, from the use of compound words of more than ordinary length, from a complicated grammatical structure, and from a protracted suspension of the governing term, it may be somewhat difficult to discover the precise meaning; yet, in general, the language is intelligible as well as elegant, and can occasion no great embarrassment to a practised scholar, while it affords him a useful example of classical prose composition.

While the language of the Daśa Kumára Charita is recommended by its general character, it furnishes also, in some of its peculiarities, an advantageous opportunity for the study of a portion of Sanskrit Grammar, of which examples are not often multiplied, particularly in metrical works. Although not written, like the Bhaṫṫí Kávya, purposely to illustrate grammatical forms, yet the writer particularly affects the use of derivative verbs, and presents a greater number of causal and desiderative inflexions than can be found in any other composition. Whether he, at the same time, purposely omitted the different tenses and persons of the intensitive or frequentative verb, tradition has not recorded; but is it very remarkable that, amidst the copiousness of the forms specified, the inflexions of the frequentative verb do not appear. Such fancies as the exclusion of certain words or grammatical forms are not unknown in Sanskrit literature, especially at the period at which this work was probably written; a period at which, although not yet wholly corrupted, an elaborate and artificial style of writing had begun to supplant the simple and more elegant models that had been furnished by the writers of the school of Kálidása.

Tradition affirms the contemporary existence of Dańḋí, the author of the Daśa Kumára Charita, and Bhoja Deva, Rájá of Dhárá, the celebrated patron of men of letters at the end of the tenth century*. The internal evidence of the work is not at variance with the traditional date, for it describes both the political and social condition of India at a period anterior to the Mohammedan conquest, and no mention is made of the Mohammedans, except as merchants or as navigators, or rather, perhaps, pirates, in which capacities the Arabs are likely to have been known to the Hindus before the establishment of the slaves of Mohammed Sám at Delhi, and the desolation of Ujjayiní, in the immediate vicinity of Dhárá, by the second of the

* [Lassen, Ind. Alt., III, 844. 50 ff. IV, 811. A. Weber (Monatsberichte d. Königl. Akademie der Wissenschaften. 1859, p. 21 Note) hints at the possibility of Dańḋí having lived under an earlier Bhoja in the 8th century. See also F.-E. Hall's strictures on the above assertions in the Preface to his edition of the Vásavadattá. Calcutta: 1859, p. 19 ff. and p. 9 ff., by which Prof. Weber's supposition is raised to certainty.]

dynasty, Altmash. In truth, the perfect preservation of the political divisions of Central India, and the consistent delineation of manners unmixedly Hindu, might warrant the attribution of a still earlier date, but that this is opposed by tradition. The style would not be incompatible with an earlier æra, as it is not more elaborate than that of Bhavabhúti, who wrote in the eighth century, although it bears, perhaps, a closer affinity to that of parts of the Mahánáťaka, a drama ascribed to Bhoja himself*.

In contradiction, however, to the date usually assigned to the work, or to any earlier æra, we have one internal proof that it is later even than the reign of Bhoja, for the last of the stories relates to a prince who is said to be a member of his race—the Bhoja vanśa—implying, necessarily, the prior existence of that prince. This would be fatal to the evidence of the tradition, as well as of the general tenor of the composition, if there were not a possibility that the story in which the Bhoja vanśa is alluded to is not a part of the original work. It is universally admitted that the Daśa Kumára Charita was left unfinished by the author, and no specification is to be found of the point at which it terminated. The story in question ends abruptly, and would so far confirm the general admission, being in that case Dańdí's own composition: but the style undergoes a change, and the language is less elevated, and the incidents are more

* [Lassen, Ind. Alt., IV, p. 817. 820 f.]

diffusely narrated. These considerations suggest some doubt of the genuineness of this portion of the work, although they are not sufficient to justify a conclusive opinion. If the work be, as it stands, the composition of Dańd'í, he must have flourished some time after Bhoja—not long, however—and in the time of some of his immediate descendants, as the mention of the Bhoja vanśa is clearly intended to be complimentary. This would not be incongruous with the priority of the author to the Mohammedan conquest; and we shall perhaps be not far wide of the truth in placing his composition late in the eleventh or early in the twelfth century.

A work on Alankára, or Rhetoric, the Kávyádarśa, is also attributed to Dańd'í. It is not often met with, but there is a copy in the Bodleian Library. It is not of great extent, but the rules are illustrated by examples, taken, it is affirmed, from different authors: unluckily the authors are not named, and it would be a work of time and labour to identify the passages cited: apparently there are some from the Mahábhárata and Rámáyańa, and from the writings of Kálidása, but there is nothing sufficiently ascertained to warrant any inference of the date of the composition.

The date of the Daśa Kumára Charita is not the only circumstance connected with it of a questionable character. The very name of the author suggests an uncertainty. Dańd'í properly designates a "staff bearer", but is commonly applied to a sect of religious mendicants, who profess to be the spiritual descendants of Śankara Áchárya, a reformer of the eighth century, and who are so termed because they carry a slender dańd́a, or wand. Many of the order have been literary characters; and it is not impossible that one of them may have amused his leisure with inventing the stories in question, however inconsistent with his religious meditations. The work would thus be that of a dańd́í, not of Dańd́í; but it is not generally so considered, Dańd́í being ordinarily regarded, in this instance at least, as a proper name, and associated with the usual honorary prefix, or Śrí Dańd́í*.

The Daśa Kumára Charita, as universally recognised, not only ends abruptly, but begins in an equally abrupt manner, introducing the reader at once to persons and events with whom he has no previous acquaintance. This defect is supplied by an Introductory Section, the Púrva Píṫhiká, or Preliminary Chapter. This Introduction is commonly ascribed to Dańd́í himself; but as it is somewhat less ambitiously written, and as the incidents related are, in one or two cases, briefly repeated in the body of the work, and with some contradictions, doubts have been started as to the accuracy of the attribution. If not the composition of the same hand, it must be one of nearly the same time and the same school, and may be regarded as the work of one of the author's disciples. Its general congruity, however, with the acknowledged composition of Dańd́í renders it not inprobably his work**.

* [See F.-E. Hall, l. l., p. 19.] ** [A. Weber, l. l., p. 19. 22.]

The same is not pretended of the Śesha, or Supplement to the Charita, a continuation and conclusion of the stories. This is the avowed composition of Chakrapáńi Díkshita, a Mahratta Brahman, and is written in a style which aspires to surpass that of the original. While, however, more laboriously constructed, and, in consequence, more difficult of interpretation, it falls very far short of its model in purity and vigour; and, as the narrative is puerile and meagre, it offers nothing to repay the trouble of its perusal. It is of considerable length, and on that account, as well as of its want of interest, it has not been thought desirable to perpetuate it by the press.

The introductory portion of the Daśa Kumára Charita has been twice remodelled and arranged, in an abbreviated form and in verse. One of these versions was made by a celebrated Dakhińí writer, Appa or Apyaya Díkshita, the author of a standard work on rhetoric, the Kuvalayánanda. He was patronised by Kŕishńa Ráya, Rájá of Vijayanágara, in the beginning of the sixteenth century*. This abridgment was printed at Serampore in 1804, along with the Hitopadeśa and the Śatakas of Bhartŕi Hari. A similar metrical abridgment of the introduction bears the name of Vináyaka, but nothing more is known of the author. Both these abridgment are sce exedingly inferior to the original in style and in interest. Neither contains more than two hundred ślokas, and they are both too

* [Lassen, IV, p. 822.]

much compressed to allow of any detailed description of the incidents narrated in the original: the narration is consequently scanty and dull, and not seldom obscure.

A writer who calls himself Mahárájádhirája Gopínátha has undertaken the bolder task of correcting or ameliorating (Sanśodhanam) the text. Like the two preceding, his introduction is in metre, and in three sections, but they contain six hundred and seventy-nine ślokas, and are therefore much more diffuse. In the body of the work the author reverts to prose, where his so-called improvement—really a disfigurement—consists in the occasional amplification or explanation of the incidents of the original, the text of which, with such occasional interpolations or substitutions, is given without any alteration. The story is also carried on to completion.

There is also a Commentary on the text of the Daśa Kumára by Śiva Ráma Tiwári*, a Brahman of Benares. It is not without utility, as explaining a few unusual terms, but it is less comprehensive than could be desired.

The subjects of the stories of the Daśa Kumára are those taken from domestic life, and are interesting as pictures of Hindu society for centuries probably anterior to the Mohammedan conquest. The portrait is not flattering: profligacy and superstition seem to be the characteristic features;—not, in general, the pro-

* [more correctly, Tripáthí; see Prof. F.-E. Hall, l. l., p. 44.]

fligacy that invades private happiness, nor the superstition that bows down before imaginary divinities, but loose principles and lax morals, and implicit faith in the power of occult rites and magical incantations. The picture does not want some redeeming traits, and the heroes are described as endowed with enterprise and hardihood, with inviolable devotedness to their friends and kindred, and with tender and constant attachment to the objects of their affection. The opportunities which are afforded to the youth of both sexes of forming connexions are of remarkable facility; and the absence of any intimation that the bonds which are so easily contracted are to be considered of brief duration, gives a character of respectability to the very informal unions which take place. The parties however, it must be remembered, are of those classes —the regal and military—among whom marriage by mutual consent, the Gándharba viváha, is a recognised legal compact.

The work presents a great number of names of cities and principalities, of which few vestiges remain. They are to be found, however, in the Puráńas, in the travels of the Chinese in the fourth and sixth centuries, and in the records of the Rájput states; and no doubt define the political divisions of the country which subsisted from a remote period until the subversion of the whole by the tide of Mohammedan invasion. In this respect the work may be considered of historical value, as adding contemporary testimony to the correctness of the political position of a considerable part of India, as derived from other sources of information. A brief sketch of the substance of the stories will best illustrate the light which they are calculated to reflect upon the social and political condition of India during probably the first ten centuries of our æra.

The introduction to the Daśa Kumára brings us acquainted with Rájahansa, king of Magadha, or South Behar, the capital of which is Pushpapura, another name for Pátaliputra, the ancient Palibothra and modern Patna, the identity of which, generally admitted, has been recently confirmed by the discovery of the course of the old bed of the Śońe river, which united with the Ganges in the immediate vicinity of the city, conformably to the statement of Arrian, that Palibothra was situated near the confluence of the Erranoboas (the Hirańyabáhu, a synonym of the Śońe) and the Ganges. For this conclusive evidence we are indebted to Mr. Ravenshaw, of the Bengal Civil Service (Memorandum on the ancient bed of the Śońe, J. As. Soc. B. No. 158). The term Pushpa-putra, the Flower-city, is synonymous with Kusumapura, and is essentially the same with what should probably be the correct reading, Pátali-pura, the Trumpet-flower city. A legend as old as the eleventh century, being narrated in the Kathá-sarit Ságara, published and translated by Mr. Brockhaus, has been invented, to account for the name Pátali-putra; but this has evidently been suggested by the corruption of the name, and does not account for it. That Patna was called Kusumapura, the Flower-city, at a late period, we know from the

Chinese-Buddhist travellers, through whom the name Ku-su-mo-pu-lo became familiar to their countrymen*.

Rájahansa, having engaged in warfare with Mánasára, the Rájá of Málava (Malwa), was, in the first instance, victorious, but was finally defeated, and obliged to take shelter in the Vindhya forests, where his wife gave birth to a son, Rájaváhana. The Rájá had three hereditary ministers (Kulámátyas)—a peculiarity in the tenure of office under Government, of which the modern history of Hindu princes affords examples —named Dharmapála, Padmodbhava, and Sitavarmá. Of these, the first had three sons, Sumantra, Sumitra, and Kámapála; Padmodbhava, the second, had two, Suśruta and Ratnodbhava; and the third, Sitavarmá, two, Sumati and Satyavarmá. Of these, Kámapála, whose habits were dissolute, Ratnodbhava, who was curious of foreign travel, and Satyavarmá, who was of an ascetic temperament, withdrew from court, and wandered about the world; the other four remained with the king, and, upon the death of their fathers, succeeded to their stations. They partook of their master's fortune, and attended him in his retreat; and when the prince Rájaváhana was born, they also had each a son: Sumantra had Mitragupta; Sumitra, Mantragupta; Suśruta had Viśruta; and Sumati, Pramati. During Rájahansa's forest abode, also, there were brought to him or to his queen, on different occasions, five other youths, making, with the sons of the

* [Prof. F.-E. Hall, l. l., p. 35 f. and in the Journal As. Soc. Bengal 1862, p. 6.]

four ministers and Rájaváhana, the Ten Kumáras. Three of these were Arthapála, Pushpodbhava, and Somadatta, the sons, respectively, of the absent ministers, Kámapála, Ratnodbhava, and Satyavarmá, and the other two were Apahároavarmá and Upahároavarmá; who were the sons of Prahároavarmá, the king of Mithilá or North Behar, and friend of Rájahansa. Coming to the succour of his friend, he had been involved in his misfortune, and, attempting to regain his country with the reliques of his force, he had been attacked by the foresters, the Savaras, and lost his baggage and attendants. His two children also fell into the hands of the barbarous tribes, and one of them was about to be offered as a victim to Chańd́í, when he was saved by the timely interposition of a Brahman. The sacrifice of human victims by the tribes inhabiting the hills and forests of South Behar is often alluded to in the fictions of this date; and the practice, we know, still prevails among some of them, although it seems to have been driven farther to the South, being most prevalent among the Khońd́s of Gumsir. It is not long since, however, that proofs of its existence on the frontiers of the Jángal Mahals were brought to the knowledge of the British functionaries.

The nine boys thus assembled were educated along with the prince, and became his constant associates. The particulars of their education present a curious detail of what were considered, no doubt, essentially princely acquirements. The use of various tongues, skill in arms, and the menagement of horses and elephants, acquaintance with tradition, with the rules of polity, with rhetoric and logic, and with music, are qualifications sufficiently appropriate; but we should scarcely have expected to find the list extended to metaphysics, law, and the Vedas, and still less to astrology, medicine, magic, to proficiency in games of skill or chance, and dexterity in thieving; yet such is the author's beau ideal of princely training, and his narratives exhibit the practical application of those accomplishments. It is worthy of observation, as part of the internal evidence of the date of the work, that, besides the specification of the Vedas, Itihása, and Puráńas, the writings of Kaut́ilya, more commonly called Cháńakya, and the Kámandaki, are specified as the authorities for the science of Níti, or polity.

As soon as Rájaváhana and his associates had attained a sufficient age, Rájahansa, in obedience to the injunctions of a pious Brahman, allowed them to set off to see the world. They departed together; but, in the course of a few days, Rájaváhana was induced by a stranger Brahman to leave his companions privately, and assist him in obtaining the sovereignty of the subterranean regions, or Pátála. The enterprise succeeds; but when the prince returns to the spot where he had left his friends, they are all gone. Alarmed by his disappearance, the youths had taken different directions in quest of the missing prince, and hence they severally met with separate adventures, the relation of which, when they at last find Rájaváhana, constitutes the matter of the Daśa Kumára Charita.

The first whom prince Rájaváhana, roaming in search of his friends, encounters, is Somadatta. This youth has been instrumental in releasing the daughter of the Rájá of Ujjayiní from the hands of the Rájá of Láťa, to whom she had been reluctantly conceded as a bride by her father; and has defeated the forces of Láťa, and killed the king in single combat; in requital of which exploits the Rájá of Ujjayiní gives his daughter to Somadatta, and adopts him as Yuvarája, his colleague and successor. He is on his way with his bride to the temple of Mahákála, when he falls in with his prince. Mahákála was one of the twelve Śiva Lingas, which were in high repute about the time of the Mohammedan invasion. The country of Láťa was better known, apparently, to ancient than to modern geography, being the Lár or Larike of Ptolemy, and applied to the country south of the Nerbudda, and along the Taptí, corresponding with Nimaur and Khándesh*.

While yet in company with Somadatta, Rájaváhana is joined by another of his companions, Pushpodbhava. This adventurer, in the course of his peregrinations, was surprised by the fall of a man from a precipice upon his head, who proved to be his father, the merchant Ratnodbhava, the son of the minister, the elder Pushpodbhava, who had been wrecked on his voyage from the island of Kálayavana sixteen years before; and having, on that occasion, lost his wife, had been miserable ever since; until at last, unable to support

* [Lassen, Ind. Alt., III, 170 ff.]

his affliction longer, he casts himself from a rock, and is picked up by his son. Presently afterwards Pushpodbhava prevents a woman from burning herself, who proves to be his mother, and having brought his parents together he conveys them to Ujjayiní. Here he falls in love with a merchant's daughter, whom he meets at the house of a friend, and she returns his affection. She is wooed, however, by the Prince of Ujjayiní, Dáruvarmá, and is apprehensive of his violence. By Pushpodbhava's advice, she gives out that her chamber is haunted by a Yaksha, an evil spirit, and that she will wed the person who shall free her from his presense. Dáruvarmá defies the goblin, and is visited by the damsel, when Pushpodbhava, disguised as a female attendant, beats him to death. The catastrophe is ascribed to the wrath of the spirit, and no further inquiry is made: the ceremony of exorcism is performed, and Pushpodbhava marries the damsel. This story turns upon a superstition common in the East, and familiar to us in the adventures of Tobias, although in this case it is employed very coolly as the pretext of murder. Dáruvarmá is represented, however, as odious for his profligacy and tyranny, and the infliction of deserved punishment is considered as justificatory of the crime.

Rájaváhana resides for some time with his friends at Ujjayiní, when he beholds, at the festival of Kámadeva, Avantisundarí, the daughter of Mánasára, the conqueror of his paternal kingdom, but who had resigned his sovereignty to his son Darpasára. He again had gone to Rájagiri to perform austere penance, and had appointed his cousins Dáruvarmá and Chandravarmá in his place during his absence. The former of these, as has been just mentioned, has been killed, and Chandravarmá reigns alone. The princess and Rájaváhana are mutually smitten, and, through the contrivance of a friendly magician, are legally married in the actual presence of Chandravarmá, the viceroy being made to believe that the scene is a mere delusion. With this incident terminates the Purva Píṭhiká, or Introductory Section.

The first section of the body of the work represents Rájaváhana as domesticated in the interior apartments of the palace as the husband of Avantisundarí. During their repose the prince and his bride are disturbed by a dream, and, on awaking, find the feet of the Prince firmly bound by silver fetters. The princess is imprudently vociferous in the expression of her terror, and the attendants echo her clamour so loudly as to alarm the guard, who enter and discover Rájaváhana. Chandravarmá commands Rájaváhana to be put to death, but the execution is prohibited by the interposition of Mánasára, who, although abdicated, exercises some influence over his son's deputy, and has no objection to Rájaváhana as a son-in-law. Chandravarmá confines Rájaváhana in a wooden cage, and refers his sentence to Darpasára, who is engaged in austerities at Rájagiri, and in the meantime marches against Sinhavarmá, the king of Anga, and besieges his capital, Champá, a name still preserved by a village in the neighbourhood of Bhagalpur. Rájaváhana in his cage accompanies the march. Sinhavarmá, sallying from Champá, is taken prisoner, and the city falls into the hands of the victor; so does the Princess Ambáliká, of whom Chandravarmá is enamoured, and whom he determines to wed.

After the action, a messenger arrives from Darpasára, commanding that Rájaváhana shall be put to death without delay. Chandravarmá accordingly orders that while he goes to solemnize his nuptials Rájaváhana shall be brought forth to be thrown under the feet of a fierce elephant. While expecting the execution of the sentence, the chain falls from the feet of Rájaváhana, and becomes a nymph of air—an Apsaras—condemned to that form by the anger of a Muni whom she had offended, and picked up by Mánasára, a genius of the air, one of the Vidyádharas, to whom Avantisundarí had been promised by her brother. Finding, in one of his nocturnal peregrinations, that the lady had chosen another lord, Mánasára imposed the fetters on Rájaváhana, and caused his detection. The time of the nymph's transformation has now expired, and she takes her departure, leaving Rájaváhana at liberty, having been previously removed from his cage.

A clamour now arises that Chandravarmá has been killed. Rájaváhana, in the confusion, mounts the elephant appointed to crush him, strikes down the driver, turns the animal towards the palace, and invites aloud the brave man who has slain the tyrant to come to him for protection. The murderer accepts the summons, rushes through the crowd, springs upon the elephant, and proves to be one of the Prince's friends Apahâravarmá. They defend themselves valiantly against the followers of Chandravarmá, until intelligence is brought of the arrival of Sinhavarmá's allies, with a host before which the troops of Ujjayiní have fled. Their safety, and that of the king of Champá, is now ensured. Among the allies of the latter, Rájaváhana finds all the rest of his old companions, and by his desire they severally relate to him their adventures.

Apahâravarmá's story forms the subject of the second book, and is perhaps the best in the collection, being more rich than the others in varied incidents. Searching for the prince, he repairs to a celebrated hermit, Maríchi, to consult him where Rájaváhana is to be found. Maríchi desires him to remain at Champá, and he will hear of his friend, and entertains him with his own adventures, having been beguiled into the love of a courtesan named Kámamanjarí, who had wagered her liberty with another of her class that she would lead the holy man into folly. She succeeds, persuades him to accompany her to the city, wins her wager, laughs at her lover, and sends him back to his hermitage overwhelmed with shame and self-reproach. The story presents a curious picture of the pains taken with the education of public women. Not only were their health, their physical development, and personal beauty attended to; not only were the graces of deportment and elegance of attire and ornament sedulously studied, but their intellectual training was an equal object of vigilance; and they were taught a variety of subjects calculated to heighten their fascination and strengthen their understanding. Dancing, music, and acting formed their profession, and they were also taught to paint, to dress delicate dishes, to compound fragrant perfumes, and to dispose tastily of flowers; to play various games; to read, to write, and to speak different languages; and they were instructed superficially, it is said, in grammar, logic, metaphysics. A remarkable picture is also drawn of the devices resorted to, to bring them into public consideration, many of which may find a parallel in the contrivances by which public performers in European countries are sometimes forced into popularity. Apaháravarmá, piqued by her cleverness, determines to humble the conceit of Kámamanjarí, and sets off to Champá.

On arriving near Champá, Apaháravarmá finds a man by the road-side apparently in great distress. He proves to be another victim of Kámamanjarí's arts, formerly an opulent merchant, but ruined by his attachment to her, and he is now an inmate of a Budhist convent. He is called, from his ugliness, Virúpaka. He repents his abandonment of the faith of his ancestors, and is desirous of returning to it. Apaháravarmá recommends him to remain as he is for a short time, until he shall be replaced in possession of his property, which he undertakes to recover. The incident is worthy of notice, as indicating the cotemporary existence of the Buddhists at the date of the work, and an additional confirmation, therefore, of its not being later than the tenth or eleventh century; as after that period notices of Buddhists by Hindu writers are rare and inaccurate.

Having proceeded into the city, Apahàravarmá enters into a gambling-house, such places being licensed under Hindu rule. Here he wins a considerable sum of money, and establishes his credit both for skill in play and for liberality, distributing half his winnings among the assistants. He then sallies forth well armed to perpetrate house-breaking, another of the accomplishments of princely education, but falls in with a young and beautiful woman, Kulapáliká, the daughter of Kuveradatta, who has run away from home to avoid a marriage with Arthapati, a rich merchant, to whom her father has promised her, having previously betrothed her to Dhanamitra, also a merchant, but who has become impoverished by his munificence. He is still the object of Kulapáliká's affection, and she is on her way to her lover when encountered by Apahàravarmá. He sympathizes with her distress, and conducts her to Dhanamitra, with whom he becomes united in most intimate friendship, and to whose union with Kulapáliká he engages to obtain her father's consent. In furtherance of this scheme they take Kulapáliká home, and with her aid plunder her father's house of every thing of value. They leave the damsel at home, and return to the house of Dhanamitra, plundering the residence of Arthapati on their way, and concealing their booty in a thicket.

The loss of property has the effect of suspending Kulapáliká's marriage, and in the meantime Dhanamitra, by desire of his friend, takes an old leather purse to the Rájá of Anga, and tells him that, having repaired to a forest to put an end to his life, in consequence of her father's refusing to grant Kulapáliká to him, he was met by a holy man, who withheld him from self destruction, and presented him with a purse, which, he said, in the hands of a merchant or a courtesan who should not have wrongfully appropriated the property of others, would prove a source of inexhaustible wealth—the purse, in fact, of Fortunatus. This he offers to the King, who not only declines to accept it, but promises to protect him in its safe possession. The story spreads, and its truth is confirmed by the return of Dhanamitra to his former profuse liberality, the funds of which are derived from the stolen property. Among others, Kuveradatta, hearing of Dhanamitra's recovered affluence, grows cold to Arthapati, and gives his daughter to her former affianced husband.

Shortly afterwards, Rágamanjarí, the younger sister of Kámamanjarí, makes her appearance as a public performer, with great success and with unsullied reputation. She and Apahâravarmá become mutually enamoured, but their union is prevented by her mother and sister, who look upon Apahâravarmá as a pauper. The objection is overcome by his undertaking to steal the "inexhaustible purse", and give it to Kámamanjarí, provided she fulfil the condition of restoring their property to those whom she had reduced to poverty. Accordingly the Buddhist Virúpaka recovers his wealth.

Dhanamitra, acting in concert with Apaháravarmá, complains to the Rájá of the loss of his purse, and after a time Kámamanjarí is called before the Rájá and accused of the theft. At the suggestion of Apaháravarmá the crime is imputed to Arthapati, who is consequently banished, and whose property is confiscated.

Apaháravarmá, in a fit of extravagant bravado, attacks the patrol, and is taken prisoner. The charge of the gaol has lately devolved on Kántaka, a vain young man, who threatens the prisoner with eighteen kinds of torture and final death, unless he restores all the wealth he has stolen, and particularly the inexhaustible purse, which he is said to have carried off. The Rájá, at Dhanamitra's request, promises him liberty if he will restore it. In the meantime Rágamanjarí and the Rájá's daughter Ambáliká have become intimate friends, and the latter is prepared to share the affections of Apaháravarmá. The latter has a rival in Kántaka, who flatters himself that the Princess loves him. He is encouraged in this belief by Śrigáliká, the nurse of Rágamanjarí, and emissary of Apaháravarmá, who also persuades him that the lines in his hand announce his elevation to the kingdom, and that if he could make his way into the interior of the palace, which adjoins the gaol, Ambáliká would wed him. Kántaka applies to Apaháravarmá, as a skilful housebreaker, to help him, promising to set him free, but secretly purposing, as he informs Śŕigáliká, to confine him again and put him to death. Apaháravarmá consents, and makes an excavation under the prison walls, by which he and Kántaka might pass into the palace; but he takes an opportunity of killing Kántaka, in anticipation of the deadly project entertained by the latter, and proceeds alone into the apartments of the Princess. He finds her asleep, delineates his portrait on the wall, with a verse imparting a hope that she may not suffer the pangs of love by which he is afflicted, and returns to the prison. He then liberates the former governor, who was also in detention there, and, with his consent, makes his escape.

Ambáliká, on waking, beholds the drawing, and reads the verse, and is enamoured of the author. Her union with him is accomplished, when Chańd́avarmá besieges Champá, and, after the capture of the Rájá, seizes the person of the Princess, and compels her submission to a public celebration of their nuptials. Apaháravarmá, having directed his friend Dhanamitra privately to assemble a party of citizens round the palace, passes into it in the garb of one of the attendants, and, as Chańd́avarmá attempts to take the shrinking hand of Ambáliká, approaches and stabs him. In the confusion he snatches up Ambáliká, and carries her to his friends, under whose protection he gains the innermost chambers, and prepares to defend himself, when he hears of the arrival of Rájaváhana, whom he joins in the manner above described. This closes the second section, constituting a large proportion of the whole.

In the third chapter the other son of the king of Mithilá, Upahúravarmá, narrates his adventures. He had repaired to his own country, Mithilá, in search of the Prince, and thus met with a female ascetic, who proved to have been his nurse who lost him in the woods in the manner related in the Introduction. His father, Prahúravarmá, on returning, found his kingdom occupied by the sons of his elder brother, with Vikaťavarmá at their head, and has been defeated by them and thrown into prison, together with his queen. Upahúravarmá determines to effect their rescue, and, through the agency of his nurse's daughter, contrives to win the affections of Vikaťavarmá's queen, offended by the dissolute manners of her husband. At the suggestion of Upahúravarmá she persuades the Rájá, who is remarkable for his ugliness and deformity, that a mystical rite has been communicated to her, by which he may be transformed into perfect symmetry and beauty. He falls into the snare, and is murdered by Upahúravarmá, who then openly assumes his throne as the metamorphosed Rájá. The intended change had been made the subject of previous report, and its possibility, through the power of magic, was not doubted —a probable illustration of the credulous superstition of the author's times. The belief of the ministers is confirmed, also, by Upahúravarmá's acquaintance with certain secret projects of his predecessors, which he had revealed to the Ráńí as a preliminary condition of his transformation. They are all of an iniquitous tenor, and are reversed by Upahávavarmá, with the applause of his counsellors. Among these was the intention of defrauding a Yavana merchant of the fair price of a very valuable diamond which he has for sale—a notice which is interesting as a proof of the intercourse of foreign traders, Arabs or Persians, with India before the Mohammedan conquest. Another was, the purpose of taking off the Rájá Prahāravarmá by poison—a crime which justifies Upahāravarmá's proceedings. He sets his parents at liberty, and places his father on the throne, receiving from him the office of Yuvarája, in which capacity he commands the army sent by the Rájá of Mithilá to the aid of the Rájá of Anga, and, consequently, meets with Rájaváhana.

The fourth chapter contains the story of Arthapála's adventures, comprising those also of his father, Kámapála, the son of one of Rájahansa's ministers, who had early disappeared from court, and who is now King of Káśí, or Benares, which city Arthapála visits. We find the celebrated ghát Mańikarńiká named; but instead of Viśveśwara, the form of Śiva now worshipped there, we have an older appellation, one found in several of the Puráńas, or Avimukteśwara*. Arthapála encounters a man in deep affliction, and, inquiring the cause, learns that he is in despair on ac-

* [e. g. Śiva Pur. II, c. 43. Matsya Pur., c. 167. A. Weber, Ind. Stud., II, 73 ff.]

count of the danger of Kámapála, late minister of the King of Kásí, who had been his benefactor. Having been struck by the strength and resolution of this man, named Púrńabhadra, in baffling and putting to flight an elephant by whom he was to be put to death for thieving, Kámapála pardoned him, took him into his confidence, and told him his adventures. Having quitted Pushpapura he came to Benares, where he beheld the Princess Kántimatí, the daughter of Chańdasinha. A love match takes place between them, the result of which is the birth of Arthapála, who is secretly removed and exposed in a cemetery, where he is found by Táráválí, a Yakshińí, who carries him to the Queen of Rájahansa, as mentioned in the Introduction. The intrigue is discovered by the Rájá, and Kámapála is seized, and is to be put to death. He makes his escape, and hides in the forests, where Táráválí, who had been his wife in two preceding births, when he bore the names of Śaunaka and Śúdraka, comes to his succour, and again becomes his bride. With her aid he gains unperceived admission into the sleeping apartments of Chańdasinha, wakes him from his sleep, and intimidates him into acknowledging him as his son-in-law, and as Yuvarája. On his death his son Chańdaghosha becomes Rájá, with Kámapála's assent, and on his dying early the latter inaugurates Sinhaghosha, the son of Chańdaghosha, as king. A faction is formed against the minister, and the prince is persuaded that he has caused the death of his predecessors, and will attempt his life if not anticipated. Kámapála is therefore seized, and ordered for execution. Púrńabhadra, in despair, is about to put an end to himself.

While Arthapála considers how he may rescue his father, a poisonous snake shews itself, which he, safe in his knowledge of mantras or charms, secures. With this he departs to where his father is led to his fate, and in the crowd throws the snake upon him, which bites him, and he falls apparently lifeless, the fatal operation of the venom being counteracted by Arthapála's magical powers. He is supposed to be dead, and is carried to his dwelling. His wife Kántimatí, privily apprised, through Púrńabhadra, of her son's device, obtains permission to burn herself with the body, and a pile is constructed in the court-yard of Kámapála's house within an enclosure, into which Kántimatí enters alone—peculiarities in the performance of the Satí unknown to the practice of later years. Kámapála, resuscitated and reunited to his wife and son, collects his friends, and puts his dwelling into an attitude of defence. The Rájá, hearing of his recovery, besieges him. Arthapála constructs a tunnel leading to the royal palace, with the intention of carrying off Chańd'aghosha: when half way through he comes upon a spacious subterranean chamber, where Mańikarńiká, the daughter of Chańd'aghosha, had been secreted by her grandfather, who destined her to be the bride of Darpasára, the son of Mánasára, king of Málava, and had shut her up that she might not make a different election for herself. Chańd'asinha had died, however, without accomplishing his object, and Mańikarńiká, with her nurse and attendants, had continued in their hiding-place, well supplied with all necessaries, but in other respects unnoticed, until she had attained a marriageable age. Arthapála, although he admires the princess, pursues his purpose, and, by the communication with the subterranean chambers, enters into the Rájá's sleeping apartment, and carries him a prisoner back to the dwelling of Kámapála, who then administers the kingdom. The Princess is married to Arthapála, who becomes Yuvarája, and leads an army to the assistance of the King of Anga.

The fifth section relates the adventures of Pramati, who is here represented as the son of Kámapála by the Yakshińí Táravalí, and not, as in the Introduction, the son of Sumati. Arthapála is there also called the son of Táravalí, while, as we have seen in the preceding narrative, he is described as the son of Kántimatí. Either the author has been nodding, or the Introduction is the work of a different writer, who has been heedless or forgetful of the narrative of his predecessor. While on his journey Pramati is benighted in a forest on the Vindhya mountains, and, recommending himself to the protection of the local divinities, goes to sleep beneath a tree. While asleep he fancies himself transported to the interior of a palace, where a princess is sleeping among her attendant damsels; that he reclines beside her; that she awakes, and they exchange looks, but fall asleep again: when he wakes he finds himself still in the forest. There presently appears to him a nymph, who declares herself to be Tárávalí, the bride of Kámapála, who had left his house in anger, and had consequently become an evil spirit for a twelvemonth. The term of her penance had expired on the preceding evening, and she was on her way to the neighbouring city of Śrávastí, when she was arrested by Pramati's invocation, and conveyed him to the chamber of Navamáliká, daughter of Dharmavarddhana, Rájá of Śrávastí. In the morning, before dawn, she brings him back to the forest, and then recognises him as her own son by Kámapála. She leaves him to seek his fortune, and he repairs to Śrávastí to endeavour to obtain the hand of the princess. On the way he stops at a cock-fight, and there contracts a friendship with an old Brahman. He then proceeds to Śrávastí, where, in a garden in the suburbs, he is noticed by one of the attendants of the princess, who has a portrait in her hand, which proves to be his own. It is the work of Navamáliká, who has delineated it in the hope of discovering the original, whom she has seen, as she supposes, in a dream. A plan is devised to effect their union. The old Brahman takes Pramati, in the dress of a female, to the Rájá, and introduces him as his daughter, who has been betrothed some time, but whose bridegroom is absent. The pretended father therefore professes to go in search of him, and asks to leave his daughter in the care of the Rájá, to which the latter consents. Pramati thus obtains access to his mistress. After a short time he contrives to make his escape and assume his own semblance, and returns with the Brahman as his son-in-law to claim his bride. The bride, however, is not forthcoming, and the Rájá, to divert the dreaded imprecation of the Brahman, consents to give his own daughter as a substitute for the missing damsel. Pramati thus becomes the son-in-law of the Rájá, and leads his troops to Anga, where he finds his prince.

Mitragupta next narrates his proceedings, in the sixth section, at Dámaliptá, in the Suhma country, the king of which is Tungadhanwá. By propitiating Vindhyavásiní he obtains two children, a son and a daughter, on condition that the former shall be subordinate to the husband of the latter, and that the daughter shall annually exhibit her skill in playing at ball, in honour of the goddess, until she meets with her destined husband, of whom she is to be allowed the free choice. She is called Kandukávatí, her brother Bhímadhanwá. Mitragupta beholds the pastime of the princess, which is described with singular minuteness of detail, and they become mutually enamoured, carrying on a communication through Chandrasená, the foster-sister of the princess, who is the object of the young prince's affection, but who is attached to a different person, one Koshadása. Mitragupta forms an intimate friendship with him, and devises schemes for their joint success, when he is seized by order of Bhímadhanwá, and thrown, fettered, into the sea. With the aid of a strong plank he floats until he is picked up by a Yavana vessel, apparently intimating an Arab ship. He has not changed his lot to advantage, and is about to be maltreated, when the vessel is attacked by another ship from the shore. Mitragupta encourages the crew to resist, and, being let loose, animates them to board and capture their assailant, the captain of which proves to be Bhímadhanwá. He is taken on board the Yavana vessel and confined, when a contrary wind rises, and carries the ship out of her course to a distant island, abounding with fruit and fresh water. They anchor, and Mitragupta goes on shore. He meets with a Rákshas, who threatens to kill him unless he answers correctly to the questions, What is that which is naturally cruel? What is the great wish of a householder? What is love? What overcomes difficulties? To which he replies severally, The heart of a woman; A virtuous wife; Determination to possess; Intelligence; and illustrates his replies by four narratives, of each of which a woman is the heroine. These narratives present some curious pictures of manners, and several incidents which are to be found in other compilations, particularly the third story, in which the wife of a merchant is made to appear, in the estimation of her husband and the Pancháyat, or Council of the city, a Dákińí, or woman who obtains supernatural powers by an impure intercourse with the spirits of ill, who haunt the ground where the dead are buried. The point of the story is found in the first narrative of the Baitál Pachsíí.

The Rákshas is pleased by the stories he hears, and promises Mitragupta his friendship. He is presently called upon to prove it. A brother Rákshas is seen in the sky, carrying off a female, evidently against her will. Mitragupta's friend ascends to the rescue, and the ravisher drops the damsel, who proves to be Kandukávatí. Mitraguptá sets sail with her, and arrives at Dámaliptá in time to save the lives of the King and Queen and all the chief citizens, who had vowed to starve themselves to death on the banks of the Ganges. He restores the Princess and her brother to their parents, and is gladly accepted by them as their son-in-law. Tungadhanwá is one of the allies of Anga, and Mitragupta has come to Champá in command of his troops.

The adventures of Mantragupta form the subject of the seventh chapter. He arrives at Kalinga, and goes to sleep on the edge of a lake bordered by a thicket contiguous to the burning-ground of the dead. He is wakened by a conversation between two goblins relating to a Siddha, an ascetic, who has acquired magical powers; and, curious to know what it means, follows them privily to where their master is seated, decorated with ornaments of human bones, smeared with ashes, wearing braided hair, and feeding a fire by dropping into it, with his left hand, seeds of mustard and sesamum. At his command the Princess of Kalinga, Karńalekhá, is brought by one of his ministering demons before him. The ascetic seizes her by the hair, and is about to cut off her head, when Mantragupta rushes upon him, and decapitates him with his own sword. He hides the head and hair in the hollow of a tree. The spirits present, wearied of the tyranny and cruelty of the magician, praise the youth for his courage, and declare themselves his servants. He desires them to convey the Princess to her apartments, but she implores him to accompany her, and they are both carried into the palace, where Mantragupta remains undiscovered.

The King of Kalinga, Kardana, moves in the hot season with his family and suite to the sea-shore, to spend a few days encamped upon the sand. While amusing himself with songs and music and merry-making he is suddenly attacked by the flotilla of the King of Andhra, and, with his wife and daughter, carried prisoner to Andhra, leaving Mantragupta overwhelmed with despair. He hears, after a short time, that Jayasinha, the King of Andhra, wooes Karṅalekhá to become his queen. A report, however, prevails that a Yaksha loves the Princess, and that unless he can be put to flight by a powerful sorcerer, the Rájá's suit cannot be safely prosecuted. Mantragupta avails himself of the hint, and sets off for Andhra in the character of a magician, dressed in the tangled hair of the Siddha whom he had decapitated, and accompanied by disciples who spread his reputation through the country. The King soon hears of his fame, and applies to him for aid. After some pretended hesitation, he desires the Rájá to plunge at midnight into a neighbouring pond, having previously had it dragged to remove all its living creatures, and surrounded it at some little distance by guards to prevent any one's approach. By doing this, and in consequence of the magic rites which he, the pretended sorcerer, has practised, he will issue forth with a person entirely metamorphosed, and such as the Yaksha will be unable to resist. With these instructions the pretended ascetic takes his leave of the Rájá, professing that he has tarried longer than was consistent with his religious observances in the same place, He accordingly sends off his followers, but secretes himself in a hollow which he has previously dug in the bank of the pond. The King conforms to the directions he has received, but, when he is under water, is seized by Mantragupta, and stifled. His body is concealed in the hollow, and his enemy comes forth from the water as representing the Rájá. The guards, deeming it impossible that any other person could have issued from the pond, acquiesce quietly in the substitution, and escort Mantragupta to the palace, where he privately communicates the truth to the princess and her parents, and, with their concurrence, marries Karṅalekhá according to the ritual. Her father, Kardana, becomes King of both Andhra and Kalinga, and sends his son-in-law to succour his ally the Rájá of Anga.

One incident of this story, the transformation of the person, is repeated from the story of Upaháravarmá; but the narrative is peculiar in the locality of the incidents, the sea-coast of Kalinga, and in making Andhra, the ancient Telingana, a maritime power. There is also an allusion to the predominance of heretical opinions, either Buddhist or Jain, in Andhra; as Mantragupta, when Rájá, orders the temples of Śiva, Yama, Vishńu, and other gods, to be reverenced, to the discomfiture and shame of the infidels or Nástikas.

The last of the narratives is attributed to Viśruta, who, while wandering in the Vindhya forest, meets with the young Prince of Vidarbha, or Berar, and extricates his solitary attendant from a well into which he had fallen while seeking to procure water for the boy, who is exhausted with hunger and thirst. The Prince is of the family of Bhoja: his grand-father, Puńyavarmá, is described as a Prince of superior merit; but his father, Anantavarmá, is led by vicious companions into habits of dissipation, which end in the loss of his kingdom and life. The arguments which are urged by one of his favourites in behalf of idle pleasures, and in detraction of grave advisers and ministers, while they speak the language of the profligate in all ages, afford some curious insight into the abuses of official authority which prevailed in Indian Governments at the time of the composition. There is also, in the account of the feudatories of Anantavarmá, whose disaffection is the cause of his death, an interesting enumeration of the principalities bordering on Berar, to the north and west. Some of them must be identical in topographical situation with the provinces of the Mahratta principality, but the name Mahratta does not occur. It is found in older writings as Mahárásht́ra; but the kingdom appears to have been broken up in the middle ages into a number of petty states, among whom the ancient name was forgotten, or it was applied to the people, not to the territory; a circumstance which is equally applicable to modern times, in which we have "the Marhattas", the people of Khándesh,. Poona, and the Konkan, not of Mahárásht́ra.

After the death of Anantavarmá, his Queen, Vasundhará, with her daughter, Manjuvádiní, and her son, Bháskaravarmá, take refuge with the half-brother of her husband, Mitravarmá, Prince of Mhishmatí. Her plots against his nephew's life, and the Ráńí sends her son into the thickets with one of her attendants. They are suffering greatly from hunger and thirst, when Viśruta encounters them, and relieves their necessities. He proves to be a kinsman of the Prince's mother, and engages to replace him in his father's kingdom. Her therefore sends her servant back to Vasundhará, to inform her of what has chanced, and desires her to spread a report that the Prince has been devoured by a tiger. He sends her also a poisoned chaplet, with which he directs her to strike Mítravarmá on the heart, exclaiming that it will prove fatal only if she has been a faithful wife; and then, washing the garland, she is to apply it to her daughter's person, when it will prove innocuous. The death of Mitravarmá is accordingly considered by the people to be the consequence of his guilt, not of any treacherous practice. The principality is taken possession of by Prachańd́avarmá, who demands Manjuvádiní in marriage; a demand with which the Queen, by Viśruta's advice, feigns to comply. Viśruta and his charge, in the disguise of Śaiva ascetics, then repair to Vidarbha, where the former attires himself as a juggler, and mixing with a crowd of dancers and posture-masters, by whom Prachańd́avarmá is surrounded, exhibits various feats of sleight of hand and activity: among other things, he plays with knives, and tossing one of them in the direction of Prachańd́avarmá, it penetrates his breast and kills him. In the confusion Viśruta escapes, resumes his garb, and hides himself with the young Prince in an old temple of Durgá, where he contrives the means of entering it unobserved, and concealing himself underneath the pedestal of the image. The Rańí, in obedience to a pretended vision, repairs to the temple, attended by all the chief people of Máhishmatí, in whose presence she has the interior examined and the doors closed. After an interval the doors are opened from within, and Viśruta and the Prince appear. The former tells the people that he is the minister of the goddess, and is commanded by her to announce to them that she was pleased, in the form of a tigress, to carry off the Prince, in order more effectually to save him from his enemies; but as they are now removed, she restores him to their homage. He is accordingly recognised as Rájá; and Viśruta marrying Manjuvádiní, he becomes the chief manager of the principality. The last incident may be regarded as evidence of the profane uses to which the divinities of the Hindus were sometimes made subservient. The new Minister proceeds to take measures for recovering Vidarbha, which has been seized by the King of the Aśmakas, and we may conclude that he is victorious; but the work terminates abruptly, and leaves the denouement to the imagination. The deficiency is supplied by Gopínátha, who not only carries on the story of Viśruta to the end, but takes the united Princes to Pátaliputra, and re-establishes Rájahansa in his kingdom. We might have annexed his supplement, but the narrative is not of great interest, and the only copy of the work available is far from accurate. It has been thought better, therefore, to close with Dańdí's own composition.

III.

(Continued from p. 276.)*

MEDICAL AND SURGICAL SCIENCES OF THE HINDUS.

From the Oriental Magazine, Vol. I (1823), p. 349—56.

HAVING established the fact of Surgical Science being known, as a distinct branch of Medicine, to the early writers of the Hindus, we come to the consideration of the extent and manner, in which it was practised. According to our own system, and to all correct principle, we should for this purpose ascertain, in the first instance, what degree of acquaintance they possessed with Anatomy, on which alone rational Surgery is founded. Such however is not their mode of conducting the enquiry, and as we are endeavouring to trace their systems, and not those of a more enlightened period, we may be satisfied to wave this topic for the present, and adopt the course their own authorities pursue.

The practical part of the subject of Surgery is pre-

* [We regret that the second portion of this Essay came too late to hand for insertion in the proper place.]

ceded by a few general remarks, in which, amidst many erroneous notions, we trace some justness of classification, and soundness of principle. "Living bodies are composed," it is said*, "of the five elements, with action or life superadded: they are produced from vapour, vegetation, incubation, and parturition, as insects, plants, birds, fishes, reptiles, and animals. All the Hindu systems consider vegetable bodies as endowed with life. Of animals, man is the chief, and in proportion to his complicated structure is his liability to disease. The disorders of the human frame are of four kinds, accidental, organic, intellectual, and natural. The injuries arising from external causes form the first class. The second comprehends the effects of the vitiated humours, or derangements of the blood, bile, wind, and phlegm. The third class is occasioned by the operation of the passions, or the effects on the constitution of rage, fear, sorrow, joy, and others; and the last is referable to the necessary and innate condition of our being, as thirst, hunger, sleep, old age, and decay.

"The judicious alleviation of human infirmities, the means of which were compassionately revealed by the gods, can only be effected by the knowledge that is to be gained from study and practice conjoined. He who is only versed in books will be alarmed and confused, like a coward in the field of battle, when he is called upon to encounter active disease. He who

* [Suśr., Vol. I, p. 4.]

rashly engages in practice, without previous conversancy with written science, will be entitled to no respect from mankind, and merits punishment from the king. Those men who, in ignorance of the structure of the human frame, venture to make it the subject of their experiments, are the murderers of their species. He alone, who is endowed with both theory and experience, proceeds with safety and stability, like a chariot on two wheels."—It is much to be regretted that these aphorisms have so little influenced Hindu practitioners.

The instrumental part of Medical treatment was, according to the best authorities, of eight kinds—*Chhedana*, cutting or scission; *Bhedana*, division or excision; *Lekhana*, which means drawing lines, appears to be applied to scarification and inoculation; *Vyadhana*, puncturing; *Eshya*, probing, or sounding; *Áhárya*, extraction of solid bodies, *Visrávańa*, extraction of fluids, including venesection; and *Sevana*, or sewing: and the mechanical means, by which these operations were performed, seem to have been sufficiently numerous. Of these the principal are the following:—

Yantras, properly machines, in the present case instruments; but to distinguish them from the next class, to which that title more particularly applies, we may call them implements; *Śastras*, weapons, or instruments; *Kshára*, alkaline solutions, or caustics; *Agni*, fire, the actual cautery; *Śaláká*, pins, or tents; *Śŕinga*, horns, the horns of animals open at the extremities, and, as well as *Alábú* or gourds, used as our cupping glasses; the removal of the atmospheric pressure through the first being effected by suction, and in the second by rarifying the air by the application of a lamp. The next subsidiary means are *Jalauká*, or leeches.

Besides these, we have thread, leaves, bandages, pledgets, heated metallic plates for erubescents, and a variety of astringent or emollient applications. The enumeration is tolerably full, and the details are curious, if not instructive.

The detailed descriptions of the Hindu instruments we have been able to meet with are not very minute or precise. As also they are not illustrated by drawings or plates,* we are deprived of any thing like ocular verification of their construction. A few instruments, and some of neat and ingenious fabric, are in the hands of native operators, particularly those for depressing cataracts; but they are not very common, and we know not how far they may correspond with those designated by early writers. We can only therefore conjecture what the instruments might have been, by adding to the imperfect description given of them the purport of their names, and the objects to which they were applied.

The *Yantras*, or implements, known to the author of the Sauśruta were one hundred and one, and are

---

* [A plate containing drawings of the 20 Śastras is inserted in Wise's Hindu System of Medicine. Calcutta: 1845, facing p. 169.]

classed as Swastikas, Sandanśas, Tálayantras, Náďíyantras, Śalákás, and Upayantras.*

The *Swastikas* are twenty four in number—they are metallic, usually eighteen inches long, having heads or points fancifully shaped like the heads of animals, the beaks of birds, &c. They are secured with small pins, and are curved or hooked at the points, and are used to extract splinters of bone or foreign bodies lodged in the bones—they were therefore pincers, nippers, or forcipes.

The *Sandanśas,* which in usual import mean tongs, were of that description. There were in the time of Suśruta but two sorts, one with and one without a ligature or noose (Nigraha?) attached. They were smaller than the preceding, being but sixteen inches in length; and were used to remove extraneous substances from the soft parts, as the flesh, skin, vessels, &c. The work of Vágbhatťa adds another sort, only six inches long, which were employed preferably for the soft parts and for fleshy excrescences.

The *Tálayantras* must have been something of the same kind, only smaller, their length being but twelve inches. They were but two, and were employed to bring away foreign matters lodged in the outer canals, as the ears, &c.

The *Náďíyantras* were, as the name implies, tubular instruments. There were twenty sorts, varying in

---

* [Suśruta I, ch. 7.]

size and shape according to their intended use. They were employed for removing extraneous bodies from deep seated canals, as the intestines, urethra, &c. for examining affections of parts similarly removed from inspection; for the introduction of other instruments, so as to enable them to be applied; and for drawing off fluids by suction, &c. The work of Vágbhaťťa specifies the number of perforations in each of these tubes, as they varied in this respect as well as others: the descriptions are however very indistinct, and we can only conclude generally, that they bore an analogy to our canulæ catheters, syringes, &c.

The *Salákás* were rods, and sounds, &c. They were of twenty-eight kinds, varying in size and shape, for extracting foreign matters, lodged in parts of difficult access; for cleansing or clearing internal canals, especially the urethra; for applying collyria, caustic solutions, and the actual cautery; and for eradicating nasal polypi, the complaint called Nakra so common and so troublesome in India, and to be alleviated by no other means than the forcible extraction of the irritating excrescence.

The *Upayantras* were, as their appellation signifies, merely accessory implements, such as twine, leather, bark skin cloth, &c.

The first, best, and most important of all implements, however, is declared to be the *Hand*.

The next division of our apparatus consists of the *Śastras*, the instruments, of which twenty different sorts are enumerated by Suśruta,* twenty-six by Vágbhaṫṫa. They were of metal, and should be always bright, handsome, polished, and sharp; sufficiently so indeed to divide a hair longitudinally. The latter authority adds, they were in general not above six inches in length, and that the blade forms about a half or quarter of that length. They are less fully described than the preceding in the Sauśruta, and we can only partially, and perhaps not very accurately, notice a few of them, as detailed in the two works referred to.

The *Maṅḋalágra* appears to be a round pointed lancet; the *Vŕiddhipatra* a knife with a broad blade; the *Arddhadhárás* are perhaps knives with one edge; the *Trikúrchaka* is a lancet with three prongs or blades; the *Vŕittágra* may be a sort of canular trochar, having a guarded point. The *Vríhimukha* is a perforating instrument, and when used is held in the hollow of the hand, whilst the point is steadied between the thumb and forefinger. The *Kuṫhárikά* appears to be a kind of Bistouri, as it is a cutting instrument to be held in the left hand, whilst it is conducted by the thumb and middle finger of the right. The *Vaḋiśa* is a hooked or curved instrument, for extracting foreign substances, and the *Dantaśanku* appears to be an instrument for drawing teeth. The *Árá* and *Karapatra* are saws for cutting through bones. The *Eshaṅí* is a blunt straight instrument,

* [I, ch. 8.]

six or eight inches long, for examining abscesses, sinuses, &c. or, in fact, a probe. The *Súchí* is a needle.

Aṅuśastras are supplements, or substitutes; such as rough leaves, that draw blood, as those of the Śephálíká, Gojí, &c. crystal, or glass; the pith of some trees, skin, leeches, caustics, &c. With these therefore, and the Yantras, the Hindu Chirurgeon was not ineffectively armed.

The means by which the young practitioner is to obtain dexterity in the use of his instruments are of a mixed character; and whilst some are striking specimens of the lame contrivances to which the want of the only effective vehicle of instruction, human dissection, compelled the Hindus to have recourse, others surprise us by their supposed incompatibility with what we have been hitherto disposed to consider as insurmountable prejudices. Thus the different kinds of scission, longitudinal, transverse, inverted, and circular, are directed to be practised on flowers, bulbs, and gourds. Incision on skins, or bladders, filled with paste and mire;—scarification on the *fresh hides of animals from which the hair has not been removed;* —puncturing, or lancing, on the hollow stalks of plants, or *the vessels of dead animals;*—extraction *on the cavaties of the same,* or fruits with many large seeds, as the Jack and Bel;—sutures, on skin and leather, and ligatures and bandages on well-made models of the human limbs. The employment of leather, skin, and even of dead carcases, thus enjoined, proves an exemption from notions of impurity we were little to expect when adverting to their actual prevalence. Of course, their use implies the absence of any objections to the similar employment of human subjects; and although they are not specified, they may possibly be implied, in the general direction which the author of the Sauśruta gives, that the teacher shall seek to perfect his pupil by the application of all expedients which he may think calculated to effect his proficiency.

Of the supplementary articles of Hindu surgery the first is *Kshára,* alkaline or alkalescent salts.* This is obtained by burning different vegetable substances, and boiling the ashes with five or six times their measure of water. In some cases the concentrated solution is used after straining, and is administered internally, as well as applied externally. For the latter purpose, however, the Śárngadhara directs the solution, after straining, to be boiled to dryness; by which, of course, a carbonate of potash will be obtained, more or less caustic according to its purity. It is not unlikely that some of the vegetable substances employed will yield a tolerably pure alkali, and in that case will afford an active caustic. Care is enjoined in their use, and emollient applications are to be applied, if the caustic occasions very great pain. At the same time these and the other substitutes for instrumental agents are only to be had recourse to, where it is necessary to humour the weakness of the patient.

* [Suśr. I, ch. 11.]

They are especially found serviceable, where the surgeon has to deal with princes and persons of rank, old men, women and children, and individuals of a timid and effeminate character.

We need not advert particularly to the nature and use of the horns and gourds, as, however rude the substitute, the principle is sufficiently obvious and correct. With respect to the bandages, also, of which fourteen kinds are described by Vágbhaťťa, it would be useless to attempt so unintelligible a detail. We shall therefore close this account of the Hindu apparatus, with a selection of some of the circumstances our authorities specify, regarding the actual cautery and leeches.

The *cautery** is applied by hot seeds, combustible substances inflamed, boiling fluids of a gelatinous or mucous consistence, and heated metallic bars, plates, and probes. The application is useful in many cases, as to the temples and forehead for headaches; to the eyelids for diseases of the eyes; to the part affected for indurations in the skin; to the sides for spleen and liver; and to the abdomen for mesenteric enlargements. As amongst the Greeks, however, the chief use of the cautery was in the case of hemorrhages, bleeding being stopped by searing the wounded vessels.

Much pains, and perhaps to but little good purpose, were bestowed upon the subject of *leeches***. It is

* [Suśr. I, ch. 12.]
** [ib. ch. 13.]

said that there are twelve sorts, of which six are venomous:—they are thus enumerated. The six poisonous leeches are the *Kŕishńá*, or black and two headed; the *Karburá*, the large bellied leech with a scaly hide: the *Alagardá*, the hairy leech; the *Indráyudhá*, which is variegated like a rain-bow, whence its name; the *Sámudriká*, which is striped yellow and black; and the *Gochandaná*. The bites of these produce excessive irritation; great itching, heat, and pain; spasms, sickness, and syncope; and that of the Indráyudhá even death. The six sorts that are fit for use are the *Kapilá*, or tawny leech, with a smooth back and glossy sides; the *Pingalá*, a similar animal, but with a redder tinge; the *Śankumukhí*, which is of a yellow colour, and has a long sharp head; the *Múshiká*, of a dun colour; the *Puńdaríkamukhí*, which is of the hue of the Mudga (Phaseolus Moong); and the *Sávariká*, which resembles the leaf of the lotus in its colour. The first six are bred in foul, stagnant, and putrescent waters, whilst the latter are met with in the vicinity of clear and deep pools:—they are all amphibious. Very minute instructions are laid down for their preservation and training; but we need not pause to extract them, as they are not very important. If the leeches, when applied, are slow and sluggish, a little blood may be drawn from the part by a lancet, to excite their vivacity; when they fall off, the bleeding may be maintained by the use of the horns and gourds, or the substitutes already mentioned, for the cupping glasses of our own practice.

The details thus concisely noticed prepare us to expect an active practice amongst those to whom they were familiar; and accordingly we find that, in the practical treatment of diseases, many of the great operations of the chiropoietic art are enjoined, such as extraction of the stone in the bladder, and even the removal of the fœtus from the uterus. The operations are rude, and very imperfectly described. They were evidently bold, and must have been hazardous:—their being attempted at all is however most extraordinary, unless their obliteration from the knowledge, not to say the practice, of later times be considered as a still more remarkable circumstance. It would be an enquiry of some interest, to trace the period and causes of the disappearance of Surgery from amongst the Hindus: it is evidently of comparatively modern occurrence, as operative and instrumental practice forms so principal a part of those writings, which are undeniably most ancient; and which, being regarded as the composition of inspired writers, are held of the highest authority. It is an enquiry connected with the progress of manners, for the persons whoever they were, who wrote in the character of Munis, or deified sages, would not have compromised that character by imparting precepts utterly contrary to the ritual or the law, or at variance with the principles and prejudices of their countrymen. In what has been already quoted from Suśruta and Vágbhaťťa, however, there is much that is utterly irreconcilable with present notions, and in other parts of their treatises that disregard is equally evinced. We must therefore infer, that the existing sentiments of the Hindus are of modern date, growing out of an altered state of society, and unsupported by their oldest and most authentic civil and moral, as well as medical, institutes.

Berlin, printed by Unger Brothers, Printers to the King.

LINGUISTIC PUBLICATIONS

OF

TRÜBNER & CO.

60, PATERNOSTER ROW, LONDON, E. C.

Alcock.—A PRACTICAL GRAMMAR of the JAPANESE LANGUAGE. By Sir RUTHERFORD ALCOCK, Resident British Minister at Jeddo. 4to., pp. 61, sewed. 18*s.*

Alcock.—FAMILIAR DIALOGUES in JAPANESE, with English and French Translations, for the Use of Students. By Sir RUTHERFORD ALCOCK. 8vo., pp. viii. and 40, sewed. Paris and London, 1863. 5*s.*

Asher.—On the STUDY of MODERN LANGUAGES in general, and of the English Language in particular. An Essay. By DAVID ASHER, Ph. D. 12mo., pp. viii. and 80, cloth. 2*s.*

Asiatic Society.—JOURNAL of the ROYAL ASIATIC SOCIETY of GREAT BRITAIN and IRELAND, from the Commencement to 1863. First Series, complete in 20 Vols. 8vo., with many Plates. Price £10; or in single Numbers, as follows:—Nos. 1 to 14, 6*s.* each; No. 15, 2 Parts, 4*s.* each; No. 16, 2 Parts, 4*s.* each; No. 17, 2 Parts, 4*s.* each; No. 18, 6*s.* These 18 Numbers form Vols. I. to IX.—Vol. X., Part 1, op.; Part 2, 5*s.*; Part 3, 5*s.*—Vol. XI., Part 1, 6*s.*; Part 2 not published.—Vol. XII., 2 Parts, 6*s.* each.—Vol. XIII., 2 Parts, 6*s.* each.—Vol. XIV., Part 1, 5*s.*; Part 2 not published.—Vol. XV., Part 1, 6*s.*; Part 2, with Maps, 10*s.*—Vol. XVI., 2 Parts, 6*s.* each.—Vol. XVII., 2 Parts, 6*s.* each.—Vol. XVIII., 2 Parts, 6*s.* each.—Vol. XIX., Parts 1 to 4, 16*s.*—Vol. XX., 3 Parts, 4*s.* each.

Asiatic Society.—TRANSACTIONS of the ROYAL ASIATIC SOCIETY of GREAT BRITAIN and IRELAND. Complete in 3 vols. 4to., 80 Plates of Facsimiles, etc., cloth. London, 1827 to 1835. Published at 9*l.* 5*s.*; reduced to 1*l.* 11*s.* 6*d.*

The above contains contributions by Professor Wilson, G. C. Haughton, Davis, Morrison, Colebrooke, Humboldt, Dorn, Grotefend, and other eminent oriental scholars.

Bartlett.—DICTIONARY of AMERICANISMS: a Glossary of Words and Phrases colloquially used in the United States. By JOHN R. BARTLETT. Second Edition, considerably enlarged and improved. 1 vol., 8vo., pp. xxxii. and 524, cloth. 16*s.*

Benfey.—A PRACTICAL GRAMMAR of the SANSKRIT LANGUAGE, for the Use of early Students. By THEODOR BENFEY, Professor Pull. Ord. of Sanskrit in the University of Goettingen, etc. etc. 8vo., pp. xviii. and 228, cloth. 7*s.* 6*d.*

Bleek.—A COMPARATIVE GRAMMAR of SOUTH AFRICAN LANGUAGES. By Dr. W. H. I. BLEEK. Will be completed in Four Parts. Part I., pp. 104, sewed. 5*s.*

Bleek.—REYNARD in SOUTH AFRICA; or, Hottentot Fables. Translated from the original Manuscript in Sir George Grey's Library. By Dr. W. H. I. BLEEK, Librarian of the Grey Library, Cape Town, Cape of Good Hope. In one volume, small 8vo. [*In preparation.*

Canones Lexicographici; or, Rules to be observed in Editing the New English Dictionary of the Philological Society, prepared by a Committee of the Society. 8vo., pp. 12, sewed. 6*d.*

Coleridge.—A GLOSSARIAL INDEX to the printed English Literature of the Thirteenth Century. By HERBERT COLERIDGE, Esq. 1 vol. 8vo., pp. 104, cloth. 5*s.*

Goldstücker.—A DICTIONARY, SANSKRIT and ENGLISH, extended and improved from the Second Edition of the Dictionary of Professor H. H. WILSON, with his sanction and concurrence. Together with a Supplement, Grammatical Appendices, and an Index, serving as a Sanskrit-English Vocabulary. By THEODOR GOLDSTÜCKER. Parts I. to V. 4to., pp. 400. 1856—1863. Each Part 6*s.*

Goldstücker.—PANINI: His Place in Sanskrit Literature. An Investigation of some Literary and Chronological Questions which may be settled by a study of his Work. A separate impression of the Preface to the Facsimile of MS. No. 17 in the Library of Her Majesty's Home Government for India, which contains a portion of the MANAVA-KALPA-SUTRA, with the Commentary of KUMARILA-SWAMIN. By THEODOR GOLDSTÜCKER. Imperial 8vo., pp. 268, cloth. 12*s.*

Goldstücker.—A Compendious SANSKRIT-ENGLISH DICTIONARY, for the Use of those who intend to read the easier Works of Classical Sanskrit Literature, By THEODOR GOLDSTÜCKER. Small 4to., pp. 900, cloth. [*In preparation.*

Grammatography. A MANUAL of REFERENCE to the Alphabets of Ancient and Modern Languages. Based on the German Compilation of F. BALLHORN. In one volume, royal 8vo., pp. 80, cloth. 7*s*. 6*d*.

The "Grammatography" is offered to the public as a compendious introduction to the reading of the most important ancient and modern languages. Simple in its design, it will be consulted with advantage by the philological student, the amateur linguist, the bookseller, the corrector of the press, and the diligent compositor.

ALPHABETICAL INDEX.

Afghan (or Pushto).
Amharic.
Anglo-Saxon.
Arabic.
Arabic Ligatures.
Aramaic.
Archaic Characters.
Armenian.
Assyrian Cuneiform.
Bengali.
Bohemian (Czechian).
Búgis.
Burmese.
Canarese (or Carnâtaca).
Chinese.
Coptic.
Croato-Glagolitic.
Cufic.
Cyrillic (or Old Slavonic).
Czechian (or Bohemian).
Danish.
Demotic.
Estrangelo.
Ethiopic.
Etruscan.
Georgian.
German.
Glagolitic.
Gothic.
Greek.
Greek Ligatures.
Greek (Archaic).
Gujerati (or Guzerattee).
Hieratic.
Hieroglyphics.
Hebrew.
Hebrew (Archaic).
Hebrew (Rabbinical).
Hebrew (Judæ-German).
Hebrew (current hand).
Hungarian.
Illyrian.
Irish.
Italian (Old).
Japanese.
Javanese.
Lettish.
Mantshu.
Median Cuneiform.
Modern Greek (Romaic).
Mongolian.
Numidian.
Old Slavonic (or Cyrillic).
Palmyrenian.
Persian.
Persian Cuneiform.
Phœnician.
Polish.
Pushto (or Afghan).
Romaic (Modern Greek).
Russian.
Runes.
Samaritan.
Sanscrit.
Servian.
Slavonic (Old).
Sorbian (or Wendish).
Swedish.
Syriac.
Tamil.
Telugu.
Tibetan.
Turkish.
Wallachian.
Wendish (or Sorbian.)
Zend.

Grey.—MAORI MEMENTOS: being a Series of Addresses presented by the Native People to His Excellency Sir GEORGE GREY, K.C.B., F.R.S. With Introductory Remarks and Explanatory Notes; to which is added a small Collection of Laments, etc. By CH. OLIVER B. DAVIS. 8vo., pp. iv. and 228, cloth. 12*s*.

Grey.—HANDBOOK of AFRICAN, AUSTRALIAN, and POLYNESIAN PHILOLOGY, as represented in the Library of His Excellency Sir GEORGE GREY, K.C.B., Her Majesty's High Commissioner of the Cape Colony. Classed, Annotated, and Edited by Sir GEORGE GREY and Dr. H. I. BLEEK.

Vol. I. Part 1.—South Africa, 8vo., pp. 186, 7*s*. 6*d*.
Vol. I. Part 2.—Africa (North of the Tropic of Capricorn), 8vo., pp. 70, 2*s*.
Vol. I. Part 3.—Madagascar, 8vo., pp. 24, 1*s*.
Vol. II. Part 1.—Australia, 8vo., pp. iv. and 44, 1*s*. 6*d*.
Vol. II. Part 2.—Papuan Languages of the Loyalty Islands and New Hebrides, comprising those of the Islands of Nengone, Lifu, Aneitum, Tana, and others, 8vo., pp. 12, 6*d*.
Vol. II. Part 3.—Fiji Islands and Rotuma (with Supplement to Part II., Papuan Languages, and Part I., Australia), 8vo., pp. 34, 1*s*.
Vol. II. Part 4.—New Zealand, the Chatham Islands, and Auckland Islands, 8vo., pp. 76, 3*s*. 6*d*.
Vol. II. Part 4 (*continuation*).—Polynesia and Borneo, 8vo., pp. 77—154, 3*s*. 6*d*.
Vol. III. Part 1.—Manuscripts and Incunables, 8vo., pp. viii. and 24, 2*s*.

Grout.—The ISIZULU: a Grammar of the Zulu Language; accompanied with a Historical Introduction, also with an Appendix. By Rev. LEWIS GROUT. 8vo., pp. lii. and 432, cloth. 21*s*.

Haug.—OUTLINE of a GRAMMAR of the ZEND LANGUAGE. By MARTIN HAUG, Dr. Phil. 8vo., pp. 82, sewed. 14*s*.

Haug.—ESSAYS on the SACRED LANGUAGE, WRITINGS, and RELIGION of the PARSEES. By MARTIN HAUG, Dr. Phil., Superintendent of Sanskrit Studies in the Poona College. 8vo., pp. 278, cloth. 21*s*.

Hernisz.—A GUIDE to CONVERSATION in the ENGLISH and CHINESE LANGUAGES, for the use of Americans and Chinese in California and elsewhere. By STANISLAS HERNISZ. Square 8vo., pp. 274, sewed. 18*s*.

The Chinese characters contained in this work are from the collections of Chinese groups, engraved on steel, and cast into movable types, by Mr. Marcellin Legrand, Engraver of the Imperial Printing Office at Paris. They are used by most of the Missions to China.

Hoffman.—SHOPPING DIALOGUES, in Japanese, Dutch, and English. By Professor J. HOFFMAN. Oblong 8vo., sewed. 3*s*.

Kafir Essays, and other Pieces; with an English Translation. Edited by the Right Reverend the BISHOP of GRAHAMSTOWN. 32mo., pp. 84, sewed. 2*s*. 6*d*.

Kidd.—CATALOGUE of the CHINESE LIBRARY of the Royal Asiatic Society. By the Rev. S. KIDD. 8vo., pp. 58, sewed. 1*s*.

Legge.—The CHINESE CLASSICS. With a Translation, Critical and Exegetical, Notes, Prolegomena, and Copious Indexes. By JAMES LEGGE, D.D., of the London Missionary Society. In Seven Vols. Vol. I., containing Confucian Analects, the Great Learning, and the Doctrine of the Mean. 8vo., pp. 526, cloth, price 2*l*. 2*s*. Vol. II., containing the Works of Mencius. 8vo., pp. 634, cloth, price 2*l*. 2*s*.

Ludewig (Hermann E.)—The LITERATURE of AMERICAN ABORIGINAL LANGUAGES. With Additions and Corrections by Professor WM. W. TURNER. Edited by NICOLAS TRÜBNER. 8vo., fly and general Title, 2 leaves; Dr. Ludewig's Preface, pp. v—viii; Editor's Preface, pp. iv—xii; Biographical Memoir of Dr. Ludewig, pp. xiii, xiv; and Introductory Bibliographical Notices, pp. xiv—xxiv, followed by List of Contents. Then follow Dr. Ludewig's Bibliotheca Glottica, alphabetically arranged with Additions by the Editor, pp. 1—209; Professor Turner's Additions, with those of the Editor to the same, also alphabetically arranged, pp. 210—246; Index, pp. 247—256; and List of Errata, pp. 257, 258. One vol., handsomely bound in cloth. 10*s.* 6*d.*

Manava-Kalpa-Sutra; being a portion of this ancient Work on Vaidik Rites, together with the Commentary of KUMARILA-SWAMIN. A Facsimile of the MS. No. 17 in the Library of Her Majesty's Home Government for India. With a Preface by THEODOR GOLDSTÜCKER. Oblong folio, pp. 268 of letterpress and 121 leaves of facsimiles. Cloth. 4*l.* 4*s.*

Markham.—QUICHUA GRAMMAR and DICTIONARY. Contributions towards a Grammar and Dictionary of Quichua, the Language of the Yncas of Peru; collected by CLEMENTS R. MARKHAM, F.S.A., Corr. Mem. of the University of Chile, Author of "Cuzco and Lima," and "Travels in Peru and India." In one vol., crown 8vo., pp. 150, cloth. [*In preparation.*

Medhurst.—CHINESE DIALOGUES, QUESTIONS, and FAMILIAR SENTENCES, literally rendered into English, with a view to promote commercial intercourse and assist beginners in the Language. By the late W. H. MEDHURST, D.D. A new and enlarged Edition. Part I., pp. 66. 8vo. 5*s.*

Morley.—A DESCRIPTIVE CATALOGUE of the HISTORICAL MANUSCRIPTS in the ARABIC and PERSIAN LANGUAGES preserved in the Library of the Royal Asiatic Society of Great Britain and Ireland. By WILLIAM H. MORLEY, M.R.A.S. 8vo., pp. viii. and 160, sewed. London, 1854. 2*s.* 6*d.*

Muir.—ORIGINAL SANSCRIT TEXTS on the Origin and History of the People of India, their Religion and Institutions. Collected, Translated into English, and illustrated by Remarks, by J. MUIR, D.C.L., LL.D. Part IV., Comparison of the Vedic with the later representation of the principal Indian Deities. 8vo., pp. xii. and 440, cloth. 15*s.*

Osburn.—The MONUMENTAL HISTORY of EGYPT, as recorded on the Ruins of her Temples, Palaces, and Tombs. By WILLIAM OSBURN. Illustrated with Maps, Plates, etc. 2 vols. 8vo., pp. xii. and 461; vii. and 643; cloth. 2*l.* 2*s.*

Vol. I.—From the Colonization of the Valley to the Visit of the Patriarch Abram.
Vol. II.—From the Visit of Abram to the Exodus.

Philological Society.—PROPOSALS for the Publication of a NEW ENGLISH DICTIONARY. 8vo., pp. 32, sewed. 6*d.*

Ram Raz.—ESSAY on the ARCHITECTURE of the HINDUS. By RAM RAZ, Native Judge and Magistrate of Bangalore, Corresponding Member of the R. A. S. of Great Britain and Ireland. With 48 Plates. 4to., pp. xiv. and 64, sewed. London, 1834. Original selling price, 1*l.* 11*s.* 6*d.*, reduced (for a short time only) to 12*s.*

Rawlinson.—A COMMENTARY on the CUNEIFORM INSCRIPTIONS of BABYLONIA and ASSYRIA, including Readings of the Inscription on the Nimrud Obelisk, and a brief Notice of the ancient Kings of Nineveh and Babylon. Read before the Royal Asiatic Society, by Major H. C. RAWLINSON. 8vo., pp. 84, sewed. London, 1850. 2*s.* 6*d.*

Rawlinson.—OUTLINES of ASSYRIAN HISTORY, from the Inscriptions of Nineveh. By Lieut.-Colonel RAWLINSON, C.B., followed by some Remarks by A. H. LAYARD, Esq., D.C.L. 8vo., pp. xliv., sewed. London, 1852. 1*s.*

Renan.—An ESSAY on the AGE and ANTIQUITY of the BOOK of NABATHÆAN AGRICULTURE. To which is added, an Inaugural Lecture on the Position of the Shemitic Nations in the History of Civilization. By M. ERNEST RENAN, Membre de l'Institut. In 1 Vol., crown 8vo., pp. xvi. and 148, cloth. 3*s.* 6*d.*

Rig-Veda Sanhita; a COLLECTION of ANCIENT HINDU HYMNS, constituting the Fifth to Eighth Ashtakas or Books of the RIG-VEDA, the oldest Authority for the Religious and Social Institutions of the Hindus. Translated from the original Sanskrit by the late HORACE HAYMAN WILSON, M.A., F.R.S., etc. Edited by JAMES R. BALLANTYNE, LL.D., late Principal of the Government Sanskrit College of Benares. Volumes IV., V., and VI. [*In the Press.*

Schlagintweit.—BUDDHISM in TIBET: illustrated by Literary Documents and Objects of Religious Worship. With an Account of the Buddhist Systems preceding it in India. By EMIL SCHLAGINTWEIT, LL.D. With a folio Atlas of 20 Plates, and 20 Tables of Native print in the Text. Royal 8vo., pp. xxiv. and 404. 2*l.* 2*s.*

Schlagintweit.—GLOSSARY of GEOGRAPHICAL TERMS from INDIA and TIBET, with Native Transcription and Transliteration. By HERMANN DE SCHLAGINTWEIT. Forming, with a "Route Book of the Western Himalaya, Tibet, and Turkistan," the Third Volume of H., A., and R DE SCHLAGINTWEIT'S "Results of a Scientific Mission to India and High Asia." With an Atlas, in imperial folio, of Maps, Panoramas, and Views. Royal 4to., pp. xxiv. and 293. 4*l.*

Sophocles.—A GLOSSARY of LATER and BYZANTINE GREEK. By. E. A. SOPHOCLES. 4to., pp. iv. and 624, cloth. 2*l.* 2*s.*

Tindall.—A GRAMMAR and VOCABULARY of the NAMAQUA-HOTTENTOT LANGUAGE. By HENRY TINDALL, Wesleyan Missionary. 8vo., pp. 124, sewed. 6*s.*

Vishnu-Purana: or, SYSTEM of HINDU MYTHOLOGY and TRADITION, translated from the original Sanskrit, and Illustrated by Notes derived chiefly from other Puranas. By HORACE HAYMAN WILSON. Thoroughly Revised and Edited, with Notes, by Dr. FITZ-EDWARD HALL. In 3 vols., 8vo. [*In preparation.*

Watts.—ESSAYS on LANGUAGE and LITERATURE. By THOS. WATTS, of the British Museum. Reprinted, with alterations and additions, from the Transactions of the Philological Society, and elswhere. In 1 vol., 8vo. [*In preparation.*

Wedgwood.—A DICTIONARY of ENGLISH ETYMOLOGY. By HENSLEIGH WEDGWOOD, M.A., late Fellow of Ch. Coll. Cam. Vol I. (A to D), pp. xxiv. and 508, 8vo., cloth. Vol. II. (E to P), pp. 570, 8vo., cloth. (Will be complete in 3 vols.) Price of each vol., 14*s.*

"Dictionaries are a class of books not usually esteemed light reading; but no intelligent man were to be pitied who should find himself shut up on a rainy day in a lonely house in the dreariest part of Salisbury Plain, with no other means of recreation than that which Mr. Wedgwood's Dictionary of English Etymology could afford him. He would read it through from cover to cover at a sitting, and only regret that he had not the second volume to begin upon forthwith. It is a very able book, of great research, full of delightful surprises, a repertory of the fairy tales of linguistic science."—*Spectator.*

Williams.—FIRST LESSONS in the MAORI LANGUAGE, with a Short Vocabulary. By W. L. WILLIAMS, B.A. Square 8vo., pp. 80, cloth. London, 1862. 3*s.* 6*d.*

Wilson.—WORKS by the late HORACE H. WILSON, M.A., F.R.S., Member of the Royal Asiatic Societies of Calcutta and Paris, and of the Oriental Society of Germany, etc., and Boden Professor of Sanskrit in the University of Oxford. Vols. I. and II.—Also under this title, ESSAYS and LECTURES, chiefly on the RELIGION of the HINDUS, by the late H. H. WILSON, M.A., F.R.S., etc. etc. Collected and Edited by Dr. REINHOLD ROST. In 2 vols., 8vo., cloth. 21*s.*

Wilson.—The WORKS of the late HORACE HAYMAN WILSON. Vols. III., IV., and V., containing Essays on Oriental Literature. Edited by Dr. REINHOLD ROST, St. Augustine's College, Canterbury. In 3 vols., 8vo., cloth. [*Nearly ready.*

Wilson.—ESSAYS on ORIENTAL LITERATURE. By the late H. H. WILSON. Edited by Dr. REINHOLD ROST, St. Augustine's College, Canterbury. In 3 vols., 8vo., cloth. [*Nearly ready.*

Wilson.—The PRESENT STATE of the CULTIVATION of ORIENTAL LITERATURE. A Lecture delivered at a Meeting of the Royal Asiatic Society, by the Director, Professor H. H. WILSON. 8vo., pp. 26, sewed. London, 1852. 6*d.*

Wilson.—SELECT SPECIMENS of the THEATRE of the HINDUS, translated from the original Sanskrit. By HORACE HAYMAN WILSON, M A., F.R.S. Second Edition. 2 vols., 8vo., pp. lxx. and 384, 415, cloth. 15*s.*

CONTENTS.

Vol. I.—Preface—Treatise on the Dramatic System of the Hindus—Dramas translated from the original Sanskrit—The Mrichchakati, or the Toy Cart—Vikrama and Urvasi, or the Hero and the Nymph—Uttara Ramá Cheritra, or continuation of the History of Ramá.

Vol. II.—Dramas translated from the original Sanskrit—Maláti and Mádhava, or the Stolen Marriage—Mudrá Rakshasa, or the Signet of the Minister—Retnávala, or the Necklace—Appendix, containing short accounts of different Dramas.

Wise.—COMMENTARY on the HINDU SYSTEM of MEDICINE. By T. A. WISE, M.D., Bengal Medical Service. 8vo., pp. xx. and 432, cloth. 7*s.* 6*d.*

ESSAYS
ANALYTICAL, CRITICAL AND PHILOLOGICAL
ON SUBJECTS CONNECTED WITH
SANSKRIT LITERATURE

ESSAYS
ANALYTICAL, CRITICAL AND PHILOLOGICAL

ON SUBJECTS CONNECTED WITH

SANSKRIT LITERATURE

BY THE LATE

H. H. WILSON, M.A., F.R.S.,

BODEN PROFESSORS OF SANSKRIT IN THE UNIVERSITY OF OXFORD, ETC., ETC.,

COLLECTED AND EDITED BY

DR. REINHOLD ROST

IN THREE VOLUMES

VOL. II

GYAN

Published by

Gyan Publishing House
5, Ansari Road
Daryaganj, New Delhi-110002
Phone: 011-47034999, 9811692060
E-mail: books@gyanbooks.com

Distribution Network
gyanbooks.com
India, USA, Canada, UK, Australia, France

ISBN : 978-81-212-4519-7 (Set)
ISBN : 978-81-212-4732-0 (HB)
First Published, 1864

2nd Impression 2020

Printed at: Gyan Press, Delhi.

Essays Analytical, Critical and Philological Vol. II
Author: H. H. Wilson

ESSAYS

ANALYTICAL, CRITICAL AND PHILOLOGICAL

ON SUBJECTS CONNECTED WITH

SANSKRIT LITERATURE.

BY THE LATE

H. H. WILSON, M.A., F.R.S.,

BODEN PROFESSOR OF SANSKRIT IN THE UNIVERSITY OF OXFORD,

ETC., ETC.

COLLECTED AND EDITED BY

DR. REINHOLD ROST.

IN THREE VOLUMES.

VOL. II.

LONDON:

TRÜBNER & CO., 60, PATERNOSTER ROW.

1864.

CONTENTS OF VOL. II.

VI.

ANALYTICAL ACCOUNT
OF THE
PANCHA TANTRA,
ILLUSTRATED WITH OCCASIONAL TRANSLATIONS.

Read June 5, 1824.
From the Transactions of the R. Asiatic Society, Vol. I, No. 2, (1825) p. 155—201.

"As the active world is inferior to the rational soul, so Fiction gives to mankind what History denies, and in some measure satisfies the mind with shadows, when it cannot enjoy the substance."—LORD BACON.

WHAT the profound observer, quoted above, pronounced generally of fiction, is peculiarly pertinent, when applied to the Hindus. The history of their progress, in the arts of civilized life, is so clouded with mythology, and overcast by time, that our efforts to penetrate the obscurity have been hitherto of little avail. As the mind, therefore, has little substantial gratification to expect from this branch of intellectual enjoyment, it may be permitted to indulge in the shadows, that are abundantly presented, and dwell with more interest, than the subject would otherwise excite, on the copious materials afforded by the mass of Hindu fable within its reach.

The elucidation, which such an inquiry promises to afford of the past manners of the Hindus, before they were metamorphosed, and degraded by the influence of foreign subjugation, constitutes an advantage of more than imaginary value. We see what they were more distinctly than through the medium of any general description; and can trust to their own pictures of themselves more confidently than to any crude and imperfect exhibitions, delineated from present experience, or circumscribed research. In this point of view, therefore, Hindu fable becomes a valuable accession to real knowledge, and serviceably supplies that want of sober history, which all Oriental inquirers have such perpetual occasion to lament.

It is not only with respect to themselves, however, that the fictions of the Hindus are calculated to add to our stock of knowledge: and the influence, which they have exercised on the state of manners in Europe, will only be duly appreciated, when we shall be better acquainted with the extent of the obligations we owe them. By whatever channel they may have been conveyed to the West, the Oriental origin of most of the tales, which first roused the inventive faculties of our ancestors, is universally admitted; but the advocates of the Gothic or Arabic origin of romance agree in referring its birth-place to the East.

It is now too late to inquire, whether we are to

consider Persia as the birth-place of fictitious narrative: for, if such narrative was cultivated there, it must have been clad in the Pehlevi language; and both body and dress are irrecoverably lost. We must, therefore, be content to admit the claims of the Hindus, amongst whom we may trace the original of much that has interested, and amused, our forefathers and ourselves.

The oldest collection of fables and tales, of the class here intended, is the work that passes by the title of the Fables of Bidpai, or Pilpay. The history of this work is too well known to require any elucidation. Mr. Wilkins, and Sir William Jones, brought to light its original, from amongst the hidden stores of Sanskrit literature; and Mr. Colebrooke gave the text itself of the Hitopadeśa to the public. The learning and industry of the Baron de Sacy have finally traced the work through all its stages; and there are few subjects of investigation, the history of which has been more successfully ascertained than the Bibliographical adventures of the solutary instructions of *Vishńu-śarmá*, or *Fables of Pilpay*.

Although the stories of the Hitopadeśa are undoubtedly identical with most of those, which are found in all the forms of Pilpay's fables, yet it has been clearly shown by Mr. Colebrooke, that it is not the source from which its successors have been directly derived. It is, in fact, itself but a scion of the same parent stock, and in common with the rest, originates, as it indeed admits, from an older collection, the *Pancha Tantra*. The text of this work is not very rare in India, and it were therefore to have been wished, that it had been selected for translation, in preference to the Hitopadeśa; but the opportunity has passed. The identity of the two works, for the greater part, renders the translation of both a work of supererogation: and, fully as the topic has been developed, it is likely that a main defect will long continue to mutilate it, at the very outset. The deficiency has, in some measure, been supplied by the sketch, given by Mr. Colebrooke, of the contents of the Pancha Tantra; but, as his chief object was only to substantiate the greater affinity between it and the Kalíla wa Damna, than between the Arabic work and the Hitopadeśa, he has not prosecuted its details farther than was sufficient to effect his purpose. In the want, therefore, of a full analysis, and in the little likelihood that exists, of a translation of the entire work being now published, it has been presumed that a more minute account of the Pancha Tantra, than has yet been given to the world, will not be an unacceptable communication to the Royal Asiatic Society of London.

In offering a detail of the contents of the Pancha Tantra, it was of course desirable to collate them with those of the Hitopadeśa, and Kalíla wa Damna, which has been accordingly effected; and to relieve the dryness of analytical detail, as well as to convey an idea of the merits of the composition, it has been thought advisable to introduce translations of a number of the stories. Some affinities have also been pointed out between the narratives of the Pancha Tantra, and those met with in popular works in Europe; but the want of access to books has necessarily limited this part of the inquiry. Some illustrations of national or literary peculiarities have also been occasionally, but sparingly, added; lest the paper should be rendered too voluminous, and under the impression that many members of the Society are better able to appreciate the extent to which such illustrations may be needed, and better qualified to supply them.

The *Pancha Tantra* is so called from its being divided into five *Tantras*, or sections, and is referred to under that name in the Hitopadeśa. It is better known, however, in common speech, by the denomination of *Panchopákhyána*, which may be rendered the "Five (collections of) Stories:" and under this appellation the work may be met with in most parts of India.

The ensuing analysis is founded upon an examination of three copies of the work; one of which was procured in Calcutta, the others in Benares. These copies agree in all essential points, although they present, abundantly, the variations to be expected in compilations of such a character; where stanzas, and even stories, are often omitted or inserted at the pleasure of the transcriber.

The invocation, with which, like all Hindu works, the Pancha Tantra commences, differs very importantly from that of the Hitopadeśa. In the latter work, it is addressed to Śiva, in the former to Saraswatí. One manuscript, indeed, calls upon all the Hindu Pantheon, on Brahmá, Rudra, Kumára, Hari, Indra,

Yama, &c. &c., the elements, the planets, the Munis, Rishis, and all the other objects of Hindu reverence, to be propitious to the reader; but this is a solitary reading, and a probable interpolation. The homage to Saraswatí is followed by a tribute of respect to the authors of ethical compositions, of whom are named Manu, Váchaspati, Uśanas (Śukra), Paráśara, Vyása, and Cháńakya.[1] It is then stated, that Vishńu Śarmá, having extracted the essence of all the most celebrated works of this class, composed the *Níti*[2] *Sástra,* in five Tantras, or chapters. We are then introduced to the

[1] Authors of very different character. The first is the Legislator, whose code has been rendered into English by Sir William Jones. The works of Váchaspati, the teacher of the Gods, and of Śukra, the preceptor of the (daityas) Titans, have not, it is believed, been found on earth.* Paráśara, the father of Vyása, is the reputed author of an institute of laws, and the chief interlocutor of the Vishńu-Puráńa. To Cháńakya is ascribed a treatise on (Níti) regal polity, which is cited by authors of some antiquity, as Dańdí, in the Daśa Kumára [p. 183.] Cháńakya was the minister of Chandragupta, and the chief agent in his elevation to the throne of Magadha. [Lassen, Ind. Alt., II, 199 ff.]

[2] Sir Wm. Jones translated the term Níti by Ethics, and he has been followed by all Sanskrit scholars, in the interpretation. This is not, however, the precise import of the term. As applied to a class of writings, or division of science, it would be, more correctly, polity, the art of regal administration, both in peace and war, inclnding the moral, as well as political, obligations of a sovereign. [Benfey, Pantschatantra. Leipzig: 1859. I, p. XV.]

* Váchaspati is the same with Vrihaspati, as Uśanas is identified with Śukra. Institutes of law, ascribed to Vrihaspati and to Uśanas, are extant.—H.T.C.

frame work of the whole, the education of the King's sons by Vishńu-Śarmá; on which occasion the apologues were composed. This is introduced in the Hitopadeśa, but with some variations; and, as it affords an example of the concurrences and disagreements of the two collections, I shall give it at length from the Pancha Tantra.

"There is a city in the Southern country, named Mahiláropyam, the king of which, learned, munificent, distinguished among princes and scholars, was named Amara Śakti. He had three sons, youths of no capacity, nor diligence: Vasu Śakti, Bhadra Śakti[1], and Ananta Śakti. Observing them averse from study, the king called his counsellors, and said to them, "you are aware that my sons are little inclined to application, and incapable of reflection. When I contemplate them, my kingdom is full of thorns, and yields me no pleasure. It is said by the wise, 'Better is a son unborn; better is a dead son, than one who is a fool. The first may cause affliction for a little while, but a fool, as long as life endures.' Again 'of what use is a cow who has no milk with her calf; of what use is a son who has neither knowledge, nor virtue? Better it is, that a wife be barren, that she bear daughters or dead children, and that the family become extinct, than that a son, endowed with your form, wealth, and family-credit, should want understanding.' If, therefore, by any means, their minds can be roused, do you

[1] In some copies, Ugra-śakti.—H.T.C[olebrooke].

declare it." On this, a counsellor replied, "Prince, the study of grammar alone is the work of twelve years, how then is a knowledge of Dharma, Artha, Káma, and Moksha[1], to be speedily conveyed?" Another counsellor, named Sumati, observed, "Prince, the powers of man are limited by his transitory existence; but to acquire a knowledge of language alone, demands much time. It is better that we think of some means of communicating the substance of each science, in a compendious form; as it is said, 'The Śabda Śástra (Philology) is a boundless ocean: life is short, and the difficulties are many; the essence, therefore, is to be taken, as the swan extracts the milk from the water.'[2] There is a Brahman, named Vishńu Śarmá, celebrated for his perfect acquisition of the sciences. To him entrust your sons, and he will render them well informed." On hearing this, the king sent for Vishńu Śarmá, and addressed him, "Venerable Brahman, confer a favour upon me, by instructing these princes in polite literature, and rendering them superior to the youths, their companions; in recompense of which, I promise you lands of large extent." Vishńu Śarmá

---

[1] The four objects or occupations of human life: Duty, Wealth, Desire, and Final Liberation.

[2] This is a popular nation among the Hindus, originating, probably, in the colour of the bird. (Or rather, because the bird seems, as the Hindus apprehend, to extract his food, by suction, from solution in water; wherefore a bird of this genus is considered to be an emblem of discrimination, as being capable of separating milk from water.—H.T.C.)

replied, "Hear, O king, my words. I am not a retailer of knowledge for lands and wealth; but if I do not instruct your sons in the Níti Śástra, I will forego my own name. There is no need to say more. I do not utter this vaunt through any desire of wealth; for wealth is useless to any one whose passions are mortified, and subdued: I wish but to gratify you, and to do the will of Saraswatí. Let it be written, therefore, that if, in six months from this day, I do not make the princes more proficient than many people, in various branches of knowledge, it shall not be allowed to me, a Brahman, to point out the way of God." The king, highly gratified by this assurance, delivered his sons to him, and retired; and Vishńu Śarmá, taking the princes with him, repaired to his own house; where, for their instruction, he composed these five chapters: Mitra bheda, dissension of friends; Mitra prápti, acquisition of friends; Kákolúkíya, inveterate enmity; Labdha praśamana, loss of advantage; Aparíkshita káritwa, inconsiderateness. Reading these, the princes were, in six months, highly accomplished; and the five Tantras became famous throughout the world. Whosoever reads this work, acquires the whole Níti Śástra, and will never be overthrown by Indra himself."

The commencement of the Pancha Tantra, which is thus given, differs materially, in some respects, from the Hitopadeśa, of which the Mitralábha, or acquisition of friends, constitutes the first, and the Mitra bheda, or dissension of friends, the second book. The arrangement of the Pancha Tantra is, no doubt, the original, as the same is observed in the Kalíla wa Damna of 'Abdallah Mokaffah, exclusive of the avowedly additional prolegomena. It may here also be observed, that in the large collection of stories, made by Somadeva in the eleventh century, and usually known as the *Vŕihat Kathá*, we have a chapter appropriated to the same stories, that occur in this section of the Pancha Tantra, following nearly the same order. I shall, therefore, refer occasionally to this series also in my remarks; and shall here state, that it begins in the same manner as the Pancha Tantra, and its Arabic translation, with the journey of the merchant, and his abandonment of his ox, Sanjívaka, in the forests, on the borders of the Yamuná.

Many varieties of minor importance occur in this part of the story, not only as related in the Hitopadeśa, but as told in different copies of the Pancha Tantra. They are, however, of no consequence. It is only worth while to observe, that most copies of the latter agree in naming Mahiláropya as not only the residence of Amara Śakti, but as the city whence the merchant departs. One manuscript has a laboured description of the splendour and strength of the town. Now, in general, in both the Pancha Tantra and the Hitopadeśa, the places named are real[1]; and there seems every

---

[1] So Agnolo Firenzuola, the Florentine translator, has laid the scenes of the several narratives in various real localities, transferred to Italy.

reason, therefore, to conclude, that Mahiláropya was a city, in the south of India, of some celebrity, when these stories were first composed. We need not be much at a loss for its identification, as the name approaches sufficiently to Mahilapur, Meliapur, or St. Thomé; where our own records indicate a city of some consequence, in the beginning of the Christian era, as the scene of the labours and martyrdom of St. Thomas, occurrences very far from invalidated by any arguments, yet adduced against the truth of the tradition. The Hitopadeśa changes the residence of the King to Pátaliputra, on the Ganges; and although it leaves the merchant's residence in the south, it alters the name to Suvarńavatí, that is, the "Golden." Hamilton calls St. Thomé, Mailapúr, "The City of the Peacock," and the import of Mayil, in the Tamul language, is a Peacock, whilst púr is the ordinary Sanskrit addition, signifying town. There is no good authority, however, for supposing this to be the original designation of Meliapúr, and it may be only a vernacular modification of the name, whilst Mahiláropya furnishes a much nearer approximation to the Maliarpha of Ptolemy, which has been hitherto supposed the same with Meliapúr, or St. Thomé.*

* [Lassen, Ind. Alt., III, 204, places Maliarpha much further north, near Masulipattana. It has also been shewn by Babington (Lassen, l. l., I, 165) that the original name of Meliapúr was Mahámalayapura, with which it would be more hazardous to identify Mahiláropya than with Maliarpha.—According to the popular etymology, Meliapúr more probably means Jasmine-town

The name of the ox that falls, and is left behind, is in all the books, Sanjívaka, whence the Arabic Shanzebeh; those of the jackals, Karaťaka and Damanaka, altered to Kalíla and Damna. The lion is uniformly termed in the Sanskrit Pingalaka; the Arabic leaves him unnamed.

The first story, in all the Hindu books, is "the monkey and the timber." It is the second in the Arabic. The story of "the man, who could not avoid his destiny," related by the merchant's servant, is an addition; being, however, grafted upon a verse, in the original, which inculcates the irresistible force of fate. "What fate protects, is safe, though it be unwatched; and that which is guarded with the greatest precaution if destiny defend it not, will surely be destroyed. One who is left without a guardian in a forest shall escape with life; whilst another perishes in the house, and in spite of every care."*

There is a very great variety in the different manuscripts, in the passages that follow. The Hitopadeśa has also the story of "the Dog and the Ass," which is not found in the Pancha Tantra, Kalíla wa Damna, or Vŕihat Kathá: the next story, in all these three, being "the Fox and Drum," which the Hitopadeśa omits.

The Hitopadeśa has again the story of "the Cat and

(mayilei) than peacock-town (mayil). See Graul, Reise in Ostindien. Leipzig: 1856. Vol. III, p. 355 and Winslow's Tamil Dictionary s. v. mayilei.]

* [Panchatantra I, p. 24. Benfey, l. l., I, § 28.]

the Lion," in which it differs from all the rest; whilst the Pancha Tantra has the story of "Dantila, a merchant of Varddhamána," which does not occur in the Arabic.* The merchant incurs the displeasure of the sweeper of the palace, who, in revenge, mutters insinuations against his character, for the king to overhear. When questioned farther, he pretends not to know what he has uttered, and to have talked in his sleep: the insinuations, however, produce their effect. When the merchant has discovered the cause of his disgrace, and reconciled the menial Gorambha, the latter takes an opportunity of venting an insinuation against the king himself, so wholly absurd, that the prince is convinced, his servant prattles unmeaningly, and he acknowledges the merchant's innocence. The object of this story is to shew, that the meanest individuals, about the person of a prince, are not to be offended with impunity.

The story of "the goblin Ghańtákarńa," is peculiar to the Hitopadeśa. That of "Kandarpaketu," agrees in the general course, although not in the first part, with the adventures of "Deva Śarmá," in the Pancha Tantra, which latter is precisely followed in the story of the Násik, or religious man, in the Kalíla wa Damna; and Tahíd, in the Anvári Soheilí. One of the incidents of this story has attracted extraordinary admiration, if we may judge by the endlessly varied copies, and

** [Benfey, l. l., § 40—41. H. Kurz ad "Esopus. von B. Waldis" Leipzig: 1862, B. I, fab. 69.]

modifications of it, which have appeared in the East, and in the West: the loss of her nose by the confidante and its supposed recovery by the intriguante, for whom she had been substituted, affording a miraculous proof of the wife's innocence, imposing upon her husband, has been retold in a vast number of ways. It is repeated, with different degrees of modification, in the "Roman and Turkish Tales," in the "Decameron" of Boccacio [VII, 8.], the "Novelle" of Malespini [140.], the "Cent nouvelles Nouvelles," [38.], the "Cheveux Coupés," a fabliau, by Guérin,* in the "Contes" of La Fontaine [I, 31.], in the "Women pleased," of Beaumont and Fletcher [Act III, Sc. 4.], and in "The Guardian" of Massinger.** The story itself, as told in the Hitopadeśa, has been versified by Hoppner; and, as narrated in the Anvári Soheili, it has been rendered into English verse, by Atkinson.***

The next story, in the Pancha Tantra, is omitted in all the works, derived from this original. It is, however, a well known story, being the same as Malek and Shírín in the Persian Tales, and the Labourer and Flying Car in the additional stories from the Arabian Nights.† It is also narrated, with some variation, in the Vŕihat Kathá [Tar. 12]. The Muhammedan con-

---

* [ap. Legrand d'Aussy, Fabliaux. Paris: 1829, Vol. II, p. 340.]

** [ed. of. 1813, Vol. IV, p. 185.]

*** [Benfey, l. l., I, p. 140–47. F. H. von der Hagen, Gesammtabenteuer. Vol. II, p. XLVIII ff.]

† [transl. by J. Scott. 1800, p. 1 ff.]

trivance of a box, and the personification of Muhammed, are rather clumsy substitutes for the fiction of the original, in which the adventurer, in love with a princess, personates Vishńu, and rides on a wooden representation of Garuda guided by a pin, and moving by magic, the prototype of the flying steed of Magellan; "the wondrous horse of brass, on which the Tartar king did ride," and other self-moving machines of celebrity, in oriental and chivalric romance.*

The story of "the Gopí and her two lovers" is here peculiar to the Hitopadeśa; but it is familiar to European story-telling. It is the third of the three fabliaux, De la Mauvaise Femme,** and occurs in Le Roman des Sept Sages,*** and the Novelle of Bandello [II, 11], Boccacio [VII, 6], Sansovino [III, 10], and other similar collections.

The next story of "The Two Crows," is common to all the collections; as is that, interwoven with it, of "The Crane, or Swan, killed by the Crab."† This portion of the original has been made great use of by the author of the Bahár Dánish, who has compiled his story of "The Mouse and Prince of Ghilán" almost wholly of extracts from the Pancha Tantra. This portion of the latter work contains a quotation of some

---

* [Benfey, l. l., I, p. 159-63. Gesammtabenteuer, I, p. CXXXV ff.]

** [Legrand d'Aussy, IV, p. 189—91.]

*** [ed. Keller, p. CL. Cf. Benfey, l. l., I, p. 163—97.]

† [Benfey, l. l., I, p. 167—79. B. Waldis' Esopus II, 26, and note.]

interest in the literary history of the Hindus. It is a passage from the astronomical writings of Varáhamihira, and occurs, without variation, in the two best manuscripts of the original. This citation is justly considered, by Mr. Colebrooke, as a proof of the astronomer's priority to the composition of the Pancha Tantra, and a satisfactory corroboration of other arguments, favourable to his existence, at the time usually assigned to him, in the fifth century of the Christian era.[1]

A striking proof occurs here, also, of the more exact correspondence between the Pancha Tantra and Kalíla wa Damna, than between the latter and Hitopadeśa. In the story of "The Two Crows," the interwoven story in both the former works is that of "The Crane, or Swan, killed by the Crab;" and it is not till the apologue of the Crows is closed, that the "Lion led into a Snare by the Hare" occurs. In the Hitopadeśa the first is omitted, and the second put in its place; and instead of a Hare, the beguiler of the forest monarch is an old Stag. The story of "The Crab and (Vaka) Crane," is not found in the Hitopadeśa earlier than the last section, or Sandhi, to which several of the fables, belonging to this part of the Pancha Tantra, are transferred.

The next story, "The Flea, the Bug, and the King," is omitted from the Hitopadeśa. It occurs in the Kalíla wa Damna, but not exactly in the same order.

---

[1] As. Res. IX. 364, and Hindu Algebra, Introd. Also Preface Sanskrit Dictionary, xiv. [Benfey, l. l., II, 392—96.]

The adventures of the Jackal, who falls into the dyer's vat, are not given in the Arabic version. They are told in the Hitopadeśa, but in a different section, that of Vigraha, or war [ed. Schlegel et Lassen, p. 91]. They are also copied in the Bahár Dánish.

The next story of "The Lion with his three Ministers (the Tiger, Crow, and Jackal), and the Camel," whom they ensnare and destroy, holds the same place in the Pancha Tantra, and Kalíla wa Damna. It is briefly told in the Hitopadeśa, but in the Sandhi section, or Chapter on Peace [p. 121].

The ensuing story of the Ṭiṭṭibha occurs in all the three works in the same place; but there is a great difference in its internal arrangements. In the Hitopadeśa [p. 72], it includes no other apologue whatever; in the Kalíla wa Damna only one, "The Tortoise and the Geese"; in the Pancha Tantra it comprehends five: "The Tortoise and the Geese"; "The three Fishes"; "The Elephant, destroyed by the Sparrow, the Woodpecker, the Fly, and the Frog"; "The Swan, creeping Plant, and Fowler"; and "The Ram killed by the Lion". In the Kalíla wa Damna the first, as observed, occurs in the same place, the second somewhat earlier, and the other three are omitted.[1]

In the Hitopadeśa the two first occur in the fourth section [p. 110]; the other three are wanting.

The story of the Ṭiṭṭibha, or Titawé, is one of the

[1] They appear to have been wanting in Mr. Sotheby's copy of the Pancha Tantra.—H.T.C.

decisive proofs of the Indian origin of these fables. The personified ocean, or Varuńa, and Garuḋa, the bird of Vishńu, are inadequately represented by the Vakíl al Bahr and the Anka, the king and lord of the feathered race. But the name of the bird is alone sufficient. The Titawé, although it is found in the Arabic lexicons, and is said to be a species of the Katá,[1] has very little appearance of an Arabic term; nor can it be resolved to any satisfactory root. It is, therefore, probably only a transcript of the Sanskrit Ṫiṫṫibha, Bengali Ṫiṫib, and Hindu Ṫiṫṫhrí: the names, throughout India, for a kind of Sandpiper,[2] very numerous on the sandy banks and shores of rivers. The strutting gait of this bird is supposed, universally, to indicate his inordinate conceit; and thence the appropriate selection of him, in the story, as defying the sea. This characteristic is so commonly attributed to the Ṫiṫṫibha,

---

[1] The Katá is described as a bird frequenting watery places. Golius and Meninski explain (قطا) Katá, avis columbæ similis magnitudine et formâ, quæ gregatim volat; et e longinquo aquam petere novit, vocem, kattá, edens, unde illi nomen. [See also S. de Sacy, Chrest. arabe, (2nd edit.) II, 368 ff.] Thére are said also to be two kinds, one much larger than the other. Burckhardt, in his Travels in Syria, calls the Katá a species of partridge, and mentions their being met with in the mountains of Belba, Kerek, Djebel, and Thera, in such flocks, that the Arab boys often kill two or three at a time, by throwing a stik at them. The Ṫiṫṫibha is encountered tn numerous flocks, but is in size unlike either a pigeon or a partridge, and is a very different bird.

[2] The Ṫaṫihrá or Ṫaṫihrí (Sansk. Ṫiṫṫibha) is a Jacana, the Parra Goensis of Gmelin, or Tringa Goensis of Latham. See Am. Dict. p. 125, and Hunter's Hind. Dict. I. 514.—H.T.C.

that it is proverbially said to sleep on its back, with its legs upwards, to prevent the sky from falling.*

This section of the Hitopadeśa, or Mitra Bheda, contains no more apologues, but closes with that of The Birds and Sea, and the engagement between the Lion and the Bull, and the death of the latter. In the Pancha Tantra, the Kalíla wa Damna, and Vṙihat Kathá, the Jackals converse together, during the contest, and narrate several stories. The first, in the former work, is that of the Lion tricked out of the Camel's flesh by the Jackal, which is not related in any of the rest, being very like that of The Lion, his Ministers, and the Camel, noticed above.**

A small cluster of stories occurs in the Pancha Tantra, which are all omitted in the other works. They are peculiarly Hindu; and, as novelties affording some relief to the dry detail hitherto pursued, we shall translate them.***

"In Ayodhyá, the capital of Kośala,[1] reigned a monarch of great splendour and power, named Purushottama. On one occasion, the Governor of the Forests came and announced to him, that the woodland chiefs were all in a state of rebellion, instigated and

---

* [A Hindustani proverb says: ṫatíhrí se ásmán thámá jácgá? i. e. will the sky be supported by the sandpiper?]

** [Benfey, l. l., I, p. 251.]

*** [Benfey, l. l., I, p. 253 ff. II, p. 142—48.]

[1] The province of Oude and its capital, the modern Faizábád, is usually identified with the ancient city in popular belief. [Lassen, Ind. Alt., I, 129.]

headed by Vindhyaka, the Rájá of the Vindhya[1] hills. The king sent his chief minister Balabhadra, to quell the rebels.

"When Balabhadra was gone, there came to the capital, at the close of the rains, a Śramaṅaka,[2] or mendicant of the Bauddha religion, who, by his skill in divination, his knowledge of hours, omens, aspects, and ascensions, his dexterity in solving numbers, answering questions, and detecting things covertly concealed,* and his proficiency in all similar branches of knowledge, acquired such fame and influence, that it might be said he had purchased the country, and it was his own. The report of his reputation at last reached the king, who sent for him, and treating him with great civility, asked him whether it was true, that sages could tell the destinies of others. The mendicant replied, Your Majesty will know by the result. They then entered into conversation, in which he so entertained the king, that his daily society became indispensible.

"One day he absented himself from court; and on

---

[1] The authority of the Kośala monarch appears to have extended much beyond the limits of the modern province of Oude: an inscription found at Ratnapur in the Chatis-ghar district, dated Śalivâhana 781, or A.D. 859, states that province to be dependent upon the sovereign of Kośala. [Journal R. As. Soc., Vol. IV, p. 5 ff.]

[2] From subsequent passages, however, it appears that the usual confusion of Bauddha and Jaina occurs in the Pancha Tantra; and that, in fact, the latter alone is intended, whichever be named.

* [Benfey, l. l., II, p. 440, Note 600.]

the next, when he made his appearance, he accounted for his absence by stating that he had been upon a visit to Paradise; and that the deities had sent by him their compliments to the king. The king was simple enough to believe him, and was filled with astonishment and delight. His admiration of this marvellous faculty so engrossed his thoughts, that the duties of his state, and the pleasures of his palace, were equally neglected.

"Things were in this condition, when the valiant Balabhadra, having reduced the forest chieftains to obedience, returned. To his surprise, he found the king in a close conference with a naked mendicant, instead of being, as usual, surrounded by his ministers. Having ascertained from the latter, the pretensions of the ascetic, he approached the monarch, and inquired, if what he had heard of the mendicant's celestial visit, was truth. The king assured him that it was, and the ascetic offered to satisfy the general's apparent scepticism, by departing for Swarga in his presence. With this intent, the king and his courtiers accompanied the Śramańaka to his cell, which he entered, and closed the door. After some delay, Balabhadra inquired of the king when they were to see the mendicant again. He answered, 'have patience; the sage upon these occasions quits his earthly body, and assumes an ethereal person, with which alone he can approach Indra's heaven.' 'If this is the case,' replied Balabhadra, 'bring wood and fire, and let us burn his cell.' 'Why so,' asked the king. 'So please your Majesty,' answered the general, 'by consuming the earthly body of the ascetic, we shall prevent his re-assuming it, and then your Majesty will always have an angelical personage in your company. A case of this kind is well known.

"In Rájagŕiha dwelt a Bráhman named Deva Śarmá. He had no children, a subject of bitter affliction to his wife, who could not look upon a neighbour's infant without tears. At last her husband desired her to desist from farther lamentation, as by the efficacy of some mystic words he had secured her having a son of eminent beauty, and auspicious destiny. Highly delighted with this prophecy (indications of the fulfilment of which soon began to appear), the Bráhman's wife anticipated eagerly the period of her delivery. What therefore was her surprise, and the horror of her attendants, when the offspring, so anxiously sighed for, and impatiently expected proved to be a snake! The assistants exclaimed, Let the monster be destroyed. But the parent, with maternal affection, interfered to preserve her progeny, and carefully protected and reared the snake.

"After a time, the nuptial festivals of a neighbour's son awoke the envy of Deva Śarmá's wife and she reproached her husband for not having thought of a suitable match for their child. He replied, I would do so, if I could get admittance to Pátála, and present my supplications to Vásuki[1]. I do not think any other so

[1] The serpent monarch of Pátála, the region under the earth, inhabited by the Nágas, or snakes.

great a fool, as to wed his daughter to a son like thine. Finding, however, his wife was sadly distressed, he proposed, in order to divert her thoughts, that they should travel; and equipping themselves plentifully for their journey, they set out. After some months, they arrived at a city, named Bhaṫṫanagara, where they were hospitably received and entertained, on the night of their arrival, by an acquaintance. In the morning the Bráhman's friend asked him why he had come, and whither he was going. The Bráhman told him he was in search of a wife for his son; on which the other offered him his own daughter, a girl of great beauty, and insisted on his taking her away with him. Accordingly, Deva Śarmá returned to his own city with his destined daughter-in-law. When the people of the city saw her, they opened their eyes in admiration of her grace and loveliness, and asked her attendants, how they could think of sacrificing such a jewel of a girl to a serpent. Their words filled her servants with distress, and they were urgent with the damsel to effect her escape. She refused, saying, It must not be; there are three things, which are final from the first: The command of a king, the vow of an ascetic, and the gift of a maiden. That too which is previously resolved by destiny, cannot fail to be, as it happened to Pushpaka, and the Ģods.

"The maiden's attendants now asked her, who Pushpaka was, and she thus proceeded:

"Pushpaka was the favourite parrot of Indra, a bird of wonderful beauty, extraordinary abilities, and prodigious learning. One day he was perched on Indra's hand, and was repeating the hymns of the Vedas, when Yama arrived. The parrot immediately flew, away abruptly. The Deities afterwards asked him why he had withdrawn; he replied, how could he face the destroyer of life. The Deities, in order to remove his fears, assured him that they would protect him; and, prevailing on him to accompany them, they returned to Yama, and begged him, at their intercession, to abstain from ever taking away the life of the parrot. Yama replied, that he knew nothing about the matter, and referred them to Kála (Time), to whom they accordingly repaired. Time referred them to Death, who, he said, was at hand: and they hastened to prefer their suit to him. They no sooner encountered the grisly terror, than the parrot fell dead. Exceedingly distressed and perplexed by this accident, they returned to Yama, and inquired of him what it meant; he replied, that Fate had fixed the parrot's life, and that no care on their parts would have been of any avail.

"Therefore, I say, whatever is foredoomed by destiny cannot fail to come to pass.

"In this manner she resisted their persuasions, and the marriage took place. She performed her duties diligently, feeding her serpent-husband during the day with milk, and keeping him in her chamber at night, in a spacious basket. One night she was alarmed by the appearance of a man in her chamber, and jumping up in terror, she ran to the door to make her escape.

The person called to her to stop, and dismiss her fears, as he was her husband; and, to assure her, reassumed his ophitic form, and crawled into the basket, whence immediately after, he again issued, in all the bloom and vigour of human adolescence, and glittering with gold and gems.

"In the morning, Deva Śarmá, who had observed what was going forward, approached the basket, before his son was risen, and seizing the deserted skin of the snake, threw it into the fire; in consequence of which the youth was constrained to adhere to his natural figure, and continued ever after to constitute the pride of his parents, and the happiness of his family."

"The king of Ayodhyá, having heard this narrative from Balabhadra, hesitated no longer to follow his advice. The mendicant's cell was therefore immediately set on fire, and he perished in the flames."

The next story in the Pancha Tantra, and Kalíla wa Damna, is that of The Monkeys and Fire-fly; and the moral is stated precisely to the same effect in both, that it is absurd to try to bend a stubborn tree, or prove a sword upon a stone.

The story of Dharma Buddhi and Dushṫa Buddhi*, the honest man and the rogue, as narrated in the Pancha Tantra, is faithfully followed in the Arabic, with the exception of an interwoven story, omitted in the latter. It is the story of the Vaka, or Crane, who tempted the Ichneumon to destroy the Snake, and

* [Benfey, l. l., I, p. 275—79.]

was afterwards destroyed by the same. The story occurs in the Sandhi section of the Hitopadeśa [p. 111].

The witty story of The Rats who eat iron, and the Hawks that carry off children, is the next in the Pancha Tantra, and Kalíla wa Damna*. It is the last of the section in the latter; but we have a few more stories in the former work, as the story of The Two Parrots who learned respectively harsh and gentle phraseology, according to their natural dispositions, to prove that merits and defects are innate.

The next story agrees, in name, with the last in the Kalíla wa Damna, being that of The King's Son and his Companions: the resemblance, however, proceeds no farther, the incidents being quite different, although some, if not all, of those in the Arabic tale, are to be found in other Sanskrit works. In the Pancha Tantra, a Prince, a Minister's, and a Merchant's Son, pass their days together in the woods and groves, hunting, riding on horses, or elephants, driving cars, and practising archery. Their fathers reproach them for their neglect of their several duties; and, in resentment, they determine to leave their home. They go to Rohanáchala, (Adam's Peak in Ceylon)**, where they find each a gem of great price; and to preserve it, on their way back, through the forests, where lay the Phellis, or Villages, of the Bhillas, they swallow the

* [Benfey, l. l., I, p. 283 f. H. Kurz ad B. Waldis' Esopus, Vol. II, p. 142. (B. III, fab. 96).]

** [Benfey, l. l., II, p. 447, Note 652.]

gems, and then convey them home in safety, although they narrowly escape being ripped open by the Pallipati, or chief of the foresters.

The Prince acquires a sovereignty of his own, and leaving to his two friends the direction of affairs, amuses himself in his palace, after his own fashion. He has a pet Monkey, as it is said "Parrots, Pheasants, Pigeons, Monkeys, and their like, are naturally the especial favourites of Kings." This Monkey he sets to watch him, as he sleeps in a pavillion, in his garden. A troublesome bee settles on the Prince's face, in spite of the Monkey's pains to drive him off, till the latter, highly incensed, snatches up his master's sword, and, making a blow at the bee, cuts off the Rájá's head.

This apologue, therefore, is a very old acquaintance, the moral is the same: a sensible foe is preferable to a foolish friend[1]. The death of Sanjívaka, the grief of the Lion, and the councils of the Jackals, close this, the first and longest division of the Pancha Tantra, in the same manner as the corresponding sections of the Kalíla wa Damna, Hitopadeśa, and Vṛihat Kathá. This first section, according to the original enumeration, comprehends thirty-one stories[2].

---

[1] The form familiar to us is the story of the Gardener, the Bear, and the Fly, in which it occurs in the Anvári Soheili, and Ayár Dánish. [Benfey, l. l., I, p. 292 ff. II, p. 538. B. Waldis II, 99, & note, Vol. II, 112.]

[2] In Mr. Sotheby's copy, only twenty-six.—H.T.C.

SECTION SECOND.

THE ACQUISITION OF FRIENDS.

The *Mitra Prápti*[1], or acquisition of friends, is the same as the Mitra Lábha of the Hitopadeśa, with the difference only of transposition. It is the same also as the seventh chapter of the Kalíla wa Damna: the sixth being a probable addition of the translator, who, in his idea of poetical justice, has put Damna upon his trial, and condemned him to death; occurrences not hinted at in the Hindu work. Neither have we the few narratives that occur in his section; nor are the moral remarks, or the judicial proceedings, of a Hindu complexion.

The Mitra Prápti opens, like the Mitra Lábha, with the description of the scene of action, placed by both in the South, with this variety, that the one states it to lie on the banks of the Godávari, and the other, that it was not very far from the city Pramadáropyam. The Crow, or Raven, Laghupatanaka, opens the business in all the copies. The fowler is very minutely described in the Pancha Tantra, as an inhabitant of the city, living by bird-catching, of an uncouth figure, with splay feet, and clumsy hands; round as a ball; sturdy, though advanced in years; clad in red

[1] It is also read Samprápti, which has the same import.

garments, with his hair bound into a knot on his head, carrying a net and staff, and followed by dogs: in short, he looked like Destiny with the fatal noose; like the personification of Sin; like the heart of iniquity; like the monitor of the wicked; like the friend of Death." This description is reduced to "like fate," in the Hitopadeśa; and in the Arabic, to "ill looks, and the net and the staff."

The Hitopadeśa [p. 10] is singular in the story told by Chitragríva, of "The Traveller and the Tiger," to dissuade the Pigeons from descending on the grain. The Pancha Tantra, again, is alone in the story, told by the same to recommend unanimity, of "the Bháruńda*," a bird with two necks, one refusing to part with a share of nectar, the other swallowed poison, and the bird died.

The other circumstances of this story are continued, alike in all, to the formation of the friendship between the Rat, and the Crow; but the discussion is much more protracted, and contains much more matter, peculiarly Hindu, in the Pancha Tantra, than in either of the other works. The Rat replies to the Crow's protestations, "I have no faith in your oaths; as it is said, 'Put no faith in a foe, who even has vowed friendship to you: Vŕitra was killed by Indra, in spite of his reiterated oaths[1].' Again, 'An enemy of the Gods is

* [Benfey, l. l., II, p. 525 suggests the form *bheruńda*. See also I, 309 & 538, and Loiseleur Deslongchamps, Essai sur les Fables indiennes. Paris: 1838, p. 45.]

[1] The story is narrated in several of the Puránas, and is al-

not to be destroyed until he places trust in them. The embryo of Diti was destroyed by Indra, only when she ceased to fear him*."

In another passage we have allusions to some traditions, which are but little known.—

"He that observes, 'I might say, I abound with amiable qualities, and no one can be inclined to do me harm,' speaks that which is ridiculous. It is related that the valuable life of Páńini (the grammarian) was destroyed by a lion; and an elephant demolished the sage Jaimini, though he composed the Mímánsá; an alligator killed the harmonious Pingala (the first writer on Prosody), on the sea-shore. Of what estimation is genius with irrational and ferocious brutes!"

Although the arguments, on either side, are continued for several pages, they are not intermixed with any narrative illustration in the Pancha Tantra, or Kalíla wa Damna. On the contrary, the Hitopadeśa inserts here the stories of the Antelope and the Jackal; and the Crow, the Cat, and the Vulture. Afterwards the several works proceed in a similar manner to the visit of the Rat and the Crow to Manthara, the Tortoise; to whom, and the Crow, Hirańyaka, the Rat related his adventures.

The commencement of this story is the same in all, but the Arabic version here is singularly close. The

---

luded to in the Ṙig-Veda. As. Res. vol. viii, p. 378. [Wilson, Ṙig-Veda, Vol. I, p. 85.]

* [Rámáy. I, 46 Schl., 47 Gorr. Vishńu Pur. p. 151 f., quoted by Benfey in "Mélanges Asiatiques," Vol. IV, p. 214.]

Hitopadeśa alone inserts the story of the young wife, who took her husband by the hair, and embraced him, to favour the retreat of her lover; a story well known in Europa, from its version by Marguerite of Navarre, in her "Stratagème d'une femme qui fit évader son galant, lorsque son mari, qui étoit borgne, croyoit le surprendre avec elle" [Nov. 6], and she borrowed it from the first story of the Mauvaise Femme*. It was made a similar use of by the Sieur D'Ouville**, Malespini [I, Nov. 44], Bandello [I, Nov. 23], and other raconteurs***. In place of this, the original, and the Kalíla wa Damna have the story of the woman, who exchanged picked for unpicked sesamum seeds, including that of the "Forester, Wild Boar and Jackal," which occurs a little farther on in the Hitopadeśa. A long train of adventures, told of a merchant's son, follows this, in the Pancha Tantra, only to shew that a man must obtain the wealth that is designed for him by fate. The close of this story is followed by one, narrated by Manthara, of Somillaka, a weaver, who is taught by some Spirits, that wealth is to be enjoyed, not hoarded; and this includes a story of the "Bull and the Jackals," to inculcate the folly of absurd expectations. These two last stories have, however, but little merit, and do not occur in the Arabic, any

* [Legrand d'Aussy, Fabliaux. Vol. IV, p. 188.]

** [Élite des contes. Rouen: 1680, p. 224.]

*** [Hitopadeśa traduit par E. Lancereau. Paris: 1855, p. 217-22. Hagen, Gesammtabenteuer, Vol. II, p. XXVII ff. Benfey, l. l., I, p. 367 f.]

more than in the Hitopadeśa. The latter story, with some variations, has given rise to an idiomatic compound in the Bengali language; and Bakáńdapratyása, indulgence in unreasonable expectation, comprises the pith of this story; the Baka, or Vaka, a crane, being substituted for the Jackal of the original. A verse of interesting resemblance follows the stories. Manthara says to the Rat, "Dismiss all anxiety regarding your lost wealth, as it is said, 'He, to whom the Swan owes her white feathers, the Parrot his green hue, and the Peacock his variegated plumage, He will provide me sustenance.'"

The addition of the Antelope to the friendly society occurs here, in the same manner, in all. The story of "the Elephant, liberated from his bonds by the Rat," of which we have a familiar version in the apologue of the Rat and the Lion, next occurs in the Pancha Tantra*. In its place, in the Hitopadeśa, we have the double story of the Prince, the Banker's Son, and his Wife, and of the Elephant and Jackal. There is none in the Kalíla wa Damna. The three works conclude with the same incident, the liberation of the Antelope from the hunter's snare, by the united efforts and devices of the Tortoise, the Crow, and the Rat.

This Tantra contains, in the original, eight stories. It is more amply illustrated in the Hitopadeśa, than in either of the other two works.

---

* [Benfey, l. l., I, p. 324 ff. H. Kurz ad B. Waldis I, fab. 14.]

SECTION THIRD.

INVETERATE ENMITY, OR WAR BETWEEN CROWS AND OWLS.

The third section of the Pancha Tantra corresponds with the eighth chapter of the Kalíla wa Damna, and the third chapter of the Hitopadeśa. In the last work, however, the belligerent powers are the peacocks and the geese. The choice of the Pancha Tantra is the genuine one, no doubt; not only from the character of the work itself, but its connection with a particular grammatical rule. The Sútras of Páńini afford a precept for the use of a particular affix, to form derivatives from compound terms, when enmity is implied[1]; and this rule is exemplified by the form Kákolúkika, in which káka, a crow, and ulúka, an owl, are compounded, to signify the natural antipathy that subsists between these birds. Now as language precedes grammar, this rule was invented to explain the purport of a word already in use; and as in all probability this word expressed a popular notion of great antiquity, its established currency influenced the author of the fables to select the owl and the crow for the purpose of his narrative. We can scarcely suppose, that it was an accidental choise, which afterwards gave rise to

[1] Páń. 4. 3. 125. [Benfey, l. l., I, p. 37. 335—39.]

the popular expression, and the introduction of the compound term; and which, consequently, would make the Pancha Tantra take precedence in date of the Sútras of Páńini. I may also add, that the substantive term Kákolúkika, which Páńini's affix (Bun) could form, appears very rarely, if ever, in the Pancha Tantra. The form used by the author of that work is more usually the attributive, Kákolúkíya, which is formed by a different affix (Chha).

The introductory matter of this section, descriptive of the quarrel between the Crows and Owls, and the consultations of the monarch of the former, with his five ministers, correspond very closely in the Pancha Tantra and Kalíla wa Damna; although they extend to a greater length in the former, and contain some matters curious in themselves, and reflecting light on several Hindu peculiarities: amongst these, the following enumeration of the officers of state, who are, or are not, to be relied upon with confidence, is quoted from the Mahábhárata, the Sabhá Parva*, in which Nárada, it is said, communicated their names to Yudhishṫhira. The full detail is, however, not given in that work, but the passage does occur, and the reference indicates, at any rate, the existence of the Mahábhárata prior to the date of the Pancha Tantra[1].

* [The enumeration does not occur in the printed edition, but is alluded to in v. 171 f.]

[1] A similar list occurs in the Bhairavi Tantra. [Kosegarten's edition has some various readings, on which see Benfey, l. l., II, p. 483 f. and Mélanges As., IV, p. 253.]

The Officers to be distrusted are eighteen.

1 Mantrí	The minister.
2 Purohita	The royal chaplain, or priest.
3 Senápati	The general.
4 Yuvarája	The young prince, associated in the empire, and designated as successor.
5 Dauvárika	Warden, or chamberlain.
6 Antarvanśika	The superintendant of the inner apartments.
7 Sannidhátryupadeshtá	A sort of master of the ceremonies.
8 Jnápaka	A master of requests.
9 Aśwádhyaksha	Master of the horse.
10 Gajádhyaksha	Master of the elephants.
11 Kosháddhyaksha	Superintendant of the treasury.
12 Baládhyaksha	Ditto of the forces, or perhaps the stores.
13 Durgapála	The governor of the fort.
14 Karapála	The ruler of the prisons.
15 Símápála	The superintendant of the boundaries, or lord of the marches.
16 Párishada	A companion.
17 Protkata bhritya	A courtier.
18 Átavikádhya	The forest chiefs, and others.

The fifteen, naturally attached to the monarch's cause, are

1 Janani	The qneen mother.
2 Deví	The queen.
3 Kanchukí	The confidential attendant.
4 Málika	The chaplet weaver, or florist.
5 Śayyápála	The bed-maker.
6 Śayyádhyaksha	The superintendant of the beds.
7 Sámvatsarika	The astrologer, or time-keeper.
8 Bhishak	Physician.
9 Jalaváhaka	The cup, or water-bearer.
10 Támbúlaváhaka	The betel-bearer.

11 Áchárya	The preceptor.
12 Anga-rakshaka	The captain of the body guard.
13 Sthána-chintaka	Quartermaster.
14 Chhatradhára	The umbrella-bearer.
15 Vilásiní	Female attendant and singer, &c.[1]

Besides these, spies were a very efficient part of the ancient Hindu regime. We have no particular enumeration of these, except its being observed, that for what is going on amongst his own party, the king's best spies are the physician, the astrologer, and the preceptor; and that men, who exhibit snakes and the like, are the best to observe the designs of the enemy.

We have then the cause of the enmity between these feathered tribes referred to the successful interference of a crow, in preventing the owl being chosen king of the birds, narrated in a similar manner in the Pancha Tantra, and the Arabic copy; it is omitted in the Hitopadeśa. That work, however, inserts two stories, those of the Birds and the Monkeys, and the Ass in a Tiger's skin, (the latter an apologue of very wide circulation); before the story, common to all three, of the Elephant and Hares, and the Reflection of the Moon.

The story of the Hare, the Sparrow, and the Cat, does not occur in the Hitopadeśa, although much of the discription of the hypocritical piety of the Cat is copied in the story of the Vulture and the Cat, in the first section of that work [p. 18]. Some of the com-

[1] It is by no means certain, that all these names are rightly interpreted, or even rightly extracted from the text; but the greater part do not admit of doubt.

ments, however, are spared. It may be observed, indeed, that a much more decisive vein of satire, levelled particulary at Princes and Devotees, runs through the Pancha Tantra, than either the Kalíla wa Damna, or Hitopadeśa: thus the Hare observes, when he sees the Cat away, as it is said, "Trust not in low persons, who exercise austerities for their own nefarious designs. Penitents are to be found at holy shrines, whose only virtue is in their vaunts."

The story of the Three Rogues, who persuade the Bráhman that his goat is something else, and so induce him to leave it to them, is the next in the Pancha Tantra, and Kalíla wa Damna: it occurs in the last section of the Hitopadeśa [p. 116]*.

An incident, rather than a story, next occurs in the Pancha Tantra, singly, that of a Snake killed by Ants. The device adopted by the king of the Crows, as narrated in the Pancha Tantra, and Kalíla wa Damna, reminds the reader of the story of Zopyrus; the councillor Chiranjíva being, at his own suggestion, stripped of his feathers, and smeared with blood, and left at the foot of the tree, in which state he is found by the Owls, and brought to their king. The discussions regarding his treatment, between the king and his ministers, are to the same purport in both works; but they are more detailed in the Pancha Tantra, and illustrated by very different stories.

The first minister, Raktáksha, who recommends the

* [For the literature, imitations &c. see Benfey, l. l., I, p. 355 ff.]

crow's being put to death, narrates, in order to shew that no confidence is to be placed in a reconciled foe, the story of the Snake and the Bráhman's Son*, comprising a brief apologue of the Swans and the strange bird. Neither of these is in the Arabic, or Hitopadeśa: and they may be therefore translated:

"In a certain country dwelt a Bráhman, who reaped no benefit from the cultivation of his grounds. As he was reposing one day in the hot season under the shade of a tree, he dreamt that he beheld a large hooded snake, coiled upon an ant-hill, at a little distance; and waking from his dream, he concluded that the snake must be the tutelary deity of the spot, who was little pleased with him, as one from whom he had never received any veneration. The Bráhman determined, therefore, to worship him; and boiling some milk, he placed it in a vessel, and carried it to the ant-hill, exclaiming as he laid the cup upon the ground, 'Lord of the soil, I have hitherto been ignorant of thy place of residence, and, therefore, only have foreborne thy worship; forgive my negligence, and accept my oblation. So saying, he left the milk and went home.'

"When he visited the ant-hill on the morning following, he found in place of the milk a Dínár[1], and this

* [Benfey, l. l., I, p. 359—61. Weber, Ind. Stud., III, p. 341 ff.]

[1] A gold coin. That there existed some connexion between this and the gold Denarius of the Romans, is not improbable, as has been shewn in another place. As. Res. XV. The indication of treasure by the presence of a snake is a common superstition among the Hindus.

was repeated daily. At last, the Bráhman having occasion to go to the village, appointed his son to present the oblation of milk in his absence. When the lad, upon the ensuing morning, found the Dínár as usual, it occurred to him, that the mound must be filled with coin; and that it would be the most eligible plan to kill its serpent-owner, and seize at once upon the whole treasure. Arming himself, therefore, with a stick, he lay wait for the snake, as he was lapping the milk, and struck him on the head. The blow failed to kill the snake, and the animal, inflamed with wrath, bit the lad with his poisonous fangs, so that he immediately died. The body was burnt by his people, who were at hand, and saw what had chanced. The father returned on the day following, and when he had heard the cause of his son's death, was satisfied that the event was not unmerited; declaring, that the vital elements will be ever snatched from those, who shew no tenderness to those living creatures, that repair to them for preservation, as happened to the Swans and their Lake. The persons present asked him to explain this allusion, and he thus replied:

"'In a certain country reigned Chitraratha, in one of whose gardens was an extensive lake, guarded by his troops. In this lake were golden swans, who moulted a feather once in every six months. A large bird, having joined them, was refused admission to their troop; they claiming the exclusive occupation of the pool by the fee of the moulted feather. After much discussion, the stranger bird applied to the king, and said, Sire, these swans have had the audacity to say, what have we to do with the king? we will not allow any one to reside here: and it was to no purpose that I expostulated with them on the impropriety of such language, and threatened to bring it to your knowledge. The king, having heard this, commanded his servants to go and kill the birds, and bring them to him; and they set off with this intent. When they approached the pool, an old swan, suspecting their purpose, persuaded the rest to fly away; and thus, although they preserved their lives, they lost the residence, which they refused to share with a guest.'

"Having related this tale, the Bráhman proceeded to worship the snake. The serpent, however, could not be tempted forth, but shewing himself at the entrance of his hole, he thus spoke: 'Avarice brings thee hither, and banishes all sorrow for thy son's fate, but there cannot be any cordiality between thee and me:' again, 'in the insane presumption of youth, your son struck me; I have bitten him, and killed him: how is it possible for me ever to forget his violence? how is it possible that you should ever forget his death? Take this jewel, therefore; depart, and never more approach this place.' Having thus spoken, and cast a gem of inestimable value to the Bráhman, he withdrew into his hole. The Bráhman took the jewel, but, considering its value much inferior to what he might have acquired by long assiduous homage, never ceased to lament the folly of his son."

The next story is also peculiar to the Pancha Tantra,

and indeed so decidedly of a Hindu character, that we need not be surprised at its omission, from the Arabic translation at least. It may be called the Fowler and the Pigeons. The fowler, having caught the female dove, is overtaken by a violent storm, and repairs for shelter to the tree inhabited by the male. Moved by the councils of his captive mate, and his own estimate of the rites of hospitality, he not only gives the fowler shelter in the hollow trunk, but collects dry leaves, and makes him a fire, and casts himself into the flames, to furnish his guest a meal. The bird-catcher liberates the dove, and she also throws herself into the fire; on which she and her lord assume celestial forms, and are conveyed to heaven in divine cars, agreeably to the text, that says, 'A widow, who burns herself, secures for herself and her husband enjoyment in Paradise, for as many years as there are hairs on the human body, or thirty-five millions[1].' The fowler becomes an ascetic, and voluntarily perishes in a burning forest.

The next story of the Husband, and his Wife, and the Thief, is translated in the Arabic, but does not occur in the Hitopadeśa. It has been imitated by the writers of Europe. The Bráhman, the Thief, and the Rákshasa, the next story, is the same with

---

[1] This text is attributed to Angiras, and forms part of the declaration or Sankalpa, pronounced by the widow at the time of her ascending the pile. — As. Res. vol. iv, p. 210. [Colebrooke, Essays, p. 71 f. Skandapuráńa, Káśikhańda IV, 59, quoted by Benfey, l. l., II, 495 & 542. I, 365.]

"the Ascetic, the Thief, and the Evil Genius of the Kalíla wa Damna.

The next story, of the Prince who had a snake in his bowels, is peculiar to the Pancha Tantra. He is cured by his wife. The eleventh fable is the same with the Husband under the Bed, of the Arabic, which occurs also in the third section of the Hitopadeśa. The next story, again, is the same in the Pancha Tantra, and Kalíla wa Damna, that of the Mouse turned to a young girl by a sage, and finally to a mouse again*. The Arabic translator, by his alterations, has lost the point of the story. He makes the sun &c. decline the marriage; but in the Sanskrit, the lady makes objections to all the proposed bridegrooms, till she sees the rat, when her natural propensities induce her to solicit her adoptive father to give her to him in marriage**.

The next story of "the Bird that voided gold with its dung" is peculiar to the Pancha Tantra; so is that of "the Fox, who detects the presence of a Lion in a cavern***:" neither tale has much point. The story of "the Snake and Frogs†" is told in all three works; but in the Pancha Tantra it is interrupted by the following: viz.

"The Bráhman and his Wife.

---

* [See the literature for No. 8–11 in Benfey, l. l., I, p. 366–73.]

** [Benfey, l. l., I, 373 ff. A. Weber, Indische Studien, III, 345. Die Fabeln des Sophos. Posen: 1859, p. LIII ff.]

*** [Benfey, l. l., I, 382. Die Fabeln des Sophos No. 45.]

† [B. Waldis, I, 17. Weber, Ind. Stud., III, 346.]

"There was a Bráhman, named Mandavisha, whose wife was a woman of loose character. She had a lover, to whom she was accustomed to carry delicacies and cates, which she prepared herself. Her husband, at last taking notice of this, inquired of her whither she took them, and to whom: she replied, I carry them as oblations to my tutelary goddess Deví, whose temple, you know, is close at hand. Pretending to be satisfied with this reply, the husband allowed her to proceed, but continued to watch her. As she found that he observed her, she went to the temple, and performed the customary oblations, and entered the building. Her husband immediately set off by another path; and getting into the edifice by a different entrance concealed himself behind the statue of the goddess. The wife, being afraid that her husband was still on the watch, determined to go through with the ceremony in earnest, and having presented the oblations, she thus prayed, "O! goddess, deign to inform me by what means my husband can be deprived of his eyesight." The husband, hearing this, disguised his voice, and answered, "Feed him daily with such cates as you have brought hither, and he will soon become blind." The wife returned home delighted, and put in practice the supposed instructions of the goddess. In a few days the Bráhman began to complain of dimness of vision, and shortly afterwards pretended to lose his sight. The wife, attributing this to the favour of the goddess, entertained no doubt of the fact; and in the confidence of not being detected, invited her gallant to come fearlessly to the house. The husband, however, now thoroughly apprised of the truth, lost no time in punishing her misconduct. Surprising the guilty pair, he beat the adulterer with his staff, till he expired; and, cutting off his wife's nose, he turned her away*."

The remainder of this section, and the destruction of the Owls by their more crafty enemies, corresponds in the Pancha Tantra, and Kalíla wa Damna.

The third section comprises seventeen stories.

SECTION FOURTH.

LOSS OF THAT WHICH HAS BEEN GAINED.

The fourth section of the Pancha Tantra, illustrative of the folly of losing what has once been acquired (*Labdha-praśamana*[1]) corresponds with the ninth chapter of the Kalíla wa Damna, which relates the story of "The Monkey and the Tortoise." The Arabic, or Pehlevi translator has, however, made rather short work with his original, and has turned the twelve tales of the latter into two.

The chief performers in this selection, and the cir-

---

* [Benfey, l. l., I, 385. In Kosegarten's text, and Benfey's translation, the name of the Bráhman is Yajnadatta, and, more appropriately, Mandavisha the name of the serpent who relates the story.]

[1] It is also read Labdha Prańaśana, and Labdha Prańáśa, but the sense is the same.

cumstances, out of which the tales arise, are the same; only, instead of a Tortoise, the treacherous friend of the Monkey is the Makara, a fabulous aquatic animal, which corresponds, in representation at least, with the Capricornus of the Greek Zodiac. The first story, narrated by the Monkey after his escape, is that of "the Snake and the Frogs." The former is introduced into his well by the King of the latter, to revenge him on his rebellious subjects. This being done, however, he devours the king's subjects, and finally the king himself. The moral is, "that hunger will be appeased, even in spite of crime*."

The next story is the only one of the section, found in the Arabic, that of "the sick Lion, the Jackal, and the Ass**."

The next story is that of "a Potter, who, having cut his forehead against some broken pots, is encountered, bleeding, by a Prince, and taken for a valiant warrior by him, in consequence of which he is enrolled amongst his guards. When the mistake is discovered, the prince orders him to withdraw: and when the potter requests that he may be allowed to stay, repeats to him the next story, that of "the two young Lions, and the young Jackal, brought up with them, but who betrays his origin by his cowardice, and is advised by the old Lioness, his adoptive mother, to withdraw

* [Benfey, l. l., I, 429.]

** [Benfey, l. l., I, 430 ff. Weber, Ind. Stud., III. 338. Die Fabeln des Sophos, p. LXXX.]

quietly, lest his foster brothers find him out and destroy him." The potter takes the hint, and walks quietly off.

The ensuing stories tend to the disparagement of the fair sex. The first is that of a Bráhman, who quits his home and family, and relinquishes half his life for the sake of a spouse, who, notwithstanding, deserts him for a lame beggar, and attempts his life: a story that is told also in the Daśa Kumára*. The next is to shew that there is no pleasing women, without complying with all their caprices; as the minister Vararuchi, to conciliate his wife, submitted to have his head shaved; and his royal master, Nanda, to gratify his queen, allowed her to put a bridle in his mouth, and mounting on his back, compel him to carry her about, neighing at the same time like a horse**.

The next story in this section is an apologue of very familiar character. "A washerman, the owner of an ass, dresses him up with the skin of a tiger, to frighten away intruders from his field: after a time the ass betrays himself by his braying, and gains a beating from the villagers." This is given in the Hitopadeśa, in the third section. [Fable 2.]***

The ninth tale is of a villager's wife, who is tempted

* [p. 150. Benfey, l. l., I, 436 ff. F. Liebrecht in Benfey's "Orient und Occident", I, 127. „Das Ausland", 1858, p. 845 ff.]

** [Benfey, l. l., I, 461 f. von der Hagen, Gesammtabenteuer, I, p. LXXV ff.]

*** [Benfey, l. l., I, 462 ff. II, 547. Weber, Ind. Stud., III, 338.]

to run away from her husband, and carry off his wealth. When she arrives, with her gallant, at a river, he persuades her to entrust him with the property, and her clothes, to convey them across; after which he is to return for her. This, however, he omits to do, and she is deserted. In this state she sees a Jackal approach with a piece of meat in its mouth. The Jackal, seeing a fish on the edge of the water, lays down the meat, to make the fish his prey: the fish escapes; and, in the mean time, a vulture carries off the meat. The deserted wife laughs at the incident, when the Jackal thus applies it to herself: "Your wisdom is double that of mine; for here you are, naked in the water, and have neither a husband nor a gallant *."

The story of "the Sparrows and Monkey," is the same as that of "the Birds and Monkeys," in the beginning of the third section of the Hitopadeśa.

The two next stories, which complete this section, are those of "the Jackal, who by his craft preserved the carcase of a dead Elephant from a Lion and a Tiger, and by his courage from another Jackal **;" and "the Dog who, in a famine, left his own town for another, but was driven back by the dogs of the strange place, and was glad to seek his own home again."

The Makara now retires, having previously been

---

* [H. Kurz ad B. Waldis I, 4. Weber, Ind. Stud., III, 339. Die Fabeln des Sophos, No. 31.]

** [taken, according to Benfey (I, 473) froh Mahábhár. I, 5567—92.]

told of his wife's death, and the invasion of his abode by an enemy: circumstances, omitted in the Arabic translation, as well as the stories to which they give rise.

There are twelve stories in this section.

SECTION FIFTH.

INCONSIDERATENESS.[1]

The fifth Tantra corresponds in purport with the tenth chapter of the Kalíla wa Damna, the Ascetic and the Weasel being intended to illustrate the folly of precipitancy. The Pehlevi or Arabic translator has, however, taken a similar liberty with his original as in the preceding section, and has reduced again twelve stories to two. The tales in the original, therefore, are mostly novel, and not very prolix. It may be observed, by the way, that in the last two Tantras of the work either the original compiler had exhausted his store, or less frequent additions have been made by subsequent hands; as the reflections and citations, which are most disproportionably interspersed in the three first sections, become now much less copious: an obvious improvement in the interest, if not in the utility, of the collection.

Vishńu Śarmá now remarked, "a man should never

---

[1] Aparíkshita-káritwa, inconsiderate conduct; acting without previous investigation.

attempt a business which he has imperfectly seen or understood, transacted or investigated, or he will meet with such mischance as befel the imprudent Barber." The Princes asking him, to what he alluded, he thus proceeded:

"In the south there is a city named Pátalipura, in which Mańibhadra, a banker, resided. Although attentive to his moral and religious duties, it was the will of fate, that he should lose his wealth, and be reduced to poverty. The insignificance, into which he consequently fell, preyed upon his spirits, and he indulged in such reflections as these:

"It is justly said, that amiable feelings, purity of manners, moderation, ability, suavity, and respectability, are qualities that shine with little lustre in the person of a poor man. Dignity, pride, discernment, conceit, or intellect are all lost, when a man is poor; as the freshness of the dewy season is dissipated by the breeze of spring. The most brilliant talents will be of little benefit to their possessor, whose thoughts are all occupied in devising means for the support of his family, and when, for the exercise of lofty fancies, are substituted clothes, rice, oil, salt and ghee. Men without wealth are of no note amongst their fellows. They perish, as they are born, unheeded, like bubbles on the stream."

"Impelled by these considerations, he determined to abstain from food, and so terminate his life. For what, he exclaimed, is the use of a miserable existence? With this resolve he fell asleep. In his sleep the

Padma-nidhi[1] appeared to him under the form of an old Jaina mendicant, and forbade him to despair. You have been, he said, a faithful worshipper of me, and I will not desert you. In the morning early, you shall see me again, as I now appear: do you then take a staff, and strike me on the head; on which I shall be changed immediately to a pile of gold. He then disappeared.

"When the merchant rose, in the morning, he recollected his vision, but could scarcely persuade himself, that it would so come to pass. He referred it to the subject of his previous thoughts; as it is said: To those who are in sickness, or in sorrow, whose

---

[1] The Nidhi is properly a treasure; and is especially a kind of wealth appertaining to Kuvera, the God of Riches. The nidhis, or their superintendants at least, are personifications; and are, as such, worshipped (See Megha Duta, in note ad v. 79). The worship is of the Tántrika description. The Śáradá Tilaka, a celebrated authority of that school, contains the following directions for adoring the Śánkha and Padma-nidhis, in conjunction with Lakshmí, the Goddess of Prosperity. "1. Let the votary worship the Śánkha-nidhi, and his spouse upon the right hand of the Goddess: him corpulent, and her full breasted: both adorned with pearls and rubies, both exhibiting gentle smiles upon their lotus-like countenances, locked in each other's arms, and each holding a lotus and a shell, both scattering showers of pearls, and each bearing a conch upon the forehead. 2. Let him adore the Padma nidhi, placed with his wife upon the left hand of the Goddess: both of the colour of minium, each in the other's embrace, and either holding a red lotus and a blue one: both employed in raining jewels, and either wearing a lotus as a crest: the male Padma nidhi corpulent, the female slender."

minds are occupied with anxiety or desire, the object of their waking wishes is presented in their dreams.

"At this time, the barber, who had been sent for by the merchant's wife, to pare her nails, arrived, and whilst he was busy at his work, the seeming mendicant appeared. Mańibhadra immediately recognized the figure of his dream, and snatching up a stick, struck him on the head; on which the figure changed to gold, and fell upon the floor. The banker took the gold to an inner apartment, desiring the barber not to mention to any one what he had witnessed. The barber promised secrecy, and went home, but could not help thinking of the occurrence. These naked mendicants, he muttered to himself, are all of one fraternity, and if one is changed into gold by a rap on the pate, why should not any other be changed in a similar manner? I will therefore invite their principals to my house, and then with a few strokes of a cudgel I shall surely get a quantity of the finest metal. These ideas he revolved in his mind the rest of that day, and all the night. When morning came, he went to the Vihára[1], and facing to the north, perambulated the Jina[2] three times. He then went on his knees, and holding up his hands with reverence, lifted up the edge of the curtain, repeating in a high tone this stanza, "Glory to those Jainas who possess the only true knowledge: and are thus enabled to traverse the wild

[1] The name of a Bauddha or Jaina convent.

[2] The deified sage who is the object of Jaina worship.

ocean of human passions." And again, "The tongue which glorifies, and the mind that is dedicated to Jina, are alone to be praised, with the hands that are busied in his adoration." Having uttered these, and similar invocations, he repaired to the chief of the convent, and kneeling at his feet, received his blessing. The barber then, in an insinuating tone, requested the favour of his coming, with his principal sages, to a slight recreation at his house. The principal replied, "How now, son; what is it you say? Are we Bráhmans, think you, to be at any one's beck and call? No, no; at the hour when we go forth to gather alms, we enter the mansions of those votaries only, who, we know, are of approved faith. Depart, therefore, nor reiterate thine offence." The Barber replied, "most venerable Lord, I shall obey, and do as you command, but I beg to mention, that I have a store of excellent cloths, for covers to our holy books; and of the materials for writing, which will be fitly disposed of, when time may serve." So saying he went home, and provided some stout bludgeons, which he hid in a corner; he then went back to the convent, and took his station at the gate; and, as the different ascetics came forth, he addressed them as he had spoken to their principal. Tempted by the wrappers for their books, they all listened to him favourably, and deserting their old acquaintances, followed the barber to his house; as it is said: The naked ascetic, who has abandoned his home, and all his possessions, is still no stranger to the desire of worldly goods. When the

Barber had introduced them into his house, he took up his staff, and struck them on the head, so that several were killed in an instant. The rest then, with broken skulls, set up so loud a clamour, that the neighbourhood was alarmed, and the town guards[1] flocked towards the spot, to see what was the matter. As they approached, they met the Jaina mendicants, fleeing with broken heads, and covered with blood, from the barber's house. Having learnt the cause of their dismay, they proceeded to lay hold of the barber, whom they bound and carried to the police. When questioned as to his conduct, he justified himself by the example of Mańibhadra: but when Mańibhadra, being sent for, and examined, revealed the extact nature of the occurrence, he was of course dismissed, whilst the barber was hanged, as a punishment for his violent and inconsiderate aggression.

"When the barber was disposed of, the judges remarked, that he had deserved his fate, as it is well said, that which has not been tried, should not be attempted, and that which is done, ought first to be well considered, otherwise repentance will follow, as in the case of the Bráhman and Ichneumon. Mańibhadra asked how that was, and they replied.

"There was a Bráhman, named Deva Śarmá, whose

---

[1] The Purakoshťapálapurusháh: The men who guarded the avenues of the city. Possibly there may be some etymological connexion between Koshťapála (Sanskrit), and Kotwál (Persian), an officer of Police.

wife had one son; she had also a favourite ichneumon[1], that she brought up with the infant, and cherished like another child. At the same time she was afraid that the animal would, some time or other, do the child a mischief, knowing its treacherous nature, as it is said, "A son, though ill-tempered, ugly, stupid and wicked, is still the source of delight to a father's heart." One day the mother, going forth to fetch water, placed the child in the bed, and desired her husband to guard the infant, especially from the ichneumon. She then departed, and after a while the Bráhman himself was obliged to go forth to collect alms. When the house was thus deserted, a black snake came out of a hole, and crawled towards the bed where the infant lay; the ichneumon, who saw him, impelled by his natural animosity, and by regard for his foster brother, instantly attacked him, and, after a furious encounter, tore him to pieces. Pleased with his prowess, and the service he had rendered, he ran to meet his mistress on her return home, his jaws and face besmeared with blood. As soon as the Bráhman's wife beheld him, she was convinced that he had killed her child, and in her rage and agitation, she threw the water jar at the ichneumon with all her force, and killed him on the spot. She then rushed into the house, where she found the child still asleep, and the body of a venomous snake torn in pieces at the foot of the bed. She then perceived the error she had committed, and beat her

---

[1] Nakula: Viverra mungo, C. [Benfey, l. l., I, 479. ff.]

breast and face with grief, for the unmerited fate of her faithful little favourite. In this state her husband found her on his return. When he had told her the cause of his absenting himself, she reproached him bitterly for that greedy desire of profit, which had caused all the mischief, forgetting, she said, the saying, "Excessive cupidity is to be avoided, although all desire of profit be not relinquished. The wheel whirls round his head, who evinced inordinate avarice." The husband asked her how that happened, and she replied:

"There dwelt in a certain town four Bráhmans, all intimate friends, and equally poor. They consulted together what was to be done; for poverty, they agreed, was intolerable. Patrons, however well attended, are dissatisfied; friends and sons desert the poor; merit is of no avail, and misfortunes multiply. Wives of the best family abandon their husbands; friends transfer their attachment to more powerful individuals. Again, let a man be brave, handsome, eloquent, and learned, without wealth, he obtains not any enjoyment, and is as a dead man amongst the living. Better death, than poverty. Again, it is said, "Arise, my friend, for a moment, and remove the burden of indigence from my fate, that I may share with you the felicity which death affords. It is better, therefore, to go to the cemetery at once, and become a corpse, than live in poverty." The friends assented to this, and agreed, that every effort should be adopted to acquire wealth, as it is said, nothing is obtained by him who has not money. Let, therefore, the wise man attach himself to its acquirement. Wealth is acquirable by six means: begging, service, agriculture, science, usury, and trade: of which, trade is the best, as its profits are most independently realized; as it is observed: "The food obtained as alms may be carried off by crows; the favour of a prince or patron may be withdrawn; agriculture is laborious; and the respect to be paid to a preceptor in acquiring knowledge is troublesome; usury brings poverty on other people; so that the only method eligible is trade. Money is made in trade in seven ways: by defective weights and measures; by false statements of price; by the lapse of deposits; by receiving the securities of friends; by managing estates for others; by dealing in perfumes; and by exporting goods for sale. In the first case, it is pretended that the measure is full, when it is not. In the second, selling a thing for more than its worth is the natural practice, even of barbarians. While a deposit is in his house, the merchant prays to the gods that the owner may die, when he will make them suitable offerings. When a trader sees an acquaintance coming to borrow, he pretends to lament his misfortune, but is inwardly delighted. In the management of estates is the reflection, I have got hold of lands full of treasure. Of all goods[1], perfumes are the best: gold is not to be compared to the article which is procured for one, and is parted with

[1] See remarks at the close of this Essay.

for a thousand. Exporting commodities is the proper business of persons already wealthy; as it is said, 'Those who are wealthy are heard of from afar.' Riches are attracted by riches, as wild elephants are caught by tame ones. Capital is multiplied twice and thrice over, in repeatedly buying and selling, by those who have knowledge, and travel to other lands. The idle and weak alone are afraid of foreign countries. 'Crows, deer, and dastards, die in their native place.'

Having thus reflected, the four friends determined to quit their home, and set off together on travel. The man, whose mind is intent on wealth, leaves his friend and family, his mother and his natal soil, and roams to foreign and ungenial lands, without a moment's hesitation. After some days, the Bráhmans arrived at Avanti (Ujjayiní), where they bathed in the Siprá, and worshipped Mahákála[1]; after which they proceeded, and met with a Yogí named Bhairavánada, with whom they formed an acquaintance, and who invited them to his abode. He inquired of them the purpose of their journey. They said, they were pilgrims in search of magic power, repairing to the shrine where wealth or death awaited them; as it is said, 'The water that falls from Heaven may sometimes flow in the realms below the earth. The force of fate is inconceivable, and man is weak against it. The

---

[1] One of the twelve great Lingas, and well known to have been especially worshipped at Ujjayini. This Linga was destroyed by Altumák, in 1231.

objects of man may be apparently attained by mortal efficacy: but that is fate; for when you speak of human qualities, you give that name to destiny; at the same time, ease is not here the source of ease, nor can it be enjoyed without exertion. The destroyer of Madhu (Vishńu) seized Lakshmí forcibly, and held her clasped in a firm embrace. Tell us, therefore, they continued, if you are acquainted with any drug of virtue, to carry us into secret chasms, and tame the imps of evil; or efficacious in the rites of charnel grounds. You, they said, are an adept; we are but novices, but we are resolute. None but the illustrious can satisfy the wishes of the worthy. The ocean alone supports the subterrestrial flame.'

The Yogí, finding them apt scholars, admitted their request, and gave them four magical balls, one a-piece, directing them to go to the northern side of the Himáchala mountains, where each, on the spot where the balls should spontaneously fall, would find a treasure. They accordingly went thither; and one of the balls soon fell on the ground. The Bráhman, to whom it belonged, with the assistance of the rest, dug up the soil, and there discovered a copper mine. He desired the rest to take as much as they liked, but they refused, determining to seek their fortunes farther. He replied, Go on, then, I shall return; taking therefore as much of the metal as he could, he went back, and the rest proceeded.

The ball belonging to another soon fell, and he dug up the spot, which proved to contain a silver mine.

Overjoyed, he exclaimed, "Let us go no farther, but take as much as we can, and then return." The other two, however, ridiculed his folly, and resolved to advance, hoping as they had at first met with copper, then silver, they should successively meet with metal still more valuable. So it proved, for the next ball that fell indicated a vein of gold, with which the man to whom the ball belonged entreated his companion to rest satisfied. The argument previously used, however, being justified by the discovery of gold, determined him to persevere, in the full confidence, that he should next come to a bed of diamonds. The discoverer of the gold mine declined accompanying him, and he went on alone—, the other promising to await his return.

The last Bráhman proceeded through solitary paths, scorched by the rays of the sun, and faint with thirst, till at last he came to a place which was whirling round, and on it stood a man, whose body was covered with blood, and on whose head a wheel revolved. He approached, and asked him who he was, and why the wheel was placed upon his head, and requested him also to shew him where any water was procurable; but he had scarcely spoken, when the wheel transferred itself from the crown of its late possessor to the head of the Bráhman. He exclaimed, How! what is this? and the stranger replied, You have taken the wheel from my head, and you must keep it, till some one like yourself shall come hither, with that magic ball in his hand, and shall address to you similar questions to those you have asked of me. The Bráhman inquired, how long a time he had passed in that plight. The stranger asked who was the present sovereign, to which the Bráhman answered, Víńávatsa[1]. The man then said, When Ráma reigned, I came hither, impelled by my poverty, and guided by the magic ball, as thou hast been: I found a man here with the wheel on his head, and asking him such questions as thou hast put, the wheel was fixed upon my head. I have been here ever since. And how did you get any thing to eat? inquired the Bráhman. The other replied, This law was fixed by the God of wealth, who fears his treasure should be plundered. His fears are known to the Siddhi Nágas[2], who send

---

[1] Udayana or Vatsa, the King of Kauśámbi, is probably intended here; he was celebrated for his skill on the Víńá, or Lute. This prince is the hero of the first chapters of the Vŕihat-Kathá, which gives this account of his descent. He is the son of Sahasráńika, the son of Śatánika, the son of Janamejaya, the son of Parikshit, the son of Arjuna. The genealogy of Arjnna's descendants, which Dr. Bnchanan Hamilton derives from the Bhágavata P., has no prince of this name. The son of Sahasráńika is termed Aśwamedhaja. The two works are also at variance, regarding the founder of Kauśámbi, the Vŕihat Kathá ascribing it to Sahasráńika, which is so far apparently most correct, that various works concur in styling Vatsa king of Kauśámbí, whilst the Bhágavata, however, calls the founder of that city Chakra, the fourth prince from Sahasráńika. Hindu genealogies, Introduction 13, and table 9. [Lassen, Ind. Alt., I, XXVI.]

[2] The Nágas are the serpents which inhabit the region under the earth. Siddhi means snperhuman power which may be ob-

men hither: but when a mortal arrives, he loses the sensations of hunger and thirst, and is exempt from decay and death. He retains alone the consciousness of solitude and pain. But now excuse me, I am released, and shell return home. So saying, he departed.

The Bráhman, who had found the gold mine, wondered why his companion tarried so long, and becoming at last impatient, he set off in quest of him. Tracing his course by the impressions of his feet, he followed him to the spot where he stood, and beheld him covered with blood, running down from his head, which was cut by the sharp edges of the wheel. To the inquiries of his friend he replied by telling him the property of the wheel—, and what he had witnessed. On which the other reproached him, saying, Did I not tell you to stop? but your lack of sense could not allow you to take my advice. It is very justly observed, 'Better sense than science; unless it improve by knowledge.' Those who want common understanding will as surely perish as did those who revived the Lion. The man with the wheel asked how that was, to which the other replied:

"There were four Bráhmans residing in the same village, all intimate friends. Three were men of great acquirements, but destitute of common sense. The

---

tained by their worship. Their being opposed to Kuvera, and desirous of encroaching on his wealth, although here stated in a popular form, is like many things in this work, no longer a familiar notion amongst the Hindus.

fourth was an intelligent fellow, but equally destitute of learning. As they were poor, they determined at one of their meetings to go to some country where learning was patronized, and where, they were satisfied, they should speedily be enriched with presents from the king. They accordingly set off, but when they had gone some way, the eldest cried out, 'It never occurred to me before, that our fourth friend here is illiterate. He is a man of sense to be sure, but that will not entitle him to any rewards from the king; we shall have, therefore, to relinquish to him a part of our earnings, and it would be fairer, I think, for him to remain at home.' The second agreed in this opinion, but the third opposed it, saying, 'we have always been friends and companions from infancy, and let him, therefore, participate in the wealth we shall acquire.' This sentiment prevailed, and they all went on in harmony.

"As they passed through a forest, they saw the scattered bones of a dead Lion. 'I have met,' said one, 'with an account of a method by which beings can be re-animated: what say you? shall we try the experiment, and employ the energies of science to restore life and shape to these bones?' They agreed. One undertook to put the bones together; the second to supply the skin, flesh, blood, &c., and the other to communicate life to the figure. When the two first had accomplished their tasks, the third was about to begin his; but the fourth stopped him; 'Consider what you are going to do,' he exclaimed, 'if you give life to the lion, the consequence will be that he will devour us.' 'Away, blockhead,' replied the sage, 'I am not to project things in vain.' 'Wait an instant, then,' replied the man of sense, 'till I get up into this tree.' So saying, he climbed up into a tree at hand, and his learned associates accomplished their undertaking. A substantial living lion was formed, who fell upon the three philosophers, and destroyed them. When he was gone, the man of common sense descended from his hiding place, and reached home again is safety."

When he had finished, the man with the wheel exclaimed: "This is very unreasonable, that destiny should destroy men of great talents, and allow simpletons to escape; as it is said, 'See where Śatabuddhi (hundred-wit) is carried on the head, and there too is Sahasrabuddhi (thousand-wit), whilst I, who am Eka-buddhi (single-wit), still may gambol in the crystal stream.' 'How,' asked he of the gold mine, 'happened that?' The Chakradhara[1] replied, 'In a certain reservoir were two fishes, one named Śatabuddhi, the other Sahasrabuddhi. They had a friend, a frog, named Ekabuddhi, with whom they were in the habit of meeting and conversing at the edge of the water. When the usual party assembled, they saw several fishermen with their nets approach, and heard them say to one another, 'this pool is full of fish, the water

---

[1] From Chakra, a wheel, and Dhara, who bears; the use of this denominative may spare some repetition.

is but shallow, we will come to-morrow morning and drag it.' They then went away. When they had departed, the frog said to his friends, 'What is to be done? had we not better make our escape?' at which Sahasrabuddhi laughed, and said, 'never fear, they have only talked of coming. Yet, if they should come, I will be answerable for your safety, as well as my own. I shall be a match for them, as I know all the courses of the water.' Śatabuddhi said, 'My friend here is very right; wherever there is a way for the breeze, for water or its tenants, or for the rays of the sun, the intellect of a sagacious person will penetrate. By following his counsel your life would be in no peril, even had you approached the abodes of the manes. Stay where you are, even I will undertake your safety.' The frog said, 'I have, perhaps, but limited talent, a mere singleness of sense, but that tells me to flee; and therefore, whilst I can, I shall withdraw with my mate to another piece of water.' The frog left the pool that night. In the morning the fishermen arrived, and the lake was so beset with nets, that all the fish, turtles, crabs, and other tenants of the water were made prisoners, and amongst them Śatabuddhi and Sahasrabuddhi, in spite of their boasted cunning, were caught and killed. The frog saw the fishermen on their return, and recognising Śatabuddhi on the head of one man, and Sahasrabuddhi dragged along with cords by another, pointed them out to his mate in the words which I cited."

The Bráhman of the gold mine answered, This may

be very true, but a friend's words are not to be despised, and you had better have listened to me, than followed the dictates of your own avarice and presumption. Well was it said, 'Bravo, uncle, you would sing your song, though I dissuaded you, and see what a splendid gem you have received as the recompense of your performance.' The Chakradhara asked, how was that? The other replied.

"In a certain village there was an Ass named Uddhata. During the day he carried the bundles of a washerman. At night he followed his own inclinations. During his nocturnal rambles he formed an acquaintance with a Jackal, in whose company he broke into enclosures, and feasted on their contents. On one occasion, when in the middle of a cucumber field, the Ass, exulting with delight, said to the Jackal, 'Nephew, is not this a heavenly night; I feel so happy that I must sing a song. In what key will you prefer it?' The Jackal replied, 'What nonsense, when we are engaged in plundering, to think of such a thing. Silence becomes thieves and libertines, as it is said, 'Let the sick man and the lazy refrain from stealing and chattering, if they would escape with life.' If your song be ever so sweet, should the owner of the field hear, he will rise, and in his rage bind and kill you: eat, therefore, and be silent.' The Ass replied, 'You can be no judge of the charms of music, as you have spent all your life in the woods. Observe, in the nights of autumn, in privacy with your love, the distant song of the singer drops like nectar into the ears.' The Jackal answered, 'may be so, but your voice is abominable, why should you let it lead you into trouble?' The Ass was highly affronted at this, and said; 'away, blockhead, do you question my musical proficiency? I know every branch of the science; for instance, there are seven notes, three scales, and twenty-one intervals, &c.[1] The scientific combination of the parts of music is particularly grateful in the autumnal season. There is no gift of the gods more precious than music. Rávańa received the boon from the three eyed god (Śiva), delighted with the rattling of dry tendons. How then do you presume to question my powers, or to oppose their exercise?' 'Very well,' replied the Jackal, 'let me get to the door of the garden, where I may see the gardener as he approaches, and then sing away as long as you please.' So it was settled; and the Jackal having provided for his own safety, the Ass opened his chaunt. The gardener was awakened by the noise, and rising immediately, repaired to the spot, armed with a stout stick, with which he fell upon the ass, knocked him down, and belaboured him till he was tired. He then brought a large clog, with a hole in it, which he fastened to his leg, and tied him to a post, after which

---

[1] The entire enumeration in the text is 7 swara, 3 gráma, 21 múrchhana, 19 tála, 3 mátrá, 3 laya, 3 sthána, 6 yatis, 9 rasa, 36 varńa, 40 bháshá, 150 gitá. See the author's remarks, at the close of this essay. Mr. Wilson reads nara for rasa, and three divisions of yatis in place of 6 yatis.—H.T.C.

he returned home, and went to sleep. The Ass came to himself, and forgot his tortures in the recollection of his home and companions. As it is said, 'On a dog, a mule, and an ass, a good beating leaves but a momentary impression.' Accordingly, springing up, he forced his way out of the inclosure, carrying the clog along with him. As he ran off, the Jackal met him, and said, 'Bravo, uncle,' &c."

The Chakradhara having heard this story, answered, What you observe is very just; but you should recollect, that a man who neither exercises his own judgment, nor follows a friend's advice, brings on his own ruin, as was the case with Manthara, the weaver.

"There was a weaver named Manthara, all the wood work of whose loom was, on one occasion, broken. Taking his axe, he set off to cut fresh timber, and finding a large Śiśu-tree, by the sea side, began to fell it. In the tree resided a spirit, who exclaimed on the first stroke of the axe, 'Hola, this tree is my dwelling, and I cannot quit it, as here I inhale the fresh breeze that is cooled by the ocean's spray.' The weaver replied, 'What am I to do? unless I get wood, my family must starve. Do you, therefore, look out for another house; quick, this I must have.' The spirit replied, 'You shall have any thing else you ask for; but not this tree.' The weaver then agreed to go home, and consult a friend and his wife, and return with his final determination.

"When the weaver returned home, he found there a very particular friend of his, the barber of the village, to whom he told what had occurred, and whom he consulted what he should request. The barber said: 'Ask to be made a king; then I will be your prime minister, and we shall enjoy ourselves gloriously.' The weaver approved his notion; but first, he added, he must consult his wife. To this the barber strenuously objected. A wise man, he argued, would confer on women food, clothing, and appropriate ornaments, but would never let them share his councils, as Bhárgava has stated, that where a woman, a rogue, or a child, had the management, the house was sure of going to ruin. A man would maintain his rank and respectability, as long as he associated with grave people, and entrusted no woman with his secrets. Women are engrossed with their own designs, and purpose only their own pleasure. They love their own children even no longer than they derive from them self-gratification.' The weaver admitted the justice of his friend's observations; but his wife, he said, had no other thoughts than for her husband's welfare, and he must take her advice. Accordingly he went to her, and related what had happened, what the barber had recommended, and asked her what she thought it would be most advantageous for him to solicit: she replied:

"'You should never listen, husband, to the advice of a barber; as it is said, 'Husbands should never take counsel with courtezans, parasites, mean persons, barbers, gardeners, and beggars. Royalty is a very troublesome thing, and the cares of peace and war, aggression and negotiation, defence and administration, never allow its possessor a moment's enjoyment. He, who is wise, will ever shun the station of a king, for which his own relations, brothers and offspring, would be armed against his life. I should recommend you, therefore, to be contented with your station, and only to seek the means of more effectually earning your livelihood. Ask for an additional pair of hands, and another head, with which you may keep a loom going both before and behind you. The profit of such a second loom will be quite sufficient to give you consequence and credit with your tribe, as we have already from those of the first quite enough for our own expenditure."

"This advice pleased the husband mightily; he repaired forthwith to the tree, and requested the spirit, as the price of his forbearance, to give him another pair of arms, and an additional head. No sooner said than done; and he immediately was possessed of two heads and four arms, with which he returned homewards, highly delighted. His new acquisitions, however, proved fatal; for as soon as the villagers saw him, they exclaimed, 'a goblin! a goblin!' and falling on him with clubs, or pelting him with stones, speedily put a period to his existence. Therefore, I say, &c."

The Chakradhara continued: Every one who is tormented by the devil of improper expectations naturally incurs ridicule, as it is said, 'He who forms extravagant hopes for the future will be as much disappointed as the father of Soma Śarmá.' How was that? asked the other Bráhman; and he with the wheel proceeded.

"There was an avaricious Bráhman named Soma Śarmá, who had collected during the day as much meal, in alms, as filled an earthen jar. This jar he suspended to a peg immediately at the foot of his bed, that he might not lose sight of it. During the night he lay awake some time, and reflected thus: That jar is full of meal. If a scarcity should take place, I shall sell it for a hundred pieces at least; with that sum I will buy a pair of goats; they will bear young, and I shall get enough by their sale to purchase a pair of cows. I shall sell their calves, and will purchase buffaloes; and with the produce of my herd I shall be able to buy horses and mares. By the sale of their colts I shall realize an immense sum; and with my money I will build a stately mansion. As I shall then be a man of consequence, some wealthy person will solicit my acceptance of his daughter with a suitable dower. I shall have a son by her, whom I will call by my own name Soma Śarmá. When he is able to crawl, I shall take him with me on my horse, seating him before me. Accordingly, when Soma Śarmá sees me, he will leave his mother's lap, and come creeping along, and some day or other he will approach the horses too near; when I shall be very angry, and shall desire his mother to take him away. She will be busy with her household duties, and will not hear my orders; on which I shall give her a kick with my foot. Thus saying, he put forth one of his feet with such violence, as to break the jar. The meal accordingly fell on the ground; where, mingling with the dust and dirt, it was completely spoiled: and so ended Soma Śarmá's hopes.[1] "

"There is a city in the north, named Madhupura, of which Madhusena was king. A daughter was born to him, who had three breasts. When the king heard this, he ordered the chief attendant to take away the infant, and expose her in the woods, so that the matter should remain unknown. The attendant, however, recommended that, as the birth of such an infant was a very extraordinary event, it would be better to consult the Bráhmans what was to be done, so that the consequence might not be the loss of both worlds; as it is said, a wise man should always inquire the meaning of what he observes, like the Bráhman, who thus escaped the grasp of the goblin. The king asked how that was, to which the attendant replied:

"Chańđavarmá, a Rákshasa, haunted a certain wood, and one day laid hold of a Bráhman, who passed, leaping upon his shoulders, and ordering him at the same time to proceed. The Bráhman, overcome with terror, obeyed; but as he went along, he observed that the goblin's feet were particularly soft and tender, and inquired of him how this happened. The Rákshasa

---

[1] A story of a monkey revenging himself on a king, who had caused a number of tame monkeys to be killed, and the marrow of their bones applied to relieve burns in his horses, scorched by the stables being burnt, here follows; and is succeeded by a tale of a monkey, a thief, and a goblin. Both are omitted, as deficient in interest; the entire fifth section being too long for insertion.

replied, I am under a vow never to walk, or touch the ground with my feet. After this, they came to a pool, where the Rákshasa said, Let me down, whilst I bathe, and perform my devotions; but beware how you leave the place till I come out of the water. The Bráhman obeyed; but when he had got rid of his load, he reflected, that now was his time to escape; for as the Rákshasa was incapacitated for walking, he would not be able to overtake the fugitive; accordingly he took to his heels, and effected his retreat in safety: therefore I said, &c."

The advice thus given by the attendant was followed by the Rájá; and having summoned the Bráhmans, he consulted them how he should act; to which they replied, "It is said, Sire, that a daughter whose limbs are defective or excessive will be the cause of death to her husband, and destruction of her own character: and a damsel with three breasts will inevitably be the source of evil to the parent, whose sight she may attract. Your Majesty should therefore take care to avoid seeing your daughter. Let any one, that will, marry her, stipulating that he leaves the country. In this way no offence will be offered to this world, or the next." The Rájá approved of this plan, and ordered the drum to be beat, and proclamation to be made, that whoever would marry the princess, and remove with her to a distant country, should receive a hundred thousand rupees. Notwithstanding this offer, no person came forward; and the princess arrived at adolescence, without any one proposing to espouse her. At last she found a husband.

In the city resided two paupers who were friends; the one was blind, and the other hunch-backed; the latter, who was named Manthara, persuaded the former to marry the princess, with whom, and the money, they should remove to a distant place, and lead a life of ease: or if by the evil nature of the princess he should die, there would at least be an end of his misery. The blind man accordingly accepted the terms of the proclamation; and having married the princess, and received the dower, set off with her, and his friend, to a distant residence.

After passing some time contentedly, the blind man giving himself up to indolence, and hunch-back conducting their domestic arrangements, the evil influence of the princess's deformity began to operate, and she intrigued with hunch-back. This couple then soon began to plot the blind man's destruction. With this intent hunch-back brought home one day a dead snake of a venomous nature, which he gave to the princess, and desired her to mince it, and dress it with proper sauces, after which she should give it to her husband, telling him it was a dish of fish. Manthara then went away, and the princess, delighted, cut up the snake, and set it to boil: then, having other matters to look after, she called to her husband, and desired him to attend to the stirring of the nice mess of fish she was cooking for his dinner. He obeyed her, licking his lips at the intimation, and stirring the vessel as it boiled. In this manner, hanging over the caldron, the fumes of the venom drew the tears so copiously from his eyes, that they gradually dissolved the film which obscured his vision, and he was restored to sight. As he looked into the boiler, he saw immediately that he was cooking the fragments of a black snake. He at once concluded what his wife's design was, but remained in doubt, who her accomplice could be. To ascertain this, he resolved to dissemble, and still affect his former blindness. Presently hunch-back returned, and the husband, watching his conduct unobserved, was soon satisfied of the good understanding that subsisted between his treacherous friend, and faithless spouse. He approached them unperceived, and suddenly seizing hunch-back by the feet, being a man of great strength, he whirled him over his head, and dashed him against the breast of the wife with such violence, that his head drove her third breast through her body to her back, and both she, and her paramour, instantly perished: therefore I said, &c.

The Bráhman who had found the gold mine then concluded, "It is well said, all prosperity proceeds from Fate; but, in compliance with Destiny, prudence is not to be disregarded in the manner in which you neglected it by not listening to my advice." He then left his friend to his fate, and returned to his own abode.

Vishńu Śarmá having thus terminated these narratives, asked the princes, what more it was necessary for him to say? The princes replied, Most worthy preceptor, we have learnt from you all that is essential to the duties of a king. Then we have only to wish, answered Vishńu Śarmá, that this Śástra may be considered as a mirror, reflecting light friendly to other sciences, and facilitating to those, who are acquainted with its contents, the acquirement of worldly wisdom.

When the king found his sons were instructed in this manner, in the course of six months, in the substance of all the Śástras, he was highly delighted with their improvement, and acknowledging that the sage had fulfilled his promise, loaded him with unprecedented wealth and favours.

The course of the narrative has interrupted our comments: it is therefore necessary to revert to them, to indicate a very few analogies which this section offers, and to notice one or two circumstances which are interesting as throwing light on a state of manners no longer known to the Hindus.

The first story, of the beggar turned to a lump of gold by a blow, occurs, with some variation, in the third section of the Hitopadeśa. It may be also considered as connected with the tale of the dervise Abounader, in the Oriental Tales*. The chief peculiarity, however, of this story is its correct de-

---

* [Cabinet des Fées, Vol. XXV, p. 150. Benfey, l. l., I, 477 ff.]

lineation of Jain customs; a thing very unusual in Bráhmanical books. The address of the barber, and the benediction of the Superior of the Vihára, are conformable to Jain usages. The whole is indeed a faithful picture: it is also unaccompanied by any sneer, or abuse; and the satire is rather levelled at the Bráhmans. The accuracy of the description is an argument for some antiquity; as the more modern any work is, the more incorrect the description of the Jainas and Bauddhas, and the confounding of one with the other.

The second story is in both the Hitopadeśa, and Kalíla wa Damna. It was an early favourite in Europe, and is found as a Fabliau, the dog being substituted for the weasel or ichneumon; an exchange in very good taste, when the scene is laid in Europe, but wholly foreign to the notions of the Hindus, amongst whom the dog has never been a domestic animal: whilst the nĕol or nakula, the viverra mungo, on the contrary, has always been a pet. The most pleasing form of this celebrated tale is the ballad of Bath Gellert*.

The passage of the third story, relative to the profits of trade, it is not very easy to render in a satisfactory

* [bedd Gelhart, i. e. the grave of Kilhart. E. Jones (Musical relics of the Welsh bards. London: 1808, Vol. I, p. 75.) mentions the common Welsh proverb: yr wy'n edivarn cymmaint a'r Gwr a laddedd ei vilgi, i. e. I repent as much as the man who slew his greyhound. See also A. Keller ad "Dyocletianus Leben." 1841, p. 53.]

manner, as the technical terms employed are no longer in use.

The Goshṫika karma appears to imply the management of lands for others, by the expression illustrative of it; but the Parichita-gráhakágama is by no means clear. One copy alone attempts to explain it. Parichitam ágachchhantan gráhakam utkanṫhayá vilokya śrehsṫhí hṙidaye hṙishyate: The merchant is delighted at heart, when with affected sorrow he sees an acquaintance coming (as a borrower)*.

The musical pretensions of the ass, and the beating they procure for him, form a fable with which all children are familiar**. The recapitulation of musical terms that occurs, is, however, rather curious, and exceeds the limits, to which Sir William Jones and Mr. Paterson*** have carried their explanation of the musical language of the Hindus. The seven notes are common to the Hindu scale, and that of Europe. The Grámas are scales. Of these, the Madhyama Gráma is identified by Mr. Paterson with the major, and the Gándhára with the minor, mode. The Múrchhanas

* [The verses quoted above are found in Kosegarten's text inserted at p. 6 & 7 (Book I, vv. 6—20.) Benfey, l. l., II, 5. translates *goshṫikakarmaniyukta* by "an agent" or "broker", and *parichitagráhaka* by "a rich buyer". The former is rendered by Böhtlingk (Mélanges Asiatiques, IV, 209.) "the partner in a joint business", the latter "a customer".]

** [Weber, Ind. Stud., III, 352. Grimm, Reineke Fuchs. Berlin: 1834, p. CCIX.]

*** [Asiat. Res., IX, 456 ff.]

he considers as the intervals of the scale. There are seven to each gráma, or twenty-one in all. Tála is the division of time; and the Mátrás and Layas refer to the same, no doubt: the first possibly implying the duration of the bars, the second that of the notes, and the third that of the rests, or pauses. Of the remaining members of the list, in their purely musical sense, I cannot here attempt an explanation[1].

The story of the weaver may remind us of the three wishes, to which, however, in point and humour, it is vastly inferior*. That of Soma-Śarmá is given in the Kalíla wa Damna, and Hitopadeśa [IV, 8]. It is in substance the same also as that of Alnaschar, in the Arabian Nights. As related in the Ayár Dánish of Abúlfazl, it is translated in the first volume of the Asiatic Miscellany**.

The story comprised within the last, of the Rákshasa who got upon the Bráhman's shoulders, contains the hint of the old man who proved so troublesome to Sindbad, in his fifth voyage; and who makes so prominent a figure also in the Hindi story of Kámarúpa and Kámalatá, translated by Colonel Franklin***. The

---

[1] As relating to vocal music, several of the terms may here be understood in their ordinary sense: mátrá refers to syllabic length, or vowel sounds; varńas are consonants; bháshá signifies language; and gitá tune or song.—H.T.C.

* [Benfey, l. l., I, 495 ff.]

** [Benfey, l. l., I, 499 ff. H. Kurz ad B. Waldis IV, 80. Grimm's Kindermärchen, Vol. III, 244.]

*** [For the literature comp. Benfey, l. l., I, 534 ff., who refers also to Mahábh. XIII, 5885—5918.]

last story of the section is absurd enough; but it has a curious bearing, although perhaps unintentionally. The malformation of the heroine might be thought a satire on a very popular legend of the south of India, traces of which may be seen in their sculptures, particularly at Madura. According to that story, the daughter of one the early Páńďyan Kings was born with three breast. She was an incornation of Deví; and the third breast disappeared, when she espoused Śiva himself, in the form of Sundareśwara, the divinity that was ever afterwards the tutelary god of the Páńďyan kingdom, and its capital, Madura. A modification of this legend is also met with in Ceylon; the fair demon Kuráńí, having been born with three breasts, one of which disappeared on her espousal of Vijaya, the prince who first led a colony to that Island.—Davy's Ceylon, 294*.

NOTE.

The Hitopadeśa is not the only Sanskrit epitome of the Panchopákhyána, or Pancha Tantra. Another abridgment of it, following the original much more closely, both in the matter, and in the arrangement of it, is the Kathámŕita-nidhi (treasure of the nectar of tales), by Ananta-Bhaťťa, who describes himself in the introductory and concluding lines of the work as

---

* [Benfey, l. l., I, 515—34.]

son of Nagadeva - bhaťťa, a Bráhman of the Káńwa branch. He professes to preserve in his epitome of the text the whole of the narrative, or story, but to abbreviate the poetical illustrations. The performance appears, so far as I have compared it with the original, to conform with the author's professed design in that respect.—H.T.C.

VII.

HINDU FICTION.

From the British and Foreign Review, No. XXI (July 1840), p. 224—274.

1. Essai sur les Fables Indiennes. Par M. A. Loiseleur Deslongchamps. Paris: 1838.
2. Somadeva's Mährchen-Sammlung, Sanskrit und Deutsch. Von Dr. Hermann Brockhaus. Leipzig: 1839.

The controversy that was carried on towards the end of the last century between the advocates of the eastern or of the northern origin of European fiction, had reference especially to a particular class of creations, — to those of chivalric romance, — to the marvellous exploits that were magnified out of the traditional achievements which might possibly have been wrought by the companions in arms of Arthur and Charlemagne, elevated to the rank of knights of the round table, or Paladins of France. These narrations, although they no doubt derived much of their martial fierceness from the songs of the bards and scalds, and much of their machinery from the more graceful and inventive fancy of the Arabs, yet took their peculiar character from the people for whom they were composed, and were moulded into the forms in which they were popular, in unison with the temper and tone of the times in which they were written, until they presented but few and uncertain vestiges of their foreign original.

This was not the case with the different class of fictions which, at a somewhat later date, formed an important accession to the literature of Europe, and which can most confidently be traced to the East. Belief in the Asiatic origin of many of the fables and tales of domestic life, which afforded instruction and entertainment to the Middle Ages, has for some time prevailed, and of late years the proofs have been multiplied by the industry of Oriental scholars. The evidence adduced has been of the most positive description. It is not built on probabilities, upon general and indefinite analogies, or on partial and accidental resemblances, but upon actual identities. Although modifications have been practised, names altered, scenes changed, circumstances added or omitted, we can still discover the sameness of the fundamental outline, and, amidst all the mystifications of the masquerade, lay our hands, without hesitation, upon the authentic individual. We can also, in many instances, follow the steps of the migration which the narratives have undergone, and determine when and by what means these Asiatic adventurers were naturalized in the different countries of Europe in which they are found. The inquiry, however, is yet in its commencement, and it seems highly probable that its further prosecution will very extensively add to the testimonies of the Eastern origin of many of the inventions, which, as Contes, Fabliaux and Novelle, constituted the light reading of the more civilized nations of the West in the fourteenth and fifteenth centuries.

Sir William Jones, in his Discourse on the Hindus *, observes that they are said to have boasted of three inventions,—the game of chess, the decimal scale, and the mode of instructing by apologues. He does not cite his authority, and it may be doubted if the Hindus ever boasted of any such discoveries. As far as relates to teaching by apologues, although there can be no doubt that it was a national contrivance, devised by them for their own use, and not borrowed from their neighbours, yet there is no sufficient reason to suppose that it was originally confined to them, or first communicated by them to other nations. It has been urged with some plausibility, that the universal prevalence amongst the Hindus of the doctrine of the metempsychosis was calculated to recommend to their belief the notion that beasts and birds might reason and converse, and that consequently the plan of such dialogues probably originated with them; but the notion is one that readily suggests itself to the imagination, and an inventive fancy was quite as likely as a psychological dogma to have gifted mute creatures with intelligence, and supplied them with a tongue. At any rate, we know that, as an article of poetical and almost of religious faith, it was known to the Greeks at an early

* [Works, III, p. 44.]

date, for Homer is authority for the speech of horses. Without affirming the apocryphal existence of Aesop, we cannot doubt that fables, such as are ascribed to him, were current even prior to his supposed date; and we have an instance of the fact in the story of the Hawk and Nightingale of Hesiod*. Other specimens of the same class of compositions are afforded by the fable of the Fox and Ape of Archilochus, of which a fragment is preserved by Eustathius; and by that of the Eagle and the Fox, which is attributed to the same writer**, and is an established member of all collections of fables, both in Asia and in Europe. Roman tradition,—it would once have been called history,—furnishes at least one well-known instance of popular instruction by fable, which Menenius was not likely to have learnt from the Hindus; and various examples of this style of composition are familiarly known as occurring in Scripture. Although the invention was very probably of Eastern origin, we cannot admit that it was in any exclusive degree a contrivance of the Hindus, or that it was imparted originally by them to other Asiatic nations. If such a communication ever did take place, it must have occurred at a period anterior even to Hindu tradition.

Although, however, instruction by apologues cannot, strictly speaking, be regarded as originally or exclu-

---

* [Erga 202—11.]

** [Comp. G. Bernhardy, Griech. Literatur. Halle: 1856, II, 1, p. 427 f.]

sively a Hindu device, yet the purposes to which the Hindus directed it, and the mode in which they employed it, seem to be peculiarly their own. Fable constitutes with them practical ethics—the science of '*Níti*' or Polity—the system of rules necessary for the good government of society in all matters not of a religious nature—the reciprocal duties of the members of an organized body either in their private or public relations: hence it is especially intended for the education of princes, and proposes to instruct them both in those obligations which are common to them and their subjects, and those which are appropriate to their princely office; not only in regard to those over whom they rule, but in respect to other princes, under the contingencies of peace or war. Each fable is designed to illustrate and exemplify some reflection on worldly vicissitudes, or some precept for human conduct; and the illustration is as frequently drawn from the intercourse of human beings, as from any imaginary adventure of animal existence; and this mixture is in some degree a peculiarity of the Hindu plan of fabling or story-telling. Again, these stories are not aggregated promiscuously, and without method, but they are strung together upon some one connected thread, and arranged in the frame-work of some continuous narrative, out of which they successively spring; a sort of machinery to which there is no parallel in the fabling literature of Greece or Rome. As far, therefore, as regards the objects for which the apologues or stories are designed, and the mode in which they are brought together, this branch of literary composition may be considered as original with the Hindus; and it was the form of their fabling that served as a model, whilst at the same time the subjects of their tales afforded materials, to the storytellers of Europe in the Middle Ages.

That the *fables of Pilpay* were of Indian extraction was known to the orientalists of Europe in the latter part of the last century. They are so described by Assemannus, Fabricius, Schultens, and other scholars. Acquaintance with Sanskrit literature had not then been attempted, and the orientalists alluded to were therefore unaware that the Indian original, in one of its forms at least, was still in existence, and was still as popular in its native country as it had been for some fifteen centuries at least. The translation of the Sanskrit work, entitled Hitopadeśa, or Friendly Instruction, by Mr. Wilkins and Sir William Jones, first added this fact to the history of Pilpay's fables, and it was confirmed by the publication of the text at Serampore, in 1804, with an interesting preface by Mr. Colebrooke, in which its relations to its Asiatic and European imitations are circumstantially particularized. The text has been twice reprinted; in London in 1810, and at Bonn in 1829. The history has been further investigated, and a very ample and interesting detail of the different translations and imitations of the Indian original is prefixed to the late Sylvestre de Sacy's excellent edition of its Arabic version, the "Calila et Dimna, ou Fables de Bidpai," published at

Paris in 1816*. The subject has been resumed in the Essais sur les Fables Indiennes of the late M. Loiseleur Deslongchamps; and all that is known respecting it has been collected by him with most commendable industry, extent of erudition and accuracy of research. His premature death has deprived not only this department, but other branches of Sanskrit literature, of a zealous and talented scholar.

The *Hitopadeśa*, although in much of its contents the same as the prototype of Pilpay's fables, is not in all respects the original. It is avowedly a compilation, and the compiler in the introductory lines specifies his having collected his materials from the *Pancha Tantra* and other books. He therefore apprises us of at least a nearer approximation to the original, if not of the title of the original. In all works of this nature, however,—in all miscellaneous collections of stories, interspersed with passages which are in most instances, and may be possibly in all, citations from other works, great liberties have always been taken, both in the East and West, by transcribers and translators, with regard to the contents of the original compilation. The outline has usually been preserved, the most striking stories have been repeated, and in general a similar succession has been followed; but new stories have been inserted, old ones omitted or

* [Comp. also Liebrecht's translation of Dunlop's "History of Fiction." Berlin: 1851, p. 194 ff. Die Fabeln Bidpai's. Uebersetzt von Ph. Wolff. Stuttg. 1837. Introduction.]

remodelled, and the intervening remarks and precepts diversified at pleasure, so as to produce infinite variety in the copies of a work nominally the same, and to render it a matter of almost insuperable difficulty to determine the priority of any particular version, in composition or in date. It would be rash, therefore, to affirm of the Pancha Tantra that it is the very work* that was translated by order of Noushirván, the king of Persia, into Pehlevi in the sixth century, although there is reason to believe that it is of high antiquity, even as now current. An analysis of its contents has been published in the first volume of the Transactions of the Royal Asiatic Society**; and from various considerations there specified it may be reasonably inferred that, in the condition in which it is still met with, it is an ancient work. In the arrangement of the chapters it conforms with the Arabic Kalíla wa Damna more exactly than the Hitopadeśa; and this is one argument in favour of its approaching more nearly to the assigned date of the original, as the Arabic translation is itself a work of the ninth century. The correspondence, however, is not complete; and as far as any inference may be drawn from its greater or less exactness, there is reason to believe, as we shall have occasion hereafter to show, that we have in the Sanskrit language another form of part of Pilpay's

* [See however Benfey's Panchatantra, I, p. 5—8.]

** [See the preceding article.]

fables, which claims precedence even of the Pancha Tantra.

A version of the Pancha Tantra, as current in the South of India, has been published in French by the Abbé Dubois, but not entire. He has given only a selection of the stories, taken from three different copies, written one in Canarese, one in Telugu, and one in Tamil. It may be doubted if his principle of selection is the most judicious that could have been adopted. "Nous avons tiré de cet ouvrage tous les apologues qui peuvent intéresser un lecteur européen, et nous avons omis plusieurs autres, dont le sens et la morale ne pouvaient être entendus que par le très-petit nombre de personnes versées dans les usages et les coutumes indiennes auxquelles ces fables font allusion*." This is in fact to omit all that is most characteristic. Enough, however, is given to show that the vernacular representatives of the Pancha Tantra in the Peninsula correspond in plan, and in most of their many details, with the Sanskrit original. Some of the stories are additions: they are classed, like the original, in five books, whence the name of the work, Pancha Tantra, meaning 'The Five Chapters;' not, as M. Dubois explains it, 'Les Cinq Ruses.'

The earliest date at which we have evidence of the existence of this collection of fables is in the middle of the sixth century. Noushirván, who reigned from a. d. 531 to a. d. 579, having heard of the work, sent

* [Préface p. VIII.]

his physician Barzúya to India on purpose to procure it. He brought it back, and by the king's command translated it into Pehlevi. He gave it the name of the Book of Kalíla and Damna, from the names of the two Jackals, who are interlocutors in the first book of the collection. The fact of the translation of an Indian collection of fables into the language of Persia, at the period spoken of, rests upon the authority of a number of Mohammedan writers, some of whom were so near to the time at which the occurrence is said to have taken place, that they cannot be very far wrong in their chronology. The story is told by Firdausí in the Sháh Náma, and by Masúdí in his history called the 'Golden Meadows*,' who both wrote in the tenth century of our era; and a similar account is given in the preface of the Arabic translation, which was made in the eighth. M. De Sacy, therefore, is fully justified in asserting, "s'il est un fait que la critique la plus rigoureuse ne puisse contester, ce seroit assurement celui-là, quand même on n'auroit à faire valoir en sa faveur que cette imposante réunion de témoignages." (Calila et Dimna, Mémoire Historique, 2.)

A difficulty that has sometimes puzzled even those who feel little doubt of the Indian origin of the Kalíla and Damna, or of Pilpay's fables, is the name of the author, which, according to the Mohammedan writers, was Bidpai, of which Pilpay is the European corruption. In the Sanskrit works, the Pancha Tantra and

---

* [Maçoudi. Paris: 1861. I, 159.]

Hitopadeśa, the author is not named. The stories are ascribed to a Brahman denominated Vishńu Śarman, who repeats them for the instruction of the sons of the king; but this is merely a part of the machinery, a dramatic impersonation. No satisfactory Indian original has been conjectured for the term Bidpai*. As Sir William Jones observes, Bid-pai in Persian means willow-footed, which is mere nonsense if applicable to a man; and Pil-pai elephant-footed, which is not much better. He is disposed, upon the authority of the author of the Anwári Soheilí, to resolve it into Baidya-priya, said by that writer, and by Abúlfazl, to denote 'friendly physician.' The character of 'physician' attributed to the first translator of the work, Barzúya, is in favour of some such etymology, and possibly the original term was merely the Sanskrit word Vaidya or Baidya, physician, or with the additional final vowel, which in Persian converts a definite into an indefinite noun, Baidya-i, a physician. It is easy to understand how this became Baidpai, for the only distinction between the two consonants is in the dots underneath them, a y having two dots, and a p three: the accidental addition of a third dot would therefore at once have changed Baidyai into Baidpai, and the mistake of a copyist will have been the source of the perplexity. According to M. De Sacy**, the original Arabic reads the name Baidaba, which he conjectures may be

* [Compare however Benfey, l. l., I, 32—35.]

** [Calila et Dimna. Mémoire historique, p. 17, Note.]

derived from the Sanskrit Vidván or Bidbán, a learned man. The common attribution of the character of physician to Bidpai is however in favour of Vaidya.

The Mohammedan conquest of Persia in the seventh century was the era of the destruction of the literature as well as of the religion and independence of the country. That the Persians had a literature is undeniable, as it is repeatedly alluded to by the earliest Mohammedan writers; and besides the reputed version of the Pancha Tantra into Pehlevi, both Tabarí and Firdausí affirm that they derived their accounts, historical and poetical, of the kings of Persia from Pehlevi (that is, from Persian) records. The total disappearance of the national compositions and popular literature of Persia prior to the Mohammedan invasion is a remarkable circumstance, and one not easily to be explained; but it is sufficient to refer to it in this place as the occasion of a very inconvenient chasm in the history of fiction. It is now impossible to determine how far the literature of the Persians was the fountain of that fabling which the Arabs transmitted, or how far it was itself merely the channel by which a stream, originally springing up in India, was conveyed to the Mohammedans, and by them to the people of the farther west. The tradition that an envoy was sent to India to procure a collection of fables, intimates, however, that the Persians were rather the importers than the fabricators of such wares. The destruction, although rapid, was not immediate, and at any rate the Book of Kalíla and Damna was spared for a season.

About a century after the subjugation of Persia it was translated from Pehlevi into Arabic by a native Persian, a convert to Mohammedanism, 'Abdallah Ibn Mokaffa', in the reign of Al Mansúr, the second khalif of the house of Abbás, who reigned from a. d. 754 to a. d. 775, the first khalif, according to Masúdí, who ordered tranlations of Persian and Greek works into Arabic to be made; amongst these was the 'Calíla et Dimna.' The Pehlevi text then shared the fate of the other writings in the same language. The Arabic version still exists, and is the work which M. De Sacy published.

The Arabic prose translation of Ibn Mokaffa' was put into verse at the end of the same century, under the patronage of Yahya, son of Jaffir the Barmekide; and another metrical version was subsequently composed. In the tenth century it was translated into modern Persian verse by Rudeghí, a celebrated poet at the court of Nasr, one of the Sámání princes; and in the twelfth century, or a. d. 1121, a Persian prose translation was made by 'Abdul Má'lí Nasr-ullah, who wrote under the patronage of one of the last kings of Ghizní, Behram Sháh. This work is still extant, and a detailed account of it is given by M. De Sacy in the tenth volume of the Notices et Extraits des Manuscrits. It has been eclipsed, however, in the estimation of the Mohammedans, by a more modern version of the Kalíla and Damna, composed about a. d. 1494 by Hosein Bin 'Alí, surnamed Al Wá'ez, who was patronized by Amír Sheikh Ahmed, surnamed Sohail, a chieftain commanding under Hosein Mirza, one of the last princes of the family of Timúr, who held his court at Herat. In honour of his patron, Al Wá'ez changed the name of his work to that of Anwári Soheilí, under which it is well known, and is deservedly popular. It has been printed repeatedly in India, and portions of it have been occasionally translated. Much of the work very faithfully translates both the tales and the moral precepts and remarks of the Sanskrit original; and it is evident that the author must have had the original Sanskrit under his eye, for the moral and practical observations of the Hitopadeśa reappear in the Anwári Soheilí much more literally rendered than in the Arabic version of Ibn Mokaffa'. The translator has, however, reset the whole in a frame of his own devising, and has made many additions to the narratives from the general mass of Mohammedan and Hindu fiction, which, at the time and in the country in which he wrote, and under the political relations that had then long subsisted between Khorasan and India, had no doubt become intimately, and in many cases undistinguishably, intermixed.

At a period long antecedent to the composition of the Anwári Soheilí in the East, the Kalíla and Damna had performed the first stage of its journey westward. It was translated from Arabic into Greek by Simeon Seth, towards the end of the eleventh century. Syriac and Hebrew versions were made probably about the same date, and from other copies of the original, as they offer discrepancies, which, although of little moment, show that different manuscripts must have been employed. From the Hebrew translation*, John of Capua, a converted Jew, executed, some time between 1262 and 1278, a version into Latin; it was printed in 1480, under the title of Directorium humane vite, alias Parabole antiquorum sapientum. This translation, as M. De Sacy remarks, is of the greatest importance in the history of the Kalíla and Damna, as it is the source from which, directly or indirectly, the translations and imitations in Spanish**, German***, Italian, French, and perhaps other languages, are derived, and is probably the channel by which the narratives and apologues originating with the Kalíla and Damna have passed into those collections of tales which became popular in the fourteenth and fifteenth centuries in Europe. An interesting specification of the different European versions, up to the latest date, is given by M. Deslongchamps.

In his résumé of the contents of the Pancha Tantra, which he has taken from the analysis of that work in the Royal Asiatic Society's Transactions, M. Deslongchamps has repeated, with several interesting additions, the identifications there intimated between the Hindu stories and their European reiterations. For these,

---

* [the tenth chapter of which was edited & translated in Benfey's "Orient und Occident", I, p. 481 ff. & 657 ff.]

** [ib., I, 497 ff. published in Vol. LI. of the Biblioteca de Autores Españoles, p. 11—78.]

*** [ib., I, 138 ff. and 383 ff.]

however, we must be content to refer to his pages, and must pass to what constitutes a greater novelty in his dissertation, his account of 'Le Livre de Sendabad'.

The *Book of Sendebad,* according to M. Deslongchamps, is an oriental romance, of which translations or imitations exist in various European and Asiatic languages. Of these he specifies three as likely to be in an especial degree derived from the original. The Arabic story of a king, his son, his favourite, and seven vizirs; the Hebrew romance of the Parables of Sendebar, and the Greek romance of Syntipas; and from one of the two last, but more particularly from the Hebrew, M. Deslongchamps derives the History of the Seven Sages of Rome, Historia Septem Sapientum Romæ, which was composed by Dam Jehans, a monk of the abbey of Haute Selve, about the beginning of the thirteenth century, and enjoyed extensive popularity in Europe for three centuries afterwards. In confirmation of his view it may be remarked, that in a MS. of the Parables of Sendebar, which exists in the British Museum, it is repeatedly asserted in anonymous Latin notes, that the work was translated out of the Indian language into Persian and Arabic, and from one of them into Hebrew. Sendebar is also described as a chief of Indian Brahmans, and Biebar, the king, as a king of India.—Ellis, Metrical Romances, vol. iii.*

* [Benfey, l. l., I, 12 ff. 38 ff. and in Mélanges Asiatiques, III, p. 188. 192. 196 ff. A. Keller's Introduction before his edition

There is no doubt that the scheme of these different works is the same. In each a young prince is falsely accused by the wife of the king to his father, who determines thereupon to put him to death. The king, however, has seven ministers, and each of them in succession undertakes to defend the prince against the unfounded accusations of the queen. The charge and defence are both supported by a variety of stories, related alternately by the queen and one of the seven ministers or sages; and in the end the innocence of the prince is established. The stories vary to a greater or lesser extent in the several compilations, but many of them agree, and are traceable to Indian sources. Many of them differ; but the identity of the general plan cannot be an accidental occurrence, and it is quite sufficient to place beyond reasonable disbelief the existence of some common original. That the native country of that original was India, appears, from the circumstances above referred to, to have been matter of tradition; and that the tradition was not unfounded there is further evidence to substantiate.

The Arabic writer Masúdí has already been adverted to as evidence for the history of the Kalíla and Damna; he is likewise available for that of the work in question. In his Golden Meadows (Murúj-az-zeheb), in the chapter on the ancient kings of India, he speaks of an

of "Dyocletianus Leben." 1841. E. Carmoly, Paraboles de Sendabar. Paris: 1849. Introduction. H. Sengelmann, Das Buch von den sieben weisen Meistern. Halle: 1842.]

Indian philosopher named Sendebád, who was cotemporary with king Kúrush, and was the author of a work entitled, 'The story of the seven vizirs, the tutor, the young man, and the wife of the king.' "This is the work," he adds, "which is called the Book of Sendebád*." Masúdí died a. d. 956. It is clear from his description, brief as it is, that the main subject of the Book of Sendebád was the same as that of the Parables of Sendebár, in which the name also is preserved, and with the Historia Septem Sapientum, where it is omitted. The Book of Sendebád, according to a more modern Persian writer, the author of the 'Mujmal at-Tawáríkh,' as quoted by M. Langles**, was written in Persia under the Arsacidan kings, and his account is confirmed by an Arabic historian, Hamza Isfahání; but they probably allude to a different work, the Adventures of Sindbád, which, although known to us as part of the Thousand and One Nights, does not properly constitute a member of that collection. However this may be, the testimony of Masúdí is quite sufficient for the determination of the Indian origin of this Book of Sendebád, in which we have no fabulous voyages or adventures, but a series of amusing illustrations of domestic manners, tending mostly to a calumnious depreciation of the female character.

---

* [Paris edition, I, p. 162.]

** [Voyages de Sind-bâd le Marin. Paris: 1814, p. 139. See also H. L. Elliot, Index to the Historians of Muhammedan India. Calcutta: 1849. I, 265—7.]

The analysis which M. Deslongchamps offers of the Greek romance of Syntipas, compared with the Parables of Sendebár and the romance of the Seven Vizirs, affords several instances of narratives familiar to Indian fiction. One of the stories of the first sage, related in Syntipas and the Parables of Sendebár, the trick practised upon the parrot by the wife, that its information of her misdeeds may not be credited by her husband, and which is repeated in the Arabian Nights, the Seven Vizirs, the Directorium humane vite, Discorsi degli Animali, Giorni of Sansovino, is of Indian currency, and no doubt Indian origin*. The story of the woman, her two lovers, and her husband, occurs in the Hitopadeśa [II, 9]. One of the two stories of the third philosopher relates the adventures of a woman who goes to market to buy 'rice.' The two stories of the fourth philosopher are both Indian: one is that of the prince and merchant's wife of the Hitopadeśa [I, 8]; the other is found in a work to which we shall have occasion to recur, the Kathá Sarit Ságara. The fifth sage relates the remarkably popular story of the man who inconsiderately slew his dog, thinking that he had killed his infant, when in truth the animal had saved the child by destroying a serpent which had approached its cradle. This story is found in the Kathá Sarit Ságara, in the Pancha Tantra [V, 2] and in the Hitopadeśa, and there is in all of them a fitness in the incidents which is wanting in the version of the tale in

* [Benfey, l. l., I, 271—275.]

Syntipas, the Parables of Sendebár, and the History of the Seven Sages, in all which also it occurs. The venomous snake is more suitable to India than to any European country; but there is a still more truly national circumstance in the description of the faithful animal by which the snake is killed, as a 'mungoose,' the fierce hostility of which creature to snakes, and its singular power of killing them, are in India so well known as to have become proverbial, and are verifiable by daily observation. It is doubtful if a dog has either any instinctive enmity to snakes, or any characteristic dexterity in destroying them. There is much more propriety in the beautiful Welsh tradition of Beth Gelert, where the slain intruder, who is killed by Lewellyn's gallant hound, is a wolf; but this is evidently an improvement upon the original narrative*. Several other tales are related in the story of Syntipas, which are indisputably of Indian origin, although modified in their details.

The analysis of the *Historia Septem Sapientum* shows that the monk of Haute Selve departed very widely from whatever form of the original may have served him for a model; and although he has adopted the plan, he has changed the persons, and either invented his fables, or borrowed them from other sources. The work is well known by the account given of it under its English form of the Seven Wise Masters, by Ellis, and it is not necessary, therefore, to allude to it

* [See above p. 76.]

more particularly. Those of its stories which are most unequivocally Indian, are that of the prince and merchant's wife; the dog, child, and snake; and the pie (or in the original, the parrot,) killed by its master for giving false witness, as he supposed, against his wife. The story of the monkey and wild boar is found, with some variations, in the Indian tales translated by Galland and Cardonne. An incident similar to that of the device adopted by Octavian to discover the friends of a dead body found in the royal treasury and suspended upon a gibbet, for the purpose of finding out who the person was, occurs in the Kathá Sarit Ságara. The story of the three corpses is evidently of the same origin as that of the hunchback in the Arabian Nights; and nothing can be more common in the fiction of the Hindus than the mutual love of two young persons utterly unknown to each other brought about by their mutual dreams, an instance of which occurs in the seventh and last story related by the queen. Although, therefore, the Seven Wise Masters, or the Historia Septem Sapientum, is undeniably indebted to other quarters for the bulk of its materials, yet some of them, as well as its general design, are as undeniably of Asiatic and Hindu invention.

Besides the migration westwards of these two works, the Fables of Pilpay and the Parables of Sendebár, in their general outline, as well as their component figments, no reasonable doubt can be entertained that various narratives of Indian origin found their way individually and unconnectedly to Europe. By what particular vehicles their transport was effected it is now unprofitable to inquire; but the intercourse with the East through commerce, literature, religion and war, was much more intimate and frequent from the early ages of Christianity down to the fifteenth century than it has ever been since the latter date, even than it is in the present day, notwithstanding the existence of the British empire in India. The greater proximity of Asia Minor to the countries of the South of Europe was one especial cause of the more intimate intercourse that subsisted between them; and the greater parity of civilization in which indeed the Asiatics had rather the advantage, was another. The political relations of the divisions of the Eastern and Western Empire necessarily preserved the provinces of either in a communication with each other, which could not speedily be forgotten; and although interrupted by the first violences of the Mohammedan conquest, it was readily renewed when the storm had passed, and the first khalifs of the house of Abbás encouraged the resort of merchants and scholars, both from the East and the West, to Bagdád. Upon their decline followed the Crusades, and the interest which they attracted to the scene of their achievements, and the numbers that, either as soldiers or pilgrims or traders, were constantly passing to and fro, continued to preserve that interest from decay, and were no doubt actively concerned in importing and disseminating the lighter oriental fictions of domestic life, as well as tales of chivalry and romance.

From the period subsequent to the establishment of the Khalifat, Europe received whatever literary articles were imported from the East through the medium of the Arabs. This did not imply that they were of Arab manufacture exclusively. The subjugation of Persia placed at the disposal of the Arabs whatever treasures they chose to spare from the destruction to which the mass was condemned; and it is upon record of the most indisputable authenticity, that the first Abbaside khalifs in the eighth and ninth centuries, from Al Mansúr to Al Mámún, patronised in an especial manner natives of India; and that Hindus of eminence in various branches of literature and science flourished at their courts. (Journal of the Royal Asiatic Society, vol. v.)

This, according to the same record, was the season at which the fictions of the Hindus were naturalized amongst the Mohammedans. It has even been asserted that *the Arabian Nights' Entertainments* had an Indian origin*; and there can be no doubt, that although in their actual form the collection has received contributions from other and comparatively modern sources, yet there existed at Bagdád a work upon a similar plan prior to the golden age of Arabic literature, and which served as the foundation of the Thousand and One Nights. For this Masúdí again is irrefragable authority. The passage was first brought to notice by the celebrated orientalist Von Hammer,

* [Lassen, Ind. Alt., IV, p. 902 ff.]

now Baron Purgstall, in the preface to his translation of some unedited portions of the Thousand and One Nights, or rather in the German translation of Von Hammer's French version by Professor Zinserling. The French translation, after passing through some adventures almost as wonderful as the original tales, was lost, on its transmission to England. As the passage did not occur in all the MSS. of Masúdí, Von Hammer subsequently published the original Arabic with a translation in the Journal Asiatique (vol. x. p. 253): the translation runs thus:—

"Many persons learned in the ancient history of the Arabs assert that these accounts (of the Garden of Irem) are romances and tales invented by persons who wished, by relating them, to conciliate the favour of their princes, and who became popular amongst their countrymen by learning and reciting such narrations. The traditions thus repeated are of the same class as the works which have come down to us translated from Persian, Indian and Greek, and they are composed in the style of the book denominated the Hazár Afsána, which is rendered in Arabic Alef Khiráfa, that is to say, The Thousand Tales; for the Arabic word Khiráfa corresponds with the Persian Afsána, and people call this book 'The Thousand Nights'. It is the story of a king and of his vizir, and of the vizir's daughter and her nurse; the two last are named Shirzad and Dinarzad. Such also is the story of Yalkand and Shimas, and the particulars which are found in it of the histories of the kings of India and their ministers, and in the story of Sindbad and other similar compositions."

There are some variations in the reading of this passage in different MSS. In the first version given by Von Hammer, he called the book 'Thousand and One Nights;' and a MS. in the British Museum confirms the translation denominating it the Alef leila wa leila, or Thousand Nights and One Night. M. De Sacy, however, in a memoir on the origin of the Arabian Nights published in the Mémoires de l'Académie, v. x, p. 30, translates it the Thousand Nights, which seems to be the correcter appellation. The difference is not very material, and the agreement is close enough to establish the Persian or Indian origin of the Arabic work. In its actual form however the latter is no doubt of much more modern aggregation. The prominent part assigned in the early stories to the Khálif Hárún Al-Rashíd could have been ascribed to him only some considerable period after his demise. In the story of the Barber of Bagdád, the barber observes that it is the 653rd year of the Hijra, a. d. 1255. The institution of Calendars, according to M. De Sacy, originated in the christian year 1150; and the title of Sultan of Egypt, which occurs in the story of Beder ud dín Hassan, was not assumed before the middle of the twelfth century. These and other considerations induced M. De Sacy to conclude that 'The Arabian Nights,' as now current, was compiled not earlier than the thirteenth or fourteenth century. The middle of the thirteenth century is the date conjectured by Galland, the original translator of these tales; but M. Caussin de Perceval, upon the authority of a MS. note, affirmed that the compiler was living in a. d. 1548. That some portions at least are as late as the end of the fifteenth century, is proved by one instance of internal evidence not yet noticed by any European critic.

In the tale of Prince Ahmed and the fairy Peri bhánu, the eldest of the three brothers, Prince Hosein, in search of some extraordinary rarity which may entitle him to the hand of the Princess Núr-an-nihár, repairs to the Indian city Bisnagar, the capital of a country of the same name, and a metropolis of extraordinary wealth and population. This is no doubt the Bijnagar of the Mohammedan historians of the South of India, and of the early European travellers in the Dekhin — the Vijayanagar of the Hindus; and we know from ancient inscriptions, as well as Indian history, that this city was not founded until the middle of the fourteenth century*. It could not have risen to a reputation which extended to Arabia earlier than the beginning or middle of the fifteenth, and any collection in which it is found must have been put together subsequently to that date.

It is not precisely determinable from the expressions of Masúdí whether the Hazár Afsána is considered by him as of Indian or Persian origin, and his translator leaves it equally undecided, although he leans to the latter,—"les mille et une nuits étaient originairement non des contes Arabes, mais des contes Indiens, ou plus probablement Persans." The appellation Hazár Afsána is Persian, and no doubt the Arabs received their first knowledge of the work through the Persian language. Another Arabic writer, since quoted by Baron Purgstall in the Journal Asiatique of August

* [Lassen, l. l., IV, 156—160.]

last, is evidence in favour of their Persian extraction. Abú Ya'kúb al Darak compiled a Fihrist, a catalogue raisonné of Arabic literature, in the Hijra year 377 (a. d. 987). Amongst a long list of romances and tales attributed to the Persians, Indians, Greeks, Babylonians and Arabs, mention is made of the Hazár Afsána as the oldest work of the kind; for it is said to have been the composition of Homai, queen of Persia, daughter of Ardeshir Dirázdast (Artaxerxes Longimanus), and a favourite book of Alexander the Great and his successors. The authenticity of these particulars may be thought questionable; but there is no disputing the proof given, that at the end of the tenth century there was translated into Arabic from Persian a collection of tales, which was the prototype of the Thousand and One Nights. The subject of the Hazár Afsána is said by Abú Ya'kúb to be the story of a king who married a damsel of royal blood, full of wit and intelligence, named Shehrazad, who was accustomed to amuse her husband by relating stories to him every night, until he interrupted her, and put off the conclusion to the following night. In this manner a thousand nights were passed. There was another female of the party named Dinarzad, who assisted the narratress. In the end the king became attached to Shehrazad, and spared her life. The author adds, that the Hazár Afsána contains a thousand nights and two hundred conversations by moonlight, and that he had several times seen a complete copy. He appears to have no great taste for the marvellous, as he concludes,

"It is in truth a book of frigid tradition." It is clear therefore that the opinion of Mr. Lane, in denying the Persian origin of the Arabian Nights, as far at least as their plan and principal performers are concerned, is wholly untenable.

That many of the stories current in Europe originated in Persian invention is not at all improbable, but unfortunately we have no means of verifying the fact. The contrary is the case with the fictions of the Hindus; for although this branch of their literature is yet imperfectly investigated, yet enough has been ascertained to determine the actual existence in Sanskrit, or in vernacular translations from it, of a very extensive literature of fiction, in which many of our European acquaintances are at once to be recognised. This is true not only of the Pancha Tantra and Hitopadeśa, but of other collections, such as the Vetála Panchavinśati, twenty-five stories of a demon; the Sinhásana Dwátrinśati, thirty-two tales of the animated images supporting the throne of Vikramáditya; the Śuka Saptati, the seventy tales of a parrot; and a variety of popular collections of a more miscellaneous description. One of the most interesting and extensive works of this class is now however for the first time made known to the European public by the industry and learning of Dr. Hermann Brockhaus, Sanskrit Professor in the University of Jena*, the Kathá Sarit Ságara, or Māhrchensammlung des Somadeva.

* [Since 1841 at Leipsic in the same capacity.]

The work of which a portion is now published in the original Sanskrit, with a German translation, the *Kathá Sarit Ságara*, or ocean of the streams of narrative, is more commonly known in India as the *Vrihat Kathá*, the great tale, or great collection of tales. The popular nomenclature is however erroneous, and the compiler of the Kathá Sarit Ságara declares expressly that his work is a compendium of a preceding and more comprehensive work, entitled the Vrihat Kathá, of which it contains the substance. It corresponds exactly with the original; there is not the least departure from it, only the style is more compressed in order to avoid the great prolixity of the primitive work. It has also been composed in verse, care having been taken to preserve the arrangement of the text and the interest of the stories. The author adds, that his object is "not a reputation for learning, but the hope of enabling the memory more readily to retain the complicated net of narrative invention."

"Mich ehrfurchtsvoll verbeugend vor Sarasvati, der Fackel um aller Worte Sinn zu erleuchten, beginne ich diese Sammlung, die das Mark der Vrihat Kathá enthält. Wie das ursprüngliche Werk, so ist auch dieses, man wird nirgends die geringste Auslassung bemerken; nur die Sprache ist gedrängter, um die zu grosse Ausdehnung des Buches zu vermeiden. Den Kräften gemäss habe ich mich bemüht, den passendsten Ausdruck zu wählen, und indem die verschiedensten Gemüthsstimmungen in den Erzählungen dargestellt worden, ist ein Werk entstanden, das zu den Gedichten gerechnet werden kann. Meine Arbeit entsprang nicht aus Begierde nach dem Ruhme der Gelehrsamkeit, sondern um leichter dem Gedächtniss das bunte Mährchennetz zu bewahren."

From this it is clear that the Vŕihat Kathá was in all essential respects the same as the present work; but inasmuch as it was written in prose, and with that minuteness of detail which is the soul of all story-telling, it was without doubt a much more animated and interesting compilation.

The period at which the original Vŕihat Kathá was compiled is uncertain, but it must have preceded the eleventh century, for that is the date at which its abridgment, the Kathá Sarit Ságara, was composed. This work derives a great part of its value from the circumstance that its date admits of positive verification; and although this is subsequent to the time at which Indian and old Persian stories first became accessible to Europe, in consequence of their translation into Arabic, yet it precedes the era of the actual migration of the stories to the West, and establishes their naturalization in India at a date anterior to the possible introduction of Mohammedan literature amongst the Hindus. Whether India was indebted for its stories to the Magian Persians is doubtful; to some extent it possibly was; at least it is very likely that under the Sassanian princes there was an active traffic in all sorts of fabrics—those of the imagination as well as of the hand—between India and Persia, making it difficult to attribute to either its own indigenous productions. However this may have been, it is very improbable, it is almost impossible, that before the inferrible date of the Vŕihat Kathá, before the actual date of the Kathá Sarit Ságara, the Hindus should have been indebted to the Arabs for any of their story-telling. In truth, until the Arabs were saturated, as their own authors acknowledge, with translations from Persian, Indian and Greek, they were not a story-telling, not a literary, not a scientific people. They had some poetry, some romance; but the poems that were suspended at the Ka'aba, and the exploits of Antar, are of a very different description from the rich and diversified pictures of social life which at first evidenced the more advanced civilisation of Persia and India, and afterwards accompanied the progress of society in Bagdád, Cairo and Cordova.

The date of the Kathá Sarit Ságara admits of being determined with very tolerable precision. At the close of it, the author, Somadeva, states that he compiled it at the desire of Súryavatí, a dowager queen of Kashmir, for the amusement and instruction of her grandson, Harsha Deva, whilst under her guardianship. Harsha Deva reigned, as Professor Brockhaus mentions, about a. d. 1125; but the Chronicles of Kashmir, the Rája Taranginí, give us more exactly the time. Harsha Deva was, according to Somadeva's genealogy of him, the son of Kalaśa, the son of Ananta, the son of Sangráma, kings of Kashmir in succession. The Rája Taranginí has the same series of descents, and both authorities designate Súryavatí as the wife of Ananta, mother of Kalaśa and grandmother of Harsha. The period assigned for the joint reigns of Harsha's three predecessors in the Rája Taranginí is seventysix years. Abúlfazl has the same names; but in Gladwin's translation of the Áyíni Akbarí the aggregate of the three reigns is but thirty-one years. The MSS. of the work are however, in the chronological tables which they contain, exceedingly incorrect. Diḋḋá Ráńí, the predecessor of Sangráma, died a. d. 1025 (Asiatic Researches, vol. xv. p. 80), and seventy-six years added to this places Harsha's accession a. d. 1101 *. According to the Kashmir Chronicle, however, Súryavatí burnt herself with her husband Ananta's dead body eight years before, or in a. d. 1093. The compilation of the Kathá Sarit Ságara must have preceded this event by some few years, so that we cannot be far wrong in assigning it to about a. d. 1088, to which therefore we fix the most modern limit of all the stories found in the compilation. The Kathá Sarit Ságara then, considered in itself, and still more especially as the representative of a still earlier composition, the Vŕihat Kathá, is the oldest extant assemblage of tales, except the Hindu original, and the first translation of the Kalíla and Damna, and it is therefore indispensable to the history of fiction to determine what it contains.

The Kathá Sarit Ságara is a large work. It consists of eighteen books, subdivided into 124 sections. The portion published by Professor Brockhaus extends to

* [Troyer (Rájatarangińí. Vol. III, p. 655) places the reign of Harsha from 1090—1102, Lassen (l. l. III, p. 1061. 1078.) end of 1091 to end of 1103. The latter places the termination of Diḋḋá's reign towards the end of the year 1007 (l. l. p. 1046,) after 24 years' reign.]

but five books, comprising 26 sections*. The Sanskrit text occupies 469 pages, the German translation but 153, but it is very closely printed in a small type. Each book comprises a number of stories loosely strung together, by being narrated for the recreation or information of the same individuals, or arising out of their adventures. These are Vatsa, king of Kauśámbí, and his son Naraváhana-datta. The marriage of the latter with various damsels of terrestrial or celestial origin, and his elevation to the rank of king of the Vidyádharas, a class of heavenly spirits, are the leading topics of most of the books; but they merely constitute the skeleton of the composition, the substance being made up of stories growing out of these circumstances, or springing from one another with an ingenuity of intricacy which, although the Abbé Dubois complains of it, is in reality one of the great charms of all such collections.

"Un autre défaut peut-être qu'on pourra reprocher encore à ces apologues, défaut dont au reste les compositions orientales présentent de fréquens exemples, c'est qu'ils s'entrelacent presque tous les uns dans les autres de sorte qu'une fable commencée donne lieu, avant qu'elle soit finie, à une seconde fable, interrompue bientôt elle-même par une troisième, et celle-ci par une quatrième**."

---

* [The text of Books VI, VII and VIII was published by the same (in Roman characters) at Leipsic in 1862, comprising sections 27—50, and an analysis of B. VI and VII in "Berichte der Kgl. Sächsischen Gesellschaft der Wissenschaften." Philologisch-historische Classe, Vols. 12 and 13.]

** [Le Pantcha Tantra. Paris: 1826. Préface p. XIII.]

This is no very grave imputation, for the Abbé admits that, "l'auteur ne manque pas de revenir à son sujet et de finir tous les récits commencés." In the Kathá Sarit Ságara the stories all wind up at the end of each book, or not unfrequently sooner. The action is never suspended for any very prolonged interval, and the complication is not of such a nature or extent as to convert variety into confusion. The stories are always characterized by the features of Hindu nationality, and are illustrative of Hindu opinions, usages and belief. They exhibit, in a striking and interesting manner, the peculiarities of the social condition of India; and in the exposure of its follies and vices furnish those delineations of the similar imperfections of all civilized society, of which the general applicability and truth have recommended their imitation to the satirists and storytellers of Europe. The greater number of them turn upon the wickedness of women, the luxury, profligacy, treachery and craft of the female sex. These attributes no doubt originate in the feelings which have always pervaded the East unfavourable to the dignity of the female character; but we are not to mistake the language of satire, or the licentiousness of wit, for truth, or to suppose that the pictures which are thus given of the depravity of women owe not much of their colouring to the malignity of men. The avidity with which this style of portraiture was adopted and improved upon in Europe, shows that either the women of Christian Europe were still more vicious than those of India, or the men were still less disposed to treat them with deference and esteem. It is in this respect that stories of domestic manners contrast so remarkably with the inventions of chivalric romance; and the homage paid in the latter to the virtues and graces of the female sex is a feature derived, in all probability, from that portion of their parentage which comes from the North, woman being ever held in higher honour amongst the Teutonic nations than amongst those of the South of Europe or of the East, and contributing, by the elevating influence she was permitted to enjoy, to their moral exaltation and martial superiority.

Although the text and translation of the Kathá Sarit Ságara are now published for the first time in a continuous form, yet a short extract from the text has been previously published by Dr. Brockhaus himself —the story of the foundation of Pátaliputra or Palibothra. A translation of a larger portion of the work was published in a Calcutta periodical, the Quarterly Oriental Magazine of 1824—25*, from which a notice of the original has been recently inserted in the account of India, which forms a number of the Edinburgh Cabinet Library. The Calcutta publication also had the merit of attracting the notice and exciting the interest of the present editor and translator, and thus leading to the publication which has given rise to our remarks.

Our readers would probably be little profited by any

* [Reprinted in the first volume of this division, p. 156—268.]

criticisms we might offer upon the result of the editorial labours of Dr. Brockhaus. It is sufficient to observe that the text is carefully printed, upon a careful collation of five entire copies and one imperfect copy. The last and three of the former are to be found in the invaluable collection of oriental manuscripts at the India House; a fourth is in the collection of the Sanskrit Professor of the University of Oxford, and a fifth was procured by Dr. Brockhaus from India. He has employed these materials with unremitting industry and judicious scholarship, and has given a very accurate typographic representation of his original. The mechanical execution of the work is creditable and the type distinct. Dr. Brockhaus has followed Professor Bopp's plan of separating conjunct words and marking the separation—a device which we think unnecessary, and one which is objectionable, as not unfrequently productive of greater uncertainty than that which it was intended to obviate. The translation appears to be in general executed with very commendable fidelity, without sacrificing to a servile adherence to the original all pretensions to elegance and spirit. For a vindication of these opinions we must refer to the book itself, whilst we proceed to offer a summary account of the whole of the original work, with reference especially to the light it may be expected to reflect on the history of fiction.

The first book is introductory, and refers the origin of the tales contained in the collection to no less a person than the deity Śiva, who, it is said, related them in private conversation with his wife, Párvatí, for her entertainment. One of the attendants of the god, Pushpadanta, took the liberty of listening, and he repeated them, under the seal of secresy, to his wife, Jayá, a sort of lady's maid to the goddess. What woman, says the author, can restrain her tongue? Jayá takes an opportunity of intimating to her mistress that she is acquainted with the stories narrated by Śiva, to the great mortification of Párvatí, who had flattered herself that they had been communicated to her alone. She accordingly complains to Śiva of his having deceived her, and he vindicates himself by discovering the truth. Párvatí thereupon pronounces an imprecation upon Pushpadanta, condemning him to be born upon the earth as a man; and she sentences his friend Mályaván, who had ventured to intercede for him, to a like destination. The infliction of this punishment is a not uncommon fate of the subordinate divinities of the Hindus, when they incur the displeasure of the Dii majores, or even of holy sages. The degradation, however, endures only for a season, and terminates upon the occurrence of some preannounced catastrophe. On the present occasion, Párvatí tells the culprits that they shall resume their celestial condition when Pushpadanta, encountering a Yaksha, a follower of Kuvera, the god of wealth, "doom'd for a certain time to walk the earth," as a Piśácha or goblin, shall recollect his own former state, and shall repeat to the Piśácha the stories he overheard from Śiva; and when Mályaván, falling in with the Piśácha, shall hear from him again the stories that his friend Pushpadanta had narrated. The recitation of the stories forms also the limit of the Yaksha's sojourn amongst mortals. This machinery is of course exclusively Hindu.

The two demigods, Pushpadanta and Mályaván, are born as two Brahmans, named Vararuchi and Guńáďhya, and their adventures as mortals constitute the subject of several tales. Some of these possess much local interest: we have in them literary anecdotes relating to celebrated works and authors, as to Páńini the grammarian; notices of historical persons and events, as of the accession of Chandragupta or Sandrocoptus; and traditions of the origin of celebrated places, as of that of Palibothra already alluded to. The circumstances of these narratives are marvellous, it is true, and are not to be received as facts. In the absence of all authentic history and biography, however, they are not without interest, and perhaps not without value; and in the place in which they are found they are evidence of the early date at which popular belief assented to legends still current.

We find also in this portion of the work various incidents and tales which are of wide dissemination. One of the best-told stories in the whole work occurs here. Upakośá, the wife of Vararuchi, becomes, during the absence of her husband, the object of the addresses of the king's family priest, the commander of the guards, the prince's tutor, and her husband's banker. She makes assignations with them all: each as he arrives is quickly followed by his successor, and is secreted only to be finally exposed and punished. The story* is the same in all essential respects as that of the Lady of Cairo and her four gallants, in Scott's additional Arabian Nights; and that of the merchant's wife and her suitors in the tale of the king, his favourite, and the seven vizirs, translated by the same orientalist. It is also that of Arouya in the Persian tales; and it is also found as a Fabliau, that of Constant du Hamel, or 'la dame qui attrapa un Prêtre, un Prevot et un Forestier,' (Fabl. de Le Grand, iv. p. 246); and it is worthy of remark, that the Fabliau alone agrees with the Hindu original in the mode of putting the suitors out of the way, by hiding them in baskets and disrobing them under the plea of a bath.

There is in this part of the work some very curious matter, the purport of which it is not easy to conjecture, unless it conceal an intimation that the stories are of inferior, if not of foreign origin. Mályaván, or Guńáďhya, in consequence of a dispute with a rival Brahman, foregoes the use of the Sanskrit, Prákrit and Deśya, or vernacular languages. He afterwards learns the Paiśáchí language, or that of the goblins, which enables him to receive the narrations as they are told him by the metamorphosed Yaksha or Piśácha. Possibly the author thought some contrivance necessary to explain how the Piśácha should be intelligible to the Brahman, and nothing more is meant than meets the

* [See above Vol. I, p. 169 ff.]

eye; but a hypothesis might be framed upon it, that the stories were translations, whence made, it would not be easy to explain, unless we call in Pehlevi, a language extinct or disused before the Kathá Sarit Ságara was compiled. However this may be, Guńáḋhya having heard the stories, extending to seven hundred thousand stanzas, wrote them with his blood, for there was no ink in the forest. He then offered the work to Sátaváhana, king of Pratishṫhána, who rejected it with abhorrence, on which the author kindled a fire in the forest, and reading it aloud, to the great edification of spirits and goblins, and birds and beasts, he burned it leaf by leaf as he finished the perusal. The news of this proceeding at last reached the king, and he repented of what he had done, and repaired to Guńáḋhya to solicit the gift of the work. The sage consented to present the king with the hundred thousand verses that had not yet been consigned to the flames. Sátaváhana took it to his capital, and having received an explanation of it from two of Guńáḋhya's disciples, he translated it from the language of the Piśáchas. Sátaváhana, as king of Pratishṫhána, it may be observed, is identifiable with the Sáliváhana, whose reign, a. d. 78, forms an epoch in the ordinary chronology of the Hindus*. It would seem as if tradition ascribed to him the patronage of this class of composition, and there is nothing very improbable in

* [See above Vol. I, p. 181.]

the supposition that the golden age of Indian fabling dates about the commencement of the Christian era.

The second book is supposed to commence that part of the original narrative which was not consumed, and records the adventures of Udayana, king of Kauśámbí, a prince of great celebrity in the plays and poems of the Hindus, and his marriage with Vásavadattá, princess of Ujjayiní. The third book describes his acquisition of a second bride, Padmávatí, princess of Magadha; and the fourth book the birth of the son of Vatsa, by Vásavadattá, Naraváhanadatta; at the same time sons are born to the chief ministers of Vatsa, and they become the companions and councillors of the young prince. The fifth book records the adventures of a mortal, who became king of the heavenly beings termed Vidyádharas, a class of spirits who reside upon the loftiest peaks of the Himálaya mountains, who possess superhuman longevity and faculties, and the knowledge of what is passing beyond their presence. They have in many cases been mortals, and are constantly connected with human beings in friendship and enmity, love and hate. The story of their king is told to illustrate the manner in which the destiny of Naraváhanadatta, who it is foretold will be king of the Vidyádharas, can be fulfilled. With this tale the publication of Dr. Brockhaus closes.

In the stories which this portion of the Kathá Sarit Ságara comprises, we have various details which are recognisable in the fiction of the West, some possibly accidental, but others of too peculiar a nature to have occurred independently to different inventors. Thus we need not identify Vatsa with Orpheus, because his musical proficiency on the lute subdues the animals of the forest to his will; nor is it necessary to refer to the tale of Troy for the origin of a contrivance by which he is taken prisoner, a hollow wooden elephant instead of a horse, in which armed men are concealed; although perhaps traces of some such stratagem were scattered over the East long before it came to Virgil. "Habebat poeta fabulam a multis tractatam et vulgarem ante se positam." The case is different with other analogies. Guhasena, a young merchant, is compelled to leave his wife, Devasmitá, for a season, on matters of business. The separation is painful to both, and the pain is aggravated by fears on the wife's part of her husband's inconstancy. To make assurance doubly sure, a couple of divine lotus flowers of a red colour are obtained in a dream, the hues of which, the married pair are told, will fade, should either prove untrue. Some such marvellous indication of unsullied honour is exceedingly common in European romance. It is not always the same. In Ariosto the test is a cup, the wine of which is spilled by the unfaithful lover who attempts to drink from it; this device also occurs in the romances of Tristram, Perceval and La Morte d'Arthur, and is well known by La Fontaine's version, 'La coupe enchantée.' Spencer has derived his Girdle of Florimel from these sources, or more immediately from the Fabliau, 'Le manteau mal taillé,' an English version of which is published in Percy's

Reliques, 'The boy and the mantle.' In the Gesta Romanorum the test is the whimsical one of a shirt which will require neither washing nor mending as long as the wearer is true. There are not wanting, however, instances of such a test as that of Somadeva. In 'Amadis de Gaul' it is a garland; in 'Les Contes à rire' a flower, and in 'Perce Forest' it is a rose, which borne by a wife or maiden of immaculate virtue preserves its freshness, but withers if the wearer is unchaste*.

Guhasena falls in with boon companions, who learning the purport of his lotus, and the virtue of his wife, set off, like Iachimo, to put it to the proof. They find an old Buddhist priestess willing to promote their designs. In order to shake the constancy of the merchant's wife, she visits her, and leads along with her a bitch held by a string, whom she takes an opportunity of feeding with a piece of meat strongly seasoned with pepper; the effect of the seasoning is to draw tears from the eyes of the animal; and when Devasmitá inquires why the animal weeps, the old woman tells her that she and the bitch were in a former life the wives of a Brahman who was frequently from home in the service of the state; during his absence she amused herself as she pleased, but the other wife was of rigid virtue and turned a deaf ear to all her suitors. They have both been born again in their actual forms, and with a recollection of their former state of existence,

* [above, Vol. I, p. 220.]

and the once faithful wife now weeps for the penalty she pays for her coldness and cruelty. Now this contrivance is quite consistent with the Hindu notion of the metempsychosis, and is clearly of Indian origin. It was nevertheless naturalized with suitable modifications in Europe, although not directly from the Kashmirian compilation, for it was introduced into the West about the same time that the Kathá Sarit Ságara was compiled. It occurs in the 'Disciplina Clericalis'* of Petrus Alfonsus, a Spanish Jew who wrote about a. d. 1106. His materials were obtained chiefly through the Arabian writers, and it must have been by way of Bagdád that the story travelled from Hindustan to Spain. It was speedily taken hold of by the conteurs and trouveurs, and appears in Le Grand's Fabliaux as 'La vieille qui séduisit la jeune fille**.' The French might almost pass for a translation of the Sanskrit. The woman gives "une chienne à manger des choses fortement saupoudréés de sénevé, qui lui picotait le palais et les narines, et l'animal larmoyait beaucoup." She then shows her to the young woman and tells her that the bitch was her daughter, "son malheur fut d'avoir le cœur dur...Dieu l'a bien vengé: voyez en quel état pour la punir il a réduit ma pauvre fille, et comment elle pleure sa faute." The story became extremely popular: it was inserted in the Gesta Romanorum as 'The old woman and her little

* [ed. F. W. V. Schmidt, No. XIV and p. 129 ff.]

** [ed. of 1829, Vol. IV, p. 50.]

dog*;" and it also has a place where we should little expect to find it,—in the Promptuarium of John Herolt of Basil, an ample repository of materials for sermons**! It is worthy of note that the European conteurs make the example effective,—female virtue yields to such a warning. The Indian narrative has a more moral dénouement. Devasmitá appears to relent, and invites her lovers to an entertainment, where they are plied with wine in which a narcotic drug has been infused, and when they fall asleep they are branded on the forehead with the mark of a dog's foot, and then turned out of the house. They return to their own country disappointed and disgraced. Devasmitá, fearing that her husband may be the victim of their revenge, follows them in the garb of a man and character of a merchant. She makes acquaintance with her husband, who does not know her in her disguise, and after a season applies to the king of the country to recover certain persons whom she denounces as her runaway slaves. These were her suitors, who are accordingly obliged to appear, and are claimed by Devasmitá as her slaves. She appeals to the brand on their brows in testimony of their servile condition; their turbans are removed, and the mark becoming manifest is

---

* [ch. 28. See Swan's translation, I, 347, and Grässe's transl. II, 259.]

** [Latin Stories, ed. by Th. Wright. London: 1842, No. XIII & p. 218. See also Loiseleur Deslongchamps, l. l., p. 107 f. and J. H. von der Hagen, Gesammtabenteuer. 1850. I, CXII ff.]

admitted as proof. Subsequently Devasmitá consents to accept a liberal ransom from them, with which she enriches her husband, to whom she makes herself known, and they return home together to be separated no more.

In the story of Śaktideva, which forms the main subject of the fifth book, we have, along with a genuine national charakter, many particulars found in other collections. The Princess of Varddhamána, when pressed by her father to marry, declares she will have no man for her husband but one who has visited the 'Golden City.' Public proclamation to this effect is made; and Śaktideva, a young and dissolute, but courageous and enterprising Brahman, undertakes to discover what no person is acquainted with, the situation of the city to which a visit is to win the hand of the princess. He first has recourse to an old hermit, who refers him to his still older brother, by whom he is sent on to a certain island—in which particulars Śaktideva resembles Mazin of Khorasan in his search after the island Wák-al-wák. In the voyages he consequently performs he is repeatedly shipwrecked, and on one occasion is caught in a whirlpool, like Ulysses, and escapes in a similar manner, by jumping up and clinging to the branches of a fig-tree,—the Indian fig-tree,—the pendulous branches of which are more within reach than those of the Sicilian fig can be, making it doubtful whether Homer did not borrow the incident from some old eastern fiction. From hence Śaktideva is conveyed by a gigantic bird, one of the race of Garuḍa, the bird of Vishńu, and prototype of the 'Roc,' to the place he is in search of. The Golden City is the residence of Vidyádharís, females of the Vidyádharas only, so Wák-al-wák is inhabited by female genie alone. The chief of the sisterhood welcomes him as her future husband; but deeming it necessary to obtain her father's consent, she and her companions depart to ask his sanction. Śaktideva is left in possession of the palace, with a recommendation not to ascend the central terrace. He of course disregards the injunction. He finds three pavilions on the terrace, enters them, and discovers to his great horror the three apparently lifeless corpses of beautiful damsels,—one of whom is the princess of Varddhamána. Quitting the last chamber he comes to a reservoir of water, by the side of which stands a horse caparisoned. Śaktideva approaches to mount him, but the steed kicks him into the reservoir. When he struggles to the surface he finds himself in the midst of a well-known pond in his native city, Varddhamána. Some similar incidents occur in the story of Mazin; and the catastrophe, more humourously but less poetically related, is that of the third Calendar in the Arabian Nights.

Again we find an analogy with the tale of Mazin, in the consequence of Śaktideva's satisfying the princess that he has been to the Golden City. She is in truth a Vidyádharí, condemned for a time to wear a mortal shape: the term has expired; she flies away to resume her proper form, which was lying seemingly inanimate in the palace of the Golden City, and thither Śaktideva sets off to recover her. On his way he meets with other two nymphs, whom he espouses: they prove to be the originals of two of the three lifeless bodies he had seen, and in fact are Vidyádharís. By his marriage with them he himself becomes a Vidyádhara, and then proceeds, without difficulty, to the island of the Golden City, where he finds the former princess of Varddhamána, as well as the queen of the female inhabitants of the island. He marries them also, and repairs with his wives to their common father, the king of the Vidyádharís, who resigns the sovereignty to him, to be exercised only until the son of Vatsa shall be born*. The occurrence of this event is the occasion of his appearance.

The main purpose of the sixth book is the marriage of the young prince with the daughter of Kalingasená, a princess sprung from a celestial nymph, and who at first had been enamoured of Vatsa, and desirous of becoming his wife. Vatsa is well enough disposed to marry her; but as he has two wives already, his chief minister suggests to him that he may be contented. A friend of the princess, a nymph of air, is also opposed to the match, and a variety of tales are recited on either side in support of the reasonings for and against the union. One of these is the story of the wife of a foolish Brahman, who liberates her husband from a bad bargain with a Piśácha or goblin, by a

---

* [See Vol. I, p. 268.]

device not of a very delicate description. The story was not the less acceptable to the conteurs of Europe, for the point is precisely the same as that of 'le petit diable' de Papefigue of Fontaine. In the end, a spirit of air, in love with the princess, assumes the semblance of Vatsa, and in his person weds her. She becomes reconciled to what is without remedy, and has a daughter, who is the bride of Vatsa's son.

In the next book Naraváhanadatta marries a Vidyádharí: the wedding is celebrated at the residence of the lady's father, on one of the snow-crowned summits of the Himálaya. When the married couple return to Kauśámbí the young bride persuades her husband to throw open the doors of the inner apartments, and allow free ingress to his friends and associates. "The honour of women," she affirms, "is protected by their own principles alone; and where these are corrupt, all precautions are vain." The object of this arrangement is not only, however, the emancipation of the women from jealous restraint, but provision for the carrying on of the series of tales, as the prince's companions are their ordinary narrators. The stories that then ensue bear hard in general upon the conduct of women; but some are told in their vindication. A king has many wives, and an elephant of celestial race. The elephant is struck dead by a bird of the Garuda breed, and the incident throws the prince into great affliction. A voice from the sky proclaims that the animal will be restored to life by the touch of a chaste woman. The king commands one of his wives to perform the operation. She puts her hand on the elephant, but there is no resuscitation; the rest equally fail. The king then turns them all off, and tries his luck elsewhere. He is invariably disappointed, and at last relinquishes his quest in despair. The moral of this story is the occasion and connecting link of the Arabian Nights, and is the burthen of that of Giocondo, as related by Ariosto*.

The eighth book is devoted to the further illustration of the mode in which the prince may attain the elevation that has been promised him, by the relation of the adventures of a prince named Súryaprabha, who became king of the Vidyádharas. The scene of action is mostly in the regions below or those above the earth, and the dramatis personæ are the Nágas or snake-gods of Pátála and the Vidyádharas of mid air. The stories have little of humanity to recommend them, and lose in interest what they gain in the wonderful. They serve to illustrate, however, the notions of the Hindus with regard to magic, and to those classes of creatures who hold a middle station between human and divine; and it seems not improbable that many of the incidents in the Thousand and One Nights, in which magicians, witches, Peris and Jins, are implicated, are traceable to these inventions of the Hindus. Beings of supernatural origin, or the possession of supernatural powers by mere mortals, have no doubt a place in every form of popular superstition, ancient

* [XXVIII, 7 ff.]

or modern; but there are some coincidences which cannot well have been derived from a mere community of imagination, and which are not very intelligible until they are traced to some one existing system. There are some peculiarities in Hindu belief which explain much of the magic in other collections. Thus the adept in the practices of the Yoga philosophy is supposed, amongst other marvellous faculties, to have that of quitting his own body and animating any other he pleases. Now this involves a doctrine of some of the Hindu psychological schools. Besides the gross external corporeal frame, the soul is invested with a subtile body, made up of the impalpable senses and rudiments of matter, and it is this vehicle of soul which migrates with it from one body to another after death, or may be made by the perfection of the Jogí in his exercises to travel at his commands. Frequent instances of this occur in Hindu tales: thus in the first book of the Kathá Sarit Ságara, Indradatta, the Brahman, takes possession of the dead body of king Nanda, recently deceased, leaving his own body in the thicket, intending to resume it. The minister, suspecting the nature of the king's recovery from apparent death, but wishing to keep him on the throne, the heir being yet an infant, commands search to be made for all dead bodies, that they may be burnt. Amongst them the deserted body of Indradatta is consumed, and he is obliged to remain in that which he had purposed to occupy only for a season. He is therefore known in tradition as Yogananda, or the magic Nanda. So in the case of the four Vidyádharís in the last book: their own bodies were left inanimate in the chambers of the Golden City, whilst they occupied persons of inferior excellence; and in this book Súryaprabha finds in Pátála a lifeless giant; he is told that it is his own proper form, and he consequently lays down the dwarfish human body he is incased in, and resumes that of his former gigantic self. There can be little doubt, that any such device occurring in the fictions of other countries is of Indian origin. There is one well-known exemplification of it in the story of Fadlallah, in the Persian tales, where the Dervish, who animates the body of the dead bird, avows he had learned the art from an ancient Brahman in the Indies. The substance of this story is given in an Italian work of the end of the sixteenth century, 'Peregrinaggio di tre giovani figliuoli del Re di Serendippo.' Translated from the Persian by M. Christoforo, Armeno. Venice: 1584. It has been thence transferred to the 'Soirées Bretonnes de Gueulette*.'

There seems no particular reason for an occasional metamorphosis, not uncommon in both Eastern and Western fiction, that of fairies into serpents, as in the story of Zobeide in the Arabian Nights. Hindu notions account for it at once. The Nágas of the subterrene regions are in their own persons serpents—demi-divine, but snakes nevertheless. They have, however,

* [Dunlop's History of Fiction. Transl. by F. Liebrecht, p. 411. Benfey, Pantchatantra, I, 125 ff. Cabinet des Fées, XIV, 326.]

the power of assuming human forms, and the snake maidens are of very slippery virtue as well as of exceeding beauty. They are very fond of paying visits to earth, where, upon an emergency, they drop the human shape and appear as snakes. Of the Vidyádharas notice has already been taken. They correspond with the benevolent Genii and Peris of Arabian and Persian fiction, whilst the malignant Genii are represented by the Rákshasas: of inferior spirits, goblins, ghouls, ogres, ogresses, and the like, there is no lack of counterparts in the Vetálas, Piśáchas, Yoginís and Dákinís, of the Hindus. Of the paraphernalia of magical machinery there is also abundance. Thus in the first book of the Kathá Sarit Ságara, Putraka, the reputed founder of Pátaliputra, or Palibothra, becomes possessed of a staff that creates what it delineates, a cup that is always full of meat and drink, and shoes of swiftness, or a pair of slippers that enables the wearer to travel speedily through the air. The latter virtue, for a given time at least, is also ascribed in the third book to certain mustard-seeds extracted from the navel of a corpse in which a goblin resided. Vidúshaka, the hero of the tale in which this occurs, possesses also a sword of sharpness, which nothing can resists. Nothing also is more frequent than for a sage, or magician, or an adventurer, to have a Vetála, a Rákshasa, or a Vidyádhara—a goblin, a giant, or a genie, for a servant or a slave. It is worthy of notice too, that the Rákshasa, who is a cannibal as well as a giant, like the 'Fee fa fum' heroes of this class, so well known in our nurseries, is as remarkable for stupidity as malevolence and cannibalism. The following story* exhibits both these characteristics:—

The Prince of Varddhamána.

"The sovereign of Varddhamána had several sons, of whom the youngest, Śringabhuja, was his father's favourite, being distinguished above his brothers for grace and beauty, skill in martial exercises, and gentleness of disposition. The partiality of the king, and the superiority of Śringabhuja, excited the envy and jealousy of his brothers, and they were not satisfied until they had devised a plan to effect his removal, and, as they hoped, accomplish his destruction, without their incurring peril or suspicion. There dwelt a Rákshas in the forests of Vaddhamána, who was the terror of the surrounding districts, appearing from time to time in the most hideous shapes, and carrying off cattle, and even human creatures, for his sustenance. Him the princes propitiated by prayers and oblations, in the hope of securing his assistance to get rid of their obnoxious brother. Their end was at last accidentally attained. In the course of his predatory excursions the Rákshas one day made his appearance on the field where the princes were engaged in the sport of archery, in the form of a large and uncouth crane. The youths proposed to try their skill upon the intruder, and directed their shafts against him, but in vain, the bird keeping at too great a distance, or, by changing his position, evading the arrows. Śringabhuja was not so easily baffled, and his weapon lodged in the wing of the crane, striking him as it seemed to the earth. The prince advanced to secure his prize, but the wounded bird contrived to retire as Śringabhuja advanced, first slowly, and as it seemed with pain, until he appeared gradually to acquire vigour, and at last flew off with the arrow adhering to his side. Śringabhuja, who had been drawn a considerable distance from the exercising ground, and unwilling to lose his arrow, followed the crane as long as he

* [VII, ch. 39; ap. Brockhaus, p. 110. Comp. R. Köhler in Benfey's "Orient and Occident," Vol. II, p. 113 ff.]

was in sight, and when the bird had disappeared, continued to trace him through the forest by the drops of blood which at intervals were visible on the leaves of the trees or on the turf beneath them.

"In this pursuit the day had elapsed, and the prince found himself at sunset in the vicinity of a spacious garden, adjoining to a place of vast dimensions and extent. Utterly unacquainted with the place he had come to, and being unable to follow the track through the gathering gloom, Śṙingabhuja determined to rest where he was for the night, and in the morning endeavour to retrace his steps. He accordingly entered the garden to learn from some of the menials of the palace the name of the person to whom it belonged, and to solicit the hospitality of its owner.

"In the mean time the princes returned home, and reported to the king that his favourite son had been carried off by the Rákshas, and had undoubtedly been made the monster's meal. The king and the mother of Śṙingabhuja were overwhelmed with affliction at this intelligence, the truth of which was confirmed by the failure of all the parties sent out in quest of the prince to discover any vestiges of him.

"After wandering some time through the garden without meeting with any individual, Śṙingabhuja came to a large and stately Baṙ tree, in the centre of a smooth grass plot, and beheld seated at its foot a nymph of uncommon loveliness, so that he was disposed to look upon her as the tutelary divinity of the grove. She was no less impressed by his appearance, and in an instant a mutual affection sprang up between them, before a syllable was interchanged. Recovering from his surprise, the prince advanced and saluted the damsel; and having informed her of his name and rank, and the circumstances which had brought him thither, inquired who she was and what she was doing there. She replied, I am named Rúpaśikhá, and am the daugther of the Rákshas, Agniśikha, who dwells in this palace, and who is the person you have wounded in the form of a gigantic crane. No archer but yourself in all the three worlds could have hit such a mark; but his wound is healed by the application of the divine remedies which he possesses, and he will no doubt welcome so heroic a prince to his castle, and hold him worthy of his alliance. The prince replied suitably to these gracious advances, and the damsel repaired to her father to annonnce their guest, declaring at the same time that she had set her heart upon having him for her husband, and that she would put an end to her existence unless her father consented to the match.

"Now Agniśikha, notwithstanding his canibalism and other fiendish propensities, was fond of his daughter, and was not over-wise, so that he could be easily coaxed or terrified into a compliance with all Rúpaśikhá's wishes. He therefore told her to conduct the prince into the palace, and promised not only that he would not eat him, but that he would accept him as his son-in-law on certain conditions: he desired her at the same time to go and bring her sisters, and the espousals should take place forthwith.

"Rúpaśikhá, who was much shrewder than her sire, perceived his drift, and contrived to intimate to the prince how it might be counteracted. The party was collected; Śringabhuja having previously bathed, and been attired by order of Agniśikha in bridal vestments. To the prince's astonishment, he beheld a hundred maidens before him, all arrayed and decorated alike, and so perfectly similar in form and features that it was impossible to discriminate one from another. The father giving the prince a chaplet, desired him to place it on Rúpaśikhá's neck, and she should be his. Śringabhuja appeared to hesitate; but his mistress, as preconcerted, had suspended a small blossom from the hair that parted on her forehead, and guided by this signal the prince selected his bride.

"Agniśikha thus discomfited, then told the prince that the wedding could not take place before the next morning, as his brother Dhúmaśikha must be present at the ceremony. 'Do you,' he continued, 'go and invite him; he lives about twenty miles off in an old temple of Śiva in the forest; ask him to be here by day-break tomorrow, but do you return without fail to-day.' Śringabhuja readily assented; but before his departure, Rúpaśikhá, who guessed her father's purpose, provided him with a fleet horse, a handful of earth, a cup of water, a few dry sticks and a match, and told him wbat to do to escape from the snare that was laid for bim; for sbe was a fairy, prescient of events and commanding the elements.

"Śriṅgabhuja set off and soon arrived at his journey's end, wbere he found Dhúmaśikba, an old monster more bideous and savage than his brother. As soon as his message was delivered, the prince abruptly witbdrew as be had been enjoined by his mistress, sprang npon bis borse, and set off at full speed. When he had ridden a few yards he turned his bead ronnd and saw tbe cannibal close behind him, on whicb, in conformity to his instructions, he threw the handful of earth upon the ground, and an immense mountain separated him from his pnrsuer. He now relaxed his speed, but soon repented of having done so, as Dhúmaśikba was again close at his heels. He therefore, as directed in such an emergency, ponred the water on tbe earth, and a broad and stately river flowed between bim and the cannibal. The prince nevertbeless urged on his horse, but to little avail, as Dhúmaśikha had traversed the stream, and was once more upon him. His last resource was his match and fuel. Setting the sticks on fire be cast tbem on the path of the Rákshas, wbo was immediately enveloped and destroyed by a mighty flame.

"Śriṅgabbuja completed his journey, and alighting from his horse annonnced to Agniśikha the delivery of his message. The Ráksbas, snrprised at his safe return, began to think the prince something more tban hnman, and to tremble for his own security. He tberefore allowed the marriage to be consnmmated, stipnlating only that Śriṅgabhuja and bis wife should continne to reside with him.

"For a time the young couple, delighted with each otber, and therefore with everything and everybody about them, lived happily in Agniśikba's palace, till at length Śriṅgabhuja began to pine for his parents and his home. His wife perceived what was passing in his mind, and readily agreed to accompany him. They departed clandestinely; bnt their flight was soon known to Agniśikha, who baving the faculty of moving through the air, overtook them before they bad completed their journey. On marking his approacb, the prince, by bis wife's desire, hid himself*, whilst she assumed the semblance of a wood-cutter, with axe and faggots in hand. As soon as the Rákshas saw the supposed woodman, he descended and asked him if he had seen a youth and damsel such as he described. Rúpaśikhá replied, 'Yes, they are further in the forest, in great grief, and are cutting faggots to burn the corpse of their father, one Agniśikha, who is just dead.' Agniśikha, alarmed to hear of his own demise, and not quite sure whether he was alive or not, immediately returned to his own palace to ascertain the fact. In the meanwhile Śríngabhuja and his wife reached the capital of Varddhamána, where they were received with rapture by the prince's parents, and spent the rest of their days in uninterrupted felicity."

In the ninth book are narrated a number of stories for the consolation of Naraváhanadatta, on the disappearance of his favourite bride Madana Manchuká, their subjects being the temporary separation and final reunion of faithful couples. They wind up with a compendious recital of the adventures of Nala and Damayantí**, known to English readers as it occurs in its primitive form in the Mahábhárata, by the version of Mr. Millman. We have therefore one limit in its chronology determined. It must be older than the eleventh century. It is no doubt very much older, but so much is certain. The next book, the tenth, is of still greater importance than any of its predecessors in the history of fiction, as the fourth section of it constitutes one portion of the fables of Pilpay, the

* [or rather, he was made invisible by his wife, cháditaṅ vidyayá.]

** [ed. by H. Brockhaus: Die Sage von Nala und Damayantí. Leipzig: 1859. It forms the latter part of ch. 56.]

first book of the Pancha Tantra and Kalíla wa Damna, the story of the Lion Pingalaka, the Bull Sanjívaka and the two Jackals Damanaka and Karaṭaka. The stories and the order in which they succeed agree better with the tales and arrangement of the Kalíla wa Damna then even the Pancha Tantra, and it would appear therefore that we have in the Kathá Sarit Ságara an earlier representative of the original collection than even the Pancha Tantra, at least as it is now met with; a comparative catalogue of the contents of each may throw some light on the relationship of the different collections *.

Stories in the Pancha Tantra, Kalíla wa Damna, and Kathá Sarit Ságara.

Pancha Tantra.	Kalíla wa Damna.	Kathá Sarit Ságara.
Merchant and his Bull, Lion and two Jackals —forming the introduction and framework.	Same.	Same.
1. Monkey and Timber.	1. Same.	1. Same.
2. Fox and Drum.	2. Same.	2. Same.
3. King, Merchant and Slave.		
4. Adventures of an Ascetic.	3. Same.	
5. Magic Garuḍa.		
6. Two Crows.		
7. Crane killed by the Crab.	5. Swan killed by the Crab.	3. Crane killed by the Crab.

* [Benfey, l. l., I, 419 f.]

Pancha Tantra.	Kalíla wa Damna.	Kathá Sarit Ságara.
8. Lion and Hare.	6. Same.	4. Same.
9. King, Flea and Bug.	8. Same.	5. Same.
10. Jackal dyed.		
11. Lion, Tiger, Crow, Jackal and Camel.	9. Same.	6. Same.
12. Tittibha and the Sea.	10. Same.	7. Same.
13. Tortoise and Geese.	4. Same.	8. Same.
14. Three Fishes.	7. Same.	9. Same.
15. Elephant and Sparrow, Woodpecker, Fly and Frog.		
16. Swan, Creeper, and Fowler.		
17. Ram and Lion. Battle between the Bull and Lion.	Same.	Same.
18. Lion, Jackal and Camel.		
19. King, General and Ascetic.		
20. Snake changed to a Man.		
21. Parrot and Death.		
22. Monkies and Fire Flies.	11. Same.	10. Same.
23. Honest Man and Knave.	12. Two Friends and Bag of Money.	11. Brothers and Bag of Money.
24. Crane, Mungoose and Snake.	4. Same.	12. Same.
25. Rats that eat Iron.	13. Same.	13. Same.
26. Two Parrots.		
27. King's Son and his Companions.	(14th Book.-King's Son and his Companions.)	
Death of the Bull.	Same.	Same.

There is only a difference of one story therefore between the contents of the Kathá Sarit Ságara in this section and of the fifth book of the Kalíla wa Damna, the four preceding books of which treat of new and introductory matters prefixed by the translator. The omitted story however is a remarkable one, and one of great popularity in Europe. It relates the adventures of a religious mendicant called Deva Śarman in the Pancha Tantra* and Hitopadeśa**, but not named in the Kalíla wa Damna, who in his wanderings puts up at the house of a barber; the barber's wife goes to an assignation with a lover, and leaves her confidante in her place. The barber, imagining that his wife is present, and provoked at her misbehaviour, throws his razor at her in the dark, and deprives her of her nose. The wife returns, and finding what has happened, prays to the gods that if she is virtuous her nose may be restored to her; and as her face is found in the morning without any defective feature, her husband is convinced of her immaculate purity, and suspects her no more. That this story jumped with the humours of our forefathers is proved by its numerous repetitions and imitations, as, with some modifications, it occurs as the Fabliau of the 'Cheveux Coupés,' the 'Une verge pour l'autre' of the 'Cent Nouvelles Nouvelles,' a story in the Decameron, in the collection of Malespini, and in the Contes of La

* [I, 4. Benfey, l. l., I, 140 ff.]

** [II, 7. Brockhaus in "Berichte der Königl. Sächs. Ges. d. Wiss." 1853, p. 198 ff.]

Fontaine, and has been dramatized in the "Guardian" of Massinger. In the East it is found in the Tooti Náma, or Tales of a Parrot, the Bahár Dánish, and other popular collections *.

In the fifth section of the same book occurs the skeleton of the first book of the Hitopadeśa, the second of the Pancha Tantra, and seventh of the Kalíla wa Damna, the Mitralábha or acquirement of friends, as illustrated by the association of the Rat, the Crow, the Tortoise and the Deer. The identity is confined to the general outline however, and none of the episodical tales are inserted. The purport of the narration is to contrast the fidelity and attachment of which animals are capable with the treachery of women, in illustration of which follows a story of a jealous husband and his wife. A man had a very beautiful wife, of whom he was so devotedly fond that he scarcely ever suffered her to be out of his sight. Having occasion to go from home he took her with him, and during his necessary absènce on business left her under the care of an old Brahman. Near the Brahman's house was a village of Bhils, foresters, and with one of them the wife eloped. The husband on his return having learnt what had happened, proceeded in quest of his wife to the Bhil village, and arriving there, whilst the men were out hunting, encountered his wife. She assured him that she had been carried away by force, and desired him to secrete himself in a cave till night, when she would

* [See above p. 14.]

escape along with him. He believed her, and hid himself; but when the lover returned in the evening the false wife betrayed her husband, and he was seized and bound to a tree in order to be offered as a human victim in the morning to the goddess Chańdí. His prayers to the goddess however moved her to free him from his bonds, and he availed himself of his freedom to kill his rival and cut off his head. The wife had still art enough to persuade him of her innocence, and accompanied him in his flight, carrying with her the head of her Bhil lover. Upon their arrival at the first city they came to, she produced the head, declared it was her husband's and gave the real husband in charge to the police as the murderer. He was taken before the king, but the investigation established his innocence and his wife's guilt. She had her ears and nose cut off, and was deserted by her husband, who was now cured of his misplaced confidence in her affection. It may be remarked that frequent mention is made in the Kathá Sarit Ságara of the sacrifice of human victims by the barbarous tribes inhabiting the woods and mountains, who, although not Hindus, seem to have adopted as their favourite divinity some of the terrific forms of Durgá, and offered to her human sacrifices: the practice still prevails amongst them when it can be perpetrated with impunity, but it is contrary to the letter and to the spirit of the genuine Hindu ritual.

The sixth section of the tenth book contains the war between the Crows and the Owls, which forms the subject of the third books of the Pancha Tantra and Hitopadeśa, the eighth book of the Kalíla wa Damna, and the fourth chapter of the Persian imitation of it, the Anwári Soheilí.

Pancha Tantra.	K. S. S.	K. D.	Anwári Soheilí.
Introduction —War of the Crows and Owls.	The Same.	The Same.	The Same.
	1. Ass in Lion's Skin.		1. The King and his Mistress.
1. Elephant and Hares.	2. Same.	1. Same.	2. Same.
2. Hare, Sparrow and Cat.	3. Same.	2. Same.	3. Same.
3. Brahman, Rogues, and Goat.	4. Same.	3. Same.	4. Same.
4. Snake killed by Ants.			
5. Snake and Brahman's Son.			
6. Swans and Strange Bird.			
7. Fowler and Pigeons.			
8. Husband, Wife and Robber.	5. The Same.	4. The Same.	5. The Same.
9. Brahman, Thief and Rákshas.	6. The Same.		6. The Same.
10. Prince with a Snake in his Belly.			
11. Husband under the Bed.	7. The Same.	5. The Same.	7. The Same.
12. Brahman and Mouse changed to a Girl.	8. The Same.	6. The Same.	8. Monkeys and Bears.
13. Bird that voided Gold.			9. The Same.
14. Lion and Fox.			
15. Old Snake and Frogs.	9. The Same.	7. The Same.	10. The Same.
16. Brahman and his Wife.			11. The two Sparrows.

Of these stories several are well known in the narrative fictions of Europe; some of the identifications are pointed out in the 'Analysis of the Pancha Tantra,' and others by M. L. Deslongchamps. Thus the first of the Kathá Sarit Ságara, which occurs in another book of the Pancha Tantra*, is a very common apologue in all collections; the third or second of the Pancha Tantra and Kalíla wa Damna has been imitated by La Fontaine in the fable of Le chat, la belette et le petit lapin**. The story of the Brahman who is persuaded to part with his goat is found in les Facécieuses nuits du Seigneur Straparole***. The fifth story, which is found in the Pancha Tantra alone, is considered by M. Deslongchamps to be the same as La Confiance perdue of Senecé†. It is also found in the collection of Marie de France, a fabulist of the thirteenth century. The husband, wife and robber, and the mouse changed into a girl, are both modernized by Fontaine; the latter he derived from the Livre des Lumières of Daniel Sahid; the former occurs in the Cent Nouvelles Nouvelles††. In this, as in the story of the bull and the lion, the Kathá Sarit Ságara agrees better than the Pancha Tantra with the Arabic work, and may, there-

* [IV, 7; above p. 46.]

** [ap. Robert, Fables inédites, II, 107. cf. Benfey, l. l., I, 350 ff.]

*** [Paris: 1857, I, XVI & p. 46. F. W. V. Schmidt, die Mährchen des Straparola. Berlin: 1817, p. 308. Above p. 37.]

† [Paris: 1855, p. 119. Le Grand d'Aussy, IV, 389. Kurz ad B. Waldis I, 26. Above p. 38.]

†† [La Fontaine IX, 7 & 15. Livre des L. p. 279. Cent N. N. 16. Above p. 41 f.]

fore, be of earlier date; at the same time the style of the stories is unequivocally that of an abridgement, and they no doubt existed in some more detailed arrangement, and very possibly associated with others not here inserted.

In the next section of this book occurs the excellent story of the monkey and Śiśumára or Porpoise. In the Pancha Tantra, the Makara, a nondescript marine animal, is substituted for the Śiśumára; and, in the Mohammedan versions of the story, a tortoise takes the place of the Hindu aquatic. There is a greater coincidence again between the Kalíla wa Damna and our text in this story than between the former and the Pancha Tantra, in which last the story includes nine others; in the Arabic work, and in the Kathá Sarit Ságara, it has but one, that of the sick lion, the jackal (or fox) and the ass. The monkeys and tortoises, so often introduced in these stories, are, as M. de Sacy remarks, evidence of an Indian origin. "Les singes et les tortues souvent mis en scène dans ces fables appartiennent plutôt à l'Inde qu'à la Perse."—Mémoire Historique, vii. But this is still more applicable to such entirely Indian animals as the Makara or Śiśumára.

We have in this section also what may be perhaps the original of another well-known Arabian story, one of the earliest in the Thousand and One Nights. Two young Brahmans travelling are benighted in a forest, and take up their lodging in a tree near a lake. Early in the night a number of people come from the water, and having made preparation for an entertainment retire; a Yaksha, a genie, then comes out of the lake with his two wives, and spends the night there; when he and one of his wives are asleep, the other, seeing the youths, invites them to approach her, and to encourage them, shows them a hundred rings received from former gallants, notwithstanding her husband's precautions, who keeps her locked up in a chest at the bottom of the lake. The Hindu story-teller is more moral than the Arab. The youths reject her advances; she wakes the genie who is going to put them to death, but the rings are produced in evidence against the unfaithful wife, and she is turned away with the loss of her nose. The story is repeated in the next section with some variation; the lady has ninety and nine rings, and is about to complete the hundredth, when her husband, who is here a Nága, a snake-god, wakes, and consumes the guilty pair with fire from his mouth.

In the commencement of the eighth section of this book we have the story of the mungoose, the snake and child (see p. 54), and in the same section is a long and not uninteresting story of two friends, Ghaṫa and Karpara. They become thieves, and break into the king's palace to plunder his treasure. While Ghaṫa keeps watch without, Karpara makes his way into the inner apartments, where the princess sees him, and falls in love with him. She gives him much valuable property, with which he despatches his companion to their home, and returns into the palace. He is surprised there, and by the commands of the king hung upon a tree. On his way to the place of execution, Ghaṭa, who, alarmed at his friend's not returning, had come back to seek for him, sees Karpara led to the gibbet. Karpara, by signs unperceived by the guards, commends the princess to the care of Ghaṭa; he by the same means expresses his promise to effect her rescue. Accordingly at night he enters the palace, liberates the princess from her bonds, and carries her off. When the king is apprised of this, he concludes the perpetrator of the deed must have been a friend of Karpara, and that it is likely, therefore, that he will attempt to obtain the body, in order to perform its funeral rites; he accordingly places guards around the tree on which the corpse is suspended, and commands them to arrest any one who shall display any particular grief on viewing the body, or shall seek to take it away. Ghaṭa determines, as the king had anticipated, to procure the body of his friend, and commit it to the flames. He disguises himself as a countryman, with one of his servants as a woman, and another carrying a jar of sweetmeats, in which the narcotic juice of the Dhattura has been infused. Pretending to have lost his way, he approaches the guards, and, entering into familiar conversation with them, invites them to partake of his sweetmeats, his wife, he says, being very famous for her skill in making them. The guards eat and fall asleep, and Ghaṭa cuts down and burns the body of Karpara. He afterwards contrives to carry off the ashes; and the king, finding precaution useless, causes it to be proclaimed that he will give his daughter and half his kingdom to the man who has done these deeds. We have in these incidents an obvious analogy to those of the story of the knight and his two sons in the History of the Seven Sages of Rome, as above intimated, and still more to some of the circumstances of the story of Rhampsinites, king of Egypt, as narrated by Herodotus, (Essai sur les Fables Indiennes,) if not to the leading incident in the tragedy of Antigone*. The Indian story continues in a strain intended to demonstrate the depravity of women. Ghaṫa is persuaded by the princess that the king's offer is merely a trap for him; and, instead of accepting it, he departs with her and a religious mendicant, his associate, to a distant country. On the journey his mistress and friend accomplish his murder. The princess afterwards abandons the mendicant, and leads a life of profligacy paralleled by similar instances, which grow out of the story of her adventures.

The eleventh book is occupied with one story only, that of Velá, a damsel married to a merchant's son; the leading incidents are their shipwreck, separation and re-union. It is only worth while to notice the frequency with which adventures by sea are narrated in this collection, and, indeed, in other works of the

* [Herod. II, 121. Keller, Dyocletianus Leben, p. 55. Keller, Li Romans des sept Sages, p. CXCIII. Liebrecht's transl. of Dunlop's History of Fiction, p. 197 & 264.]

same, or an earlier date, showing that at the period in question the Hindus were not accustomed to regard sea-voyages as either unlawful or unusual.

The twelfth book presents several examples of the transformation of human persons to animals, of which instances are so frequent in the Arabian Nights, although it may be doubted if the notion be an article of Mohammedan superstition. With the Hindus it is but the second step in the doctrine of the metempsychosis, as the belief that men and women become animals in a future life readily reconciles them to the admission of the possibility that they may assume brute forms even in this. They have also exemplifications of it in their mythology; and Vishńu himself, in three of his incarnations, is a fish, a tortoise and a boar. In the first section of this book of the Kathá Sarit Ságara, Vámadatta has a wife who becomes possessed of magical powers; he detects her in some of her vicious practices, and is about to put her to death, when she throws some dust into his face, and he is turned to a buffalo, in which state he is sold by his wife, and becomes a beast of burthen. Another female sorceress discovers his true nature, restores him to it, and gives him her daughter in marriage; she enables him also to transform his wife to a mare, in which form he inflicts upon her daily chastisement. There is no hesitation in recognising in the story the leading incidents in the stories of the old man and his two dogs, and of Zobeide and her two sisters, and particularly in the story of Syed Naoman in the Thousand and One Nights; in the latter of these the wicked wife is transformed also into a mare. In the fourth section again of this same book we have some transformations which call to mind the adventures of Apuleius in the Golden Ass, or the still more ancient metamorphoses of Circe. Bhímaparákrama, coming to Ujjayiní, puts up in the house of a woman, who receives him hospitably. He goes to rest; but, waking in the night, sees his hostess busy in preparing some dishes of fried barley-meal, and muttering charms over them. Suspecting her to be a sorceress, he watches his opportunity, and transfers the meal to some other plates, whilst he replaces it with meal he finds set apart. The sorceress invites him to breakfast with her, and, unwittingly eating the barley she had bewitched, is changed to a she-goat. Bhímaparákrama sells her to a butcher. The butcher's wife is a sorceress also; and, although unable to save her friend, determines to revenge her; she therefore finds the youth when asleep, and, by tying a thread round his neck, changes him to a peacock. He is found in this condition, and liberated by his friend Mŕigánkadatta, prince of Ayodhyá. The connecting chain of the whole of the twelfth book is the marriage of Mŕigánkadatta with the princess of Ujjayiní; but before this can be effected the prince incurs the displeasure of his father, and is banished with his ten companions, the sons of his father's ministers. They set off together for Ujjayiní. In passing through a forest they find an ascetic sitting under a tree; they inquire of him his purposes in such a solitude, to which he replies that underneath the tree is the dwelling of a Nága, a snake god, who is master of a miraculous sword, the holder of which enjoys superhuman powers; that this sword is to be forced from its possessor by incantations, in which he asks them to give him aid. They assent; his magic compels the nymph of the sword to issue from the tree, but her beauty so bewilders him that he pauses in his process, and forgets his art. The Nága avails himself of the opportunity, appears, and destroys the magician, and condemns the inconsiderate youths to a temporary separation from each other. They are ultimately re-united with the prince, and repeat to him their several adventures. The scheme of this series of narratives is similar to that of a very excellent and popular Hindu work, ascribed to Dańdí, a writer of the ninth or tenth century, the Daśa Kumára, the Ten Princes, in which a prince and his nine companions are separated for a season, and recount what has happened to each when they meet again. The stories, however, are different. There are in the eighth section of this book incidental passages of some interest in the history of Sanskrit literature: the adoption of names, persons and incidents, and even the plagiarism of expressions found in well-known compositions, as the dramas of Mádhava and Málati, and Vikrama and Urvaśí, and the poem of the Megha Dúta, or cloud-messenger, a work of Kálidása, to the prior celebrity of which they therefore bear testimony.

The ninth section of the twelfth book also is of

importance in the same respect, in its subservience to the history of Sanskrit writings, as it contains the plan and details of a collection extremely popular in India, existing both in Sanskrit and in all the vernacular dialects that have any literature, Hindee, Bengali, Mahratta, Telugu, Tamil, and the rest. This is the Vetála Panchavinśati: twenty-five tales of a Vetála, being related by a sprite, who haunts cemeteries and animates dead bodies, to Vikramáditya, king of Ujjayiní, according to the usual version, to Trivikrama Sena, king of Pratishṫhána or Pythan, on the Godávarí, according to the Kathá Sarit Ságara. The king receives for a long time from a religious mendicant daily presents of a fruit, which he hands over to his treasurer; at last a pet monkey takes the fruit, and breaking it open, a precious jewel falls from it. The treasurer being questioned as to what he had done with the fruits previously presented, reports that they had been thrown behind a door, where they still are; but being desired to produce them, discovers that they have all decayed, leaving a pile of valuable jewels on the spot where they had been cast. The king inquires of the mendicant how he became possessed of these gems, on which it appears that he is a Yogí or ascetic, engaged in rites for the acquirement of superhuman faculties, for the accomplishment of which a dead body is necessary; and he has been propitiating Trivikrama in order to induce him to aid his operations, a man of undaunted resolution being alone capable of conveying a corpse, or in fact a body in which a malignant spirit abides, from the tree where it is suspended. The king undertakes the exploit, braves with unshaken intrepidity the horrors of the charnelground, cuts down the body, and lifts it on his shoulders. He is surprised, however, to find it address him, and propose to beguile the way by a series of narratives. It is essential to the safe conveyance of the Vetála that it should be effected in silence, and he therefore cunningly contrives that the Rájá shall not observe the condition. At the end of each story he proposes to the Rájá some question, arising out of what he has narrated; Vikrama replies; the body flies back to the tree, and the Rájá has the trouble of returning, and again endeavouring to secure it. The Vetála at last, subdued by the prince's perseverance, becomes his servant, and apprises him that the ascetic has a plot against his life, which he instructs the Rájá how to frustrate. The spirit being placed before the ascetic is worshipped by him, and he then desires the Rájá to perform a reverential prostration to the Vetála. The Rájá answers he knows not how to do it properly, and begs the ascetic to show him. The ascetic accordingly casts himself prostrate on the ground, when the Rájá cuts off his head. He then returns to his palace, and ever afterwards commands the services of the Vetála. The Vetála Panchavinśati has appeared in an English dress, having been translated by Rájá Kálí Krishńa, a native gentleman of Calcutta, and printed there*. Some of the stories have been imitated in the literature of other countries. There is one remarkable tale, however, found in the Hindu version, which does not occur in this setting of the stories. This is the story alluded to by Gibbon, as accounting for the disgrace into which the empress Eudocia, the wife of Theodosius the younger, fell. A Brahman presents a beautiful fruit to the king Bhartŕi Hari; he gives it to his queen; she transfers it to a gallant; he hands it to a courtezan, by whom it is again brought as a present to the king, who thus detects his wife's infidelity. According to the story, and to popular tradition, Bhartŕi Hari, disgusted with the world, abandoned, in consequence of this occurrence, his throne, and retired to a religious life. The French translation of Moreri, relating the story as applicable to Eudocia, says: "L'empereur se chagrina au sujet d'un fruit qu'il lui avait donné, dont elle fit présent au Paulin et que ce dernier rapporta à ce prince, ce fruit fut une vraie pomme de discorde." The authority for the story is Theophrastus, whose history of the Roman empire closes in the beginning of the ninth century. From the literature of the lower empire the story became familiar to that of Europe, and is dramatized by Massinger in his Emperor of the East. The probability of its Asiatic origin is confirmed by its being incor-

* [Bytal-Puchisi. Calcutta: 1834.]

porated into the Thousand and One Nights, under the title of the Three Apples *.

The thirteenth book is short, and recounts the adventures of two young Brahmans, who effect secret marriages with a princess and her friend. The incidents are curious and diverting, but they are chiefly remarkable from being the same as the contrivances by which Mádhava and Makaraṅda obtain their mistresses in the drama entitled Málatí and Mádhava, or the Stolen Marriage. (See Specimens of the Theatre of the Hindus.) The two next books, the fourteenth and fifteenth, are of less general interest than the preceding, the scene of action being laid chiefly amongst the fabulous regions of the Vidyádharas. In the first, the prince Naraváhanadatta makes an addition to his domestic arrangements of five Vidyádharí wives. In the second he is crowned emperor of the Vidyádhara race.

The connecting thread of the series of tales should here terminate; but in the next book, the sixteenth, we have an account of the death of Vatsa, who resigns his throne to Gopálaka, the brother of his wife Vásavadattá, and, accompanied by his wives and ministers, goes to Mount Kálanjana, where a heavenly chariot descends, and conveys them all to heaven. Gopálaka, inconsolable for the loss of his brother-in-law, soon relinquishes his regal state, and making over Kauśámbí to his younger brother, Pálaka, repairs to the White

* [Nights 18—24.]

Mountain, and spends the rest of his days in the hermitage of Káśyapa. We have then an account of the son of Pálaka falling in love with a young girl of low caste, a Cháńḋálí, and different stories illustrative of unequal matches, some of which have been told before. A very convenient doctrine is maintained by Pálaka's ministers, that the very circumstance of the prince's being enamoured of the Cháńḋálí is a proof that she cannot be truly of so base an origin, but that she must be a princess or goddess in disguise; otherwise it were impossible that she should have attracted the affections of any noble individual. They therefore counsel the king to demand the nymph of her father. The father consents, on condition that the Brahmans of Ujjayiní eat in his house. Pálaka issues orders that the Brahmans, to the number of eighteen thousand, shall dine with the Cháńḋála. They are of course in great alarm, as this is a virtual degradation, and loss of caste, and they apply to Mahákála, the form of Śiva especially worshipped in Ujjayiní, to know what to do. He commands them in a dream to comply, as Matanga, the supposed Cháńḋála, is in truth a Vidyádhara. He had conspired against the life of Naraváhanadatta, in order to prevent his becoming emperor of the Vidyádharas, and had been therefore condemned by Śiva to live in Ujjayiní with his family as Cháńḋálas. The curse was to terminate when eighteen thousand Brahmans should eat in his house; and this being accomplished, he is restored to his rank, and his daughter is a fit bride for the son of the king.

The principal feature in this tale deserving of notice is its intimation of an indignity offered to the Brahmans of Ujjayiní by a king named Pálaka, a circumstance which is either derived from an ancient play, the Mŕichchhakaťí, or taken, as well as the drama from some historical tradition.

The two last books are composed of narratives told by Naraváhanadatta, when on a visit to his uncle Gopálaka at the hermitage of Káśyapa. He repeats those stories which were communicated to him when he was separated from Madanamanchuká, to console him under the anguish of separation. The first book treats entirely of the loves of Muktáphala Ketu, a prince of the Vidyádharas, and Padmávatí, daughter of the king of the Gandharbas. The former is condemned by a holy person to become a man, and he is thus for a season separated from the latter. He is, after a short time, restored to his station and his wife. The story is not without merit, but it is tedious, and relieved by no episodical tales. The last book is of a more diversified description, and has Vikramáditya or Vikramaśíla, son of Mahendráditya, king of Ujjayiní, for its hero, and describes his victories over hostile princes, and his acquirement of various princesses. These are interspersed with love adventures, some of which reiterate the calumnies against women, and with stories relating the tricks of professed cheats. Several of them have some curious matter, but nothing that reflects any particular light upon the migrations of storytelling.

The sketch thus given of the contents of the Kathá Sarit Ságara will show that it has been judiciously selected by Dr. Brockhaus for publication and translation. It is impossible that so voluminous a compilation should be without a due proportion of tediousness and insipidity, and the spirit of the narrations is not improved by the substitution of verse for prose. The verse is in general of very simple construction, and the style is upon the whole sufficiently easy; the metrical arrangement, however, involves a formality and sententiousness which are inconsistent with the freedom that gives animation to narrative. The work, however, is full of interest, as abounding with pictures of national manners and feelings, and as offering the oldest extant form of many of the tales which were once popular in Europe. It is not necessary to suppose that the West was, in the middle ages, barren of invention; that the novelists and fablers of Europe were destitute of imagination. Many of these fictions are no doubt "native, and to the manner born"; but it is equally indubitable that they were indebted to the East for many of their "findings", and that the Hindus occupy an early and a prominent place in the History of Fiction.

VIII.

EXTRACTS FROM THE DAŚAKUMÁRA, OR THE TEN PRINCES.

From the Quarterly Oriental Magazine, Vol. V, (1826), p. 297–314: Vol. VI, p. 106–124 & 211–227; Vol. VII (1827), p. 279–294; and Vol. VIII (1828), p. 69–83.

FIRST SECTION.

In Pushpapurí, a city of Magadha, ruled Rájahansa, an excellent and accomplished monarch; his queen was named Vasumatí. He had three ministers, Dharmapála, Padmodbhava, and Sitavarmá, who were the royal councillors by hereditary succession; of these Sitavarmá had two sons, Sumati and Satyavarmá. Dharmapála had three, Sumantra, Sumitra, and Kámapála; and Padmodbhava two, Suśruta and Ratnodbhava.

Satyavarmá, the son of Sitavarmá, becoming disgusted with the world, went upon a pilgrimage to foreign lands. Kámapála, the son of Dharmapála, attaching himself to low company, parasites, actors, and women, led a vagabond life; and Ratnodbhava who was engaged in traffic spent much time in distant voyages:

the other brothers succeeded to the ministerial situations held by their sires.

It happened that a war broke out between Rájahansa and Mánasára, King of Málava, in the course of which the former led a powerful host against his enemy; he was encountered by the King of Málava, and a furious conflict ensued in which Mánasára was defeated, and taken prisoner. The king of Magadha was of too generous a character, to wreak his vengeance on a captive prince, and far from treating Mánasára with rigour, he immediately restored him to his liberty and his kingdom.

Rájahansa now ruled the whole world without a rival, or anxiety; still he was not happy: he grieved that his union had not been blessed with progeny, and to obtain children was the subject of his constant supplications to the Creator of the universe, Náráyańa. His prayers were not in vain: his principal Queen shortly afterwards conceived, on the anouncement of which happy event Rájahansa, inviting all his royal and princely friends, celebrated with great splendour the Símanta festival. On this occasion whilst seated on the Throne, the Chamberlain informed the King, a holy man had arrived at Court, who begged admittance to the presence; permission was granted. As soon as he appeared, Rájahansa recognised him through his disguise as one of his own confidential emissaries, and dismissing the Courtiers he withdrew with his ministers, and enquired smilingly what news the spy had brought. The spy replied: 'In obedience to your Royal commands I entered the capital of the Prince of Málava: his late overthrow rankling in his heart he addressed himself to Maheśwara in the shrine of Mahákála, and by the fervour of his devotion obtained a divine boon, a club endowed with the certain power of slaying one individual: armed with this weapon, confident of victory, and anticipating your destruction Mánasára is levying forces to march against your Majesty.' When the Ministers heard this intelligence, they advised the King to retire into the Fort, and resign to them the conduct of the war; but he disdained their council, and determined to meet the enemy in person. Mánasára advanced into Magadha, and the Ministers prevailed upon Rájahansa to send the women to a place of security in the Vindhya Mountains. The armies met on the confines of the Province, and an obstinate engagement took place. In the battle the Princes encountered, and Mánasára directed the fatal mace against the head of the King of Magadha; he missed his aim, but the blow killed the Charioteer, and left the King senseless; the horses being without a master ran off frightened towards the Hills, and carried their unconscious Lord into the thickets, which had given shelter to his household.

The troops of Magadha, seeing their Sovereign's fate, fled in every direction; and the king of Málava, now victorious, overran the Country, and established his own residence at Pushpapurí. The Ministers of Rájahansa had all been left on the field, covered with wounds, but not dead, and having recovered a little with the fresh breeze of the morning, their first effort was to seek for the body of the king: the search proving fruitless, they repaired to the retreat in the mountains, which concealed the Queen, and reported to her the misadventures of the conflict, and the disappearance of her husband. Vasumatí was resolved not to survive her Lord, but was dissuaded by the Ministers, especially as she would thus frustrate the decrees of the stars, which had predicted her giving birth to a lovely, valiant, and illustrious Prince.

The Queen was silenced by this opposition: she held her peace, but kept her purpose, and at midnight she stole forth to the neighbouring thicket, where, fastening her veil round her neck, she attempted with it to suspend herself from the branch of a Beŕ tree, exclaiming "May that Lord whose beauty was as the flowery bow of Káma be again my husband in a future life." At that moment the king who had been hurled out of his car on that very spot, and now recovered, heard and recognised the voice of his Queen: he called to her, and she hearing his accents, hastened to him agitated with doubt and alarm. Delighted to find him still alive, she loudly called for assistance, when the servants of the Rájá approached, and seeing their master, joyfully prostrated themselves at his feet: they then prepared a tent, had his wounds healed without delay, and to console him cited the example of Hariśchandra and other Princes who, after experiencing adversity, had again obtained an imperial dominion. After a time Rájahansa went with his attendants to visit Vámadeva, a holy sage, who resided in the adjoining thickets, and having spent a short time with him, requested his aid to recover his kingdom. The sage recommended him to remain tranquil, assuring him that his Queen was about to give birth to a son, who would revenge him on all his foes. Vasumatí shortly afterwards bore a Prince, who was named Rájaváhana, and at the same time it happened that there were born sons to the King's four Ministers, the son of Sumati was named Pramati; of Sumantra, Chitragupta; of Sumitra, Mantragupta; and of Suśruta, Viśruta; these grew up together, the playfellows and friends of the Prince.

One day a Brahman approached the King, and delivering a young boy to him thus said:

TALE.

Sire, being one day on my travels through a forest, I saw a young woman in ragged and foul attire, weeping bitterly. Moved by compassion, I asked, why thus alone in a dreary forest she was wandering, and in grief. She replied, as well as her sobs would permit her: "Prahúravarmá, Prince of Mithilá, came to Pushpapurí, when the Kings were assembled at the Símantiní ceremony of the Queen of Magadha, and afterwards accompanying the King against his enemy, the Prince of Málava, shared the defeat of his Ally: making his escape from the field, he marched towards his own country with such of his followers as survived the engagement, but proceeding through a wood was unexpectedly attacked by the Śavaras, and most of his people were slain: with great difficulty he effected his escape, and secured the retreat of the females of his family, guarded by a select corps. I and my daughter who were the nurses of the Prince's two twin sons were unable to keep up with him in his flight; we were lost in the wood, and whilst thus deserted, a fierce tiger rushed open-mouthed upon me. I attempted to fly, but in my terror fell, and with me fell the boy I bore in my arms; he scrambled away, and hid himself beneath a cow, that lay dead near us. The tiger seized the carcase and was dragging it along, when an arrow from a Forester streched the monster lifeless on the ground. The forester pleased with the child's appearance took him up, and carried him away, whither I knew not, nor did I know where to seek my daughter and her charge: overcome with agitation and fatigue I became insensible, and was found in that state by a Cowherd, who conveyed me to his hut, and gave me food and shelter. Thus recovered I have issued forth to search for my nurseling, or to return at least to my Lord to inform him what has so sadly chanced." Thus having said she left me. Sympathising with the distress which the Rájá of Mithilá would suffer, I determined to seek his children. On my search I beheld a stately Temple of Chańdiká, and approaching it, beheld a number of mountaineers collected, amongst whom was a fair child, whom they had resolved to sacrifice to the Goddess, in gratitude for their late victory, and for the propitiation of the deity in future. They differed as to the manner of killing their victim; some proposing to suspend him to the branch of a tree, and strike off his neck with a sword; some to set him as a mark for their arrows, and some to let him loose, and chace him with dogs. I approached and addressed them, saying: valiant Foresters, I am an old Brahman, who some days ago missed my way as I passed through your woods with my young son. I left him in the shade, whilst I went to recover the track, and when I returned I had lost my boy; Have any of you, worthy Sirs, encountered a stray child? They were pleased with my address, and producing the young Prince, asked if the boy was mine, I pretended that he was, and they resigned him to me. I received him and took my leave, and have brought him to you for protection.

The Rájá grieving for his friend Praháravarmá's misfortunes gladly took charge of the Prince; he named him Upaháravarmá, and brought him up as if he had been his own.

On one occasion as Rájahansa was travelling to holy places, he came to a village of Foresters, when he observed one of the women accompanied by a child of extraordinary beauty, and enquired of her who he was; she replied that, when her people defeated the troops of the Mithilá Prince, her husband brought this boy to her from the field, which was very near the village. The King on hearing this was satisfied it was his friend's son, and prevailed on the woman to relinquish the child; carrying him to his residence, he called him Apahâravarmá and brought him up with his own son.

The pupil of the sage Vámadeva one day brought a boy to the King and said: Prince, on one occasion, when I had bathed at Rámatírtha and was returning, I encountered in a forest an elderly woman bearing a child new born. I asked who she was, why in that lonely place, and what she was doing with the babe; she said: "In Kálayavana Island dwelt Kálagupta, a wealthy merchant: he had a daughter named Suvŕittá, who was married to a man of great wealth and abilities, the son of the minister of the King of Magadha, Ratnodbhava; in due time the wife became pregnant, and her husband being anxious to return to his own country set off with her privately for that purpose: the ship they embarked in was caught in a storm, and dashed to pieces: fortunately Suvŕittá and myself, who attended her as her nurse, got upon a plank, and were borne to land; what became of the crew and Ratnodbhava we knew not: the fright brought on premature pains, and in this wood my mistress has just been delivered of this child: she lies by the side of a pool under a tree senseless with her sufferings, and I have left her, to seek for assistance, bearing with me the infant, as the mother is unable to take care of it. The old woman had scarcely finished when a wild elephant sprang forth: she dropped the child, and ran away: I hid myself in a neighbouring clump whence I could see what chanced: the elephant picked up the infant with its trunk, when a fierce lion rushed upon the animal: the elephant in alarm cast the infant from its uplifted trunk towards the boughs of a tree, where an ape seeing the child, and taking it for some sort of fruit, caught it in his arms; finding his mistake the monkey laid the infant upon a net-work of the crossing branches, and bounded away, and the lion having killed the elephant likewise disappeared. I then ventured from my hiding place, took the child from the tree, and went in quest of its mother or nurse. Having sought for them through the thicket in vain, I brought the child with me to my superior, by whose desire I transfer him to your royal care.

The King was much astonished at the strange fortunes which had brought together the children of his friends, and his own, and was deeply grieved for the loss of his early associate Ratnodbhava: the brother of that chief, Suśruta, was equally afflicted for the loss of the father, and consoled by the preservation of the child; and to him the King consigned the boy, naming him Pushpodbhava, and directing him to be brought up with the Prince and his young companions.

One day Rájahansa observed the Queen nursing a strange infant, and approaching her he asked whose the child was. The Queen replied: I was awakened in the night by a celestial female, who delivered to me this infant, saying, I am the beloved of Kámapála the son of your Minister Dharmapála; my name is Tárávalí, the daughter of Mańibhadra, and by the command of the King of the Yakshas, I bring you this my son to be a servant to your son, whom future fame awaits, your Rájaváhana. So having said she disappeared, before I had recovered from my astonishment, and left the infant in my hands.

Rájahansa was not less astonished by the Queen's relation, and receiving the child he named him Arthapála, and gave him in charge to his uncle Sumitra to be brought up with the other Princes.

On another occasion one of Vámadeva's pupils brought a most lovely boy to the presence of the King, and said: I went, oh Monarch, in pilgrimage to the Káverí River, and there I saw an old woman on the bank with a child in her lap weeping violently. I asked the cause; she replied: formerly Satyavarmá, the son of Sitavarmá, minister of Rájahansa King of Magadha, came to this holy spot, and taking up his abode in a neighbouring Agrahára[1], he married Kálí the daughter of a Brahman: she proving barren, he espoused her younger sister Gaurí, by whom he had a son: the elder sister conceived a violent hatred for the child, and one day

[1] A sort of secular convent; lands and houses granted to Brahmans and their families.

seized an opportunity of pushing me, who am its nurse, along with the infant, into the stream. I supported myself and the child as well as I could, till we reached a floating tree, clinging to which we were borne along with the current to this place: on the tree was a black snake, by which I was bitten, and the poison spreads through my frame, so that I cannot long survive, and then what is to become of my child? so I thought, and as I thought, I wept.

She had scarcely finished, when she fell on the ground lifeless. I endeavoured with charms and drugs to arrest the venom, but it was too late; then committing her body to the flames, I took the child, and not knowing where to find the abode of its parents, I have brought him to your Majesty.

The King accordingly received the boy, and gave him to be reared under his uncle Sumati, naming him Somadatta, and directing him to be educated with the Prince and his companions.

So these boys were associated and went through their education together: they were taught to write and speak various tongues; the Holy Sciences, Policy, Rhetoric, History, and sacred Record (Puráńas), Metaphysics, Astrology, Law, and the morals of Princes, according to Káuťilya, and the Kámandakíya; and to play on many Instruments, and the sciences of Music, Medicine, and Magic; to manage the Horse, Elephant, and Car, to use various weapons; to excel in thieving, gaming and other such practices; and the King seeing their youth, and skill, and valour, felt proud of his juvenile band, and confident of triumphing with their aid over every danger.

SECOND SECTION.

On one occasion Vámadeva approached the King, surrounded by these Princes, each as lovely as Káma, and valiant as Kárttikeya; he returned the King's salutation with his benediction, the prostration of the Princes with his embrace, and thus addressed the King: "The time is arrived for your son to set forth to conquest: let Rájaváhana attended by his companions depart." Accordingly Rájaváhana, attended by his associates appointed to the various offices of state, took leave of his father in a propitious hour, and directing his course by the auspices he noticed, entered the Vindhya forest: there he saw a man covered with scars, with a body as hard as iron, and of hideous aspect; by his cord he seemed a Brahman, but in all other respects a Barbarian. Rájaváhana, receiving his respects, said, "How is it you reside in this lonely spot, fit only for the deer? why wear you this sacred cord, and yet by these wounds appear a savage woodman?" To this the stranger replied:

In this wood, oh! Prince, resided many Brahmans who followed the usages of the barbarians, and ate with them; foregoing the study of holy writ, the observances of their tribes, and their moral and social duties; of one of these I am the son, my name is

Mátanga: on one occasion with a party of savages I harried the neighbouring country. We bound the old men and the women, and brought away wealth and captives, and destroyed all else. On our return I observed a party of my associates menacing a Brahman with death. I commanded them to forbear, but they reviled, and fell upon me, and left me dead. I went to the city of Souls, and beheld its mighty King seated upon a lofty throne studded with splendid jewels. I bowed before him; he looked at me, and calling to Chitragupta said: 'This man's hour is not yet come. He dies in defence of a Brahman. That one virtuous act effaces all his former sins. Let him behold the penalty paid by the wicked, and then restore him to his former body.' Chitragupta then shewed me where the wicked were beaten with red-hot clubs, hurled into caldrons of scalding oil, pulverized with pestles, or pealed with adzes, and then giving me friendly counsel he dismissed me. Restored to my former body, I found the Brahman I had rescued sprinkling me, as I lay apparently fainting, with cool water; my friends who had heard of my encounter then arrived, and carried me home, and dressed my wounds, and the grateful Brahman still staid with me, and gave me instructions: he taught me to read, to understand the sacred Books, and to look on Śiva with the eye of wisdom. He then left me. After his departure, I abandoned my former life, quitted my family and home, and came to abide here, in undisturbed meditation upon the one God of all worlds. Something I have to say to you, but alone; follow me. The Prince withdrawing with him, he thus continued: Last night Śiva imparted to me a dream, saying, 'On the bank of the River of the Dańdárańya forest, behind the Sphaṫika linga, is a stone marked with the feet of the daughter of the Mountain Monarch: near that is a Chasm: in it is a Copper-plate, on which is written the means of making you sovereign of Pátála: your associate in this must be the Prince who to-day or to-morrow will come hither. You have come as he foretold, and now give me your aid. The Prince assented, and at midnight, leaving his friends asleep, accompanied Mátanga to a distant thicket: when his followers woke and missed him, they sought him in every direction, but their search proving vain, they agreed to separate, and after prosecuting their enquiries for some time, rendezvous finally at Ujjayiní.

Mátanga aided by the Prince, entered the Chasm, obtained the Talisman, and penetrated the path to Pátála. On arriving near a city they paused in a grove on the edge of a Pool where, agreeably to the directions of the plate, Mátanga made a fire, and offered Ghee, whilst the Prince stood watch against intrusion. Whilst thus employed, he was surprised to see his companion cast himself into the flames, and thence again rise in an angelic form. On this a damsel richly arrayed, and numerously attended, approached the grove: she presented to the Brahman a splendid jewel, and to his enquiry who she was replied in tones of exquisite sweetness,—

I am the daughter of the King of the Asuras: my name is Kálindí. Vishńu, impatient of my father's fame, destroyed him. A Saint, in compassion of my sorrow for his loss, announced that some heavenly-formed being would become my husband, and cherish these domains. I have awaited your coming, as the Chátaka expects the rain, and hearing of your arrival, I have come with the concurrence of my council, and the guidance of my desires, to offer the kingdom and myself, twin wives, to your espousal. Mátanga readily assented, married the Damsel, and became the King of Pátála. Rájaváhana took leave of him, receiving his thanks, and the jewel given him by Kálindí, which had the property of dispelling thirst and hunger: he returned by the Chasm to the place where he had left his followers, and finding no trace of them, set off to seek them. In his peregrinations he arrived in the city of Ujjayiní, and entering a Garden saw a man borne in a litter with his wife, and attended by his followers, approach. When they met the Prince, the man sprang from the litter exclaiming, my master! and fell at his feet. The Prince at last recognising him embraced him, and said, 'Somadatta, where have you been so long; what has befallen you; where do you go now; and who is this Damsel? declare.' Somadatta, after recovering from his agitation, thus replied:

THIRD SECTION.

SOMADATTA'S STORY.

"Whilst wandering in quest of your Highness, I arrived oppressed with thirst on the borders of a tank; as I stooped to drink the cool water, I saw a most brilliant diamond on the sand. I picked it up, and went on my way. After some time, I entered for shelter and rest into a Temple, where I saw an old man with several boys, whom I respectfully saluted. He said, 'you see me living here with these orphans in this dreary place, and subsisting by charity.' I enquired of him who was the sovereign encamped in those tents I beheld, his name, and what was the cause of his coming hither. The old man answered:

'The camp belongs to Mattakála, King of Láta; the King of this country is Víraketu; his daughter Vámalochaná was celebrated for her beauty, and this coming to Mattakála's ears, he demanded her in marriage. Her father refused to assent, but was compelled by Mattakála's superior force, and gave her up. Mattakála now takes her with him to his own country to espouse her there, and is on his way, but halts here to hunt. Mánapála, the minister of Víraketu appointed to guard the Princess with a strong escort, encamps separately, and mourns his master's disgrace.' Finding the old man so intelligent, and pitying his state, I gave him the jewel I had found; he accepted it with many blessings, and departed with his scholars. Overcome with fatigue I fell asleep and was awakened by a loud outcry of "this is the thief," when looking up, I found the old man bound and guarded; the guard quitted him and seized me, and without listening to my defence carried me off, tied hand and foot, and threw me into prison, amongst a number of people they called my confederates. I learned from my fellow prisoners that they were the servants of the minister, who at their master's instigation had broke by night into the apartment of the King of Láťa, hoping to kill him, but he was not there, and missing him, they plundered the apartment, and carried off the valuables into the woods: the next day they were overtaken, and brought back with their spoil, excepting one gem of great price, which was not to be found, and which was accidentally the one I had met with. The identity of our fate produced a friendship between us, and taking an opportunity we broke out of our prison, and fled to the camp of Mánapála. When he heard my story from his people, he treated me with kindness. The King of Láťa sent to reclaim us by an insolent message, which still more incensed the minister; "who is this King, he cried; what have we to do with him," and he sent back the messengers with disgrace; their report inflamed Mattakála to rage, and although slightly attended, he immediately attacked our camp, where Mánapála, who expected and desired the contest, was fully prepared to receive him; he provided me with arms, a chariot and steed, and directed his troops to follow me, confiding in my prowess. We rushed to the encounter. I met the King of Láṭa, struck him from his chariot, and cut off his head; his troops fled, and we plundered their camp. The minister welcomed me with honour: the King who had beheld the conflict rewarded my exertions with his daughter's hand and adopted me into the empire as Yuvarája. Nothing was wanting to my happiness but your presence, and I was now on my way to the shrine of Mahákála, where a Seer predicted I should find my lost friend." Whilst thus engaged in converse, they saw a man advancing who proved to be Pushpodbhava; they hastened to embrace him, and after their first greetings had passed, he thus related his adventures.

SECTION FOURTH.

STORY OF PUSHPODBHÁVA.

When we found that your Highness did not return, we set off severally in search of you. After I had passed some time in the pursuit I one day rested myself in the shade of a tree, at the foot of a mountain, when suddenly a speck appeared, and a man fell upon me; he lay senseless awhile, till I brought him to himself, when I enquired his story. He thus replied:

'My name is Ratnodbhava, I am the son of Padmodbhava, the minister of the King of Magadha. I went as a merchant to Kálayavana Island, where I married a merchant's daughter. I was returning with her, when we were wrecked near shore, and all were drowned except myself. The loss of my wife, however, overwhelmed me in the depths of despair; and although the counsel of a holy Seer, whom I encountered, led me to hope her recovery, at the end of sixteen years, I threw myself from off a precipice.' At this moment his story was interrupted by the sound of a female voice, exclaiming; "why throw yourself into the flames, when sixteen years will restore your husband and son!" On hearing this I said, 'Father, you have much to say, but stay awhile, and let me see what this means.' I accordingly ran off to where I beheld a blazing fire, and a woman about to throw herself into it; I seized her, and her attendants, and brought her to my father. I then asked them, what they were doing in this lonely wood; the oldest replied: this is Suvŕittá, the daughter of Kálagupta, merchant of Kálayavana. When she was coming back with her husband, our vessel was wrecked near the shore, and I her nurse, and she, escaped upon a raft. Being near her time, she was delivered of a son in the forest, but the boy was carried off from me unhappily by an elephant. A Seer told us, sixteen years would restore us to her child and husband; we have resided that time in a holy house, but the patience of my mistress being now exhausted, she has determined to cast herself into the flames. Knowing that this was my mother, I prostrated myself at her feet and pointed to my father. My parents recognized each other, and mutually rushed into each other's arms, when blessing and embracing me they sat down in the shade of a tree, and I related to them all that had befallen me. Leaving them in the cell of a sage, I prosecuted my search for you. Wandering through the Vindhya Forest, I came to some ruins, where I observed the signs of buried treasures, I dug them out, and found a heap of Dínárs; thence going into a camp, I bought oxen and bags, and returning to the spot, loaded them with the treasure. I thence rejoined the camp, and forming a friendship with a merchant's son, travelled in his company to Ujjayiní. I brought my parents thither and, with the assent of the King of Málava obtained by the aid of Bandhupála my friend's father, lived there. I made frequent excursions in search of you, but my friend Bandhupála at last advised me to forbear, as they were fruitless, and that he would impart to me signs of your near approach. In expectation of this I visited him daily, and here saw Bálachandriká, a lovely maid whose beauties struck me to the heart; she herself was not unmoved, and by her looks expressed the emotions of her bosom. I was, therefore, encouraged to form a plan for our union. On one occasion I accompanied Bandhupála to a garden in the suburbs of Ujjayiní, to watch for omens of your coming, where, whilst he listened to the language of the birds, I wandered through the groves, and coming to the bank of a pool beheld Bálachandriká. I approached her and avowed my love, and sued for its return; and encouraged by the privacy of the place, she banished her diffidence, and thus addressed me: 'Youth, Mánasára, when advanced in years, crowned his son Darpasára sovereign of Ujjayiní: he in the hope of overcoming the world has gone to Rájagiri to practise austerities, leaving the Government to the sons of his paternal aunt Dáruvarmá and Chandravarmá. Dáruvarmá, disregarding the restraint of his elder brother Chandravarmá, commits all sorts of atrocious acts, and seizes the wives and wealth of his people: he has seen me, and professes such love as you offer me: as, however, I have discouraged his suit, and he is regardless of feminine purity, he seeks to appropriate by violence the person he will not gain by affection. In constant alarm of his attempts, I live wretched. So saying she wept bitterly. I dried her tears, and soothed her apprehensions, vowing to effect the death of Dáruvarmá. I desired her therefore to circulate a report that a Yaksha was a candidate for her charms and occupied her chamber, and to promise that, if any would encounter, and overcome the Goblin, he should be rewarded with her hand. If Dáruvarmá hearing this should desist, it would be well; and if he persevered, her friends should say to him that it would not be proper for the minister of Darpasára the King of the world to suffer violence in their mansion, and that he should take Bálachandriká to his own dwelling in the presence of the people, and there dispose of her as he pleased. If he consented to this as he probably would, I undertook to accompany her as a female attendant, dressed in a woman's garb, and thus having gained admission, I would kill him with my hands and feet: then, still in the capacity of an attendant, follow her fearlessly forth; after which we would apprise the family of our mutual love; and they no doubt would consent to our marriage. She agreed to what I proposed, and reluctantly departed. On returning to Bandhupála he told me to expect your return in thirty days, and we then repaired home, and things occurring as I had expected, I accompanied Bálachandriká to the chamber of Dáruvarmá, where I fell unexpectedly upon him, and pummelled him to death, then rushing forth called loudly for assistance. The people thinking he had been killed by the Goblin, and censuring Dáruvarmá's rashness in incurring such peril, entered in crowds, full of alarm and curiosity, and in the bustle we withdrew. When some days had passed we went through the ceremony of exorcism, and I espoused the damsel. On this day, as announced by Bandhupála, I came forth to seek you, and have found you."

The Prince now narrated to Pushpodbhava his own adventures and those of Somadatta, and they all repaired to Ujjayiní, where the Prince passed for the son of Pushpodbhava's preceptor, and was soon distinguished for his eminent acquirements.

SECTION FIFTH.

The season of spring had now arrived, and the youths and damsels of Ujjayiní celebrated the festival of the deity of amorous desires. On this occasion, Avantisundarí, the daughter of Mánasára, attended by her friend Bálachandriká and female train, went forth to the gardens of the suburbs, and worshipped Káma at the foot of a Mango tree. Desirous of beholding the Princess, Rájaváhana, accompanied by Pushpodbhava, entered the gardens, and after roaming through its pleasant paths, came to where the Princess stood. Beckoned by Bálachandriká they approached, and the figure of Rájaváhana made an immediate impression on the bosom of Avantisundarí. She thought him Káma approaching to grant a boon in person to his worshippers, and trembled with emotion, like a creeper waving in the breeze. He was no less struck by her charms. The Princess asked her friend to tell her who the youth was, but unwilling to declare the truth before so many witnesses, she answered generally, that he was a young Brahman of great learning, valour, skilled in magic, and entitled to her reverence. Hearing this the Princess was highly delighted, and bade him to be called, when giving him a seat she offered him the customary homage. Rájaváhana immediately recognised the Princess as his wife in a former birth, then named Yajnavatí, and took occasion to recall the circumstances to the recollection of the Princess: she remembered it, and all her ancient love revived.

Whilst thus engaged, the Queen of Mánasára, attended, came to view her daughter's pastimes. Bálachandriká gave the signal to her husband, and he and Rajaváhana hid themselves amongst the trees; after a short time the Queen returned, and her daughter attended her to the palace. The affection of Rájaváhana and the Princess continuing to become more intense, they sought anxiously for an interview, which at last was thus effected: walking in the garden, where Rájaváhana first saw the damsel, he encountered a Brahman of sumptuous apparel, and splendid appearance: they exchanged salutations, and the stranger called himself Vidyeśwara, a magician: they soon formed a friendship, and he engaged to assist Rájaváhana to obtain his mistress. On the ensuing morning Vidyeśwara, well attended, went to the palace, and was announced by the Chamberlain; he was invited by the Prince into the inner Court, where after song and music he beguiled all the spectators with the whirls of his wand, so that the Prince and all his Court were confounded, and imagined they perceived strange sights, as if innumerable snakes rolled along on all sides, and vultures darted down, and bore them away in their beaks: he then exhibited the story of Hiraṅyakaśipu as torn by Nṙisinha, and filled the Rájá with surprise: at the end he offered to exhibit him still more pleasant sights, and to perform a marriage by spirits, between the seeming Princess, and the Prince destined to be her lord.

The King assented, and the imagination of the courtiers being deceived, Rájaváhana and the Princess, who were ready to play their parts, were married in their presence, with all the customary rites: at the close of the ceremony, the magician ordered audibly all his attendants to disappear, and the Princess and Rájaváhana withdrew unnoticed into the inner apartments. There, whilst spending his time in enjoyment, the Prince related to his spouse the secrets of the fourteen worlds.

Having heard the description of the universe from the Prince, Avantisundarí replied, 'What return can I make my Lord for the delightful entertainment and instruction I have received from him? I have nothing to requite such favour with, but my permission for him to share undisturbed by my jealousies, or doubts, the embraces of Saraswatí[1].' In such conversation and mutual enjoyment they passed their time. On one occasion they beheld in their dreams a Swan, and wakened at the vision: on waking the Prince found his feet fast tied together by a silver chain, like the lotus bound with lunar beams. The Princess perceiving it screamed with apprehension; her screams were echoed by her attendants; their cries brought the guards to see what had chanced, and they discovered the Prince: not daring however to approach him, appalled by his royal radiance, they hastened to

[1] The Goddess of Literature and the Arts.

communicate the circumstance to Chandravarmá. He came, foaming with fury, like the flame of fire, and seeing the Prince, recognised him as the friend of Pushpodbhava, the husband of Bálachandriká, for whose sake his younger brother had perished: 'how, he exclaimed, can Avantisundarí have thus forgotten her rank to treat such as we are with disdain, and decline to such a base and false adventurer as this! But this must be remedied: she shall see her new Lord this very day exalted to the dignity of the gibbet.' Rájaváhana, finding resistance hopeless, submitted to his fate, and recommended patience to his wife, reminding her, that the Swan had foretold a period of two months as the limit of this ill fortune. He was sent to prison. When the old King and Queen of Málwa heard the story, and considered that Rájaváhana, by whatever means, was now their son-in-law, they opposed the execution of the sentence, and threatened to put an end to their own lives if it were accomplished. Chandravarmá persisting in his purpose, but unwilling to cause the destruction of the elder Princes, wrote to Darpasára for his commands, and in the mean time seized Pushpodbhava also, with all his family, threw him into prison, and confiscated his effects. The Prince like a young Lion was secured in a wooden cage, and would have been starved to death, had he not been preserved from the distress of hunger, and thirst, by the magical jewel he had formerly received; and which he had preserved in his hair. Chandravarmá being engaged in an attempt to compel the King of Anga to give him his daughter in marriage, proceeded against that Prince, carrying Rájaváhana incaged along with the army, with which Champá was invested. The King of Champá, Sinhavarmá, issued with his forces, impatient of aggression, and unable to await the arrival of his numerous allies. Notwithstanding their valiant exertions, the army of Sinhavarmá was defeated, and himself taken prisoner. Chandravarmá detained him, but ordered him to be taken care of; not purposing his death through the love he bore his daughter Ambáliká, also named Abaláratna, whom, she having likewise fallen into his hands, he resolved in conformity to the calculations of the Astrologers to espouse that evening. During the celebration, a Courier arrived from the Northern Mountains with the reply of Darpasára, which ran thus:—"Fool! what respite shall be granted to the violator of the secret chambers? Why listen to the imbecility of age? let me hear that the love-crazed Idiot is put to death with the tortures he deserves; as to the girl, throw her into chains, and let my younger brother Kírttisára share the same fate." On receipt of this, Chandravarmá ordered Rájaváhana to be brought before the palace gate next morning, and his own elephant also to attend; intending that the criminal should be crushed to pieces by the elephant; after which he would proceed to encounter the allies of the King of Anga. The dawn arrived: Rájaváhana was led forth, and the elephant was brought. At that instant, the silver chain fell spontaneously from the Prince's ancles, and assuming the semblance of one of the Nymphs of Heaven, stood before him, and thus addressed him: "Prince, condescend to hear me; I am a Nymph of Heaven, the daughter of Somaraśmi; and Suratamanjarí is my name: once I traversed the Mandodaka Lake, in the bosom of Himálaya: my course was impeded by a flight of Swans: to make my way amongst them I waved my hand, and in the act of waving my hand, my bracelet slipping off fell upon the head of Márkańdeya Muni, as he stooped to perform his ablutions in the wave. Incensed by the affront, he denounced a curse upon me, and sentenced me to take a metallic form; then relenting, he limited my transformation to a period of two months, during which I have been attached to your feet, as the chain from which you are just liberated. After my transformation I was found, and known for what I was, by the Vidyádhara Víraśekhara, the son of Mánasavega, the son of Vegaván, a Prince of the family of Ikshwáku. Víraśekhara had formed an alliance with Darpasára, in enmity of Naraváhana, the grace of the lineage of Vatsa, and Darpasára had agreed to give him his sister Avantisundarí in marriage. The Vidyádhara, anxious to see his intended bride, descended one night upon Ujjayiní, and entering the palace unperceived beheld the Princess sleeping in your arms: enraged at the sight, he determined to expose your person to the fury of the Prince of Ujjayiní, and with this view passed me as a fetter round your feet. To day my curse expires;

I have been your servant for two months. Is there any thing I can do to oblige you?" The Prince replied: Go, bear the news of my liberation to my other life, and cheer his sinking spirits! And then dismissed the nymph.

When the Apsará had disappeared, a sudden cry arose, that Chandravarmá was killed, stabbed by a single thief as he took the hand of Ambáliká, and that a hundred others had fallen by the same hand, as he was resolutely forcing his escape. On hearing this Rájaváhana leaped upon the elephant, knocked down his driver, and forcing the animal into the press, called to the valiant youth to join him, promising to aid his retreat: the youth advanced, and before he could be prevented sprang on the elephant. Rájaváhana, with no less joy than surprise, recognised in him his friend Apaháravarmá, who also knew him: after a momentary embrace they seized the weapons which the elephant carried, and fought their way through all opposition, levelling Chandravarmá's chieftains with the ground. At this time another army made its appearance, and fell upon the host of Chandravarmá. After some interval, a person on a swift elephant advancing to the friends, announced to Apaháravarmá, that the host now engaged was that of the allies of the King of Anga, whose advance he had been sent to accelerate, and whose efforts were attended with success, as the army of Chandravarmá was broken, and dispersing. Apaháravarmá then presented the person to Rájaváhana as his friend, and other self, Dhanamitra.

Dismissing Dhanamitra then to liberate the King of Anga, and dispose of the spoil, Apahâravarmá and the Prince withdrew from the city, and alighting from the elephant sat down on the border of the Ganges under the shade of a Rohin tree. While thus seated, a splendid Troop advanced, whom on their near approach Rájaváhana knew to be his friends, Upahára-varmá, Arthapála, Pramati, Mitragupta, and Viśruta, attending the King of Mithilá, Prahâravarmá; the King of Káśí, Kámapála; and the King of Champá, Sinhavarmá. The Prince rose to receive them, and after their first congratulations were exchanged, he narrated to them at their request his own adventures, and those of Somadatta and Pushpodbhava. His other friends in turn recounted to him the incidents which had severally befallen them, Apahâravarmá thus commencing:

STORY OF APAHÁRAVARMÁ.

When we dispersed in search of your Highness, I took the direction of Anga, and arrived at the Ganges, near Champá. At a short distance from the city resided a holy Saint named Maríchi, of whose wonderful powers I heard frequently from passengers on the road. I was therefore desirous to see and consult him respecting your fate, and repairing to his hermitage beheld under the shade of a young Mango tree a wild looking Devotee: sitting down by him, I asked him respectfully where the great Seer Maríchi was, of whom I wished to enquire the destinies of a dear friend. The Seer, for it was he himself, thus spoke: There was such a sage formerly, in this retirement; a Damsel named Kámamanjarí once approached him; large tear-drops fell like stars upon her breast, and as she bowed in homage to the holy man, her long dishevelled tresses swept the ground. She had scarcely attempted to impart her grief, when a vast crowd, led by the Damsel's mother filled with apparent rage, arrived, and thronged around the hermitage. The sage moved with pity addressed the Damsel, and demanded the cause of her distress.—She thus replied: 'these people round me would best accomplish this world's desires; mine seek the world to come, and therefore I prostrate myself at your feet, the asylum of the afflicted.' The mother here interrupted her, bowing to the ground: 'great Sage! permit your slave to say without offence, that in this I follow the duties of my profession. With women of my cast if we have daughters, we cultivate their beauty from their birth; we carefully nourish them with choice viands, and from five years of age they never see a man, not even a father. On their birth day, and every festival, we celebrate auspicious rites: we train them thoroughly in foreign literature; we instruct them to read and write, and express themselves with elegance and wit, we rear them to understand flowers, perfumes, and confectionery, and accomplish them in drawing, painting, dancing, singing, in playing musical instruments, and in dramatic representation: we have them instructed in grammar, in logic, and astrology, and teach them to earn a livelihood, to excel in sportive graces, to be skilled in games of chance or strife, to appear in gay and elegant raiment at public festivals, to speak in praise of public characters, to recommend talent to patronage, and want to charity. When this is accomplished, we grant them to one whom they may love, to one who may passionately love them, or to such as are amiable, respectable, learned, skillful, and above all, who are independent: to such we deliver them for a price proportioned to their means, but if we have given them to be trained by others, the teacher shares the remuneration. In all circumstances, however, the mother or grandmother must never be disobeyed. Now this Damsel has abandoned the duties prescribed by her fate; she has fallen in love with a young Brahman whose form is his whole fortune, and has at her own expense indulged her passion; her admirers are repulsed and enraged, her family ruined; from my reproaches she has fled to take up her abode in the woods, and if so, then what is to become of us, who depend upon her for subsistence?' She ended with a flood of tears.

The Ŕishi then addressed the Damsel:—"a life of devotion is a life of suffering; its object is either absorption or paradise: the first is only attainable by the perfection of wisdom, a thing not easily effected; the second is within the reach of all who discharge the duties of their station. It were well therefore that you return to obedience, and your mother." To this she replied: 'if I find not protection from you, I shall have recourse to the Lord of flame.' The Muni finding her determined, recommended her friends to leave her alone for a few days, in which time she would grow weary of an ascetic life, and return to her home, and they obeyed, and left the Damsel. A very little time had elapsed before her charms, her devotion, her graceful accomplishments, and elegant and serious conversation, made an impression on the Sage's heart. On one occasion he addressed her: "say, child, in what degree does Dharma (virtue), excel Artha (wealth), and Káma (pleasure)?" She replied, 'you mock me to ask my opinion, yet as it may be only a proof of your kind wish to hear me prattle, I will speak.

Without Dharma the other two properties are unproductive, but without regard to them Dharma alone is the creative cause of final happiness: it is the object of the soul, attainable by meditation, whilst unlike Artha and Káma it is not affected by external agents: where there is a fund of moral merit, that is not injured by the occasional prevalence of the other properties, or if affected, it is recovered by a little exertion, and eradicating the fault secures not a slight reward.

Hence the passion of Pitámahá for Tillottamá; of Śiva for the Muni's wife;, of Kŕishńa for his sixteen hundred concubines; of Prajápati for his own daughter; of Súrya for a mare; of Anila for a lioness. These acts of the Gods were worthy of Demons alone, but by the virtue of divine wisdom they did not destroy the moral worth of the individuals: a mind that is purified by piety admits no soil, any more than the atmosphere can be defiled by dust. I therefore hold that Artha and Káma are not to be regarded as comparable in the hundredth degree with Dharma.'

Having heard this, the passion of the Sage was augmented, and he replied, "Damsel, you have spoken well; the piety of those who know what truth is is not incompatible with earthly enjoyment, but we from our birth are unable to judge of the real merits of Artha and Káma. It is necessary to note what are their natures, their circumstances and their results." She replied, 'of Artha the essentials are accumulation, increase, and conservation, the concomitants agriculture, pasturage, trade, and government, and its consequence devout duties and alms. Káma is the various intercourse of the sexes, yielding pleasure to the passions; its concomitants earthly splendor, and beauty; its fruit mutual gratification, delightful recollections, self-satisfaction, supreme and present pleasure. The duties of an ascetic are severe, and imply liberal gifts, perilous conflicts, and crossing deep waters.' Hearing this, the Muni, overcome by fate, her eloquence, and his own infirmity, forgot his devotions, and became her prize. She prevailing on him to accompany her ascended a car, and with him at her side returned to her own house by the high street. As they passed, the Criers announced the next day as the festival of Káma. In the morning she made the ascetic discard his usual attire, bathe, and perfume himself, and put on a flowery garland, to appear as a votary of the

God of love, and led him, who could not bear to be separated an instant from her, by the public and most frequented roads through the bands of Káma's votaries to the gardens in the suburbs, where the King sat, surrounded by hundreds of Damsels. On her approach the King said, "Damsel, sit down with the Sage." She paid her obeisance smilingly, and sat down, on which one of the train rose, and addressed the King: 'Sire, I confess myself vanquished, and own myself the Damsel's slave.' A general murmur of applause followed: the Damsel was then rewarded by the Prince with valuable jewels and dresses, and with the applause of the citizens she returned home. On the way she thus spoke to the Sage; "grave Sir, accept my thanks, your servant has been favoured; now so please you, return to your pious purposes." As if struck by a thunderbolt, he heard her, and replied: "fair Damsel, what means this? whence this indifference? where is the affection you professed?" She smiled and replied: "Sir, the Damsel who in the assembly confessed herself defeated formerly defied my being able to conquer your affections; I accepted the challenge, and it was agreed upon between us, that the loser should become the servant of the other. By your favor I have won the wager." The Seer, when he heard this, was filled with surprise, and mortification, and falling as it were from the clouds, he recovered his senses, and returned to his solitary dwelling. That same Ŕishi, shamed by a girl, behold, brave youth, in me; the passion I then felt once subdued, my devotion has been rendered more intense. The question you would ask I shall in no long time be able to answer, and in the meanwhile do you abide in yonder city, Champá, the capital of Anga." At this time it was sunset, and with the Muni's assent I passed the night at his hermitage, listening to his conversation, till we fell asleep. In the morning when the first red rays glowed above the eastern mountain, I paid my homage to the Lord of day, and preceeded to the city. As I advanced, I passed a Vihára[1], where seated under an Aśoka tree, in a grove by the road side, I beheld a miserable Bauddha mendicant: the tears fell down from his filthy breast.—I sat down by him, and asked him, 'what is this penance and why these tears? if not a secret let me know the cause.' He answered: "my name is Vasupálita, I am the eldest son of the Banker Nidhipálita, an inhabitant of Champá, where I was destinguished by the epithet of the Ugly; there was another youth, called the Handsome, he was as clever as beautiful, but possessed of little wealth, and as I was opulent, the ill-disposed made these properties the cause of enmity between us. After much dissension and mutual abuse we agreed at last that the merit of a man was not to be decided by beauty or fortune, but its surest test was woman's love, and he who could win the choicest of our Damsels should be owned the victor. Of all our girls Kámamanjarí was the most distinguished, and we therefore

[1] A convent of Bauddha ascetics.

both addressed ourselves to her: my advances were most fovourably received, and she became the mistress of my house, my heart, my wealth, and my existence. She availed herself of her influence to appropriate all my means, and leaving me not even any clothes to wear, turned me out of my own mansion. Unable to face the ridicule and contempt of my fellow-citizens, I came and took my abode in this Jaina convent where under the tuition of a holy Sage I sought the path to final felicity. I fear I have mistaken the road, and in deviating from the faith and observances of my progenitors I follow an impure track, as if it were that of virtue; disregarding the Vedas and Smŕitis (Codes of law), abandoning the distinction of my caste, and constantly listening to blasphemy against the Gods. On this account I seek these shades, to bewail my hapless lot in privacy." Moved to pity for his grief, I advised him to be patient, and promised I would endeavour to redeem his property for him. I then left him, and entered the city, preparing to encounter the tricks and frauds of the rogues with which Champá notoriously abounded, and to reduce some of them who had enriched themselves at their neighbour's cost to their primitive poverty.

I therefore early entered the gambling houses, and associated with the gamesters, and was never satisfied with observing them skilled in the twenty-five sorts of games, knowing how to cog a die, and shift a card without being perceived; to reply to any reflection on their play with abundant abuse, to engage in affrays as prodigal of life, to admit the faith of their President, to argue or contend in order to enforce payment, to wheedle the resolute, and bully the timid; able to make partisans, to profess or proffer secret advantages, to disclaim a bet, to divide peremptorily the spoil, to mutter abuse. I laughed at one who made a blunder in his play: his partner swelling with rage said, 'what do you, who seem so fond of laughing, pretend to teach us? let him alone, he is but a novice; but if you are disposed, you shall find your match in me.' The Chairman assenting to this, we played. I won 16,000 Dínárs of him, half of which I gave to the President and the Assembly, and with the other half I rose to go into the town: the party were loud in my praise, and the President requested me to put up at his house, where I was splendidly entertained. He, on whose account I had first played, put great faith in me, and looked upon me as his other self; his name was Vimardaka, and by his means I became most thoroughly acquainted with the city. On a night as dark as the throat of Śiva, putting on a black jacket, and a sword under my arm, with a scoop, a whistle, tongs, a sham-head[1], magic powder, a magic light, a measuring thread, a wrench[2], a rope, a lamp, a beetle in a box[3], I went to the house of a celebrated usurer. I found his strong box, and

[1] Or perhaps a mask.

[2] Called Karkaťaka, a Crab.

[3] [or a box containing winged insects] to put out the light.

brought it away. As I passed along the main road, I saw a sudden blaze like the fall of lightning, and on nearing the object I met a lovely Damsel, richly attired, who I thought at first was the presiding Goddess of the city. She stopped alarmed. I asked her who she was, and whence, to which she hesitatingly replied: "A merchant lives in this city, named Kuveradatta. I am his daughter: my father betrothed me from my very birth to Dhanamitra, the son of a wealthy man in this city, but he upon his death purchased with profuse liberality the condition of a pauper, and although he has thus gained the epithet of munificent, yet being now destitute, my father refuses to give me to him for a wife: he is now desirous of marrying me to a merchant of great opulence, named Yathártha: the marriage is fixed for to-morrow morning, and to avoid this union, agreeably to a promise formerly made to my beloved, I have deceived my father, and am making my escape to my lover's house. I learnt the way in my early youth, and have love to attend my steps: let me pass, and take this casket." So saying she put it into my hands, but pitying her state, I said, 'come on, fair maiden, I will lead you to your lover;' and proceeded a few steps, when we saw by the light of their torches the city-watch all armed, and numerous, approaching. The Damsel was alarmed. I told her not to fear; my sword was to be trusted, but that for her sake I would have recourse to stratagem. 'I will affect to sleep, as if overcome by poison, do you say to these people thus: We entered the city this night: my husband here was bitten by a snake in this place: if any one of you know a charm to remove the poison, have pity on my desolate condition, and restore my Lord to life.'

The Damsel, whose own terrors fitted her to enact this part, did as I desired; I assumed the appearance of profound fainting: one of the train professing himself an adept tried his skill upon me, but in vain, and he proclaimed me defunct: 'there is no hope, he said to the Damsel, be of good cheer, we will burn the body to-morrow; who can oppose fate!' So saying they passed on. When they were off, I rose and accompanying the maiden to her lover, thus addressed him: I am by profession a thief, and in my travels encountering this maiden coming to you with no companion but her affection, I have attended her through compassion hither. I resign to you also this casket of splendid gems. He replied: 'youth, you have brought me a present, for which I have not words to thank you; I cannot speak my wonder at what you have done, and yet it seems marvellous to yourself. You have made me your slave. What folly do I utter! how can I propose so worthless an object as this body for the gift of my love:—a body that is your present; for had I not obtained her, I should have soon parted with it in death.' So speaking he fell at my feet. I raised him, embraced him, and enquired his intentions; he replied he could not continue to reside in the city with safety, upon marrying his mistress without the concurrence of her parents, and therefore purposed leaving Champá that very night, unless I should disapprove of it. I replied that change of country was nothing to a man of talents and spirit, but that he should consider the tender age, and timid disposition of his future bride rendered foreign travel, and separation from her first home, painful tasks to her, and that it did not appear impossible for him to stay at home with impunity. Follow my advice, I said, let her conduct us to her own house, and do as I direct. He assented, and we repaired thither; she served as a spy and guide, and we stole every thing except the earthen pans. Leaving the Damsel, we went and hid our booty, and then proceeding, we encountered a party of citizens, but just before they reached us we found an elephant resting by the road side, whose rider we dismounted, and ascended ourselves. The elephant it happened was a savage beast, and tore and trod on all he approached. We arrived at the house of the lady's lover, and passing on into a grove, caught hold of the branches above, by which we held till the animal passed away, when going home we bathed and reposed till sun-rise, when after the performance of our customary rites we went abroad to hear of the stir we had made. The merchant had sent some cash to his intended father-in-law Kuveradatta on hearing of the robbery, but had put off the marriage for a month. I then advised Dhanamitra to take a handsome leather bag, and go to the King, and say: 'your Majesty knows that I am Dhanamitra, the sole heir of Vasumitra: being reduced to poverty, I was despised of men, and

Kuveradatta who had promised his daughter to me, whilst wealthy, now retracted his promise; in grief for which I repaired to a neighbouring wood, and was about to cut my throat, when an ascetic of the Śaiva faith prevented me, and rebuked me for my despair, saying, there were many ways of recovering lost wealth, but none to redeem lost life; that he was perfect in the art of multiplying treasure, and possessed a purse, which would yield any sum I might want, and which, as he no longer required it, he would give me; that, if I should be ever under the necessity of relinquishing it, I must recollect, it would be available only to merchants, and courtezans, and that, should any wish to benefit by it, they must first restore whatever they might have dishonestly gained to the right owner, and give what they possessed to the Brahmans: after which, performing worship to the bag, and depositing it at night in a secure place, they would find it in the morning full of treasure. So saying he gave it me, and vanished. I have not thought proper however to retain it without leave from your Majesty.' The King being pleased by the offer, will desire you to do with it as you please, and then do you ask the Prince to protect you against it being stolen, after which go home, and give away every thing you have. Afterwards fill the bag by night with some of the stolen booty, and in the morning take it out before all the people. When Kuveradatta hears this, he will esteem his present intended son-in-law as nothing, and will himself give you his daughter.

Yathártha will be affronted, and in his rage he will endeavour to ruin Kuveradatta, but you should anticipate him, and reduce himself to rags.

So it happened: in the mean time Vimardaka the gambler by my instructions excited the wealthy lover's enmity against Dhanamitra, whilst Kuveradatta wished to give the latter his daughter, and still more incensed the former.

At this time Rágamanjarí, the younger sister of Kámamanjarí, being to sing at the public rooms, the people in their best garbs were collected: when the dance began I was struck with admiration and love, and how it happened I know not, but I caught her attention, and she smiled significantly on me as she withdrew. I returned home and under pretence of a head-ache went to bed. Dhanamitra knew by his own experience the truth, and comforted me by expatiating on her good qualities, and the certainty of our coming together. He told me that she had declared her determination to be won only by merit, and to become no man's expect by marriage: that her sister and mother had applied to the King to complain of her, and prevailed upon him to declare, that any one who should carry her off without their assent, should be punished as a thief: hence without wealth she was not attainable from her kindred, nor without merit from herself. I therefore opened a negociation with Kámamanjarí by her principal agent, a servant who was a female mendicant of the Bauddha order, and promised to steal Dhanamitra's purse, and give it to her, if she would give me Rágamanjarí: accordingly I wedded the latter. By my directions a violent quarrel took place in the exchange between Vimardaka and Dhanamitra, in which the former, as the friend of Yathártha, told the latter to look to his magical bag, or he might lose it: accordingly, the bag having disappeared, Dhanamitra complained to the King, and he summoned Yathártha, and desired him to produce Vimardaka, but the latter was not to be found, for I had sent him in search of you to Ougein, and the suspicions of the King being thus confirmed, the merchant was sent to prison.

After a time Kámamanjarí, being desirous of availing herself of her prize, restored the property of Virúpaka to him, and he abondoning the society of ascetics returned to his own profession again. Kámamanjarí then gave away all that remained of her own effects. Dhanamitra, instructed of this by me, informed the King of it, and stated what he suspected must be the cause of such liberality in so covetous a person. She was accordingly summoned, and being advised by me of the probable motive, it was a question what was to be done: at last her mother suggested that they should assert that they received it from Yathártha, with whom, it was known, they were on intimate terms. The King hearing this accusation ordered him to be put to death, but was prevented by Dhanamitra, in consequence of whose intercession the King contented himself with confiscating all his wealth, and banishing him from his dominions; some of his treasures were made over to the luckless Kámamanjarí, and I took Rágamanjarí to a house full of gold and jewels.

Man, however ingenious, cannot avoid his fate. I was one day enjoying the pleasures of the table with my mistress, till I was completely intoxicated, and as drunken people follow the practices to which they are naturally or customarily addicted, I promised to fill the house that night with the collected spoil of the city. In spite of her entreaties I set off, armed only with my sword; at her desire her nurse Śrigáliká followed me: my manner attracting the notice of the guard, they arrested me, and after a very feeble resistance I fell. Śrigáliká came up as I was bound, and the tumult dissipating my drunkenness, I considered what was to be done. I therefore called out to Śrigáliká, 'away, you old devil, you are disappointed in your plans to bring that covetous Rágamanjarí and my false friend together, having borne off his bag, and your daughter's ornaments, I am now ready to die with pleasure.' She took the hint, and addressing the guard with tears and sobs, said: "very true, Sirs, all my property has been stolen of late, pray let me ask this fellow some questions." They desired her to approach, and she prayed me most pitifully to tell her what had become of her daughter's property, and threw herself at my feet. I pretended to relent, and stooping to raise her, whispered to her what was to be done. On which she blessed me aloud, and withdrew. I was carried to the guard.

The next day Kántaka, the chief magistrate, who had lately succeeded to his father's place, and who was young, silly, arrogant, and vain of his person, threatened me, if I did not restore Dhanamitra's purse, and the property of the people I had robbed, I should see the end of the eighteen punishments, and death. I laughed at him, and told him that, though I might give up all the other wealth I had stolen, I would never restore my false friend's magical purse, and I was accordingly punished with stripes, but in vain, as I defied my judge. In this manner, sometimes threatened, and sometimes soothed, several days passed, during which my wounds were neglected and spread. At last, one evening, Śrigáliká with a smiling countenance, and handsomely dressed, approached me, as my guards were a little removed, and embracing me said: "you are fortunate, your plans have not been neglected; I spoke to Dhanamitra as you desired me, he accordingly complained to the King, that in a fit of jealousy you had stolen his purse, and your wife's casket, and run away, in which you had been seized by the watch; that you had restored the casket, and might be prevailed on to give up the purse, in which case he solicited the King's mercy for you. I also, procuring the necessary means from Rágamanjarí, secured the interest of Mangáliká, the nurse of the Princess Ambáliká, and became soon a very great favourite with the latter. One day the flowers in her ear being loose, I pretended to adjust them, but let them fall, and then picking them up, and pretending to throw them at the pigeons, I threw them upon Kántaka who was entering the prisons which are below the female apartments. He thinking it a mark of kindness looked up to our window, and was confirmed in his fancy by the smiles of the Princess, and my signs; so he went away, deeply wounded with the venomed shaft of love. In the evening I took a basket sealed with the Princess's signet, containing perfumes, pán, a dress, and ornaments, from her to Rágamanjarí, but conveyed it instead to Kántaka's house, who, plunged in passion's ocean, hailed me as his friendly bark. I augmented his passion by describing in most piteous terms the condition of the Princess, and pretending that she had sent him these tokens of her affection. I said to him: your signs of auspicious elevation are not likely to be in vain. A neighbour of mine, a cunning man, has told me, this kingdom shall fall into Kántaka's hand; he bears the marks of it: and accordingly the Princess, the only child of the Rájá, has fallen in love with you: however much the King may be displeased, he must, through fear of his daughter's death, consent, and you will then be Cæsar at least, and what will not follow? how are you to get into the apartments? I will tell you: there is not above three spans between the prison, and the palace wall. Do you procure some skillful hand to aid you alone in making a hole through the wall; once in, I will be answerable for our guards and her attendants, who are all well affectioned. 'Well said,' he replied; 'there is a thief equal to the sons of Sagara at a mine; if I can secure him, the job is done. Who should that be, and why not procurable? I enquired. 'It is the man,' he answered, 'who stole Dhanamitra's magic purse.' I tell you what, said I, go swear you will liberate him if he does the work properly, then fetter him again, and representing his obstinacy to the King, you will get him out of the way: so that your object will be gained, and there will be no fear of the secret being discovered. He was pleased with my council, and has sent me to communicate with you, whilst he remains without." I praised Sŕigáliká's address, and desired her to introduce the judge: he entered, and took a faltering oath for my liberation. I understood his sense, and swore never to divulge the secret. He set me at liberty, and had me well fed and taken care of for some days: we then set to work to break the palace wall; beginning in a dark corner, I made a hole with a crow (snake-headed). Whilst employed thus, I considered that the purport of his oath was to murder me, and that I was therefore fully justified in effecting his destruction. Having made the breach, as he extended his hand to help me through, I kicked him on the breast, and then knocking him down dispatched him with my knife. I then desired Śrigáliká to shew me the way into the inner apartments, that my labour might not be wholly unprofitable, and I might carry off something of value. I entered the chamber, and found the Princess sleeping securely on a white couch, like lightening on the fleecy clouds of autumn. The sight arrested my attention, and instead of plundering the apartment I was robbed of my heart. I did not dare to wake her, lest her alarm should summon her attendants to her aid, and I should be apprehended, and put to death. I picked up a pencil, therefore, and with the smoke of the lamp sketched her sleeping, and myself kneeling at her feet, with this motto:

Your slave, thus kneeling at your feet, implores you.
Sleep not, but wake, for him who here adores you.

Then finding some superior betel, I extracted the juice, and cast it upon a pair of Chakwas painted on the wall. After which I took off her ring gently, and exchanged it for my own, and then effected my retreat: repairing to the prison I went to Sinhaghosha, one who had been a chief of Police, but afterwards was my fellow captive, by which we became friends, and I recommended to him to say as the means of being enlarged, that he had detected Kántaka breaking into the palace, and in edeavouring to arrest him had killed him. I then set off with Śrigáliká. On our way we encountered the watch: I could easily have escaped, but what was to become of the old woman. After a moment's thought I assumed an attitude of rushing upon them, and called out: If I am a thief do you seize me, but let this poor old woman go. Śrigáliká guessed my purpose and said: 'my good friends, this is my son, he has been long afflicted by a demon, and has been taking medicine: being something recovered yesterday, I gave him better food, his best clothes, and let him go to day where he pleased;

at midnight he was again seized by the fiend; he has killed Kántaka, and exclaiming, he would have the Princess for his bride, he ran off into the public road: I followed him as fast as I could. Pray, pity my trouble, bind him, and give him over to me.' As she thus exclaimed, I cried out: away old woman! who shall fetter the wind? shall the crows presume to pounce upon the hawk? absurd! And away I ran: she then abused them for letting me escape, and crying and scolding followed me. Thus we arrived at home, when I cheered Rágamanjarí who had pined in so long an absence. In the morning I saw my friend Dhanamitra, after which I went to the Sage Maríchi, whose cause I had avenged, and who having resumed his holy practices, and recovered his superhuman knowledge, announced to me your approach. Sinhaghosha was placed in the situation of Kántaka by the King, who was pleased with the service he was supposed to have rendered. The passage into the interior of the palace was still open to me, and by the agency of Śŕigáliká I obtained possession of the Princess. In those days Chańdavarmá being refused the daughter of Sinhavarmá, and being highly enraged, besieged the city. The King Sinhavarmá, impatient of the outrage of the enemy, and mistrusting his friends, marched out of the city, and he was defeated by the superior numbers of the enemy, and taken prisoner. The Princess Ambáliká was likewise seized and carried to the palace of Chańdavarmá, where the marriage was to be solemnized at the close of the night. I had also prepared the nuptial bands to be bound at the house of Dhanamitra. I told him that the allies of the King of Anga were close at hand, and that he should collect the chief men of the city, and joining them unobserved bring them as fast as possible, when they should find the enemy without a head. He set off for this purpose: I remained, and taking advantage of the confusion, and crowd assembled at the wedding, I slipped in, armed, along with the Brahmans, when seizing the hand of Ambáliká, whilst Chańdavarmá invoking the fire to witness, according to the Atharvańa rite, put forth his arm to take her, I dragged her aside, and stabbed him in the belly with my dagger: then baffling those who sought to seize me, I made my retreat to this place, bringing with me the Damsel, whose fear I dissipated with my endearments, and bore her to a private apartment. At that moment I heard your voice, as welcome as the muttering clouds laden with the first dews of the season. What ensued you already know.

Rájaváhana, having heard of this narrative, addressed Apaháravarmá, and acknowledged that he had acquired such proficiency in so difficult a practice as to overcome Karńísuta: he then desired Upaháravarmá to relate his adventures, who bowed and thus obeyed.

STORY OF UPAHÁRAVARMÁ.

During my peregrinations I came to Videha, and just without the city of Mithilá rested myself at the threshold of a temple, when an ancient female devotee gave me welcome, and water for my feet; she looked at me attentively, and after a time burst into tears, of which I enquired the occasion. She replied: Prahá-ravarmá was the King of the city of Mithilá, and the particular friend of Rájahansa, King of Magadha; their Queens Vasumatí and Priyamvadá were equally attached to each other. The latter with her Lord went to visit her friend, upon the birth of her first child. Whilst at Pushpapura, a war broke out between Rájahansa, and the King of Málava, in which the former was utterly overthrown. When Praháravarmá returned to his country, and found that the throne had been seized by Vikaṭavarmá and the other sons of his elder brother Śankara, he resolved to repair for assistance to his sister's son, the King of Suhma. With this intent he entered the forests, and was there attacked by the Barbarians, and plundered of every thing. I fled with the youngest child in my arms, and to avoid the shower of arrows, plunged into the thicket; the child was there knocked from my grasp by a tiger; he hid himself in the carcase of a cow; the tiger was killed by the arrow of a forester, and the child carried off by the Barbarians, whilst I remained insensible. A cow-herd found me, and conveyed me to his hovel, where he dressed my wounds, and tended me, until I had nearly recovered. As I regained my strength, I became impatient to rejoin my master, and was meditating how to effect this purpose, when my daughter with a youth arrived at my dwelling. She related to me her adventures, the defeat of the troops, the loss of the young Prince, her captivity by a forester who sought to win her affections, and his attempt to put her to death when she refused to listen to his suit, her preservation by the youth in her company and who had subsequently espoused her. The youth was a servant of the King; and attended by him we overtook Prahâravarmá and Priyaṁvadá, and afflicted them with the loss of the Princes. Prahâravarmá was baffled in his efforts to recover his dominions, and he and his Queen were both made prisoners. Their misfortunes affected me so strongly that I determined to adopt a mendicant life, whilst my daughter in despair took service with Kalpasundarí. Had the sons of Prahâravarmá lived, they would have been of your years, and the oppression of their parents would not be attempted with impunity. So saying, she wept violently. When I heard her story I told her to be comforted, and reminding her of the Muni to whom she had applied in the forest, [I told her how he had applied in the forest,] I told her how he had found and brought up the child, and that in fact I was that infant. I then vowed to destroy Vikaṭavarmá but it was necessary to proceed with caution as he had many brothers, and the people were generally attached to him, whilst on the other hand even my parents did not know me, much less any other persons. I therefore resolved to wait for a favourable opportunity of executing my designs.

I now entered the temple where my old nurse provided me with every necessary, and kept me from observation. I passed the night in meditation on the means of procuring access to the inner apartments of the royal palace, as the fittest scene for my intended operations, and enquired of my nurse, as soon as the day had dawned, whether she were acquainted with the secrets of the Harem. I had scarcely spoken, when a female appeared. The old woman as soon as she saw her exclaimed. See, my dear daughter, our master's son. She welcomed my recovery with tears of joy, and when the feelings excited by our interview had subsided, began to tell us the state of affairs in the palace. The Queen, she said, was highly displeased with her Lord: her name was Kalpasundarí: she was the daughter of Kalindavarmá, King of Kámarúpa, and excelled the Apsarasas in beauty and accomplishments. Vikaťavarmá was excessively attached to her alone, although he had many other women in his palace.

On hearing this, I told her to carry to the Princess garlands prepared by me, and to inflame her resentment still more against her Lord, by citing to her the example of Vásavadattá, and other distinguished females, who obtained Lords of equal value with themselves, and bringing to her knowledge whatever private favours the King had bestowed on other females of his establishment. After which she should come, and report the results to me. My agents, both mother and daughter, diligently promoted my designs, and in a few days my nurse told me that the Queen considered herself as ill-matched as the lovely Mádhaví to the bitter Nimba, and was plunged in despair. What, said she, is now to be done? I gave her a picture of myself, and desired her to put it in the way of Kalpasundarí: she did so, and the Queen was immediately struck by the performance, conceiving it to be a work of fancy, and highly creditable to the painter's skill. My old nurse told her that the world was large, and handsome as was the picture, she did not doubt the reality might prove as charming; but she enquired, supposing that such a youth were found, with talents, graces, and rank to correspond, what might he expect. Kalpasundarí replied: 'Nothing, for what have I to offer worthy of such a prize? my body, heart, and being, were of infinitely less value; but if this be not a fiction, let me at least behold the original.' To this the old woman replied, "It is no fiction: there is such a youth, the son of a King, who having beheld you at the vernal festival was penetrated with the arrows of Káma. He applied to me to procure him access to your presence, and conceiving you to be made for each other I promised him my aid. The Chaplets I bring you are the work of his hands, and this his picture is painted by himself. If you are desirous of beholding him, his talents and valour will make way to you, and I have no doubt you will see him this very day." The Queen reflected a little, and then replied:

'Mother, I can have nothing to conceal from you. My father was the attached friend of Prahváravarmá, and my mother equally devoted to his Queen: these two agreed that, when they should have children of a different sex, their offspring should be married. As it chanced, however, that the sons of Priyamvadá were lost, my father gave me in marriage to my present husband, a wretch of cruel and unjust temper, misshapen body, and uncultivated mind, a boasting liar, a forfeiter of his word, and vain only of his ferocious valour. I hate him not the less that he passes his time with my rivals, especially a low and miserable creature, Ramayantiká, a woman who has the audacity to measure her state with mine, and whom he has dared to decorate with flowers plucked from the Champa that I had planted, and reared as if it had been my child. I hear these things from my faithful attendant Pushkariká. The man is detested, and I am scorned: what more is necessary? the fear of futurity is obscured by present sufferings, and the female heart can ill restrain the passion love inspires, when its gratification is impeded only by duty to one we hate. Let your friend therefore come this day to the Mádhaví bower in the garden.' My nurse promised that I should, and having communicated the conversation to me, I had only to accomplish her engagement.

When the night set in, and the vapours rose in the west round the setting sun, as from the fume of a vast and red hot coal dipped in the ocean, I retired to repose, and to reflect that, if I sinned in intriguing with another's wife, I might claim some extenuation in the important objects which induced me to it, the recovery of my birthright, and liberation of my parents. In such meditation, and in considering how my friends, and Prince would judge of my conduct, I sank into repose. In my sleep Ganeśa appeared, and encouraged me to persist; and I rose, determined to proceed. Káma, unoccupied that day elsewhere, plied me with his shafts, so that by the evening I was impatient to see the Queen. As soon as it was dark I repaired to my assignation, clothed in dusky raiment, grasping my trusty sword, and prepared with all implements necessary for my purpose. When I arrived at the palace I crossed the ditch by a bamboo ladder concealed previously near the spot by Pushkariká, and which again served me to scale the wall. I let myself down on the other side by the projecting steps of the Masonry. I then slowly passed the Bakula bower, and Champaka avenue. I heard at a little distance the cries of the Chakwas. I then turned to the north by the Bignonias, and having leaped over the canal that ran to the palace, proceeded on a gravel walk bordered by red Aśoka trees and Jasmines. I again turned to the west by a Mango grove, and there distinguished the Mádhaví bower, shining gently by the lustre of the gems that gleamed from an open casket upon an inlaid couch in the centre. I entered an inner appartment, separated by a wall of flowers, and branches, and a door of the same materials. There I found a couch of flowers, caskets of Lotus leaves, an ivory-handled fan, and vases filled with fragrant waters. I sat awhile inhaling the odours about me, when I heard the gentle tread of feet approach: leaving the Chamber I hid myself behind a tree. Kalpasundarí now arrived and not finding me there, broke out into the most passionate regrets at her disappointment, calling upon Kámadeva to know what crime she had committed, that he thus exposed her to the flames of despair, and yet refrained from reducing her to ashes. I then appeared and consoled her distresses: we soon felt implicit confidence in each other, and how impossible it was ever more to separate. I therefore instructed her what plan to pursue.

By my desire she was to shew my portrait to the King, and ask him whether he did not think it surpass mere mortal beauty: 'to this, I continued, he will say yes: then do you tell him that an old female devotee has instructed you, how by particular charms, and sacrifices, to become invested with this very form, but it must be done at night, and alone, presenting to Fire a hundred sticks of sandal, Aguru, and handfuls of camphire, and silk garments, preceding it in the day by a public offering to the same element, with all due ceremonies: then you are to sound a bell, on hearing which your husband is to come, when if he will acknowledge to you all his secret purposes and plans, have his eyes bound, and embrace you, this form shall be transferred from you to him, you becoming the same as you were before. Tell this to the King, and leave it to him to determine, advising him to call his counsellors, and people together, and be guided by their advice. There is no doubt he will comply. When the royal sacrifice is performed in these garden walks, and the smoke of the oblation fills the air, I will enter and secrete myself in this bower.' I told her also to reproach him in seeming sport with his infidelity, and threaten him not to fulfil the rite, and desired her to let me know his reply. I then left her, Pushkariká effacing the marks of my footsteps as I retired. In a short time every thing turned out as I expected, and the rumor run through the city that the Rájá was about to obtain, by the magic skill of the Princess, a most celestial figure, and that there was no trick in this; for it was to take place in the garden of the palace, in the presence of the chief Queen, and had received the concurrence of the ministers. The efficacy of jewels, charms, and drugs was pronounced wonderful. So it took place, and when clouds of smoke spread from the palace adding gloom to the shade, I entered the garden. Kalpasundarí soon hastened to me, and told me that she had addressed the King, as I had told her to do, on which, falling at her feet, he vowed, that he never more would seek the love of any other woman. I have now come here, she continued, your bride, the former evidence of our marriage was Káma, but now let these sacred flames bear witness to our union. I desired her to withdraw, whilst I completed our plan. I then struck the bell, and she muttered in low sounds, like the herald of fate. The King approached; she then retired, and I remained, engaged apparently in the oblations when he arrived, and as he stood in fear and doubt, I said, declare again, and take the holy fire to witness, you will never when you assume this form prove unfaithful to me. This dissipated his doubts; he was satisfied it was the Queen, and no imposition; and therefore began to make such a vow. I then smiled, and stopped him, saying: I will not exact your oath. What woman need I fear? and if the Apsarasas be attracted, follow your inclinations. Now then reveal your secrets, and having uttered them take this form. He replied: I have plotted with my ministers to convey poisoned food to my father's younger brother Praháravarmá, who is in prison, intending to give out that he has died of an old disease. My own younger brother Viśokavarmá I am about to send with an insufficient army to Puńdra, where he must perish. An old merchant of Panchála, and Paritráta, my merchant, are employed by me to get from Khanati, a Yavana, a jewel of inestimable value for a little price, and my managing man Śatahali has been authorised by me to destroy Anantasíra, a powerful landholder, by exciting troubles on his estates, and leading a force to support them.

Having heard his secrets thus related, I said to him: receive the reward of your actions! On which I drew my sword, and cut him in two, and making a copious offering of ghee to the Lord of flame, threw his body into the blaze, where the whole was speedily reduced to ashes. Then cheering my mistress who with the timidity of her sex was agitated with apprehension, I took her by the hand, and returned with her to the palace, where summoning all the attendants I received their homage. I then retired to rest in the royal apartments along with my bride, from whom I learned the customary practices of my predecessor. In the morning, after bathing, and the usual auspicious observances, I repaired to council, and addressing my ministers, said: 'With my figure, Sirs, I have changed my temper. Let my uncle be liberated, and restored to his Sovereignty, and I will shew that obedience I owe him.' Sending for my younger cousin, I told him, 'The people of Puńdra at present have been urged to despair by distress, whilst we are in plenty; it is only necessary to protect our harvests from their depredations, and it is needless for you to march against them.' To the jewel dealers I sent, and told them that I thought it but just, that a suitable price should be given for an article of value, and directed them to pay the owner of the diamond the price he demanded. I then called Śatahali, and said, as the chief fault of Anantasíra was his attachment to Praháravarmá he was no longer an object of resentment, and as my uncle was restored to dignity we should desist from all aggression upon his friends. By these orders the Officers of my Government were satisfied of my identity, and delighted with the amendment of my character. My parents were set at liberty, and re-seated on the Throne. After a short time my nurse, by my instructions, revealed the whole truth to my parents, and I had the happiness of prostrating myself at their feet. I was also installed in the Yuvarájya by my father's commands. It only now remained to complete my felicity, to be reunited to your Highness, and I was meditating the means of finding you, when letters from Sinhavarmá, my father's ancient friend, solicited my aid against the hostile advances of Chańḋavarmá. I was united with him in the command, and arrived at this place, now rendered illustrious by your auspicious presence.

Having thus concluded, Rájaváhana observed that the important objects his friend had accomplished excused his single deviation from moral rectitude, and that the schemes of the prudent were certain of success. Then turning to Arthapála, with an encouraging look, the Prince requested him to relate his adventures.

STORY OF ARTHAPÁLA.

I engaged with our other friends in search of your Highness, and after some time spent in traversing this sea-encircled earth I arrived at Káśipurí, Váráńasí, where I bathed in the pure transparent waters of Mańikarńiká, and paid my adoration at the shrine of Avimukteśwara the foe of death. I then proceeded south of the city, where I met a man of stout, robust make, tightly girded, and his eyes red with incessant weeping. It appeared strange to me that a man of such singularly powerful make should give way to despair, and determined to ascertain the cause of his affliction. I therefore addressed him, saying, 'Brother, your appearance indicates some desperate purpose; if not a secret, I should be gratified to know what has caused your evident grief, and whether I can be of use to you.' He looked at me awhile, and then said: "I have no objection to relate my story to you." We accordingly sat down under a Karavíra tree, and he thus proceeded: "I am the son of a man of property, and my name is Púrńabhadra. I was accustomed always to follow my own inclinations, and in spite of my father's cares addicted myself as I grew up to the profession of a thief. Being detected robbing the house of a trader in this city, I was confined, and sentenced to death. I was accordingly led forth in front of the palace gate, and in the presence of Kámapála, the chief minister, a wild elephant was let loose upon me, and approached amidst the clamour of the multitude, clattering his bells still louder, and curling his trunk to seize me. I was not accustomed to fear, and encountering the animal I struck him with the uplifted logs in which my arms were wedged: he reeled and retreated. His driver enraged had recourse to abuse, and the liberal application of his heel and his goad, and at last again forced the elephant to the encounter. I repeated my blow with greater violence, and the animal, who was for a moment stunned, no sooner recovered, than he turned tail, and fled: his driver brought him up a third time, but he retreated again as soon as he saw me preparing to attack him, and all his guide's efforts were now in vain. When the minister observed this, he sent for me and said: 'The elephant you have discomfited has been hitherto as irresistible as death himself. So much valor merits not so vile a fate. Desist therefore from the unworthy practices you have followed, and adopt a more creditable life: what say you? Will you enter into my service?' With all my heart, I replied. I accordingly attached myself to him, and he treated me as a friend. When he felt confidence in me he one day communicated to me his story at my request.

Dharmapála was the minister of Ripunjaya, the King of Kusumapura, a man of profound understanding and great learning: his son, equal to him in all respects, was named Sumitra. I am his younger brother by a different mother. As I spent much of my youth amongst improper persons, my elder brother reprimanded me for it. I did not much relish his reproofs, although they were kindly urged, and therefore withdrew from my home. Wandering about the world, I came to this city, Káśi, where I saw Kántimatí, the daughter of Chańdasinha, the King, playing at ball with her damsels in a grove dedicated to Káma. I was the prize of her beauty, and in time effected a private union with her. The fruit of our secret love was a son, of whom she was privately delivered: her attendants, apprehensive that the infant might lead to a discovery, told the mother it was still born, and carrying it away, exposed it on a mound, whence a woman of low caste was employed to carry it to a cemetery. As she returned along the road by night, she was seized by the guard, and being threatened with severe punishment unless she gave a satisfactory account of herself, she betrayed our secret. The King was immediately informed of it, and by his commands the woman led him to the place of my concealment, the grotto below the artificial mound, where I lay unsuspectingly asleep. I was immediately seized and carried off to the place of execution. The executioner aimed the fatal blow at me, but fate so willed it that he missed the mark, and only cut asunder the cords that bound me: before he could recover, I sprang upon him, wrested the sword from his gripe, and dispatching him and several of his assistants made my escape. As I wandered alone without shelter, I was addressed as I passed through a forest by a damsel of celestial beauty, attended by a train of females, but seemingly immersed in grief. She approached me, and decorating her lovely forehead with the tiara radiance of her hands she invited me to sit down with her at the foot of a stately Banian tree. I accepted the invitation, and asked her the motives which induced her to detain me; who she was, and where was her abode. In a honied stream of eloquence she replied:

"I am named Táráválí, and am the daughter of Mańibhadra, King of the Yakshas. Having paid a visit to the venerable Lopamudrá, the wife of Agastya, I was returning from the Malaya Mountains, when I saw in a charnel ground at Benares an infant weeping. I took him up and feeling compassion for his helpless condition conveyed him to my father. My father carried him into the presence of the Lord of Alaká. The friend of Śiva sent for me, and said, 'daughter, how feel you for this infant?' As if I had given him life,

I replied. The God said, 'the poor child speaks the truth,' and then he related to us a long narrative from which I found that Śaunaka, Śúdraka, and Kámapála were one person in different lives, and that Bandhumatí, Vinayavatí and Kántimatí were also the same individual; other wives of these persons were in like manner reborn, amongst whom in the time of Śaunaka I was named Gopakanyá. When you were Śúdraka, I was again your wife in infancy; but when you grew up, your affection was chiefly given to Vinayavatí, who was thence born again as Kántimatí, whilst I was born again in my present form. After relating these events, Kuvera directed me to take the child to the wife of Rájahansa, where he might be brought up along with Rájaváhana, and by the advice of my elders I have come to lay myself at the feet of one, who by the will of fate has so often overcome the power of death." When I heard this narrative I embraced her, shedding tears of delight, and spent some time with her in a palace suddenly reared in the forest, and in the midst of more than mortal enjoyment. After a few days I expressed to Táràvalí my desire to be avenged on Chańdasinha for the jeopardy in which he had put my life. My new spouse smiled, and said, 'you shall see Kántimatí, I will bring her here.' Accordingly, at midnight, the palace of the King of Káśi was transported to us, and entering his chamber I took up the sword lying at his pillow, and woke him from his sleep, saying: 'behold your son-in-law; I gained possession of your daughter without your concurrence, and am now come to wipe away my fault.' In terror of his life, the King bowed down to me, and said: "The fault was mine, who like an idiot, or one possessed, repaid with death the honor you had conferred upon me; now deign to dispose of my daughter, my kingdom, and my life, at your pleasure." His submission appeased me, and being restored to his Capital, he celebrated publicly my espousal of his daughter, Táráválí, repeated to Kántimatí the different transmigrations we had undergone, and we lived happily together; the King conferring on me the station of Yuvarája, and placing in my hands the chief administration of affairs.

Kámapála having thus finished his story continued to shew me the same regard: at last, time that consumes every thing summoned his royal father-in-law to heaven. He then elevated to the Throne the youngest son of the late King, Sinhaghosha, a child of five years of age, his elder brother Chańdaghosha being reduced to premature decay by his debaucheries. When the boy attained the years of puberty, the inconsiderateness of his age induced him to listen to the insinuations of evil counsellors, and they persuaded him that Kámapála had violently obtained the person of the Princess, had extorted the concurrence of the late King through his fears for his life, had taken off the young King's elder brother by poison, and would, no doubt, get rid of him in the same manner the moment he should assert his claim to independent rule, unless he were anticipated. In this way his enmity was excited against Kámapála, but the protection of the Yakshiní defeated all schemes against her Lord.

At this time the chief Queen, Sulakshańá, said with seeming affection to Kántimatí, she was sure she was not as happy as formerly, and begged her to relate the truth. She replied, that her friend and fellow-wife Táràvalí had gone away in displeasure, because her husband had mentioned Kántimatí's name at an unsuitable season, and no entreaties had been able to pacify her, that her husband was much grieved by her disappearance, and that she herself was distressed to observe his sorrow. This Sulakshańá told the King, and he now fearlessly plotted the destruction of the minister. Accordingly whilst engaged at the palace in affairs of state, he was recently seized by men stationed for the purpose, and thrown into confinement. Charges against him have been publicly promulgated, and in consequence his eyes are to be put out, but in such a manner that death shall ensue. When I heard this news, I was overcome with grief, but at last drying my tears, I have resolved to precede my friend and patron on the road to death. This is the cause of my present affliction."

The stranger, having finished his narrative, left me no less afflicted than himself to hear of my father's peril. After checking my emotion, I told him who I was, and we concerted the possibility of effecting my father's release. Whilst thus employed, a large venomous snake thrust his head out of a hole in the wall. I immediately secured him by the power of charms, and told my new friend that thus assisted I would seek for my father, and privily loosing the snake would let him bite with such restraint on the venom that it should not be mortal; although he should drop, as if he was dead. In the mean time he should hasten to my mother, and apprise her of our situation: she would come to us with all speed; but he should tell her this, 'Let her send you fearlessly to the King, to say to him on her part: It is a soldier's duty to suppress his foes, without regard to kindred, or alliance; but it is a woman's duty to share the fortunes of her husband in honor or in shame. I will therefore accompany my Lord upon the funeral pile, agreeably to the ritual, if you will give me his body. The King will of course assent; do you then take the body to your house, and in a retired place inclosed with canvas screens prepare a pile covered with a layer of Darbha grass, as if for the wife to ascend it after her husband's death. I will come to the spot, and you will give me admittance; when restoring my father to perception, we shall be all happily reunited.' When my father's follower had received my instructions, he immediately set off. I repaired to the place of proclamation, and ascending a tamarind tree secreted myself among the branches. An immense crowd soon assembled, and presently my father, with his hands bound behind him, and attended by a guard like a thief, appeared; when the executioner, as usual having stopped, thrice proclaimed his imaginary crimes, charging him with having caused the death of Chańdaghosha, and plotted the destruction of the King himself by a column filled with combustibles: 'he has been sentenced therefore, he continued, to lose his eyes, and should any be wicked enough to imitate his offences, they will meet with the like reward.' When he had ceased, and the crowd began to move, I cast the snake from the tree unperceived upon my father, and then quickly descending approached him, and anticipated the fatal effect of the venom. The snake in rage and alarm bit my father, so that he immediately dropped, and to all appearance was dead. The people thought it was the act of destiny. Kántimatí, being apprised by Púrńabhadra of what was going forward, hastened to the spot, and taking my father's head on her lap, sent word to the King: 'This is my husband; whether he has offended against you, heaven must judge, not I. This alone is my business to accompany him in death, to whom my hand, in life, was pledged, or I shall disgrace our common origin. Give permission that I may ascend the funeral pile.' The King was pleased with the application, and readily gave his assent, directing all due honors to be paid to his brother-in-law. The rest happened, as I had arranged it, and when my mother had gone through the form of assuming violent affliction, taken leave of her friends, and repeatedly refused to listen to their tears and entreaties, she entered alone the chamber, which contained the corpse; admitted by Púrńabhadra, as agreed upon, I soon restored animation to the body by the Vainateya process, and when my mother found my father alive, she fell at his feet, and then embraced me, repeatedly expressing her joy in a flood of tears, and convulsive sobs; now congratulating herself on my recovery; now blessing my filial exertions which had saved a father; now vehemently accusing Táráválí for having so long separated us, and then in a passion of grief and joy throwing herself upon my neck; and bathing me with tears. My father in the mean time, having heard the whole story from Púrńabhadra, contemplated me with proud delight, and felt himself happier than the Lord of Heaven. When our mutual emotions had subsided, I asked my father, how we should next proceed. He replied: 'There is no occasion for secrecy; my palace is strong and well stored with arms. Many leaders of note are in my service, and most of the Chiefs of people are ill satisfied with my treatment. Let us therefore retire home, and endeavour to inflame the public resentment and dissatisfaction; when ripe for insurrection, we will assemble and arm our friends, and lead them against the abettors of the tyrant.' This was put in execution. When the King found us so secure from his power, he was vexed at what had passed, but employed all the hostile stratagems against us that he could devise: his agents however were daily cut off by our party. At last, having learned the situation of the Royal chamber, I determined to effect a subterraneous passage to it from our own palace: beginning at the angle of a turret wall, I followed it up some distance, mining below the foundation. The passage opened at last on an excavated chamber, where I was surprised to see a number of Damsels of beauty calculated to make earth a paradise. At that moment one of surpassing loveliness entered the cavern: her charms irradiated these subterraneous realms with more than mortal light: she looked like the personified earth, the abode of the flower-armed God, or the genius of the empire secreting her splendour from iniquitous monarchs under ground. As she advanced, dissipating the gloom, she resembled an image of burnished gold. When she and the other Damsels saw me, they trembled like fragrant sandal creepers agitated by the breeze of Malaya. In that assembly there was an aged woman, who resembled a tuft of white-headed Káś: she fell at my feet, and solicited my forbearance, as if I was a deity descending to battle with the denizens of the infernal shades. I replied: relinquish your fears; you see in me a mortal, the son of Kámapála and Kántimatí, who seek by these unwonted paths access to the palace. But declare, who you are, and why inhabiting a place like this. The old lady answered:

'Prince, we are fortunate in being favoured with the sight of so much dignity and grace; you shall hear. Your grandfather had by his Queen Lílávatí two children, Kántimatí your mother, and the Prince Chańḋaghosha. The young Prince, when scarcely arrived at manhood, brought on a consumption by his excesses, and died before his father. He left his wife Ácháravatí pregnant: she was delivered of a daughter, Mańikarńiká, whom you here behold, and died soon afterwards. The grandfather Chańḍasinha then sent for me, and privately informed me, that he was pledged to give his grand-daughter in marriage to Darpasára, the son of his friend the King of Málava; but after the late events in which your mother Kántimatí was involved, he was apprehensive the example might have a mischievous effect, and to guard against accidents he had determined to rear Mańikarńiká with the greatest care and secrecy. There was a suite of rooms, he said, underground, in the heart of an artificial elevation, constructed as an asylum against the fury of a triumphant enemy; it consisted of many extensive apartments fitted up with every splendid decoration, and provided with stores for a century's consumption, and he proposed that I should bring up his grand-daughter in this recess, attaching to us a suitable train. When he received my assent, he opened a trap door in the wall, fastened by a bolt, and leading from the square of his own apartments. Into the passage it opened to he made us all enter. Twelve years have since elapsed: my ward is now a woman; but the King seems to have forgotten us. It is probable that his promise of her to Darpasára will never be fulfilled, and better were it that she became the bride of one so nearly allied, and in fact betrothed to her before her birth by a secret agreement between your mother and her's, in case the latter bore a female child.' The Princess seemed nothing loth; but I interrupted them by saying, I must first accomplish what I proposed in the palace, when I should return to them.

Receiving from the matron a lamp, and following the passage from the cavern, I came to the secret entrance to the Royal chambers. At midnight I opened it, and entered the apartment where lay Sinhaghosha asleep: darting upon him, as an eagle pounces upon a snake, I seized him, and dragged him off, before he could call for succour, to the secret passage; when securing the door, I bore him to the cavern, and thence to my own dwelling. I put him in fetters, and exhibited him a captive to my own parents. I also narrated to them the adventure of the subterraneous chamber. They heard the story with great satisfaction, and detaining the King in confinement, brought the Damsels home. I married the Princess, by which I acquired a claim to the now vacant throne, and exercised the functions of royalty. In this state of things we heard of the attack upon the King of Anga, our Ally, and hastened to his assistance. The result it is unnecessary to repeat; but as we have been so fortunate as to meet with your Highness, let the unworthy Sinhaghosha share the general satisfaction, and wipe away all his offences by the penance of prostration at your feet. Rájaváhana assented; but in the mean time desired Pramati to relate his adventures. Pramati bowed and thus obeyed.

STORY OF PRAMATI.

After having wandered some time in search of your Highness, I came to a forest near the skirts of the

Vindhya mountain. There evening overtook me, and the beauty of the West was decorated with the crimson blossoms of the last rays of the sun. I refreshed myself in a limpid pool. Being unable to distinguish the irregularities of the road, levelled now by the gloom, I determined to halt, and collecting a quantity of dry leaves, I made a bed with them at the foot of a stately tree, where having recommended myself to the tutelary Dryad, I composed myself to rest. After a short interval it appeared to me, that my limbs reposed on some softer material than the ground, and sensations of exquisite delight pervaded my whole frame. I felt my right arm throb, and I thought I looked up, and beheld a white canopy, that screened me from the beams of the moon. As I cast my looks to the left, I saw the walls of a lofty apartment, along the foot to which a number of Damsels lay asleep on painted couches. I then directed my gaze to the right, and beheld a most lovely maiden, as graceful as a creeper of Indra's garden, rent from its prop by Airávata, and bowed in sleep like the Lotus when it shuts its petals on the amorous bee. She looked, as lying on the pure white couch, like the earth reclined on the ivory tusks of Ádivaráha, whilst a pearly robe, like the milky ocean, floated loosely over her well turned shoulders. The change filled me with astonishment, and I lay wondering what had become of the forest, and my leafy couch; what building was this, on whose lofty turret rose the spear-crowned figure of the martial God (Kártikeya), shaded by banners floating in the sky; how had I been transported to my present situation, and who the maidens could be, by whom I was surrounded. But the Damsel, who appeared their chief, and resembled the Goddess that bears the Lotus, was the especial object of my meditations. A mortal she certainly was, for the eyes were fast closed in sleep, like the Lotus in the lunar beams; drops of perspiration stood on her cheeks like tears of amber from the snapped branches of the mangoe, and parts of her raiment lying about were discoloured with dust*. Whilst I meditated whether I should disturb her slumbers, methought she gently opened her eyes, and surveyed me with more affection than alarm; after appearing as if she would call her attendants, she seemed to abandon the intention, and drawing herself up, and retiring to the further part of the couch, she lay watching me with half-shut eyes till again she fell asleep. I felt the same power overcome my passion, and was once more plunged into profound repose. After a time I awoke, and looking about me, found myself still at the foot of the tree, in the same place where I had lain down. It was dawn, and I arose, but recurring to the vision of the night, I could scarcely persuade myself it was a dream, and I determined to take up my residence on the spot, and spend my whole life there if necessary, until I should ascertain the truth. I had scarcely formed this determination, when a woman approached: she was of a graceful appearance, but emaciated with care,

* [Nalop., V, 25. Naishad., XIV, 19 ff.]

and clad in ragged attire; her eyes were red with weeping; her hair was bound up in a plait, and her whole semblance indicated one who had suffered the pangs of absence and separation. She ran up to me, and throwing her arms about my neck, expressed every mark of maternal affection. At last, as well as her sobs would allow her, she spoke thus:

"My dear child, behold in me the person who entrusted, as you must have heard, the infant Arthapála to the care of the Queen of Magadha. I am the daughter of Mańibhadra, the wife of Kámapála, the son of Dharmapála, and your mother: having allowed myself to feel displeasure with my husband, and having therefore quitted him in anger, I was cursed in a dream by some one in the form of a Rákshasa, who said: 'I take up my abode in you, oh! violent woman, for a year.' The year, as long as a thousand years, expired last night. I purposed, after attending the Assembly held at the festival of Tryambaka, in the city of Śrávastí, to reseek my Lord, and I was on my way, when I beheld you here, and heard you solicit the protection of the Dryad: the effects of my curse prevented me from properly recognising you, but I could not abandon you in the forest, and I accordingly transported you with me: as we approached the city, I considered that I could not take you to the meeting, and as it chanced we were near the apartments of the Princess Navamáliká, the daughter of Dharmavarddhana, King of Śrávastí, I determined to leave you there; it was an open terrace on the roof of the house where the Princess and her attendants were sleeping. I left you among them, whilst I repaired to the heavenly Assembly. When the ceremonies were over, and the Assembly broke up, I took my leave of my friends, and paid my homage to the Lord of the three worlds, and then offered my respects to the Goddess, to whom my heart is most devoutly attached. She smiled upon me, and said: do not fear, your period of absence is expired, go and be happy with your husband. Thus favoured, I returned to you, and being restored to my proper nature, knew you now to be my son, and the dear friend of Arthapála. I knew also the events of the night, and that you and the Princess had beheld and were enamoured of each other, and although fear and shame had withheld you from any communication, yet a feeling of love deterred the damsel from alarming her attendants. I resolved by some means to bring the event to a favourable conclusion, but was then obliged to carry you back to the forest. I must now hasten, and prostrate myself at your father's feet." So saying, she once more embraced me tenderly, and then departed, whilst I took the road to Śrávastí. On the road I came to a Bunjara camp, where a great crowd was collected to behold a cock-fight. I looked on for a time, and could not suppress a smile. An old Brahman who sat near me, noticed it, and in a low tone asked the reason. I said to him: this is absurd, how could the people have thought of matching that large strong cock of the cocoanut breed with one of the Valáka[1] tribe. He said: you are right, but they are not up to it, so mum: and thus saying, he offered me betel from his box, and entered into discourse with me. The Valáka cock was beaten, and the Brahman to whom the other belonged, was highly pleased with his victory, and my connoisseurship: he invited me to his house, and treated me with every mark of attention. When I took leave of him the next day, he begged me not to forget him, and to depend upon his friendship, if ever I had occasion for it. I left him after due acknowledgement of his kindness, and proceeded to Śrávastí. Being fatigued with the length of the way, I stopped at a garden in the suburbs, and lay down to rest at the foot of a tree, when I was suddenly roused by the musical clank of female anklets, and looking up beheld a damsel approach. When she came opposite to me, I observed that she had a picture in her hand, with which she evidently compared my features, and having done so, appeared to express delight and surprize: having looked at the picture, and recognised the resemblance it bore me, I begged of her to stop, and sit down. She accepted of my invitation, and sitting down entered into conversation with me, giving me an account of the country; at last, perceiving, she said, I was a traveller, and looking as if wearied by my journey, she asked me to rest at her house. I ac-

[1] The Valáka, white, long-necked, long-winded, but dunghill (Skhalamána).

cepted the invitation, and followed her home, where I was regaled in a princely manner. In the course of conversation she enquired of me, what I considered as the most marvellous circumstance that had befallen me in my travels. The question inspired me with hope, and I entertained no doubt that the picture was the work of the Princess, to explain to her attendants the cause of that change in her appearance, which her passion had inflicted. I therefore replied: allow me to look at the picture. She gave it me, and taking it I delineated the Princess as she slept, and then said, 'I saw in a dream as I thought such a maiden as this, as I slept once in a forest, but it was not merely a dream.' When the Damsel saw this she was highly delighted, and begged me to explain the whole, with which request I complied. She then related to me the sufferings of her friend, and we consulted by what means our union might be effected. I told her it was necessary for that purpose I should quit her for a few days. I accordingly took my leave, promising to return as soon as I had matured my scheme. I went to the old Brahman, with whom I had formed an acquaintance, who was astonished to see me back so soon, and enquired the cause. I told him I had received a deep wound from the eyes of the Princess, and depended upon him to extract the dart: he agreed readily to assist me, and this was the plan we adopted.

He disguised me in female apparel, and I passed as his daughter: then taking me with him, he went to the King as he held public audience, and said to him: 'Sire, this is my only daughter, her mother died, whilst she was a child, and she has been reared by my cares alone. A young Brahman, connected by marriage, went some time since to Ujjayiní to earn her dower. I have promised to give her to him: but as he delays returning, and as she is now a young woman, I purpose going myself to bring him hither, and transferring to his charge the anxious trust, thence forward lead a religious life: for the care of a full-grown daughter is at all times arduous; much more so is it, when there is no mother. In the mean time I must solicit your Majesty, the parent of your subjects, to allow her to repose in the shadow of your protection, until I return with the bridegroom.' The King complying with his petition, made me over to his daughter, and I thus obtained the means of gratifying my passion. On the ensuing Phálgun, the inmates of the female apartment celebrated a festival, when all the women repaired to bathe in the river, at an Island on which stood a Temple of Kártikeya. Here, whilst sporting heedlessly in the stream, I dived and disappeared, coming up in a retired place, where my friend awaited me with male apparel. The women thought I was drowned; the Princess exclaimed, she would not survive me, and a scene of grief and alarm ensued, which spread to the city, and excited the attention of the King. Whilst vainly searching for me, the Brahman appeared with me as his intended son-in-law, and expatiating on my acquirements, my knowledge of the four Vedas, six Angas, sixty-four Kalas, of the four branches of tactics, and the use of weapons, and of every branch of Science and Literature, demanded his daughter. The King was overwhelmed with confusion and grief, and unable to answer; the chief attendants, relating what had chanced, endeavoured to console and pacify the supposed father, but he was not to be silenced, and insisted, that in reparation for his loss, and my disappointment, the King should give me his own daughter. To this request no attention was paid, and we were at last forced out of the hall: we were not however to be so easily baffled, but collecting a quantity of wood, which we piled up at the palace gate, my friend, the Brahman, threatened to set fire to, and ascend it, unless his requests were granted: he was seemingly about to put his threats in execution, when the King attended by his chief Counsellors, entreated him to desist, and agreed to his conditions. Thus I obtained the hand of the Princess, and after a time the King finding my fitness, retired from the cares of Government, and placed it in my hands.

At this time Sinhavarmá solicited my aid, and I advanced in consequence to Champá, where I have been so fortunate as to find my Prince. Rájaváhana expressed the pleasure he had received from the account of his friend's ingenuity and fortune, and then requested Mitragupta to narrate what had befallen him.

STORY OF MITRAGUPTA.

Whilst engaged in the same object as my companions, and in quest of your Highness, I came to a city in Suhma called Dámalipta, in the skirts of which, in a stately grove, I found a crowd collected in observance apparently of some festival. I observed also in a bower of Atimukta creepers a young man sitting by himself playing on his Víńá, and approaching him I enquired what celebration was going forward, and why he sat thus apart from the rest. He replied:

Tungadhanwá, King of Suhma, had no progeny: he addressed his prayers to Vindhyavásiní, who had forgotten in her residence at this place her passion for her abode at Vindhya, and obtained from her favour two children: the Goddess appeared to him in a dream, and announced to him the birth of a son and a daughter: the former she said, should be the servant of the husband of the latter; and she directed, that the girl from the age of seven until her marriage should worship her every month on the Kŕitika Nakshatra by playing at ball in public, and further, she should be allowed to marry any one whom she should choose. The festival was to be called the Kandukotsava. In a short time the prophety of the Goddess was fulfilled, and a son and daughter were born to the King: the Damsel was named Kandukavatí, and she comes abroad to-day to play in public. Her foster sister and dear friend Chandrasená is prevented from coming with her by her wish to avoid the young Prince Bhímadhanwá, who teazes her with a suit, to which she prefers mine: her absence is the cause of my solitude and affliction.

He had scarcely ended, when we were startled by the tinkling of anklets near us, and a female entered the bower, whom as soon as the youth beheld he tenderly embraced, and making her sit down introduced her to me as his other life. After condoling with each other upon the danger and uncomfortableness of their situation, they spoke of making their escape to some other country, and the youth appealed to me, to inform him which of the places I had visited was the most fertile and civilized. I told him that there was no dearth of pleasant regions in the world, where he might find a suitable habitation, but that it was not impossible, perhaps, for them both to be happy where they were: if it was, I would show them the way. Before I could explain myself, the sound of female ornaments was distinctly heard, and the damsel sprang up in a hurry, and said to us: the Princess Kandukavatí approaches, doing honour to the Goddess in her sports. A sight of her on these occasions is allowed to all; come and behold her, and may the result be fortunate; I must attend her. So saying she departed. I followed and beheld the Princess seated in an open pavilion of great splendour. The moment I saw her my heart received the impression of her beauties. As I gazed upon her with intense love and admiration, she rose gracefully, and touched with the tips of her lovely fingers the footstool of the Goddess as she hastily paid her devotions. She then took the ball like the red eye of love when moved to wrath. She first let it gently strike the ground, and as it slowly rose beat it down with her open hand, till at last, catching it at the rebound on the back of her hand, she threw it up as high as she could, caught it in its descent, and tossed it up again. As long as it kept good time she struck it gently, but when it slackened reiterated the blows without mercy: occasionally she kept it fluttering in the air like a bird, hitting it up alternately with either hand, in a straight line above her, whilst at others, when it descended obliquely, she sprang forwards, backwards, and sideways to catch it. Thus sporting gracefully she attracted the gaze and applause of the people collected around the pavilion. As I stood, leaning on the shoulder of my new friend, lost in admiration, I drew her notice, and then first she felt the power of Kandarpa, communicated by a glance, and with her sighs repelled the bees that were attracted by the fragrance and beauty of her Lotus cheeks. Increasing in her speed, and driving the ball in a circle, she stood as it were, as if abashed by my gaze, in the centre of a flowery cage: she then followed the game in every direction, and stooping, rising, shrinking, watching, standing, and running pursued her sport. After this, she united her companions in the pastime, and one ball traversing the space between heaven and earth seemed as if it were fifty. She then closed her exercises by repeating her homage to the Goddess, and withdrew, followed by her attendants, and by my whole soul, darting at me as she passed sidelong looks as fatal as the chosen shafts of the flower-armed deity, and reverting as she retired her moon-like face, as if she sought to reclaim the heart she had deposited in mine. Being quite beside myself with love, I readily accepted the invitation of Koshadása to take up a temporary abode at his house: and he treated me most hospitably. In the evening Chandrasená appeared, and having saluted me inclined herself close to her lover for a little, and then sat down. Koshadása smiled and said to me: may I always find favour in your sight. I asked him what he meant: whether any unguent had been applied to the eyes of his rival, so as to induce him to cast his looks in a different direction, and regard Chandrasená as a monkey. She replied laughingly: 'your humble Servant is much obliged to you, if in this life you convert her from a human being to an ape; so be it, for thus only our desires will be gratified. The Princess was so much struck by your appearance at the festival that she immediately became the prey of the foe of Hara. This was at once perceived by me, and I shall tell my mother of it: she will inform the Queen, who will certainly communicate it to the King. He must consent to give his daughter to you, and the Prince will then become your dependant, for so the pleasure of the Goddess was announced. When the Kingdom is your's, Bhímadhanwá will no longer be able to disturb our happiness; only wait here for three or four days.'

So having said she embraced her lover and went away. Koshadása and I spent the night discussing what she had told us. In the morning after we were dressed, I went again to the grove where I had seen the Princess. I was there met by the Prince, who shewed me great civility, and pressing me to accompany him, took me with him to his tent, where I was treated exactly like himself: when I retired to rest, the charms of my mistress visited my slumber. I thought I was locked in her embrace, as I was awakened from my sleep by the clasp of iron fetters, and the grasp of a number of sturdy hands. The Prince thus addressed me: Hark ye, Sirrah! This old woman appointed by me to watch that hussy Chandrasená overheard your fine discourse with her, and her impertinent swain. So, you are the object of Kandukavatí's amiable affections; I am to be your servant; am I? and you are, in my despite to give Chandrasená to Koshadása. Then turning to an attendant, he said: go, toss the scoundrel into the sea. He obeyed, and I was carried off and thrown into the waves. As I had the use of my arms, I swam, as it chanced, till I came luckily across a piece of timber sent by destiny to my aid. I got upon it, and floated about till daylight, when I saw a Ship at a little distance. The crew were Yavanas; when they saw me, they made for me, and hoisting me in gave information to their Captain named Rámeshu, who ordered me to sprinkle a thousand raisins in an instant as I was strong enough. At that moment a galley surrounded by a number of vessels bore down upon us. The Yavanas were alarmed at seeing so many Ships advancing to assail them, like dogs rushing upon a boar. Escape was impossible, and the crew gave themselves up for lost. Observing their despondency, I addressed them, and told them that, if they would take off my chains, I would show them the way to victory. They set me free, and I made them seize their arms, and hurl a shower of darts and arrows at the foe: then grappling with the foremost Ship, we sprang upon the deck, and presently clearing it of its defenders took the Commander alive. Who should this be but Bhimadhanwá. I made myself known to him, and desiring him to meditate on the vicissitudes of destiny gave him over to my followers, by whom he was fettered with the chains which I had borne. The rest of the enemy dispersed, and a contrary wind springing up, we were blown off to an Island in the ocean, where we anchored. We landed in search of fresh water, fruit and herbs, and found an abundant supply. I came to a lofty mountain, the pleasantness of whose brow induced me to ascend, and I held on my way, without observing the distance, till I found myself unexpectedly on the summit: there I discovered a spacious reservoir, to which led steps of precious stones, and whose waters were decorated with Lotus flowers. I seized the opportunity of performing my ablutions, and sipped the juice from the stalks of the Lotuses: then throwing the flowers on my shoulders, I proceeded, and met a Goblin of hideous aspect.—

He stood before me, and enquired in a menacing manner, who I was, and whence I came. I replied undauntedly to his enquiries, and related my adventures. He then said: answer the questions I shall put to you, or I devour you. I bid him propose them, and this conversation ensued:

Rák.—What is the most cruel of all things?

Mitr.—The heart of woman.

Rák.—What constitutes domestic happiness?

Mitr.—The attention of a wife to the gratification of her husband.

Rák.—What is love?

Mitr.—Desire.

Rák.—What overcomes difficulties?

Mitr.—Ingenuity.

I then added, 'I will give you examples of these in the anecdotes of Dkúminí, Gominí, Nimbavatí, and Natambavatí.' He desired me to narrate them, and I proceeded to

THE STORY OF DHÚMINÍ *.

In the city of Trigartta lived three brothers, Dhanaka, Dhányaka and Dhanyaka. It happened that a terrible dearth took place; there was no rain for 12 years. The grains were withered; the pools were beds of earth; the streams were dried up; religious rites fell into disuse; thieves and rogues multiplied;

* [Benfey, Pantschatantra, I, 436.]

the people ate one another; and the villages and towns were almost depopulated. The three brothers had consumed every thing belonging to them, even to their families, and the wife of the youngest named Dhúminí was the only eatable article left. She was accordingly devoted to the same fate as her predecessors; but as her husband Dhanyaka was too much attached to her to assent to her sacrifice, he determined to fly with her to a distance, and they set off that night into the forest, allaying their thirst with his own blood. On their way they found a miserable man deprived of nose, feet, and hands, lying by the road side. Dhanyaka, in pity of his sad plight, took him on his back, and carried him along with them, until they discovered a cave suited to their purposes. Here they halted, and finding in the vicinity a supply of roots, and some herds of deer, they took up their abode. When the party had somewhat recovered their health and strength, the evil passions of the female began to acquire activity, and as Dhanyaka was often absent in quest of game for their support, Dhúminí was left alone with the cripple, whom she compelled to comply with her desires. Hating the man she had thus injured, she next conspired her husband's death, and taking advantage of his stooping to recover a rope, which she had purposely dropped into a well, she came behind him, and pushed him over into it. She then quitted the place, carrying her mutilated lover on her back. He passed for her husband wherever they came, and the people admiring her conjugal devotedness worshipped her as a Saint. In this manner they came to Avanti, where the circumstances being brought to the notice of the King he gave them a comfortable maintenance as the recompense of so much virtue. Soon after the fall of Dhanyaka into the well, it chanced that a caravan halted on that spot, and the merchants repairing to the well to procure water, they extricated Dhanyaka from his perilous situation, and took him along with them. Amongst other places, they visited Avanti, and Dhúminí meeting her husband, exclaimed—"that is the wretch by whom my husband was so barbarously mangled. He was in consequence immediately seized, and ordered to be put to death. Dhanyaka however requested, that he might be first confronted with the cripple; admitting that, if he should confirm the accusation, he ought to be considered guilty. The cripple was brought, and as soon as he saw his preserver fell at his feet, acknowledging the obligations he owed him, and revealing all the wickedness of his wife. When the King heard this, he was highly incensed, and ordered the woman to be punished, as she deserved. This story of Dhúminí proves my assertion that the most cruel of all things is woman's heart. I shall now relate to you

THE STORY OF GOMINÍ.

In Drávira is a celebrated city called Kánchí. A young merchant of considerable wealth, named Śakti Kumára, resided there. He was unmarried at the age of eighteen, and considering that there was no real happiness in a single life, as also that felicity in wedlock depended upon the wife's character, he determined to set off in search of a spouse; adopting therefore the character of a fortune-teller, and carrying with him a Prastha of rice bound up in his cloth, he proceeded on his travels. Wherever he went, those who had daughters brought them to him, and when he met with a girl whose appearance pleased him, he terminated his prognostications by asking her as a favour to shew him how well she could cook his rice. Some laughed, and some were angry, but all sent him away without complying, and he went from house to house in vain. Having arrived in a town of the Śivis on the Southern side of the Káverí, he came to a house, where making his usual application, a Damsel was brought out by her nurse, her parents being both deceased. As he looked at her, he observed, that she was perfect, her limbs were neither too long nor too short, too slight nor too stout; her hands were marked with all the lucky signs, as the fish, lotus, vase, &c. her fingers were straight, and the palms ruddy; her ankles were clean and even, and her feet well turned, and fleshy, with small and scarcely visible fibres; her legs were straight and symmetrical, and well set; and her knees were small, delicate and even; her hips prominent and well rounded; her waist was slender; her body gently inclined; her breasts were protuberant, and divided by a narrow interval; her arms were long, fleshy, smooth and soft; her neck was graceful and well turned, and surmounted by a lovely countenance, where the pouting lips were of a most brilliant red; the chin was elegant, and not small; the cheeks were firm and round; the nose was like the budding sesamum flower; the eyes were of the darkest jet, rolling in the most crystalline white; and the forehead as radiant as the moon, shaded by curling locks of deep sapphire hue. Śakti Kumára was subdued by these charms, and with an agitated bosom proposed his ordinary test. She smiled, as she looked archly at her attendant, and taking the rice desired the guest to sit at the threshold, where she washed his feet. She then steeped the grains a little in water, dried them in the sun, and rubbing them gently in the ground, removed the awn without breaking the grain. She then said to the nurse, 'this bran will be acceptable to the goldsmiths to clean their jewellery: go, sell it to them, and purchase with the price fuel, an earthen boiler, and two platters.' Whilst the old woman was gone on this errand, the Damsel brayed the grain in a mortar of arjuna wood with a pestle of khayar headed with iron, she then winnowed it with the basket, and having well washed it, set it to boil in five times its quantity of water, worshipping the chimney as she placed the boiler. When the rice was swollen up properly, she took the boiler from the fire, and separated the scum, then replacing it, kept stirring it till it was quite boiled; after which she placed the boiler with the mouth downwards, and extinguishing the fire with the cold water, sent the old woman to dispose of the coals which were unconsumed; with the price procured for them buying vegetables, ghee, curds, oil, myrobalans, and tamarinds. These she seasoned with condiments. She then placed the scum of the rice-water in a new saucer, and cooling it with a fan, added to it perfumes evaporated on the coals. She then pealed the myrobalan, and added to it Lotus perfume, when she directed her nurse to desire Śakti Kumára to bathe. When he was bathed, and had rubbed himself with oil and myrobalan, she laid a plank on a part of the floor well swept and levelled, on which he sat down: she then placed before him on a well trimmed plantain leaf two platters. Having given him some water to drink, she served him with two spoonfuls of rice, to which she added ghee and sauce, the rest of the rice he ate with spices, curds, butter, milk, and rice gruel. She finally brought him water to drink pure, cool, and fragrant in a new jug, perfumed with agallochum. The old woman then removed the fragments, and cleaning the ground with fresh cowdung, spread her garment upon it, on which he went to sleep. When he awoke he expressed his satisfaction, and being contented to seek no further, he married the Damsel, and took her along with him, when she found herself unexpectedly a woman of wealth and consequence. She nevertheless continued to worship her husband as a God, to pay the most assiduous attention to his household affairs, and to superintend the regulation of her family. In this way she acquired the entire confidence of her spouse who, leaving all his domestic concerns to her care, tasted in his corporeal form the joys of Paradise. I shall now relate to you

THE STORY OF NIMBAVATÍ.

In the kingdom of Sauráshtŕa, in a city called Valabhí, there dwelt Gŕihagupta, a Ship-owner, who was possessed of great wealth. He had a daughter named Ratnavatí, who was married by Balabhadra, a Merchant's son. Soon after their espousal the husband, finding the young bride indifferent to his endearments, conceived so violent a dislike to her, that he could not bear the sight of her; to all his friends and retainers he gave her the nickname of Nimbavatí. After some time had elapsed, and when she sorrowfully meditated on the conduct she should pursue, an old female devotee, who was like a mother to her, brought to her flowers from the idol, and noticing her distress enquired its cause. Ratnavatí informed her of her husband's aversion, and begged her to befriend her, declaring, if she could not recover that regard, which was the only happiness and honour of a woman of respectable birth and station, she would no longer suffer so hateful an existence. The old woman promised to give her whatever aid she could, and desired her to suggest a plan for the purpose. She said: "There is a neighbour, a merchant, of immense wealth and consequence; his daughter Kanakavatí is very like me in person, and of my age; she is also my particular friend. I will go to visit her, and take an opportunity of amusing myself on the terrace of her house, splendidly attired. Do you contrive to bring my husband to the place, with the assent of my friend's mother, which we will obtain. As you approach, I will let a ball fly in your direction, as if by accident; pick it up, and give it him, and tell him, 'this Damsel Kanakavatí, the daughter of Kuveradatta, is the friend of your wife, and is vehement in her abuse of you: this ball is hers, and you should not relinquish the property of an enemy?' Looking up, he will think me to be Kanakavatí, and when I descend to claim the ball, will at my request conveyed through you return it to me. From this opening his regard will be attracted, and in all probability he will become enamoured of me in the person of my friend. As he cannot expect that the haughty merchant will consent to our wedding, he will concert through your mediation measures for carrying me off, which of course I shall consent to, and we will fly together to another country." So it happened, and as the old devotee reported that Balabhadra had expressed his regret for his past neglect of his wife, her friends concluded when she disappeared that she was gone with him. On the road Ratnavatí bought a female slave, and with her they settled at a small town, where Balabhadra who was well skilled in trade soon made a large sum at a little cost, and in time became the chief man in the city, and retained a number of slaves. He now treated his first female servant with great indignity, and by his ill-behaviour to her excited her resentment.

In her rage she promulgated, as much as she thought she knew of his secret history, as she had learnt it from her mistress. This coming to the ears of the mayor, he reported it to the seniors, and Balabhadra was denounced as a disgrace to the city, having stolen the daughter of Kuveradatta. Balabhadra when he heard of this was excessively alarmed, but Ratnavatí encouraged him, desiring him to say, she was not Kanakavatí but Ratnavatí, the daughter of Gŕihagupta of Valabhí, given him by her father in marriage, and to desire them, if they doubted him, to send a messenger to ascertain the truth. Balabhadra said, as she had desired him, and the elders sent to Valabhí. When Gŕihagupta heard of his daughter's existence, he set off with her mother to her residence, and was overjoyed to find his Ratnavatí again. Balabhadra now perceived that he had been taken in; but Ratnavatí had become too dear to him for him to regret the deception. Therefore I say that Love is Desire. I shall now relate to you

THE STORY OF NITAMBAVATÍ.

In Śúrasena is a city called Mathurá, where dwelt a youth of family, who was addicted to loose pleasures, and vicious society, and being a lad of spirit he was so often entangled in broils, that he was called Kalahakańtaka. One day he saw in a painter's possession the picture of a female, with whose charms he became violently enamoured. After some solicitation he prevailed on the painter to tell him, who the original was, and having learnt that she was the wife of Anantakírtti, a merchant of Ujjayiní, and her name Nitambavatí, set off in the disguise of a mendicant for that city. Having got access to the house, under pretence of soliciting alms, he obtained a sight of the lady, and found her still more fascinating than her picture. With a view to effect his projects he solicited and obtained the care of the cemetery, and with the clothes of the dead he attached to his interests a female Śramańiká or Bauddha devotee. This woman he employed to convey a message from him to Nitambavatí, inviting her to come and see him, to which she sent back an angry and indignant reply. He was not discouraged, but desired his messenger to return to the merchant's wife, and say to her, as from herself: 'Persons like us, who are fully acquainted with the insufficiency of life, and only desirous of final emancipation, cannot be suspected of entertaining any purpose adverse to the reputation of women of respectability. The message I lately conveyed to you I only intended to try your merit, as I was afraid such youth and beauty could scarcely be satisfied with a man so advanced in years as your husband. I was mistaken, and the result has so much pleased me, that I am anxious to confer upon you a proof of my esteem. I should wish to see you a mother, but the planet under which your husband was born, has hitherto opposed it. This evil influence however may be counteracted, if you will be content to assist. Accompany me to a grove at night, where I will bring you a seer versed in incantations; you must put your foot in his hand, whilst he conveys into it his charms. Then, as if angry, kick your husband on the breast, when the evil influence will be expelled, and you will be blessed with progeny, and your husband will venerate you as a Goddess. There is nothing to be afraid of.' Nitambavatí with some little difficulty consented, and being apprised of her intentions, the false Saint awaited her at the appointed place. She came, as was directed, and put her foot into his hand; he pretended to rub it, muttering imaginary charms all the time, until he had taken off her golden anklet, when making a sudden cut at her thigh with a knife, which he had covertly prepared, he inflicted a gash in the upper part of it, and then quickly withdrew. Nitambavatí full of pain and terror, reviling herself for her own folly, and ready to kill the Śramańiká for having exposed her to such peril, returned home, and privately dressing her wound, kept her bed for some days. The rogue in the mean time offered the anklet to Anantakírtti for sale. He knew it to be his wife's, and enquired, how the vender had come by it. He refused to tell; the merchant threatened him with punishment, on which Kalahakańtaka professed himself ready to communicate the truth to the Guild, (or Committee of merchants). He was accordingly taken before them, when he desired the merchant to send for his wife's anklets. She replied, she had lost one of them; it was large, and had slipped off, but she forwarded the other. The anklet in the possession of the supposed mendicant being compared with this was found to correspond, and there remained no doubt of their owner. The ascetic then being questioned as to the circumstances, under which he gained possession of it, replied thus: "You are aware, Gentlemen, that I was appointed to take charge of the graves of the deceased. As some people wished to deprive me of my fees, by burning the bodies by night, I kept watch at all hours. Last night I saw a dark-complexioned female dragging the half-burnt fragments of a dead body from the funeral pile, when to punish her horrible attempt I made a cut at her with my knife, and wounded one of her thighs, as she turned to escape; she ran off however, dropping one of her anklets as she fled, and I thus became possessed of it." The account thus given inspired all the auditors with horror. Nitambavatí was unanimously pronounced a Śákiní or witch; she was turned out of his house by her husband, and rejected with abhorrence by all the citizens. In this distress she repaired to the cemetery, where she was in the act of putting a period to her life, when she was prevented by her lover. He threw himself at her feet, and told her that, unable to live without her, he had adopted this contrivance to obtain her person, and entreated her to rely upon the fervour and faithfulness of his regard. His entreaties and protestations were at last successful, combined with the consciousness of her helpless situation, and Nitambavatí rewarded his ingenuity with her affection. Therefore I say that ingenuity accomplishes the greatest difficulties.

When I had finished my narratives, the Brahma Rákshasa expressed himself highly pleased with me; but he had scarcely so spoken, when several pearls mixed with drops of water fell from the sky. I looked up, and saw a Rákshasa in the air, carrying along with him a female who struggled to free herself from his grasp. I assailed him with reproaches, but could not more actively punish his violence, as he held his course in the air. My Rákshasa friend however felt as I did, and called to the other to stop, rising at the same time to intercept him. The ravisher, obliged to defend himself, threw down his lovely burthen, intending to dash her to pieces. She dropped, like a blossom shaken from a tree of heaven, and I fortunately caught her in my arms. I held her fainting, without noticing her countenance, my gaze being quite fixed upon the conflict in the air, where the contending demons hurled vast trees, and mountain peaks against each other. To shun the falling fragments, I hastened from the spot, and carrying my gentle load to the reservoir, imagine my delight, when I found I pressed my dear life Kandukávatí to my heart. I sprinkled her with the cool wave; she recovered her senses, immediately recognised me, and suffered herself to be encouraged by my endearments. She told me that, when she heard I was drowned by order of her cruel brother, she determined not to survive my loss; she contrived accordingly to deceive her attendants, and get out to the grove alone, with an intent of there putting an end to her life. Whilst thus engaged, she was observed by the Rákshasa who, attracted by her person, had endeavoured to allay her distress, and engage her regard: but finding his efforts unavailing, he had recourse to violence, and carried her off, when he was prevented as already narrated. When Kandukávatí had finished her narrative, I conducted her on board-ship, and we set sail. Contrary winds however drove us from our destined course, and carried us again to Támaliptá. When we landed, we heard that Tungadhanwá with his Queen were so deeply affected by the disappearance of their son, and the loss of their daughter, that they had gone to the banks of the Ganges, intending to abstain from all food, and die there. As the chief citizens were warmly attached to their King, and contemplated his death with sincere grief, their sorrow gave place to joy when they found that the Prince and Princess were returned. I conducted his children to the King, who received them with rapture, and to requite my services bestowed on me the hand of his daughter, and the first place in the state. The young Prince now very willingly submitted to my superiority, and assented to the union of Chandrasená with Koshadása. We were living happily together, when our alliance with Sinhavarmá brought us to his succour, and procured me the happiness of again beholding my honored Lord.

Mitragupta having thus concluded, Rájaváhana, after expressing his admiration of the marvellous incidents his friend had encountered, requested Mantragupta to repeat his adventures: he thus obeyed.

STORY OF MANTRAGUPTA.

The direction, which I had taken in quest of your Highness, brought me to the country of the Kalingas. When I approached Kalinga the capital, I stopped at a short distance, and rested on the borders of a reservoir adjoining to the public obsequial ground. I fell asleep. When I awoke, I found it was midnight, the surrounding objects were plunged in gloom, the chilly dews fell heavily, and the cold breeze sighed sorrowfully amidst the trembling leaves. All the world was at rest, save where the imps of mischief hovered in the murky air. Whilst my eyes were scarcely open, I distinctly heard one goblin say to another: 'What orders has the parched up magician to give, what abominable desire to gratify, that he commands our attendance? I wish that some one of power adequate to the task would destroy the Aṅaka chief.' These words excited my curiosity, and I determined to follow them, and see the person of whom they spoke. I rose, therefore, and cautiously followed the spirits to a spot, where I beheld a man decorated with ornaments made of human bones, stained all over with the ashes of burnt wood, and bearing a braid of hair of a lightning hue, busily feeding with his left hand a devouring fire with Sesamum and mustard seeds. The goblin I had followed presented himself with joined palms before the seer, and respectfully asked, what duty he was to perform. The stern magician replied: 'Go, bring hither Kanakalekhá, the daughter of Kardana, King of Kalinga.' The imp vanished, and in an instant re-appeared with the Princess, half dead with terror; she called out sobbing with low broken tones on her friends and parents, till the magician enraged seized her by her lovely tresses escaped from the burst fillet in one hand, whilst he raised with the other a sharpened sword, with an intention to strike off her head. This was not to be witnessed. I sprang upon him, and in a moment, wresting the sword from his grasp, struck off the villain's head, and tossed it with its clotted hair-band into the hollow of a tree. The goblin who had brought the maiden praised the act, and rejoiced at being liberated from a master as tyrannical as savage, one, he said, who never slept himself, and never allowed his slaves a moment's repose. In his gratitude, he offered to perform whatever I should order, and requested me to appoint him some task. I commanded him to carry the Princess back to the palace whence he had conveyed her. As he was about to execute this commission, the Princess, who had surveyed me sometime askance, as she stood, as if abashed, beating the ground with her feet, and whilst the cool drops fell from her eyes upon her bosom, and a soft sigh like the shaft of love escaped from her lips, entreated me in most melodious accents, not to desert her, nor, after rescuing her from the hands of fate, to leave her to perish in the depths of passion. She declared, she considered herself as my slave, begged that I would regard her as an atom of the lotus dust which was allowed to rest upon my feet, and finally proposed, if I could unite my destiny to hers, that I should accompany her to the palace, where I might live with her in security, as from the faithful attachment of her attendants I might be confident that our secret would never be divulged. It needed no persuasion to gain my assent, wounded as I felt myself by the shaft of the heart-born archer, and I desired the spirit, if he was inclined to do me a service, to carry us both wherever the Princess should direct. He bore us to the palace, where I resided for some time in uninterrupted delight.

When the vernal season had set in, and the air was scented with the breezes of Malaya, and musical with the Koil's song, the King of Kalinga went with all his household and attendants, to pass a fortnight on the sea shore, where the wind cooled by the spray of the ocean attempered the fierceness of the Solar rays. Here, whilst engaged in every kind of elegant diversion, the whole party was suddenly surprised, and carried off by the King of Andhra, Jayasinha, and a body of troops, which landed unexpectedly from the flotilla, with which he scoured the coasts.

When I heard of the captivity of the Princess, I

was overcome with despair, and vainly meditated on the means of effecting her recovery. At last a Brahman who came from Andhra reported that Jayasinha, who had at first intended to put Kardana to death, was diverted from his purpose by the charms of Kanakalekhá, whom he had espoused; that the Princess, however, was possessed by a spirit, who kept at bay the King, and could not be expelled by the skill of the physicians. This account inspired me with hope, and I determined to repair to Andhra immediately. Before going thither I went to the cemetery, where I took the old conjurer's tufted locks from the tree, and his patched robe, with which I disguised my person, and collecting some disciples about me I kept them in good humour with the presents we obtained from the villagers for the tricks we practised on their credulity. In a short time we approached Andhra. I took up my abode in a grove, on the edge of a spacious lake lovely with lotus flowers, and lively with flocks of wild geese. When I was settled here, my disciples spread themselves abroad, and reported my miraculous skill and universal knowledge, and asserted also that I could answer all questions, solve all secrets, and had all the Śástras upon the tip of my tongue. Full credit was given to these reports, and my fame at last reached the King, as the only person capable of expelling the demon who had taken possession of his bride. He accordingly came to visit me, and day after day presented himself before me, treating me with the most profound reverence, and gratifying my followers with liberal presents. After some time he stated he had something to say to me. I appeared to be lost in a fit of abstract meditation, and suddenly as it were recovering said, 'Son, I know what you would say, and worthy of you is the desire to possess that damsel the pearl of maidens, and asylum of all excellences. There are means of obtaining for you the Goddess Lakshmí, who wears a necklace of a thousand streams, and a girdle of the milky sea. This Yaksha cannot bear that one should ever look on that lotus-eyed. Have patience therefore for three days, I will do what is necessary.' The King departed highly pleased; in the mean time I laboured every night to form an excavation in the bank of the lake, opening into it on the surface of the water, taking care to avoid observation; the outer mouth of this I covered with rubbish and stones, so that it was not observable, and worshipped daily here with prostrations and red lotus flowers the God of the thousand rays, who wears the planets as a gorgeous necklace, the lion that destroys the elephant of darkness, the witness of every act of good or ill. When three days had elapsed, and the blaze of light was veiled by the red peak of the Western mountain, and the sun looked like the bosom of twilight smeared with ruddy sandal, the King came, and stood before me, hiding his tiara in the dust at my feet. I said: 'When fate befriends us in this world, fortune does not take up her abode with the indolent; prosperity is in the hands of the active. This reservoir must be cleaned thoroughly by your most respectable servants who are to perform the task with zeal and faith; after that, you will bathe in it to-night, and at midnight, after bathing, float on the water with suppressed breath as long as you are able; on this certain sounds will be heard by your attendants as if the bank had fallen, and as if the wild geese mourned the wounds they received from the lotus stalks; that sound having subsided, you will come forth with dripping garments, and red eyes, and in a form in which you will be the delight of all eyes; the Yaksha will not be able to stand before you, and you will instantly become the master of the maiden's heart. With regard to thy bride, the earth, when you come forth you will find a circle in your hand that shall annihilate all your foes. If you wish, you may cause the lake to be carefully examined by those in whom you confide with nets, and surround it with your troops for thirty fathoms, for who can tell what device an enemy may employ?' I was confident these precautions would not detect the hole I had made, and was sure he would attend to my instructions out of his excessive passion. I then said to him: 'King, we have tarried here too long; it is not our custom to remain any time in one place. When your purposes are attained, you will not see me more: we could not depart till we had done something to serve you, having gleaned in your kingdom: now the motive of our stay ceases. Go home, bathe in fragrant water, perfume your person, put on a white garland according to your state, make presents to the Brahmans, and at night, illuminating the gloom with thousands of lamps, advance to the attainment of your desires.' The King was penetrated with gratitude, but lamented my purposed disappearance, as invalidating the favour I had bestowed. As my will was not to be disputed, however, he took his leave, and went to prepare for his visit to the lake. I went forth at night alone, and entered the hole, where I listened attentively to what was going forward. At midnight the King, having set guards all round, approached, and having had the pool examined was satisfied of his security, and plunged into the water. As he floated, with his hair loose, and breath suppressed, I cast my scarf round his neck as a noose, and drew him down, and pummelling him to death in an instant, thrust his body into the hole; after which I ascended from the water. The attendants were astonished at the surprising change of the King's person, but suspected nothing; and ascending the royal elephant I returned with all the pomp and splendour of sovereignty to the palace, where in an assembly of all the Chiefs, collected by my order, I seated myself on a throne glittering with gems, and observing that they were struck by my altered appearance, I thus addressed the Court: 'Observe the power of the Saint by whose will such a transformation of our person has been wrought. Let the heads of infidels be now bowed down in shame. Let all honour be paid to the shrines of the Gods, and the song and dance proclaim their praise, and let wealth be distributed to the poor, and dissipate all their cares.'

The Ministers exclaimed: glory to the Prince! may the ten regions own his power, and his fame eclipse that of all other Kings! Repeating these wishes, they left me to obey my orders. I now noticed one of my wife's most attached servants; calling her to me I desired her to look at me, and asked her if she had ever seen me before. As soon as she looked at me, she recognized me, and while tears of transport startled from her eyes, she restrained her emotions, and replied: 'If this is not the work of magic, I know whom I behold,' and then begged me to explain to her, how I came there. I told her the story, and sent her to impart it to our friends. Having thus set the captive King at liberty, I was united without hindrance or disguise to his daughter by his consent, and in a short time communicating the truth to my father-in-law I made over to him the Kingdom, and Kardana reigned over the united dominions of Andhra and Kalinga. His ancient alliance with the King of Anga brought him hither, and led to this delightful meeting.

Rájaváhana having complimented his friend on the success with which he had sustained the saintly character, and the miracles he had wrought, seriously praised his ingenuity and courage. Then turning to Viśruta, requested him to proceed with his story. He thus complied:

STORY OF VIŚRUTA.

Whilst travelling in search of our Prince, I came to the Vindhya forest, and one day encountered by the side of a well a boy about eight years of age, who was weeping bitterly, and in great distress; as soon as he saw me, he cried to me to help him to rescue his friend, and ancient guardian, who had fallen into the well. I immediately lent my aid, and with the stalks of long creepers we succeeded in extricating from the chasm a venerable old man, after which, knocking down with stones the fruit of some tall Likucha trees, and drawing up some water in a bamboo, we recruited our strength as we sat down together at the foot of a tree. When our hunger and thirst were appeased, I asked the old man to relate his story, with which request he readily complied.

Puńyavarmá was the king of Vidarbha; he was the ornament of the race of Bhoja, an incarnation of the God of Justice, liberal, wise and affable, the protector of his people, and the terror of his foes. When he was numbered amongst the immortals, Anantavarmá succeeded. This Prince was graced with every excellence, but held the science of Politics (Dańďaníti) in little esteem; one of his Ministers, Vasurakshaka, reproved him for this neglect, in terms more severe than respectful: 'Sire, he said, I observe that you are not inferior to your ancestors in merit, but, unfortunately, your mind is chiefly engrossed by the trivial amusements of music, dancing, painting and poetry.

The intellect, that is not exercised in worthy studies, is like gold that has not been refined in the fire; and the Prince, whose understanding is uncultivated, is unable to anticipate how far his own elevation may be surpassed by others, or to judge of the objects to be effected, or means by which they are to be attained. Being unfit to judge of affairs, his orders are disregarded by his own servants and by strangers, and the commands of a Prince personally contemned are but of little weight, even when the purpose be public good. This contempt of authority soon leads to general demoralisation, and the corruption of public morals is ruinous to a monarch both in this world and the next. Abandon, therefore, mere external accomplishments, and study those sciences by which your authority will be respected, and your power extended throughout the sea-encircled world.' When the King had heard this address, he said, "You counsel wisely; it shall be looked to," and then withdrew to the inner apartment, and communicated what had passed to Vihárabhadra. This man was one of the Ministers, and associates of the King's pleasures: he was well skilled in singing, dancing and playing, thoroughly acquainted with the town, of witty fancy, of licentious tongue; he had a peculiar tact in finding out a person's weak side, could excite laughter, and recommend scandal; was a Pańdit in craft, a Pilot of libertinism, and a Professor of all vicious arts. Having heard the Prince's account, he smiled, and thus proceeded:

"Sire, whenever by the favor of fate a person is blessed with prosperity, there will always be found men forward to assail and teaze them, without a why or a wherefore, merely that the rogues may accomplish their own designs; thus some advise him to place his hopes on the goods of the life to come, they shave his head, gird him with straw, clothe him in skins, smear his body with butter, and send him to sleep without his supper, in return for which they consent to take all his property: nay, there are others still more heinous, who are persuaded to relinquish children, wives, and even life. If the person these men have to deal with be too cunning or too covetous to let his goods slip out of his hands, they attack him in another manner. They profess they can convert a gross of cowries to a lac of gold, they can destroy our foes without weapons, and they can make this mortal body that of an Emperor, provided those they address are ready to follow the path they will shew. If any one ask what path is that, they will reply: 'There are four branches of royal knowledge, Trayí, Vártá, Anvíkshikí, (Logic) and Dańđaníti, (or Policy); of the three first the fruits, though important, are slowly matured: let them alone therefore, and study the Dańđaníti, as recently composed by the learned Vishńugupta in six thousand stanzas, for the use of the King Maurya. This, though but an epitome, will require its true time, but it must be studied.' So the King sets to work, and reads and listens, till he grows old. One Śástra is connected with another; unless all are read, nothing is known; so be it, be the time long or short; still read. Well, the student is accomplished; what has he learnt? The first lesson is, never trust to wife or child. The next is, so much water is required to boil so much rice, and so much fuel to heat that water; let them be measured before they are served out. When a King has risen, and has washed his mouth, he must devote the first watch of the day to the examination of the day's receipts and expenditure; he must not let a handful, nor half a handful escape him, and yet even whilst he hears, the superintendant will cheat him twice as much as ever. Cháńakya has detailed forty modes of defrauding; but servants, by the force of their own ingenuity, multiply these a thousand fold. In the second watch the Prince, whose ear is to be assailed with the squabbles of contending subjects, lives a most wretched life; on that account let judges and others, who thrive by litigation, dispose of the suits as they please, consulting their own advantage, and leaving all the sin and shame to their sovereign. In the third watch he finds leisure to bathe and eat, and until his food is digested, he lives in dread of poison. In the fourth he rises to stretch forth his hands to receive gold. In the fifth he is plagued with the schemes of his Counsellors, who like indifferent and impartial umpires are agreed amongst themselves to pervert merits and defects, misstate the reports of the spies, misrepresent possibilities and impossibilities, and confound all distinctions of place and time, confirm the friends of themselves and others in their appointments, excite the King's rage in private, and allay it in public, and leave their master not to be depended upon. In the sixth the Prince is attended by the ministers of his amusements, and is his own master for an hour and a half. In the seventh watch he reviews his troops. In the eighth he has to listen to the ambitious projects of his friends, the Generals. Evening is now arrived; in the first watch of the night he must receive his secret emissaries, and appoint these ferocious fellows to their work of fire, sword, and poison. In the second, after eating, he must begin like a Vaida Brahman to con his book. In the third he is sent to sleep with the sounds of the trumpet. In the fourth and fifth he may enjoy a three hour's slumber, if his poor thought-labouring brain will allow him to repose. In the sixth he must begin to prepare for the duties prescribed by the Śástras. In the seventh he must consult with the ministers regarding the dispatch of agents and emissaries; for these fellows, who get rich by presents on both sides, and the privileges granted to their traffic, will make work if there be none. In the eighth the Purohita and others assembling must relate to the King the troubled dreams they have had, the lowering of the planets, and the unlucky omens they have noted, to avert which threatened misfortunes propitiatory rights must be performed. So be it; the essential of all oblations is gold. Then there are those Brahmans, each like Brahmá himself, if they will pray for the King's prosperity, it will be augmented. They are poor men, have large families, are constant in devotional rites, and ascetic practices; they have yet received no bounty; whatever is given to them will be paid with long life and good fortune and happiness fit for heaven: and thus having persuaded the King to entrust them with liberal gifts, these worthy Gentlemen pocket the purchase of Paradise themselves. Thus by a life of unremitted labour and care, and without a moment's enjoyment, night or day, why should a politic Prince think of becoming an Emperor, when his own little district is with difficulty preserved? If mistrust of all is to be entertained, what is the prosperity of a state? But in those things, for which Policy provides not, the world will take care of itself: the infant needs no instructions from the Śástras to drain the maternal breast. Abandon then all absurd restraints, and follow your own inclinations. These sages, who say that the senses are to be subdued, six foes to be shunned, the expedients of pacification, &c. to be perpetually observed, questions of peace and war to be eternally discussed, and not a moment's relaxation admitted—these hypocritical counsellors only lay in wait to carry off your wealth and spend it amongst their harlots. Who are those beggarly fellows that shew such stern virtue, and lay down the laws so sagely? Your Śukra, Angiras, Viśáláksha, Báhudantiputra, Paráśara and others. What foes did they subdue? what Śástras did they acknowledge? did they foresee all the consequences of what they did, when they began to do any thing? Those who are deeply read are often taken in by the ignorant. Is it not the act of the Gods, that you have rank, youth, beauty and wealth? why vex your thoughts with cares of state? are all unavailing, ten thousand elephants, three lac of horse, and countless infantry, and the treasuries filled with jewels and gold beyond your utmost expenditure, even if life be lengthened to ages? is all this insufficient, that there should be occasion to labour for more? The life of Mortals lasts but three or four days, and we should therefore make the most of it. Those are fools, who whilst they are accumulating perish, and reap no benefit from what they have collected. But enough of this. Leave the load of empire to those who have your confidence, and are adequate to the task, and do you enjoy your corporeal existence, amongst the lovely damsels of the palace, in the song, the dance, and the convivial cup, whilst the season serves."

So saying, he prostrated himself on the ground, and thus remained. The denizens of the haram smiled applause; the King was also pleased, and said, 'Rise, your advice is sound, I acknowledge you to be my Guru, and who shall disobey my Preceptor's counsels?' So saying, he raised him, and resumed his amusements with greater zest than ever.

The old minister who had given such unprofitable advice, was soon sensible of an alteration in the King's behaviour: he was never entrusted with any confidential matters; he was never addressed with a courteous smile; he was never asked after his family; he never received any friendly presents, nor was he invited to the inner apartments. On the other hand, he was employed on the most disagreable duties; his suggestions were listened to in silence, or treated with ridicule; his presents, however valuable, received with contempt; and his actual enemies were always secure of the King's favor. In this dilemma he considered what was to be done: he could not abandon a Prince to whom he was attached by the ties, which had long connected their mutual ancestors, and he was yet desirous of rendering the Prince sensible of the importance of neglecting the councils he had given. He concluded that if the Kingdom were in the hands of Vasantabhánu, the ruler of Aśmaka, a Prince of policy, its present ruler would suffer a heavy calamity, and determined, that it were better to support the neglect he suffered, that he might be able to serve the King more effectually, when the occasion should arrive.

In this state of affairs, it happened that Chandrapálita, the son of Indrapálita, minister of the King of Aśmaka, being professedly expelled his father's palace for his profligate conduct, but, in truth, being sent by the king of Aśmaka, came to Vidarbha with a numerous train of dissolute retainers. An intimate friendship was soon formed between him and Vihárabhadra, and they concerted a plot for subverting the Government by leading the King on gradually to the commission of various vices. With this view Vihárabhadra confirmed the King in every idle purpose, and eulogised each amusement that was casually suggested. When hunting was the theme, he recommended it as calculated to strengthen the constitution, improve the appetite, and render the frame strong, active, hardy: he expatiated also on the utility of pursuing the deer, and the wild cattle to punish them for the mischief they did for the crops, and of rendering the roads safe and free, by destroying the wolf and the tiger: he described also the pleasure of beholding various regions, and traversing the mountains, and the forests, but above all he argued the importance of the satisfaction thus afforded to such a Prince's subjects, as tenanted the wilds, and the intimidation such proofs of an active spirit necessarily impressed upon hostile chiefs. When gambling was spoken of, he called the loss of wealth that of so much trash, and was warm in his praise of unbounded munificence. Play taught persons, he said, not to be elated with success, nor depressed by ill luck, to acquire the power of confining their thoughts to a fixed object, to exercise determined perseverance and unremitted acuteness in its prosecution, disregard for persons and perils, and a noble disdain of individual danger. With respect to sexual gratification he maintained it was the end and recompense of wealth and virtue, a perpetual school for eloquence and ingenuity, in gaining the damsel loved, preserving her when acquired, enjoying her when preserved, pleasing her when possessed, pacifying her when offended; but above all in the generation of progeny it was the source of supreme felicity both here and hereafter. Wine, he said, was the medicament of a variety of diseases, the preserver of perpetual youth, and the dissipation of every care: it befriended love, it appeased resentment, and delighted all with the undisguised language it inspired, it prolonged enjoyment, conferred beauty, and lavished grace; as it rendered man also insensible to fear and pain, it was highly serviceable in war. He further always recommended harshness of speech, and severity of punishment, as a King, he said, was not to imitate the apathy of a Saint, if he expected to govern mankind, and keep his foes in awe.

The ascendancy of Vihárabhadra was now fully established, and the King adopted all his lessons. The people, imitating their betters, threw off all restraint, and became universally licentious; their Governors neglected their duties; the channels of the royal revenue were closed, and those of the expenditure opened to all abandoned characters. Drinking parties were publicly held by the most eminent persons, and all castes openly abandoned their observances. The women of the city, despising all reserve, intrigued with their lovers openly, even before their husbands: then affrays became frequent, the weak were assaulted by the strong, the rich were plundered by the poor, neither life nor property was secure, and general dissatisfaction and murmuring prevailed.

When this disorganization had become general, the secret enemies of the King began to carry their plots into effect: if the King went a hunting, they contrived to destroy his people in great numbers: if his men entered a cave to chace the deer, they had dry sticks and leaves collected, and setting fire to them at the only entrance, stifled both men and beasts; others were compelled to charge the tigers, to whom they fell a sacrifice; some were sent away from the places, where water was at hand, to others at a distance, so that they sank under thirst and fatigue; some were snared in pits covered over with straw and leaves; some were destroyed by poisoned knives, used to take the thorns out of their feet, and many were purposely slain with arrows, which were apparently levelled at the scattering herds of deer. In like manner, the numerous agents of the King of Aśmaka were actively employed in the capital to promote affrays in all the public meetings, foment private enmities, abet or commit assassinations, and by spreading in every way death and terror amongst the citizens to undermine the power of Anantavarmá.

Vasantabhánu now excited Bhánuvarmá, a forest Prince, to make war with Anantavarmá; the latter, therefore, having resolved to march against him, commanded his dependent Princes to meet him with their forces on the borders of the kingdom. Vasantabhánu advanced immediately to join him with his chiefs, and was admitted for his alacrity to the particular friendship of the King. The other subsidiary chiefs arrived successively on the banks of the Narmadá. It happened that a principal chief, Avantideva, ruler of Kuntala, had a female dancer in his train, of such superior accomplishments, as to be an Urvaśí on earth *. This girl attracted the notice of Anantavarmá, and being pleased with her he seized her, and carried her off. The King of Aśmaka excited the Chief of Kuntala to revenge this insult: 'this haughty tyrant, he said, dares to violate our females, how much longer is it to be borne? You have five hundred elephants; I have one hundred; let us unite, and we shall, I know, be joined by Vírasena, Chief of Murala, Ekavíra of Richíka, Kumáragupta of Konkańa, Nágapála of Śáśikya, alike impatient of this tyranny. The forest monarch is my friend; whilst he encounters the despot in front, let us assail him in the rear; we shall thus master his treasures and baggage.' The Konkańa Chief readily entered into the plot, and with presents and persuasions induced others to associate with them. On the next day Anantavarmá was the victim of the confederacy. Vasantabhánu, who had possessed himself of the treasure and animals, then proposed to the rest, that they should share amongst them in proportion to their effects and strength, professing to be content with any thing they should be disposed to give him. This led, as he expected, to a general dispute, which ended in the ruin of all, except the crafty proposer, who consequently appropriated the whole booty to himself, presenting a small portion of the spoil to his forest ally. He then established himself in the vacant government of Anantavarmá.

* [or, Kshmátalorvaśí by name].

The old minister, Vasurakshita, having contrived with the aid of some ancient servants of the King, to rescue the youth Bháskaravarmá, and his younger sister Manjuvádiní, along with the Queen Vasundhará, their mother, effected his retreat, but died soon after of grief. The Queen was conveyed with her children to Máhishmatí, and consigned to Mitravarmá, her late husband's brother by another mother, for protection. He soon formed improper views on his Sister-in-law, and was repulsed with severe reproof, but apprehending that in revenge he might oppose the elevation of the young Prince to his late father's throne, or form designs against his life, she requested me to convey him secretly to some place where he would be in safety, and let her know privately where we were, when we had secured an asylum. I set off with the Prince, and plunged into the Vindhya forests, to keep clear of the emissaries of the King; fatigue and thirst having oppressed my young charge, I was endeavouring to procure him some water from this well, when overreaching myself I fell into it, and must have perished but for your timely succour."

After repeating his thanks to me, I enquired the family of the Princess, and found that she was the daughter of Kusumadhanwá, King of Kośala, by Ságaradattá, daughter of Vaiśravańa, a merchant of Pátaliputra: his mother and my father were therefore descended from a common maternal grandfather; Suśruta, my father, being the son of Sindhudatta. Having, therefore, an additional motive to interest myself in my young kinsman's behalf, I vowed I would not be satisfied until I had replaced him on his throne and overturned the usurpation of the King of Aśmaka. In the meanwhile it was a consideration, how we were to appease our hunger.

At this moment appeared two deer, chased by a huntsman, who expended three shafts on them in vain. I made him give me the bow, and two remaining arrows, and presently shot the animals. One I gave to the hunter, the other I skinned and cleaned, removing the entrails, and cutting off the feet, and spitting it with a stake I roasted it at a fire. We made a hearty meal upon the flesh. The forester was highly pleased with my skill, and kept us company. I asked him if he had heard any news from Máhishmatí. He replied, he was just come from thence, having been there to sell a tiger-skin, and that great preparations were making for the marriage of Prachańḋavarmá, the younger brother of Chańḋavarmá with Manjuvádiní, the daughter of Mitravarmá. On hearing this, I took the old man aside, and thus spoke: 'I understand the plot; by treating the daughter as his own child Mitravarmá wishes to gain the confidence of the mother, and the person of the Prince, whom he may then put to death. This must be prevented: go back to the Queen, and tell her, what has chanced, in private. Then in concert with her give out that the Prince has been killed by a tiger: news that will be highly pleasing to Mitravarmá, although he may assume the outward semblance of distress. After this let the

Queen appear to be disposed to listen to his addresses, and so give a fresh impulse to his affections. Then let her rub her necklace with this poison, Vatsanága, and taking an opportunity strike him on the breast with it, saying, If I am faithful to my Lord, may this necklace be as a sword to thee. Let her then wash the necklace well with water and present it to the Princess, who by wearing in safety what was fatal to her uncle will prove the purity of the Queen. The Queen may then promise to give her daughter and the kingdom to Pracháńďavarmá, and invite him for that purpose: in the mean time we will arrive in the disguise of Kápálika mendicants, receive alms from the Queen, and take our station in the cemetery. Let the Queen call the old ministers and chief citizens together, and tell them in private, the Goddess Vindhyavásiní has appeared to her in a dream, and assured her, that the Prince is still alive, having been carried off by the Goddess herself in the form of a tigress, in order more effectually to protect him; that in four days Pracháńďavarmá will die. On the fifth her son will be found in company with another youth in a lonely temple of the Goddess on the bank of the Revá river, when his companion shall re-establish him in the Sovereignty, and you shall give him in recompense the hand of the Princess, but let her add this is to be a profound secret till we see what chances.'

The old Courtier approved of my plans, and leaving his charge to me set off to his mistress. In a few days the general rumour spread, that the marvellous faculty of conjugal fidelity had converted a necklace into a sword fatal to Mitravarmá, but otherwise innocuous, being actually worn by the young Princess. Upon this we presented ourselves, disguised as mendicants, to the Queen. When the Queen saw us, although she was prepared for our visit, she could scarcely suppress her emotions, as she spoke to us; she said, she had had a vision, the result of which was yet to be proved; but if her fate was favourable, she was no longer destitute.

Having made Manjuvádiní, whose looks evinced the interest she felt in me, pay her obeisance, she continued smilingly: "If your appearance is assumed, I shall lay my hands on this youth and detain him to-morrow." I cast an expressive glance on Manjuvádiní, and said, 'so may it be!' We then received alms, and went, having previously given a sign to Nálíjangha to follow us. When alone, I asked him where Prachańdavarmá was. He told me, that, being quite sure of the Sovereignty, he occupied the royal palace, where he amused himself with the company of dancers. The Prince I left in an empty temple, not far from the wall, and told him to keep close. I then entered the throng, and exhibiting as a dancer attracted the notice of Prachańdavarmá. When it was sun-set, I performed in various styles of dancing and singing, imitated different voices, and assumed different postures, as those of a scorpion, Makara, and fish. I then borrowed the daggers of the standers by, and fixing them in my body displayed feats not easily described. Whilst thus engaged I struck Prachańd̄avarmá, although he was at the distance of twenty yards, on the breast with a knife, exclaiming, May Vasantabhánu live a thousand years! One of the attendants attempted to seize me, but I shook him off senseless; then looking disdainfully on the frightened crowd I leaped over a wall of the height of two men, and then plunged into a neighbouring grove, whilst Nálíjangha following me levelled the marks of my footsteps. I continued my flight so as to beguile pursuit, and at last leaping the ditch, got safe out of the palace, and came to the temple where I had left my young charge, resuming my mendicant garb. We then set out again, and having passed through the crowds collected about the palace gate, with difficulty reached the cemetery. In the temple of Durgá, which stood there, I had formerly practised a small cavity leading from the outside to below the pedestal of the image, and concealed the outer entrance with a large slab of stone, which I had taken out of a part of the wall where it was loose. At midnight, having put on suitable dresses gorgeous with costly gems, brought us by a confidential messenger from the Queen, we entered the chasm. The Queen having caused the funeral ceremonies for Prachańd̄avarmá to be performed, and spread the report that his death had been contrived by the ruler of Aśmaka, came the next day, as had been concerted, to the temple and worshipped the Goddess, throwing open the shrine to all people, that they might satisfy themselves it was occupied. After which they retired, closing the door, but keeping near the building, and on the outside awaited the results, whilst the drums beat loudly. On this I lifted up the image, and its iron base upon my head (no easy labour), and setting it on one side, issued forth with the Prince. I then replaced the image as before, and the doors being again opened, we were accordingly found in the temple to the great delight and astonishment of the people. I immediately addressed them and said, 'Hear and believe what the Goddess declares to you through me. The tiger that bore off the Prince was myself, and I have adopted him as my son; receive him, and dread my power; respect me as his protector, and acknowledge my protection by giving me his sister.' They all exclaimed with delight: The offspring of the race of Bhoja is given us by the Goddess for a ruler! No words could express the joy of the Queen, who made me happy that day with the hand of her daughter. I took care to fill our hiding place in the temple, and as no trace of our contrivance was discovered, the people believed me to be some superhuman personage, and were not therefore to be diverted from respect to me by any malignant divinations or underhand contrivances. The Prince was generally known as Áryáputra, or the son of the Goddess. In order to enable him to complete his political studies, I conducted the affairs of state. Government is an arduous matter; it has three principles, Council, Authority and Activity. These mutually assisting each other dispatch all affairs; Council determines objects, Authority commences, and Activity effects their attainment. Policy is a tree, of which Council is the root, Authority the stem, and Activity the main branch, the seventy-two Prakŕitis are the leaves, the six qualities of royalty the blossoms, Power and Success the flowers and the fruit. Let this shade protect the King. There was a person at Court, named Áryaketu, who had been the minister of Mitravarmá; he was a skilful counsellor, and well-disposed to the Queen, being from the same country, Kośala. It was very desirable to secure his attachment, and I therefore taught Nálíjangha to say to him thus, as it were, in confidence: 'Tell me, wise Sir, who is this man of marvel that appropriates the prosperity of the state? shall this snake be suffered to swallow the Prince, or compelled to re-gorge him?' The answer of Áryaketu my agent was to bring to me, and this and similar conversations he held with him, but in vain. The other replied, "Speak not in this manner. The qualities of this person are most admirable, and I equally venerate his prudence and amenity, his prowess and skill. When the kingdom shall be in a state of security, and its inveterate foes appeased or eradicated, I have no doubt we shall see the young Prince duly installed in his father's throne, and the Prince of Aśmaka, wise as he thinks himself, deprived of his possessions." Having thus ascertained the friendly disposition of Áryaketu, I entered into an intimate confederacy with him, and attached to myself him, and all his friends, men of fidelity and skill, by whose assistance I governed all the Kingdom, and maintained justice and religion within its boundaries.

IX.

ON THE ART OF WAR AS KNOWN TO THE HINDUS.

(Read before the R. As. Society, June 17, 1848.)

HOWEVER unsuccessful in their contests with foreign invaders, the inferiority of the Hindus in the art of war arose from no want of cultivation of it as a science, and in theory, though not in practice, they were probably superior to those by whom they were overcome.

A supplementary portion of the sacred institutes of the Hindus, or the Vedas, was appropriated to the subject of military science under the appellation of *Dhanur-veda,* the Veda or institutes of Archery. The original treatise so termed is not known to exist, and is probably lost. A short tract entitled Dhanur-veda in Mr. Colebrooke's collection is a modern composition, and is of little value: a more detailed treatise and one much more ancient occupies several chapters of the *Agni Puráńa,* as that Puráńa is met with in some parts of Upper India. The chapters do not occur in either of two copies of the Puráńa in the India House Library. They have a place in a copy in my possession*; but unfortunately the MS. is mutilated and incorrect in many passages of the chapters on the military art, and the information derivable from the work is in most respects fragmentary and uncertain: from these two sources however, from original Lexicons, and from incidental notices in the heroic poems, especially the Mahábhárata, a variety of interesting particulars of the ancient art of war amongst the Hindus may be gleaned.

The use of the term *Dhanush*, or in composition Dhanur (as Dhanur Veda), as synonymous with arms in general is at once characteristic of Hindu warfare. The *bow* was the weapon on which they principally depended. So also the words Dhánushka and Dhanwin, signifying literally a bowman, are always used to denote a warrior or soldier. Hence perhaps one of the elements of Indian inferiority in the field, as the arrow, however formidable as a missile, was but a feeble instrument in close combat, and its use was calculated to impair the courage of the combatant by habituating him to shun rather than to seek the contiguity of his foeman. Although the favourite weapon however, it was by no means exclusively employed, and other missiles, as the discus, short iron clubs and javelins, were in general use. The troops were armed also with swords, maces, battle-axes and spears, and

* [Aufrecht, Catal. Codd. MSS., I, p. 7.]

were defended from the weapons of the enemy by shields, helmets, quilted jackets or iron armour, and coats of mail.

According to the best authorities, the component parts of an Indian army were four: Elephants, chariots, cavalry, and infantry.

These were arranged in bodies of various strength, but theoretically at least in always the same proportion. The smallest division was termed a *Patti* and consisted of one elephant, one chariot, three horse and five foot. The next, the *Senámukha,* was formed of three elephants, three cars, nine horse and fifteen foot. The larger bodies, companies, regiments, brigades, and armies, were made up in the same ratio, each component part becoming successively of thrice the strength of that which belonged to the preceding aggregate. The whole of the specifications are the following:

	Elephant.	Chariot.	Horse.	Foot.
Patti	1	1	3	5
Senámukha	3	3	9	15
Gulma	9	9	27	45
Gańa	27	27	81	135
Váhiní	81	81	243	405
Přitaná	243	243	729	1215
Chamú	729	729	2187	3645
Aníkini	2187	2187	6561	10935

An *Akshauhiňí*, or complete army, comprised ten Aníkinís, or 21.870 elephants, as many chariots, 65.610 horse and 109.350 foot. It is asserted in the

Mahábhárata that eighteen Akshauhińís were destroyed in the series of battles fought in the country between Hástinapura and Indraprastha, or the upper part of the Doáb near Delhi, between the sons of Páńdu and their kinsmen of the race of Kuru for the sovereignty of India.

Independently of the extravagant numbers assigned to the larger divisions, it is obvious that armies so composed can have existed only in imagination, and that thousands and tens of thousands of elephants could never have been brought at one time into action. In smaller bodies the proportion may have been observed, and three horsemen and five footmen may have been the complement of a single elephant or chariot as long as the corps did not exceed the strength of the *Gulma*. As the companies increased, the proportion must have been altered. In one place in the Agni Puráńa it is enjoined that fifteen foot soldiers should be attached to each elephant, and this is a more likely proportion than five. Even then we cannot admit the possibility of the ratio, as the numbers of cars and elephants augmented, or in fact of the numbers themselves. No army was ever accompanied by 20000 elephants, and even a twentieth part were questionable, although, as we know from the Greek historians of Alexander's expedition, the Indian armies did present a formidable array of these powerful animals: according to one account there were two hundred in the army of Porus. The enumeration however is valuable as presenting characteristic features of Hindu warfare and expressing the importance in their system of elephants and chariots as the most essential portions of the army.

Notwithstanding the prominence thus given to these two arms, there is a great and characteristic distinction in their application. It is remarkable that in the heroic poems a hero is very rarely represented riding on an elephant, and never on a horse: his appropriate station is the chariot, and hence a leader and a warrior of note is most commonly designated as a *Rathin*, a rider in a car, or an *Atiratha* or a *Mahá-ratha*, a rider in a great car. There are however some instances of a chieftain's moving through the army upon an elephant or even going to battle so mounted, and the Grecian accounts of Porus on his elephant are therefore not without warrant. Thus Duryodhana in the first encounter with the Páńďavas rides through his own ranks on an elephant*. Bhagadatta, Vinda and Anuvinda, three of his allies, are described in the review of his army as riding on elephants. Bhíshma, praising his grandnephews Duryodhana and the rest, says of them that they are able to fight equally well on an elephant's shoulders or the floor of a chariot: and in the first day's battle Uttara, the son of Viráťa, mounted on an elephant, attacks king Śalya in his chariot. The elephant kills the horses, but Śalya launches a javelin at Uttara and kills him. It would seem as if the warrior who fought on an elephant also guided him; for it is said by the poet that, as Uttara

* (Mahábhárata, Bhíshma Parva [v. 747]).

fell, he quitted hold of both javelin and goad,—he fell pramuktánkuśatomara. The *ankuśa* is the instrument still used to direct the elephant's course.

The more usual riders on elephants were soldiers of a lower grade, several of whom were placed on the animal's back in a kind of chair or howdah, and were armed with bows and arrows and other missiles. According to Megasthenes, as quoted by Strabo*, each Indian elephant carried three archers besides the driver, and his account agrees well enough with what may be inferred from the incidental notices of Sanskrit writers. Besides the detriment inflicted by the archers on the enemy, the especial service of the elephants was to act as pioneers upon a march, clearing away such impediments as small trees and shrubs, and in battle to oppose the elephants of the enemy and break in upon and scatter his array.

The *chariot* was in a still greater degree than the elephant characteristic of Indian warfare; but, as above observed, it was the especial vehicle of the chiefs and leaders. That it bore a large proportion to the whole force is confirmed by *classical* authority, as according to Curtius** there were three hundred chariots in the first line of Porus's battle. He says that each chariot held six men, two bearing shields, two bowmen, and two armed drivers. This however does not seem to be correct. Other classical authorities state the

* [XV, 1, 52. Lassen, Ind. Alt., III, 332.]
** [XIII, 13. Lassen, l. l., II. 147.]

number of persons carried by the war-car at three, or two warriors and the driver. This may have been occasionally the case, but in general, according to the heroic poems, there were in the Hindu chariot as in the Grecian at the siege of Troy but two individuals, the combatant and his charioteer. The latter also as amongst the Greeks was no ordinary person: he was a warrior and at least the confidential attendant and friend of the chief. On particular occasions heroes of renown did not disdain to take the reins in company with an equal. Thus Karńa, the prince of Anga, drives the car of Śalya, king of Madra, and Kŕishńa acts as the charioteer of his friend Arjuna. The car was drawn by two horses in general, but sometimes by four, and one object of attack seems to have been the destruction of the horses, compelling the rider to quit his car and fight on foot. This however he frequently did without being so compelled, whenever apparently his arrows and darts failed, and he had recourse to his sword, axe or mace. The facility with which this is effected shews that the chariot was open either all round or behind and at no great elevation above the ground. There is otherwise no description of its form, although many of its parts are specified in lexicons. One part of its decorations was the banner of the chief, a flag with a device peculiar to the individual. Thus Arjuna's banner bore the monkey Hanumán, Bhíshma's a palm tree, Duryodhana's a serpent, Kŕipa's a bull.—The car was not armed in any way, as were those of the Persians and

Scythians with scythes. The use of war chariots and the mode of employing them seems to have been common to the Asiatic Greeks, the Egyptians and the Hindus, and in early times at least neither of these nations was equestrian. The chariot, if ever employed by the European Greeks, amongst whom it would have been of little advantage owing to the nature of the country, soon fell into disuse. On the level plain of Egypt it continued much later, and in this as well as in the importance attached to the bow there is an evident resemblance between the Egyptians and Hindus. At the same time it is obvious that no intercourse could have subsisted between them, or the former would have learnt from the latter the management of the elephant. The animal was close at hand in the wilds of Africa, but no delineation of it, tame or wild, in peace or war, appears in the numerous representations which have been discovered of battles, sieges or processions. As with the Greeks so with the Hindus the horse came to supersede the chariot. There is no mention of the latter in the accounts given by Mohammedan writers of their first engagements with the Hindus. Its use is characteristic of antiquity, and its exchange for the horse may not improbably be ascribed in some degree to the infusion of Scythian tribes and manners from the west about the commencement of our era.

Whatever was the distribution of the combatants, it does not appear that there was much difference in the weapons which they wielded. The bow and arrow, the mace, the javelin, a club either made of iron altogether or in part, the sword and shield seem to have been the principal arms of the chiefs, whilst in addition to these spears and axes of different forms and missiles of various kinds were employed by their followers and occasionally by themselves. Detailed descriptions of some of these weapons are given in the Dhanur-veda, Agni Puráńa and commentaries on the Amarakosha and Mahábhárata. They do not always agree, but they sometimes afford curious particulars.

Thus of *Bows* it is said that they may be made of metal, horn or wood, the bowstring of cord made from hemp, flax, the pát or lute plant, from the fibres of bark, or from animal membrane, especially of the deer, buffalo or ox. The kinds of horn preferred are those of the buffalo and Rauhisha, a sort of deer. Different kinds of wood, whether of trees or twining plants, are used; but the best bows are constructed of the Bambu, cut at the end of autumn. The length of a bow varies from one as long as a man's arm to one of four cubits or six feet: the latter is declared to be the best. The *arrows* also vary in length from three feet to five or six: they should be smooth and tough, be made of wood or of bambus, feathered at the bulk and tipped at the head with steel points variously shaped, needle or lance-pointed, semicircular, dentiform, double-edged or jagged like a saw; they should be greased or anointed with various substances to facilitate their action, but no notice of poisoned arrows as used in battle occurs. Such arrows were sometimes employed in the chase. Besides the arrows commonly used the Dhanur-veda describes two other kinds, the Náráchа entirely of iron, and the Nálíka made of a reed. The latter was intended for a long flight and is therefore said to be most appropriately used for sieges. Curtius perhaps alludes to the Náráchа when he says, some of the Indian archers shot with arrows which were too heavy to be very manageable. The arrows were carried in a quiver on the right hip. Part of the archery practice of the Hindus consisted in shooting a number of arrows at once, from four to nine at a time.

Swords were of various shapes and sizes. The best are said to be brought from countries with which we are unacquainted, that is, if the names be rightly given, from Kháťi Vaťtara and Súryavaka. Those made in Bengal and Behar are commended as tough and capable of taking a fine edge. Those are fabricated of the best steel which ring sharply on being struck. The best-sized sword is one fifty fingers long, having the handle guarded by an iron netting: this must have been a two-handed weapon.

The technical classification of weapons is most usually fivefold,—or 1. Missiles thrown with an instrument or engine, *Yantramukta,* as arrows from bows; 2. Missiles hurled by hand, *Hasta-mukta,*—stones, clubs, darts, discuses; 3. Weapons which may be thrown or not, *Muktámukta,* javelins, tridents, spears, clubs; 4. Those which are not thrown, *Amukta,* swords, axes, maces;—and 5. Natural weapons, as the fists. In the commentaries on Lexicons and Poems we have explanations of a variety of the individual weapons composing these classes; but their descriptions do not always agree. Thus the commentators on Amara call the *Bhindipála* a short arrow either cast with the hand or blown through a tube, or it is a short club hurled by the hand; the commentator on the Mahábhárata says, it is the instrument called by the Mahrattas Gophan, which is interpreted a sling. The former identify the *Tomara* with the Śavalí, which in Hindi and Bengali is the name of an iron bar or crow; the latter says it is a dart with a long stick or a javelin, and its use, as noticed in the text, is most in accordance with his explanation. According to him also the *Nárácha* is a large arrow with a broad blade, but the others agree in asserting that it is an arrow entirely of iron. One of the commentators on Amara calls the *Prása* a Chákí, a sort of quoit or discus still thrown by the Sikhs; the rest generally explain it by the terms konch, kunta and neza, which imply a lance or spear; the commentator on the Mahábhárata calls it the Saintí, a javelin with a string fastened to it, so as to recover it after it has been cast. These differences indicate the imperfect acquaintance possessed by later writers amongst the Hindus with the weapons familiar to their forefathers, and the same inference may be drawn from their vague and imperfect notices of other implements mentioned in the heroic poems, as the *Rishti* said to be a short dart thrown by the hand, the

Paṭṭiśa, which appears to have been a kind of bill or halberd; the *Kṛipáṅa* and *Kshepaṅi* are missiles, but of what nature has not been ascertained. The *Páśa*, which is specified in the Agni Puráṅa amongst military weapons, is any sort of noose or binding, and the *Yantra*, which has also a place in the same enumeration, denotes any sort of machine, implement or engine.

A question of great historical interest is the knowledge possessed by the Hindus in early ages of any such combustible as gunpowder or of its application to military purposes. It is one to which no satisfactory answer can be yet given: our research into Hindu antiquity is yet too superficial, our acquaintance with Hindu literature and science too imperfect to warrant our replying in the negative, because we have not yet found any positive mention of such an article in the passages which have been consulted. The Hindus, as we find from their medical writings, were perfectly well acquainted with the constituents of gunpowder—sulphur, charcoal and saltpetre,—and had them all at hand in great abundance. It is very unlikely that they should not have discovered their inflammability either singly or in combination. To this inference a priori may be added that drawn from positive proofs, that the use of fire as a weapon of combat was a familiar idea, as it is constantly described in the heroic poems. The *Agni-astra* or Fire-arm is, it is true, the element itself wielded by some superhuman hero or demigod, who exercises a miraculous command over fire; but the notion might have originated in some mere mortal device for the production of flame and smoke. *Rockets* appear to be of Indian invention and had long been used in native armies when Europeans came first in contact with them: whether they are mentioned by Sanskrit authorities, has yet to be determined. It is commonly said by the Paṅḋits that the Rocket is intended by the *Śataghni*, a weapon named by the poets. The term means the destroyer of hundreds; according to some explanations it was a ball of stone or metal studded with spikes; but if so, it could scarcely have been thrown by hand*. Amongst ordinary weapons again one is named the *Vajra*, the thunderbolt, and these specifications seem to denote the employment of some explosive projectile, which could not have been in use except by the agency of something like gunpowder in its properties. That the Hindus had something like Greek fire is also rendered probable by Ctesias who describes their employing a particular kind of inflammable oil for the purpose of setting hostile towns and forts on fire**.

The subject of *Tactics* was not omitted in Hindu military science, and a great variety of modes of array are mentioned in the Agni Puráṅa and the heroic poems. They are not described however sufficiently in detail to give us very precise ideas of their several dispositions.

* [Cf. Śabdakalpadruma s. v., and Note II. "On the early use of gunpowder in India", in Sir H. Elliot's Index to the Historians of Muhammedan India. Calcutta: 1849, especially p. 358 ff.]

** [Sir H. Elliot, l. l., p. 370 ff. Lassen, Ind. Alt., II, 641 f.]

The component divisions of an army in array are variously enumerated as three, four, or seven. In the first we have the *Uras*, the breast or centre, the *Kakshas*, the flanks, and the *Pakshas*, literally as with ourselves—the wings. The second classification adds to these the *Pratigraha*, the reserve. In the larger number* we have also the *Koṫi*, a van or body in advance, the *Madhya* or middle, a second line or centre behind the breast, and the *Pŕishṫha*, the back, a third line between the Madhya and the reserve. These divisions however are considered to be more than ordinarily necessary, and Vŕihaspati, an old authority on all matters of regal administration, civil or military, whose works are no longer extant, is quoted in the Agni Puráńa as holding the four-fold disposition to be sufficient for all useful purposes.

Of the *order of march* we have these particulars in the Agni Puráńa: "After due deliberation with his council the king or general should set forth with his elephants, chariots, cavalry, infantry, and treasure. Whenever unusual danger is apprehended in consequence of having to traverse rivers, mountains or forests, or to pass by fortified posts, the army should proceed in order of battle. The scouts with a strong vanguard should lead the way. The king with his women, his baggage and his treasure should be stationed in the centre, supported immediately by the elephants; on the right and left of them should move

* [Kámandaki, XIX, 30.]

the chariots, and the horse should cover the extreme flanks. The forest or irregular bands and auxiliaries should bring up the rear. The order is to be diversified according to the direction from which an attack may be anticipated."

"When the contending parties are fairly matched, hostilities should be carried on openly and honourably. If one be much weaker than the other, he may allowably have recourse to stratagems, such as making a show of battle in the front of the enemy whilst the real assault is covertly directed against his rear, or as falling upon the rear of an enemy with one part of the army whilst another previously placed in ambuscade assails the van during the confusion. It is also permitted to take advantage of the ground, and to attack hostile troops whilst embarrassed in a defile or in a broken country, or to commence an action with inferior troops, so as to exhaust the enemy's strength, and then to fall upon him with fresh forces of the best description, or to surprise the enemy's camp when the troops are unprepared or asleep."

"The especial offices of the elephants are, on a march to make way through thickets in an attack on fortified places, to force open the gateways or pull down palisades, and in action to lead the charge, especially against compact divisions. The drivers of the chariots are also to head a charge and penetrate through the enemy's line, so that the horse and foot may follow. They are also intended to bear off the wounded from the field and to afford means of escape to the chiefs if defeated. They bear the bravest and most illustrious warriors to every part of the field, where their presence is most needed, and they are to drive through and disorder the enemy's ranks in every direction."

"A *commander in chief* should be careful to select his position according to the composition of his forces. Plains of considerable extent and of tolerably level surface are best adapted for the evolutions of both infantry and cavalry. If intersected by hills, it is not material, provided they be of no great elevation and inequality. Level ground free from trees, bricks, stones and mud is best suited to chariots. Elephants act to advantage in a similar situation, but brushwood and thicket, if consisting of only small trees and creepers, are no obstructions to them. In every case care should be taken to provide ample space for the movements of the different bodies, and that neither en masse nor individually the troops be inconveniently crowded."

"The general of an army is to remain in rear of his forces, attended by his chief officers and guarded by a strong reserve. He is never to expose himself to personal danger, for the general is the soul of the army, and deprived of him it cannot escape destruction."

The array of forces in action is termed generally *Vyúha*. The different kinds of array are sufficiently numerous: they are designated by appellations having reference to their supposed figures; but the tersm are for the most part too fanciful to express any very definite signification. In the Amara Kosha* it is said, the Vyúhas are the Dańđa and others. *Dańđa,* literally a stick or staff, is explained to signify the army in line. The commentator Ráya Mukuṫa particularises three of the other Vyúhas, the *Bhoga* or column, the *Mańđala* or hollow circle, and the *Asanhata* or detached arrangement of the different parts of the force, the elephants, cars, horse and foot severally by themselves. Each of these Vyúhas is subdivided into many modifications: there are seventeen varieties of the Dańđa, five of the Bhoga, and several of both the Mańđala and Asanhata. Their names are enumerated in the Agni Puráńa, and an attempt is made to describe a few of them, but the description is rarely intelligible without plans or diagrams; indeed details of this nature must almost always be indistinct, even when minutely particularised. In the authority referred to however the particulars are few and by no means precise. Some Vyúhas are named from their object. Thus the *Madhyabhedí* is intended to break the centre of the enemy's array, the *Antarbhedí* to penetrate between its divisions. Most commonly however the nomenclature is derived from a supposed resemblance of the array to some real or imaginary figure. Thus the *Makaravyúha* is the army drawn up like the Makara, a fabulous marine monster; the *Śyenavyúha*

* [II, 8, 2, 47; and Kámandaki XIX, 41—43, with the commentary.]

is the array in the form of a hawk or eagle with its wings spread. In the *Sakaṭavyúha* the army is arranged in the shape of a waggon, and in the *Arddhachandra* in that of a half moon; *Sarvatobhadra* is the hollow square or disposition of the troops facing every way outwards, and *Gomútrika* is said to be a diagonal disposition, a sort of arrangement in echellon*. In short, as the original observes, the Vyúha should assume every possible shape which may be best fitted to oppose the disposition and strength of the hostile force. Some further and perhaps more particular illustration of this subject may be derived from the heroic poems in their descriptions of battles. Thus in the Mahábhárata** in the first encounter of the opposing armies Yudhishṭhira, in consequence of finding himself very inferior in numbers to the Kurus, suggests to his brother Arjuna the adoption of the *Súchímukha*, the needle-pointed array. Arjuna recommends the *Vajra* or thunderbolt array for the same reason. It is easy to conceive what is meant by either, especially as the purport of the Páńḍavas is offensive rather than defensive: a narrow front or close column is to be formed with a view to break the enemy's line. Accordingly Duryodhana, the commander of the Kurus, is apprehensive of being attacked, and arranges his army in the *Abhedya*—the impenetrable—array, in which the different parts of the army, or the

* [See the commentary on Kámand. XIX, 48 ff.]

** [VI, 699. 729.]

foot, horse, cars and elephants, are so intermingled as to support each other. There are many such incidental notices in the Mahábhárata, but in a work of such extent it would be a task of much time and trouble to collect them.

Nothing is said in the Agni Puráńa of the *encampment* of an army, but that this subject received due attention appears from various passages in the heroic poems. With one of these this imperfect notice of Hindu military science may be concluded. It is taken from the Udyoga Parva of the Mahábhárata*.

"Then Yudhishthira led the army to a level and fertile spot abounding with fodder and fuel, taking care not to trespass in the march upon funeral grounds, temples, places of pilgrimage or the hermitages of holy men, and commanded his troops to halt on a place that was commodious, agreeable and well watered. After a short interval of repose the prince went forth, followed by many of his leaders and attended by a strong detachment, and having driven back the hostile squadrons of Dhŕitaráshtra, examined the ground in every direction carefully, assisted by Kŕishńa. In obedience to his orders Dhŕishtadyumna, the son of Parvata, Sátyaki, the skilled in chariots, and the hero Yuyudhána caused the ground to be measured for the site of the encampment, and carrying it on one side along the sacred river of Kurukshetra, the Hirańvatí, which was flowing with

* [vv. 5170—87. See also Kámandakíya nítis., ch. 16.]

pure and salubrious waters undefiled by mud and sand, Keśava directed a deep ditch to be dug on the other sides for the greater security of the camp. The army was then marched into the inclosed space and arranged agreeably to the precepts which regulate the practice of encampment. Whatever it was proper to do on such occasion Keśava commanded to be executed. Store of fire-wood and of all necessaries for eating and drinking was provided. Large and handsome huts like the spacious vehicles of the gods were erected severally for the chiefs. Artificers dexterous in various handicrafts were there in numbers, and skilful Surgeons were in attendance, well furnished with the means of healing wounds. Quantities of honey and ghee and resin and fuel and piles of bows and arrows and armour were heaped up like mountains, and Yudhishṫhira took care that in every tent fodder, fuel and water should be abundantly provided. Great engines of war, iron shafts, spears, axes, bows, arrows, quivers and elephants like mountains armed with spikes and covered with housings of iron mail were beheld in the camp by hundreds and thousands. When the Páńdavas knew that their friends had taken up their respective quarters, they moved with their own divisions to their several stations; and the Kings their allies, in order to secure their triumph observed in their encampment the strict rules of self-denial, liberality and religion."

X.

THE MEGHA DÚTA OR CLOUD MESSENGER:

A Poem in the Sanskrit language, by Kálidása.

Translated into English verse, with notes and illustrations.

Preface to the second edition. London: 1843.

The Translation of the Megha Dúta was the first attempt made by me to interest European readers in the results of my Sanskrit studies. It has the imperfections of a juvenile work; and the Translator has no doubt sometimes not only departed from his original further than was necessary, but further than was justifiable; and has occasionally mistaken its meaning. Some of the mistakes I have corrected; and in some instances have altered the arrangement of the lines, so as to adhere more nearly to the order of the original. I have not cared, however, to render the version much closer or more faithful; as even had I been inclined to take the trouble, the circumstance of the book becoming a class-book would have deterred me from the attempt: but it is very possible, that whatever poetical fidelity the version may possess, might have been injured by verbal approximation, and that the attempt to give a more literal likeness of the poem of Kálidása would only have impaired the similitude of its expression.

I have gone over the Notes with more attention, and have continued the information they convey to the present time. I have added some, and omitted some, especially those which were designed to place the parallel passages of European poets in contiguity with the language and sentiments of the Indian bard. Such analogies will readily suggest themselves to well-educated minds; and it cannot be necessary to endeavour to prove to them, that Imagination, Feeling, and Taste, are not exclusively the products of the Western Hemisphere.

The Megha Dúta, or Cloud Messenger, is recommended to a Student of Sanskrit by its style and by its subject. The style is somewhat difficult, but the difficulty arises from no faults of conception or construction. There must, of course, be some unfamiliar imagery, some figures of purely local associations, in every foreign—in every Oriental composition; but, with a few possible exceptions, the Megha Dúta contains no ideas that may not be readily apprehended by European intellect. It has no miserable conceits, no enigmatical puzzles, which bewilder a poetic reader, and overwhelm a prosaic one with despair; and which, when the riddle is solved, offer no compensation for the labour of solution. The language, although remarkable for the richness of its compounds, is not disfigured by their extravagance: the order of the sentences is in general the natural one, with no more violent inversion than is indispensable for the convenience of the rhythm. The metre combines melody and dignity in a very extraordinary manner; and will bear an advantageous comparison, in both respects, with the best specimens of uniform verse in the poetry of any language, living or dead.

The subject of the poem is simple and ingenious: a Yaksha, a divinity of an inferior order, an attendant upon the god of riches, Kuvera, and one of a class which, as it appears from the poem, is characterized by a benevolent spirit, a gentle temper, and an affectionate disposition, has incurred the displeasure of his sovereign, and has been condemned by him to a twelvemonths' exile from his home. In the solitary but sacred forest in which he spends the period of his banishment, the Yaksha's most urgent care is to find an opportunity of conveying intelligence and consolation to his wife; and, in the wildness of his grief, he fancies that he discovers a friendly messenger in a cloud*—one of those noble masses which seem almost

* [Wilson's transl. of Málatímádhava, Calc. ed., p. 110 f., Sanskrit text, p. 150 f.]

instinct with life, as they traverse a tropical sky in the commencement of the Monsoon, and move with slow and solemn progression from the equatorial ocean to the snows of the Himálaya. In the spirit of this bold but not unnatural personification, the Yaksha addresses the Cloud, and entrusts to it the message he yearns to despatch to the absent object of his attachment. He describes the direction in which the Cloud is to travel—one marked out for it, indeed, by the eternal laws of nature; and takes this opportunity of alluding to the most important scenes of Hindu mythology and tradition;—not with the dulness of prosaic detail, but with that true poetic pencil which, by a few happy touches, brings the subject of the description vividly before the mind's eye. Arrived at the end of the journey, the condition of his beloved wife is the theme of the exile's anticipations, and is dwelt upon with equal delicacy and truth; and the poem terminates with the message that is intended to assuage her grief and animate her hopes. The whole of this part of the composition is distinguished by the graceful expression of natural and amiable feelings, and cannot fail to leave a favourable impression of the national character; whilst the merely descriptive portion introduces the student to a knowledge of a variety of objects of local, traditional, and mythological value, with which it is his duty to become femiliar; and which he will when in India contemplate with additional interest and pleasure, from his previous acquaintance with the verses of Kálidása.

Little is known of the literary history of the Megha Dúta. It is, by common assent, attributed to Kálidása, a celebrated poet, who is reputed to have been one of the ornaments of the Court of Vikramáditya, king of Ujjayiní, whose reign, used as a chronological epoch by the Hindus, is placed 56 years before the Christian æra. There is no reason to dispute the truth of these traditions*. The poem undoubtedly belongs to a classical period of Hindu Literature; and that period, there is reason to believe, did not long survive the first centuries of Christianity. At a later date, the Poets were men of more scholarship than imagination, and substituted an overwrought display of the powers of the language for the unforced utterance of the dictates of the feeling or the fancy. This is not the case with the Megha Dúta; and although it is rather of a more sustained elevation of language than other works attributed to the same author, particularly his dramatic compositions, Śakuntalá, and Vikrama and Urvaśí, yet there is a community of character in them, a similar fidelity to nature, a like delicacy and tenderness of feeling, and the same felicity of description, gracefulness of imagery, and elegance of expression,

* [Lassen (Ind. Alt. II, 1158 ff.) places the age of Kálidása about the commencement of the 3rd century a. D.; Weber (Málaviká und Agnimitra. Berlin: 1856, p. XXVI—XL.) between the second & fourth; and Bháo Dájí (Journal Bombay Br. R. As. Soc., VI, 19 ff. & 207 ff.) about the middle of the sixth.]

which leave it sufficiently probable that they are the works of the same master-hand. There are, indeed, in the Vikrama and Urvaśí especially, passages which call the Megha Dúta to recollection; and in one place, where the deserted monarch inquires of the passing Cloud whither Urvaśí has fled*, we have the germ of the perhaps later poem, the Cloud Messenger. Of the other works attributed to Kálidása, the Ritu-sanhára, Raghuvanśa, Málavikágnimitra, Kumára-sambhava, Śŕingára-tilaka, Praśnottara-málá, Hásyárńava, and Śruta-bodha, some of them are certainly not of his composition.

WHERE Rámagiri's cool, dark woods extend,
And those pure streams, where Sítá bathed, descend; 2

* [IV, str. 74.]

Verse 1. Rámagiri] Is a compound term signifying The mountain of Ráma, and may be applied to any of those hills in which the hero resided during his exile or peregrinations. His first and most celebrated residence was the mountain Chitrakúta in Bundelcund, now known by the name of Comptah, and still a place of sanctity and pilgrimage. We find that tradition has assigned to another mountain, a part of the Kimoor range, the honour of affording him, and his companions, Sítá and Lakshmańa, a temporary asylum, upon his progress to the south; and it is consequently held in veneration by the neighbouring villagers: see Capt. Blunt's journey from Chunarghur to Yertnagoodum, Asiatic Researches, vii. 60. An account of a journey from Mirzapore to Nagpore, however, in the Asiatic Annual Register for 1806, has determined the situation of the scene of the present poem to be in the vicinity of the latter city. The modern name of the mountain is there stated to be Ramtéc: it is marked in the maps, Ramtege; but I understand that

Spoiled of his glories, severed from his wife,
A banished Yaksha passed his lonely life: 4
Doomed, by his lord's stern sentence, to sustain
Twelve tedious months of solitude and pain.

---

the proper word is Rámtenka, which, in the Mahratta language, has probably the same import as Rámagiri, The hill of Ráma. It is situated but a short distance to the north of Nagpore, and is covered with buildings consecrated to Ráma and his associates, which receive the periodical visits of numerous and devout pilgrims.

Verse 2. Where Sítá bathed.] In his exile Ráma was accompanied by his younger brother, Lakshmańa, and his faithful consort Sítá, or, as she is called in the original, the daughter of Janaka, until the latter was carried off by the demon or giant Rávańa: see the Rámáyańa. The performance of her ablutions in the springs of the mountain is here stated to have rendered their water the object of religious veneration.

Verse 4. A Yaksha] Is a demigod, of which there exists a Gańa or class. They have few peculiar attributes, and are regarded only as the companions or attendants of Kuvera, the god of wealth. The word is derived from यक्ष 'to worship'; either, because they minister to Kuvera, are reverenced themselves by men, or are beloved by the Apsaras, the courtezans of Indra's heaven. They have, however, their own female companions, or wives; as appears by the poem. One writer, cited and censured by a Commentator on the Amara Kosha, derives the name from जक्ष 'to eat,' because he says they devour children. [For another etymology proposed by Weber see his "Indische Studien", II, 185, and "Omina and Portenta". Berlin: 1859, p. 326.] Occasionally, indeed, the Yakshas appear as imps of evil; but, in general, their character is perfectly inoffensive.

Verse 5.] The lord of the Yakshas is Kuvera, who, in Hindu mythology, performs the functions of the Grecian Plutus. He is the god of wealth, and master of nine inestimable treasures. His capital is situated on mount Kailása, and inhabited by Yakshas, Kinnaras,

To these drear hills through circling days confined,
In dull unvaried grief, the god repined;
And sorrow, withering every youthful charm,
Had slipped the golden bracelet from his arm;
When with Áshádha's glooms the air was hung,
And one dark Cloud around the mountain clung;

---

and other inferior deities. He has a variety of appellations alluding to these circumstances, but is most commonly designated by the one here employed. The term is expressive of his deformity, being derived from कु 'vile', and वेर 'body'; and he is described as having three legs, and but eight teeth. No images of him occur, nor is any particular worship paid to him; and in these respects there is a considerable analogy between him and his Grecian parallel. Plutus is described as blind, malignant, and cowardly; and seems to have received but very slender homage from Greek or Roman devotion. The term "sentence", here used, is, more literally, 'curse.' The text also states that it was incurred by a neglect of duty, the Yaksha having been heedless in his office, स्वाधिकारप्रमत्तः. According to the Commentators, he was the warder of the gate of Kuvera's garden; and, quitting his post for a season, allowed Indra's elephant to commit a trespass, and trample down the flower-beds.

Verse 10. Had slipped the golden bracelet from his arm.] This is a favourite idea with Hindu poets, and repeatedly occurs: thus, in the elegant drama of Śakuntalá, [Str. 61 B., 66 W.] Dushmanta says:

इदमशिशिरैरन्तस्तापाद्विवर्णमणीकृतं
निशि निशि भुजन्यस्तापाङ्गप्रसारिभिरश्रुभिः ।
अनभिलुलितज्याघाताङ्कं मुहुर्मणिबन्धनात्
कनकवलयं स्रस्तं स्रस्तं मया प्रतिसार्यते ॥

or, in Sir William Jones's version, "This golden bracelet, sullied by the flame which preys on me, and which no dew mitigates, but the tears gushing nightly from my eyes, has fallen again and again on my wrist, and has been replaced on my emaciated arm."

In form some elephant, whose sportive rage
Ramparts, scarce equal to his might, engage.
Long on the mass of mead-reviving dew
The heavenly exile fixed his eager view;
And still the melancholy tear suppressed,
Though bitterest sorrow wrung his heaving breast.
For e'en the happy husband, as he folds
His cherished partner in his arms, beholds

Verse 11. When with Áshádha's glooms.] The month Áshádha or Ásharha comprehends the latter part of June and the commencement of July, and is the period about which the south-west monsoon, or rainy season, usually sets in.

Verse 13. In form some elephant.] Thus, in the Puráńa Sarvaswa, clouds are described as महिषाश्च वराहाश्च मत्तमातङ्गरूपिणः: 'Shaped like buffaloes, boars, and wild elephants.' In Chapman's Bussy D'Ambois they are said to assume

> In our faulty apprehensions
> The forms of dragons, lions, elephants.

And Shakspeare, although he omits the elephant, gives them, with his usual overflow of imagery, a great variety of shapes:—

> Sometime we see a cloud that's dragonish,
> A vapour sometime like a bear or lion,
> A tower'd citadel, a pendant rock,
> A forked mountain, or blue promontory,
> With trees upon 't, that nod unto the world,
> And mock our eyes with air.

ANTHONY & CLEOPATRA [IV, 12.].

Verse 20. For e'en the happy husband.] The commencement of the rainy season being peculiarly delightful in Hindustan, from the contrast it affords to the sultry weather immediately preceding it, and the refreshing sensations it excites, becomes, to the lover and the poet, the same source of love and tenderness, as the season of Spring is to the young and poetical in Europe.

This gathering darkness with a troubled heart:
What must they feel, whom fate and distance part!
Such were the Yaksha's thoughts; but fancy found
Some solace in the glooms that deepened round;
And bade him hail amidst the labouring air
A friendly envoy to his distant fair;
Who, charged with grateful tidings, might impart
New life and pleasure to her drooping heart.

Cheered with the thought, he culled each budding flower,
And wildly wooed the fertilizing power;
(For who, a prey to agonizing grief,
Explores not idlest sources for relief;
And, as to creatures sensible of pain,
To lifeless nature loves not to complain?)
Due homage offered, and oblations made,
The Yaksha thus the Cloud majestic prayed:—

Verse 35. And oblations made.] The oblation of the blossoms of the Kuṭaja, 'a small tree", (Wrightea antidysenterica) is called Argha (अर्घ) in the original, a religious rite, which seems to be analogous to the libation of the earlier periods of the Grecian ritual. अर्घ, in the Amara Kosha [III, 4, 27], is described as a species of worship, and is perhaps more properly the act of offering a libation to a venerable person, or to a deity; although it also implies the oblation itself, otherwise denominated अर्घ्य. This oblation, of which water forms the basis, is presented in a cup, a shell, or any metallic oblong and boat-shaped vessel. [See Mrs. Belnos' "The Sundhya", pl. XIII.] The vessel in the spoken dialects is called by a similar name ارگھا 'Arghá'. Indeed, Mr. Wilford states, Asiatic Researches, iii. 364, and viii. 274, that Argha, in Sanskrit, means 'a boat'; whence he deduces the ship Argo, &c.; and whence, with Mr.

Hail, friend of Indra, counsellor divine,
Illustrious offspring of a glorious line! 38

Bryant's assistance, we may deduce the Ark of Scripture. The Sanskrit word, however, has not been found in any of the vocabularies of the language with the import Mr. Wilford has assigned to it.

The oblation called Argha or Arghya, generally considered, comprises eight articles, thus enumerated:

आपः क्षीरं कुशाग्राणि दधि सर्पिश्च तण्डुलाः।
यवाः सिद्धार्थकं चैव अष्टाङ्गार्घ्यं प्रकीर्त्तितम्॥

"The eight-fold Arghya is formed of water, milk, the points of Kuśa-"grass, curds, clarified butter, rice, barley, and white mustard." In the Áchárádarśa of Śrídatta [Benares edition p. 91], in a passage quoted from the Deví Puráńa, they are stated somewhat differently; thus,

रक्तबिल्वाक्षतैः पुष्पैर्दधिदूर्वाकुशैस्तिलैः।
सामान्यः सर्व्वदेवानामर्घोऽयं परिकीर्त्तितः॥

"The general Argha, proper for any of the gods, consists of saffron, "the Bel, unbroken grain, flowers, curds, Dúrba-grass, Kuśa-grass, "and Sesamum." Water is not mentioned here, being considered as the vehicle of the whole: the same author adds, that should any of these not be procurable, they may be supplied by the imagination:

अभावे दधिदूर्वादेर्मानसं वा प्रकल्पयेत्॥

Besides the Argha common to all the gods, there are peculiar ones for separate deities: thus we find a few new-blown buds are sufficient for a cloud; and in the Sarvaswa Puráńa the Argha for the Sun is thus enumerated,

चन्दनोदकसम्मिश्रं दत्वार्घ्यं कुसुमं रवेः॥

"Having presented an Arghya to the Sun, of water mixed with "sandal, and flowers": and an oblation to the same planet, as given by Mr. Colebrooke, Asiatic Researches, ch. v. 357 [Essays. 1858, p. 84.] is said to consist of Tila, flowers, barley, water and red sanders. Water alone is also sufficient to constitute the Argha. In the articles which form the Argha of the Hindus, as well as in the mode of presentation, that of pouring it out, or libating, we trace

Wearer of shapes at will, thy worth I know,
And bold entrust thee with my fated woe:

---

its analogy with the ancient libation. Of course, wine could never enter into Hindu offerings of this kind; but we find that the Greeks had their *νηφάλια ἱερά* or 'sober sacrifices,' from which wine was excluded. These were of four kinds: *τὰ ὑδρόσπονδα*, 'libations of water,' *τὰ μελίσπονδα*, 'of honey,' *τὰ γαλακτόσπονδα* 'of milk,' and *τὰ ἐλαιόσπονδα* 'of oil;' which liquors were sometimes mixed with one another. According to Porphyry [Abstin. II, 20.] most of the libations in the primitive times were *νηφάλιοι*. See Potter's Antiqnities of Greece. We have here, then, three of the fonr fluid substances of an Argha, as first enumerated above, if we may compare the clarified butter with the oil: honcy would, of conrse, be omitted on the same acconnt as wine, being a prohibited article in Hindu law. With respect to the solid parts of the offering, a reference to the same authority will shew that they consisted of green herbs, grains, fruits, flowers, and frankincense; analogons to the grasses, rice, barley, flowers, sandal, &c. of the Sanskrit formulæ.

Verse 37. Hail, friend of Indra!] Indra is the sovereign deity of Swarga, or the Hindu Olympns. The cloud is here considered as his friend or counsellor, in allusion to his functions as regent of the atmosphere, where he appears in the character of the Jupiter Tonans or *Νεφεληγερέτα Ζεύς*. The appellative मघवत्, used in the original, is considered, by Etymologists, as irregularly derived from the passive form of मह्, 'to adore,' 'to worship'.

Verse 38. Illustrious offspring of a glorions line.] According to the original, "Descended from the celebrated line of the Pushkarávarttakas," translated, in a prose version of this passage, "Diluvian Clouds:" see Colebrooke on Sanskrit and Prakrit Prosody, Asiatic Researches, Vol. X. Clouds, agreeably to the Brahmáńda Puráńa, are divided into three classes, according to their origin from fire, the breath of Brahmá, or the wings of the mountains, which were cut off by Indra (पक्ष). These latter are also called पुष्करावर्त्तक, being especially the receptacles of water. Thus, in the Puráńa Sarvaswa,

For better far, solicitation fail
With high desert, than with the base prevail.

Thou art the wretch's aid, affliction's friend;
To me, unfortunate, thy succour lend: 44
My lonely state compassionate behold,
Who mourn the vengeance of the god of gold;

पुष्करा नाम ते मेघा वृहतस्तोयमत्सराः
पुष्करावर्त्तकास्तेन कारणेनेह शब्दिताः ॥

"The clouds called Pushkara are those large clouds which are in-"satiable of water; and, on that acconnt, they are called in this "world, Pushkarávarttakas." So also it is said, upon the authority of the Váyu, Linga, and Matsya Puráńas, "The third class of clouds "is that of the Pakshaja, or those, which were originally the wings "of the mountains that were cut off by Indra. These are also term-"ed Pushkarávarttakas, from their inclnding water in their vortices. "They are the largest and most formidable of all; and those which, "at the end of the Yugas and Kalpas, pour down the waters of the "Deluge." Vishńu Puráńa, p. 231, note.

Verse 39. Wearer of shapes at will;] Or Kámarúpa; from काम 'desire,' and रूप 'form,' 'shape': thns Socrates, in the "Clouds:"

Σω. Γίνονται πανϑ' ὅτι ἂν βώλωνται.

Soc. Why, then,
Clouds can assnme what shapes they will, believe me!

CUMBERLAND's Translation.

Verse 40. For, better far, solicitation fail &c.] This is a sentiment of rather an original strain, and indicates considerable clevation of mind. Something of the same kind occurs in Massinger's play of the "Bondman;" where Pisander says,

I'd rather fall under so just a judge,
Than be acquitted by a judge corrupt
And partial in his censure.

Verse 46. The god of gold,] Kuvera. See above.

Condemned amidst these dreary rocks to pine,
And all I wish, and all I love resign.

Where dwell the Yakshas in their sparkling fields,
And Śiva's crescent groves surrounding gilds,
Direct thy licensed journey, and relate
To her who mourns in Alaká, my fate.
There shalt thou find the partner of my woes,
True to her faith, and stranger to repose;
Her task to weep our destiny severe,
And count the moments of the lingering year:
A painful life she leads, but still she lives,
While hope its aid invigorating gives;
For female hearts, though fragile as the flower,
Are firm, when closed by hope's investing power.

Verse 50. Where Śiva's crescent realms surrounding gilds.] The crest of Śiva is the new moon, which is sometimes described as forming a third eye in his forehead. The Himálaya mountains, amongst which we shall hereafter find Kailása to be situated, are Śiva's favourite haunts. He also resides occasionally on that mountain, and is represented as the particular friend and frequent guest of Kuvera.

Verse 52. I have here taken a liberty with the order of the original, and brought the description of the Yaksha's wife a little in advance, in order to preserve the description which follows, of the Cloud's progress, more connected. The Hindu poets are not very solicitous in general about arrangement; but it is possible that in this case I may not have improved upon that of Kálidása. The 10th stanza of the Sanskrit corresponds with these lines.

Verse 53. Alaká is the capital of Kuvera, and the residence of his dependent deities.

Still, as thou mountest on thine airy flight,
Shall widowed wives behold thee with delight,
With eager gaze, their long locks drawn apart,
Whilst hope re-animates each drooping heart:
Nor less shall husbands, as thy course they trace,
Expect at hand a faithful wife's embrace;
Unless, like me, in servitude they bend,
And on another's lordly will depend.
The gentle breeze shall fan thy stately way,
In sportive wreathes the Cranes around thee play;

Verse 70. Valáká (बलाका) is said, in Mr. Colebrooke's Amara Kosha, to mean a 'small crane.' The word is always feminine, and perhaps therefore means the female bird only. Indeed, some of the Commentators on this poem call it the female of the Vaka (बक), Ardea Torra and Putea. The rainy season is that of their gestation; which explains their attachment to the Cloud, and the allusion to its impregnating faculty mentioned in the text of the original, गर्भाधानक्षणपरिचयम्.—The periodical journeys and orderly flight of this kind of bird have long furnished classical poetry with embellishments: they are frequently alluded to by Homer, as are the wild geese, of which mention is also made below:—thus, in the Iliad, Book ii. 459:

> Τῶν δ', ὥστ' ὀρνίθων πετεηνῶν ἔθνεα πολλὰ,
> Χηνῶν, ἢ γεράνων, ἢ κύκνων δουλιχοδείρων,
> Ἀσίῳ ἐν λειμῶνι, Καϋστρίου ἀμφὶ ῥέεθρα.
>
> Not less their number than th' embodied cranes,
> Or milk-white swans in Asia's watery plains,
> That o'er the windings of Cayster's springs
> Stretch their long necks and clap their rustling wings. POPE.

The translator has omitted the geese. Milton also describes the flight of these birds:

Pleased on thy left the Chátaka along
Pursue thy path, and cheer it with his song; 72
And when thy thunders soothe the parching earth,
And showers, expected, raise her mushroom birth,

So steers the prudent Crane
Her annual voyage, borne on winds.

PARADISE LOST, vii, 436.

And again, line 442:

Others on silver lakes and rivers bathed
Their downy breast.——
——Yet oft they quit
The dank, and, rising on stiff penons, tower
The mid aërial sky.

Verse 71. The Chátaka is a bird supposed to drink no water but rain-water: of course he always makes a prominent figure in the description of wet or cloudy weather. Thus in the rainy season [II, 3.] of our author's (ऋतुसंहार) 'Ṙitu Sanhára,' or Assemblage of Seasons:

तृषाकुलैश्चातकपक्षिणां कुलैः
प्रयाचितास्तोयभरावलम्बिनः ।
प्रयान्ति मन्दं नववारिधारिणो
बलाहकाः श्रोत्रमनोहरस्वनाः ॥

The thirsty Chátaka impatient eyes
The promised waters of the labouring skies,
Where heavy Clouds, with low but pleasing song,
In slow procession murmuring move along.

The Chátaka is the Cuculus Melanoleucus. The term वाम is rendered by the Commentators in general 'left,' on the left side; but Rámanátha Tarkálankára interprets it 'beautiful'; and maintains that the cry of birds, to be auspicious, should be upon the right side, not upon the left. Bharata Mallika, however, cites astrological writers to prove that the Chátaka is one of the exceptions to this rule:

बर्हिश्चातकचाषा ये च पुंसञ्ज्ञिताः खगाः ।
मृगा वा वामगा दृष्टाः शिवसम्पत्फलप्रदाः ॥

The Swans for mount Kailása shall prepare,
And track thy course attendant through the air. 76
Short be thy farewell to this hill addressed,
This hill with Ráma's holy feet imprest;

"Peacocks, Chátakas, Cháshas (blue jays), and other male birds, oc-"casionally also antclopes, going cheerfully along the left, give good "fortune to the host." The Greek notions agreed with those of Rámanátha, and considered the flight of birds npon the right side to be auspicious: the Romans made it the left; bnt this difference arose from the situation of the observer, as in both cases the auspicious quarter was the east; the *οἰωνοπόλος* facing the north, and Aruspex the south. In general, according to the Hindns, those omens which occur upon the left side are unpropitions.

Verse 75. "The Rájahansas, desirous of going to the lake Má-"nasa, shall accompany thee as far as Kailása, having laid in their "provisions from the new shoots of the filaments of the stalk of the "lotus." This is the closer reading of the text. Kailása is, properly speaking, a mythological mountain; but the name is also applied to the lofty range that runs parallel with the Himálaya, on the north of that chain. The lakc Mánasa lies between the two ranges: and it is quite true, that it is the especial resort of the wild grey goose at the beginning of the rainy season; "Those birds finding in the "rocks bordering on the lake an agreeable and safe asylum, when "the swell of the rivers in the rains and the inundation of the plains "conceal their usnal food." Moorcroft's Journey to Mánasarovara: Asiatic Researches, xii. 466. The Rájahansa is described as a kind of goose with white body and red legs and bill; whence Mr. Ellis affirms that it is properly applicable to the Phoenicoptcros or flamingo. Asiatic Researches, xiv. 23, note.

Verse 78. With Ráma's holy feet imprcst.] In the original text we have, "marked with the steps of Raghupati, vcnerated of men." This appellation is given to Ráma, as the most distinguished, the lord or master as it were, of the line of Raghu, an ancestor of that warrior, and himself a celebrated hero and sovereign. Ráma is

Thine ancient friend, whose scorching sorrows mourn
Thy frequent absence and delayed return.

Yet ere thine ear can drink what love inspires,
The lengthened way my guiding aid requires:
Oft on whose path full many a lofty hill
Shall ease thy toils, and many a cooling rill.
Rise from these streams, and seek the upper sky;
Then to the north with daring pinions fly.
The beauteous Sylphs shall mark thee with amaze,
As backward bent thou strik'st their upward gaze,
In doubt if by the gale abruptly torn
Some mountain-peak along the air is borne.

---

hence also termed Rághava (राघव), a regular derivative from Raghu, implying family descent. The exploits of the two heroes form the chief subject of another poem by our author, entitled Raghuvanśa (रघुवंश), or The race of Raghu.

Verse 85. We now begin the geographical part of the poem; which, as far as it can be made out through the difference of ancient and modern appellations, seems to be very accurately conceived. The two extreme points of the Cloud's progress are the vicinity of Nagpore, as mentioned in the note on Verse 1, and the mountain Kailása, or rather the Himálaya range. During this course, the poet notices some of the most celebrated places, with the greater number of which we are still acquainted. In the first instance, we have here his direction due north from the mountain of Rámagiri; and we shall notice the other points as they occur.

Verse 87. Literally, the wives of the Siddhas. The Siddhas are originally human beings, but who, by devout abstraction, have attained superhuman powers, and a station apparently intermediate between men and gods. They tenant the upper regions of the air,

The ponderous Elephants, who prop the skies,
Shall view thy form expansive with surprise;
Now first their arrogance exchanged for shame,
Lost in thy bulk their long unrivalled fame.

Eastward, where various gems, with blending ray,
In Indra's bow o'er yonder hillock play,
And on thy shadowy form such radiance shed,
As Peacocks' plumes around a Kŕishńa spread,
Direct thy course: to Mála's smiling ground,
Where fragrant tillage breathes the field around;

Verse 91. Each of the four quarters, and the four intermediate points of the compass, has, according to the Hindus, a regent or presiding deity. Each of these deities also has his male and female elephant. The names of them all are enumerated in the following verse of the Amara Kosha [I, 1, 2, 3.]:

ऐरावतः पुण्डरीको वामनः कुमुदोऽञ्जनः ।
पुष्पदन्तः सार्वभौमः सुप्रतीकश्च दिग्गजाः ॥

Airávata, Puńdaríka, Vámana, Kumuda, Anjana, Pushpadanta, Sárvvabhauma, and Supratíka, (are) the elephants of the sky.

Verse 95. A reference to the map will shew that it was necessary for the Cloud to begin the tour by travelling towards the east, in order to get round the lofty hills which in a manner form the eastern boundary of the Vindhya chain. It would otherwise have been requisite to have taken it across the most inaccessible part of those mountains, where the poet could not have accompanied it; and which would also have offended some peculiar notions entertained by the Hindus of the Vindhya hills, as we shall again have occasion to remark.

Verse 96. Indra's bow is the rainbow.

Verse 97. The body of Kŕishńa is represented of a dark blue colour; and the plumes of the peacock are frequently arranged upon the images of this deity. Allusion is especially made to Kŕishńa in his juvenile character, as a cow-herd in the groves of Vrindávana.

Thy fertile gifts, which looks of love reward,
Where bright-eyed peasants tread the verdant sward.

Thence sailing north, and veering to the west,
On Ámrakúťa's lofty ridges rest;

Verse 99. It is not easy, after the lapse of ages, to ascertain precisely the site of several places enumerated in the poem before us. The easterly progress of the Cloud, and the subsequent direction by which he is to reach the mountain Ámrakúťa, prove that the place here mentioned must be somewhere in the immediate vicinity of Ruttunpoor, the chief town of the northern half of the province of Cheteesgarh, and described in Captain Blunt's tour, Asiatic Researches, Vol. vii., and also in that of Mr. Colebrooke, published in the Asiatic Annual Register for 1806. The ouly modern traces that can be found of it are in a place called Máldá, a little to the north of Ruttunpoor. In Ptolemy's map there is a town called Maleta, and sitnated, with respect to the Vindhya monntains, similarly with the Mála of our poet. I shonld have supposed that the Mála mentioned from the geography of the Puráńas by Mr. Wilford (Asiatic Researches, viii. 336) was the same with the place allnded to in the text of Kálidása: if, however, that gentleman is correct in applying the name to the Malbhoom of Midnapoor, it will be much further to the east than will do for onr present purpose, and must be an entirely different place. There is little reason to think that either of these Málas are the country of the Malli, who are mentioned by Pliny; and who are more probably the samé with the Μαλλοὶ of Arrian, and the inhabitants, as is stated by Major Rennell, of the province of Multan.

Verse 104. The course pointed out to the Cloud, aud an allusion which follows to the vicinity of the Narmadá river, furnish us with reasons for supposing that the mountain here mentioned is that more commonly designated by the name of Omerkuntnk. The change of sound is not more violent than it is in a number of evident corruptions from the Sanskrit language, now current in the dialects of India. The term Ámrakúťa means the Mango Peak, and refers to

Oft have thy showers the mountain's flames allayed,
Then fear not wearied to demand its aid.
Not e'en the basest, when a falling friend
Solicits help it once was his to lend,
The aid that gratitude exacts denies:
Much less shall noble minds the claim despise.
When o'er the wooded mountain's towering head
Thy hovering shades like flowing tresses spread,
Its form shall shine with charms unknown before,

---

the abnndance of mango-trees in the incumbent and surrounding forests. Shonld this conjecture be correct, it will invalidate the derivation assigned with some ingenuity to the word Omerknntuk, in a prefatory note to a pleasing little oriental poem published in England, called the Metamorphosis of Sona. The author of that note imagines the proper name to be Omer Khandaka; and he is happy in the affinity of the sound, though not in his definition of the sense, as "the district of Omer" is exceedingly unmeaning, and erroneous. Amara Khandaka might mean the "immortal portion," but I do not know of any reason for assigning such an epithet to the mountain in question.

Verse 107. The Hindus have been the object of much idle panegyric, and equally idle detraction. Some writers have invested them with every amiable attribute, and they have been deprived by others of the common virtues of humanity. Amongst the excellencies denied to them, gratitude has been always particularized; and there are many of the European residents in India who scarcely imagine that the natives of the country ever heard of such a sentiment. To them, and to all detractors on this head, the above verse is a satisfactory reply; and that no doubt of its tenor may remain, I add the literal translation of the original passage. "Even a low man, when his friend comes to him for assistance, will not turn away his face, in consideration of former kindness;—how, therefore, should the exalted act thus?"

That heavenly hosts may gaze at, and adore,
This earth's round breast, bright swelling from the ground,
And with thy orb as with a nipple crowned.

Next bending downwards from thy lofty flight,
On Chitrakúta's humbler peak alight;
O'er the tall hill thy weariness forego,
And quenching rain-drops on its flames bestow;
For speedy fruits are certain to await
Assistance yielded to the good and great.
Thence journeying onwards, Vindhya's ridgy chain,
And Revá's rill, that bathes its foot, attain;

Verse 117. The mountain here mentioned must be in the vicinity of Omerkuntuk, and part of the same range: the name signifies, "the variegated or wonderful peak," and is applied to a number of hills: the most famous hill of this name, as was mentioned in the first note, is situated in Bundelkund.

Verse 123. The Vindhya range of mountains holds a very distinguished station both in the mythology and geography of Hindustan: these points are both discussed at some length in the tour from Mirzapore to Nagpore, already cited; and, as in those passages which I have been able to investigate I find a perfectly accurate statement, I shall here transcribe the words of its author.

"Bindh, in Sanskrit named Vindhya, constitutes the limit between Hindustan and the Deccan. The most ancient Hindu authors assign it as the southern boundary of the region which they denominate Áryabhúmi or Áryávarta. Modern authors, in like manner, make this the line which discriminates the northern from the southern nations of India. It reaches almost from the eastern to the western sea; and the highest part of the range deviates little from the line of the tropic. The mountainous tract, however, which retains the appellation, spreads much more widely: it meets the Ganges in sev-

Whose slender streams upon the brown hill's side,
Like painted streaks upon the dusky hide 126

---

eral places towards the north; and the Godávarí is held to be its sonthern limit.

"Sanskrit etymologists deduce its name from a circumstance to which I have just now alluded: it is called Bindhya, says the anthor of a Commentary on the Amarakosha, because people think (आयपन्ति) the progress of the sun is obstructed (वैन्ध) by it. Suitably to this notion, the most elevated ridge of this tropical range of mountains is found to run from a point that lies between Chhoṫa Nagpore and Palamu, to another that is situated in the vicinity of Ongein. But the course of the Narmadá river better indicates the direction of the principal range of the Vindh hills. From Amrakúṫa, where this river has its source, on the same spot with the Śońe and the Hatsu, to the gulf of Cambaya, where it disembogues itself into the sea, the channel of the Narmadá is confined by a range of hills, or by a tract of elevated gronnd, in which numerous rivers take their rise; and by their subsequent course towards the Śońe and Jamuná on one side, and towards the Taptí and Oodaver on the other, sufficiently indicate the superior elevation of that tract through which the Nermadá has forced its way." [For a better etymology compare Lassen, l. l., I, 81.]

"The vast extent of this mountainous tract, contrasted with the small elevation of these hills, viewed from the plains of Hindustan, has furnished grounds for a legend to which the mythological writings of the Hindns often allude. Vindhya having once prostrated himself before his spiritual guide, Agastya, still remains in that posture, by command of the holy personage. This humiliation is the punishment of his presumption, in emulating the lofty height of Himálaya and Meru. According to this legend, Vindhya has one foot at Chunar; and hence the real name of that fortress is said to be Charańádri (चरणाद्रि): his other foot is, I think, placed by the same legend in the vicinity of Gayá: the vulgar, very inconsistently, suppose the head of the prostrate monntain near the temple of Vindhya Vásini, four miles from Mirzapore."

Of the tall Elephant—in bright display,
Through stones and rocks wind slow their arduous
way.

Here the soft dews thy path has lost resume,
And sip the gelid current's rich perfume,
Where the wild Elephant delights to shed
The juice exuding fragrant from his head.

Verse 124. The Revá is a name of the Narmadá river, which, as we have seen in the preceding note, rises from the mountain Ámrakúṫa or Omerkuntuk. It may be here observed, that the rivers are always personified by the Hindus, and are, in general, female personifications. Thus we have Gangá, the daughter of Jahnu; Yamuná, the daughter of the Sun; and Revá, or Narmadá, the daughter of Himála, as is said in the hymn translated from the Váyu Puráńa, and given by Captain Blunt, Asiatic Researches vii. 103. The names of the Narmadá river are thus stated in the Amara Kosha. [I, 2, 3, 32]:

रेवा तु नर्म्मदा सोमोद्भवा मेकलकन्यका

"Revá, Narmadá, Somodbhavá, and Mekala-Kanyaká;" which are explained by the best Commentators [e. g. Bhánndíkshita] thus, "who flows, who delights, who is descended from the line of the moon, and who is the daughter of Mekala." The last term is applied either to the Vindhya mountain, or is considered to be the name of a Ŕishi or saint, and progenitor of the river-goddess. Tradition has assigned to this river a very Ovidian kind of tale; which is related in Captain Blunt's tour, and which has been repeated in verse, with much elegance and spirit, by the author of the Metamorphosis of Śońa.

Verse 131. The juice exuding fragrant from his head.] It is rather extraordinary that this juice which exudes from the temples of the elephant, especially in the season of rut, should have been unnoticed by modern writers on natural history, until the time of Cuvier (Règne animal), although mention of it is made by Strabo

Then swift proceed, nor shall the blast have force
To check with empty gusts thy ponderous course.
Reviving nature bounteous shall dispense,
To cheer thy journey, every charm of sense;
Blossoms, with blended green and russet hue,
And opening buds, shall smile upon thy view.
Earth's blazing woods in incense shall arise,
And warbling birds with music fill the skies.

Respectful Demigods shall curious count
The chattering Storks, in lenghthening order mount;
Shall mark the Chátakas, who in thy train
Expect impatiently the dropping rain:
And, when thy muttering thunders speak thee near,
Shall clasp their brides, half ecstasy, half fear.

Ah! much I dread the long-protracted way,
Where charms so numerous spring to tempt delay:
Will not the frequent hill retard thy flight,
Nor flowery plain persuade prolonged delight?

---

from Megasthenes. The author of the Wild Sports of the East states, that "on each side of the elephant's temples there is an aperture about the size of a pin's head, whence an ichor exudes;" but he does not appear to have been aware of its nature. Indeed his descriptions, though entertaining, are frequently defective, owing to his extreme ignorance of the languages, the literature of which he so liberally devotes to the flames. In the Amara Kosha [II, 8, 37], this fluid is termed मदः and दानम्; and the elephant, while it flows, is distinguished by the terms प्रभिन्नः, गर्जितः, मत्तः from the animal out of rut, or after the juice has ceased to exude, and which is then called उद्वान्तः or निर्मदः. All these names are expressive

Or can the Peacock's animated hail,
The bird with lucid eyes, to lure thee fail? 152

---

of the circumstances. The exudation and fragrance of this fluid is frequently alluded to in Sanskrit poetry. Its scent is commonly compared to the odour of the sweetest flowers, and is then supposed to deceive and attract the bees. These circumstances occur in this passage from a work already referred to, the Ṙitu Sanhára [II, 15]:—

वनद्विपानां नवतोयदस्वनैर्मदान्वितानां स्वनतां मुहुर्मुहुः ।
कपोलदेशा विमलोत्पलप्रभास्सभृङ्गयूथैर्मदवारिभिः श्रिताः ॥

Roars the wild Elephant inflamed with love,
And the deep sound reverberates from above;
His ample front, like some rich lotus, shews
Where sport the bees, and fragrant moisture flows.

Verse 151. Or can the Peacock's animated hail?] The wild peacock is exceedingly abundant in many parts of Hindustan, and is especially found in marshy places. The habits of this bird are, in a great measure, aquatic; and the setting in of the rains is the season in which they pair. The peacock is therefore always introduced in the description of cloudy or rainy weather, together with the Cranes and Chátakas, whom we have already had occasion to notice. Thus, in a little poem descriptive of the rainy season &c., entitled Ghaṫakarpara (घटकर्पर), [v. 2] the author says, addressing his mistress—

नवाम्बुमत्ताः शिखिनो नदन्ति मेघागमे कुन्दसमानदन्ति ॥

O thou, whose teeth enamelled vie
With smiling Kunda's pearly ray,
Hear how the Peacock's amorous cry
Salutes the dark and cloudy day!

And again, in one of the Śatakas or Centos of Bhartṙi Hari, [I, 42] where he is describing the same season—

शिखिकुलकलकेकारावरम्या वनान्ताः ।
सुखिनमसुखिनं वा सर्वमुत्कण्ठयन्ति ।

When smiling forests, whence the tuneful cries
Of clustering pea-fowls shrill and frequent rise,

Lo! where awhile the Swans reluctant cower,
Daśárńa's fields await the coming shower.
Then shall their groves diffuse profounder gloom,
And brighter buds the deepening shade illume;
Then shall the ancient tree, whose branches wear
The marks of village reverence and care,

Teach tender feelings to each human breast,
And charm alike the happy or distrest.

Verse 154. Daśárńa's fields await the coming shower.] No traces of this name are to be found in modern maps: [according to Lassen (I, 117), however, it corresponds to the modern Dossan; cf. also III, 160 f.] It is enumerated in Major Wilford's lists from the Puráńas, Asiatic Researches, vol viii. amongst the countries situated behind the Vindhya mountains; and corresponds, according to him, with the Dosarene of Ptolemy and the Periplus. Ptolemy's map has also a Dosara and Dosaronis Fluvium; and in the Pauránik list of rivers, there is also a Daśárńá river, which is said to rise from the mountain Chitrakúta. It may possibly correspond, at least in part, with the modern district of Chetcesgerh, as the etymology of both words refers to similar circumstances. [According to Dr. F. E. Hall (Journal Am. Or. Soc. VI, 521) it was situated to the east of Chandeyree.] Cheteesgerh is so named from its being supposed to comprise Thirty-six forts; and according to Bharata, the Commentator on our text, Daśárńa is derived from Daśa (दश) Ten, and Ŕińa (ऋण), a strong hold or Durga, the Droog of the Peninsula, and thence means the district of the Ten citadels. [See the Petersburg Dictionary, s. v., and Weber's Ind. Stud., I. 209.]

Verse 157. Then shall the ancient tree, &c.] A number of trees receive particular veneration from the Hindus; as the Indian fig, the Holy fig tree, the Myrobalan trees, &c. In most villages there is at least one of these, which is considered particularly sacred, and is carefully kept and watered by the villagers, is hung occasionally with garlands, and receives the Prańám or veneratory inclination of the head, or even offerings and libations. The birds mentioned in

Shake through each leaf, as birds profanely wrest
The reverend boughs to form the rising nest.

Where royal Vidiśá confers renown
Thy warmest wish shall fruit delightful crown:
There Vetravatí's stream ambrosial laves
A gentle bank with mildly murmuring waves;
And there her rippling brow and polished face
Invite thy smiles, and sue for thy embrace.

Next o'er the lesser hills thy flight suspend,
And growth erect to drooping flowerets lend;

---

the text by the epithet गृहबलिभुज् are the Vakas or Cranes. The term signifies, "who eats the food of his female"; गृह commonly a house, meaning, in this compound, a wife. At the season of pairing, it is said that the female of this bird assists in feeding the male; and the same circumstance is stated with respect to the crow and the sparrow, whence the same epithet is applied to them also.

Verse 161. Where royal Vidiśá confers renown.] Vidiśá is described as the capital of the district of Daśárńa. It appears to be the modern Bhilsá, in the province of Málwa. It is still a place of some note; and is well known in India for the superior quality of the tobacco raised in its vicinity. [Another etymology is proposed by F. E. Hall in the Journal As. Soc. Bengal for 1862, p. 112.]

Verse 163. The Vetravatí is the modern Betwah. It rises on the north side of the Vindhya chain; and, pursuing a north-easterly course of 340 miles, traverses the province of Málwa and the south-west corner of Allahabad, and falls into the Jamná below Kalpee. In the early part of its course, it passes through Bhilsá or Vidiśá.

Verse 167. Next o'er the lesser hills thy flight suspend.] The term in the text, नीचैराख्यं गिरिं, is explained by the Commentators to signify either the hill named Nichais, a mountainous range, of little note, or of little elevation. It is of no great moment; but perhaps the latter, which meaning we select, is the most satisfactory.

While sweeter fragrance breathes from each recess,
Than rich perfumes the hireling wanton's dress.

On Naga Nadí's banks thy waters shed,
And raise the feeble jasmin's languid head; 172
Grant for a while thy interposing shroud
To where those damsels woo the friendly Cloud;
As, while the garland's flowery stores they seek,
The scorching sunbeams singe the tender cheek, 176

Verse 168. And growth erect to drooping flowerets lend.] This passage, more literally rendered, is, "That hill which with upright flowers is like the body with its hair on end." The erection of the hairs of the body is, with the Hindus, constantly supposed to be the effect of pleasnre or delight.

Verse 171. On Naga Nadi's banks.] Some of the Commentators notice various readings of the name of this river, which occurs, as given in the translation, Naga Nadi (नगनदी), 'the mountain stream'; Nava Nadí (नवनदी), 'the new river;' and Vana Nadi (वननदी), ,the forest river.' It is probably one amongst a number of small streams falling from the Vindhya range of hills; and, indeed, the whole province of Málwa abounds in water; so that, as is stated in the Ayeen Akbery, "you cannot travel two or three cose without meeting with streams of good water, whose banks are shaded by the wild willow and other trees, and decorated with the hyacinth and other beautiful and odoriferous flowers." Gladwin's Translation, vol. ii.—I have given the preference to the Naga Nadí as above, from finding a river west of the Betwah, which we have crossed, named the Parbatty; and which, rising in the Vindhya chain, runs north-west, till it joins another called, in Arrowsmith's Map, the Seprá; and the two together fall into the Chumbal. The word Parbatty, or Parvati, means, 'sprung from the mountains'; and Naga Nadi, as I have mentioned, bears a similar import; so that they possibly are synonyms of the same stream.

Verse 175. As, while the garland's flowery stores they seek.]

The ear-hung lotus fades: and vain they chase,
Fatigued and faint, the drops that dew the face.

What though to northern climes thy journey lay,
Consent to track a shortly devious way;
To fair Ujjayiní's palaces and pride,
And beauteous daughters, turn awhile aside.
Those glancing eyes, those lightning looks unseen,
Dark are thy days, and thou in vain hast been.

The use of garlands in the decoration of the houses and temples of the Hindus, and of flowers in their offerings and festivals, furnishes employment to a particular tribe or caste, the Málakáras or wreath-makers. The females of this class are here alluded to.

Verse 181. Ujjayiní, or the modern Oujein, is supposed to have been the residence of our poet, and the capital of his celebrated patron, Vikramáditya. Few cities, perhaps, can boast of a more continuous reputation; as it has been a place of great note from the earliest periods of Hindu tradition down to the present day. It is now in the possession of the family of Scindiah, and is the capital of his territories. A full and highly-interesting account of it is to be found in the Sixth Volume of the Asiatic Researches, in the Narrative of a Journey from Agra to this city, by the late Dr. Hunter,—a gentleman, the activity of whose mind was only equalled by the accuracy of his judgment, and the extensiveness of whose acquirements was only paralleled by the unwearied continuance of his exertions.

Verse 184. Dark are the days.] The expression of the poet is simply, "If you do not enjoy the glances, &c., you are defrauded" (वञ्चितो ऽसि), and the Commentators explain it by adding, "of the "object of your life." That is, if you have not seen these beauties, you might as well have been blind, or not have existed at all. This compliment is rather hyperbolical; but we are acquainted with it in Europe: and the Italian proverb, "He who has not seen Rome has not seen any thing", conveys a similar idea.

Diverging thither now the road proceeds,
Where eddying waters fair Nirvindhyá leads,
Who speaks the language amorous maids devise,
The lore of signs, the eloquence of eyes;
And seeks, with lavish beauty, to arrest
Thy course, and woo thee to her bridal breast.

The torrent passed, behold the Sindhu glide,
As though the hair-band bound the slender tide;
Bleached with the withered foliage, that the breeze
Has showered rude from overhanging trees:

Verse 186. Fair Nirvindhyá leads.] This stream has not been found by name in the maps; but a number of small rivers occur between the Parbatty and the river mentioned below, the Siprá, one of which must be the Nirvindhyá of the poet. The four following lines, descriptive of the female personification of the current, are englished rather with respect to the sense than the words, the plainness of which might perhaps offend European fastidiousness. There is not, however, any one of Kálidása's river-ladies who behaves so indecorously as several of Drayton's similar personifications; and there is not one of them possessed of speech at all, to say nothing of such speech as is made use of by the Hayle, and other like "lusty nymphs," of that author's Poly-olbion.

Verse 191. Behold the Sindhu glide.] This is a stream also, with which the maps are not acquainted by name. As, however, it is the nearest river to Oujein, it may probably be the same with that now called Ságurmuttee. The river having been diminished by the preceding hot weather, the poet compares it to a long single braid of hair; and, conformably to the personification of it as a female, he supposes the braid to have been bound, in consequence of the absence of the Cloud, after the fashion in which the hair is worn by those women whose husbands are absent;—a custom we shall again be called upon to notice.

To thee she looks for succour, to restore
Her lagging waters, and her leafy shore.

Behold the city whose immortal fame
Glows in Avanti's or Viśálá's name!
Renowned for deeds that worth and love inspire,
And bards to paint them with poetic fire;

Verse 197. The synonyms of Oujein are thus enumerated in the Vocabulary of Hemachandra [976]:

उज्जयिनी स्याद्विशालाऽवन्ती पुष्पकरण्डिनी ।

Ujjayiní, Viśálá, Avantí, and Pushpakaraṅdiní.

Verse 199. Renowned for deeds &c.] I have here taken some liberty with the text, the literal translation of which is "famous for the story of Udayana, and the number of its learned men." The story of Udayana, or Vatsarája, as he is also named, is thus told concisely by the Commentators on the poem:—Pradyota was a sovereign of Oujein, who had a daughter named Vásavadattá, and whom he intended to bestow in marriage upon a king of the name of Sanjaya. In the mean time, the princess sees the figure of Vatsarája, sovereign of Kusha Dwípa, in a dream, and becomes enamoured of him. She contrives to inform him of her love, and he carries her off from her father and his rival. The same story is alluded to in the Málatí Mádhava [p. 38.], a drama by Bhavabhúti; but neither in that, nor in the Commentary on the Megha Dúta, is mention made of the author, or of the work in which it is related. Mr. Colebrooke, in his learned Essay on Sanskrit and Prákrit Prosody, in the Tenth Volume of the Asiatic Researches, has stated, that the allusion by Bhavabhúti was unsupported by other authority; not having, perhaps, noticed the similar allusion in this poem. [Comp. however, Hindu Theatre, Vol. I, 89, Vol. II, Mál. Mádh. p. 32, F. E. Hall's Vásavad., p. 2 ff., and A. Weber in "Zeitschrift der D. Morg. Ges.", VIII, 530 f.] He has also given an abstract of the Vásavadattá of Subandhu; a tale which corresponds, in many points, with that of Udayana, as here explained. Udayana is also

The fairest portion of celestial birth,
Of Indra's paradise transferred to earth;
The last reward to acts of virtue given;
The only recompence then left to Heaven. 204

---

the hero of part of the Kathá Sarit Ságara; and his marriage with Vásavadattá is there related in nearly a similar manner as that just described. The story was evidently popular; and the text might be rendered Ujjayiní, "great or illustrious by the number of those skilled in the tale of Udayana."

Verse 204. The only recompence then left to Heaven.] To understand this properly, it is necessary to be acqnainted with some of the Hindu notions regarding a future state. The highest kind of happiness is absorption into the divine essence, or the return of that portion of spirit which is combined with the attributes of humanity to its original source. This happiness, according to the philosopher, is to be attained only by the most perfect abstraction from the world, and freedom from passion, even while in a state of terrestrial existence: but there are certain places, which, in the popular creed, are invested with so much sanctity, as to entitle all who die within their precincts to final absorption or annihilation. One of these is Oujein, or Avantí; and they are all enumerated in this verse:

अयोध्या मथुरा माया काशी काञ्ची अवन्तिका ।
पुरी द्वारावती चैव सप्तैता मोक्षदायिकाः ॥

"Ayodhyá, Mathurá, Máyá, Káśí, Kánchí, Avantiká, and the city "Dwárávati, are the seven places which grant eternal happiness." [Cf. Káśíkańda, c. 7.]

Besides this ultimate felicity, the Hindus have several minor degrees of happiness; amongst which is the enjoyment of Indra's Swarga, or, in fact, of a Muhammedan paradise. The degree and duration of the pleasures of this paradise are proportioned to the merits of those admitted to it; and "they, who have enjoyed this lofty region of Swarga, but whose virtue is exhausted, revisit the habitation of mortals." The case now alluded to seems, however,

Here, as the early Zephyrs waft along,
In swelling harmony, the woodland song,
They scatter sweetness from the fragrant flower
That joyful opens to the morning hour.
With friendly zeal they sport around the maid
Who early courts their vivifying aid;
And, cool from Siprá's gelid waves, embrace
Each languid limb and enervated grace.

Here should thy spirit with thy toils decay,
Rest from the labours of the wearying way:
Round every house the flowery fragrance spreads;
O'er every floor the painted footstep treads;

---

to be something different from that so described by Sir William Jones. It appears, by the explanation of the Commentators, that the exhausted pleasures of Swarga had proved insufficient for the recompence of certain acts of austerity, which however, were not such as to merit final emancipation: the divine persons had therefore to seek elsewhere for the balance of their reward; and for that purpose they returned to Earth, bringing with them the fairest portion of Swarga, in which they continued to live in the discharge of pious duties till the whole account was settled, and their liberated spirits were re-united with the great, uniform, and primeval essence. The portion of Swarga thus brought to Earth was the city Avantí; whose superior sanctity and divine privileges are here alluded to, and thus explained by the poet.

Verse 211. The Siprá is the river upon the banks of which Oujein stands, and which is called Sipparah in the maps. In Arrowsmith, however, there is another stream with a similar name, the Siprá, which appears to be a continuation of the Sagarmuttee, considerably to the north-east of Oujein. There can be no doubt of the position of the river mentioned by the poet.

Breathed through each casement, swell the scented air,
Soft odours shaken from dishevelled hair;
Pleased on each terrace, dancing with delight,
The friendly Peacock hails thy grateful flight: 220
Delay then! certain in Ujjayin to find
All that restores the frame, or cheers the mind.

Hence, with new zeal, to Śiva homage pay,
The god whom earth and hell and heaven obey: 224
The choir who tend his holy fane shall view
With awe, in thee, his neck's celestial blue:

Verse 216. The painted footstep.] Staining the soles of the feet with a red colour, derived from the Mehndee, the Lac, &c., is a favourite practice of the Hindu toilet. It is thus elegantly alluded to in the Ode to one of the Female Personifications of Music, the Rágini Asauveree:

The rose hath humbly bowed to meet,
With glowing lips, her hallowed feet,
And lent them all its bloom.

Hindu Odes, by John David Paterson, Esq., published in the New Series of Gladwin's Oriental Miscellany, Calcutta.

Verse 223. The Commentators have thought proper, in explaining this verse and the preceding, to transpose the order of the explanations;—I do not see for what reason, and have therefore conformed to the text.

Verse 224. The god whom earth and hell and heaven obey.] "Lord of the three worlds" in the expression of the original text: the worlds are, Swarga or heaven, Pátála or hell, and Bhúmi or the earth.

Verse 226. With awe, in thee, his neck's celestial blue.] The dark blue of the Cloud is compared to the colour of the neck of Śiva, which became of this hue upon his swallowing the poison

Soft through the rustling grove the fragrant gale
Shall sweets from Gandhavatí's fount exhale:
Where with rich dust the lotus-blossoms teem,
And youthful beauties frolic in the stream.

Here, till the sun has vanished in the west,
Till evening brings its sacred ritual, rest;—
Then reap the recompence of holy prayer,
Like drums thy thunders echoing in the air.
They who, with burning feet and aching arms,
With wanton gestures and emblazoned charms,

---

produced at the churning of the ocean. The story is thus related in Wilkins's Translation of an Episode of the Mahábhárata, affixed to his Bhagavad Gítá:—"As they continued to churn the ocean more than enough, that deadly poison issued from its bed, burning like a raging fire; whose dreadful fumes in a moment spread throughout the world, confounding the three regions of the universe with its mortal stench, until Seev, at the word of Brahmá, swallowed the fatal drug, to save mankind; which remaining in the throat of that sovereign Dew of magic form, from that time he was called Neelkant, because his throat was stained blue."

Verse 232. Till evening brings its sacred ritual, rest.] There are three daily and essential ceremonies performed by the Brahmans, termed Sandhyás (सन्ध्या), either from the word Sandhi (सन्धि), 'junction', because they take place at the joinings of the day as it were, that is, at dawn, noon, and twilight; or as the term is otherwise derived from सम् 'with,' and ध्यै, 'to meditate religiously'. When the ceremonies of the Sandhyá are of a public nature, they comprehend the ringing of bells, blowing the conch, beating a tabor, &c.; and this kind of sound the Cloud is directed by the Yaksha to excite, as an act of devotion.

Verse 235. They who, with burning feet and aching arms.] The female attendants upon the idol.

In Mahádeva's fane the measure tread,
Or wave the gorgeous chowrie o'er his head;
Shall turn on thee the grateful-speaking eye,
Whose glances gleam, like bees, along the sky,
As from thy presence showers benign and sweet
Cool the parched earth, and soothe their tender feet.
Nay, more,—Bhavání shall herself approve,
And pay thy services with looks of love;

Verse 238. The gorgeous chowrie.] The Chowrie, or more properly Chounri (چونری), is a brush of Peacock's feathers, or the tail of a particular kind of cow, &c., set in a handle of such materials as suit the fancy or the means of the proprietor. It is used for a fan, or to whisk off flies and other insects; and this piece of attention is always paid by the Hindus to the figures of their gods.

Verse 240. Whose glances gleam, like bees, along the sky.] Although this allusion may be new to European imagery, it is just and pleasing. The consequence of the glance is well conveyed by the sting of the bee, while its poetically radiating nature is not unaptly compared to the long flight of a line of these insects. The lengthened light of a glance is familiar to us; for Shakspeare speaks of "eyes streaming through the airy region": and the continuous flight of bees was noticed so long back as the time of Homer, who describes them as proceeding in branches, a circumstance which his translator, Pope, has omitted:—

Βοτρυδὸν δὲ πέτονται ἐπ' ἄνθεσιν εἰαρινοῖσιν. [Il. II, 89.]

Branching, they fly abroad o'er vernal flowers;

Or, as in Pope,

Clust'ring, in heaps on heaps, the driving bees &c.

Verse 242. And soothe their tender feet.] It is to be recollected that these ladies are dancing bare-footed: divesting the feet of the shoes is a mark of reverence or respect paid to sacred places, such as the interior or vestibule of a temple, which has been from the remotest times practised in the East, as we know from the authority of Scripture.

When, as her Śiva's twilight rites begin,
And he would clothe him in the reeking skin,

Verse 243. Bhaváni shall herself approve.] Bhaváni is one of the many names of the consort of Śiva. The reason of her satisfaction, and indeed the whole of this passage, although familiar to a Hindu, and although much amplified in the translation, requires a little explanation to be rendered intelligible to the English reader. Śiva is supposed to be dancing at the performance of the evening Sandhyá, and to have assumed as his cloak the bloody skin of an elephant formerly belonging to an Asura destroyed by him. As this is no very seemly ornament, Bhaváni is delighted to find it supplied by the Cloud; which being of a dusky red, through the reflexion of the China roses now abundant, and being skirted, as it overhangs a forest, by the projecting branches of trees, resembles the elephant hide in colour, and its dangling limbs as well as in its bulk, and is mistaken for it by Śiva in his religious enthusiasm. The office performed by the Cloud has often been assigned to it in the West: thus, Horace, Ode II. Book I.:

Nube candentes humeros amictus
Augur Apollo.——

Or come Apollo, versed in fate, and shroud
Thy shining shoulders with a veiling cloud.

So Milton, in his Penseroso, speaking of the Morning, describes it as

Kerchief'd in a comely cloud.

Lee invests sentiments of the mind with a similar garb, and has—

For true Repentance never comes too late;
As soon as born, she makes herself a shroud,
The weeping mantle of a fleecy cloud.

And a Poet of later day, but of no inferior name, has made a very fine use of this figure:

I've known her long, of worth most excellent;
But in the day of woe she ever rose
Upon the mind with added majesty;

He deems thy form the sanguinary hide,
And casts his elephant attire aside;
For at his shoulders, like a dusky robe,
Mantling, impends thy vast and shadowy globe;
Where ample forests, stretched its skirts below,
Projecting trees like dangling limbs bestow;
And vermil roses, fiercely blooming, shed
Their rich reflected glow, their blood-resembling red.
Amidst the darkness palpable, that shrouds,
Deep as the touchstone's gloom, the night with clouds,

As the dark mountain more sublimely towers,
Mantled in clouds and storm.

MISS BAILLIE'S De Montfort.

The action, the elephant skin, and other attributes of Śiva, are well described in a passage cited by Mr. Colebrooke, in his Essay on Sanskrit Prosody, from the Drama of Bhavabhúti, though there assigned to a form of his consort Durgá:

प्रचलितकरिकृत्तिपर्य्यन्तचंचन्नखाघातभिन्नेन्दुनिस्यन्दमानामृत-
श्च्योतजीवत्कपालावलीमुक्तचण्डाट्टहासत्रसद्भूरिभूतप्रवृत्तस्तुति:

The elephant hide that robes thee, to thy steps
Swings to and fro; the whirling talons rend
The crescent on thy brow; from the torn orb
The trickling nectar falls; and every scull
That gems thy necklace laughs with horrid life.
Attendant spirits tremble and applaud.

[Málatimádh., p. 81. Calc. ed.]

Verse 255. Amidst the darkness palpable, that shrouds.] So Milton's celebrated expression,

And through the palpable obscure find out
His uncouth way.——

The literal interpretation of the original passage is, "the darkness that may be pierced with a needle."

With glittering lines of yellow lightning break,
And frequent trace in heaven the golden streak:
To those fond fair who tread the royal way,
The path their doubtful feet explore betray;
Those thunders hushed, whose shower-foreboding sound
Would check their ardour, and their hopes confound.

On some cool terrace, where the turtle-dove
In gentlest accents breathes connubial love,
Repose awhile; or plead your amorous vows
Through the long night, the lightning for your spouse.
Your path retraced, resume your promised flight,
When in the east the sun restores the light,
And shun his course; for with the dawning sky
The sorrowing wife dispels the tearful eye,
Her lord returned;—so comes the sun, to chase
The dewy tears that stain the Padma's face;
And ill his eager penitence will bear,
That thou shouldst check his progress through the air.

Now to Gambhírá's wave thy shadow flies,
And on the stream's pellucid surface lies,

Verse 275. Now to Gambhírá's wave.] This river, and the Gandhavatí in the vicinity of the temple of Śiva, which lately occurred, are probably amongst the numerous and nameless brooks with which the province of Málwa abounds.

Like some loved image faithfully imprest
Deep in the maiden's pure unsullied breast:
And vain thy struggles to escape her wiles,
Or disappoint those sweetly treacherous smiles,
Which glistening Sapharas insidious dart,
Bright as the lotus, at thy vanquished heart.

Verse 281. Which glistening Sapharas.] The Saphara is described as a small white glistening fish; which darting rapidly through the water, is not unaptly compared to the twinkling glances of a sparkling eye. Assigning the attributes of female beauty to a stream, ceases to be incongruous when we advert to its constant personification by the Hindus: and it is as philosophical as it is poetical, to affiance a River and a Cloud. The smiles of rivers, nay, of the Ocean itself, have often been distributed by poetical imagination: thus Lucretius, invoking Venus, says,

Tibi rident æquora ponti.
The ocean waves laugh on you:

for his late translator, Mr. Good, is very angry at the conversion of this laugh into a smile, as effected by less daring of his predecessors. Milton again gives to the Ocean nose as well as dimples:

Cheered with the grateful smell, old Ocean smiles,

And Metastasio, in his beautiful Ode to Venus, has,

E i flutti ridono
Nel mar placati.
The waves now placid play,
And laugh amidst the deep.

All these, however, as well as our author, are far surpassed by Drayton, in his Poly-olbion; where hill and dale, forest and river, are constantly described with male or female attributes. With respect to the streams, he is not satisfied with wedding them to various objects, but fairly subjects them to the pains of parturition. The instances are frequent; but we may be content with the follow-

What breast so firm unmoved by female charms?
Not thine, my friend: for now her waving arms,
O'erhanging Bayas, in thy grasp enclosed,
Rent her cœrulean vest, and charms exposed,
Prove how successfully she tempts delay,
And wins thee loitering from the lengthening way.

Thence, satiate, lead along the gentle breeze
That bows the lofty summits of the trees;
And pure with fragrance, that the earth in flowers
Repays profuse to fertilizing showers;
Vocal with sounds the elephants excite,
To Devagiri wings its welcome flight.

---

ing, especially as it is explained and defended by his very learned illustrator:—

> When Pool, quoth she, was young, a lusty sea-born lass,
> Great Albion to this nymph an earnest suitor was,
> And bare himself so well, and so in favour came,
> That he in little time upon this lovely dame
> Begot three maiden Isles, his darlings and delight.

"As Albion (son of Neptune), from whom that first name of this Britain was supposed, is well fitted to the fruitful bed of this Pool, thus personated as a sea-nymph, the plain truth (as words may certify your eyes, saving all impropriety of object) is, that in the Pool are seated three isles, Bruntsey, Fursey, and St. Helen's, in situation and magnitude as I name them. Nor is the fiction of begetting the Isles improper, seeing Greek antiquities tell us of, divers in the Mediterranean and the Archipelagus; as, Rhodes, Delus, Hiera, the Echinades, and others which have been, as it were, brought forth out of the salt womb of Amphitrite." Selden's Illustrations.

Verse 294. Devagiri is the mountain of the deity, and may perhaps be the same with a place called in the map Dewagur, situated

There change thy form, and showering roses shed,
Bathed in the dews of heaven, on Skanda's head; 296
Son of the Crescent's god, whom holy ire
Called from the flame of all-devouring fire,

---

south of the Chumbul, in the centre of the province of Málwa, and precisely in the line of the Cloud's progress; which, as we shall hereafter find, has been continued nearly due north from Oujein. This hill is the site of a temple of Kártikeya; which, as well as that of Śiva described above, we must suppose to have enjoyed, in the days of antiquity, considerable reputation, or they would not have been so particularly specified in the poem.

Verse 296. Bathed in the dews of heaven.] "Moistened with the waters of the Mandákiní", the celestial Ganges. Skanda, or Kártikeya, is the son of Śiva and Párvatí, and the Mars of Hindu mythology. There are various legends respecting his birth, one of which is presently noticed by the poet.

Verse 297. Several instances of the solitary production of offspring occur in the Hindu as well as in the Grecian mythology. Thus, as Pallas sprang from the brow of Jupiter, we have Skanda generated solely by the deity Śiva: Gangá springs from the head of the same deity, and Ganeśa is the self-born son of the goddess Párvatí. The miraculous birth of the warrior deity, Skanda, was for the purpose of destroying Táraka, an Asura or demon, who, by the performance of continued and severe austerities, had acquired powers formidable to the gods. [Váráha Pur. 25, Vámana Pur. 57 ff. Káliká Pur. 66.] The excentric genius of Southey has rendered it unnecessary, by his poem, 'The Curse of Keháma,' for me to explain the nature or results of these acts of devotion. The germ of Skanda was cast by Śiva into the flame of Agni, the god of fire; who, being unable to sustain the increasing burden, transferred it to the goddess Gangá: she accordingly was delivered of the deity, Skanda; who was afterwards received and reared, among thickets of the Śara reed (Saccharum Sara), by the six daughters of a king, named Kṛittiká; or according to other legends, by the wives of

To snatch the Lord of Swarga from despair,
And timely save the trembling hosts of air.

Next bid thy thunders o'er the mountain float,
And echoing caves repeat the pealing note;
Fit music for the bird, whose lucid eye
Gleams like the horned beauty of the sky;
Whose moulting plumes, to love maternal dear,
Lend brilliant pendants to Bhavání's ear.
To him whose youth in Śara thickets strayed,
Reared by the nymphs, thy adoration paid,
Resume thy road, and to the world proclaim
The glorious tale of Rantideva's fame,
Sprung from the blood of countless oxen shed,
And a fair river through the regions spread.

---

seven great Ŕishis or Saints. In either case, they form in astronomy the asterism of the Pleiades. Upon his coming to maturity, Skanda encountered and killed the demon, who had filled the region of Indra with dismay:—

> Emissumque imâ de sede Typhoëa terrâ,
> Cœlitibus fecisse metum.

Verse 305 &c. Whose moulting plumes, to love maternal dear.] Skanda, or Kártikeya, is represented mounted upon a peacock; and Bhaváni we have already seen is the wife of Śiva, and half-mother to this deity. We have also noticed the frequency of the allusion to the delight the peacock is supposed to feel upon the appearance of cloudy and rainy weather.

Verse 310. Rantideva is the son of Sankŕiti, and sixth in descent from Bharata. Vishńu Puráńa, p. 450 [IV, 19, 9.].

Verse 311. Sprung from the blood of countless oxen shed.] The sacrifice of the horse or of the cow, the गोमेधा or अश्वमेधा, appears to have been common in the earliest periods of the Hindu

Each lute-armed spirit from thy path retires,
Lest drops ungenial damp the tuneful wires.

---

ritual. It has been conceived that the sacrifice was not real, but typical; and that the form of sacrificing only was performed upon the victim, after which it was set at liberty. The text of this passage, however, is unfavourable to such a notion, as the metamorphosis of the blood of the kine into a river certainly implies that blood was diffused. The expression of the original, literally rendered, is, "sprung from the blood of the daughters of Surabhi", that is, 'kine'; Surabhi being a celebrated cow produced at the churning of the ocean, and famed for granting to her votaries whatever they desired. "Daughter of Surabhi" is an expression of common occurrence, to denote the cow.

Verse 312. And a fair river through the regions spread.] The name of this river is not mentioned in the text of the poem, but is said by the Commentators to be the Charmanvatí; and such a name occurs in Major Wilford's lists, from the Purāńas, amongst those streams which seem to arise from the north-west portion of the Vindhya mountains. The modern appellation of the Charmanvatí is generally conceived to be the Chumbul, which corresponds with it in source and situation; and which, as it must have been traversed by the Cloud in its northerly course, would most probably have been described by the poet. It may be curious to trace the change of Charmanvatí into Chumbul; which seems very practicable, notwithstanding their present dissimilarity. Tavernier, describing the route from Surat to Agra by way of Brampore, calls this river the Chammelnadi; the possessive termination Vatí (वती) having been confounded with the Nadi (नदी) 'a river': Chammelnadi is, therefore, the Chammel river. Again, the addition Nadi being regarded as superfluous, it has been dropped altogether, and we have the Chammel, or Chambel. The word Chammel may readily be deduced from Charman; as, in the dialects of Hindustan, the letters N and L are constantly interchangeable, and careless pronunciation may easily convert Charmel into Chammel, or Chambel. [Lassen, I, 116.]

Celestial couples, bending from the skies
Turn on thy distant course their downward eyes,
And watch thee lessening in thy long descent,
To rob the river's scanty stores intent;
As clothed in sacred darkness not thine own,
Thine is the azure of the costly stone,
A central sapphire in the loosened girth
Of scattering pearls, that strung the blooming earth.

The streamlet traversed, to the eager sight
Of Daśapura's fair impart delight;
Welcomed with looks that sparkling eyes bestow,
Whose arching brows like graceful creepers glow,

Verse 314. These two lines occur a little earlier in the Sanskrit; but as they seemed more connected with the two following, and to be rather awkward in their original position, they have been introduced here.

Verse 319. In sacred darkness not thine own.] Being of the same dark blue colour as Kríshńa; a hue the poet charges the Cloud with having stolen.

Verse 321. A central sapphire &c.] This comparison, when understood, is happily imagined; but to understand it, we must suppose ourselves above the Cloud, and to be looking obliquely downwards upon its dark body; as shining drops of rain form a continuous line on either side of it, and connect it with the earth.

Verse 324. Daśapura, according to its etymology, should mean a district, that of the ten cities. It is said however by the Commentators to be the name of a city; and by one of them, Mallinátha, to be that of the city of Rantideva: if he is correct, it may possibly be the modern Rintimpore or Rantampore; especially as that town, lying a little to the north of the Chumbul, and in the line from Oujein to Tahnesar, is consequently in the course of the Cloud's progress, and the probable position of Daśapura.

Whose upturned lashes to thy lofty way
The pearly ball and pupil dark display;
Such contrast as the lovely Kunda shows,
When the black bee sits pleased amidst her snows.
Hence to the land of Brahmá's favoured sons,
O'er Kuru's fatal field, thy journey runs.
With deepest glooms hang o'er the deadly plain,
Dewed with the blood of mighty warriors slain.
There Arjun's wrath opposing armies felt,
And countless arrows strong Gáńdíva dealt,

Verse 329. Such contrast as the lovely Kunda shews.] The Kunda (Jasminum pubescens) bears a beautiful white flower; and the large black bee being seated in the centre of its cup, they afford a very delicate and truly poetical resemblance to the dark iris, and white ball of a full black eye. [Śakunt. 120. W.]

Verse 331. Hence to the land of Brahmá's favoured sons.] Brahmávartta (ब्रह्मावर्त्त) is the abode of Brahmá, or the holy land of the Hindus. It is thus described by Manu, ii. 17:

सरस्वतीदृषद्वत्योर्देवनद्योर्यदन्तरम् ।
तं देवनिर्मितं देशं ब्रह्मावर्त्तं प्रचक्षते ॥

"Between the two divine rivers, Saraswatí and Dríshadwatí, lies the tract of the land which the sages have named Brahmávartta, because it was created by the gods." [Lassen, I. 1., I, 91. 126.]

Verse 332. Kuru-Kshetra (कुरुक्षेत्र), the Field of the Kurus, is the scene of the celebrated battle between them and the Páńdus, which forms the subject of the Mahábhárata. It lies a little to the south-east of Tahnesar, and is still a place of note and pilgrimage. It is not far from Pannipat, the seat of another celebrated engagement, that between the assembled Princes of Hindustan, aud the combined strength of the Mahrattas. This part of the country, indeed, presenting few abtacles to the movement of large armies, has in every period of the history of Hindustau been the theatre of contention.

Thick as thy drops, that, in the pelting shower,
Incessant hurtle round the shrinking flower.

O'er Saraswatí's waters wing thy course,
And inward prove their purifying force;
Most holy, since, oppressed with heaviest grief,
The ploughshare's mighty Lord here sought relief;

Verse 335. Arjuna was the friend and pupil of Kŕishńa, and the third of the Páńdava Princes. He has been long ago introduced to European readers, especially in Sir Charles Wilkins' able translation of the Bhagavad-Gítá; and appears, in the opening of that poem, in a very amiable light:

अहोबत महत्पापं कर्त्तुं व्यवसिता वयम् ।
यद्राज्यसुखलोभेन हन्तुं स्वजनमुद्यताः ॥ ४४ ॥
यदि मामप्रतीकारमशस्त्रं शस्त्रपाणयः ।
धार्त्तराष्ट्रा रणे हन्युस्तन्मे क्षेमतरं भवेत् ॥ ४५ ॥

"Alas! that for the lust of the enjoyments of dominion we stand "here ready to murder the kindred of our own blood. I would "rather patiently suffer that the sons of Dhŕitaráshŧra, with their "weapons in their hands, should come upon me, and, unopposed, kill "me unguarded in the field."

Verse 336. As the horses and swords of chivalry received particular names, so the weapons of the Hindu knights have been similarly honoured. Gáńdíva is the bow of Arjuna.

Verse 339. The Saraswatí, or, as it is corruptedly called, the Sursooty, falls from the southern portion of the Himálaya mountains, and runs into the great desert, where it is lost in the sands. It flows a little to the north-west of Kuru-kshetra; and though rather out of the line of the Cloud's progress, not sufficiently so to prevent the introduction into the poem of a stream so celebrated and so holy.

Verse 342. We have here the reason why the waters of the Saraswatí are objects of religious veneration. Balaráma is the eldest brother of Kŕishńa. He is called (लाङ्गली) Lángalí, (हलभृत्) Ha-

No longer quaffed the wine cup with his wife,
But mourned in solitude o'er kindred strife. 344

Thy journey next o'er Kanakhala bends,
Where Jahnu's daughter from the hills descends;

---

labhrít, &c., from his being armed with a plonglishare; which he is said to have employed as bills were formerly used, for pulling his enemies down from their horses, &c., which enabled him then to dispatch them with his club. Although Kríshńa took an active part in the warfare between the Kurus and Páńdus, Balaráma refused to join either party; and retired into voluntary seclusion, filled with grief at the nature of the contest: 'deserting', the poet says, 'his favourite liquor marked by the eyes of Revati';—that is, emulating their brightness as she shared the revels of her husband. Vishńu Puráńa, p. 510, 604.

Verse 345. The name is Kalakhala in the original, but it more properly is as given above. The meaning of the word, agreeably to a forced etymology, is thns explained in the Gangádwára Máhátmya section of the Skanda Puráńa:

खलः को नात्र मुक्तिं वै भजते तत्र मज्जनात्
अतः कनखलं तीर्थं नाम्ना चक्रुर्मुनीश्वराः ॥

"What man (कः) so wicked (खल) as not to obtain (न) futnre happiness from bathing there? Thence the holy sages have called this Tírtha by the name of Kanakhala."

It also occurs in this passage of the Hari Vanśa portion of the Mahábhárata:

गङ्गाद्वारं कनखलं सोमो वै यत्र संस्थितः ॥

"Gangádwára, Kanakhala, and where the moon impends": and, in both instances, is applied to the place where the Ganges descends into the low ground of Hindustán. The name is still retained; as appears from the testimony of an impartial witness, Lieut. Webb, in his Survey of the Sources of the Ganges; a survey which has essentially improved the geography of those regions:—"The party arrived at Haridwára, and encamped at the village of

Whose sacred waters, to Bhagírath given,
Conveyed the sons of Sagara to heaven. 348

Kanakhala" (Kankhal), on the west bank of the Ganges, at the distance of about two miles from the fair." Asiatic Researches, xi. 449. The Ganges does not now descend at Kankhal; and it is a question for geologists to solve, whether the Ganges has, in the course of nineteen centuries, so corroded the skirts of the mountain, as to have thrown back the gorge through which she passes, a distance of two miles. See note on a view of Kankhal, Oriental Portfolio.

Verse 346. Where Jahnu's daughter from the hills descends.] Jahnu's daughter is Gangá, or the Ganges; which river, "after forcing its way through an extensive tract of mountainous country, here first enters on the plains." It is rather extraordinary that Kálidása should have omitted the name of Haridwára (Hurdwár), and preferred Kanakhala, especially as the former occurs in the Puráńas, in the Skanda Puráńa, as mentioned in the note, page 450, vol. xi. of the Researches; and in this passage from the Matsya Puráńa, cited in the Puráńa Sarvaswa:

सर्वत्र सुलभा गङ्गा त्रिषु स्थानेषु दुर्लभा ।
हरिद्वारे प्रयागे च गङ्गासागरसङ्गमे ॥

"The Ganges is everywhere easy of access, except in three places, Haridwára, Prayága, and her junction with the sea." Jahnu is the name of a sage, who, upon being disturbed in his devotions by the passage of the river, drank up its waters. Upon relenting, however, he allowed the stream to re-issue from his ear; and the affinity of Gangá to the saint arises from this second birth.

Verse 348. Conveyed the sons of Sagara to heaven.] The Ganges, according to the legend, was brought from heaven, by the religious rites of Bhagíratha, the great-grandson of Sagara; who, as well as that king, had engaged in a long series of acts of austerity, for the purpose of procuring the descent of the river to wash the ashes of Sagara's 60,000 sons. The youths had been reduced to this state by the indignation of Kapila, a saint, whose devotions they had disturbed in their eager quest of the horse that was to be the victim

She, who with smiling waves disportive strayed
Through Śambhu's locks, and with his tresses
played;
Unheeding, as she flowed delighted down,
The gathering storm of Gaurí's jealous frown.

Should her clear current tempt thy thirsty lip,
And thou inclining bend the stream to sip;
Thy form, like Indra's Elephant, displayed,
Shall clothe the crystal waves with deepest shade;

---

of an Aśwamedha by their father. Their misfortunes did not, however, cease with their existence, as their admission to Swarga depended, according to the instructions of Garuḍa, upon the use of the water of the Ganges in the administration of their funeral rites. At this period the Ganges watered the plains of heaven alone; and it was no easy undertaking to induce her to resign those for an humble and earthly course. Sagara, his son Anśumán, and grandson Dilípa, died without being able to effect the descent of the heavenly stream: but his great-grandson, Bhagíratha, was more fortunate; and his long-continued austerities were rewarded by the fall of the Ganges, the bathing of the ashes of his ancestors with the holy water, and the establishment of them in the enjoyments of Swarga. The whole story is told in the First Book of the Rámáyaṅa, [from the 41st to the 44th section S., 42–45 G., 40–44 Madras ed.]

Verse 349. She, who with smiling waves disportive strayed.] The earth being unable to bear the sudden descent of so great a river as the Ganges, Śiva was induced, at the intercession of Bhagíratha, to interpose his sacred head. Accordingly, Gangá first alighted on the head of the deity, and remained for a considerable period wandering amongst the tresses of his long and entangled hair, to the extreme jealousy and displeasure, according to Kálidása, of the goddess Gaurí or Párvatí, Śiva's consort.

Verse 355. Thy form, like Indra's Elephant.] We have already

With sacred glooms the darkening waves shall glide,
As where the Jamná mixes with the tide.

As Śiva's Bull upon his sacred neck,
Amidst his ermine, owns some sable speck;
So shall thy shade upon the mountain show,
Whose sides are silvered with eternal snow;
Where Gangá leads her purifying waves,
And the Musk Deer spring frequent from the caves.

---

noticed that presiding deities are attached to the various points of the compass, and that each of these deities is furnished with a male and female Elephant. Amongst these, the most distinguished is Airávata, the Elephant of Indra, in his capacity of Regent of the East.

Verse 358. As where the Jamná mingles with the tide.] The waters of the Jamná, or Yamuná, are described as much darker than those of the Ganges at the point of their confluence, from the circumstances of the stream being less shallow and less discoloured with clay or sand. Occasionally, indeed, the waters of the Ganges there are so white from the diffusion of earthy particles, that, according to the creed of the natives, the river flows with milk. The confluence of rivers always forms a sacred spot in India: but the meeting of the Ganges and Jamná at Prayága or Allahabad, from the sanctity of both the currents, and from the supposed subterraneous addition of the Saraswatí, is a place of distinguished holiness.

Verse 359. As Śiva's Bull upon his sacred neck.] The Bull is the vehicle of Śiva, and the animal of the god is always painted of a milk-white colour.

Verse 364. And the Musk Deer spring frequent from the caves.] This animal is what is called the Thibet Musk; "but its favourite residence is among the lofty Himalley (Himálaya) mountains, which divide Tartary from Hindustán." See the best account of the Musk Deer yet published, in Gladwin's Oriental Miscellany, Calcutta 1798,

From writhing boughs should forest flames arise,
Whose breath the air, and brand the Yak supplies; 366

---

accompanied with accurate drawings by Mr. Home, of the figure, teeth, hoofs, &c.

Verse 365. Should forest flames arise.] The conflagration of the woods in India is of frequent occurrence; and the causes of it are here described by the poet. The intertwining branches of the Saral (Pinus longifolia), of the Bambu, and other trees, being set in motion by the wind, their mutual friction engenders flame. This spread abroad by the air, and, according to the poet, by the thick tails of the Yak of Tartary or Bos Grunniens (from which Chowries are made), readily communicates to the surrounding foliage, dried up by the heat of the sun, and exceedingly inflammable. The burning of a forest is so well described in the 1st book of the Ŕitu Sanhára, that I cannot avoid citing the passage, although its length perhaps requires an apology:

पटुतरवनदाहात् प्लुष्टशष्पप्ररोहाः परुषपवनवेगात् क्षिप्तसंशुष्कपर्णाः ।
दिनकरपरितापात् क्षीणतोयाः समन्तात् विदधति भयमुच्चैर्वीक्ष्यमाणा वनान्ताः ॥ २२ ॥

विकचनवकुसुम्भस्वच्छसिन्दूरभासा परुषपवनवेगोद्धूतवेगेन तूर्णम् ।
तटविटपलताग्रालिङ्गनव्याकुलेन दिशि दिशि परिदग्धा भूमयः पावकेन ॥ २४ ॥

ध्वनति पवनविद्धः पर्वतानां दरीषु स्फुरति पटुनिनादः शुष्कवंशस्थलीषु ।
प्रसरति तृणमध्ये लब्धवृद्धिः क्षणेन क्षपयति मृगवर्गं प्रान्तलग्नो दवाग्निः ॥ २५ ॥

बहुतर इव जातः शाल्मलीनां वनेषु स्फुरति कनकगौरः कोटरेषु द्रुमाणाम् ।
परिणतदलशाखादुत्पतत्याशु वृक्षाद् भ्रमति पवनधूतः सर्वतो ऽग्निर्वनान्ते ॥ २६ ॥

Which, omitting a few repetitions and excrescences, may be thus translated:

The forest flames—the foliage, sear and dry,
Bursts in a blaze beneath the torrid sky.
Fanned by the gale, the fires resplendent grow,
Brighter than blooming Safflower's vermil glow,

Instant afford the aid 'tis thine to lend,
And with a thousand friendly streams descend.
Of all the fruits that fortune yields, the best
Is still the power to succour the distrest.

Shame is the fruit of actions indiscreet,
And vain presumption ends but in defeat.
So shall the Śarabhas, who thee oppose,
Themselves to pain and infamy expose;
When round their heads, amidst the lowering sky,
White as a brilliant smile, thy hailstones fly.

Next to the mountain, with the foot imprest
Of him who wears the crescent for his crest,

Brighter than Minium's fierceness, as they wind
Around the branch, or shoot athwart the rind:
Play through the leaves, along the trunk ascend,
And o'er the top in tapering radiance end.
The crackling Bambu rushing flames surround,
Roar through the rocks, and through the caves resound.
The dry blade fuel to their rage supplies,
And instant flame along the herbage flies,
Involves the forest tenants in its sphere,
And in its rapid course outstrips the deer.
Like palest gold the towering ray aspires,
And wafting gusts diffuse the wasting fires:
Wide fly the sparks, the burning branches fall,
And one relentless blaze envelopes all.

Verse 373. The Śarabha is a fabulous animal, described as possessing eight legs, and of a fierce untractable nature. It is supposed to haunt these mountains especially.

Verse 376. White as a brilliant smile.] It is remarkable that a laugh or smile is always compared to objects of a white colour by Hindu writers.

Devoutly pass, and with religious glow
Around the spot in pious circles go:

Verse 377. Next to the monntain, with the foot imprest.] The fancied or artificial print of some saint or deity on hills or detached stones is a common occurrence in the creeds of the East. The idea is not confined to the inhabitants of Hindustán; but is asserted similarly by those of Nepal, Ceylon, and Ava; as may be seen in Turners Journey to Nepal, Symes's Embassy to Ava, &c. The Mussnlmans also have the same notion with respect to many of the Prophets; for they believe that the marks of Adam's feet remain on a mountain in the centre of Ceylon; and that those of Abraham were impressed npon a stone which was formerly at Mecca, and which he had used as a temporary scaffold in constructing the upper part of the primary Kaaba. A number of similar stories may be fonnd in Mirkhond, and other Mohammedan anthors. The Himálaya monntains are the scene of most of Śiva's adventures, his religious abstraction, his love, marriage &c.; and the place here mentioned may have some connexion with the Ghát, and neighbouring hill at Haridwára, mentioned in Capt. Raper's account of the survey of the Ganges, by the name of Haraká Pairi, 'the foot of Hara or Śiva.'

Verse 380. Aronnd the spot in pious circles go.] Circumambulating a venerable object, or person, is a nsual mark of profonnd respect. Thus, in Śakuntalá [p. 160 W.], Kańwa thns addresses his foster-danghter, on the eve of her departure:

वत्से इतः सद्यो हुताग्नीन्प्रदक्षिणीकुरुष्व ।

"My best beloved, come and walk with me ronnd the sacrificial fire."

And again, in the Rámáyańa, we have the same ceremony described thus:

जनकस्य वचः श्रुत्वा पाणीन्पाणिभिरस्पृशन् ।
चत्वारस्ते चतसृणां वशिष्ठस्य मते स्थिताः ॥
अग्निं प्रदक्षिणं कृत्वा वेदिं राजानमेव च ।
ऋषींश्चापि महात्मानः सहभार्या रघूद्वहाः ॥

"Hearing the words of Janaka, the four supporters of Raghn's race,

For there have Saints the sacred altar raised,
And there eternal offerings have blazed,
And blest the faithful worshippers; for they
The stain of sin with life shall cast away,
And after death a glad admittance gain
To Śiva's glorious and immortal train.
Here wake the chorus:—bid the thunder's sound,
Deep and reiterated, roll around,
Loud as a hundred drums;—while softer strains
The swelling gale breathes sweetly through the canes;
And from the lovely songsters of the skies
Hymns to the victor of Tripura rise.

"previously placed according to the direction of Vaśishtha, took the "hands of the four damsels within theirs, and, with their spouses, "circumambulated the fire, the altar, the king, and the sages."

Rámáyaňa, with Translation, I, 60, 37. [I, 73, 32 f. S. 75, 24 f. G. 73, 34 f. Madras ed.]

A somewhat similar practice seems to have been in use amongst the Celtic nations. The Highland leech, who is called to the aid of Waverley, "would not proceed to any operation until he had perambulated his couch three times, moving from east to west, according to the course of the sun." And Sir Walter Scott observes, in a Note, that "the Highlanders will still make the 'deasil'" (the circumambulation, or 'pra-dakshiňa') "around those whom they wish well to." [Comp. also J. F. Campbell's Tales of the West Highlands, IV, 314 ff.]

Verse 391. The lovely songsters of the skies] are the females of the Kinnaras, or demigods, attendant upon Kuvera, and the musicians of Swarga.

Verse 392. Hymns to the victor of Tripura rise.] Tripura is the name of a city, or rather, as its etymology implies, three cities col-

Thence to the snow-clad hills thy course direct,
And Krauncha's celebrated pass select;
That pass the swans in annual flight explore:
And erst a Hero's mighty arrows tore. 396

---

lectively: these formed the domain of a celebrated Demon, or Asura, destroyed by Śiva, and were reduced to ashes by that Deity. [See the quotations in Weber's Ind. Stud., II, 310.] According to the Commentators, we have here a full and complete concert in honour of Mahádeva.

Verse 394. And Krauncha's celebrated pass select.] I have not been able to make any thing of this pass or hole (क्रौञ्चरन्ध्र). The original text states it to be on the very skirt (उपतट) of the snowy mountain; and calls it also हंसद्वार, 'The gate of the geese', who fly annually this way to the Mánasarovara lake. Krauncha is described as a mountain, in the Mahábhárata [Hariv. 942]; and, being personified, is there called the son of Mainâka. A mountain also called Krauncha Meru occurs in Mr. Wilford's lists, amongst those mountains situated in the north. It must lie at some distance from the plains; and perhaps the Poet, by using the term उपतट, implies its relative situation with the loftiest part of the range or proper snow-clad mountains.

Verse 396. And erst a Hero's mighty arrows tore.] The Krauncha pass, or defile, in the Krauncha mountain, is said to have been made by the arrows of Bhṙigupati, or Paraśuráma, who was educated by Śiva on Mount Kailása, and who thus opened himself a passage from the mountains upon the occasion of his travelling southwards to destroy the Kshatriya or military race. Paraśuráma is an Avatár, or descent of Vishńu, in the person of the son of the Saint Jamadagni; and this Saint being also descended from the celebrated sage Bhṙigu, his son is named Bhṙigupati, or, Chief of that race. See Legend of Paraśuráma, Vishńu Puráńa, p. 401 [transl. from Mahábh. III, 11071—12010]. The fissure in the Krauncha mountain is, in the Váyu and Vámana [57 ff.] Puráńas, ascribed to Kártikeya. Ibid, p. 169, note 10.

Winding thy way due north through the defile,
Thy form compressed, with borrowed grace shall smile:
The sable foot that Bali marked with dread,
A god triumphant o'er creation spread.
Ascended thence, a transient period rest,
Renowned Kailása's venerated guest;

Verse 399. The sable foot that Bali marked with dread.] The story of Bali and the Vámana, or dwarf Avatár, was first told by Sonnerat, and has since been frequently repeated. As the former is a good specimen of the style in which Hindu legends were narrated by European travellers in the last century, it may be here inserted. "The fifth incarnation was in a Bramin dwarf, under the name of Vamen: it was wrought to restrain the pride of the giant Bely. The latter, after having conquered the gods, expelled them from Sorgon: he was generous, true to his word, compassionate, and charitable. Vichenou, under the form of a very little Bramin, presented himself before him while he was sacrificing, and asked him for three paces of land to build a hut. Bely ridiculed the apparent imbecility of the dwarf, in telling him that he ought not to limit his demand to a bequest so trifling;—that his generosity could bestow a much larger donation of land. Vamen answerd, that being of so small a stature, what he asked was more than sufficient. The prince immediately granted his request; and, to ratify his donation, poured water into his right hand; which was no sooner done, than the dwarf grew so prodigiously, that his body filled the universe! He measured the earth with one pace, and the heavens with another; and then summoned Bely to give him his word for the third. The prince then recognised Vichenou, adored him, and presented his head to him: but the god, satisfied with his submission, sent him to govern the Pandalon; and permitted him to return every year to the earth, the day of the full moon, in the month of November."

Sonnerat's Voyages in the East Indies, Calcutta edition, vol. I, p. 22.

That mount, whose sides with brightest lustre shine,
A polished mirror, worthy charms divine; 404

Verse 402. Kailása's venerated guest.] Kailása, as it here appears, a part of the Himálaya range, is in fable a mountain of costly gems or of crystal, the site of Kuvera's capital, and the favonrite haunt of Śiva. I shall borrow, from the notes to Southey's 'Curse of Keháma', a description of it from Baldæus, curious enough in itself, but still more so for its strange medley of accuracy and incorrectness, and its uncouth transformation and commixture of the Sanskrit names. "The residence of Ixora (Íśwara or ईश्वर) is upon the silver mount Kalaja (Kailása or कैलास), to the south of the famous mountain Mahameru, being a most delicious place, planted with all sorts of trees, that bear fruit all the year round. The roses and other flowers send forth a most odoriferous scent; and the pond at the foot of the mount is enclosed with pleasant walks of trees, that afford an agreeable shade; whilst the peacocks and divers other birds entertain the ear with their harmonious noise, as the beautiful women do the eyes. The circumjacent woods are inhabited by a certain people called Munis or Rixis (Ŕishis or ऋषि), who, avoiding the conversation of others, spend their time in offering daily sacrifices to their god.

"It is observable, that though these Pagans are generally black themselves, they do represent these Rixis to be of a fair complexion, with long white beards, and long garments hanging cross-ways, from about the neck down over the breast. They are in such high esteem among them, that they believe whom they bless are blessed, and whom they curse are cursed.

"Within the mountain lives another generation, called Jexaquinnera (Yaksha or यक्ष, and Kinnara or किन्नर), and Quendra (Indra or इन्द्र), who are free from all trouble, and spend their days in continual contemplation, praises, and prayers to god. Round about the mountain stand seven ladders, by which you ascend to a spacious plain, in the middle whereof is a bell of silver and a square table, surrounded with nine precious stones of divers colours: upon this table lies a silver rose, called Tamarapua (?[ताम्रपुष्प]), which contains two

Whose base a Rávaṅ from its centre wrung,
Shaken, not sundered, stable though unstrung;
Whose lofty peaks to distant realms in sight
Present a Śiva's smile, a lotus white. 408
And lo! those peaks, than ivory more clear,
When yet unstained the parted tusks appear,

---

women as bright and fair as a pearl: one is called Brigasiri(?), *i. e.* 'The lady of the mouth;' the other Tarasiri(?), *i. e.* 'The lady of the tongue:' because they praise God with the mouth and tongue. In the centre of this rose is the triangle of Quivelinga (Śiva-linga); which, they say, is the permanent residence of God." BALDAEUS. The latter part of this description is quite new to the Pandits, and I suspect is rather Mohammedan than Hindu. Little is said of Kailása in authentic Hindu legend. See Vishńu Puráńa, p. 172.

Verse 406. Shaken, not sundered, stable though unstrung.] This alludes to a legend of Rávańa's having attempted to remove the mountain from its situation; although he did not succeed as well as Satan and his compeers, when,

> "From their foundations loosening to and fro,
> They plucked the seated hills."

He considerably unhinged its foundations. The story perhaps originates with the curious vibrating rock at Mahábalipuram; of which it may be said, as is observed by Selden of Mainamber, *i. e.* Ambrose's stone in Cornwall, not far from Penzance, that "it is so great, that many men's united strength cannot remove it, yet with one finger you may wag it."

Verse 407. Whose lofty peaks to distant realms in sight.] The lofty peaks of the Himálaya range of mountains are very justly stated by the poet to be visible to surrounding regions (प्रतिदिशम्). They are seen, in the south, from situations more remote than those in which any other peaks have been discerned; and the supposition of their exceeding even the Andes in elevation has been confirmed by recent inquiries.

Beam with new lustre, as around their head
Thy glossy glooms metallic darkness spread;
As shews a Halabhṙita's sable vest
More fair the pallid beauty of his breast.
Haply across thy long and mountain way
In sport may Gaurí with her Śiva stray;

Verse 412. Thy glossy glooms metallic darkness spread.] The expression in the original (स्निग्धभिन्नाञ्जनाभे) may be rendered, "shining like glossy powdered antimony", a preparation used for darkening the eye-lashes or the edges of the eye-lids, a practice common to the females of the East. It is also explained to mean merely, "black divided antimony"; and the shining greyish-blue of the sulphuret of antimony, the substance alluded to, may often be observed in the hue of heavy clouds. ["Antimony mixed with oil." Schütz.]

Verse 413. Halabhṙita is a name of Balaráma; and implies, as has been before explained, his use of a ploughshare as a weapon. He is represented of a white colour, clothed in a darkblue vest; and is thus alluded to in the introduction [v. 12] to the Gita Govinda of Jayadeva:

वहसि वपुषि विशदे वसनं जलदाभं हलहतिभीतिमिलितयमुनाभम् ॥
केशव धृतहलधररूप जय जगदीश हरे ॥

Thus translated by Sir William Jones, in his Essay on the Chronology of the Hindus: "Thou bearest on thy bright body a mantle "shining like a blue Cloud, or like the water of the Yamuna trip-"ping towards thee through fear of thy furrowing ploughshare, O "Cesava! assuming the form of Balaráma, be victorious O Heri! "Lord of the Universe."

Verse 416. In sport may Gaurí with her Śiva stray.] I have already noticed that these mountains are the scene of Śiva's loves and sports: they may still be considered as his favourite haunts, for some traces of him seem to start up in every direction amongst them. See the late Travels to the Source of the Ganges, and Col. Hardwicke's Tour to Sirinagur.

Her serpent bracelet from her wrist displaced,
And in her arms the mighty god embraced.
Should thus it fortune, be it thine to lend
A path their holy footsteps may ascend;
Close in thy hollow form thy stores comprest,
While by the touch of feet celestial blest.

Then shall the nymphs of heaven, a giddy train,
Thy form an instrument of sport detain;
And with the lightning, round each wrist that gleams,
Shall set at liberty thy cooling streams.
But should they seek thy journey to delay—
A grateful solace in the sultry day—
Speak harsh in thunder, and the nymphs shall fly
Alarmed, nor check thy progress through the sky.

Where bright the mountain's crystal glories break,
Explore the golden lotus-covered lake;

Verse 424. Thy form an instrument of sport.] Literally, "They shall take thee as being the abode of an artificial water-work"—a jet-d'eau, or shower-bath; or, according to some of the Commentators, a vessel for sprinkling water, either a common syringe or squirt, or the more elegant Asiatic apparatus in use for sprinkling perfumed waters, especially rose-water—a Guláb-pásh.

Verse 425. And with the lightning, round each wrist that gleams.] The diamond and thunderbolt, according to Hindu notions, are of one substance, and are called by the same appellation (वज्र). As the fall of the thunderbolt is usually followed by rain, and may thus be considered as its cause; the propinquity and the mutual friction of the same substance upon the wrists of our young ladies is, in like manner, supposed to occasion the dispersion of the fluid treasures of the Cloud.

Imbibe the dews of Mánasa, and spread
A friendly veil round Airavata's head;
Or, life dispensing, with the Zephyrs go,
Where heavenly trees with fainting blossoms blow.

Now on the mountain's side, like some dear friend,
Behold the city of the gods impend;
Thy goal behold, where Gangá's winding rill
Skirts like a costly train the sacred hill;

Verse 433. Mánasa, Mánasarovara, or commonly Man-sarour, is a celebrated lake situated in the centre of the Himálaya mountains, and was long said to be the source of the Ganges and Brahmaputra rivers: with respect to the first of these, the statement has been found to be erroneous; and we have no positive proofs of its accuracy with regard to the latter. When the passage in the text was translated, the chief information regarding the latter was derived from the vague reports of Hindu Pilgrims. Since then, Mánasarovara was visited by that enterprising traveller, Moorcroft. He has not yet had a successor. [A. Gerard, Journal of the A. Soc. of Bengal, XI, 363—88.]

We here take leave of the geographical part of the poem, which is highly creditable to Kálidása's accuracy; and now come to the region of unmixed fable, the residence of Kuvera and his attendant demigods.

Verse 434. A friendly veil round Airavata's head.] Indra's Elephant, ut supra, verse 355.

Verse 436. Where heavenly trees with fainting blossoms blow.] Literally, the Kalpa trees, one of the five kinds which flourish in Indra's heaven. They are thus enumerated in the Amara Kosha [I, 1, 50]:

पञ्चैते देवतरवो मन्दारः पारिजातकः ।
सन्तानः कल्पवृक्षश्च पुंसि वा हरिचन्दनम् ॥

Verse 438. The city of the gods impend.] Alaká, the capital of Kuvera.

Where brilliant pearls descend in lucid showers,
And Clouds, like tresses, clothe her lofty towers.

There every palace with thy glory vies,
Whose soaring summits kiss the lofty skies;
Whose beauteous inmates bright as lightning glare,
And tabors mock the thunders of the air;
The rainbow flickering gleams along the walls,
And glittering rain in sparkling diamonds falls.

There lovely triflers wanton through the day,
Dress all their care, and all their labour play;

Verse 449. I have availed myself of the aid of the Commentators to make out this passage rather more fully than it occurs in the original, and consequently more intelligibly to the English reader. The poet describes the toilet of the Yakshiṅís, or female Yakshas, through the six seasons of the year, by mentioning as the selected flowers those peculiar to each period. Thus the Lotus blooms in Śarat or the sultry season, two months of our autumn; the Kunda (Jasminum pubescens) in Śiśira or the dewy season; the Lodh, a species of tree (Symplocos recemosa, Rox.), is in blossom in Hemanta or winter; the Kuruvaka (Gomphræna globosa) in Vasanta or spring; the Śirísha (Mimosa Śirísha) in the hot months, or Grishma; and the Nípa or Kadamba (Nauclea Kadamba) at the setting in of the rains. It is to the Commentators also that I am indebted for the sole occupation of the goddesses being pleasure and dress. The fact is,

——To sing, to dance,
To dress, and troll the tongue, and roll the eye,

constitutes a very well-educated female, according to the customs of Hindustan. We cannot help, however, being pleased with the simplicity and propriety of taste which gives to the graceful ornaments of nature so prominent a part in the decoration of feminine beauty.

One while, the fluttering Lotus fans the fair,
Or Kunda top-knots crown the jetty hair.
Now, o'er the cheek the Lodh's pale pollen shines,
Now midst their curls the Amaranth entwines.
These graces varying with the varying year,
Śirísha-blossoms deck the tender ear;
Or new Kadambas, with thy coming born,
The parted locks and polished front adorn.

Thus graced, they woo the Yakshas to their arms,
And gems, and wine, and music, aid their charms.
The strains divine with art celestial thrill,
And wines from grapes of heavenly growth distil.
The gems bestrew each terrace of delight,
Like stars that glitter through the shades of night.
There, when the Sun restores the rising day,
What deeds of love his tell-tale beams display!
The withered garlands on the pathway found;
The faded lotus prostrate on the ground;
The pearls, that bursting zones have taught to roam,
Speak of fond maids, and wanderers from home.

Verse 462. And wines from grapes of heavenly growth distil.] So MILTON, Paradise Lost, v. 426:

——In heaven, the trees
Of life ambrosial fruitage bear, and vines yield nectar.

And again, line 835:

——Rubined nectar flows,
Fruit of delicious vines, the growth of heaven.

Verse 464. Like stars that glitter through the shades of night.] Thus B. JONSON:

The starres that are the jewels of the night.

Here filled with modest fears, the Yaksha's bride
Her charms from passion's eagerness would hide;
The bold presumption of her lover's hands
To cast aside the loosened vest, withstands;
And, feeble to resist, bewildered turns
Where the rich lamp with lofty radiance burns;
And vainly whelms it with a fragrant cloud
Of scented dust, in hope the light to shroud.

The gale that blows, eternally their guide,
High over Alaká the clouds divide
In parted masses, like the issuing smoke
Of incense by the lattice-meshes broke:

Verse 470. Speak of fond maids, and wanderers from home.] I have already mentioned that the Hindus always send the lady to seek her lover, and they usually add a very reasonable degree of ardour and impatienee. Our poet, in another plaee, compares the female so engaged to a rapid current. Thus, in the Ŕitu Sanhára [II, 7]:

निपातयन्त्यः परितस्तटद्रुमान् । प्रवृद्धवेगैस्सलिलैरनिर्मलैः ॥
स्त्रियः प्रकामा इव जातविभ्रमाः । प्रयान्ति नद्यस्त्वरितं पयोनिधिम् ॥

Fast flow the tnrbid torrents, as they sweep
The shelving valleys to rejoin the deep:
Impetuous as the maid whom passion warms,
And drives impatient to her lover's arms,
Along they bound with unresisted force,
And banks and trees demolish in their course.

Verse 478. Of seented dust.] She easts npon it a handful of Chúrna: whieh means not only any powdered or pounded substanee, but especially aromatie powders; which we may suppose to eonstitnte part of an Indian lady's toilet, as they did in the last century of those of Europe, when the toilet of a belle was equipped

With patches, powder-box, pulvil, perfumes.

Scattered they float, as if dispersed by fear,
Or conscious guilt spoke retribution near; 484
Their just award for showers that lately soiled
Some painted floor, or gilded roof despoiled.

Ere yet thy coming yields opposing gloom,
The moon's white rays the smiling night illume, 488
And on the moon-gem concentrated fall,
That hangs in woven nets in every hall;
Whence cooling dews upon the fair descend,
And life renewed to languid nature lend. 492

What though while Śiva with the god of gold
Delights a friendly intercourse to hold;
The Lord of Love, remembering former woe,
Wields not in Alaká his bee-strung bow: 496

Verse 486. Some painted floor.] It is customary amongst the Hindus, upon festival occasions, to smooth and paint the ground on which worship is to be performed, or the assembly to be held. As this spot is generally in an open area within the walls of the house, a shower of rain is of course very hostile to such decoration.

Verse 489. The moon-gem, or Chandrakánta (चन्द्रकान्त), which is supposed to absorb the rays of the moon, and to emit them again in the form of pure and cool moisture. [St. Julien Mémoires sur les contrées occidentales. Paris: 1858, II, p. 145.]

Verse 495. The Lord of Love, remembering former woe.] This alludes to the fate which befel the Hindu Cupid upon his assailing Śiva, whom, at the desire of the gods, he inflamed with the love of Párvatí. Śiva, in his wrath, reduced the little deity to ashes, by a flame from the eye in his forehead; and, although he was subsequently restored to animation, he is here supposed to remain in dread of his former enemy. The whole story is spiritedly told in Sir William Jones's Hymns to Camdeo and to Durgá.

Yet still he triumphs: for each maid supplies
The fatal bow with love-inspiring eyes;
And wanton glances emulate the dart,
That speeds unerring to the beating heart. 500

Northward from where Kuvera holds his state,
Where Indra's bow surmounts the arching gate;
Where on rich boughs the clustering flower depends,
And low to earth the tall Mandára bends; 504
Pride of the grove, whose wants my fair supplies,
And nurtures like a child—my dwelling lies.

Verse 499. And wanton glances emulate the dart.] The eye darting arrows is an idea familiar to English poetry; as in these instances:

> Her eye darted contagious fire. MILTON.
>
> Her eyes carried darts of fire,
> Feathered all with swift desire.
> GREENE'S "Never too late."
>
> I mote perceive how in her glancing sight
> Legions of loves with little wings did fly,
> Darting their deadly arrows fiery bright.
> SPENSER. Sonnet 16.
>
> And those love-darting eyes shall roll no more.
> POPE'S Elegy.

Verse 504. The tall Mandára.] The Coral-tree, Erythrina Indica.

Verse 506. And nurtures like a child.] Tender attachment to natural objects is one of the most pleasing features in the poetical compositions of the Hindus. It is very frequently expressed, and perhaps in few places with more beauty than in the drama of Śakuntalá, where, upon departing from the bower of her foster-father, she bids adieu to the plants she had carefully tended, and the orphan fawn she had reared. The whole of this scene must be read

There is the fountain, emerald steps denote,
Where golden buds on stalks of coral float;
And for whose limpid waves the Swans forsake,
Pleased at thy sight, the mount-encircled lake.
Soft from the pool ascends a shelving ground,
Where shades devoted to delight abound;
Where the cœrulean summit towers above
The golden circle of a plantain-grove:
Lamented haunts! which now in thee I view,
As glittering lightnings girt thy base of blue.

See where the clustering Mádhaví entwines,
And bright Kuruvaka the wreath confines;
Profuse, Aśoka sheds its radiant flower,
And budding Keśara adorns the bower;
These are my rivals; for the one would greet,
As I would willingly, my charmer's feet;

---

with pleasure; and may be classed with the departure of Goldsmith's village family from Auburn, and the farewell of Eve to the bowers of Paradise.

Verse 517. The Mádhavi entwines.] This Creeper (Gærtnera racemosa, or Banisteria Bengalensis) is often alluded to by the Poets, for its superior elegance, and the beauty of its red blossoms.

Verse 518. Kuruvaka is the crimson Amaranth. The Sanskrit name is also applied to a blue species of Barleria.

Verse 519. Profuse, Aśoka sheds its radiant flower.] Jonesia Aśoka; speaking of which, Sir William Jones says, "The vegetable world scarcely exhibits a richer sight than an Aśoka tree in full bloom."

Verse 520. And budding Keśara.] A tree yielding a strong-smelling flower (Mimusops elengi).

And, with my fondness, would the other sip
The grateful nectar of her honeyed lip.

A golden column on a crystal base,
Begirt with jewels, rises o'er the place.
Here, when the evening twilight shades the skies,
The blue-necked Peacock to the summit flies,
And moves in graceful circles to the tone
My fair awakens from her tinkling zone.
These be thy guides—and faithfully preserve
The marks I give thee: or e'en more, observe,
Where painted emblems holy wealth design,
Kuvera's treasures—that abode is mine.

Verse 521. These are my rivals, &c.] These allusions refer to some particular notions of the Hindus respecting the Keśara and Aśoka, which plants are said to blossom upon being touched respectively by the face or foot of a female: the story is probably, originally poetical. [Stenzler od Raghuv. VIII, 61, and Kumáras. III, 26.]

Verse 528. The blue-necked Peacock to the summit flies.] The wild Peacock, although it lays its nest upon the ground, is said, by Captain Williamson, to roost constantly on the loftiest trees.

Verse 530. My fair awakens from her tinkling zone.] A girdle of small bells (क्षुद्रघण्टिका) is a favourite Hindu ornament; also silver circles at the ankles and wrists, which emit a ringing noise as the wearer moves.

Verse 534. Kuvera's treasures.]

> Thick with sparkling oriental gems
> The portal shone.——
>
> Paradise Lost, B. iii. 507.

For such Kuvera's nine treasures are sometimes supposed to be. Rámáśrama [and Bhánudikshita] commenting upon Amara [I, 71], thus enumerates them, from the Śabdárṅava:

Haply its honours are not now to boast,
Dimmed by my fate, and in my exile lost. 536

पद्मो ऽस्त्रियां महापद्मः शङ्खो मकरकच्छपौ ।
मुकुन्दनन्दनीलाश्च खर्वश्च निधयो नव ॥

"The Padma, Mahápadma, Śankha, Makara, Kachhapa, Mukunda, Nanda, Níla, and Kharva, are the nine Nidhis." The Śabda Ratnávalí also has the same reading. In Hemachandra [v. 193], and the Śabda Málá, कुन्द is substituted for नन्द. Nidhi (निधि) is the generic name; but how it should be rendered into English, I am not prepared to say. Mr. Colebrooke calls the particular Nidhis, 'auriferous gems'. See his translation of the Amara Kosha. Some of the words bear the meanings of precious or holy things: thus, Padma is the Lotus; Śankha the shell or conch. Again, some of them imply large numbers; thus, Padma is 10,000 millions, and Mahápadma is 100,000 millions, &c.; but all of them are not received in either the one or the other acceptation. We may translate almost all into things: thus, a lotus, a large lotus, a shell, a certain fish, a tortoise, a crest, a mathematical figure used by the Jainas. Níla refers only to colour; but Kharva, the ninth, means a dwarf. Mr. Kindersley, translating through the medium of the Tamul [probably from the Márkańdeya Puráńa, c. 68.], has called eight of Kuvera's gems, the coral, pearl, cat's-eye, emerald, diamond, sapphire, ruby, and topaz. The ninth he leaves undetermined. In Dr. Hunter's Dictionary, I find one only of the nine in the Hindoostanee Language, نیلم or نیل من Neelum or Neelmun, derived from नीलमणि 'a blue gem', and interpreted the Sapphire. पद्मराग Padma-colour, means a Ruby; and possibly the Padma may be the same: perhaps कच्छप, the tortoise, means tortoise-shell; and Makara may be an error for Maraka or Marakata, an Emerald, or it may imply the same stone from the green colour of a fish: these, however, are mere conjectures. Agreeably to the system of the Tántrikas, the Nidhis are personified, and upon certain occasions, as the worship of Lakshmi, the goddess of prosperity, &c., come in for a share of religious veneration. They have also their peculiar mantras, or mystical verses.

For when the sun withdraws his cheering rays,
Faint are the charms the Kamala displays.

To those loved scenes repaired, that awful size,
Like a young elephant, in haste disguise;
Lest terror seize my fair one, as thy form
Hangs o'er the hillock, and portends the storm.
Thence to the inner mansion bend thy sight,
Diffusing round a mild and quivering light;
As when, through evening shades, soft flashes play
Where the bright fire-fly wings his glittering way.

Verse 538. The Kamala is a name of the lotus.

Verse 546. Where the bright fire-fly wings his glittering way.] The fire-fly presents a very beautiful appearance, as its soft and twinkling light is contrasted with the deep shade of the bushes, in which it may be seen in great numbers during the wet season. The phænomenon is common to the East and the West Indies; and it may be amusing to see the effect produced by it on different persons and at different periods. Moore, meeting with it in America, writes some elegant stanzas on the subject; and adds to the lightness of his verse the solidity of prose in the authority of this note: —"The lively and varying illumination with which these fire-flies light up the woods at night gives quite an idea of enchantment. Puis ces mouches se developpant de l'obscurité de ces arbres, et s'approchant de nous, nous les voyions sur les orangers voisins, qu'ils mettoient tout en feu, nous rendant la vue de leurs beaux fruits, que la nuit avoit ravie, &c.—L'Histoire Des Antilles." See Moore's Odes and Epistles. We have now to hear the description of a Traveller of 1672, the learned and very devout Johannes Fryer, M. D.

"The next day, at twelve o'clock at noon, we struck into our old road at Moorbar, from whence before we were misguided: we packed hence by five in the afternoon, and left our burnt wood on the

There, in the fane, a beauteous creature stands,
The first best work of the Creator's hands; 548

---

right-hand; but entered another, which made us better sport, deluding us with false flashes, that you would have thought the trees on a flame, and presently, as if untouched by fire, they retained their wonted verdure. The Coolies beheld the sight with horror and amazement, and were consulting to set me down and shift for themselves; whereof being informed, I cut two or three with my sword, and, by breathing a vein, let Shitan (the Devil) out, who was crept into their fancies; and led them, as they do a startling jade, to smell to what their wall-eyes represented amiss; where we found an host of flies, the subject both of our fear and wonder, which the sultry heat and moisture had generated into being, the certain prodromus of the ensuing rain, which followed us from the hills. This gave my thoughts the contemplation of that miraculous bush crowned with innocent flames that gave to Moses so pleasant and awful a prospect; the fire, that consumes every thing, seeming rather to dress than offend it."

Verse 548. The first best work of the Creator's hands.] Literally, the first creation of Brahmá: and 'first' may refer to time, or to degree: it most probably here means 'best.' So Milton, speaking of Eve:

> "Oh, Fairest of creation! last and best
> Of all God's works."——
>
> Paradise Lost, B. ix. 896.

We now enter upon perhaps the most pleasing part of this elegant little poem, the description of the Yaksha's wife. I may perhaps come under the denomination of those who, according to the illiberal and arrogant criticism of such a writer as a Mr. Pinkerton, prove, "That the climate of India, while it inflames the imagination, impairs the judgment;" when, standing in very little awe of such a poetical censor, I advance an opinion, that we have few specimens, either in classical or modern poetry, of more genuine tenderness or delicate feeling.

Whose slender limbs inadequately bear
A full-orbed bosom, and a weight of care;
Whose teeth like pearls, whose lips like Bimbas
show,
And fawn-like eyes still tremble as they glow. 552

Lone as the widowed Chakravákí mourns,
Her faithful memory to her husband turns,

Verse 551. Whose lips like Bimbas show.] The Bimba (Bryonia grandis) bears a red fruit, to which the lip is very commonly compared.

Verse 553. The Chakravákí is the ruddy goose (Anas Casarca), more commonly known in India by the appellation Brahmany Duck or Goose. These birds are always observed to fly in pairs during the day, but are supposed to remain separate during the night. [Śakuntalá, ed. Williams, p. 129.] In the Hindoostanee Philology of Messrs. Gilchrist and Roebuck, an amusing account of the popular belief on this subject is thus given: "This bird, in the poetry of the "Hindus, is their turtledove, for constancy and connubial affection; "with the singular circumstance of the pair being doomed for ever "to nocturnal separation, for having offended one of the Hindu di- "vinities (Munis or Saints), whence,

چكوا چكوي دو جني ان مت مارو كوي
يه ماري كرتار كي رين بيچاره هوي ✿

"Mark Heaven's decree, and man forbear
"To aim thy shafts, or puny thunder
"At these poor fowls, a hapless pair,
"Who pass the lonely nights asunder.

"If we believe popular tradition and assertions, the cause is so far "confirmed by the effect observable in the conduct of these birds to "the present day, who are said to occupy the opposite banks of a "water or stream regularly every evening, and exclaim the live-long "night to each other, thus:

And sad, and silent, shalt thou find my wife,
Half of my soul, and partner of my life, 556

چکوي مَين آؤن؟ نہين نہين چکوا —
چکوا مَين آؤن؟ نہين نہين چکوي

"Say, shall I come, my dear, to thee?
"Ah no, indeed, that cannot be.—
"But may I wing my love to you?
"Nay chuck, alas! this will not do."

Verse 556. Half of my soul, and partner of my life.] So MILTON:

Part of my soul, I seek thee; and thee claim,
My other half.—

जीवितं मे द्वितीयम्, "My second existence", are the words of the original; and the other expression, "my half", is not more uncommon in Sanskrit than in Western poetry. Thus these tender, and, as Mrs. Malaprop thinks, profane expressions of endearment seem to have obtained a very extensive circulation. 'My life', 'my soul', are common to most of the European languages; and the most frequent epithet by which a mistress is addressed in Persian or Hindoostanee, جان, is of a similar import. Amongst the Romans, 'vita' and 'anima' were used in the same manner, or even in the temperate warmth of friendship; as Horace calls Virgil:

Animæ dimidium meæ,
Half of my soul!

And Propertius, addressing his Mistress, calls her his Life:

Æratas rumpam, mea Vita, catenas.
I'll burst, my Life, the brazen chains.

We may suppose the Romans derived these pretty words from the Greeks; and indeed, as we learn from Juvenal, vi. 194, they were very fond of employing, though not in the most becoming manner, the original terms *Ζωὴ καὶ ψυχή*, the English translation of which has been given at some length by Mrs. Tighe, in her poem of Psyche; and, with some addition, by Lord Byron, in his Anglo-

Nipped by chill sorrow, as the flowers enfold
Their shrinking petals from the withering cold.
I view her now! Long weeping swells her eyes,
And those dear lips are dried by parching sighs.
Sad on her hand her pallid cheek declines,
And half unseen through veiling tresses shines;
As when a darkling night the moon enshrouds,
A few faint rays break straggling through the
Clouds.

Now at thy sight I mark fresh sorrows flow,
And sacred sacrifice augments her woe.
I mark her now with Fancy's aid retrace
This wasted figure and this haggard face.

Greek song, the burthen of which is the old sentiment in a modern antique shape, or 'My Life, I love you', in the *Ζωή μου, σᾶς ἀγαπῶ*, of the Greek of the Morea.

Verse 566. And sacred sacrifice augments her woe.] Thus Laodameia to Protesilaus, in Ovid:

Thura damus lacrymamque super.
We offer incense up, and add our tears.

The Commentators, however, are not agreed how to interpret this passage in the original text, बलिव्याकुला nor the expression निपतति पुरे, "She falls before thee": they seem, however, to conceive it means, that the approach of the Cloud reminding her of its being the period at which absent husbands usually return home, she recollects that the return of her own lord is proscribed; and therefore either falls in a swoon, or with excess of affliction. The sacrifice is to be performed to render the gods propitious, or it is a sacrifice called काकबलि, usually performed by women at the beginning of the rainy season. Some interpret पुरे "In the city", not "Before, in front." [C. Schütz: "when thy glances fall on the city."]

Now from her favourite bird she seeks relief,
And tells the tuneful Sáriká her grief;
Mourns o'er the feather'd prisoner's kindred fate,
And fondly questions of its absent mate. 572
In vain the lute for harmony is strung,
And round the robe-neglected shoulder slung;

Verse 570. The Sáriká (Grakula religiosa) is a small bird, better known by the name of Mainá. It is represented as a female, while the parrot is described as a male bird [See J. E. Hall in his edition of the Vásavadattá, p. 35]: and as these two have, in all Hindu tales, the faculty of human speech, they are constantly introduced, the one inveighing against the faults of the male sex, and the other exposing the defects of the female. They are thus represented in the fourth story of that entertaining collection, the Baitál Pachísí:

मैना बोली कि पुरुष अधर्मी पापी दग़ाबाज़ स्त्रीहत्या करने वाले होते हैं । यिह सुनकर तोते ने कहा कि नारी भी दग़ाबाज़ झूठी बेवकूफ़ लालची हत्यारी होती है ॥ ["The mainah said, 'Men are devoid of religion, sinful, treacherous and murderers of women.' The parrot having heard this replied, 'Woman is also deceitful, false, silly, avaricious and a murderess.'"]

Ladies have always been distinguished for maintaining pet animals; and the fancy seems to have been equally prevalent in the East and West, and in ancient or modern times. The Swallow of Lesbia, 'Passer deliciæ meæ puellæ', may rival the Sáriká of the wife of the Yaksha, and Bullfinch of Mrs. Throckmorton. See Cowper's Poems.

Verse 573. In vain the lute for harmony is strung.] The lute is here put for the Víñá or Been, a stringed instrument of sacred origin, and high celebrity amongst the Hindus. In Bengal, however, players on this instrument are very rarely met with; and amongst the natives of this province the English fiddle is its substitute. In the Játras, or dramatic performances still current amongst them, I have seen the entrance of Nárada, the traditionary inventor of the

And faltering accents strive to catch in vain
Our race's old commemorative strain:
The falling tear, that from reflection springs,
Corrodes incessantly the silvery strings;
Recurring woe still pressing on the heart,
The skilful hand forgets its grateful art,
And, idly wandering, strikes no measured tone,
But wakes a sad wild warbling of its own.

At times, such solace animates her mind
As widowed wives in cheerless absence find;
She counts the flowers, now faded on the floor,
That graced with monthly piety the door.
Thence reckons up the period, since from home,
And far from her, I was compelled to roam;
And deeming, fond, my term of exile run,
Conceives my homeward journey is begun.

Víńá, bearing in its stead a violin. The Víńá is much the most harmonious and scientific of all the Hindu instruments of music. A description of it may be found in the First Volume of the Asiatic Researches.

Verse 574. "Robe-neglected" is here put for मलिनवसने, 'dirty clothes.' So Laodameia says:

> Et quâ possum squalore tuos imitare labores, &c.
> And with my squalid vesture ape thy toils.

Verse 576. Our race's old commemorative strain.] "The verse made in honour of my kindred": a circumstance that points out some affinity to the songs of the ancient minstrels and family bards.

Verse 586. That graced with monthly piety the door.] The Hindus pay a species of adoration to many inanimate objects. Amongst others, the door-way, or door-post, receives such homage as is rendered by hanging up a flower or a garland there once a month.

Lightened by tasks like these, the day proceeds;
But much I dread a bitterer night succeeds,
When thou shalt view her on the earth's cold breast,
Or lonely couch of separation rest,
Disturbed by tears those pallid cheeks that burn,
And vision of her dearer half's return.
Now seeking sleep, a husband to restore;
And waking now, his absence to deplore;
Deprived of slumber by returning woes,
Or mocked by idle phantoms of repose;
Till her slight form, consumed by ceaseless pain,
Shews like the moon, fast hastening to its wane.
Crisp from the purifying wave, her hair
Conceals the charms, no more her pleasing care;
And, with neglected nails, her fingers chase,
Fatigued, the tresses wandering o'er her face.

Firm winds the fillet, as it first was wove,
When fate relentless forced me from my love;
And never flowery wreaths, nor costly pearls,
Must hope to decorate the fettered curls;
Loosed by no hand, until, the law divine
Accomplished, that delighted hand is mine.

Verse 591. In this, and some of the following passages, considerable liberty has been taken with the order of the original.

Verse 607. Firm winds the fillet, as it first was wove.] The Veńi is a braid into which the long hair of the Hindustani women is collected, when they have lost their husbands. [So Sítá in Rámáy. V, 15, 24 (Madras ed.)] The dancing-girls also wear their hair in this manner.

Dull as the flower when clouds through æther sweep,
Not wholly waking, nor resigned to sleep,
Her heavy eyelids languidly unclose
To where the moon its silvery radiance throws 616
Mild through the chamber: once a welcome light;
Avoided now, and hateful to her sight.

Those charms that glittering ornaments oppress,
Those restless slumbers that proclaim distress, 620
That slender figure worn by grief severe,
Shall surely gain thy sympathizing tear.
For the soft breast is swift to overflow,
In moist compassion, at the claims of woe. 624

The same fond wife as when compelled to part,
Her love was mine, I still possess her heart.
Her well-known faith this confidence affords,
Nor vain conceit suggests unmeaning words. 628
No boaster I! and time shall quickly teach,
With observation joined, how just my speech.

O'er her left limbs shall glad pulsations play,
And signs auspicious indicate the way; 632

Verse 616. To where the moon.] The moon is supposed to be the reservoir of amŕita or ambrosia, and to furnish the gods and manes with the supply. "It is replenished from the sun, during the fortnight of the increase. On the full moon, the gods adore that planet for one night; and for the first day, all of them, together with the Pitŕis and Ŕishis, drink one kalá or digit daily, until the ambrosia is exhausted." Váyu Puráńa.

Verse 631. O'er her left limbs shall glad pulsations play.] Palpitations in the left limbs, and a throbbing in the left eye, are here

And like the lotus trembling on the tide,
While its deep roots the sportive fish divide,
So tremulous throbs the eye's enchanting ball,
Loose o'er whose lids neglected tresses fall.

Soothed by expected bliss, should gentle sleep
O'er her soft limbs and frame exhausted creep,
Delay thy tidings, and suspend thy flight,
And watch in silent patience through the night.
Withhold thy thunders, lest the awful sound
Her slumber banish, and her dreams confound;
Where her fond arms, like winding shrubs, she flings
Around my neck, and to my bosom clings.

Behold her rising with the early morn,
Fair as the flower that opening buds adorn;
And strive to animate her drooping mind
With cooling rain-drops and refreshing wind;
Restrain thy lightnings, as her timid gaze
Shrinks from the bright intolerable blaze;

---

described as auspicious omens, when occurring in the female: in the male, the right side is the auspicious side, corresponding with the ideas of the Greeks, thus described by Potter:—

"The third sort of internal omens were the *Παλμοὶ* or *Παλμικὰ οἰωνίσματα*, so called *ἀπὸ τοῦ πάλλειν*, 'from palpitating.' Such were the palpitations of the heart, the eye, or any of the muscles, called, in Latin, 'saltationes', and *βόμβος*, or 'a ringing in the ears', which in the right ear was a lucky omen: so also was the palpitation of the right eye, as Theocritus telleth us:

Ἄλλεται ὀφθαλμός μοι ὁ δεξιός.
My right eye twinkles."

And murmuring softly, gentle sounds prepare,
With words like these to raise her from despair:—

'Oh, wife adored! whose lord still lives for thee,
'Behold his friend and messenger in me;
'Who now approach thy beauteous presence, fraught
'With many a tender and consoling thought!
'Such tasks are mine:—where absent lovers stray,
'I speed the wanderer lightly on his way;
'And with my thunders teach his lagging mind
'New hopes the braid of absence to unbind.'

As beauteous Maithilí with glad surprise
Bent on the Son of air her opening eyes,
So my fair partner's pleased uplifted gaze
Thy friendly presence with delight surveys.
She smiles, she speaks, her misery foregoes,
And deep attention on thy words bestows;
For such dear tidings happiness impart,
Scarce less than mutual meeting to the heart.

Verse 660. 'The braid of absence' is the Veńí: see Note on verse 607.

Verse 661. Maithilí is a name of Sítá, derived from Mithilá, the place of her nativity, and the modern Tirhut. The allusion relates to the discovery of her in Lanká, by Ráma's envoy, Hanumán, the Monkey chief, said to be the son of the Wind. [Rámáy. V, 34.]

Verse 668. Scarce less than mutual meeting to the heart.] They have a proverb similar to this in the Hindustanee language, "A letter is half a meeting." The expression is common in the poetry of the Rekhta, and occurs thus in a Ghazal by Jirat:

كهتي هَين كه مكتوب بهي هَي نصف مُلاقات

Being, of years protracted, aid thy friend,
And with my words thine own suggestions blend!
Say thus: 'Thy lord o'er Ráma's mountain strays,
'Nor cares but those of absence blight his days.
'His only wish by me his friend to know,
'If he is blest with health, that thou art so:
'For still this fear especially must wait
'On every creature of our passing state.

'What though to distance driven by wrath divine,
'Imagination joins his form with thine.
'Such as I view, is his emaciate frame;
'Such his regrets; his scorching pangs the same;
'To every sigh of thine his sigh replies,
'And tears responsive trickle from his eyes.

'By thee unheard, by those bright eyes unseen,
'Since fate resists, and regions intervene,
'To me the message of his love consigned
'Pourtrays the sufferings of his constant mind.

It also exists in the Arabic language; and is thus given in one of the Exercises of Captain Lockett's Translation of the Mi'at Ámil, and the Sharah Mi'at Ámil, or an Arabic Grammar and Commentary:

المُراسَلاتُ كما قيْلَ نصفُ المُلاقات

"Correspondence, they say, is half an interview."

Verse 675. For still this fear especially must wait.] It is to be recollected here, that even these heavenly Beings are of a perishable nature, and subject to the infirmities of existence. The whole are swept away at each Mahá-pralaya, or destruction of the Universe,

Which, like the baseless fabric of a vision,
Leaves not a wreck behind.

'Oh! were he present, fondly would he seek
'In secret whisper that inviting cheek;
'Woo thee in close approach, his words to hear,
'And breathe these tender accents in thine ear:'

"Goddess beloved! how vainly I explore
"The world, to trace the semblance I adore.
"Thy graceful form the flexile tendril shews,
"And like thy locks the peacock's plumage glows;
"Mild as thy cheeks, the moon's new beams appear,
"And those soft eyes adorn the timid deer;
"In rippling brooks thy curling brows I see,
"But only view combined these charms in thee.

Verse 695. Mild as thy cheeks, the moon's new beams appear.] Comparing a beautiful face to the moon has been supposed peculiar to Oriental Poets. Instances, however, may be found in English verse: perhaps that passage in Pope, where, speaking of an amiable female and the moon, he says, "Serene in virgin modesty she shines", may not be exactly in point, although the general idea is similar. Spenser, however, is sufficiently precise:

> Her spacious forehead, like the clearest moon,
> Whose full-grown orb begins now to be spent,
> Largely displayed in native silver shone,
> Giving wide room to beauty's regiment.

Verse 698. But only view combined these charms in thee.] This turn of the compliment, closely faithful to the original, conveys a high idea of the gallantry of a Hindu Bard, and as this gallantry cannot be the ten times repeated retail of romantic folly or chivalrous phrensy, it may be considered as the natural expression of unsophisticated tenderness. We have in these lines a complete description of beauty, agreeably to Hindu fancy; and I do not think the series of comparisons will much suffer by being contrasted with any similar series in classical or modern writers.

" E'en in these wilds our unrelenting fate
" Proscribes the union, love and art create:
" When, with the colours that the rock supplies,
" O'er the rude stone thy pictured beauties rise,
" Fain would I think, once more we fondly meet,
" And seek to fall in homage at thy feet;—
" In vain;—for envious tears my purpose blight,
" And veil the lovely image from my sight.

" Why should the god who wields the five-fold dart
" Direct his shafts at this afflicted heart;

Verse 701. When, with the colours that the rock supplies.] "Having painted you with mineral colours" (धातुरागैः), that is, according to the Commentators, with 'red chalk', &c. Our very limited acquaintance with the high land which is the scene of the Yaksha's exile prevents our specifying the mineral substances which he may be supposed to have employed. The expression in the text, however, is one of many circumstances that render it probable that the mountains which run across the northernmost part of the Peninsula are rich in the objects of mineralogical inquiry. We know that copper mines have been discovered in the eastern extremity of them, the ore of which is very productive. The Sálagrám stones, or Ammonites, are found in the Narmadá; and the several kinds of Makshikas, a class of ores not yet investigated, are usually called नदीज and तापीज, or 'River-born', and 'Taptí-born', in reference to their being found in the course of the Taptí river.

Verse 707. Why should the god who wields the five-fold dart.] Kámadeva, the Hindu Cupid, is represented as the Eros of the Greeks, armed with a bow and arrows. These weapons are of peculiar construction, and most poetically formed. The bow is of sugar-cane; the bow-string consists of a line of bees; and the arrows are tipped each with a separate flower. The weapons and application of the allegory will be best explained by a verse in Sir William Jones's Hymn to this deity:

" Nor spare to agonize an aching breast,
" By sultry suns and banishment oppressed?
" Oh, that these heavy hours would swiftly fly,
" And lead a happier fate, and milder sky!

" Believe me, dearest, that my doom severe
" Obtains from heavenly eyes the frequent tear;
" And where the spirits of these groves attend
" The pitying drops in pearly showers descend,
" As oft in sleep they mark my outstretched arms,
" That clasp in blissful dreams thy fancied charms,
" Play through the air, and fold in fond embrace
" Impassive matter and etherial space.

He bends the luscious cane, and twists the string,
With bees how sweet, but, ah! how keen their sting!
He with five flowrets tips the ruthless darts,
Which through five senses pierce enraptured hearts.
Strong Chumpa, rich in odorous gold;
Warm Arka, nursed in heavenly mould;
Dry Nagesar, in silver smiling;
Hot Kriticum, our sense beguiling;
And last, to kindle fierce the scorching flame,
Love shaft, which gods bright Bela name.

In the Romaunt of the Rose there is something of a similar allegory: Cupid is armed with "ten brode arrows"; of which, "five were shaven well and dight", and of a nature to produce virtuous attachment; while the other five, "also black as fiend in hell", were 'Pride', 'Villaine', &c., and of pernicious properties.

Verse 715. And where the spirits of these groves attend.] Sthalí Devatás are, literally, 'the deities of the soil'; so completely has Hindu, like Grecian faith, peopled inanimate nature.

" Soft and delightful to my senses blows
" The breeze that southward wafts Himálaya's
snows,
" And rich impregnated with gums divine,
" Exuding fragrant from the shattered pine,
" Diffuses sweets to all, but most to me;—
" Has it not touched? does it not breathe of thee?

" What are my tasks?—to speed the lagging night,
" And urge impatiently the rising light:
" The light returned, I sicken at the ray,
" And shun as eagerly the shining day:
" Vain are my labours in this lonely state;
" But fate proscribes, and we must bow to fate.

" Let then my firmness save thee from despair,
" Who trust myself, nor sink beneath my care:

Verse 733. Let then my firmness save thee from despair.] We are scarcely prepared for this sudden fortitude of the Yaksha; but it is not by any means unnatural. The task of consoling partners in affliction necessarily diverts the mind from its own distress.

Reference to the principle is very frequent in the writings of the Hindus. The Átma Bodha, or 'Knowledge of Spirit', a small treatise which contains the ethical part of the Vedanta philosophy, and which has been translated and published by Dr. Taylor, concludes with this stanza [v. 67]:—

दिग्देशकालाद्यनपेक्ष्य सर्व्वगम् । शीतादिहृन्नित्यसुखं निरञ्जनम् ॥
यः स्वात्मतीर्थं भजते विनिष्क्रियः । स सर्व्ववित्सर्व्वगतोऽमृतो भवेत् ॥

"He who has made the pilgrimage of his own spirit, a pilgrimage in which there is no concern respecting situation, place, or time; which is everywhere; in which neither cold nor heat are experienced; which bestows perpetual happiness and freedom from sor-

"Trust to futurity; for still we view
"The always wretched, always blest, are few:
"Life like a wheel's revolving orb turns round,
"Now whirled in air, now dragged along the ground.

"When from his serpent couch, that swims the deep,
"Śárangí rises from celestial sleep;

---

row; he is without action, knows all things, pervades all things, and obtains eternal beatitude." [C. Graul, Bibliotheca Tamulica. Lipsiæ: 1854, Vol. I, p. 195, agreeing with the Madras edition.]

A fine passage inculcating the same feeling occurs in Manu ch. viii. 84, where the legislator exhorts a witness to speak the truth:—

आत्मैव ह्यात्मनः साक्षी गतिरात्मा तथात्मनः ।
मा ऽवमंस्थाः स्वमात्मानं नृणां साक्षिणमुत्तमम् ॥

"The soul itself is its own witness; the soul itself is its own refuge: offend not thy conscious soul, the supreme internal witness of men." Sir WILLIAM JONES's Translation.

Verse 737.] Plutarch, in his 'Consolation to Apollonius', has a similar idea, in similar words:

Τροχοῦ [γὰρ] περιστείχοντος ἄλλοθ' ἡτέρα
Ἁψὶς ὕπερθε γίγνετ', ἄλλοθ' ἡτέρα.

The wheel of Life is ever on the round,
While one side's up, the other's on the ground.

Verse 740. The serpent couch is the great snake Ananta, upon which Vishńu, or, as he is here called, the Holder of the bow Śárnga (the horn-bow), reclines, during four months, from the 11th of Áshádha to the 11th of Kártik; or, as it has occurred in 1813 (the year in which the first edition was printed), from the 23d of June to the 26th of October. The sleep of Vishńu, during the four months of the periodical rains in Hindustan, seems to bear an emblematical relation to that season. It has been compared to the Egyptian Hieroglyphical account of the sleep of Horus, typical of the annual overflow of the Nile, by the late Mr. Paterson, in his ingenious Essay on the Origin of the Hindu Religion. Asiatic Researches, vol. viii.

"When four more months, unmarked, have run their course:
"To us all gloom—the curse has lost its force;
"The grief from separation born expires,
"And Autumn's nights reward our chaste desires.

"Once more I view thee, as mine eyes unclose,
"Laid by my side, and lulled by soft repose;
"And now I mark thee startle from thy sleep,
"Loose thy enfolding arms, and wake to weep:
"My anxious love long vainly seeks reply;
"Till, as the smile relumes that lucid eye,
"Thy arch avowal owns, that jealous fear
"Affrighted slumber, and aroused the tear.

"While thus, O goddess with the dark black eyes!
"My fond assurance confidence supplies,
"Let not the tales that idle tatlers bear,
"Subvert thy faith, nor teach thee to despair.
"True love no time nor distance can destroy;
"And, independent of all present joy,
"It grows in absence, as renewed delight,
"Some dear memorials, some loved lines excite."

Such, vast Dispenser of the dews of heaven!
Such is my suit, and such thy promise given:
Fearless, upon thy friendship I rely,
Nor ask that promise, nor expect reply.

Verse 764. Nor ask that promise nor expect reply.] We cannot help pausing here, to remark the ingenuity of the Poet in the con-

To thee the thirsty Chátakas complain;
Thy only answer is the falling rain:
And still such answer from the good proceeds,
Who grant our wishes, not in words, but deeds.

Thy task performed, consoled the mourner's mind,
Haste thy return these solitudes to find;
Soar from the mountain, whose exalted brow
The horns of Śiva's bull majestic plough,
And, hither speeding, to my sorrowing heart,
Shrunk like the bud at dawn, relief impart,
With welcome news my woes tumultuous still,
And all my wishes tenderly fulfil!
Then to whatever scenes invite thy way,
Waft thy rich stores, and grateful glooms convey;
And ne'er may destiny, like mine, divide
Thy brilliant spouse, the lightning, from thy side!

---

duct of his work. He sets out with excusing the apparent absurdity of the Yaksha's addressing himself to a Cloud as to a rational being, by introducing a pleasing and natural sentiment: see Verse 32. The Cloud has now received his charge; and something is expected by way of reply, expressive either of refusal or assent. To have given the Cloud any thing like the faculty of speech, would have been straining probability overmuch; and we see in the above lines with what neatness Kálidása has extricated himself from the dilemma.

Verse 773. Thus Ovid, in his Tristia:—

Prospera sic vobis maneat Fortuna, nec unquam,
Contacti simili sorte, rogetis opem.

So may on thee propitious fortune wait,
Nor may'st thou need such aid, nor mourn so sad a fate!

This said, he ceased:—the messenger of air
Conveyed to Alaká his wild despair.
The god of wealth, relenting, learnt his state;
And swift curtailed the limit of his fate, 784
Removed the curse, restored him to his wife,
And blest with ceaseless joy their everlasting life.

Vol. V, containing also the Index for Vols. III - V, will be published in June.

ESSAYS
ANALYTICAL, CRITICAL AND PHILOLOGICAL
ON SUBJECTS CONNECTED WITH
SANSKRIT LITERATURE

ESSAYS
ANALYTICAL, CRITICAL AND PHILOLOGICAL

ON SUBJECTS CONNECTED WITH

SANSKRIT LITERATURE

BY THE LATE

H. H. WILSON, M. A., F.R.S.,

BODEN PROFESSORS OF SANSKRIT IN THE UNIVERSITY OF OXFORD,
ETC., ETC.,

COLLECTED AND EDITED BY

DR. REINHOLD ROST

IN THREE VOLUMES

VOL. III

GYAN

Published by

Gyan Publishing House
5, Ansari Road
Daryaganj, New Delhi-110002
Phone: 011-47034999, 9811692060
E-mail: books@gyanbooks.com

Distribution Network
gyanbooks.com
India, USA, Canada, UK, Australia, France

ISBN : 978-81-212-4519-7 (Set)
ISBN : 978-81-212-4733-7 (HB)
First Published, 1865

2nd Impression 2020

Printed at: Gyan Press, Delhi.

Essays Analytical, Critical and Philological Vol. III
Author: H. H. Wilson

ESSAYS

ANALYTICAL, CRITICAL AND PHILOLOGICAL

ON SUBJECTS CONNECTED WITH

SANSKRIT LITERATURE.

BY THE LATE

H. H. WILSON, M.A., F.R.S.,

BODEN PROFESSOR OF SANSKRIT IN THE UNIVERSITY OF OXFORD,
ETC., ETC.

COLLECTED AND EDITED BY

DR. REINHOLD ROST.

IN THREE VOLUMES.

VOL. III.

LONDON:
TRÜBNER & CO., 60, PATERNOSTER ROW.
1865.

CONTENTS OF VOL. III.

XI.

CONSIDERATIONS ON THE HINDOO LAW, AS IT IS CURRENT IN BENGAL,

by the Honorable Sir FRANCIS WORKMAN MACNAGHTEN, Knt. One of His Majesty's Justices of the Supreme Court of Judicatüre at Fort William in Bengal.

"Misera est servitus, ubi jus est vagum aut incertum." 4th Inst.

Serampore Mission Press, 1824.

From the Quarterly Or. Magazine, Vol. III (1825), p. 171—240.

A WORK on the Laws of the Hindus by the eminent authority which had long administered them, excited our highest expectations, and we opened the volume with the fullest confidence of its yielding us the most satisfactory information. No common motives had operated on the learned author to induce him to become thoroughly master of his subject: the rights of individuals depended upon his accurate interpretation of the institutes on which they rested, and with the known intelligence and feeling of an English judge, we felt assured that he would never have been satisfied with the hurried or partial investigation of those arguments by which such important decisions were to be justified to the public and himself.

How far our expectations have been realised will appear, as we proceed; but the preface is of evil augury: it is wholly occupied with charges of inconsistency, and uncertainty against the Hindu code. We should have thought these qualifications would have pleaded in its favour with an experienced practitioner in our own jurisprudence, and should scarcely have supposed them serious grievances to one to whom the glorious uncertainty of English law must have afforded, in earlier life, no unfrequent opportunities for the display of acumen and research. The case, however, is otherwise, and Sir F. Macnaghten complains that "the contradictions of Hindu law reduce it to a nullity; that there is hardly any question that may not be either affirmed or denied under the sanction of texts which are held to be equal in point of authority; and that research is productive of little more than perplexity, for the conflict of lawgivers is endless, and they can never be reconciled."

To these assertions, however, we must confess we hesitate in giving unqualified assent. That conflicting authorities may be cited on many subjects may be conceded, but their being held to be of equal weight is by no means universally the case, although a mere English lawyer may be unable to determine which should preponderate: neither is it in our estimation so arduous a task as the learned judge seems to apprehend, to appreciate the reasons why lawgivers disagree, or to reconcile their differences. If that is impracticable, it is seldom difficult to give them that consideration to which they are justly entitled, upon reference to common sense, to obvious analogies, and the unquestionable and, in general, rational principles of Hindu Law. Again, the history of the authorities, the probable dates of their existence, the conditions of Hindu Society to which their institutes apply, and the local character of their influence, ought all to be taken into account in estimating the value of their dicta. Now all this, the criticism of Hindu Law, appears to us to form no part of the studies of the Calcutta Court, and we cannot wonder that its brightest ornaments should often be sadly puzzled. It is quite impossible that it should be otherwise as long as pleaders and judges are wholly at the mercy of the Pańḋits.

Sir Francis Macnaghten seems rather reluctant to admit the unfavourable testimony of Sir William Jones; as, although he cites that really learned Judge's opinion, that the Pańḋits have it in their power to mislead the court whenever they please, he holds that "the translated Hindu law-books contain enough, without being aided by the craft or cunning of a Pańḋit, to mislead any man." This is rather a singular mode of defending the Pańḋits, but if it be the case, of which by the way we are not at all assured, it must be from other causes than that stated by Sir Wm. Jones. In a translation, the reader has an opportunity of seeing the texts of the law in their proper places, applied to what they relate to, bearing upon the subject to which they belong, and corroborating or contradicting others of a similar tendency; but, as Sir Wm. Jones observes, "*a simple obscure text,* as explained by the Paṅḋits themselves, might be quoted as express authority, though perhaps in the very book from which it was selected it *might be differently explained, or introduced only for the purpose of being exploded.*" In a translation, the entire passage of the original is given, whilst in a Paṅḋit's *vyavasthá* it is not unfrequently perverted by incomplete or garbled citation, so as to bear a totally different meaning from that which it really conveys. We have no desire, more than the learned judge, to cast any reflexion upon the Paṅḋits of the Supreme Court, or of any other court, but we have seen too much of them, not to be satisfied that they are the authors of many of the irreconcileable contradictions of Hindu law.

The circumstances in which the Hindu legal advisers of the courts of justice in this country are situated, are perhaps not so familiar to many of our readers as to preclude the necessity of our offering some remarks upon the subject. A Paṅḋit, attached to a court in that capacity, is placed in it by personal favour entirely, without being subjected to any examination, and without producing any credentials;—who shall say then that he is 'learned in the law'? There is every probability against it, for until very lately neither means nor encouragement were offered to the Brahmans to study their own laws, and the assistance latterly given is much too recent to have produced any effect. There are no public establishments amongst the natives themselves, and they are too poor to pay for education: a teacher must feed as well as instruct his scholars, and such 'virtue is no longer extant.' In fact, an instructor was formerly enabled to maintain his pupils, and to glean a surplus for himself by the bounty of Rájás, and even of Nawábs, who gave him a village or two for that purpose, but grants of this description have long been out of fashion: without education there can be no learning, and as Pańđits are at best but indifferently taught, they are very rarely indeed learned men.

If the uncertainties of the English law are less perplexing than those of the Hindu law, we doubt if its *delays* are not something more interminable. A long time elapses before a cause comes for decision, and abundant opportunity therefore is afforded for the traffic of underhand negociation, intrigue and corruption; it is needless to cite instances to prove the consequences, or to make any individual application: public events have rendered the fact notorious. It can scarcely be otherwise. The Pańđits are in all cases ill paid, and the sums offered to their acceptance are in general equal to many years' purchase of their salaries: they are but men, and where the temptations are so great, they must be more than men to resist them. But is not every opinion to be received with reasonable distrust, emanating from parties over whom, whether proven or not, we cannot doubt undue influence operates, when a cause comes to be adjudged, and when the Paṅḋits are desired to report their opinions on the points of Hindu law?

Besides the opinions of the court Paṅḋits, given in reply to the queries of the court, it seems to be the practice of the Supreme and Sadr Courts at least, to receive the opinions of other Paṅḋits on either part. Need we wonder that these differ? What are counsel retained for in English courts? If opinions on the law were uniform, at least if the utterance of them were never to vary, what would become of the bar? The Paṅḋit in such a circumstance is an advocate, feed to make out the best story he can for his client, to adduce whatever can be pleaded in his favour, and overturn or explain away whatever appears to make against him. This trial of skill matters nothing with us, because we have Judges who know the law as well as the pleaders. In Hindu law, however, unluckily, the case is otherwise, and the Judge who is to decide the cause, knows nothig *per se* of the merit of the arguments which are to regulate his decision, not even of the language in which they are enforced. As long as this is the case, and every judge cannot be a Sir William Jones, we need not be surprised at the difficulty which attends the reconciliation of the contending doctrines of the Hindu law.

The mere question of the consistency of the Hindu law would be a matter of little importance, but that it leads to the serious consideration of the expediency of maintaining that law in force. If it be a nullity, as the learned judge remarks, what advantage follows its administration? At the same time, he recognises the policy and equity of governing the Hindus by their own laws, and consequently advocates a perseverance in the present plan, recommending however means "by which we may hope in time to cleanse the system of its aggregate corruptions and to *defecate the impurity of ages.*" And what are these means? The decisions of the Supreme Court; an appeal from Hindu law to an English bench; a preference of the opinion of foreign judges, and those but superficially conversant with the subject, to the laborious discussions of native law-givers, and scholars; and the substitution of common for written law, of that law which the historian of British India pronounces oral, traditionary, and barbarous, and describes as "any thing which the judges choses to call law, under no other restriction than certain notions, to a great degree arbitrary, of what has been done by other judges before them." We doubt very much whether the Hindus will not fare better amongst the contradictions of their own texts, admitting that they exist, than the frequently conflicting decisions of different judges, and the very commonly opposite awards of the Sadr Díwání, and Mufassal Courts, in which we believe the judgements of the Supreme Court are regarded as any thing but infallible. At any rate, before hazarding such an experiment, we should be desirous to behold one much more obvious put to the test, and before the Hindu law is irreprievably condemned, we should wish to see it studied.

There are many other assertions in this preface which we think much too generally, if not incautiously and erroneously, advanced. We shall satisfy ourselves, however, with adverting to but one more, that we may not disproportionately delay our examination of the work itself. Sir F. Macnaghten, speaking of the translations that have been made, observes: "that they admit of different explanations it would be folly to deny, because there is hardly a passage in any one of them which has not been differently explained." We must be guilty of the folly of denying the inference, as we have no proof whatever of the fact. By whom have these passages been differently explained? certainly not by different translators, for we have no one work on Hindu law translated by two different hands. We are not aware that the translators are at variance with themselves, and although obscure sentences, no doubt, occur in which variety of translation might be defensible, yet these are comparatively few, and unimportant. The leading texts, which are repeated in different works are almost always short, simple, and precise, and are rendered in a similar manner wherever they occur. Upon what proof therefore the learned judge's assertion is founded, we are wholly at a loss to conjecture: unless he refers to the explanations of the Pańḍits; and then indeed we concede the fact, although we are at issue as to the cause. The unfavourable impression of translations, which the learned judge seems inclined to convey, appears to us wholly unmerited, and, if implicitly credited, calculated to do much harm. We can have no expectation that the Gentlemen of the Calcutta Bar will waste their valuable hours upon the unprofitable study of Hindu law-books in the original Sanskrit: and upon translations therefore they must depend for any knowledge of Hindu law: but if they are told from high authority that these translations are only calculated to mislead them, and that the interpretations are in almost every passage disputable, they will of course not think it worth their while to consult such defective guides, and will prefer ignorance to error. In this, however, they will err most egregiously. The translations of Jones, Colebrooke, Wynch, and Sutherland are fully entitled to their confidence, and if read with attention and rendered familiar by frequent reference, they will convey very accurate notions both of the determined, and the doubtful points of Hindu law. Sir F. M's appropriation of the two last chapters of his own book to the publication of part of the translation of the Mitákshará by his son, Mr. W. Macnaghten, is rather at variance with the opinion he would seem to inculcate of the worthlessness of translations.

The first chapter of Sir F. Macnaghten's work is dedicated to the law of inheritance, and starts oddly enough with a paragraph declaring, once for all, that a widow cannot claim any property in right of her husband, of which he was not actually possessed. We have no objection to the law of the declaration, but its abrupt appearance in the van of the laws of inheritance is rather a violent and unnecessary dislocation.

The learned judge next lays down the following as the course of Inheritance.

1st. The primary rules of Inheritance are these—A (the original acquirer) shall be succeeded

1st. By his son, or sons—if no son, by
2d. His widow, or widows—if none, by
3d. His daughter, or daughters—if none, by
4th. His daughter's son or sons—if none, by
5th. His Father—if dead, by
6th. His mother—if dead, by
7th. His uterine brother or brothers—if none, by
8th. His brother or brothers of the half blood—if none, by
9th. Sons of uterine brothers—if none, by
10th. Sons of brothers of the half blood—if none, by
11th. Grandsons of uterine brothers—if none, by
12th. Grandsons of brothers of the half blood.

Here the succession in this line ceases. A's Estate will now go-back to the son or sons of his sisters, and their heirs; failing them, to his paternal grandfather,—then to his paternal grandfather's widow,—then to the paternal grandfather's sons and their heirs.

The order of succession, thus laid down by the learned Judge, appears to us to be very far from full or precise. The first article, for instance, states that the deceased is succeeded by his son or sons, and the second, if no son, by his widow or widows; but unless the term son implies also grandson, and great grandson, the statement is exceedingly inaccurate; for a widow inherits only if neither son, grandson, nor great grandson be in existence.*

The list, also, is much more brief than the detail

* [See Sir W. H. Macnaghten's Principles of Hindu and Mohammedan Law. London edition (1860), p. 18.]

required, and the learned Judge admits this, as upon closing it he states, he believes he has set forth a sufficient number of reversioners for all the purposes of utility, and refers to Mr. Wynch's table *, a very useful one no doubt, for the rest of the course; but it is in remote succession that disputes chiefly originate, and opinions differ: and in a work emanating from such a quarter we should have expected to have found such cases less summarily disposed of.

Upon the line of inheritance the learned judge observes, it is perhaps less disputable than any other part of the Hindu law, and this admission is rather irreconcileable with his previous assertion, that the whole is a nullity. In truth all authorities are agreed in the main series of inheritance, and the chief contradictions and incongruities arise out of what must be allowed to be an ample field for their occurrence, partition of property. As far, however, as the claimants are immediate, and exclusive, there is no more conflict of opinion amongst Hindu law-givers than our own: the same may be safely said on every other subject, and in all the leading features, in whatever light the learned Judge may have contemplated them, the aspect of the Hindu code is very reasonably uniform, and consistent.

With respect to the law of inheritance amongst the Hindus, it is regulated generally by the performance of funeral oblations: these consist in the first degree

* [Translation of the Dáya Krama Sangraha. Calcutta: 1818, ad ch. I.]

of the presentation of a cake of rice and meat to the manes of a father, grandfather, and great-grandfather, and the individual who offers the gift to all or any of these bears the same proportionable degree of affinity to the deceased. A son, for instance, offers them to all three, a grandson to two, a great-grandson to one, and a great-great-grandson to none, for which reason the direct line of succession does not come to him, a peculiarity noticed but not explained by our text.

2d. There is a peculiarity in the *Hindoo* law, as it relates to descent in the right line. The estate cannot descend to a *great-great*-grandson, unless there be an intermediate heir, through whom it may be conveyed. For instance, If A have a son B, B have a son C, C have a son D, and D have a son E; E will then be the *great-great*-grandson of A. Supposing then B, C, and D to die in the life time of A, E shall not upon A's death take the estate—nor shall he ever take it, if it does not come to him through a long course of reversioners. Yet if D had survived A, D would have taken as A's great-grandson, and E would have taken as D's son. If C had survived A, C would have taken as A's grandson, and E would have taken as C's grandson —or if B had survived A, B would have taken as A's son, and E would have taken as B's great-grandson.

The principle does not seem indeed to have been familiar to the learned judge, and he has therefore been led into ambiguity and error in his 28th rule: (p. 8) he says that

It does not follow that a person whose duty it is to perform the *śrdddha*, or funeral rites, shall succeed as heir to the estate; or that the person succeeding to the estate shall have the duty of performing the *śrdddha* cast upon him—

An assertion in which we believe all Hindu writers to be at variance with him—except that we may suppose him to intend to say, the heir is not obliged to give the funeral offering to the deceased. That is by no means necessary, but he must share in some of those which the deceased should have offered, as to the father or grandfather, or even more remote kinsmen: the relationship involving the presentation of a funeral cake extending to seven persons, and that of offering libations of water comprehending fourteen. Under one or other of these denominations, therefore, it is highly probable that the heir will come, and he will consequently perform *Funeral rites.*

In illustration of his remark, Sir F. states that the

> Sons of a sister may succeed to the estate, but they cannot perform the *śráddha* except in the absence of relations in the male line, or except in a case in which it may be performed by any person of the same *caste* or tribe. So if there be sons of a sister, the sons of a male cousin cannot succeed to the estate, and yet it will be their duty to perform the *śráddha* in preference to the sister's sons.

But this passage is far from accurate. The sons of a sister in Bengal inherit before the son of a male cousin, precisely because they do offer funeral oblations in closer connexion with the deceased than the latter, as stated in the *Dáya Krama Sangraha*, where accordingly the following rules are expressed:

"On failure of the brother's grandson the succession goes to the father's daughter's son, for he presents *three* funeral oblations", D. C. S. p. 18;—again,

"Failing the uncle's son, the uncle's grandson succeeds, for he presents *one* oblation",—Ibid. 21.*

* [Calcutta edition (1828), p. 8 & 9.]

A rigid regulation of the right to succession by the funeral oblations is, however, peculiar to Bengal, having been adopted as a general principle by Jímútaváhana. In other parts of India the criterion is admitted only partially, and in the very case under examination is not allowed to regulate the order of the inheritance. The law, therefore, as stated by the learned Judge, is defined as loosely as the principle, for it is *only in Bengal* that a sister's son succeeds in preference to the son of a male cousin.* The authorities of the Benares and Maithilá schools do not admit the claims of a sister's son, and remove him very far from the succession. In fact, his rights are not noticed at all, and can only come under the class of cognate or remote kinsmen—those sprung from a different family, but connected by funeral oblations. The reason why a sister's son is thus excluded is, that he belongs to a different family: at the same time the participation in funeral rites, and the argument of analogy induce some of the commentators on the text of the Mitákshará, as Bálambhaṭṭa, and Nanda Paṇḍita, to endeavour to explain away the omission of a sister's son by supposing the term Brother's sons to imply sister's sons also: the rationale however of the opposite arrangement is sufficiently obvious, and no doubt of the real purport of the authorities can be entertained: a sister's son carries the property of the family away from it into that of her husband; whilst by a descent in the male

* [Dáyabhága. Calcutta: 1829, p. 326.]

line it accompanies the name and direct derivation,—and although, therefore, in harmony with provincial and modern notions, the learned Judge's definition of the law of succession in this case, as connected with a share in the funeral rites, appears to have been founded on an imperfect and partial view of both questions.*

The remainder of this chapter is occupied with the discussion of the question as to the rights of a widow over property to which she succeeds upon the death of a husband, illustrated by the answers of the Puńdits to the enquiries of the court. It is stated, that by former decisions the widow took *moveable* property *absolutely*, and *immoveable* property *for life only*, but it has been since thought, that there is not any ground for such a distinction, and that the widow takes but a life estate in moveable as well as immoveable property. There is no doubt of the object of the law, which declares that a widow succeeding to her husband's estate shall enjoy it until her death, and that the husband's heirs are to succeed to it; nor have we any objection, nor is there any in the *spirit* of the Hindu law for the court to interfere, to control the widow's expenditure of her property**: at the same time we are not satisfied that this assumption of power is warranted by the *letter* of the law.

* [Sir Th. Strange, Hindu Law. London: 1830, I, 146 f.]

** [ib. I, 134. 176. 246 f. II, 250 ff. Sir W. H. Macnaghten, l. l., 19 ff.]

There are but two ancient texts which bear positively on the widow's power over the property which she inherits as her husband's sole heir. One is attributed to Kátyáyana, and states "Let the childless woman preserving (inviolate) the couch of her lord, and obedient to her spiritual guide, enjoy, resigned, her husband's wealth until her death: afterwards let the heir take it."* The other is from the Mahábhárata, which as law, by the bye, is no authority at all. "Enjoyment is the fruit which women derive from the heritage of their Lords,—on no account should they make away with the estate of their lords."[1] Such are the ancient injunctions; which can scarcely be interpreted to mean, that if a widow gives away or sells her estate, such gift or sale is invalid. Even the later writers who entertained less reverence for the female character than the ancient sages, have stopped short of such declaration, and Jímútaváhana is content to say that "a widow shall only enjoy the estate; she *ought not* to give it away, mortgage or sell it."† He

---

[अपुत्रा शयनं भर्त्तुः पालयन्ती गुरौ स्थिता
भुञ्जीतामरणात्क्षान्ता दायादा ऊर्द्धमाप्नुयुः ॥
Víramitr., 194, r, 7. Vivádachint., p. 140, 7. Dáyakramasangraha, p. 2.]

[1] Apahri, Take off or away: it is translated in the Digest and elsewhere, "waste", which perhaps scarcely renders its due import. [According to the Dáyakramasangraha the passage is taken from the Dánadharma of the Anuśásanaparva (?):

स्त्रीणां स्वपतिदायस्तु उपभोगफलः स्मृतः ।
नापहारं स्त्रियः कुर्युः पतिदायात्कथञ्चन ॥]

† [See Dáyabhága, p. 265.]

allows her also, if unable to subsist otherwise, to mortgage or even to sell it, and to make presents to her husband's relatives and gifts or other alienations for the spiritual benefit of the deceased. It is not till we come to the third generation of lawyers, the commentators on the commentators, that the restriction is positive, and Śrí Kríshńa Tarkálankára expounding Jímútaváhana's text declares, "a widow shall use her husband's heritage for the support of life; and make donations, and give alms in a moderate degree for the benefit of her husband, but not dispose of it at her pleasure like her own peculiar property." The utmost that can be inferred from all this, is, that originally the duty of the widow was only pointed out to her, and she was left in law as she was in reason, a free agent, to do what she pleased with that which was her own; but that in later times attempts of an indefinite nature have been made to limit her power. The eagerness with which this latter doctrine is urged by the Scholiasts of the present day is ascribable in all probability to that contempt for the female sex which they have learned from their Mohammedan masters. The willingness with which it has been admitted by English Lawyers is owing no doubt to a conviction of the expedience of the doctrine, unbiassed, we trust, by prejudices either of Indian or English growth.

The learned judge observes, that with regard to immoveable property, so far as a widow is concerned, he has been unable to trace any distinction in Hindu law. We agree with him in as far as her *absolute* right is admitted over *both;* but if this is not conceded, then there is a very easily traceable distinction, for it is made by the same authorities, the modern lawyers, and it is on the very same grounds, those of analogy, that the limitation of a right over immoveable, and absolute right in moveable property, are maintained. The author of the Vivàda Ratnákara, and Vivàda Chintámańi, for example, assert that a wife may give moveable effects, gems, and the like, devolving on her by succession to her husband. Jímútaváhana is only *supposed* to hold a different opinion because he uses the word *Dhanam,* wealth in general, in restricting the widow's authority over wealth she inherits to a life interest; to which, however, as noticed, he admits the exception of charitable donations, and actual necessity: but the chief argument made use of against a widow's aliening her husband's estate is a law attributed to Nárada, that she may enjoy at her pleasure property *given her* by her husband, *or give it away* after his death, *except land or houses;* therefore, say the lawyers, *she cannot give away land or houses which she inherits.* Of course, if the exception applies to both cases, the permission holds equally good in both, and the same analogy that restricts the widow in immoveable effects recognises her right over moveable or personal property: notwithstanding, therefore, the court thought proper to reverse their own decree in the case of Hurasundari and Casinath Baisakh, and after acknowledging in 1814 her absolute interest in the moveable property of her husband, rescinding that admission in 1819; and notwithstanding the opinion declared from the bench that with respect to a widow's right there is no distinction between moveable and immovable property, and that she has no more than life interest in either, we believe it to be established by undeniable analogy, and the declared opinion of at least equal authorities, that there *is* a distinction between moveable and immoveable property, as regards a widow's rights, and that if we are guided by the old Hindu law, unsophisticated by modern subtlety, and forced analogies, a widow has *an absolute interest* in both. As to the Vyavasthá on which the opinions of the court, we presume, were formed, we never saw more superficial law nor palpable contradiction in any we ever perused. It may be worth while to examine it at some length.

1. The Court Pańdits asserted that "the Dáyabhága and *other* Śástras current in Bengal make no distinction between moveable and immoveable property." Without knowing what these other Śástras are, we cannot estimate the value of this reply: we have no objection to admit that Jímútaváhana makes no distinction.

2. "A widow has a life interest in both." The texts of ancient sages are equally current everywhere, and as far as their obvious acceptation extends, of which we have as good a right to judge as Jímútaváhana, they do not oppose the widow's absolute right over both: consequently,

3. "A widow is entitled to dispose of the same by

"gift, mortgage, sale, or otherwise for the benefit of "her husband's soul."

4. "It is incumbent upon a widow to act as her hus-"band's kinsmen direct."

The Viváda Bhangárńava, a Bengal authority, declares "a widow has no lord, and may therefore do as she likes."

5. "The gift of immoveable property is not valid "against herself or the next heir: the same of move-"able property and jewels which might be recovered "by her, or the next heir, the same as money."

Now this we deny in toto—whatever a widow may be recommended not to do, as she is not commanded not to do, she may do, and a breach of a moral injunction is punishable only in the breakers: the person who receives the donation, having received that of which the alienation is not expressly forbidden, has done no wrong: why punish him? the gift of the whole estate, therefore, is valid. The learned judge observes very correctly that it seems exceedingly absurd, that persons should be able to make a valid disposal of property which they have no right to dispose of at all, and that that which is immoral, and sinful, and prohibited, should still be good in law. We wonder it never occurred to him that the *validity* of the gift was an argument in favour of the *legality*: but this is really the case.

The old lawyers have said, 'let a widow enjoy a husband's wealth, afterwards let the heirs take it': what obligation does this involve that she *must leave it?* But she is told she should not waste it,—granted: but suppose she sells it, is that waste? Now as to the gift, the same authorities, from whom there is no appeal, define what things are alienable as gifts and what are not. Amongst the things not alienable no mention is made of a widow's inheritance. The *whole* estate of a man, if he have issue living, or if it be ancestral property, he cannot give away, without the assent of the parties interested, and this may indeed be thought to apply to the *immoveable* property inherited by a widow, but it is the only law that can be so applied: there being, therefore, no law against the validity of her donation, it follows that she has absolute power over the property: at least such was the case, till a new race of law-givers, with Jímútaváhana at their head, chose to alter it; but they only tampered with the law of inheritance, and the law respecting legal alienation being untouched, remains to bear testimony against their interpretation of a different branch of the law.

6. "A widow has not absolute interest in either "moveable or immoveable property. She has not an "uncontrolled interest, she can do nothing of her own "authority."

This last position is contradicted by a Bengal authority, as we have seen, and by the daily practice of all India. Who controlled Ahalyá Bháí?

7. "The widow has a right to the *possession of the* "*moveable property*, to which she succeeds, subject to "the control before mentioned."

We presume by possession is meant having it in her hands, or at her command. How else can she enjoy it. There is nothing that can be tortured into an assertion that her husband's relations, or any other individuals, private or public, have a right to withhold from the widow's own coffers whatever jewels or money she inherits—and, having such property in her hands, who is to prevent her making away with it? Such are the absurdities in which an attempt to limit a widow's absolute right over 'moveable' property has involved the modern Hindu law: the ancient lawgivers were too wise to attempt impossibilities—they gave the widow good advice, but abstained from legislating what it was impossible to enforce.

8. "The relations of her husband cannot dispossess "her of that property, but they may control her in the "use of it."

If they cannot do the one, they cannot do the other: if they cannot take the money from her, how is it possible they can prevent her spending it? By an injunction of the *Supreme Court*, indeed, and the consignment of the funds to the care of the *Master*, it may be, and has been done: this we know: but we have yet to learn that it is *Hindu* law.

9. "There *is no difference* in the interest taken by "a woman in property derived from partition with her "sons, and what she inherits upon her husband's death "without issue." On this point we shall join issue presently—in the mean time, see what immediately follows.

10. "We are of opinion that the most eligible mode "would be to consider it as *Stridhana.*" That is *property over which a woman has absolute power.*

These learned sages, therefore, in the course of half a dozen replies, assert that a widow has a life interest only over property which she solely inherits, and an absolute interest in property which she divides with her sons, and *yet there is no difference.* Oh wise and consistent expounders of the law, we have done with your Vyavasthá!

Next came a knot of five Bengali Pańdits, who are made to say: The Pańdits of the Court have quoted the Dáyabhága as their authority; *therefore we differ from them in opinion.* Now really we cannot conceive these Pańdits ever used any such expression: the Dáyabhága is unquestionably very high authority in Bengal, and for a Pańdit of this province to make its citation the ground of dissent surpasses our conception. They might indeed decline to admit its authority as far as inconsistent with older works, as would seem to be implied in what follows. "There are older treatises of law by which donation of property by a person who has not uncontrolled authority over it is declared void." Granted, but to what except moral control is a widow subjected? In fact, they admit that, although a widow ought not to aliene her husband's property, yet that the disposal is valid, and they also assert the widow's absolute power over the moveable part of the property.

Two other Pańdits agreed with the Court Pańdits:

that is, they admitted there was no difference between life interest, and absolute interest; they asserted, however, that a gift was not valid against the heir—"who might reclaim it". We should like to know upon what authority.

We quite agree with the learned judge, that with such guides it was not easy to arrive at the right conclusion: but this was not the fault of the Law. The spirit and the text of the original law, in our estimation, recognise the widow's absolute right over property inherited from a husband, in default of male issue.* In Bengal the authorities that are universally received have altered this law and restrict a widow to the usufruct of her husband's property. They have not, however, provided for its security, nor for its recovery if aliened, and by such neglect have virtually left the law as they found it, or the power if not the right of alienation with the widow: it is open to the court, therefore, to make what regulations on this subject they please, as far as their jurisdiction extends, and as far as they are authorised by the Charter; and the regulation most conformable to reason, to analogy, and the spirit of the Hindu code, would be to give the widow absolute power over personal property, and restrict her from the alienation of the estate, except with the concurrence of her husband's heirs.

The second division of Sir F. Macnaghten's work

* [Mitáksh. ad Yájn. II, 135. Vivádachintámani, p. 151. Víramitrod., p. 193, a. Vyavahára Mayúkha, IV, 8, 2 ff.]

treats of the partition of property, made amongst the parties themselves,—partition amongst others, by the sole owner in possession, being, in our opinion not very methodically, transposed to a future chapter. The learned judge then seems to take it for granted the subject is familiar to his readers; for, without stating either the law or the practice, he begins with considering a case which he admits he does not know ever to have occurred, the right of a great-grandmother to share with her great-grandsons,—on which after a discussion, which appears to us very unprofitable, and very unnecessary, he allows the old lady a share, provided some more immediate descendant is a party. It is scarcely worth while to discuss the case, but it seems to us very easily settled. If the partition is made of a husband's property, his widow and his mother have a right to their shares,—but whenever the character of that property is changed by transmission to persons not inheriting of the deceased husband in the degree of son or grandson, their right ceases. There is another criterion, too, by which the question may be settled, "partition is co-ordinate with the gift of the funeral cake,"* and that extends to the great-grandson. A great-grandson taking a share of his great-grandfather's undivided property, of course implies the great-grandmother's participation, and then she will share as he does. The learned judge does not seem

* [Yájnav., I, 132. Dáyabh., p. 326. 157. पिण्डदोंऽशहरः, पिण्डप्रत्यासत्तिक्रमेणाधिकारः, and the like.]

to have been put in possession of the principle, nor even of the letter of the law by the Pańdit of the court, who in reply to his queries, "invariably said the law is silent." For the author of the Digest propounds and answers the very question. "When property left by "the paternal great-grandfather is divided, should not "a share be allowed to his wife? That is admissible "from parity of reasoning, and the particle in the "phrase, "and wives of the grandfather", connects the "terms with what is understood but not expressed": 3, 24. The case, however, is of very unlikely occurrence, and to legislate for improbabilities is a work of supererogation. It seems, however, to be a favourite topic with the learned judge, for he twice recurs to it in this chapter, in rules 13 and 27, and after all, in our estimation, gives the law incorrectly.

The learned judge then proceeds to examine the rights of a woman derived from partition with her sons, and declares it as his opinion, that they are of precisely the same description as those with which she is invested as sole heir, and that she has but a life interest in both moveable and immoveable property so acquired.

In the case of the widow's sole inheritance, we have granted that the Bengal lawyers limit her in all respects to a life interest, whilst the *Mithilá* writers maintain her absolute right in moveables, and the old law authorities oppose nothing to her absolute right in every kind of property. In the case of property, however, acquired by partition, the arguments in favour of absolute right are infinitely stronger, in as much as the Bengal authorities lean to the same view of the subject. Jímútaváhana starts no objection to such power, his remark being confined entirely to the case of sole inheritance, and the Viváda Bhangárńava concludes a long and satisfactory discussion of the question by the corollary, "Therefore a wife's sale or donation of her own share is valid." We are, therefore, very much at a loss to conceive upon what grounds the learned Judge has assimilated a widow's rights as derived from inheritance or partition, or on what the "Supreme Court has considered them on the same footing." We cannot help being amused with the additional remark, "if it ever had been doubted, the "two decisions of which I have spoken are sufficient "to set the question at rest." (p. 45.) For what are those decisions? "That the parties take both moveable and immoveable property—*according to the rules of the Hindoo law*;" leaving the task of establishing the Hindu law for another law-suit. If these are the decisions that are to take the place of Hindu law, Heaven help the litigants.

It is asserted, indeed, that a husband's heirs succeed to such property in preference to a woman's own heirs, and therefore her enjoyment of it is only for life: but the postulate is supported only by analogy, not by any positive law, and therefore the inference is by no means proved: besides, even if admitted, preference of succession does not imply restriction of right in possession: our law of primogeniture does not preclude, under ordinary circumstances, the father's right to sell, give, or bequeath his property as he pleases; and why should any order of succession exercise such influence here, when not specially provided for? "Heritage, and partition" are included by the text of the Mitákshará, which is good law in every part of India, even in Bengal, amongst the constituents of "woman's property", and a woman is acknowledged by all to be mistress of her own wealth. It is argued, that lands and houses *given by a husband* to his wife must not be aliened by her after his death: *therefore,* a share of land and houses *given by his sons* on partition of his wealth, must not be made away with by their mother; but this is surely a different case. A husband, in undue fondness, might bestow upon a wife the *heritage of his sons,* and they would be deprived of that patrimony in which *they have a joint interest with the father:* it is not unwise, therefore, to secure to them the reversion of such effects. In the case of partition, however, they are already secured: they cannot be left destitute, and if the property is ample, as it always is in contested causes, they are fully provided for by the possession of their respective shares. Again, as the partition is their own act, a mother cannot enforce it, although it cannot be made without her consent. In acquittance then of her claims, in order to induce her to forego her lien upon the whole, the sons give her up her part: they then only become fully masters of their own shares, and it would be an unfair bargain if they did not admit the mother's free disposal of what may be considered the purchase money of their privileges.*

Sir F. Macnaghten admits that if it could be considered as an act of free will, the widow's share in a partition might be recognised as the gift of her sons, and consequently "as the gift of kind relations" would be placed at her absolute disposal: but he observes, she may be influenced by one son in contradiction to the will of the rest, and as partition takes place at the desire of any one of the co-heirs, they will then be compelled to relinquish the mother's share against their consent. This may be granted as a possible evil resulting from the law, but it does not alter the character of the law, and therefore, whatever may be the case in a widow's sole inheritance, we see no grounds whatever for restricting her interest in the property which she derives from partition, to a life interest only, whether the property be real or personal. It is absurd to say that a woman was not intended to be a free agent, because the old Hindu legislators have indulged in general declarations of her unfitness for that character. Manu, it is true, says of women "Their fathers protect them in childhood, their husbands protect them in youth, their sons protect them in age. A woman is never fit for independence":** but what does this prove in respect to their civil rights? Nárada goes farther, and asserts, that "after a husband's decease the nearest kinsman should control a widow, who has *no*

---

* [See also Sir T. Strange, l. l. I, 246 ff.] ** [XI, 3.]

sons, in expenditure and conduct."* But as we have observed this is neither the law, nor the practice of the present day. Besides it does not apply to the case of partition, as there the widow has sons, and they surely abandon a right to control property which they themselves have given. To sanction any other mode of procedure would only tend to perpetuate the degraded condition of the female sex in India. Admit that at present widows are generally unfit to be entrusted with the absolute disposal of property that devolves upon them by virtue of partition with their sons. Is not that to be mainly ascribed to the restrictions with which they are already fettered? Accustom them to consider themselves as likely to be invested with important trusts; accustom their kinsmen and parents to contemplate them in the same capacity, and all parties will become interested in qualifying them to discharge with ability and conscientiousness the duties to which they may be called. Sir F. M. thinks that "a life interest will secure to the mother a greater degree of peace, and contentment than she is likely to enjoy after having a proportion of the family property at her own absolute disposal." If neglect be essential to peace and contentment, she may certainly expect their enjoyment: her sons and grandsons, secure of the reversion of the principal upon her death, will think it very immaterial how they treat a mother during life who has no power to reward affection or punish undutiful-

* [quoted in the Dáyabhága, p. 269.]

ness: the bands of domestic life are already too lax in India to be further unloosed with advantage, and the authority of parents, particularly that of the mother, is too tottering to be further undermined without being utterly subverted. Although, therefore, we give the learned judge full credit for the humanity of his intentions, we think he has adopted a hasty and partial view of a mother's rights, and that the restriction to the extent he proposes would be productive of infinitely more evil than good.

A number of rules, affecting chiefly the rights of females in the case of partition, then follow. In general we believe the law is correctly stated, although there is any thing but distinctness in the detail or method in the arrangement; the rules seem to have been laid down at random, with little regard to order, and with abundant carelessness of repetition. Thus we have the same question as to a great-grandmother's rights discussed in three different places, as we have already noticed, and the argument of the identity of a widow's rights by inheritance, or partition, which had twice been most fully discussed, p. 11, to 27, and p. 31, to 37, is again the subject of animadversion in p. 73, 74, and 93, 97. We shall not imitate the learned judge's example, nor again go over the principles, on which we offer his doctrine. We are satisfied that in the cases in which the decisions of the court, awarding an absolute interest in moveable property to a widow sharing on partition, have been reversed, the tenor of authority, the guide of analogy, and the spirit of the law, have been entirely misconceived.

The laws of partition amongst the Hindus have been always the fruitful source of family dissension. The perusal of this section of Sir Francis Macnaghten's work removes all astonishment at this circumstance; for the conflicting claims become in time so complicated, that it is almost impossible to unravel them. It is evident, however, that the difficulty really arises not from the mere law of partition, but the delay of the practice. It is the attempt to maintain unanimity that engenders disputes; if Hindu families would take our advice, they would never attempt to hold property in common, but make an absolute and final division, the moment they became possessed of it. It is quite impossible as descendants multiply, that they should not disagree, and in proportion to their number, and variety of relation, is the intricacy of their pretensions. Then, as Sir F. remarks of the cause of Govindchurn Baisakh, *v.* Casinath, Ramnath, and Bishonath Baisakh, "come bills, cross bills, and pleadings, in every variety of litigation, and the contest only ceases with the funds of the litigants." That cause, for example, began in 1808, and is still carried on between the sons of Govindchurn and their Cousins, with unabated pertinacity. The following case is illustrative of the complex interests involved in these disputes.

IN EQUITY.

Sree Moottee Jeeomony Dossee, the widow and legal representative of *Gungachurn Ghose*, deceased, and *Sree Moottee Dossee Dossee*, widow and legal representative of *Buddenchunder Ghose*, complainants,

AGAINST

Attaram Ghose and *Callachund Ghose*, defendants.

The bill stated, and it was proved, that *Corrunnamoyee Dossee* and *Luckapriah Dossee* were resident at *Chandernagore*, and not subject to the Jurisdiction of the Supreme Court.

The prayer of the bill was for an account and partition of the state of *Kissenmohun Ghose*, deceased,—and that one-fourth equal part or share of the said state might be allotted to each of the complainants.

The bill also prayed an account and partition of the estate of the said *Kissenmohun Ghose*, as against the defendant *Callachund Ghose* in particular,—and of all profits and purchases made by *Callachund Ghose*, with, or out of the estate of, *Kissenmohun Ghose*, since the death of the said *Kissenmohun Ghose*; and that each of the complainants be decreed one-*third* equal part or share of the said last mentioned estate, to be held in severalty by them the said complainants.

The state of the family was as follows:—*Kissenmohun Ghose* died in the Bengal year 1192, leaving two widows, viz. *Corrunnamoyee Dossee* and *Luckapriah Dossee*, who are still living.

By *Corrunnamoyee Dossee*, *Kissenmohun Ghose* left three sons, viz. *Gungachurn Ghose*, who died in the month of *Bhadur* in the Bengal year 1207; *Buddenchund Ghose*, who died in the month of *Joistee* in the Bengal year 1216, and *Callachund Ghose*, who is still living and one of the defendants. By *Luckapriah Dossee* he left *Attaram Ghose*, who is still living and the other defendant.

Gungachurn Ghose had married two wives, first *Joyah Dossee*, who died in the life time of her husband, and in the Bengal year 1201. She left one son, *Sumboochunder Ghose, who survived* his father *(Gungachurn)* and died in the month of *Shrabun*, in the Bengal year 1215. The other wife of *Gungachurn* is the complainant, *Jeeomonee Dossee*. She had a daughter *Roopah Dossee* by *Gungachurn*, and *Roopah Dossee* is since dead.

Buddenchund Ghose left one widow, the complainant *Dossee Dossee*, by whom he had one daughter only *(Doyamoyee Dossee)*. *Doyamoyee Dossee* is still living and married to *Kissenchunder Cowar*. *Callachund*, the other son of *Kissenmohun* by *Corrunnamoyee*, and *Attaram*, the *only* son of *Kissenmohun* by *Luckapriah*, are the two defendants.

The defendant *Attaram Ghose* not only refrained from opposing the partition as between him and the other claimants under *Kissenmohun*, but alleged that a partition had already been actually made.

An account and partition of the estate of *Kissenmohun* was in the first place ordered as between the other claimants uuder *Kissenmohun* and him *(Attaram)*, he being declared entitled to one-fourth part or share thereof as one of the four sons of *Kissenmohun*. *Attaram*, then, being *solely* entitled to a *fourth separate* part of the estate of *Kissenmohun*, it was understood and admitted, that his mother *Luckapriah* was *not* entitled to any separate property upon a partition made between her *only* son and his three half brothers, and that she was to look to him for her maintenance.

If *Sumboochunder*, the son of *Gungachurn* and *Joyah Dossee*, had died in the life time of his father, it seemed to be agreed, *(Joyah Dossee* having died before her husband,) that *Jeeomonee* the surviving wife of *Gungachurn* wonld have been entitled to his estate; but *Sumboochunder* haviug survived his father, it was held that his father's estate vested in him, and that *Jeeomonee*, (not being his mother, although the wife of his father) could not take from him, *(Sumboochunder)* but that his *father's mother*, *(Corrunnamoyee)* was his heir.

It was also declared that *Dossee Dossee*, the widow of *Buddenchund*, he *(Buddenchund)* not having left a son, succeeded as his heir, and was in his right entitled to one-fourth part of *Kissenmohun's* estate.

It was therefore ordered that a partition be made of the estate of *Kissenmohun*, that it be divided into four equal parts or shares and that *Attaram*, the only son of *Kissenmohun* by *Luckapriah*, do take one of the said *four* parts or shares in severalty.

Of the other three parts it was ordered that *Corrannamoyee* do take one as the heir of her grandson *Sumboochunder*, that *Dossee Dossee* do take one as the heir of her husband *Buddenchund*—and that *Callachund* do take one as the survivor of *Kissenmohun's* son.

This partition having been made, it was further declared *Corrunnamoyee* was entitled to a *fourth* part of the *three* which had been so divided, the *third* part which she had taken upon partition contributing to make up the said *fourth* part. It then stood thus,—*Corrunnamoyee*, the representative of *Sumboochunder*, *Dossee Dossee*, the representative of *Buddenchunder*, and *Callachund*, the surviving son of *Kissenmohun*, having come to a partition—*Corrunnamoyee* as mother of *Sumboochunder's* father, as mother of *Dossee Dossee's* husband, and as mother of *Callachund*, became, upon a partition, entitled to a share equal to that of the several partitioners.

The *three* parts were therefore again to be consolidated and then divided into *four*, of which *Corrunnamoyee* as mother was to have one,—the same *Corrunnamoyee* as representing her grandson, one—*Dossee Dossee* as representing her husband, one—and *Callachund* in his own right, one.

Supposing then the three parts (*Attaram* having taken the fourth) to be divided into *twenty-four* parts, *Corrunnamoyee* would have eight, *Dossee Dossee* eight, and *Callachund* eight;—*Corrunnamoyee* then for the purpose of converting the *three twenty-fourths* into *four twenty-fourths* must contribute *two* parts out of the *eight* she had taken,—and *Dossee Dossee* and *Callachund* must each contribute *two* parts out of their *eight*. Then each (*Corrunnamoyee* in her different characters being considered as two) will have *one-fourth* or six twenty-fourth parts. The result will be, that two-eighths of the share of *Dossee Dossee* and two-eighths of the share of *Callachund* will be added to the eight twenty-fourths of *Corrunnamoyee*, who will thereby have eight twenty-fourths and four twenty-fourths, or one half of that part of *Kissenmohun's* estate which went immediately from *Kissenmohun* to her own sons. She is now entitled to twelve twenty-fourths or one half of three parts of *Kissenmohun's* estate.

It was also ordered that *Corrunnamoyee* (not being a party to the suit) be at liberty (if she shall please to do so) to come in as a complainant before the Master in taking the account, and before the commissioners in making a partition of *Kissenmohun's* estate.

It is to be observed that on the death of *Dossee Dossee* her daughter *Doyamoyee* will succeed through her *(Dossee Dossee)* to the estate of her *(Doyamoyee's)* father *Buddenchund.*

As to *Jeeomonee*, she has a right to maintenance out of her husband's estate, and may follow it for the purpose of obtaining her right into the hands of *Corrunnamoyee;* but from what has been already said, it is needless to state that she may now, if she has just cause, require security as to her rights—or perhaps the Court would have been, at the hearing, justified in ordering her maintenance to be secured. It was not asked, and she having gone for a specific proportion, and having failed in that, was I presume not apprehensive of the want of a maintenance during her life. If she has grounds for fear, she may yet come in for it upon petition.

Another case which arose out of disputes in Muddun Baisakh's family is cited in this chapter as illustrative of the effect given to a will, in the Supreme Court, and the right of a widow as heir to a husband: it is of considerable interest, but too long to be cited. We notice the result for the "grave and important question" it involves, as stated by the learned judge. Sentence was given in favour of the widow Hura Sundari, and she was declared entitled to her husband's estate, to be possessed, used, and enjoyed by her in the manner prescribed by Hindu law. Accordingly it was ordered that the principal, and accumulated interest then in the hands of the Accountant-general should be paid over to her. Her husband's brothers appealed against the decree for various reasons, but chiefly "because the decree declared Hura Sundari *entitled* to the *possession* of her husband's estate, whereas, she being entitled to the *use* and *enjoyment* only, it ought to be secured *in the hands of an officer of the court*, or *deposited with the relations* of Bishonath, who will after the death of Hoorasoondaree be entitled to it", assumptions that speak for themselves, as it is clear the Hindu law could not recognise *an officer* of an *English* court of justice, and common sense would deprecate the consignment of property to interested relations.

The Supreme Court, however, thought differently, and,

> The petition of appeal having been filed, it became necessary, if she took the money, to give security for its restoration in case the order should be reversed. She did not do so, and the principal sum with its accumulations up to the date of the order are still in the Accountant General's hands.

The learned judge observes,

> That it has been usual to give a widow, or a mother, *possession* of the property to which she may succeed, must be admitted —and that the money of her husband's estate would, had it not been for the appeal, have gone into the hands of *Hoorasoondaree Dossee,* is certain. Yet the right of her husband's heirs to it after her death is indisputable, and the justice of restraining her from waste is a necessary consequence of this right.
>
> What then is to be done? Possession will enable her to do all the mischief, before any restraint can be applied.

In our opinion this case is conclusive of a widow's rights to moveable or personal property. If it is not to be placed in the widow's own hands, to whom is it to be entrusted? certainly not to those, who are interested in dispossessing her of it. Does the Hindu law enact that it shall be deposited with any other person?—if not, it follows it must go to the widow herself, and she must have the power to do what she pleases with it. The original Hindu Legislators never brought themselves into such a dilemma: they conceded a right where they could not prevent its exercise. Lands and houses could not be made away with without formalities that admitted the interposition of authority, but money and jewels could not be restrained, and therefore they did not attempt to legislate for their appropriation. The learned Judge argues that the discipline of Hindu widows is relaxed, and that they are not under the same control as formerly: what proof have we of this, and even if true what right has the Supreme Court to legislate for this new state of things? They are to administer justice to the Hindus according to the laws and usages of the Hindus, and we believe it would be difficult to fancy any allusion in either to a Master in Chancery or Accountant General. If the laws are bad, abrogate them: substitute English Law at once; but it is mockery to regulate decisions by institutions and arrangements wholly foreign to the Hindu system, and call the hybrid monstrosity Hindu Law.

The learned Judge observes that the reversioner's right is as well founded as that of the widow; but he has by no means proved the nature of that right. In our estimation it is not absolute, but contingent. The law is simply "after her death let the heirs take it." So with us it is said "inheritance shall lineally descend to the issue of the person, who last died, actually seized", but does not therefore render it imperative that the property must be transmitted to the heirs. The rule in either case applies to property left, and cannot be said to give to the reversioners a right or control over the acts of the possessor.

Again who are these reversioners whom the learned Judge is so anxious to protect? and in answering this question we do not wish to dispute the equity, but the necessity, of their being made the objects of legal protection. Where a widow inherits as sole heir, there can be no nearer heir than a daughter, who in the constitution of Hindu society, we may be well assured, is married or will be at the mother's charge: she is therefore in her own person provided for, and if the property goes to her, it is transferred to another family, unconnected probably by name or descent with that of the deceased. In this case we should think it very immaterial whether the integral inheritance was preserved or not, as far as the interests of general society, the only interests that should be looked to, are concerned.

If there be no daughter nor daughter's sons, the estate will go to the husband's brothers: here it remains in the family, but what necessity is there for the apportionment? The brothers should not be in want, as they have already divided during the life time of the owner the patrimonial property, and have received a share severally equal to that of which the posthumous apportionment is in question: it will be no very great hardship upon them, therefore, to be excluded from a remotely contingent share in that, to which as a whole they had long before foregone all claim.

The same argument applies to a widow's rights upon partition. The sons and grandsons, and even great-grandsons, have had their shares, and the final alienation of a fraction, to which they assented for their mother's life, cannot expose them to distress—unless, indeed, the certain reversion of additional property at the end of the mother's life time, an event which they will be then tempted to desire, if not to expedite, should render them less careful of what they actually possess, and thus operate as a bounty upon extravagance. On the ground, therefore, of necessity, and in our estimation of expediency also, we deny the claim of the reversioners to that peculiar protection, which the learned judge is inclined to extend to them.

In page 56 the learned judge has explained the law relating to the portions of sisters, and concludes that they have a claim rather than a right. In page 97 he reverts to the subject thus:

> I do not expect that the value of what I now add will compensate for the irregularity of introducing it here. After my *manuscript* had gone to the press, I prepared this to be introduced at page 56, but it was mislaid; and when discovered, the printing had advanced too far to admit of its insertion in the proper place.

His conclusions are to the same effect, and whatever

may be the law, we admit the practice: originally, however, a sister claimed a fourth of a son's share. The commentators have made this simple law very indistinct by their explanation, supposing it to be necessary first to set apart a son's share, and then to give a daughter one fourth of that: thus they say in the case of a brother and sister sharing, the estate shall be divided into two equal parts: the son shall take one of these; the other is to be again divided into four, and one of those subdivisions shall go to the daughter; the rest shall devolve upon the son: consequently he will have seven-eighths, and the sister one-eighth, but we cannot conceive the law to sanction any such clumsy construction. It is true it does not authorise a sister's sharing in the whole estate to the extent of one fourth: because, in that case supposing six sons, and one daughter, the son would only take one-eighth, or half as much as the least worthy. Now this would be quite contrary to the spirit of the Hindu law. Again, a daughter cannot be said to take only one-fourth of one actual share equal to that of a son, because in the case of there being five or more daughters, all above four would go without any share at all. The inconsistencies of the law as thus understood are too obvious to have escaped the learned judge's notice; he has accordingly detailed them at considerable length, but he has offered no solution of the difficulty, nor attempted to explain, what is evidently the purpose of the law, and what involves no absurdity nor contradiction. A sister shall have the fourth part of a brother's own share: that is she shall divide with a brother in the proportion of one to three, or to state it more distinctly, a brother shall take seventy-five in the hundred, and the sister twenty-five. It is clear that, be the number of sisters, or brothers, what it may, this principle is of unvarying and ready application, and it is not the law, but the arithmetic of the case that has created any perplexity. We shall not dwell upon the subject here, as we shall have again occasion to advert to it, when we examine the similar principle which regulates the portion of adopted after the birth of natural sons. We may observe that, if the Court were to do what Sir F. M. supposes (p. 104) it might by virtue of the laws of Manu*, it would be just as bad arithmetic as that of the Hindu Scholiasts, and worse law: he states that, if there were three brothers, and one sister, and the estate 24,000 rupees, the court would declare the sister entitled to one-fourth or 6,000, placing the female heir on a par with the male in contradiction to the spirit of both English and Hindu law; the purport of which latter is clearly, that the brothers in such a case should receive each 7,200 rupees, and the sister 2,400 rupees. We have a mighty simple rule called Single Fellowship, which is the best comment upon the Hindu law that can be offered.**

* [IX, 118. Yájnav., II, 124.]

** [Sir W. H. Macnaghten, I. I., p. 54. Sir T. Strange, I. I., I., p. 173,]

The next division of Sir F. M.'s work is upon reunion, the return of a separated brother to the co-parcenary enjoyment of property: in fact, however, the chapter treats only of one circumstance connected with reunion or the rights of a separated uterine brother and united half-brother to inherit; it being held by some lawyers, that a connexion by blood confers priority of right whether united or separated, and by others, that reunion places a half-brother on a par with a whole brother and entitles him to an equal division of the inheritance. The learned judge admits that he knows no instance of such reunion, and the chief object of the section seems to be an attack upon the digest of Jagannáth, an exceedingly useful work, although it does not profess to save those who consult it the trouble of judging for themselves. As little practical benefit would result from the investigation of this subject, we shall not dwell upon it further.

The next section treats of a subject of great importance in Hindu law as giving rise to almost daily discussion, *Adoption*. A Hindu *must have* a son to extricate himself and his ancestors from a kind of purgatory, and if he have no children of his own he must adopt one. It is said indeed by Manu, that "amongst several brothers if one have a son they are all pronounced fathers of a male child"*, and it might be supposed unnecessary, therefore, for the uncles to adopt sons for themselves. Upon this Sir F. M. observes,

* [IX, 182, quoted and discussed in the Dattakamímánsá, II, 29 ff.]

Upon this particular point, the sum of all I have been able to collect out of books, or from living authorities, is, that in the three superior classes, if there be *brothers of the whole blood*, a son of *one* of them, *for religious purposes*, will be the son of *all;* and that, while this son exists, the childless brothers by the same father and mother need not adopt one for the performance of *sacred rites*. But that, in a secular point of view, a male child is not considered as the son of his father's brethren—and that to take the heritage *as a son* of his uncle, he must be adopted; that, temporally considered, he does not, as a son, derive any benefits from them, and that the son of a brother is *recommended*, in preference to all others, for adoption.

I find this explained, and I think satisfactorily, in an opinion given by *Govardhana*, some time since a *Paṅḍit* of the Supreme Court. He quotes *Vṛihaspati* as follows*:—If among several *uterine* brothers *one* have a son born, the *whole* are considered as fathers. These authorities declare a nephew even as a son to a childless uncle—*effecting, as a son would do,* the relief of his soul from the hell called *put*. It therefore follows that the adoption of any other son during the existence of such nephew *ought not* to take place, and that *he ought* to be preferred. *It must not* however be inferred that, because such nephew be equal to a son in *this one respect*, he is so in *any other without being qualified by adoption*—as, according to the following stanza of *Yájnavalkya*, *his title* to *inherit* his uncle's estate comes *after* that of the widow, daughter, daughter's son, father, mother, and uncle—whereas, *were he adopted,* he would *precede all these.*

There is another view of the subject, however, to which neither Govardhana nor the learned Judge has adverted, and which appears to us to afford a much more satisfactory conclusion, even than the arguments of the former. The son of a brother is only in a subordinate or subsidiary capacity of benefit to his uncle

---

* [See the Dattakamímánsá. Calcutta: 1834, p. 15, II, 71.]

in his own person, in the matter of religious rites. That is, he offers no funeral cake to his uncle's spirit, except under a special rule, the exact purport of which is not admitted, but is supposed to imply only a confirmation of the undisputed doctrine that the son of a brother should be preferably adopted: he benefits his uncle mediately in as far as he offers cakes to his grandfather and great-grandfather, the common ancestors of his father and his uncle. In these oblations the latter has a share, but if he die without a natural or adopted son, he loses the certainty of his own oblation, and will consequently run the risk of purgatory. To escape this chance, from which it is doubtful if the oblations of a nephew can secure him, he must adopt a son for himself, and it is therefore not only on secular but religious grounds that such adoption is imperative.* The text of Manu does not contradict this view of the case, and the expression occurs merely in illustration of the figurative application of the term *Son* to an adopted son, who can bear such relation *actually* only to his natural father, although he is considered to bear it *legally* to his adoptive parent. The conclusion affecting the right of uncles to adopt sons is Kullúka Bhaťťa's, not Manu's, and in this case and every other it may be observed, that the remarks of a scholiast, however high his character, do not debar the exercise of independent reasoning. A Pańďit of the present day, who should bring superior talent to

---

* [Sir T. Strange, l. l., I, p. 84 ff. Dattaka Chandriká I, 21 ff.]

the task, would be entitled to a preference over all preceding expositors. As to the legend from the Káliká Puráńa cited by Sir F. M. from the Dattaka Mímánsá*, it does not seem to us to bear materially on the question, and if it did it would signify little; for the *Puráńas* are not authorities in law. They may be received in explanation or illustration, but not in proof.

The right of an adopted son, to inherit collaterally, which has been the subject of much difference of opinion amongst the Pańdits, and variety of decisions in the courts, is next discussed by the learned Judge: with his usual disregard to arrangement however, he has made the same topic the subject of discussion in his preface, whilst in the same chapter, after some interval, he narrates the case of Gourbullukh *v.* Jagannath Prasad in which this subject was the question at issue, and illustrates it in the appendix by the opinions of 51 Pańdits belonging to the different Courts. We agree with him in his conclusions, that an adopted son, or the son given, has the right of collateral succession, and that its ever being contested shewed but a partial appeal to the authorities or the principles of Hindu law. The following is the view of the question we are disposed to advocate.

Twelve kinds of sons are enumerated by Manu and other writers. These sons are divided into two classes: those who are heirs and kinsmen (Dáyádás and Bán-

* [See Orianne, Droit Hindou. Paris 1845, p. 274. Dattakamimánsá. Calc. 1834, p. 11 f., and Sutherland's notes ad II, 45.]

dhavás), and those who are not heirs but kinsmen. It is agreed that a son of one kind or other, there being no son of a superior class in his way, takes the inheritance of his adoptive father, and the specification of them as heirs does not apply to his wealth, but to that of such persons as the father would be heir to in the event of their deaths; as "uncles and the rest", according to Maheśwara, and as Sapiṅḍas, or the paternal grandfather and others connected by the funeral cake, according to Jímútaváhana. There is no difference of opinion on these subjects, but the question is, which of the adopted sons inherit thus collaterally, and which do not, and here we have some difference of classification. We have taken some pains to ascertain the notions of the different authorities with respect to the comparative grade of the different sorts of adopted sons, and they seem to us to run as follows*:

AUTHORITIES.	*Manu.*	*Kátyáyana.*	*Baudháyana.*	*Vámana Pur.*	*Káliká Pur.*	*Yájnavalkya.*	*Yama.*	*Hárita.*	*Devala.*	*Nárada.*	*Vishnu.]*
The natural son (Aurasa) ..	1	1	1	1	1	1	1	1	1	1	1
A daughter's son(Putrikáputra)	0	0	2	0	0	2	3	5	2	3	3
Son of a wife (Kshetraja) ..	2	2	3	2	2	3	2	2	3	2	2
A son given (Dattaka)	3	3	4	3	3	7	9	7	9	9	8
A son made (Kṙitrima)	4	5	5	4	4	9	10	9	11	11	12

* [See Sir T. Strange, l. l., II, 194 ff. Manu IX, 166 ff. Yájnav. II, 128 ff. with the Mitákshará. Dattakachandriká, p. 60. Vivádachint., 147, 5. Vyavahára Mayúkha IV, 41 ff. Víramitrod., p. 184, v., 6 ff. Sir W. H. Macnaghten, l. l., p. 65 ff.]

AUTHORITIES.	Manu.	Kátyáyana.	Baudháyana.	Vámana Pur.	Kálika Pur.	Yájnavalkya.	Yama.	Hárita.	Devala.	Nárada.	Vishńu.
Son of unknown parentage (Gúdhotpanna).......	5	9	6	5	5	4	6	6	5	6	6
Son rejected (Apaviddha). , .	6	7	7	6	6	12	7	12	6	8	11
Son of an unmarried Girl (Kánina) .....,....	7	8	8	7	7	5	5	4	4	4	5
Son of a pregnant bride (Sahodha)...........	8	10	9	8	8	11	8	10	7	5	7
Son bought (Krita)	9	4	10	9	9	8	11	8	12	10	9
Son of a remarried widow (Paunarbhava).......	10	11	11	10	10	6	4	3	8	7	4
Son self-given (Swayamdatta)	11	6	12	11	11	10	12	11	10	12	10
Son of a Śúdra or a Slave (Śaudra)..,........	12	12	13	12	12	0	0	0	0	0	0

This enumeration extends to thirteen kinds of sons, but they are regarded usually as but twelve, a daughter's son, or a son by a female Śúdra, being excluded from some of the lists. It is immaterial, however, to adjust the scale throughout, for in the present age there are but three descriptions of sons admitted, the natural son, the son given or Dattaka, and in some places the Kŕitrima or son made. The learned judge in concluding (p. 132), that there are but two kinds known at present to Hindu law, the son begotten in wedlock, and the son given in adoption, seems to have lost sight of the case he had particularised but a few pages before, and which he states in p. 128 was a Kŕitrima adoption. This mode of adoption, however, is of restricted currency, and limited in Gangetic Hindustan, at least, to Mithilá; it is therefore sufficient here to fix the place of the *Dattaka* or the son given.

On the above authorities, four concur in placing him the third on the list, and besides these Gautama, Vasishtha and Vrihaspati as quoted in the Digest, assign him the same place. Baudháyana, who makes him fourth, does so only by inserting the daughter's son, and a text of the Vedas, an authority that should be final, as cited in the Dattaka Chandriká, assigns him a similar grade.* The weight of authority therefore clearly recognises the classification of the Dattaka amongst the first six, or those who are declared to be heirs to collateral kinsmen, as well as to their adoptive father.

There is no doubt that the worthiest sons are entitled to the highest privileges. This is conformable to common sense, as well as the manifest purport of the authorities. That the Dattaka is amongst the most respectable, is admitted even by some of the authorities, who seem to give a preference to others in their enumeration; and Vishńu who places him below the son of an unmarried girl**, &c. states [?] that they are not reputable (Apraśasta), and share neither the funeral oblation nor estate. The very acknowledgement of the Dattaka, or son given, as co-existing almost, if not quite alone, with the son begotten in wedlock, in the present age, is an admission favourable to his character, and consequently to his claims.

* [V, 26.] ** [ch. XV.]

Notwithstanding these considerations, however, a text of the sage Devala is adduced by Jímútaváhana* unfavourable to the collateral succession of the Dattaka, and he seems to have been usually considered, in Bengal, as classed with sons who are kinsmen but not heirs. An opinion so opposite to that which is derived from the text of Manu and other legislators is certainly startling, and it might be supposed impossible to offer any satisfactory explanation of such a difference, or any attempt at the reconciliation of these contradictory positions. To us, however, it appears by no means difficult to understand how the difference of doctrine has arisen, or to solve the inconsistency of Devala's text with principles that are uncontested, and to shew its utter inapplicability to the existing circumstances of Hindu Society.

The classification of the Dattaka, or son given, below several of the others, by which he is reduced to the lowest grade, depends upon a principle more subtle than just, and one contrary to established doctrines. It is argued that, whilst the son given, and his like, may be of *a different caste* from the adoptive father, the son of an unmarried daughter, of a widow remarried, and of concealed birth, may be, by the female side at least, of *the caste of the deceased*, and are *possibly* his own sons. The affinity, however, is not proven, and if it were, what would be the result? they would as bastards be excluded from all class and tribe what-

* [Dáyabhága, p. 227. Dattakachandriká, p. 61.]

ever: it is on this account in all likelihood that Manu ranks them lowest in the scale, Vishńu calls them Apraśasta, or not reputable, and Vŕihaspati* declares they are contemned by all good men. Kátyáyana* is more explicit, for he declares that they are Asavarńas, not of the same Varńa or caste with the father, and the author of the Mitákshará observes "that although they may be deemed of the same class through their natural father, yet they are not so in their own character, for they are not within the definition of tribe and class**." In fact, as far as the question turns upon this point, and it is the only thing like an argument in the way, it may be easily settled. Whatever might have been the difficulty in ancient times, there is none now; for whilst the mere possibility of affinity of tribe gave the three sorts of sons above named a contingent advantage over the son given, to whom such an affinity might not apply, that is not the case at present, as the Dattaka's being of the same caste is in the present age an indispensable condition of the validity of the adoption.

The principle, on which the opposition, therefore, to the collateral succession of a son given rests, being fallacious, or inapplicable, the objection grounded on it becomes unsubstantial, and there can be no doubt, that the Dattaka inherits mediately as well as immediately from his adoptive parent: he stands in fact in every respect in the place of a natural son; he presents

---

* [Dáyabhága, p. 229.] ** [XI, 39.]

the funeral cake to his adoptive father and his ancestors, and he foregoes all claims upon his peculiar birthrights. On the ground of equity and of equivalent, therefore, his claims are further corroborated, and the decision of the court in the case of Gourbullubh &c. was perfectly consonant with the reason and spirit of the Hindu law.

The learned Judge next proceeds to consider other contingencies of the act of adoption, and discusses the right of the adopted son in the event of a natural son being born after his adoption. In that case he says, it is the general if not the universal opinion of the Paṅdits, that the adopted son is entitled to a third part of the estate; upon a text of Devala who lays it down that the adopted son shall in this case take one third, and the begotten son two thirds of the estate.

In quoting texts of law, it is very necessary to adhere to the precise expressions as any partial change may alter the colour of the whole. Now neither in the original nor translation is there a word about the *estate*, or the two thirds to be taken by the begotten son: neither is the law so generally admitted as the learned judge seems to imagine. If it were, indeed, what is the meaning of the next page and a half, complaining of the uncertainty of Hindu law and abusing Jagannáth's digest? At the same time, setting aside the texts of Manu regarding a fifth or sixth share as no longer applicable, we believe the only difference in the law in this case arises, like that in the case of a sister's portion, from want of a knowledge of the elements of arithmetic.

Devala says, adopted sons after the birth of a natural son are dividers of *a third share**, which Jímútaváhana explains, a third part of the share of a natural son.** According to our notions of computation this does not mean *a third of the whole*, but a part equal to *one third of the portion* of the natural son, and consequently *a fourth* of the *whole* dividend: accordingly, the Mitákshará*** awards a fourth share upon the authority of Vasishṫha, and the doctrine is precisely the same as that of Devala, according as the application is made; for it is clear that, if out of 100 parts the natural son takes seventy-five and the adopted son twenty-five, he may be said to take a fourth or a third share, according as the assertion is absolute or relative. In no case, however, can it be argued that the adopted son is to have one-third, and the natural son two-thirds: the proportion is not as *two to one*, but as *three to one*, and conclusions to the former effect are not warranted by any interpretation of the law; the supposed inconsistency of which lies, in our estimation, not in the law, nor even its commentators, but its living interpreters.

The next consideration is the age at which a boy may be adopted, and which the learned judge con-

---

* [औरसे पुनरुत्पन्ने तेषु ज्यैष्ठ्यं न विद्यते ।
तेषां सवर्णा ये पुत्रास्ते तृतीयांशभागिनः ॥]

** [औरसपुत्रभागस्य तृतीयांशभागी.]

*** [I, XI, 24.]

ceives Hindu authorities to have limited to that of five years. He cites however a decision of the Sadr Dewání, in which the adoption of a boy of eight was declared valid, and he expresses a hope, that henceforth that may be acknowledged as the limit, because it has once been so decided: a very odd reason, supposing the decision to have been incorrect.

The real spirit of the Hindu law, however, leaves the age of the boy a matter of perfect indifference. It is true, that authorities founded on a contested passage of the Káliká Puráńa prohibit the adoption of a boy whose age exceeds that of five years; but even if the passage be authentic*, we deny its competency to constitute the ground-work of a positive law. But the text of the Puráńa does not prohibit the adoption; it says, "after the fifth year sons given, and the rest are not sons but slaves"—and why? because a son, having been initiated under the family name of his own father unto the ceremony of tonsure inclusive, does not become the son of another man: "the ceremony of tonsure and other rites of initiation being indeed performed under his own family name, sons given, and the rest may be considered as issue, else they are termed slaves."—Even on this very authority, therefore, the initiatory ceremonies are all that is essential, and the age of five years is specified only, because it

* [Colebr. ad Mit. I. XI, 13. Vyavahára Mayúkha, IV, 5, 20. Sutherland's transl. of the Dattaka Mímánsá. Madras: 1825, p. 225 f. 237.]

is taken for granted that by that age tonsure, which should be performed in the 2d or 3d year, must have been performed. But here again the authority invalidates its own assertion, that tonsure in the family of the adopted father is essential to adoption, for that rite will be performed probably in the 3rd year at latest, and the period of adoption is extended to five, or *after* tonsure is performed. These inconsistencies, however, arise from chusing to consider the passage as law: it is no such thing, it is merely an exposition and recommendation of the practice, and should no doubt be thus understood: initiation completed in the natural family disqualifies a boy for adoption into any other, and the greater the number of initiatory rites performed in the family into which he is adopted the better; he cannot therefore be adopted at too early an age, and it is very desirable that he should be adopted before tonsure is performed; but if that is not possible, then the age of five may be regarded as a fair average limit, because that anticipates the period of investiture with the sacrificial string, which would be a disqualification. Although the upanayana is performed usually in the eighth year from the conception of a Bráhmańa, it may be, and not unfrequently is, anticipated in the fifth. On the other hand it may be delayed till the sixteenth year, and accordingly adoption may be proportionately extended. The Hindu law refers here to a positive principle, and is neither inconsistent nor contradictory. As to the arguments in favour of early adoption suggested by the learned judge, (p. 145) they are manifestly exotics,—the growth of an English, not of an Asiatic soil. We are not aware either of the necessity, or the existence of any distinction in the age of a son who is adopted, whether he is nearly related, or not, to the adopter.

In rule 8th Sir F. M. lays it down, that the gift of an only son is absolutely prohibited, acknowledging, however, that an only son may be so given, the donor being content to suffer the consequences. Those consequences relate to his condition after life, and no Hindu will, very readily, incur them. The evil, however, is only to the prepetrator, and as the measure does not affect the peace or well-being of Society, it seems rather superfluous to have legislated upon the subject—except that it gives the learned judge an opportunity of impugning an extra judicial opinion of the Recorder of Madras. Sir F. M. has not adverted here to the allowable arrangement, by which a case of the kind is provided for, and an only son, though not absolutely given in adoption, may be affiliated as the son of two fathers—fulfilling the double capacity of a son to his natural, as well as to his adoptive father.

The law of adoption, as it stands in the Hindu code, is of itself a sufficiently fertile source of dissension, but it appears that in practice it has become still more so, and that the decisions of the courts have authorized innovations not contemplated, and therefore not only prohibited by Hindu law, but foreign to its objects, and productive of additional intricacy and doubt.

A man requires a son, to perform his funeral ceremonies, and save him from purgatory. This being done, the necessity for adoption ceases, and his *multiplying* adopted sons is an act of supererogation. It has, however, been recognised in a decision of the Sadr Court, founded chiefly on the doctrine that "many sons are desirable, and that the wish for many is meritorious"; but such an admission can scarcely constitute law. The practice may be suffered, because it is not prohibited, but the principle will equally authorise adoption, where natural sons exist, and in many respects is likely to produce mischievous results;—to lay it down as a rule, as is done by the learned judge, (rule 23d) is only likely to promote litigation.

Again the adoption is for the benefit of the father, and where a widow adopts a son, she does so under his instructions, and as his representative, and in no case is she supposed to adopt a son *for herself*, though permitted by her husband so to do, except, agreeably to the form of adoption practised in Mithilá, that of the Ḱritrima, or son made, which is especially for the purpose of performing the woman's Sapińdí Karańa. In this case a husband's assent is not necessary, and the widow therefore acts for herself, not as a husband's representative, as she does under all other circumstances: the three rules therefore, advanced (p. 156) upon the authority of the Sadr Dewání reports, tend only to sanction anomalies incompatible with the spirit of the Hindu law.

Another contingent perplexity attached to the subject arises out of the innovation of wills, by which the regulation of adoption is made the matter of posthumous caprice. We shall have more to say on the subject of wills hereafter, and it may be sufficient here to remark that, if the Hindus are to be authorised to make wills, they should be instructed how to make them, and not be suffered to bequeath absurdities, or to make the arrangements which they contemplate subject to improbable or impracticable conditions.

Finally another source of perplexity is the arbitrary interference of the Courts.

The following case singularly illustrates the mischief of all these innovations.

*Luckinarain Tagore** (a *Brahmin*) died possessed of considerable property, *moveable* and *immoveable*; mostly, I believe, *ancestorial*; but that circumstance was not relied upon in any stage of the cause. Three wives, viz. *Sree Mootee Taramonee Dabee, Sree Mootee Bhagabuttee Dabee, Sree Mootee Dagumbaree*** survived him; and at the time of his death, he had not a child.

Luckinarain made a will, by which he left 5000 rupees to each of his wives, and 1000 rupees, in addition to the 5000, to his second wife *Bhagabuttee*.

In his will he recited the pregnancy of his younger wife *Dagumbaree*, and declared that her *(son or daughter)* should be the possessor of his wealth. He constituted *Juggomohun Mullick**** his executor; *Juggomohun Mullick* some time after this died, having made a will, and constituted *Bustom Doss Mullick* † his executor. In this state of things it was assumed, and received as a matter of course, that *Bustom Doss Mullick* became the executor of *Luckinarain Tagore*. I am particular in noticing this, because

* [लक्ष्मीनारायण ठाकुर.]

** [श्रीमोतीतारामणि देवी, श्रीमोतीभागवती देवी, श्रीमोतीदिगम्बरी.]

*** [जगन्मोहन मालिक.] † [वैष्णवदास मालिक.]

it may serve to show the extent to which the wills of *Hindoos* are recognized in the Supreme Court.

Juggomohun, as executor of *Luckinarain*, had possessed himself of *Luckinarain's* property-- and *Bustom Doss*, as executor of *Juggomohun*, possessed himself of it, after *Juggomohun's* death.

On the 7th of November, 1818, and thirteen days after the death of *Luckinarain Tagore*, his youngest wife *Dagumbaree* was delivered of a *son*. This son died in seventeen days after his birth.

If *Luckinarain* had died intestate, this son must have succeeded to his property as *heir at law;* and *Dagumbaree*, his mother surviving him, would incontestably have succeeded to the property as his heir. *Luckinarain*, however, made a provision by his will, in case of the death of this child with which his wife was *enceinte*. In the event of its death, he directed that his *widows* should *adopt a son*. If they conld not *all* agree in the selection of a boy for adoption, he directed that one should be chosen by his *first* and *second* widows, *Taramonee* and *Bhagabuttee*. If the *first* and *second* widows could not agree in the selection, he then directed that a boy shonld be chosen by his *second* and *third* widows, *Bhagabuttee* and *Dagumbaree*. It will be seen, that the *second* widow, *Bhagabuttee*, was in any case to have a voice in the selection of a son for adoption. From this provision, and from the additional thousand rupees which he gave to her, it clearly appears that she was the favorite, and the one in whom he had most confidence.

In 1818, *Dagumbaree*, the youngest widow, and mother of the child, of *Luckinarain*, filed her bills against *Taramonee* and *Bhagabuttee*, the other two widows, and against *Bustom Doss Mullick*, the executor of her husband's execntor.

By this bill the complainant, *Dagumbaree*, affirmed her right to the estate of her late husband, in conseqnence of her having had a son by him, whose heir she stated herself to be by the *Hindoo* law. She prayed an account and to be put into possession of the estate of her hnsband, *Luckinarain*.

To this bill an answer was put in by *Bustom Doss Mullick*, admitting that as the executor of *Juggomohun*, who was execntor of *Luckinarain*, he, *Bustom Doss*, did possess himself of *Luckinarain's* estate, and that he was then in possession of it. He admitted also the birth of a son, and his death, as the bill set forth; but he denied that the complainant was entitled to the estate of *Luckinarain*, and he *relied upon the will* by which the adoption of a son was directed. He denied the complainant's right to an account of *Luckinarain's* estate, and insisted that no person had a right to such an account, except a son to be adopted *according to the terms of Luckinarain's will.* The other two defendants put in a joint answer to the same effect with that of *Bustom Doss Mullick.*

The will was established, and directions were given for the adoption of a son according to its provisions. Such vexation as might have been foreseen was the consequence. The widows could not be brought to concur in the selection of a boy for adoption. A reference was then made to the master, who was directed to enquire and report to the Court concerning the fitness of a boy to be adopted as the son of *Luckinarain Tagore.* The master reported in favour of *Taracomar Surmono** who had been nominated for adoption by the *second* widow *Sree Mootee Bhagabuttee Dabee. This boy was the son of Bhagabuttee's* UNCLE.

The Master's report was confirmed, and this furnished matter for further contention. The boy *Taracomar* was to be adopted; but the question was, which of the three widows had a right to *receive* him in adoption. The law is clear, and was undisputed. The boy could not be received by the *three widows jointly.* He must be received by *one* of them—and would then be considered as the son of *Luckinarain and the widow by whom he had been received*: about this there was not, because there could not be, any dispute.

Had it not been for the *natural* relation in which the child stood to *Bhagabuttee*, the second widow, the Court, considering the preference which had been given to her by her husband, might probably have declared her the properest person to act as adopting mother. But it was a family of *Brahmins,* and her claim was impugned upon the ground of relationship, it being argued that she could not without incest be the mother of her uncle's son.

---

* [ताराकुमारशर्मण.]

The argument was supposed to be conclusive, for she withdrew her pretensions.

There was no dispute as to the eligibility of this boy. He might have been adopted by *Luckinarain* himself, *but not as the son of Bhagabuttee*, who was his first cousin.

The first widow, *Taramonee*, founded her claim to receive this child upon seniority. The *third*, *Dagumbaree*, founded hers upon the fact of her having borne a son to her deceased husband.

The Master reported in favor of the *first* widow, and the Court confirmed his report; not from a *conviction* of its having been right, but because it was not opposed, and because it did not appear that the *third* widow ought to have been preferred.

I have added the will of *Luckinarain*, the Master's report, and the opinions which were given by the *Paṅdits* in his office, to the appendix. If those opinions do not impart knowledge, satisfy curiosity, or remove doubt, they will at least prove the deplorable state in which ministers of justice are placed, when they have recourse to *Paṅdits* for an exposition of the *Hindoo* law in a depending cause.

We shall content ourselves with a few remarks on this case.

The learned judge admits, that if Luckinarain had died intestate, the infant would have succeeded to the property, and Digambarí, his mother, would incontestably have succeeded to his property as his heir; the will therefore on the learned judge's own showing violated the law of inheritance.

The learned judge states also that the greater part of the estate was ancestorial property. In the following chapter on unequal distribution, he endeavours, it is true, to maintain a father's right to assign immoveable ancestorial property unequally *to his sons;* but admitting this, which is more than doubtful, he has *no right to give it away to others:* consequently the will of Luckinarain could not invalidate his own infant's claim to the ancestorial immoveable property at least, and the decree that gave it away from his heir was a violation of the law.

The idea of compelling two of the widows to agree in the choice of a son was an absurdity, and as it was a condition that could not be enforced, it ought of itself to *have invalidated the will*, in which case the whole of the property, subject to deduction for the maintenance of the other widows, would have reverted to the younger widow.

No *two* of the widows agreeing, the court assume the power of sanctioning *one* to adopt. Did this assumption emanate from the will, or from the Hindu law?

The widow makes a choice, and it is declared to be within the proscribed degree of consanguinity: to whom? not to her husband on whose behalf, and for whose benefit she acts, but herself: a matter wholly irrelevant in regard to property on which she has no claim.

This adopted son is then declared by the court not to be the adopted son of the mother who adopted him, but the adopted son of the mother, who did not adopt him: a stretch of power that we certainly can find nothing in Hindu law, nor we imagine in English law, to justify.

"Those who acted for the second widow would have held fast by her claim, if they had not known it to be untenable", so says the learned judge near the bottom of page 172: at the top of page 173, however, we have, "I now hear that the right of Bhagabuttee to receive the child in adoption was not abandoned by her adviser",—quære how long an interval had elapsed between the penning of these two passages.

"Dagumbaree being excluded, however, the second widow forbore to oppose the judgment of the court."

But allowing to the will of the deceased the power, which it cannot have in law or reason, of subverting the most positive and undoubted provisions of the Hindu code, has it not been virtually cancelled by the authoritative interposition of the court in enforcing an arrangement *contrary to the terms* of the will, and in that case has not Digambarí a right to inherit as she would have done, if no such will had existed?

The adopted son has since died: without issue it may be presumed from the date of his adoption and his age at the time. Who has succeeded to the inheritance? if the elder widow be held to be his adoptive mother, she now claims the whole succession, and if Bhágavatí's advisers have not been long-sighted enough to anticipate such a contingency they have very imperfectly advocated her interests.

Sir F. M. seems to anticipate a new adoption on the part of the widows and suggests the question of its validity (p. 175). He has forborne from answering it, but it may be safely asserted, that the Hindu law has not provided for the case; the widows have no authority from their husband to make a second choice, and in Bengal they cannot adopt without such authority*: it might be argued upon the reason of the case, that "if a man desires one son to be adopted, this is clearly expressive of his wish to be at all events represented, and that the adoption is therefore to proceed toties quoties, until this object shall have been finally accomplished." But it is not so written in the bond, and we are not aware, that the courts of judicature are authorised to make the constructive wishes of deceased parties law. If the adoption is tenable, the mother, whichever it may be, is heir, and she will have very good grounds therefore to resist a second adoption. The cases referred to by Sir F. M. as proving the validity of successive or several adoptions, do not bear upon this, as in them special authority from the husband was established; that authority being held legal, of course, the acts emanating from it were legal also.

Above 40 pages are next occupied with a critical review of a dicision by Sir Thomas Strange, in the case of Virapermah Pillay *v.* Narain Pillay. and we shall content ourselves with this reference, as we have already dwelt too long on this chapter. It is impossible however to avoid drawing a very important inference from the result of the investigation. The Chief Justice of Bengal declares that a decision pronounced and argued with great pains by the Chief Justice at Madras *will mislead those by whom it may be followed, and that the doctrines which it inculcates are con-*

* [See Sutherland, l. l., p. 233 ff. Notes VI & VII.]

trary to law (p. 229). Can we then wonder that Paṅḍits differ, or can we consent to take the decisions of the judges as substitutes for Hindu law?

At the end of this section, we have "Addenda to the chapter on inheritance", the insertion of which in this place is thus adverted to:

Although I ought, perhaps, to apologize for the great defect in point of arrangement, which will be found throughout my pnblication, I hope an acknowledgement of the fault will be deemed sufficient from a gratnitous labonrer—from one whose thoughts mnst have been chiefly directed to other avocations, and who has hardly had a single day which he could devote to this work with nndivided attention.

The next chapter on gifts and unequal distribution regards the father's absolute power over his property, or his right to divide or bequeath it unequally amongst his sons. The learned judge admits, that the law is tolerably precise with regard to property acquired by a person himself, and the moveable portion of his patrimonial inheritance. Of this there is little question, although a distribution of such effects dictated by prejudice or partiality is considered immoral. He endeavours however to shew, that the unequal distribution of ancestorial immoveable property, if not legal, is not valid, and he here avails himself of the doctrine which he sturdily resisted as applicable to the rights of a widow, *quod fieri non debet, factum valet:* he endeavours (p. 301) to make out a difference in the nature of the cases, but we think without success.

When I noticed it first, I was npon a subject very different from the present. There the question was, whether or not a woman (who was certainly entitled to no more than a life interest in the property she possessed) could lawfully deteriorate that property to the prejudice of him, who had an unquestionable title to succeed to it after her death. Here the question is, whether or not the man in possession of *ancestorial immoveable* property, has a right to dispose of it according to his own will. If I could venture to draw a conclusion, it would be that he is invested with the temporal right, subject to the spiritual consequences, of its exercise.

If a man has this right, why has not a woman? because, it is said, she has no more than a life interest in the property. But how is this proved? because others have an unquestionable right to it after her death. But who are these others? the *husband's remote heirs* Surely a son has a more unquestionable right to it than they, and the rights of a son in ancestorial property being unquestionable, the rights of the father are as much restricted to a life interest in it as those of a widow, and by the very same course of reasoning adopted by the learned judge the same absolute power must be conceded to or withheld from both.

But the fact is that the father's control over ancestorial property *is* restricted by positive texts, whilst that of the widow or mother is only limited by analogy and general declarations, as we trust we have satisfied our readers. On the contrary the authorities are clear and consistent with respect to a father's power, and although they do not invalidate *unequal* distribution, they declare that the gift of the *whole* is illegal and invalid. We shall cite a few of these texts.

What is bailed for delivery, what is lent for use, a

pledge, joint property, a deposit, a son, a wife, *and the whole estate of a man who has living issue*, the sages have declared unalienable, even by a man oppressed with grievous calamities, and what has been promised to another. *Nárada.**

The prohibition of giving away is declared to be eight fold, a man shall not give joint property, nor his son, nor his wife, nor a pledge, nor *all his wealth, if he have issue living. Vrihaspati.***

A wife, or a son, or *the whole of a man's estate*, shall not be given away or sold without the assent of the persons interested. *Kátyáyana.*

Joint property, deposits for use, bailments, in the form called Nyása, pledges, a wife, her property, deposits for delivery, bailments in general, and the whole of a man's estate, if he have issue alive, are things which the learned have declared unalienable even in times of distress. *Daksha.*

The ample support of those who are entitled to maintenance is rewarded, but hell is the portion of that man, whose family is afflicted with pain by his neglect. Therefore let him maintain his family with the utmost care. *Manu.****

Even those who are born or yet unborn, and they who exist in the womb, require food for subsistence;

---

* [Vyavahára Mayúkha IX, 2.]

** [F. E. Sicé, législation Hindoue. Pondichéry: 1857, p. 130.]

*** [quoted in Dáyabhága, p, 57. Cf. Man. IX, 202 and Víramitr. p. 221, v.]

the deprivation of the means of subsistence is reprehended. *Nárada.**

We might multiply these citations abundantly, and of whatever modifications or qualifications they may be susceptible, they leave no doubt that a man has neither temporarily nor spiritually an absolute command over the whole of any description of his property: he may certainly make away with a great part of it, but there is a limit, although the learned judge thinks it difficult to assign one. That limit is an adequate provision for his family, and we can conceive no more difficulty as to the determination of this provision by the court, than there is in the ascertainment of the sum a widow is entitled to for her maintenance.

In the above texts also is to be understood the existence of no distinction between self-acquired and inherited property, and they all apply to a man's wealth generally, making it imperative upon him to secure provision for his family before he alienates even self-acquired wealth. With this reservation, he may dispose of property he has gained during his own life time, as he pleases, as according to Kátyáyana "except his whole estate and his dwelling house, what remains after the food and clothing of his family, a man may give away **." Food and clothing are however not to be understood in their literal acceptation only, but imply maintenance, as appears from other texts.

---

* [Dáyakramasangr. IV, 25.] ** [Vyavah. May. IX, 4.]

With regard also to moveable ancestorial property, there is authority for considering that to be at the father's disposal, according to the text of Yájnavalkya: "Of precious stones, pearls and corals, the father is master of the whole, but of the whole immoveable property neither father nor grandfather is master"*. The text of Vishńu, however, goes further and declares that "the father and son have equal ownership in the whole of the grandfather's wealth." As however the control over moveable property, consisting at least of money or jewels, is a nullity, the distinction may be admitted, and the power if not the right of a father to dispose of such property at his pleasure is in general undisputed; at the same time it may be safely said that the alienation of this property, like that of self-acquired wealth, is only allowable after provision made for the family, and that the unequal partition of both amongst sons, which is authorised by special considerations, may be set aside, if the least favoured son can establish undeniably, that he has been deprived of a due share of his father's wealth by that father's unjust anger towards himself, or undue partiality for another son. We think the dialogue between the learned judge, and the court Pańdits on the subject quite inconclusive. It proceeds in the first place upon the inaccurate assertion of the latter, that a father may give a larger share of the ancestorial immoveable

* [quoted from the Mitákshará in the Vyavahára Mayúkha IV, 1, 5, Dáyakramasangraha, VI, 19 f., and Dáyabhága, p. 56.]

property to one son than to another, and that he may do this on account of being better satisfied with that son's conduct, of which, the learned judge observes, the father alone can judge, and that accordingly the act must be taken as proof of the equity of the preference. The first position is certainly contrary to the conclusions even of the Bengal lawyers, and the second is unfairly stated. The mere satisfaction of the father is not receivable in proof. Where all his sons have notoriously acted towards him in the like manner, and have been treated by him, during life, with no marked difference, he would not be justified in making unequal distribution; but if it could be proved in justification, that the son preferred had alone discharged his filial obligations to his father, and that his brethren had been notorious for contumaciousness, and had been known to have incurred the father's severe displeasure, the unequal partition of the father's own property should be upheld. In like manner, if the son excluded from a due share of his patrimony could shew, that he had never deserved the displeasure of his father, he would have a good right to such addition to his portion, as should provide for his support. There are other conditions, under which unequal distribution is allowable, but all are succeptible of proof, and this proof should be required, where the proportions are wholly inadequate. The mere unequal distribution of self-acquired or inherited moveable property by which one gets more and another less, but in which all are provided for, is not matter of litigation.

The learned judge states truly (p. 247), that the right to make an unequal partition of ancestorial immoveable property is unequivocally denied. He asks, 'will such a partition be valid, if made'? and he adds in the course of the chapter decisions and opinions, to shew that 'factum valet' has overcome the law, that the whole ancestorial lands were given to one son, that the illegality of the act was admitted, that it was declared to be immoral and sinful, but that having been done it was valid; and throughout the whole of the argument he evidently leans to an opinion founded on what he admits to be an absurdity, that a man may make what disposition he pleases of his property both ancestorial and self-acquired, and personal or real: a doctrine which is wholly at variance with the letter and spirit of the whole Hindu law, whether as laid down by Manu, and ancient legislators, or as expounded by modern Scholiasts. It is therefore worth while to examine this doctrine of the validity of illegal acts.

In the first place then, where is the distinction found? In the most recent commentators, and those of a peculiar province only, those of Bengal, whose explanation is founded on a general position laid down by Jímútaváhana; "therefore, since it is denied that a gift or sale should be made, the precept is infringed by making one: but the gift or transfer is not null, for a fact cannot be altered by a hundred texts."* This remark refers, however, to the alienation of property

* [Dáyabhága, p. 60.]

of which the aliener is undoubted proprietor, as a father, of immoveable property if self-acquired, or a coparcener of his own share before partition: but he himself concludes that a father cannot dispose of the ancestorial property, because he is not sole master of it. "Since the circumstance of the father being lord of all "the wealth is stated as a reason, and that cannot be "in regard to the grandfather's estate, an unequal dis-"tribution made by the father is lawful only in the in-"stance of his own acquired wealth." Nothing can be more clear than Jímútaváhana's assertion of this doctrine, and the doubt cast upon it by its expounders Raghunandana, Śrí Kŕishńa Tarkálankára and Jagannátha is wholly gratuitous. In fact the latter is chiefly to blame for the distinction between illegal, and invalid acts.

The distinction has clearly arisen from a confusion between the notion of acts, and rights: to say that an act is not altered by a hundred texts is an obvious truism, as Raghunandana illustrates it; "it is highly criminal to kill a cow; but if she be killed, the deed is done." That is incontestable, but there was no *right* to kill her, and the killer may be punished. So though a thing be immorally given, the person had no right to make the gift, and the misdemeanour must be dealt with accordingly. There arises something like a difficulty in determining who is the object of punishment. The donor is the culprit, but by revoking the gift the donee who has committed no crime is punished. Revocation of gift, however, is obviously the most ready mode of preventing such alienations, and the enforcement of this is fully justified by the sort of discretionary power confided in this case to the ruling authority, as "he who foolishly receives what is deem-"ed ungiven, and he who gives what may not be le-"gally aliened, should be punished by a king who "knows the law." *Nárada.* And "he who receives a "thing which ought not to be given, and he who be-"stows it, both these are to be punished as thieves, and "amerced in the highest penalty." *Mitákshará.* The *Viváda Chintámańi, Víra Mitrodaya,* and other works of authority, declare also that illegal gifts shall be resumed.* Besides this the ruling power is specially enjoined to enforce the observance of the legal code, and of all local usages or institutes not in contradiction to that code, and it is absurd to say, therefore, that the judge is to acknowledge as valid, or to permit the validity of, that which sacred institutes and universal feeling denounce as immoral and illegal. That the practice has been authorised and decisions passed accordingly, has arisen from a mistaken delicacy as to the right of authority to interpose. The only argument of any weight adduced has been this: the law certainly prohibits the practice, but it has not provided for its prevention or punishment, and therefore being done, it must be recognised. But this is a very incorrect view of the case, and would, as observed by

* [Mitáksh. ad Yájn. II, 176. Vivádachint., p. 35—61. Viramitrod., f. 121 r. ff.]

Sir F. M., authorise the perpetration of a vast variety of crimes. The law has not been so improvident. It has stated what ought and what ought not to be done, and has left the enforcement of its prescriptions to the discretion of the executive power. We are confident, that the question between illegality and validity would never have been agitated under a Hindu administration.

Notwithstanding, therefore, "the right of a man to make any unequal distribution amongst his sons of *ancestorial immoveable* property seems never to have been doubted in the Supreme Court" (p. 268,) we cannot admit, that it exists, and the learned judge acknowledges that the law cannot be considered as finally settled. We cannot admit either, that the owner has more than a contingent right to make a very unequal distribution of any description of his property, without satisfactory cause. The onus of disproving such cause, it is true, rests with the plaintiff, and unless the proof were too glaring to be deniable, it would not of course be allowed to operate. We only mean to aver that it is at the discretion of the court to determine, whether an unequal distribution has been attended with such circumstances of caprice or injustice as shall authorise its revisal. It should never be forgotten in this investigation, that wills, as we understand them, are foreign to Hindu law; for there is clearly a bias in favour of full testamentary power in the practice of the Supreme Court, and in the arguments of Sir F. M., which cannot fail to introduce many innovations into the law, and many new and vexatious sources of perplexity and litigation which are unknown to the Hindus, in the unsophisticated condition of their native code. The following case was a clear violation of the law under this feeling.

Soorjeecomar left a widow, but no child; and he made a will by which all his property, consisting in part of *ancestorial immoveable* estate, was given to his brothers. By this will he had made a provision, which he considered to be a suitable one, for his widow.

The will set up was alleged to have been forged, and upon that ground alone it was contested by the widow. It was found to have been duly executed, and here the case ended.

But why should it have ended thus? The widow's advocate was not staunch to her cause, unless indeed he felt, that it was vain to dispute the determination of the court to maintain a will at all hazards. Then he acted wisely; but his prudence does not justify the sentence. Nothing is more positive in Hindu law, than that a widow shall succeed to her husband's estate, in failure of direct issue. Here is no inconsistency nor perplexity; the law is precise and positive, and yet the will of an individual is to be maintained against it; that is, he is to subvert the whole system of succession. It is a farce to say, that the Hindus have any law of inheritance, if its most unquestionable injunctions are to subsist upon the breath of individual caprice. The learned judge's reasoning here is wholly irrelevant; he observes:

If it had been established as law, that a man cannot make a gift or an unequal distribution of *ancestorial immoveable* property to the prejudice of any of his *descendants*, it might not have followed that he, being childless, would be held under the same

restraint, when giving to his brothers, where the widow is to be prejudiced by the gift.

But it did not signify in this case what the property was, for whatever he might have done with it wholly or in part during life, he *could not control its disposition after his death.*

With regard to the decisions of the Sadr, we have some on both sides of the question. In that of Eshand Chand Rai *v.* Eshorchand Rai, the gift of a whole estate to an eldest son was confirmed chiefly on the doctrine that though the gift was sinful, it was not invalid; whilst in the case of Bhawanicharn Bunhoojea *v.* the heirs of Ramkant Bunhoojeea the gift of the whole of the ancestral property was declared to be invalid. The last decision was most conformable to the spirit of the law, and most consistent with the duty of the Court, empowered as that is both by common sense, and the purport of the Hindu code, to *make* that *valid* which is *legal, moral* and *right,* in the estimation of all the authorities. In our opinion this is a much more dignified course, and one which will do more to prevent litigation than that which the learned judge seems disposed to recommend, when he would wish to recognise the principle of "factum valet." He says, "this principle, whatever we may think of it, we must desire to see in the most active operation where it can be most beneficially applied"; that is, he would connive at immoral acts, if he thought they led to useful results. This is very like 'the end sanctifying the means' a principle, we trust, we shall never see introduced into English morality, nor even into English law.

We have so fully discussed the doctrine of alienation by widows that we need not advert to the cases illustrative of grants made by them. There is clearly a difference between the situation of a widow inheriting, and a father in possession, because the sons and grandsons have a direct lien upon the estate, which remote heirs have not: although, however, the law might be held to permit a widow's alienation of property to which she succeeds as heir, yet the obvious analogy of the case, and the general impression on the subject, operate to prevent her alienation of fixed property and chattels, and therefore the decisions of the Sadr Dewání in the cases of Mahoda *v.* Kalyani and others, and Vijaya Devi *v.* Annapurna Devi, may be admitted as law, the authority of the Court having been interposed, as we have recommended it should be in every case, to *make* that invalid which was considered immoral.

The next chapter treats of wills, and as the doctrine, on which the right of a Hindu to make a will has been recognised in the supreme Court, has been founded in a great measure upon the opinion of Mr. Colebrooke, we shall cite it, as quoted by Sir F. M.

Upon the right of a *Hindoo* to dispose of his property by will, I have seen the opinion of *Mr. Colebrooke*, and I need not add that there is not any man whose opinions may justly command a greater degree of deference.

He says, "According to the authorities of *Hindu* law which prevail in *Bengal*, a member of an undivided family may *give away* or *otherwise aliene* property to the extent of his *own share* of the joint wealth, and I conceive his disposal of property by will would be here maintained (i. e. within the limits of that province,) in conformity with *Jímúta Váhana's* doctrine, that the *gift* or *other alienation*, by an *unseparated co-heir*, may be an *immoral* act, but it is not an *invalid* one.—*Dáyabhága*, *Chapt. 2, Sect. 28.*—*Jagannátha's Digest. vol. 2, Pages 57 and 290.* It would be otherwise in the rest of the provinces."

Again *Mr. Colebrooke* says, "When writing a few days ago, I stated that I thought a *Hindoo's will* must be governed and controlled by the general rules concerning *gifts*. It will hold good, I think, for the same things for which a *gift* made in his life time would do so, and not otherwise. I should have added, however, that his *legacies to his family must be controlled by the rules regarding partition made by the father of* the family. The principle I would lay down is, that a man cannot confer either on a stranger, or on one of his family, *by will* (which I consider to be a donation in contemplation of death) what he could not bestow, either by deed of gift, or partition of patrimony during his life time. The utmost that can be said is, that he may do that by *will* which he could have done by *partition* or *donation* between living persons."

He proceeds, "Upon the principle which I have stated, a *Hindoo* in *Bengal* may leave by will *all his own acquisitions;* but is restricted, if he have sons, from distributing *ancestral property according to his own pleasure*. In countries, in which the doctrines of the *Mitákshará* prevail, he is restrained from giving away *immoveables*, and from making any other partition of his possessions among his male descendants, but such as the law has sanctioned; consequently, on the principle before explained, he would be restricted from distributing *immoveables* in a mode not sanctioned by law, but may dispose of *moveables*, of which the law permits him to make gifts on account of affection; not however to the amount of the whole property. If there be no *sons* or *male* descendants, and the property be not shared by a co-heir, *the whole of his pos-*

sessions, being his separate and distinct property, may be disposed of by will *as he pleases.*" *

It would be presumption in us to say we concur with Mr. Colebrooke, and still more to dispute his doctrine, but we confess, we demur to the last clause of the above, as it might operate to the exclusion of the widow, the daughter, the daughter's son, and all the heirs who by the positive laws of inheritance succeed in default of male descendants. It may be said indeed that the question of a man's being master of his property has never been agitated, except where there are sons or grandsons, who have a part right of ownership, and that during his life he may give, or otherwise aliene it without control. In what he does, during his life, however, it may be supposed a wife exercises some influence, and may by expostulation or endearments, or by the interference of friends, escape being deprived of all share in her husband's wealth. But when he is dead, the operation of a will would be final, and in proportion as the provisions of that will are unfavourable to her acknowledged claims, so far must the deceased have exercised a power not altogether analogous to that which he enjoyed whilst alive. In addition therefore to the clause laid down by Mr. Colebrooke, that his legacies to his family *must be controlled by the rules regarding partition made by the father of the family*, we would add, *and by the estab-*

* [Sir T. Strange, l. l., II, p. 431. 435 ff.]

lished course of inheritance after his death. These provisions might be thought to obviate the necessity for any bequests at all, and we do not see any objection to this contingency; for the practice is an innovation in the law, a very frequent violation of it, and a constant channel for the dissipation of the greater part of the bequests in interminable and demoralizing litigation.

The Supreme Court, Sir F. M. observes, will support the devise or bequest of a Hindu, if it be made of such property as the testator could lawfully have disposed of by gift in his life time, but many considerations may influence bequests which would not have any effect upon a person, during his life, in making donations. He adds, the court never professed to go further than to permit that to be effected by will, which might have been done "inter vivos." But can a man alter during his life time the course of succession to his property after his decease? If he is allowed to do this by will; if he is allowed to bequeath to a remote kinsman that which ought after his death to go to his widow, his daughter, or his brother, he does what he could not have done during life; he defrauds them of their just rights, and the court in supporting such a will makes itself a party to the violation of the law, and infringement of the rights of individuals. We are at a loss to reconcile this confident announcement of the practice of the court with a variety of sententious positions laid down by the learned judge in various parts of his book. "I do not recommend innovation, far from it. I desire to adhere to the law in its substance, and to give to every body that which he is entitled to claim" (p. 36). "If one be entitled to the immediate, and the other to the ultimate enjoyment of property, it is reasonable and just, that they should have equal protection, according to their several rights" (p. 90). The interest of him in remainder is as well worthy of the law's protection, as the interests of him in possession (p. 97). In opposition to these texts, we have every where the greatest innovation ever made in Hindu law strenuously advocated, and the rights of heirs completely kept out of view, by the support of a power to leave away from them, what every Hindu lawgiver declares they shall inherit. It does appear to us, that there is nothing so contradictory in the Hindu code, or so inconsistent in the opinions of the Paṅdits, as may be found in the learned judge's notions of the rights of heirs, when a widow succeeds to the property, and when the deceased owner leaves a will.

Again, we have the following statement of the practice relating to the administration of the law by the Supreme Court.

In many instances the wills of *Hindoos* have been recognised and established in the Snpreme Court.

It is *Mr. Colebrooke's* opinion that their right to dispose of their property by will is maintainable in the province of *Bengal*, in conformity with *Jímúta Váhana's* doctrine, that the gift or other alienation of property by a *Hindoo* is *not an invalid*, although it may be an *immoral*, act. In the words *"other alienation" Mr. Colebrooke* supposes alienation by *Will* to be included.

However this may be, it is certain that the Supreme Court grants probate of the wills of *Hindoos*, and administration to the next kin, when it is applied for in the case of an intestate.

We presume the learned judge prefaced this citation with the following passage for the sake of contrast, or to shew that the Supreme Court pays as much respect to acts of Parliament as to the Institutes of Manu.

The Stat. 21st, Geo. 3d, Ch. 70, provides, "That their *Inheritance* and *succession to lands, rents and goods*, and all matters of contract and dealing, between party and party, shall be determined in the case of *Mahomedans* by the laws and usages of *Mahomedans*, and in the case of *Gentoos* by the laws and usages of *Gentoos*.

The determination of the Supreme Court to uphold the wills of the Hindus is, we observe from the acts of the court, very oddly evinced, and the disposition, if not to set them aside, to tamper with them, and re-model them, is singularly conspicuous. Now the Hindus are to make wills, or they are not. If they are to exercise this power, their bequests are to be fulfilled. If they are not, why deceive a dying man with an erroneous impression? for how their wills have been fulfilled, the following cases will shew.

Goculchunder Corformah left all his property, with the exception of a bequest to his step-mother, to the family idol. The will, with that exception, was declared *wholly inoperative*.

Goculchunder Mitter devised that his heirs should succeed conjointly to his estate, and should never have the power to divide, and share the same.

Partition was decreed by the court.

In the will of Nemychurn Mullick it was directed, that the bulk of the family property should remain joint undivided family property under the management of the two elder brothers.

On an appeal to the King in Council, it was ordered, that partition should be made, and the property held in severalty.

In the will of Luckinarain Tagore, as we have seen, the deceased made the concurrence of two of his widows essential to the choice of an adopted son.

The court committed that election to *one* of the widows, and because, they inferred, *she had been her husband's favorite.*

The will of Raja Nobkissen was set aside in favour of an agreement *previously* granted by him, relating to the same purpose, the share of his adopted son, which the will professed to render less than the agreement.

In his will Jugut Adie directed his property to be equally divided, in absolute ownership, between his widow and his son.

The court ordered that the widow's right to her moiety should be that of *a life interest only.*

Now in some of these revisals we do not mean to question the wisdom, or the benevolence of the court; but it is obvious, that such intermeddling with the intentions of the testator is far from compatible with the spirit of the English law, which provides that "the construction be favourable, and as near the minds and apparent intents of the parties as the rules of the law will admit", and that when "the words offer no ambiguity there shall "be no interpretation contrary to their literal import." As to Hindu law, the whole proceeding is an anomaly. The learned Judge would seem to infer the legality of wills in the estimation of Hindus themselves, because very frequently the right of the testator to make particular bequests is not disputed; but we think, this is a very unsatisfactory proof of the legality of the document in Hindu law, although it exhibits a sensible acquiescence in the decisions of the court in which the cause is to be adjudged. The parties forbear to dispute the force of the will, because they know it will be in vain: they are informed, that the court is determined to uphold wills, whatever it may do with their clauses, and therefore very prudently submit to what they cannot help. But let it be understood that the court will receive arguments against the validity of wills, and there will be no lack of objectors nor objections. That they are often gross violations of Hindu law, the learned judge is compelled to admit: thus he says of the will of Sonatun Mullik, "*if it had not been for that will*, it is clear that Bidyamani (his widow) would have been entitled to the whole of his estate for her life, and that after her death it would have gone to her daughters" (p .366), and he observes of another case, "From this state of the family, if Joogul Kishore had died intestate, it is quite clear that his son Nundololl would have succeeded him", instead of which an only son, the undisputed heir of his father's whole property, was restricted to half. As to the intricate and unreasonable enravelments to which the wills of Hindus lead, we have abundant proofs of them in the two cases of Hura Sundari and Lukhinarain Thagore, which we have cited from the pages of the learned judge: and under a conviction, that wills are in the present constitution of Hindu society a mischievous innovation, we rather lament the determination of the Supreme Court to uphold the practice: at any rate, if still permitted, we think, that clear and positive rules should be laid down for their construction, and that none should be capable of being proved which are manifestly incompatible with the provisions of the Hindu law.

The next chapter treats of *contracts* and is made up almost entirely of the reprint of the texts collected in Jagannátha's Digest, translated by Mr. Colebrooke. We shall transcribe the concluding remarks as explanatory of the learned judge's object, and as vindicatory of a part of the Hindu code, at least, from the reproaches of absurdity and inconsistency so abundantly charged against it in other parts of the volume.

Although it is declared by statute, that all matters of contract and dealing, between parties, shall be determined in the case of *Hindoos* by the laws and usages of *Hindoos*, I never knew, or heard of, an instance in which the Supreme Court was called upon in a case of contract to decide by such laws and usages. I did not, therefore, consider a chapter upon contracts to be *necessary* in this work, but I conceive that the texts which I have collected, and brought together, will be thought interesting and curious.

Those who may take the trouble of reading *Jagannátha's* commentaries upon this particular subject, will wonder perhaps, at the indefatigable industry with which he has endeavoured to make simplicity complex, and to render that which is obvious *unintelligible.*

I have merely given some of the leading texts which relate to the law of contracts, and to my mind the system (generally speaking) appears to be rational and moral. No less moral, and possibly more rational, because it is, in a great degree, abstracted from the *Hindoo* religion, and dependent upon ethics alone; upon principles which are universally admitted, which are immutable in themselves, and which cannot but be eternal in their duration.

Whatever may be said by metaphysicians of the moral sense, it is plain that good faith and fair dealing are required by the institutes of all civilized people; and although there are offices, the performance of which must depend upon the feelings and the consciences of individuals—although duties must still be distinguished by those of perfect, and those of imperfect, obligation; honesty and rectitude are enforced in all civil polities, if they can be enforced by a legislative sanction.

The merit of having been founders of their jurisprudence cannot be denied to this people; and those, who are at all conversant with the decisions of our own Courts, will acknowledge the analogy which exists between some of their doctrines, and some of the texts which I have cited from the *Hindoo* law. Where this is not to be found, a comparison may, in several instances, be made without disadvantage to the *Hindoos.*

But I must restrain myself, for it is not my purpose to run into a dissertation.

There are certainly extravagancies, although I have not brought them forward, even in this part of the system; but if a prevalence of common sense is to be discovered in the laws of the Hindoos, it must be sought for in that portion of them, containing the precepts by which dealings between one man and another are to be regulated.

The next two chapters on *judicial proceedings* and *evidence* are translations, by Mr. W. H. Macnaghten, of the two first sections of the Mitákshará. That they are highly valuable, the merits of the original and learning of the translator are sufficient guarantees: they are rather however part of the text than considerations on the law. We should wish to see the rest of the Vyavahára portion of the Mitákshará translated by the same hand and published entire, for as given by Sir F. M. it has lost much of its value by compression. It is unnecessary for us to offer any detailed comments upon this part of the publication, as the law there laid down is not reduced to practice, and is so far matter rather of curiosity than use; at the same time, the Hindu System is to be regarded as a whole to be properly appreciated, and the laws of inheritance can scarcely be thoroughly understood without acquaintance with other and, in appearance, remotely connected branches of law. For this reason the institutes of Manu are particularly valuable, and the chapter of the Mitákshará on the Áchára or daily rites, and usages, would equally contribute to the illustration of the parts by conveying a view of the whole. We think the work of the learned judge has been less satisfactory than it might have been, in consequence of his enquiries having confined him to a partial investigation of the subject. There are two topics also, upon which we regret the learned judge should have abstained from offering any opinion, particularly as there is no doubt that they have a practical bearing; these are, title from possession, and the rules of evidence, at least as far as the administration of an oath is concerned: this latter we know to be a daily question of painful interest, and the other we observe from a case recorded by the learned judge has been made the subject of discussion in the Sadr Dewání. In the absence of any remarks from the learned judge we shall offer a few observations on what we conceive of the law as it appears in the translated chapters of the Mitákshará, and other authorities.

In the case of Bhawanicharn Banerjea, and the heirs of Ramkant Bunhojea (p. 283), a deed of partition was declared by the judge to be invalid, because possession was not actually taken; the elder son having instituted a suit to disprove the legality of the apportionment.

The deed was invalid on other grounds, as we have had occasion to observe; but the two Pańđits Chaturbhuj, and Śubha Śástrí, two of the ablest Pańđits we have encountered, disagreed with regard to the effects of actual possession. The former stated that the Hissanáma could not be available without possession, and Śubha Śástrí urged much more rationally that the gift was valid though possession was not taken, as that, being obstructed by the suit instituted by the plaintiff, argued no neglect nor relinquishment of right on the part of the defendants. We have no doubt of the correctness of his conclusion according to Hindu law.

Possession is in Hindu law, as well as in English, a very substantial title, no doubt; but Chaturbhuj himself admits that, to become a valid one, it must be in sight of the adverse party, and without molestation on his part, and that even possession for three generations is not sufficient, if not in sight of the adverse party, and with his acquiescence. Upon his own shewing, therefore, mere possession does not constitute right. One would think the converse of this must naturally follow, and that the absence of possession could not invalidate what its presence could not bestow. No, this would not have answered his object, and therefore he proceeds, "a title-deed *unaccompanied by possession* must be disallowed as evidence of right." Where did he find this to be the law?

In Mr. Macnaghten's translation from the Mitákshará we find "Loss accrues to him, who for twenty years observes his land enjoyed by another *without interfering*, and in the case of moveable property for ten years."* In such a case it would be reasonable, certainly, to infer relinquishment of right or defect of title; but this is very different from the delay of possession arising out of a *disputed claim.* Even in such case, however, it would appear that, if right could be ultimately established, it might be claimed; for no length of enjoyment, without title, can constitute property, as "He who *enjoys without right*,** even for many hundred years, the ruler of the earth should inflict on that sinner the punishment of a thief" (p. 424).

At the same time it may be admitted, as the Mitákshará argues, that there may be some difficulty in

* [ad Yájn. II, 27.]

** [अनागमम् Mit. I. 1.]

reconciling these texts, and although in the latter case a right is not created, yet it is forfeited by long protracted neglect, unless adequate cause be shewn; as, supposing the parties to be minors or incapable of acting for themselves, or to have been absent from the country, then the property is open to recovery, otherwise a certain period, that of three uninterrupted descents, for example, is sufficient to confirm the right of a fourth, although he have no better title to produce. This applies to fixed property; in the case of moveables the term will be limited by their nature, the difficulty of their recovery, and their liability to decay.

The main arguments in favour of the necessity of possession are the following:

"What is obtained by partition, purchase, or inheritance, or what is received from a king, is secured by possession, and lost by neglect." *Vṙihaspati.*—"Ownership lost by neglect is not resumable at will." —*Dáyatattwa.* "Possession without a deed, and not a deed without possession, but proof is firmly established by the union of both."—*Brahma Sanhitá.* "A title to land *may be* established by possession alone, or by an incontrovertible deed, if it is established by the concurrence of both, no otherwise."—*Vṙihaspati Sanhitá.* All this, however, only proves, that *wilful neglect* may forfeit right, and that title-deeds and actual possession confirm each other.

The strongest text, however, is that of Nárada: "Though there be a writing, though there be living witnessess, yet in the matter of immoveables especially, such as is not possessed is not confirmėd."* Not *Sthira* stable, firm. The purport of this law turns very much on the meaning of the word *Sthira*, and in its most obvious acceptation is does not mean that the right is lost; but that it is less secure, writings and witnesses being proofs of an inferior description to possession. That the latter does not convey right, the same authority positively declares, "Nárada has said, possession with a clear title, affords evidence, but possession constitutes no evidence if unaccompanied by a clear title"** (p. 430): this must be understood, it is true, of the first acquirer of property; but it leaves no doubt of the real intentions of the lawgiver.

Again we have a text from Yájnavalkya:*** "A deed is not strong where there is not a little possession"; but what does this imply? The title requires one of its conditions to be rendered indisputable. This being wanting, it is so far weak. Mr. Macnaghten translates this "where there is not the least possession, "there a title is not sufficient"; but this *might* be understood to signify what the law does not propose, the text being literally as we have given it, and being

---

* [Víramitr., 65 r., 4.]

** [Mitáksh. ad Yájn. II. 27. Víramitr., 63 r., 3. Vyav. May. II, 2, 1.]

*** [आगमेऽपि बलं नैव भुक्तिः स्तोकाऽपि यत्र नो । Yájn. II, 27. "acquisition by title is of no avail without possession for a short time." Dr. Röer's translation.]

explained by the commentator that "the strength in the deed is not entire." The same indeed with its context explains clearly its purport; the author states that "deeds, witnesses, and possession are the three kinds of proof; that deeds are of more weight than possession, except where possession has been hereditary; and that deeds are weak where there is no possession whatever." That is, the commentator observes, of three persons the first may plead the deed of gift, and the last may urge possession; the second may plead the gift, and the 'little' possession, the family has had of it. The term 'little' here, although literal, is therefore to be understood in the sense of 'limited' and as applied to individuals, or to time, not to a portion of the thing possessed. The Vyavahára Mátriká, however, argues upon the literal sense, and concludes that, "as the law declares the occupation of a part of a field &c. granted by a royal edict to be the virtual occupation of the whole, so the possession of no part is the relinquishment of the whole", fonnding this on one of the above cited texts, that the neglect of fixed property is its relinquishment. This conclusion, however, implies voluntary indifference or abandonment, and does not regard the delay of possession occasioned by adequate cause.

It is, therefore, in our estimation quite clear, that the Hindu law and common sense go hand in hand. A man may forego his rights, if he pleases, and any capricious abandonment of them for an unreasonable time is to be punished by their forfeiture. But he is not to be deprived of what is really his, because legal proceedings, interested opposition, accident, distance or disease, debar him from taking possession of it when it first becomes his due.

The other question which calls for a few observations is the practice observed in the courts, of taking evidence upon oath: the usual form is that of placing a copper vessel of Ganges water with a leaf of the *Tulasí* plant in it in one hand, whilst the witness touches the water with the other, and utters the following or similar declarations.

"Having touched Gangá water, copper, and Tulasí, I swear that I will truly answer the questions put to me: if I utter untruth, may I perish in a future life", or "may I perish both in this world and the next."

Popular feeling in Bengal is decidedly hostile to this practice, and it is considered highly disreputable to have taken such an oath. The disgrace attaches to a man through life, and is made a serious subject of reproach, even by his friends and connexions. Accordingly, no man who has any regard for his character will enter a court of Justice, if he can possibly avoid it, and few decent individuals will subpœna respectable witnesses, however essential to their cause; they will rather pay high and multiply the false testimony, that is to be had for hire. When subpœnaed, a man of any reputation is painfully distressed, and he secretes himself or flies beyond the jurisdiction of the court, until the suit is decided. These circumstances are too notorious to be questioned, and it can be as little doubted that they are unfavourable to the ends of Justice, as they banish from the court the only individuals from whom veracity might be expected.

The objections of the people are so far well founded, that the practice does not appear to be authorised by any of the works *on law*, ancient or modern; the provisions of which in the first stage of investigation at least are summed up in the following translation from the Mitákshará (p. 447):*

Manu has propounded a rule to be observed in taking the depositions of *Brahmins* and others. "Let the Judge imprecate a priest by his veracity; a soldier by his horse, elephant, and weapons; a merchant by his kine, grain, and gold; a mechanic, or servile man, by imprecating on his own head, if he speaks falsely, all possible crimes." The meaning is, he shall adjure the *Brahmin* by saying, if you speak falsely, your truth will be destroyed; a *Kshatriya* by saying, your horse, elephant, weapons, will become useless; a *Vaiśya*, your cattle, seeds, and gold, will be unproductive; a *Śúdra*, if you speak falsely, all sins will be on your head.

"Regenerate men, who tend herds of cattle, who trade, who practise mechanical arts, who profess dancing and singing, who are hired servants, or usurers, let the Judge exhort and examine, as if they were Śúdras."

The Vyavahára Mayúkha** adds this text from *Vríhaspati*: "Truth, carriage, arms, kine, seed, and gold, the feet of gods, and Brahmans, the head of a wife or of a child, these are declared to be oaths of efficacy in matters of minor concern, but in oaths of

* [Man., VIII, 113. 102.]

** [III, 3. Vyavahára Tattwa, 57. Víramitr. 88, v., 12.]

the highest importance the truth must be established by ordeal." The Ordeal is of five kinds,—scales, water, fire, poison and sacred libation. An interesting account of each is to be found in the Asiatic Researches (vol. I.),* but in no stage of the evidence is touching the Ganges water or any other sacred object made a test of the truth of evidence by any legal authorities.

As however the practice was introduced throughout all the courts, both civil and military, under the British Government, it is impossible to suppose that the measure was adopted without due enquiry, or that it was an innovation unwarranted by the code or customs of the country: accordingly it may be defended by the practice of the act, as alluded to in the Puráńas and Tantras, and by local usages.

In the villages of Bengal, in the case of private disputes or arbitrations, the feet of a Brahman or the head of a child are the most usual attestations of assertion; the same are commonly referred to in the western provinces. But the sacred poems, the Tulasí leaf, Śálagrám stone, Gangá water, and even spirituous liquors, are in more extensive use, and they are not unusual though less frequent in Bengal; the practice is therefore perfectly consistent with the customs of the country.

In the Tantras, *Śiva* appeals to the Gangá, which is supposed to flow from his head in proof of his asser-

---

* [See also Stenzler, "die indischen Gottesurtheile", in Zeitschrift der d. morgenl. Ges., IX, 661-82.]

tion. Thus he observes: "How is it possible to doubt the truth of my words when uttered in contact with the Ganges, the Snake, and the Bull?"

The chief authority for the practice is, however, the Brahma Vaivartta Puráńa, and this declares various hells to be the portion of those who utter untruth after touching the Śálagrám, the Tulasí, or the Gangá.

"Whoever, having taken the Tulasí leaf in his hand, "does not adhere to his engagement, is punished in "the hell *Kálasútra*, as long as the Sun and Moon "endure. Whoever takes a false oath by the Tulasí "leaf, is sentenced to the *Kumbhípáka* hell for the "reigns of fourteen Indras. Whoever, holding the "Śálagrám stone, utters a lie, suffers in the *Kúrma-"danshtra* hell for the life of Brahma. Whoever touch-"ing the Śálagrám stone breaks his promise, is con-"signed to the *Asipatra* hell for a hundred thousand "Manvantaras."

"Having heard the words of Brahma, the lord of "wisdom, the chief of the wise took the water of the "Gangá in his hand, and pledged his faith: if any one, "having touched the water of the Ganges, utters a "false assertion, he is punished in the Kálasútra hell "during the existence of Brahma."

These texts therefore shew that the practice was no innovation, and their authority, although not law, will scarcely be denied by any class of Hindus. At the same time, they are really very worthless, and apply to a state of things wholly foreign to the primitive systems both of religion and law. The Tantras are the authorities of the worshippers of Śiva and Śakti; the Brahma Vaivartta is a decided Vaishńava work. Most of the Tantras are modern, and the Brahma Vaivartta is of very recent date, being a collection of absurd legends relating to Kŕishńa and Rádhá, objects of veneration as conjoined not more than four or five centuries old. Under any circumstances, the Tantras and Puráńas cannot be received in opposition to the Śruti and Smŕiti, the religious and legal codes, and in this instance the individual works appealed to are of the worst description. Although, therefore, there is authority for the form of oath administered by the English courts to Hindu witnesses, it is still unquestionably foreign to the spirit of the law, neither does it derive any weight from being a rite of popular practice, for its observance chiefly prevails amongst the inferior castes, and rather loses than gains respectability from its popular adoption. We should therefore wish to see some other system introduced, and are confident that, wherever the form was objected to, a simple affirmation subject to the penalty of perjury would be much more conducive to the ends of public justice than the existing usage.

The importance of the subject must plead our excuse for devoting so large a portion of our pages to the examination of this work: we now take leave of it. Upon the whole we cannot deny the general utility of the Considerations on Hindu Law, and in the information it unfolds of the objects and practice of the Supreme Court it will be a most serviceable record:

at the same time it will not answer the purpose of its publication, as the conclusions are too loose, and, as we have presumed to argue, are in many instances too inaccurate to entitle it to become a safe and sure guide in matters of Hindu law. The utility of the work is also much impaired by the utter want of arrangement which prevails throughout, and for which the learned judge pleads in extenuation the haste with which the work was put together, as we have cited his apologies to prove. But what occasion was there for so much precipitancy? Why could not the materials have been taken home, and digested by the learned Judge in the *otium cum dignitate*, he is about to enjoy? We might then have had a work worthy of his known powers and long experience, and which would have entitled Sir F. Macnaghten to the permanent gratitude of the profession, and of the public.

XII.

REVIEW

of

BHAGAVAD GITA,

id est

ΘΕΣΠΕΣΙΟΝ ΜΕΛΟΣ,

sive Almi Krishnæ et Arjunæ Colloquium de Rebus divinis Bharatæ Episodium. Textum recensuit et interpretationem latinam adjecit AUGUSTUS GUILIELMUS SCHLEGEL.

BONN (1823), 1 vol. 8vo.

From the Oriental Quarterly Review. Calc. 1825. Vol. III, p. 1-51.

THE cultivation of Sanskrit by the Scholars of the Continent is no pretended nor unprofitable pursuit: they have not engaged in it merely to acquire the repute of mastering a venerable and difficult language, or to familiarise themselves with a new branch of literature for their private gratification, but they have come forward to exhibit public proofs of their proficiency, and have enriched the community of letters with the spoils of individual research. Amongst the foremost is AUGUSTUS WILLIAM SCHLEGEL, a name long known in the highest departments of literature, and one particularly dear to Englishmen, as that of the enthusiastic and able commentator of Shakespeare.

To an almost universal conversancy with the languages of ancient and modern Europe, Schlegel has superadded a very extensive knowledge of the Sanskrit language, proofs of which attainment have been for some time before the public, in his Indische Bibliothek, particularly in his elaborate and masterly review of Wilson's Sanskrit Dictionary. He has however now adduced one still more convincing in his edition of the text of the Bhagavad Gítá with a Latin translation and critical annotations, and he is about to furnish still more ample testimony in the text and translation of the Rámáyańa. How far he is equal to this latter undertaking may be inferred from the success of the present, of which we shall proceed to offer some account. The learned translator has a right to demand this at our hands, as the worthy rival of our countrymen in a path they have hitherto almost monopolised: the monopoly is theirs no longer, and Frank, Bopp, Chezy, and Schlegel have all preferred respectable claims to participation in the walk of Sanskrit literature; claims which it is to be hoped will only serve to animate our zeal, and urge us to prove that we have not been indebted for distinction only to the absence of competitors.

The first object of Schlegel, in publishing the Bhagavad Gítá, was the wish to employ in a becoming manner the fount of Nágarí types presented by the King of Prussia to the university of Bonn. This fount was executed at Paris under the professor's inspection, and is a creditable specimen of typographic art. We are not disposed, however, to admire exceedingly the forms of the letters: the vowels, which occur above and below the lines, are inelegantly engraved and clumsily connected, many of the conjunct consonants are much too slight, and the heads of the letters are too square. Such as they are however, the characters are neatly executed, and, with the advantage of Europe ink and printing, make the handsomest book, except the Nalus of Bopp, which has yet been published in the sacred language of the Hindus.

The text of the Gítá has been printed from a copy made by Schlegel himself from four Manuscripts in the Royal Library at Paris; three of these were described by Hamilton in his catalogue, the fourth is a recent addition from the collection of Col. Polier. Schlegel's copy was also compared with the Calcutta Edition of 1808, which it appears is no longer procurable even in England, and which Schlegel obtained from a friend. The text now printed, it must be admitted, is singularly correct, much more so than that of the Calcutta edition: a circumstance not very surprising, however, as the latter was the work of Native Editors without any assistance from European superintendance.

Of the translation we shall speak in detail, and shall particularise such passages, as seem to be erroneously rendered. In doing this, however, we must observe that particular exceptions are not to be regarded as detracting from the merits of the whole: on the contrary, as the objections are almost entirely verbal, and few mistakes or misconceptions of any moment occur, the necessity of seeking for blemishes in matters of so little moment is the highest compliment that can be paid to the accuracy and knowledge of the translator.

That the translation made by Mr. Wilkins in 1787 was of essential service to the present translator is fully acknowledged by him. "In interpretatione Bhagavad Gitæ elaboranda interpretationem v. cl. Caroli Wilkins magno mihi adjumento fuisse, non modo non diffiteor, sed ultro gratoque animo id agnosco:" he adds however, what is correct, that he has occasionally deviated from the steps of his predecessor, and that, if the original translator were now to revise his performance, he would no doubt authorise such deviations. In this we are disposed to concur with him, as there are several passages in Wilkins's translation, which might be amended; on the whole however it is very correctly executed, and with reference to the early period of Sanskrit study, at which it was accomplished, and the absence of all assistance from Grammars and Dictionaries, a publication of singular merit. Some of Schlegel's variations are very justifiable, and he might have made them more numerous still, as we think in some places he has been misled by the English version. Occasionally, however, his variations are not warranted by the text, as we shall have occasion to observe.

The Bhagavad Gítá, as is well known, is a treatise on theology, communicated by Kŕishńa to his friend and pupil Arjuna during a short suspension of the engagement between the Páńdava and Kuru armies. It is a section of the Mahábhárata and, as observed by Schlegel, is proved by the concurrence of the Parisian manuscripts, the printed text of Calcutta, and the translation of Wilkins, to be a genuine and unadulterated work. Schlegel and Wilkins both regard it as a composition of high antiquity; but this requires proof. We may admit with the former, that the origin of philosophy amongst the Hindus is remote, "sine dubio valde antiqua fuit apud Indos philosophiæ origo", and that the Brahmans of India investigated subjects of theological philosophy long before Plato or Pythagoras; but, upon examining the doctrines of the Bhagavad Gítá, we shall find many as foreign to the theology of the Vedas as to philosophical speculation, and indicative of a deviation from the primitive system, which we shrewdly suspect is the work of a comparatively recent date.

The original Hindu system comprised a two-fold division, and inculcated the worship of the minor deities by works, or sacrifice, gifts, and penance, and the knowledge of the great universal spirit by abstract and secluded meditation. These two divisions were not incompatible: works were proper for men engaged in active life, and who had to discharge the positive duties of their caste and condition. But when they arrived at an age, at which they could no longer take a useful share in social pursuits, it was enjoined them to leave the world, and in the silence and solitude of the hermitage to devote themselves to the cultivation of divine knowledge, performing in the first stage of this course the essential ceremonies, but finally depositing, as it is quaintly expressed, the holy fires in the mind, or discarding further attention to the ceremonial offices of religion. With the natural tendency of enthusiasm it soon happened, that the period of seclusion was accelerated, and men adopting the notion, that works were altogether unworthy of human attention, deserted their active duties for ascetic contemplation. It may be doubted, however, whether this was the spirit of the Vedas,* and it may be most probably referred to a period subsequent to those works, prior however to the Grecian invasion; for at that time a number of sects were already in existence, as the Gymnosophists, Sarmanes or Germanes, and Hylobii, all of the ascetic class.

* Manu permits the householder to become a Sannyási at once, or to pass over the intermediate stage of the hermit with attention to ceremonies. His commentator adds, a Brahman may proceed from the *first order*, or the student, to the state of a Sannyási, but this is quite at variance with the text, which declares that, if a Brahman have not read the Vedas, begotten a Son, and performed sacrifices, and yet aim at final beatitude, he shall sink to a place of degradation. These are called the three debts—to the sages, the manes, and the gods; and it is repeatedly declared that the man who has not acquitted himself of those obligations shall not pretend to supreme felicity, or to divine wisdom derived from contemplative devotion. The text is therefore entirely consistent with the old system: the comment interpolates more modern ideas.—Manu, Ch. vi, v. 25. 35. 38; also 94. 95. [Lassen, I, 580.]

In compliance with the purport of the Vedas, the Vedánta philosophy, though it did not prohibit works, countenanced them only so far as they prepared the soul for that state, in which it should be capable of acquiring divine knowledge, and when purified from all mundane illusion it might be fit to recognise its identity with the Supreme. The union with the supreme spirit resulting from this identification, and the consequent exemption from returning to any human form, are, according to the Vedánta, attainable by divine knowledge alone, and at all events, such knowledge being attained, the performance of rites and the observance of ceremonies became objects of comparative indifference, as*—"If purificatory rites be considered essential, (it may be said) they are indifferent, for if Janaka and others observed rites and ceremonies, yet wise men have offered no sacrifice with fire", *Brahma Sútra* 3, 4, 9. And the doctrine was further extended to the neglect of all instituted observances whatever: "If it be said, the attainment of (divine) knowledge cannot be without the observance of the stated orders, (as student &c. and the ceremonies incident to caste,) that is not the case—it may be attained in them, that is obvious: but it may be attained out of them, as well as in them, as was seen with Raikka and others, and it is also confirmed by the law, for

---

* आचारदर्शनादिति चेत्तुल्यं तु दर्शनं जनकादेर्यथा कर्माचारदर्शनम् । विद्वांसोऽप्यग्निहोत्रं न तु हवामहिरे. [The author has omitted to mention, which of the many commentaries on the Brahma Sútras he follows in these quotations. It is not Śankara's.]

the sacred codes relate that Samwartta and others, belonging to no instituted order, attained perfection." Ibid. 3, 4, 36.* Passages from the Upanishads also may be adduced, undervaluing the ritual. "Nothing obtained through perishable means can be eternal, hence what use of rites?" "Neither can he (the Supreme) be conceived by the help of austerities or religious rites." "All votaries who repose on God alone their firm belief, originating from a knowledge of the Vedánta, and who by forsaking religious rites obtain purification, being continually occupied in divine reflections during life, are at the time of death entirely freed from ignorance, and absorbed into God. "*Muńďaka Upanishad*,** *translated by Rammohun Roy*."

In permitting however the practice of the ritual, even after divine knowledge is obtained, the Vedánta makes a wide distinction between its ceremonies, and positively interdicts all those performed for any particular objects, as sacrifices supposed to be the means of obtaining power, wealth, progeny, and other worldly goods: the only works authorized are the Nitya and Naimittika, the constant and occasional rites incumbent on every order of Hindus, as the daily Sandhyas, oblations with fire, and libations to the manes. In these also the performer must propose to himself no

---

* अथानाश्रमिणां सर्वथा विद्यानधिकार इति चेन्न । अन्तरा-चापि तु तद्दृष्टेः । आश्रममन्तराद्विनापि च ज्ञानं स्यात्॥ रैक्वादिवाद्दर्श-नादपि च स्मर्यते ॥ अनाश्रमे सम्वर्त्तकादीनां सिद्धिश्रुतौ स्मर्यते ॥

** [III, 1, 8. 2, 6.]

benefit, and must observe them merely in conformity to the directions of the Śástras. With such a reservation, recommendation of the observance of certain ceremonies is not unfrequently urged. "Those rites, the prescription of which wise men found in the Vedas, are truly the means of producing good consequences." *Muńḋaka Upan.* "All acts are to be regarded, before knowledge is obtained, for the purification of the intellect, as a steed to convey a traveller to his home." *Brahma Sútra.**

"The duties of the order are to be discharged, according to the text: that is, it is said in the Kaushárava—Beholding this as himself, let him perform rites without hesitation,** meaning that the individual, possessed of divine knowledge, shall discharge the duties of his order, not those which do not appertain to his caste." *Ibid.*—The work we are about to examine also admits, though rather reluctantly, the superiority of divine knowledge and contemplative exercise over works and faith. Thus Arjuna is directed to fix his mind on Kŕishńa: if he cannot do that at once, he must endeavour to effect it by practice; if that is above his strength, he is to perform works, abandoning their fruit; and if that is still too great an effort, he is to put his trust in Kŕishńa. The subsequent

* सर्वापेक्षा च यज्ञादिश्रुतेरश्ववत्. [III, 4, 26.]

** विहितत्वाच्चाश्रमकर्मापि । ३२ । पश्यन्निममात्मानं कुर्यात्कर्मा-विचारयन्निति कौषारवश्रुतौ विहितत्वादाश्रमस्य अपि नावर्णस्य च कर्म ज्ञानी कुर्यात् ॥

passage in a great manner disarranges this series, but the scope of the section corroborates its tenor, and it harmonises with the general spirit of Hindu theology.

It may therefore be concluded, that the Vedánta philosophy, although it places the ritual as subordinate to divine knowledge, rather inclines to the performance of disinterested acts of devotion, and recommends those ceremonies, which propose no particular fruit to the performer. This is not the case with somé other philosophical divisions of the Hindus, and as observed in the Gítá, "some learned men have taught that acts should be shunned as faulty." *Lect.* 18, 3.* This, as *Sankara* and *Srídhara Swámí* observe, refers particularly to the Sánhhyas, who object to all the sacrificial ceremonial of the Vedas, and declare that all acts are to be relinquished: although, however condemning the ritual of the Vedas as sanguinary and futile, the Sánkhyas do not exclude all attention to outward observances, and they enjoin particular postures, modes of breathing, and looking, which they profess contribute to constrain the wanderings of the spirit, and force it into a conjunction with its primitive source.

These practices are properly the invention of a different School, the Pátanjala, in which in like manner they are substitutes for the ceremonies of the Vedas. They effect the *Yoga*, or Union of the individualised with the universal spirit, and hence the system by

* त्याज्यं दोषवदित्येके कर्म प्राहुर्मनीषिणः ।

which they are inculcated is called the Yoga Śástra. The like identification, however, or consequent exemption from transmigration, is the great object of all the philosophical sects, and the term is, therefore, familiar to them, as well as to that to which it is particularly applied. They have also adopted more or less extensively the ceremonial of the yoga, or the contrivances by which intellectual aberration is to be restrained, and the mind forced into exclusive meditation on spirit. In this light the Bhagavad Gítá is a Yoga work, and the different divisions treat of various kinds of *Yoga*, or the various means by which union with the supreme spirit is to be attained.

Whether the ritual of the Vedas be observed or not, there is no reason to conclude, that either the Sánkhya or the Vedánta School admits the compatibility of divine knowledge with the discharge of active social duties. Up to the period of seclusion, the student or the householder may be preparing himself by a tranquillised mind, and indifference to the objects of human solicitude, for that perfect calm in which knowledge is alone attainable, but it is not possible that a man engaged in worldly occupations should accomplish the requisite condition of quiescence. Hence the institution of the different degrees or áśramas, and particularly those of the Vánaprastha and Bhikshuka, or Hermit and Beggar, as indispensable stages in the scale of perfection.

In the course of time it was probably found, either that the encouragement given to ascetic devotion was injurious to social happiness, or that it was considered an unfair monopoly of emancipation, and a kind of compromise was admitted, by which the acquisition of divine knowledge should be placed within the reach of all whom it was worth while to conciliate. Hence the practice of mortification and penance came to be discountenanced,* and the discharge of social duties according to station and caste of the individual to be insisted on, at the same time that emancipation was pursued. Indifference to the result was all that was stipulated for: men were to adore, as Epicurus worshipped, nulla spe, nullo pretio inductus: the doctrine of the Vedas, that those works especially which propose some benefit should be abandoned, was strained into the position that no works should be abandoned, but that the fruit or consequence of all should be disregarded, and that this disregard of consequences was alone the real abandonment of works.** This principle

---

* In the Gítá the practisers of austere penance and mortifications are denounced as followers of a demoniac faith.

अशास्त्रविहितं घोरं तप्यन्ते ये तपो जनाः। दम्भाहंकारसंयुक्ताः कामरागबलान्विताः॥ कर्षयन्तः शरीरस्थं भूतग्राममचेतसः। मां चैवान्तःशरीरस्थं तान् विद्ध्यासुरनिश्चयान्॥

Those men who, filled with pride and hypocrisy, perform horrid penance, undirected by the ritual, and characterised by violence, passion and desire, are fools who torment the aggregated elementary essence of the body, and me who am present in it: know them to put their faith in fiends. 17, 5. 6.

** सर्व्वकर्म्मफलत्यागं प्राहुस्त्यागं विचक्षणाः 18, 2. The wise declare the abandonment of fruits to be abandonment. अनाश्रितः कर्म्मफलं कार्य्यं कर्म्म करोति यः। स संन्यासी च योगी च न निरग्नि

was applied not only to the ceremonial of religion, but to the duties of origin and profession, and even to the faculties and organs of the body.* In this enlarged interpretation of the doctrine of the Vedas the Puráńas were chiefly instrumental, and amongst the principal agents was the Mahábhárata or at least the Bhagavad Gítá.

The doctrine thus promulgated might be considered to deviate from the original faith only as far as the interpretation was questionable. It was still founded on the text of the Vedas, and might be held by some interpreters to be no more than what was fully warranted by those works. The Puráńas, however, did not stop here: they superadded a dogma wholly at variance with the spirit and letter of the Vedas when they made Faith—implicit reliance on any one deity—sufficient for emancipation. In this new sentiment the Bhagavad Gítá stands pre-eminent, and it is re-

---

चाक्रियः 6, 1. He who performs proper acts without regard to the consequences of acts, is the real Sannyási and Yogi, not he who is without a sacred fire or abstains from acts.

* यज्ञदानतपःकर्म न त्याज्यं कार्यमेव तत् Sacrifice, alms and penance are acts never to be relinquished, but to be performed. 18, 5.

स्वे स्वे कर्मण्यभिरतः संसिद्धिं लभते नरः A man attains perfection by the diligent discharge of his peculiar duty. [18, 45.]

कायेन मनसा बुद्ध्या केवलैरिन्द्रियैरपि। योगिनः कर्म कुर्वन्ति सङ्गं त्यक्त्वात्मशुद्धये॥

The adepts perform acts in body, heart, and mind, and with the simple organs, for the purification of the spirit, abandoning desire. 5, 11.

peatedly declared in it that trust in Kŕishńa is of itself exemption from all return to worldly existence.* Such assertions are a clear proof that the work which maintains them is the production of a more modern and degenerate Hinduism.**

According to all the systems of Philosophy derived from the Vedas, the most assiduous worship of the Gods of the Hindu Pantheon can only elevate the worshipper to equal rank with them. "Those observers of ceremonies who perform the adoration of celestial Gods as well as the worship of the sacred fire and oblation to sages, ancestors, men and other creatures,

---

* सर्व्वधर्म्मान्परित्यज्य मामेकं शरणं व्रज Abandoning all duties take refuge with me alone, 18, 66. मय्यावेश्य मनो ये मां नित्ययुक्ता उपासते। श्रद्धया परयोपेतास्ते मे युक्ततमा मताः॥ Those who have imbued their minds with me, and worship me constantly, being endowed with firm faith, are held most perfect by me [XII, 2].

भक्त्या त्वनन्यया शक्य अहमेवंविधोऽर्ज्जुन। ज्ञातुं द्रष्टुं च तत्त्वेन प्रवेष्टुं च परन्तप॥ I am such, oh Arjuna, that by faith placed in me, and in no other, alone may men know, behold, and be absorbed in me, subduer of thy foes. 11, 54.

** The worship of particular deities for particular purposes is the main purport of the practical portion of all the Vedas, but no one divinity occupies more than his share or swallows up the rest: neither is mere faith, trust without worship, enjoined: formulæ are however produced from the Atharvańa or fourth Veda, which differ very essentially in this respect from the hymns and prayers of the other three. The authenticity of these is rather questionable, and even if proved establishes but little, as the history and character of this Veda are far from being ascertained: the style of the fragments is much more modern than that of the other Vedas.

will by means of the latter surmount the obstacles presented by natural temptations, and will attain the state of the celestial Gods through the practice of the former." *Íśopanishad, translated by Rammohun Roy.** The Bhagavad Gítá admits this of all the Gods except Kŕishńa, conforming to the sectarial character which is peculiar to the Puráńas. "Those who worship the Gods go to the Gods,—those who worship the Progenitors go to the Progenitors,—those who sacrifice to the Ghosts go to the Ghosts,—those who worship me go to me." [IX, 25.] And again, "Those born of sinful wombs who diligently depend on me, Women, Vaiśyas and Śúdras, obtain supreme felicity." 9, 32. The doctrine is carried *ad absurdum*, but precisely in the spirit of the Puráńas. "Whosoever worships me exclusively, although addicted to unholy practices, he shall be held sanctified and well addressed: he quickly becomes of a virtuous spirit and attains eternal rest, for be assured, Kaunteya, no one who trusteth in me perisheth." 9, 30, 31,** and this is called union (with the supreme) by the *royal* knowledge, the *royal mystery*.***

---

* [Śankara ad Íśop. 11.]

** अपि चेत्सुदुराचारो भजेत मामनन्यभाक्। साधुरेव स मन्तव्यः सम्यग्व्यवसितो हि सः॥ क्षिप्रं भवति धर्म्मात्मा शश्वच्छान्तिं निगच्छति। कौन्तेय प्रतिजानीहि न मे भक्तः प्रणश्यति॥ 9, 30, 31. The mischievous tendency of the doctrine is evident, and that no doubt of it might be left, the popular works represent, in legendary adventures, the commission of various crimes as matters that are easily expiated, by firm belief in Kŕishńa, Bhagavad or Mahádeva.

*** Śankara Swámi, indeed, asserts that the Gítá teaches eman-

From these observations the character of the Bhagavad Gítá will now be understood, and it was the more necessary to offer some such preliminary view, as the learned translator has abstained from commenting upon the philosophy of his text. He pleads want of leisure for the undertaking, having been anxious to publish the book without delay. He urges also in further excuse the absence of the best commentaries. We doubt whether he would have received that aid from the commentators he seems to have anticipated: —they are far from explicit, and make extensive use of previous and collateral knowledge, the references to which they rarely explain. In addition to their glosses, therefore, it would be necessary to enter more deeply, than perhaps the means attainable in Europe permit, into the systems of Hindu theology, to do full justice to the speculations of the Gítá. We do not think, indeed, that they deserve the labour, as they are of too popular and spurious an origin, and we should rather see such acquirements and acumen as Schlegel's exercised upon some of the more abstruse and unadulterated performances of the Vedánta and Sánkhya schools.

---

cipation from knowledge only, and not from works nor faith, availing himself of Kŕishńa's injunctions to take refuge with him alone, and identifying Kŕishńa with the Supreme: he labours very assiduously to prove also that works are only recommended as the means of obtaining knowledge, but his arguments are more subtle than satisfactory, and he is evidently influenced by the popularity of the Gítá in the attempt to derive from it that support to his own doctrines which it does not afford.

Having thus taken a general view of the doctrine of the Bhagavad Gítá, we shall now enter upon an examination of the work in detail, with accompanying reference to the Translation. The work is divided into eighteen adhyáyas or lectures, each in the original described by its appropriate denomination. These Wilkins has translated—Schlegel has left them untouched, in consequence of entertaining some doubts of their being the work of the author of the text. We do not see any reason for the doubt, as the titles invariably occur in the manuscripts, and are sufficiently applicable to the subject of each section.

The Bhagavad Gítá opens with the report made to Dhŕitaráshtra, the father of the Kurus, by Sanjaya, his charioteer, of what has recently occurred at Kurukshetra, where the hostile hosts of the Páńdavas and Kauravas are assembled. Previous to the engagement, Arjuna, observing kinsmen and connexions in either army, expresses to Kŕishńa, his friend and charioteer, great reluctance to engage in a contest so unnatural. Kŕishńa, to overcome this feeling, enters upon a dissertation on the nature of spirit, his own divinity, the merit of various kinds of worship, and the propriety of discharging religious and moral obligations; in consequence of which Arjuna consents to fight. This is the business of the episode. Arjuna's regret, *Arjuna-vishdda*, forms the subject of the first *adhyáya*, rendered lecture by Wilkins, and lectio by Schlegel.

It has been the avowed object of the translator to be as literal as possible, and he has therefore translated most of the epithets,—thus he renders *Mahára-tha*, the common title of the leaders, signifying one fighting in a chariot, magno curru vectus; and *sarva-mahárathát́* omnes æque magnis curribus vecti: although *mahá* does mean great, it does not bear that acceptation only in these places, and might have been omitted or modified without any violation of fidelity.

V. 10. Schlegel has substituted non satis idoneus [impar, 2nd ed.] and idoneus, for Wilkins's translation of *Aparyáptam* and *Paryáptam*, innumerable and numerable. The commentators differ in their explanation of these terms. Śrídhara Swámí explains them by *Asamartha* and *Samartha*, which authorises Schlegel's translation. Nílakańt́ha however prefers *Bahu* and *Alpa*, which agree with Wilkins. The sense of the passage renders Wilkins's translation preferable in our opinion, as it would be rather inconsistent in Sanjaya to detract from his own friends, of whom he is actually speaking, by asserting that they were unable to face the enemy. The readings may be reconciled by considering the expression elliptical, as suggested by the second named commentator; *Aparyáptam* meaning, not capable of being surrounded or opposed by the enemy, and not, unfit to contend with them.

V. 13. *Pańava* and *Ánaka* are here translated cymbala et cornua; for the sake of variety, we presume, as they signify no such things; but merely differently formed drums. Wilkins has avoided all dispute here by grouping them as warlike instruments.

V. 15. The conch shell is the favorite instrument of the Hindus, both in war and sacrifice. In the Mahábhárata, we find every hero provided with his conch, and in general it bears a distinct appellation:—in this place several are enumerated, and we mention it to show how well the Latin Language translates these denominations, and how dexterously Schlegel has adapted the terms: thus *Pánchajanya*, once the shell of Panchajanya a giant, he renders Gigantea: *Devadatta*, Theodotes: *Paúńdra*, from its being of the colour of sugar cane, Arundinea: *Anantavijaya*, Triumphatrix: and *Sughosha* and *Mańipushpaka*, literally Dulcisona and Jemmiflorea.

V. 30. *Bhramatíva cha me manas* is rendered mens mea quasi titubat. This translation is scarcely correct, for titubo does not signify to wander or whirl round, the sense of *bhramati*: perhaps torquet or vagatur would have been preferable, or perturbatur would have been closer to the purport, if not to the letter of the expression.

V. 38. *Lobha* is rendered libido, but we think cupiditas would have been less ambiguous: Arjuna's remark is that the minds of the opposite party are distracted by the desire of supremacy and wealth, or, as Wilkins expresses it, by the lust of power.

V. 40. Some indistinctness pervades the translation in this and the following verses with regard to the term *Kuladharmáh́*, rendered by sacra gentilitia, and *Játidharmáh́*, by *familiarum* [ordinum] sacra. *Dharma* is not merely sacred or religious, but moral and social duty,* the obligation contracted by birth, and station: in this sense *Kuladharmáh́*, should be rather familiarum munera or officia. Wilkins renders these terms "family virtue, and virtue of a tribe", but virtue is too general a term. The service of Brahmans is the *Dharma*, the duty, of Śúdras, for instance, but it could scarcely be called either piety or virtue. The sense of the original would be tolerably well conveyed by the ritus familiæ patrumque of the old Roman Law.

In the same passage the term *kulastriyah́* is rendered feminae nobiles by Schlegel, women of a family by Wilkins; neither is quite correct, as *kulastrí* means a woman of character, a chaste and respectable woman, one who preserves a family, attends to its duties, and adds to its reputation; being explained कुलरक्षिका, चलन-कुलधर्म्मा and कुलकीर्त्तिकरा by different commentators on the Amara Kosha, where the term occurs synonymous with कुलपालिका, the preserver of a race.

V. 47. *Sankhye*, in acie, is more acccurately rendered by Wilkins, "in the war."

In the second Lecture Kŕishńa undertakes to prove the unreasonableness of Arjuna's reluctance to combat with his relations in the Kuru ranks, and draws his arguments chiefly from the *Sánkhya* philosophy, hence the section is denominated *Sánkhya Yoga*, Spiritual union according to the Sánkhya doctrines. Wilkins has translated it, "Of the nature of the soul, and spe-

---

* धारणाद्धर्म्मः, Dharma is so named from upholding, preserving mankind, and the universe.—Haradatta on Gautama's aphorisms.

culative doctrines"; but the principles of the Sánkhya are no more speculative than those of any other school. Schlegel, as observed, avoids translating these titles, but in the body of the text, when the term Sánkhya occurs, he renders it Ratiocinium, and Scientia rationalis,—terms as little applicable as specific designations, as speculative, and founded probably upon the previous employment of that word. It is true that it is not easy to render the meaning of the original. Śrídhara Swámí defines it etymologically* as the real nature of spirit made manifest by perfect knowledge. Śankara explains it discrimination between matter and spirit, or Prakŕiti and Purusha: and it is elsewhere defined as the doctrine of enumeration, or in which the sage proceeds by regularly enumerated steps to perfection: *sankhyá* meaning number, enumeration.** It had better therefore we think, have been left untranslated, in the same way as we use the denominations of the Greek schools, Stoic, Platonic, &c. with little or no modification. As employed in the Gítá, the followers of the Sánkhya doctrines mean those who disclaim works, as opposed to those who observe them, who are called Yogís, a term which is likewise calculated to create some perplexity: thus Śankara

---

* सम्यक्ख्यायते प्रकाश्यते वस्तुतत्त्वमनयेति संख्या सम्यग्ज्ञानं तस्मिन्प्रकाशमानमात्मतत्त्वं साङ्ख्यं ॥ [v. 39.]

** सङ्ख्यायते यस्मिञ्शास्त्रे तत्साङ्ख्यं ॥ [See Professor Goldstücker's "Pániní". London: 1861, p. 151, and Professor F. E. Hall's Preface to his edition of the Sánkhyapravachanabháshya. Calc. 1856, p. 1-6.]

says the Sánkhyas are those who are possessed of knowledge, arising from discrimination between that which is spirit and that which is not; who, abandoning works from the period of studentship, have acquired certainty in the understanding of the Vedánta; who are known as mendicants and hermits, and stand firm in Brahma. The Yogís, as mentioned in the text of the Gítá, he contents himself with calling *Karmís*, those performing karma or acts. It might have been preferable, therefore, when speaking of the disciples of these systems, to have distinguished them as Contemplationem colentes, and Ritus asservantes, instead of Scientiæ rationalis and Operum devoti.

V. 5. *Bhunjíya bhogán* is translated much too literally, 'vescar dapibus', as it implies, 'I should enjoy enjoyments'. The preferable reading attaches the epithet *Arthakámán* to *Bhogán*, signifying the enjoyments arising from pleasure and wealth; hence Wilkins renders it, "I should partake of possessions, wealth and pleasures." Schlegel has added the epithet to *Gurún*, the elders of the Kurus, desirous of wealth, Magistris opum avidis, and this is allowable.

V. 7. *Dharma-sammúdha-chetáh*: Arjuna says of himself, his mind is bewildered as to his duty; that is whether as a warrior he ought to fight the enemy, or whether as of kin to them he ought to avoid the combat. This idea is far from being correctly conveyed by the expression 'religione mentem attonitus'. Wilkins has preserved the thought, though he has not expressed it very happily, "my understanding is confounded by the dictates of my duty:" the note he adds, however, shews that he perfectly understood it.

V. 14. *Mátrásparśáń*, elementorum contactus, is a palpable mistake, committed too in the face of the more correct translation of Wilkins, "sensibility of the faculties", at least with regard to the first of the two terms: *Mátrá* is explained by both Śankara and Śrídhara, as he renders it, Faculties: the *Mátrás* they say are those, by which the objects of sense are measured or perceived;* they constitute the *Vŕitti*, the peculiar practice or faculty of the organs of perception. *Sparśa* again, though literally touch or contact, has not that limited sense here: it is the exercise of the faculties or their being acted upon** by the objects of their exercise. So far Wilkins's translation of the word by sensibility is objectionable, as it is not ability, but action, that is intended.

V. 39. Kŕishńa, having exposed the folly of Arjuna's regret by arguments drawn from the Sánkhya doctrine of the eternity and imperishableness of both matter and spirit, now proceeds to combat his sentiments with the doctrines of the Yoga School. "This knowledge thus expounded to you is derived from the Sánkhya,—now hear what the Yoga declares, being possessed of which knowledge you shall laugh at the bonds of action." Yoga in the Gítá most usually implies the performance of works, as subsequently ex-

---

* मात्रा आभिर्मीयन्ते शब्दादयः Śankara Bháshya.

** मात्राणां स्पर्शाः शब्दादिभिः संयोगाः ॥

plained, being only so far modified that the absence of all desire of benefit is indispensable.* Śankara asserts that the *Samádhi Yoga*, or performance of certain meditative acts, is also comprised. *Sánkhya*, as already noticed, is explained by Schlegel Ratiocinium, in our estimation much too loosely, and in like manner we object to his rendering *Yoga*, Devotio; although he follows Wilkins, who renders it Devotion. As we however understand devotion, we can scarcely conceive it to be identifiable with the performance of religious ceremonies, pro forma, with an utter disregard of consequences. Ritibus Assensus would perhaps better convey the sense of the term, and A ritibus Dissentio, the opposed purport of the Sánkhya; but as these phrases would still only convey a partial impression

---

* सिद्ध्यसिद्ध्योः समो भूत्वा समत्वं योग उच्यते Being alike indifferent to the attainment or non-attainment (of the object of the act), that equality (or indifference) is termed Yoga, v. 48.

Yoga is also said to be the absence of pain दुःखसंयोगवियोगं योगसंज्ञितं 6, 23. Sejunctionem a doloris conjugio sciat devotionis nomine designari. Again Śankara calls Yoga आत्मनो घटनं योगैश्वर्यसामर्थ्यं सर्व्वज्ञत्वं योगजं योग उच्यते "Restraint of spirit; faculties derived from the accession of superhuman power; omniscience derived from abstract exercises: that is called Yoga", and again he describes it as the exercise by which the intellect is delivered up to the supreme deity for the purpose of union, ईश्वरार्पणबुद्ध्यानुष्ठीयमानं योगार्थत्वाद्योग उच्यते. In the Linga Puráńa, *Yoga* is considered *Nirváńa*, final emancipation, or identification with Śiva; it is there said also that it cannot be expounded by the learned, but the knowledge of it is easily obtained by discipline, or the practice of those personal and mental restraints which coerce the senses, and purify the spirit.

of the purport of the terms, we should prefer, as we have before observed, the use of themselves to any translation.

In the same stanza also we object to the translation of *Buddhi* by Sententia: it is not merely the doctrine or opinion of either school that is communicated to Arjuna, but the result, the knowledge of the divine nature of spirit and matter. *Buddhi* therefore is in this place considered by Śankara as synonymous with *Jnána*, a word we should rather have translated by Sapientia, than Scientia, usually preferred by Schlegel, and which, though literally correct, is exceptionable from its extended and in a manner indefinite application: on the contrary Sapientia, as a term of the schools, is precisely equivalent to *Jnána*: 'Sapientia autem est, ut a veteribus philosophis definitum est, rerum divinarum et humanarum caussarumque, quibus hæ continentur, scientia.' Cic. de officiis, 6. 2.

V. 42. *Vedavádaratáh́, Pártha, nányad astíti vádinah́*, "Librorum sacrorum dictis gaudentes, nec ultra quidquam dari affirmantes." We are rather at a loss to understand what the translator intends in this place. The original contains not a word about 'giving'. The passage is simply, "Those who are attached to the doctrines of the Vedas assert, that there is nothing else:" that is, they maintain, that the Vedas offer the only path to salvation; sacrifice and prayer are all; there is no other path to heaven. There is considerable obscurity in the rest of this stanza, and some faulty translation. *Swargapará* is not "sedem apud superos finem bonorum prædicantes", but sedem apud superos summam felicitatem existimantes, those who hold the paradise of Indra to be the supreme happiness. The translator is also so far wrong, in rendering *Janma-karmaphalapradám* insignes natales tanquam operum præmium pollicentem, that the phrase is general, not restrictive, and "lofty birth" and "reward" are not the simple senses of *Janma*, and *Phala*, which signify only 'birth' and 'fruit or consequence'. The dogma alluded to is said to be one, "assigning birth as the consequence of acts:" that is, according to the act of an individual in a previous existence, he is born again either to misery or happiness.

V. 45. The Hindu system arranges all the attributes of spirit in action under three heads or qualities—the *Sattwa*, *Rajas*, and *Tamas*: the first comprises the presence of all good and absence of all evil; the last the presence of all evil and absence of all good: and the middle one is a mixed quality, in which the operation of the affections and passions is strongest, and gives occasional predominance to good and ill. In this verse Kŕishńa recommends to Arjuna to eschew the two latter qualities, and to cultivate the first alone; to be *Nirdwandwa*, exempt from the double alternatives of existence, as pleasure or pain &c. and to be *Nitya-sattwastha*, always firm in *Sattwa*, the quality of Sattwa, which is perhaps best rendered purity or excellence. Schlegel however translates it essentia, a sense the word bears as derived from *Sat*, *ens*, being, but certainly not applicable to it as one of the three *guńas.* That the quality is intended, is obvious from the context, as Śankara explains the term accordingly, सदा सत्त्वगुणाश्रितो भव. What the *Sattwaguńa* is, is equally indisputable, as we may learn from the following definition, सत्त्वं निर्मलत्वात्प्रकाशकमनामयं, the Sattwa from its purity is light and tranquillity, 14, 6. Śrídhara and Nílakańtha, it is true, interpret *Sattwa* by *Dhairya*, firmness, fortitude, but they intend the same thing in fact with the Sattwa quality, or the mens solida of the upright man who is unmoved by ignorance and passion. It appears to be the same as the Temperantia or Tranquillitas of the Stoics, whilst the *Rajas* might be expressed by Perturbatio, and *Tamas* by Intemperantia.

In the same stanza, *Niryogakshemo bhava* is rendered, expers sollicitudinum esto, following no doubt Wilkins's "Be void of care." The compound admits of such a translation, it is true, but it is not very precise. *Yoga* means here acquisition, and *Kshema* preservation, and Krishńa recommends to Arjuna to be neither desirous of obtaining what he does not possess, nor of preserving what he possesses.*

V. 48. The word *Sanga* is we think rather injudiciouly interpreted by ambitio: as well observed by the translator, it signifies the attachment of the French, "studium vel affectus quo animus vehementer tenetur",

---

* [अनुपात्तस्योपार्जनं योगः। उपात्तस्य रक्षणं क्षेमः। See Śankara and Śrídhara ad 9, 22. Benfey's Sáma Veda Gl. p. 155. Colebrooke's transl. of Mitákshará I, 4, 23.]

the eagerness evinced in the attainment of any object, or the close and intense connexion that subsists between the individual and the thing affected. It is accordingly rendered in the Trikáńda Śesha *Gŕidhnutá*, cupidity, greediness. In the note attached to this passage, Schlegel objects to the etymology of *Sanga*, as given in Wilson's Dictionary, सम्, with, and गम, to go, with the affix ड; and the etymology there is so far defective, that it applies only to the leading sense of the word, i. e. "meeting, encountering", and to the two last, "union, joining, and the confluence of rivers" —in the remaining sense, "desire, cupidity", it would have been as well if the root षञ्ज, to be attached to, had been also inserted. Schlegel however mistakes when he concludes, that *Sanga* so formed must necessarily be an adjective, for it is given by Amara* as a synonyme of सङ्गम or, as explained by Kŕishńa Swámí, सङ्गति, both of which are substantives, and nouns, of the act or action, not names of the agent. Again Schlegel proposes to derive *Sanga* from षस्ज; in preference to *Shanja*, on the principle that the latter root occasionally drops the nasal;—that is true, but whence does षस्ज ever derive a nasal? for, unfortunately for his theory, all the lists of roots, and the Siddhánta Kaumudí, explain षञ्ज by सङ्गे 'embrace, association', and षस्ज by गतौ 'going, motion'. He has taxed the author of the Dictionary with confounding

* [Bhánudikshita ad Amarakosha III, 3, 29, and Lassen's note on the passage in question.]

these two roots, but we suspect the charge is urged against the wrong quarter: the Kaumudí, the first grammatical authority current, confirms precisely what is there stated, and षञ्ज सङ्गे makes सजति in the 3d person present, while षस्ज गतौ in the same tense and person makes सज्जते and सज्जति. We are unable to see any perplexity here, or any deviation from indisputable guides.

V. 52. A wide difference occurs here in the reading of the two translators, and Wilkins calls *Nirveda* 'knowledge', whilst Schlegel makes it 'ignorantia [neglectus']. It is clear that they cannot both be right, and to a certain extent both are wrong. We apprehend, however, that, although Wilkins's translation of the whole passage is no doubt faulty, yet *nirveda* is rather knowledge than ignorance. Schlegel's error arises partly out of a spirit of system to which the learned of Europe are too ready to incline:—a Pańdit however eminent is content to follow established authorities, and admits the law that they have laid down; a European scholar is suspicious of authorities, and carries this so far as not unfrequently to question them without cause. Now Amara, Maheśwara, Hemachandra, Mediníkára, and every other Lexicographer of note, have explained the particle *Nir*, (निर् निश्चयनिषेधयोः) 'certainty, and negation', it being sometimes an affirmative, and sometimes a privative particle. We think this might satisfy the most scrupulous, as, although the senses are opposed, the interpretation is positive. Schlegel however endeavours sometimes to explain away the sense of affirmation, as we shall have occasion hereafter to notice, and at others, as in the present case, alters the sense. Now all the commentators* agree to interpret *Nirveda* by वैराग्य, the absence of passion properly, but here, indifference. But of what nature is this indifference? it is the result of ascertained knowledge (from *Nir*, certainty, and *Veda*, knowing) of the futility of the dogmas of the Vedas; Kŕishńa telling Arjuna, that, when his understanding shall overpass the glooms of infatuation, he will have attained independence, or the knowledge, which will make him independent of all that he has heard, or may have to hear.** To say that he shall have attained ignorance of what he has heard or has yet to hear, would be a strange step towards perfection. *Srotavya* and *Sruta* imply the lessons of the Vedas: that which is to be heard, or is heard. Schlegel has made a rather unwarranted addition in explaining it by "disputable doctrine." "Pervenies ad ignorantiam omnium quæ de doctrina sacra disputari possunt vel disputata sunt." He must know that the Vedas collectively are called *Śruti*, the knowledge heard, in opposition to *Smŕiti*, Law, the knowledge remembered—the one being preserved by traditional communication, from sage to sage, the other being the recollection of previously divulged codes: there is no allusion therefore to dis-

* [See also Śankara ad Muńdaka Up. I, 2, 12.]

** यदा ते मोहकलिलं बुद्धिर्व्यतितरिष्यति । तदा गन्तासि निर्वेदं श्रोतव्यस्य श्रुतस्य च.

putatious matters. The whole of Kŕishńa's arguments have been directed against the assertors of the sacrificial injunctions of the Vedas, and in the same spirit he assures his friend, that, when he becomes wholly indifferent to the consequences of acts, he will possess a knowledge to which the wisdom of the Vedas will be foolishness.

V. 89. This stanza is at best rather obscure: Wilkins has by far the best notion of it, but has rendered it too literally. Schlegel has mistaken the whole purport of the passage, the verse is—विषया विनिवर्त्तन्ते निराहारस्य देहिनः । रसवर्ज्जं रसोऽप्यस्य परं दृष्ट्वा निवर्त्तते ॥

"The hungry man loseth every other object but the gratification of his appetite, and when he is become acqainted with the supreme, he loseth even that."—*Wilkins.*

"Res sensibus obviæ recedunt a mortali abstinente, temperantia ejus insigni animadversa ipse appetitus recedit." *Schlegel.* The first half of this version might be allowed to pass unquestioned, but abstinens should be taken in its widest acceptation, as implying one who is engaged in self-denial, and refraining from every hind of gratification. The latter portion however is altogether erroneous, and not very intelligible: temperantia occurs nowhere in the original, and so far from its leading to the supreme, ascetic practices are said in the text, and in the commentary, to be characteristic of a fool or a fiend. The translator has here lost sight of the spirit of his original apparently, or he would have adhered closer to his English guide, who errs only in making that special which is general, being misled by the double sense of *Niráhára*, which means *without food*, or *without seizure or possession*, that is, of the objects of sense. The doctrine laid down is, that, however much a person may restrain his inclination towards the natural tendency of the senses, the attractive quality of sensual objects still exists; they continue to be temptations still, successfully a man may resist them: but let him once obtain a knowledge of supreme spirit, a correct view of his own nature, and that of the divinity, and he is not only able to resist temptations, but in fact he is exposed to none, every thing that made them seductive wholly disappearing. Kŕishńa accordingly says in this stanza —"The objects of sense recede from the incorporated spirit, which refrains from their enjoyment, the taste for them excepted (i. e. it remains); but this taste or flavour, (affecting the) individual ceases altogether, when he has seen the supreme."*

There are several other passages in this Lecture to which we might take exception, but not to be too minute in our comments, we shall allow them to escape animadversion, and not to confine our remarks to blemishes, shall cite the following passage** in this book as one specimen of many that might be adduced of accurate and spirited interpretation: many of the

* [This construction, proposed by Śrídhara Swámí, is against the diction of the Bhag. Gítá.]

** [II, 17–25.]

ideas forcibly recall the language of Scipio's dream. "Indelebile autem, hoc scias, est illud, a quo Universum hoc expansum: deletionem inexhausti istius nemini efficere licet. Caduca hæc corpora dicuntur, immutabili spiritu animata, indelebili atque immenso: quare pugna, o Bhârata! Qui eum arbitratur occisorem, quive eundem censet occisum, hi ambo non recte intelligunt; neque occidit ille, neque occiditur. Non nascitur moriturve unquam; non ille exstitit, exsistitve, non exstiturus: innatus, immutabilis, æternus ille, priscus, non occiditur occiso corpore. Qui novit indelebilem, æternum illum, innatum, inexhaustum, quomodo is homo quempiam occidendum curet, vel ipse occidat? Perinde ac obsoletis vestibus abiectis, novas sumit homo alias, sic abiectis corporibus obsoletis, alia ingreditur nova spiritus. Non illum penetrant tela, non illum comburit flamma, neque illum perfundunt aquæ, nec ventus exsiccat. Impenetrabilis ille, incombustibilis ille, imperfusibilis ille, nec non inexsiccabilis, perpetuus, omnivagus, stabilis, inconcussus ille atque aeternus, invisibilis ille, inenarrabilis ille, immutabilis ille declaratur. Quare, quum talem cognoveris, non luctu eum prosequi te oportet."

Lecture 3. If knowledge is superior to works, or the active discharge of moral and religious obligations, then Arjuna very pertinently enquires why Kŕishńa should urge him to a deed so horrible as the slaughter of his relations. Kŕishńa replies to his question in this chapter, and shews from positive precept, the impulses of nature and other arguments, that man must necessarily discharge active duties, taking care only to hold himself indifferent as to their results, and endeavouring, with more subtilty than truth, to establish, that such indifference is the only real abstinence from these actions; a doctrine which, as we have already observed, it is one of the two great objects of the Gítá to promulgate. We shall not enter so minutely into the questionable passages of the translation of this and the following chapters as we have done in the preceding, as we should otherwise make a very disproportionate claim upon the attention of our readers: indeed the celebrity of the translator is our only excuse for devoting so great a portion of our pages to the analysis of this translation.

V. 15 is explained very differently from the acceptation, in which the commentators concur: *Karma Brahmodbhavam* is rendered by Schlegel opus e numine ortum, but *Brahma** does not mean here *numen*, but the *Veda*: works originate with the Veda. Again, *Brahmáksharasamudbhavam* is not numen e simplici et individuo ortum, a translation the purport of which is not very intelligible, any more than the grounds on which it rests, but "the Veda originates with the Imperishable". The line thus expresses a clear and connected sense which is quite lost in the translation.

V. 16. *Iha* does not mean in hoc sæculo, but in hoc mundo, and *Agháyuh*, leading a sinful life, is strangely rendered by 'incaste ævo transacto'.

* [According to Śankara and Śrídhara.]

V. 18. *Arthavyapáśraya* is not so much ullius commodi expectatio as 'the object on which he may place dependence' of Wilkins: *Vyapáśraya* is the means or aid, the commodum itself, not the expectation of it.

V. 35. *Śreyán swadharmo viguńaḱ paradharmát swanushṫhitát* is rendered, satius est suo officio, etsi deficientibus viribus, fungi, quam alienum officium accurate implere. The translation is not correct: *Viguńaḱ* is an epithet of *Dharma*, implying void of *Guńa*, quality or merit; *Swanushṫhitát* is also an attributive of *Dharma*, implying well or excellently regulated: the passage therefore conveys the doctrine, that a man's own duty, although inferior in degree, is, with respect to himself, superior to another of a more lofty description: as, for instance, the servitude of a Śúdra is preferable for a Śúdra to study, which is the peculiar province of the Brahman.

In a note on the 10th verse of this section Schlegel has very justly called in question the accuracy of the form *Prasavishyadhwam*, propagabimini, as such an inflexion is unknown to the verb: at the same time all the manuscripts concur in the reading, and it is therefore considered as a poetical license, the word being properly *Prásavishyadhwam*, the first long vowel being made arbitrarily short for the adaptation of the metre.*

* [Schlegel, in the second edition, calls it "formam, quam definire possis terminationem et vim imperativi ad futurum secundum

Lecture 4. In this discourse Kŕishńa enters upon further explanation of the union of spirit by means of divine knowledge, and endeavours to prove, that it is but that indifference to the consequence of actions, of which he had before treated. The performance and non-performance of works, intending in this section social duties, is therefore the same, and disregard of their results is virtually their relinquishment; as in the 20th verse: "He who, having abandoned every desire of fruit, is always satisfied and independent, although he may be engaged in action, verily doeth nothing."

V. 10. *Manmayá* is better rendered by Wilkins "filled with my spirit", than by Schlegel 'mei similes', the affix मयट् implying made or consisting of, so that *Manmaya* literally means consisting of me, or one with me: it is explained by Śankara, those who see no difference in Íśwara, or supreme spirit, ईश्वराभेददर्शिनः.

V. 17. and 18, profess to explain what *Karma* or action, and what *Akarma* or inaction are, and which have, as Kŕishńa declares in the stanza preceding, puzzled the wisest. His definitions, however, are calculated to fasten rather than untie the knot, and are good specimens of the style, in which the Gítá throughout evades the question between social and ascetic practices, the merits of sacrifice, or the claims of ab-

---

translatam." The commentators on this passage and on Rámáy. I, 29, 25 explain it by the Imperative. Modern languages, e. g. Bengali and Hindi, present similar formations.]

straction. The passage is somewhat obscure, and it is not wonderful therefore that the translation is not very distinct: it is rendered however less clear than it might be by one or two mistakes. Schlegel renders the first verse 'ad ipsum opus est attendendum, attendendum quoque ad secessionem ab opere,* attendendum tandem ad otium; obscura est operis ratio.' Now in the first place, the *Karma* here discussed refers to active occupation, the duties of social life or of caste; actio would therefore, we think, have been preferable to opus. In the next place *Bodhavyam* is not attendendum, it is intelligendum rather, and refers to a noun understood, *Tattwam*, the real nature or character of action, inaction &c. Again *Vikarma* is erroneously rendered by secessio ab opere, as it means, as Wilkins correctly translates it, 'improper works', deeds that are prohibited by the Śástras; *Akarma* is secessio ab opere or inactio. Otium is a rather equivocal word. The second of these two stanzas is thus rendered: 'Qui in opere otium cernit, et in otio opus, is sapit inter mortales; is devotus, cunctis operibus peragendis aptus est.' Otium and opus are both very objectionable here, as they do not convey the spirit of the original, and therefore heighten the obscurity. There is but one position in both assertions, and the doctrine implied is, that, as there is no such thing as individual spirit, those who think they are performing deeds of which they must singly reap the fruit, or those who

* [2nd ed. ad opus haud rite impensum.]

in like manner think they abstain from works in their individual capacities, are both mistaken. The actions of the first lead to nothing, and the expectations of the latter put them on a level with the former: both are blinded by terrestrial illusion.

V. 23. *Yajnáyácharataḣ karma samagram pravilíyate*, Hominis sacrificii gratia sese accingentis opus integrum quasi evanescit. The translation is literal enough, but it is rather too close to convey the sense of the original, which states that, when a man freed from all desire performs sacrifices, merely to *promote their observation by others*, or preserve them in the world, then those acts are annihilated together with their fruits, that is to say they are not to be considered as acts at all.

V. 25. Divorum porro alii devoti religionem colunt, in theologiæ igne alii religionem ipsa religione denuo sacrificant. The translation here by no means conveys the sense of the original: we doubt indeed whether in this as in many of the doctrinal passages, particularly where verbal subtleties occur, the translator has entertained a precise idea of what he would express. In this passage he has further contributed to the obscurity of the original by rendering *Yajna*, Religio. It is, as he has frequently translated it in other places, sacrifice, and although it may be extended to every ceremonial rite of religion, it cannot be applied in the widest sense of that term. The translator has also lost sight of the antitheses of the two lines, the one of which alludes to the performers of rites for specific purposes, and the other to the cultivators of divine knowledge who observe rites only as the *means* of its acquirement. The sense of the stanza in this point of view is, 'Some observers of acts address sacrifice to the Gods, whilst others* offer up sacrifice with sacrifice in the fire that is identical with spirit,'—that is to say, in the performance of ceremonies they seek only the means of acquiring divine knowledge, and *that* being obtained, they yield or relinquish to it the benefit of all ceremonies, to be consumed by it, as it were by fire.

Lect. 5. Arjuna, and he is not singular perhaps, is now completely puzzled, and begs Kŕishńa to inform him which is really the best, the performance or abandonment of works. Kŕishńa replies to his question by stating that there is no real difference between them, according to the predominant doctrine of the whole treatise: that the abandonment of consequences is the real abandonment of works, and that, although the bodily or intellectual functions may be discharged, yet as long as no interest is felt in them the spirit is wholly inactive.

V. 2. On the word *Niśśreyas*, final emancipation, Schlegel has a note in support of his theory of the meaning of the particle *Nir*, in opposition to the etymology in Wilson's Dictionary (निः for निर्) implying eternity or certainty, and श्रेयस् best, अच् added. He

---

* [Śrídhara: अपरे तु ज्ञानयोगिनो ब्रह्मरूपेऽग्नौ यज्ञेनैवोपायेन ब्रह्मार्पणमित्याद्युक्तप्रकारेण यज्ञमुपजुह्वति यज्ञादिसर्वकर्माणि प्रविलापयन्तीत्यर्थः ।]

maintains that श्रेयस् is not the superlative, but the comparative, and that *Nir* prefixed has a negative sense: the compound implying "*That*, than which nothing is better". We should have no great objection to this explanation in this place, although it is probably more ingenious than just. *Śreyas* is constantly used in the superlative sense, and in the very passage of Amara* referred to in the Dictionary *Śreyas* occurs, uncompounded, as one synonyme of final beatitude. It cannot there be regarded as possessing only the force of the comparative degree. Again, of the commentators on Amara, Rámáśrama explains *Nir* in *Niśśreyas* by *Nitarám*, perpetually, eternally, and Ráya Mukuṭa by *Niśchitam*, certain, ascertained, whilst Kshíra Swámí** explains *Śreyas* by *atiśayena praśastam*, or most excellent. We must confess a disposition to lean to authorities like these in preference to the theory of a novice, however plausible it may appear, or however dexterously it may be maintained.

The sixth Lecture continues to explain the identity of the relinquishment of works with their performance independent of desire. It also recommends the exercise of those practices which constitute the technical Yoga, or postures and gestures by which attention to outward objects is restrained, and the mind devoted to the undisturbed consideration of its own nature. Some indication of the other chief doctrines of the

---

* [Amarak. I, 1, 4, 15. See also Śank. ad Kaushít. Up. II, 14.]
** [ad Am. K. III, 58.]

Gítá are also introduced, establishing the importance of faith in Kŕishńa, and making him one with the Supreme Universal Spirit. Kŕishńa observes:*

'Qui me cernit ubique et universum in me cernit, ex eo ego non evanesco, neque is ex me evanescit: omnibus animantibus immorantem qui me colit, unitati intentus, quocunque tandem modo versetur, devotus ille mecum versatur.' There is nothing in this section of the translation, that calls for particular remark,—we might contest some verbal translation, and we are disposed to think the explanation of *Niváta* in the note** a little too refined; but the extent of our comments must compel us to waive any more particular notice in this place. The section prosecutes the doctrine of Kŕishńa's identity with the Supreme spirit, and the union of those who worship him with him, eventually, whilst those who worship the Divinities reap only the inferior kind of fruition which their respective degrees in the regions above the earth are calculated to afford, and which besides being of a sensual description, involve the necessity of a return to life, and future transmigrations in a mortal frame.

[VII,] v. 11. contains in the translation a misconception of one term, and ambiguous equivalent for another. Kŕishńa says, "He is the strength of the strong and that desire in beings which is not contrary to the

* यो मां पश्यति सर्व्वत्र सर्वं च मयि पश्यति। तस्याहं न प्रणश्यामि स च मे न प्रणश्यति॥ सर्व्वभूतस्थितं यो मां भजत्येकत्वमास्थितः। सर्व्वथा वर्त्तमानोऽपि स योगी मयि वर्त्तते॥ [VI, 30f.]

** [ad v. 19.]

laws;" *Dharmáviruddhaḱ kámo'smi.* The first Schlegel renders by Robur robustorum, but this does not convey the idea of moral strength which the epithet attached to it, 'void of passion or desire', implies. The next is however more important, as the sense has the appearance of being the reverse of that which the original intends. Nulla lege refrenata* in animantibus Libido sum: the desire restrained by no law may indeed be admitted to signify that which there is no law to restrain, but the first impression is that it is desire which does not acknowledge moral control. Wilkins renders the passage with tolerable correctness, "I am desire regulated by moral fitness"; it is however rather desire not opposed to moral fitness than regulated by it. Śankara explains it as the natural desire by which the body is preserved, the natural wants, as hunger, thirst and the like: Śridhara gives us in illustration of it the procreation of legitimate offspring.**

The close of this section furnishes the subject of the next. Kŕishńa states that those who put their whole trust in him, and seek for liberation from infirmity and death, are acquainted with the *Brahma,* the *Adhyátmam, karma, adhibhútam, adhidaivam,* and the *adhiyajnaḱ*: and Arjuna asks for an explanation of these terms. The explanation is brief, but as they all resolve themselves into Kŕishńa as the *Paramaḱ*

* [Lege non impedita, 2nd ed.]

** [Śank.: देहधारणमात्रार्थो ऽशनपानादिविषयः कामो ऽस्मि।
Śridhara: स्वदारेषु पुत्रोत्पादनमात्रोपयोगी कामो ऽहम् ।]

Purushaħ, he proceeds to explain the meaning of that expression, which forms the subject of the 8th Lecture.

The explanation of these terms is of importance, as conveying a summary of the whole system: the literal translation of *Brahma* is the imperishable and supreme: *adhyátmam* is the innate disposition, the individuated portion of the soul: *karma* is that letting go of the divine particles, which produced the substance of the elements: *adhibhútam* is the property of dissolution: *adhidaivatam* is Purusha, the embodied male supreme being who occupied the universe before creation: and *adhiyajnaħ* is declared by Kŕishńa to be himself; that is, he as one with all the gods is the object of all adoration. We do not think the following translation very accurately conveys these ideas: "Essentia simplex ac individua est summum numen. Indoles supra spiritum dicitur; animantium genituræ efficax emanatio operis nomine significatur; super animantia est natura dividua; Geniusque supra divos; supra religiones ego ipse sum."* The attempt at closeness is injurious not only to perspicuity but accuracy; for though *adhi* in all the compounds means supra, *adhyátmá* does not mean supra spiritum; it is rather spiritus qui præest, or corpori individuo præsidens.

* [2nd ed.: "indoles intimus spiritus dicitur; animantium genituræ efficax emanatio operis nomine significatur; anima animantium est natura dividua, Geniusque numen deorum; auctor religionum ego ipse sum". See on these terms Goldstücker's Sanskrit Dictionary s. vv. *adhibhúta* and *adhyátma*; Johaentgen, "Ueber das Gesetzbuch des Manu", Berlin: 1863, p. 57 ff.]

The translation of *Purusha* by Genius, we look upon as happy, although it is not perhaps exactly the sense. It conveys however the spirit of the term, and we prefer that in all cases to the letter.

Lect. 9. contains the pith of the whole doctrine, the royal knowledge, and prince of mysteries, or in other words, as we have already observed, the superior efficacy of faith in Kŕishńa over every other system of worship, or tenor of belief. Śankara admits that this is the scope of the section, or that the sum of the argument is *Vásudevaḱ sarvam*, Kŕishńa is all. Kŕishńa, however, he per force renders *Íśwara*, the supreme, or *átmá*, spirit, and then asserts that the Gítá harmonises with the text of the Vedas, *Idam sarvam eva adwiťiyam*, 'Spirit was this universe without a second.' There is nothing in the translation to call for any particular remark.

The tenth chapter continues the subject of Kŕishńa's supremacy, or the pre-eminent conditions in which he is to be contemplated, in association with existing objects, as the sun amongst the planets, Kŕishńa amongst the gods, Meru amongst mountains, Gangá amongst rivers, the soul of all beings, and the beginning, middle, and end of all things. These identifications are called *Vibhútayaḱ*, varieties of supreme being, or as Wilkins translates it, "the diversities of the divine nature". Schlegel seems to have been undecided in his choice of an equivalent, and calls *vibhúti* sometimes majestas, sometimes virtus, and at others miraculum, neither of which is precisely applicable.

V. 7. presents the terms *Vibhúti* and *Yoga*, both rather stumbling blocks, but particularly the latter. However in this place it has clearly no reference to connexion with works, and is confined to the mysterious relation between supreme and individuated spirit. Kŕishńa says, एतां विभूतिं योगं च यो वेत्ति तत्त्वतः । सोऽविकम्पेन योगेन युज्यते नात्र संशयः ॥ which Schlegel translates, Qui hanc meam majestatem et facultatem mysticam novit penitus, is indefessa devotione sese devovet* sine ullo dubio. This is by no means the purpose of the stanza; the sense of which is that, whoever knows the various conditions of spirit and its connexion with that of the universe, becomes united with mystic powers which identify him with the deity. The *Yoga* of the first stanza, being the power resulting from the possession of union, may be called the mystic faculty, but in the second place it implies the same thing, and is therefore very inaccurately expressed by devotio.

The 11th Section prosecutes the same subject in a manner singular enough. Kŕishńa desires Arjuna to look into his mouth, which having done the latter beholds there the whole of creation. The metre changes here to the *Upajáti* species of the *Trishtubh* verse, a more stately measure, and whatever may be thought of the ideas, there is no disputing the magnificence of the style, the majestic, and at the same time exquisite melodiousness of the verse. In general the translation is close and correct.

---

* [2nd edit.: inconcussa devotione imbuitur.]

Lecture 12th is introduced with a question from Arjuna, pertinent enough, 'which class of worshippers is preferable, those who adore Kŕishńa in his visible or invisible form?' The reply which occupies the whole section is after all evasive: however, it appears that there are four modes of attaining final emancipation, absolute knowledge, the exercise of contemplation, the practice of works independent of desire, and simple faith; the latter is placed the lowest in the scale, but the gradation is regulated by the ability of the mortal, for as the result is but one, they are of course equally efficacious. The section is short and the translation calls for no remark.

Lecture 13th is chiefly occupied with the explanation of the distinction between matter and spirit as intended by the terms *Kshetra*, (क्षेत्रं) the body, *Kshetrajna*, (क्षेत्रज्ञः) that which knows its nature, *Jneya*, (ज्ञेयं) the object to be known, *Jnána*, (ज्ञानं) true knowledge, and *Purusha*, (पुरुषः) the active, and *Prakŕiti*, (प्रकृतिः) the passive principle of creation. There is in this section much that is very indistinct and equivocal, and it has given *Śankara* no small trouble to reconcile the doctrines it obscurely expresses with the pure Adwaita theology, in which one only object is admitted. Thus in the 13th verse, *Prakŕiti* and *Purusha*, matter and spirit, are declared to be both without beginning, a doctrine involving the eternity of matter, as maintained by the Sánkhyas and Naiyáyikas. To get rid of this, Śankara asserts that their eternity is understood of them only as attributes or manifestations of

Íśwara, the supreme eternal being, as parts of whose nature, without beginning or end, they may also be called interminable and from the first: an explanation which is clearly an evasion, not a solution, of the difficulty.

Kshetra, which implies properly a field, expresses the bodily aggregate, rather than the body, or the site of the elementary matter, the senses, the feelings, the passions, and the understanding: it is not badly rendered therefore by Terrenum. *Kshetrajna* is literally Terreni gnarus, spirit being understood.*

V. 4. We doubt if *Hetumadbhir viniśchitaiń* is correctly rendered by 'circa principia rerum versantibus, clare demonstratis': the expression is of a more technical character, and refers to the logical predicates of the texts inculcating divine wisdom, which comprehend motives and proofs. Wilkins is more near this sense of the original in his "including arguments and proofs".

In V. 5. an exception may be taken to the translation of *Avyaktam* by invisibile, although it is literal; but the order of the series in the original leaves no ambiguity, whilst the unfamiliarity of the subject in the translation involves considerable uncertainty. Kŕishńa enumerates the eight parts that compose bodily substance, or the five elements, individuality, divine intellect, and the invisible portion. This invisible portion we should naturally infer to be spirit,

* [See Johaentgen, l. l., p. 30.]

but then an obvious perplexity arises in considering as one predicate of the *Kshetra* or body that, which is declared to be the faculty by which it is known; the Terreni gnarus as separate from the Terrenum. In fact no such confusion is made in the original: the *Avyaktam* is not divine spirit, it is the *Múlaprakŕiti*, the primeval delusion by which terrestrial substances and acts appear to be real, the illusory or passive principle which we may call nature, and which before creation was, and in fact still is, an attribute or portion of the supreme. Schlegel has elsewhere termed this principium naturæ, and had he employed the same in this place, all uncertainty would have been avoided.

V. 6. Amongst the properties or constituent parts of the *Kshetra* here enumerated are *Sangháta* (संघातः), *Chetaná* (चेतना), and *Dhŕiti* (धृतिः). Those are rendered, multiplex conditio, cogitatio, pertinacia; but these are by no means close interpretations, *Sangháta* meaning aggregation, *Chetaná* sensation, the collection of the organs and faculties or susceptibility of impressions, and *Dhŕiti* is the principle by which the whole are preserved from decay, the vis conservatrix naturæ. In the long list of terms that ensues, several others might be questioned.

We doubt whether the translator has understood the definition V. 20. of *Prakŕiti* or nature by *Kárya-kárańa-kartŕitwe hetuh́*, which he renders In actu ministerii rerum agendarum principium.* The literal

* [2nd edit.: in actione ministerii corporalis principium.]

translation would be, the principle that operates in the agency of the instrumental causes of action: but this would be scarcely more intelligible, and the sentence required to have been analytically or paraphrastically rendered: the purport being that *prakŕiti*, nature, is the principle, or rather the cause, by which the combination of passions and feelings with the elementary particles of matter was effected, and the universal frame independent of spirit was evolved; the passions and perceptions incident to the human being would however be inert without the presence of spirit; they therefore still constitute the passive principle which requires association with the active principle before their influences are felt or exerted; this active spirit is the *Purusha*, the male or genius, the subsequent description of which is very well rendered in the following passages.*

Genius in doloris ac voluptatis perceptione principium declaratur. Genius naturæ infusus nimirum particeps fit naturalium qualitatum: propensio erga qualitates causa est generationum ejus e bono vel malo uterò. Spectator monitorque, sustentator, perceptor, magnus dominus, summus spiritus quoque dicitur in hoc corpore Genius ille eximius.

The 14th Section treats of the three *Guńas* or properties of nature, the *Sattwa*, *Rajas*, and *Tamas*,

* पुरुषः सुखदुःखानां भोक्तृत्वे हेतुरुच्यते ॥ पुरुषः प्रकृतिस्थो हि भुंक्ते प्रकृतिजान्गुणान् । कारणं गुणसङ्गो ऽस्य सदसद्योनिजन्मसु ॥ उपद्रष्टानुमन्ता च भर्त्ता भोक्ता महेश्वरः । परमात्मेति चाप्युक्तो देहे ऽस्मिन्पुरुषः परः ॥

translated by Schlegel Essentia, Impetus, and Caligo, on which we have already had occasion to comment.*

In the 6th verse *Nirmalatwam* as the predicate of the *Sattwa Guńa* is rendered sinceritas, but *nirmala* means exempt from stain or soil, and the property is illustrated by that of transparent crystal.** Again *Anámayam* is translated Sana, which is the literal sense, it is true, but as applicable to the *Sattwa Guńa* it means gentle, dispassionate, being explained by *nirupadrava* and *śánta*.

V. 14. *Dehabhŕit* is very loosely rendered mortalis; it is that which cherishes or upholds the body or, in other words, spirit: a mortal body is too well disposed of after dissolution, to obtain the region of purity, and spirit under all circumstances is immortal.

The 15th Section discriminates the different kinds of *Purusha*, or active spirit, according to its various conditions of being, as special, or general, or supreme: the first exists in all bodies from Brahma to a stone; the second exists detached from body; and the third is paramount, thence denominated *Purushottama*. This Purushottama is of course Kŕishńa or Vishńu, of whom it is one of the most familiar appellations in a popular and less mystic sense.

This book opens with the expansion of an idea derived from the Vedas, that the world is a fig tree whose roots grow above and the branches below,

* [See also Johaentgen, "Ueber das Gesetzbuch des Manu", p. 39 ff.] ** [Śridhara: स्वच्छत्वात्स्फटिकमणिरिव.]

whose leaves are the Vedas, &c. Wilkins has mistaken the object of the comparison, and has substituted the "incorruptible being" for 'the world': he was probably misled by the term *Avyayam,* unexpended, perpetual, which however is only an epithet of the tree, as meaning the *Sansára* or world. Schlegel has assigned the adjective to its proper substantive, but his translation affords no clue to the purport or object of the simile; he calls the tree Ficum religiosam *quandam,* the last condition being an accessory to his text, and shewing that he was not quite certain what the resemblance referred to: besides this, there is considerable mysticism in the whole section, and though rendered literally enough, and with a few exceptions accurately enough, by the translator, it is still very unintelligible from the want of annotations.*

The 16th Section is upon the difference between good and evil natures, and an attack upon the professors of an adverse creed rather than any further elucidation of the doctrine of the Gítá. It is entitled *Daivásura-sampad-vibhága-yoga,* the doctrine of the apportionment of divine and demoniac condition. Wilkins renders it good and evil destiny, and Schlegel, following him most probably, explains it divina et dæmoniaca sors. The latter term is no doubt preferable, for it may be questionable how far destiny is properly in-

* [These have been amply supplied in the 2nd edition. See also A. Knhn, "Die Herabkunft des Feuers". Berlin: 1859, p. 198 ff. W. Mannhardt, "Germanische Mythen". Berlin: 1858, p. 553 ff.]

tended, as the good or evil consequences resulting from these different designations are necessarily the result of the characteristics of good and evil creations, which, as (V. 6.) Kŕishńa observes, divide the world.

V. 2. *Alolatwam** should have been interpreted 'indifference to objects of sense', rather than alienus a lascivia animus.

V. 6. *Sarga* is rendered *natura***, but it is properly creation or class of creatures.

V. 7. *Pravŕittim cha nivŕittim cha janá na vidur ásuráh́*, neque agendi nec cessandi rationem norunt homines dæmonii; but what is the ratio of acting or desisting? In giving the literal meaning of the terms, the translator has here, as in many places, lost sight of the conventional sense they bear. *Pravŕitti* means the discharge of active duties, *nivŕitti* their abandonment at the proper season: the first implies the discharge of the obligations of caste and station, the performance of rites and observance of ceremonies, whilst the second expresses addiction to contemplative meditation alone. The man of the demoniac creation, it is said, regards neither the one nor the other of these duties, or, in other words, is neither a follower of the Vedas nor a worshipper of Vishńu. It is clear from the subsequent passage that the Bauddhas are especi-

* [See also Lassen's note in 2nd ed. Śrídhara's reading अलोलुप्त्वं, which he considers as an archaistic form for अलोलुपत्वं (अवर्णलोपस्त्वार्षः), is also expressed by Galanos' translation αἰτάρκεια.]

** [indoles, 2nd ed.]

ally intended as the beings of the demoniacal order. Śankara states them to be the members of the Lokáyatika sect, a sect which was a division of the Bauddhas.*

The 17th Section is upon the three kinds of faith, or faith as influenced by the prevalence of the three Guńas severally; and all acts, whether of the ceremonial or abstractive class, performed without faith, are declared to be *Asat*, non existent and null.

The question put by Arjuna which leads to this exposition is, what is the condition or classification of those who worship in faith without regard to the rules of the Śástras? *Nishthá*, rendered Statio by Schlegel, and guide by Wilkins, is rather *Avasthá*, or *Áśraya*, manner or place of being, and the 'Legis scriptæ præceptis neglectis' conveys perhaps more than is intended by the text, as it is the inattention to forms or ceremonial rites, rather than to legal or moral precept, that is alluded to.

In V. 10 we think the term *Yátayáma* is imperfectly rendered by vapidum: it is literally that of which the time is past, but is described as signifying food ill-dressed, or that which has been suffered to get half cold before it is eaten. *Paryushitam*, stale, is omitted altogether, and it is similarly left out, or at least misplaced, in the English translation.

V. 19. *Múd̄hágraheńa* is the person, not the thing;

* [? Comp. Colebrooke's Essays, p. 259, and Zeitschrift der Deutschen morgenl. Ges., XIV, 520.]

it is he who assents to a foolish doctrine, and not ex inepto commento only.

In V. 26 we are disposed to question the translation of the explanation given of the term *Sat*, which is there said to signify the properties of what is real and righteous and all excellent acts. It is not therefore merely said or used 'de veritate ac honestate', but it actually imports the abstract properties of being and excellence, and the term essentia, which has been rather exceptionally applied to the *Sattwa Guńa*, would have been very correctly substituted in this place for veritas: whilst, in lieu of honestas, præstantia would have been more apposite. Again, *praśaste karmańi* should be 'in', not 'de', laudabili opere, for in the marriage ceremony and other rites the formula '*Om tat sat*' is repeated, and it is the repetition of *Sat* on such occasions that is here especially alluded to, conformably to the tenor of the two preceding stanzas. In the following stanza *Karma tadarthíyam* is of disputable translation: the word *tat*, that, being applicable either to what has gone before, sacrifice, &c., or to *Brahma* or supreme spirit. Schlegel follows the first, Wilkins the second interpretation: we are rather disposed to prefer the latter.

The eighteenth and concluding section is a summary of the doctrines of the Gítá, and explains particularly what is intended by the abandonment of works. This is, as before, resolved into relinquishment of consequences, and it is declared, that acts of worship, mortification, and charity are not to be forsaken, neither are the duties of caste and condition to be neglected: it is only indispensable, that all hope of benefit from the discharge of these obligations shall be utterly discarded, and this, with trust in Kŕishńa as the supreme, secures emancipation from corporal existence.

V. 13. The word *Kŕitánta* has not been understood by the translator. He has rendered *Sánkhye kŕitánte proktáni* by 'rationali demonstrationi explicata'; but *Kŕitánte* is not an epithet of *Sánkhye:* it is the denomination of a different school of philosophy, or as Wilkins accurately translates the passage, 'declared in the Sánkhya and Vedánta Śástras', *Kŕitánta* meaning literally the end of works, or the Philosophy which crowns the previous observances enjoined by the Veda.

In the following stanza again *adhishťhánam* has been misunderstood: it does not mean regimen,* but site, receptacle, or in other words the body as the seat of the elements and faculties: five instrumental causes being necessary, it is said, to the accomplishment of all acts, viz. place, agent, instrument, active effort, and the will of God, not as Schlegel writes, fatum.

In the specification of the different kinds of knowledge in verse 21 and 22, the translation is far from distinct or correct. Knowledge is affected by the three guńas: in conjunction with the *sattwa guńa* it recognises the universality and identity of spirit in all states; this is the doctrine of the Vedánta and of the Gítá. When influenced by the *rajo guńa*, it contemplates

* [2nd ed. "ditio".]

spirit as individualised by eternal impressions; and when associated with the *tamo guńa*, it limits spirit by its connexion with matter, and gives it only local and temporary existence: the stanzas conveying these notions relatively to the two last qualities run thus. "That knowledge which by the individuality of bodies conceives distinct properties and forms (of spirit) in all being, that is knowledge influenced by passion. But that knowledge which attaches itself to a single object as to the whole, which springs from no cause, which possesses not the truth, and is contemptible, that is considered as the knowledge that is affected by darkness." The passage is thus rendered in the Latin translation: Singulatim autem quæ cognitio varios existendi modos peculiares novit in omnibus quæ existunt, hanc cognitionem scias esse impetuosam. Quæ vero ad singulum negotium applicata est, quasi sit universitas rerum, principiis carens, veri summæ haud consentanea atque angusta, ea cognitio caliginosa nuncupatur.

An emendation is made in the last stanza of the poem, and Schlegel reads the second line *Tatra śrír vijayo bhútir dhruváńíti matir mama*, hic faustitas, victoria, principatus; cuncta ea stabilia. Sic stat sententia. The last phrase would at any rate be so far incorrect that it omits 'mea'. Sanjaya, the speaker, giving it only as *his* conviction that all the blessings enumerated result from Kríshńa's presence. Instead of *dhruváńíti*, stabilia, however, the common and no doubt correct reading is *dhruvá*, Fortitudo, and *nítir*,

Consilium; *níti* being detached by all the commentators, and explained by its cognate synonyme *naya*, royal leading, state policy or the wisdom of administration. Although, therefore, the emendation is plausible, and according to European taste might be an improvement in the construction of the sentence, it cannot be admitted in the face of all concurrent testimony against its necessity.

We have now completed our survey of Schlegel's translation of the Bhagavad Gítá. It will be seen that we have been able to point out many questionable and defective passages in the translation, and we might, if so disposed, have extended their number. With very few exceptions however the criticisms are merely verbal, and the instances in which the sense of a passage is materially misapprehended are by no means frequent: that this should be the case, is we think highly creditable to the translator. The subject is abstruse, and the manner of treating it not always perspicuous, and that the translation should have been so generally correct, is therefore matter of more surprise, than that it should have been occasionally erroneous. Schlegel also mentions that he was, as we have noticed, not possessed of any commentaries on the work, and this is evident, for many of the faulty passages would no doubt have been given correctly if he could have had the advantage of the light thrown upon their purport by the observations of the annotators. In some of the latter books we can trace a partial reference to Śrídhara Swámí, the circumstances of which are explained in the preface to the translation, but the references are not frequent and leave to the translator the merit of independent interpretation. On the whole therefore we are of opinion, that the translation of the Bhagavad Gítá is not unworthy of Schlegel's reputation, and that he is entitled to that rank amongst oriental scholars, which he has long enjoyed amongst the scholars of the west.

In entering so largely as we have done upon the analysis of the doctrines of the Gítá, we have not had in view only the necessity of their being understood in order that the character of the work might be duly appreciated, but we have wished to direct the attention of our readers to those suggestions which the Hindu dogmas are calculated to inspire. It is impossible to avoid noticing in the double doctrine of the Gítá an analogy to the double doctrine of the early Christian church, and the same question as to the merits of contemplative and practical religion engendered many differences of opinion and observance in the first ages of Christianity. These discussions, it is true, grew out of the admixture of the platonic philosophical notions with the lessons of Christianity, and had long pervaded the east, before the commencement of our era: it would not follow, therefore, that the divisions of the Christian Church originated the doctrine of the Hindus, and there is no reason to doubt that in all essential respects the Hindu schools are of a much earlier date: at the same time, it is not at all unlikely that the speculations of those schools were re-agitated and re-modified in the general stimulus which Christianity seems to have given to metaphysical enquiry, and it is not impossible that the attempts to model the ancient systems into a popular form, by engrafting on them, in particular, the vital importance of faith, were indirectly influenced by the diffusion of the Christian religion. It is highly desirable that this subject should be further investigated, as besides the illustration of the history of the Hindu religion and literature to be derived from it, it is of some importance to the early annals of our Church, and still more to the history of philosophy.

XIII.

PREFACE

TO THE

SANSKRIT DICTIONARY

(1st edition. Calcutta: 1819).

The cultivation of the Sanskrit language by European scholars has been hitherto much impeded by the absence of such assistance as that which is now proffered them. The elements of the language have been fully and distinctly developed and explained, and they have been studied, in a few instances, with a zeal proportioned to the difficulty of the task, and a success that could scarcely have been anticipated from the arduousness of the attempt and inadequacy of the means: in general, however, the want of a Dictionary has tended to deter application, and retard advancement, and has proved a serious obstacle to the intimate and extended acquirement of a language, which holds a most important place in literary history, and should be an object of primary interest to all who are charged with the government and happiness of Hindus.

To supply a deficiency as fatal to nascent curiosity, as embarrassing to study more advanced, the present translation of an extensive original compilation has been prepared. The original work was commenced shortly after the institution of the College of Fort William, for the use of which it was designed, being evidently connected with the objects and interests of that excellent establishment. Having been necessarily entrusted to native scholars, and being a task not very familiar to their literary habits, it is not surprising that much time should have been expended upon its execution, and that a delay more than commensurate with the extent and value of the work should have occurred: it was not finished till the year 1809, under the final superintendence of the late Raghumańi Bhaṫ-ṫáchárya; and then constituted, although far from complete, the only compilation in the Sanskrit language to which the name of Dictionary could with propriety be applied.

The Koshas of the Sanskrit Lexicographers, of which the best, the Amara Kosha, has been published with a translation by Mr. Colebrooke, are with a few exceptions mere vocabularies: their contents are classed according to analogy of import, and distributed into sections or chapters, according to the judgment or fancy of the author, and the synonymes of each signification are then strung together in a metrical combination, in which they take the situation that rhythm and quantity prescribe. The inconvenience of this arrangement is obvious: it is not always easy in the first instance to know in what division of the work the word we are in quest of is to be found; when this is ascertained, the discovery of the stanza or line in which it occurs is an occupation of some time and trouble, and when in imagination we have reached the goal, and attained the situation where the object of our search should be, the amalgamation of Sanskrit vocables by the laws of Sandhi, or the euphonous combination of letters, frequently renders the extraction of the individual term a task that requires more skill and experience than a student, nay even a Pańdit, is found to possess. This last difficulty is of invariable occurrence, but in some Koshas, and in the *Nánártha* chapters of all, or those chapters which treat of words possessing various senses, an approach is made to an alphabetical arrangement and the form of a Dictionary. The alphabetical arrangement, however, is in some cases only partial, as in the Amara Kosha, where words terminating with the same final letter are contiguously placed, but they are then disposed at random: in others, as in Ajayapála, the initial letter is the connective characteristic, but there, as in the former case, the arrangement goes no farther. In the Mediní again, which is exclusively appropriated to homonymous terms, a methodical system is adopted, perplexing from its fastidious exactness. The vocables are in that compilation arranged first according to their final letters; they are then classed agreeably to the number of syllables they contain, and they are then placed in an order, which is in general strictly alphabetical. The method adopted in the Mediní, of arranging words according to their final letters and syllabic extent, is the prevailing plan of the Nánártha Koshas, but that work, and the last chapter of Hemachandra, are the only ones in which much attention is paid to their subsequent disposition, and these vocabularies therefore, although consulted with more facility than those which are described above, still present many difficulties to the practised scholar, and are of little value or advantage to the early student.

The Sanskrit vocabularies still in use are in considerable number: they repeat each other of course, but each has in general made some additions to the labours of its predecessors, and is consequently deserving of reference: the words of the language are thus scattered through a variety of authorities, none of which can be readily consulted or understood with ease.

To collect these different authorities into one compilation, and arrange their united contents in an accessible shape, were the objects of the work undertaken for the use of the College; and to these were added the citation of the authority, and the synonymes there given, the specification of the genders of nouns, and the etymological analysis. It was written in the Bengálí character, and occupied four large folio volumes.

A copy of the Dictionary thus described came into my possession shortly after I commenced my Sanskrit studies, and I anticipated the most valuable assistance to them from such a source. I found, however, that it comprehended in its etymological details, and lengthened quotations of synonymes, much more than I then required, and that from its unwieldy size it was inconvenient and embarrassing in use. I therefore effected its conversion into a more commodious form, and prepared a translation of its abbreviated contents for my private reference. I state these circumstances to obviate the charge of presumption in engaging at so early a period, and with such inadequate powers, in a task of this nature, and for undertaking which at all this explanation will account.—I may further add, that even at this time I was encouraged in the attempt by the approbation of the late zealous and accomplished Orientalist Doctor John Leyden, whose own unwearied ardour in the prosecution of Asiatic literature delighted to cherish in others the faintest dawn of a congenial spirit.

Upon the completion of my task, circumstances led to the communication of its results to Mr. Colebrooke, a name which in Hịndu literature and science carries with it a weight and authority that all must bow to, and by his advice I was induced to revise my labours, and to hope that they might be rendered serviceable to the study of Sanskrit lore. How far that hope is likely to be realized, depends now upon the opinion of the Public, but it may be necessary to the accuracy of its decision to be apprised of the intentions I proposed to effect, and the means I had of executing them; so that I may not be unjustly censured for failing in a project I never entertained, or imperfectly accomplishing a task that my materials were incompetent to perform.

The preparation of the Dictionary as it now appears rendered my first work of no practical utility, especially as in the course of the first translation it had not occurred to me to question or verify the correctness of my original. I had therefore to recommence my labours, and carefully to collate the compilation of Raghumańi with the authorities on which it rested, and it soon appeared that accuracy was no part of the Compiler's merits: the mistakes were innumerable, and of every kind; words incorrectly written and erroneously interpreted, fanciful etymologies covering and sanctioning those errors, passages wrongly cited, and the names of the original vocabularies constantly confounded, met me in every page, and the adjustment of these inaccuracies, added to the difficulty inseparable from a reference to such unmethodical guides as the Sanskrit Koshas, has rendered the business of collation the most laborious and harrassing portion of my task. Fortunately it was a duty in which my native assistants were best employed, and they have been especially so occupied. To those who are acquainted with the character of these assistants it is needless to expatiate upon the necessity of vigilantly superintending and revising whatever they do, and it would be difficult to convey to a person not acquainted with them any conception of their carelessness and indolence, and of the limited dependance to be placed upon native research, when not sedulously and unremittingly controlled. I have had in the course of my labours the aid of many Pańdits of high credit and respectable acquirements, and regret much, that

I cannot associate the name of any one of them with my own, as a partner in the little credit I may hope to derive from the present publication.

The plan of the original compilation, including the contents of the vocabularies alone, left the work exceedingly defective: the Roots of the language are all excluded from those collections, as are most technical terms and words of common occurrence, and none of these accordingly were comprised in Raghumańi's Dictionary. I am disposed, indeed, to question the expedience of the primary plan, and to conceive that a more useful Lexicon might have been drawn up from the classical compositions of the best Hindu writers, instead of deriving it from the Koshas only. At the same time, as these last are the received authorities of all India, and as the interpretations resting on general writings may be contested; as they are also perpetually cited in the ablest commentaries, and their omission might have given undue importance to their supposed contents, it was absolutely necessary to comprehend within the scope of the work as many of them as were procurable. To have added to these authorities the general body of Hindu compositions would have involved an amount of labour, cost and time, and a voluminous extent of preparation, which the state of Sanskrit study does not yet require, and perhaps does not permit, and it is therefore with some hesitation that I suggest any objections to the original plan. To remedy its deficiencies at all was obviously not incumbent upon one who appeared in the humble character of Translator only, and I should have been justified therefore in confining the limits of my Translation to those of the original. As some of its omissions were however of importance, I felt myself bound to supply them, and I have made very considerable additions to the original work. These additions were such as were most obviously useful, and particularly include the whole number of the *Radicals* of the language. But I shall not pause here, to offer a more detailed notice of them, as their specification will more consistently occur under the description I shall now proceed to give of the sources whence not only they, but the contents of the entire work, are derived. The authorities cited in the original compilation, and collated in the course of translation, are for the greater part the same as those enumerated in the preface to Mr. Colebrooke's translation of the Amara Kosha. The text of that work employed on the present occasion is that of his very accurate edition, and I have been indebted to him for the copies of the different commentaries consulted by him in his translation, and which were handed over to me, with the ready liberality which has always characterised that distinguished scholar. To his account, therefore, of these works I might be contented to refer; but, as I hope to add something to the limited knowledge we possess of the author of the Amara Kosha, and as I have to notice several works not adverted to by Mr. Colebrooke, I have thought it advisable to include the whole in the enumeration of my authorities, and thus bring into one view all the information we possess at present of those writers who are celebrated as lexicographers by the Hindus.

The *Amara Kosha*, or vocabulary of Amara Sinha, is a compilation too well known in Europe to need any particular description. It is in India the vocabulary most generally celebrated, and of the widest circulation, being a work of unquestionable authority in all the schools, and with every sect. The author, by his appellation *Sinha,* would seem to have belonged to the *Kshatriya* or military tribe, but it may merely designate his eminence, in which sense it is often conjoined to words: in like manner, though in Amara Deva, another appellation by which he is known, the latter term is a Brahmanical surname, yet it may be merely an epithet alluding to his superior or divine merit. He is generally, and apparently with reason, considered to have been a follower of *Buddha*, although this is denied by one of his late commentators, Rámáśrama, and all tradition concurs in enumerating him amongst the learned men who, in metaphorical phraseology of the Hindus, are denominated the "*nine gems*" of the court of Vikramáditya.

The era at which the author of the Amara Kosha flourished, connected as it is by these long and universally current traditions with a period of peculiar splendour in the literary annals of India, is an object of profound interest: to ascertain it within any reasonable bounds would fix the date of a number of celebrated compositions, whose age is involved at present in utter obscurity, and would determine the time and existence of a monarch, of whom, notwithstanding he furnishes an epoch by which Hindu dates are still regulated, the accounts are contradictory and perplexed. How far it is practicable to effect this object, will best appear from the following considerations, the extent of which will find a sufficient excuse in the important associations which are involved in the result. Authorities which assert the contemporary existence of Amara and Vikramáditya might be indefinitely multiplied, and those are equally numerous which class him amongst the "*nine gems*". The specification of these worthies, including the name of Amara Sinha, occurs however in a verse which appears in a great measure traditionary only, as I have not been able to trace it to any authentic source, although it is in the mouth of every Paṅdit, when interrogated on the subject. It has been published by Mr. Bentley, in his Essay on the Hindu systems of Astronomy, in the 8th volume of the Asiatic Researches, and as it is sufficient for the purposes of the present enquiry I shall here insert it.*

धन्वन्तरिक्षपणकामरसिंहशङ्कु-
वेतालभट्टघटखर्प्परकालिदासाः।

---

* Asiatic Researches VIII, 242. It may be observed that in this verse, as printed in the Researches, the name of Ghaṫakarpara is misspelt, Ghaṫakarpúra: the name is itself a poetical one, and the meaning of it with the passage in which it originally occurs are given in Mr. Colebrooke's Essay on Sanskrit and Prákrit Poetry, Asiatic Researches X, 402. [Misc. Essays, II, 75.]

ख्यातो वराहमिहिरो नृपतेः सभायां
रत्नानि वै वररुचिर्नव विक्रमस्य ॥

"Dhanwantari, Kshapańaka, Amara Sinha, Śanku, Vetála Bhaťťa, Ghaťakarpara, Kálidása, the celebrated Varáhamihira, and Vararuchi, were the nine gems in the court of the Monarch Vikrama."

From the identity of some of the names, contained in the above stanza, with some which occur in a work entitled the *Bhoja Prabandha*, a collection of literary anecdotes relating to the prince of Dhárá named *Bhoja*, and from its being undoubtedly true that the term Vikrama is a title rather than a proper name, and applied in Indian history to many different princes, it has been inferred that the Vikrama mentioned in the stanza is either Bhoja himself, or his immediate successor whose name is said to have been Vikrama, and that the "*nine gems*" flourished during the reigns of these two princes, being first in the council of Rájá Bhoja, and afterwards in that of Vikramáditya, his successor.* The reign of Bhoja is placed by Mr. Bentley at the end of the tenth, and beginning of the eleventh century, or from 982 to 1082;† and by Major Wilford Bhoja's death is placed in the year 977 or 982 at latest.‡ In either case, if Amara, and the other writers enumerated in the verse, were contemporary with Bhoja, the golden age of Hindu literature will be transferred from the century preceding the

---

* Asiatic Researches VIII, 243. † Asiatic Res. VIII, 243.

‡ Asiatic Researches IX, 157.

Christian era to which it is usually referred, or the commencement of the era of Vikramáditya, to a comparatively modern period, and be not much more than eight centuries remote.

The accuracy of this conclusion, opposed as it is by the concurring and consistent traditions of the country, and by a belief that has existed, unaltered and unassailed, for many centuries, cannot be unhesitatingly admitted, especially when upon investigation it appears to have been advanced upon grounds of a slight and frail texture in themselves, and loosely or partially examined.

The first subject of doubt is the authenticity and weight of the stanza, which is given to us, as the authority for the contemporary existence of the individuals it particularises; no mention is made of the work whence it is extracted, nor the writer to whom it is ascribed, nor are we furnished with any data by which to judge of the claims it possesses on our credit.* In truth, it appears to be little more than traditionary, as although familiar to every Pańdit, I never met with one who could tell me its origin or author. It is attributed by some to the *Vikrama Charitra*, but they have only asserted this upon report, and I have not been able to procure a copy of that work in order to

* [Prof. F. E. Hall was the first to assign the verses in question to the author of the Jyotirvidábharańa, a modern composition. See his edition of Wilson's Vishńupuráńa, I, p. VII-IX; comp. also Bháu Dáji in Journal As. Soc. Bombay, Vol. VI, p. 25 ff.]

verify the assertion; it may be doubted indeed whether the entire work exists, as Major Wilford at Benares could not meet with it, and was indebted to extracts supplied by Colonel Mackenzie from an imperfect manuscript procured in the Peninsula.* If the statement be correct, however, it adds but little strength to the argument, as the *Vikrama Charitra*, like the *Sinhásana Dwátrinśati*, and *Vetála Panchavinśati*, is a collection of mere fables, and of no historical weight. As a composition of apparently modern date, it is probably a mere transcript of some popular tradition in the list of Vikramáditya's "*nine gems*"; and we are therefore obliged to assail this tradition with the instruments itself supplies, and derive from traditionary evidence our only proof, that all such evidence is unworthy of belief. If the verse under discussion be a proof that Amara was the contemporary of any of the literary characters there named, it proves also that he was contemporary with *Rájá Vikrama*, and in order to be consistent in the argument which reduces Amara's antiquity, it becomes necessary to affix the name of the monarch to some other than the original Vikramáditya to whom it is usually assigned. That the enumeration is not entirely accurate, may be inferred from its comprising Vararuchi as well as Amara; as the former is considered by the commentators as one of Amara's authorities, and necessarily

* Asiatic Researches X, 30. [Mackenzie Collection I, 343 ff. Journal Asiatique, IVme Série, VI, 288 ff. Lassen, Ind. Alt., II, 759.]

therefore his predecessor, but as it is consistent with general belief, we need not place any stress on this exception. That by Vikrama however is intended either *Rájá Bhoja* or his successor, may confidently be denied.

The principal argument for placing the nine writers in the court of Bhoja is supposed to be furnished by the *Bhoja Prabandha,* a work in which it is said, that the "*nine gems*" are stated to have flourished under that prince, and that they are specified as the very persons named in the list above cited: assertions of which the first is untrue, and the second but partially correct.

The *Bhoja Prabandha* is a work of no estimation nor authority: its purport is the commemoration of the liberal patronage which men of letters experienced from Bhoja, the sovereign of Dhárá or Dhar in Málwá, and it introduces a number of the most celebrated writers in India as interlocutors in short dialogues with each other, or with the prince, in which they are supposed to display peculiar readiness of wit, brilliancy of imagination, or beauty of expression.* It might have been conceived to hold the character of a Sanskrit Anthology, or a collection of 'Elegant Extracts', had not the author neglected the variety of characteristic selection for the sameness of original

* [Prof. F. E. Hall justly observes: "It is high time to give up speaking of this prince as a great patron of literature. His pretensions to be so considered rest on the frailest foundation possible." Bengal Journal for 1862, p. 13.]

composition. According to Mr. Bentley it was written by *Vallála Sena*,* a prince who lived in the twelfth century.† Mr. Ward says, it was written by Bhoja himself, which is an evident inaccuracy.‡ One copy in my possession agrees so far with the first of these statements, as to term the writer *Vallála Pańđita;* but another, and a more correct copy denominates him *Vallabha Pańđita*. The last is a name of no note, nor are any data given for conjecturing his age; but from the names of authors contained in the work, whose dates are ascertained, it is clear that Vallabha Pańđita, if a correct appellation of the writer, could not have composed it earlier than the age of *Vallála Sena*, and neither of these authors therefore can be supposed peculiarly well qualified to report conversations, which they describe as having been held some centuries before; and the whole is a fiction of no historical value. If any weight can be attached to it, it can only be supposed as intended to give an account of the writers who were distinguished in the three or four centuries preceding the Author's own time, and cannot be admitted as an accurate notice of those of any particular age or reign. We have proofs of this indeed in the contemporary association of individuals, who we know lived at distant intervals; and Maheśwara whose date is A.D. 1111, and Mádhava who

---

* Asiatic Researches VIII, 244. † Ibid. V, 64.

‡ Ward on the History, Religion, and Literature of the Hindus, I, 516.

wrote about A. D. 1340, are both present in the court of Bhoja, who himself died at the latest in 1082: such being the consistency and the accuracy of a record, which has been supposed to establish for the works of "Varáha, Amara Sinha, Káḷidása, and Vararuchi an antiquity of little more than seven hundred years."*

The general unfitness of the Bhoja Prabandha to be regarded as an authority, which has thus been pointed out, might be sufficient to show, that no inference of Amara's existing at Bhoja's court as drawn from the Bhoja Prabandha is entitled to our attention; but as an object of literary discussion, and to shew the spirit in which some part of this enquiry has been conducted, I must be permitted to dwell a little longer on the subject.

The most correct copy of the work I have been able to procure, and which was brought by my friend Captain Price from Benares, I have perused with the closest attention. In no part of it is it asserted that there were "nine gems" at Bhoja's court, nor do the names of more than two of those *nine gems* occur in it. Individually and successively introduced as interlocutors in the dialogue, the different writers are very

* [See Journal As. Soc. Bombay, VI, 23; Prof. Hall in the preface to his edition of the Vásavadattá, p. 7, who calls the author of the Bhoja Prabandha *Ballála Miśra*; Lassen, Ind. Alt., III, 836 ff. Prof. Aufrecht (Catal. Sanscr. MSS. I, 151) places the Bhojaprabandha at the end of the 16th century, which is more probable than the 13th to which M. Pavie (Journal Asiatique, Vme Série, IV, 429) assigns it.]

numerous, but amongst them the only name that occurs in the stanza above given is that of *Kálidása*: we have however in the following enumeration of Bhoja's learned men one other appellative which may be identified with one in the verse:

अथ धारानगरे न कोऽपि मूर्खो निवसति। क्रमेण पञ्चशतानि सेवन्ते विदुषां श्रीभोजम्। वररुचिसुबन्धुबाणमयूररामदेवहरिवंशशङ्करकलिङ्गकर्पूरविनायकमदनविद्याविनोदकोकिलतारेन्द्रप्रमुखाः।*

"Then there was no blockhead in the city Dhárá, but five hundred learned men severally attended on Śrí Bhoja, as Vararuchi, Subandhu, Váńa, Mayúra, Rámadeva, Harivanśa, Śankara, Kalinga, Karpúra, Vináyaka, Madana, Vidyávinoda, Kokila, Tárendra, and others,"—a very different series of names, and authors, from the 'nine gems' we have enumerated, with the single apparent exception of Vararuchi.

It is now perfectly well understood, that in India identity of name is by no means identity of person, and that the celebrity of any particular denomination is the cause of its being assumed by many besides its original possessor. In the history of the Mogul empire in Hindustan many Vikramádityas or Bickermajits are found amongst their tributary Rájás, and at this moment many *Kálidásas* are to be met with in India as poets at the courts of men of opulence and rank, as if they expected to inherit with these attributes of their

* [In M. T. Pavie's edition p. 21 and v. l. p. 131. Journal Asiatique, l. l., p. 396.]

illustrious prototype some spark of his divine spirit. That there were at least *two* eminent bards of this name, is the general opinion of Hindu scholars, and the belief is borne out by the internal evidence of the compositions ascribed to Kálidása, which have every mark of having been written at different periods, both of time and taste. The existence of a Kálidása at the court of Bhoja is therefore no argument against Amara's being contemporary with another bard of that name, or to their both having flourished long anterior to the reign of that prince.*

That the name of *Vararuchi* has in like manner been applied to different individuals, might fairly be inferred from the practice thus described; but we have in this case a remarkable confirmation of our conjectures, and find, from the varying statements of several writers, that two, if not three, persons of this denomination are celebrated in the literary history of the Hindus.

In the *Kathá Sarit Ságara*, the same work in substance as the Vŕihat Kathá, and by the same author Somadeva, who declares that his abridgement has omitted no essential part of his own original, the ancient Grammarian *Kátyáyana* is said to be the same person as Vararuchi, and to be called indiscriminately by either name. The opening of this work, in the usual style of Hindu story-telling, introduces us to

* [See Journal Bombay As. Soc. Vol. VI, 19 ff.; 207 ff. Lassen, Ind. Alt., II, 1157 ff. Weber's "Málaviká und Agnimitra". Berlin: 1856, Introduction.]

superhuman agency: a demi-god named Pushpadanta, an attendant upon Śiva, has incurred the displeasure of his irascible mistress Durgá, and is condemned to expiate his offence by wearing for a certain time the human form; in obedience to this sentence, he appears upon earth as a learned Brahman, named indifferently Kátyáyana or Vararuchi, ततः स मर्त्यवपुषा पुष्पदन्तः परिभ्रमन् । नाम्ना वररुचिः किञ्च कात्यायन इति श्रुतः ॥*

Proceeding a few pages, we find Kátyáyana narrating his story to the Brahmans Vyáḍi and Indradatta, and he tells them that his birth was proclaimed by a voice from heaven, in the following stanza:

एकश्रुतधरो जातो विद्यां वर्षादवाप्स्यति ।
किञ्च व्याकरणं लोके प्रतिष्ठां प्रापयिष्यति ॥
नाम्ना वररुचिर्लोके तत्तदस्मै हि रोचते ।
यद्यद्वरं भवेत्किञ्चिदित्युक्त्वा वागुपारमत् ॥†

"A Śrutadhara is born who shall acquire knowledge from Varsha (a foolish Brahman so named), and shall give perfection to grammatical science amongst men: something of whatever is excellent (varam) shines (rochate) in him, and therefore he shall be known in the world by the name Vararuchi. Having thus spoken the voice ceased."

That Vararuchi, alias Kátyáyana, was a different person from the Vararuchi of Bhoja's court, will scarcely be disputed: the latter is regarded as the Purohita, or family priest, of the monarch, and is little known as an author. He is said to have written the

* [Tar. II, 1.] † [Tar. II, 69. 70.]

Bhoja Champú in conjunction with his royal master, and to have completed the work after that prince's death. He is also known as the maternal uncle of *Subandhu,* the author of the Vásavadattá, a tale which that author appears to have modernised, and which in its older form, and with different names, is told in the Vŕihat Kathá, and is also alluded to by Kálidása* and Bhavabhúti, who consequently are prior to Subandhu, and who might have been contemporary or nearly so with his uncle. This Vararuchi must therefore be a very different character from Vararuchi or Kátyáyana, the grammarian, one of Páńini's earliest commentators, the author of the Várttika, of the Prákŕita Manorama, and possibly of the work which is enumerated by the commentators on Amara amongst the authorities of that vocabulary. *They* indeed reckon amongst those authorities Kátyáyana also, and consequently make a distinction between these two writers. It is possible that they are correct, but the discrepancy that thus occurs between the two accounts is favourable to the present enquiry, as it renders it possible that we have *three* Vararuchis instead of one, and at least furnishes a positive proof, that the name is far from being the exclusive property of the person noticed in the Bhoja Prabandha.

It may indeed be asserted, that the Kathá Sarit Sá-

* Megha Dúta with translation, 36 and note [p. 341 in Vol. II of this division of Prof. Wilson's works]: also Asiatic Researches X, 451. [Colebrooke's Misc. Essays, II, 134.]

gara, or rather Vṙihat Kathá, is not a much better guide than the Bhoja Prabandha, and that a collection of idle stories is bad historical evidence. It must be remembered, however, that those tales are not of Somadeva's invention: he has only the merit of telling them in his own way, and of having collected them together from various quarters. Thus we have most of the legends relating to Vikrama, which constitute the Sinhásana Dwátrinśati, and Vetála Panchavinśati, and we have also a very considerable portion of the Hitopadeśa, or Panchatantra, comprised in this selection: such as the tales are, therefore, they are of remote origin and existence, and are at least faithful records of the state of popular belief many ages ago. The compilation itself is of some antiquity. Major Wilford states that it is to be considered to be between 6 and 700 years old, and this antiquity is corroborated by the mention* of the work made by *Govarddhana*, the author of the *Sapta Śati*, who flourished probably in the twelfth century. Now seven centuries would bring the Vṙihat Kathá very near to the reign

---

* Catalogue of oriental works presented to the Royal Society by Lady Jones, No. 15. Sir William Jones' works XIII, 409. The original verse is:

श्रीरामायणभारतबृहत्कथानां कवीन्नमस्कुर्मः
त्रिस्रोता इव सरसा सरस्वती स्फुरति यैर्भिन्ना ॥

thus rendered by Sir William Jones, "we do homage to the poets who composed the Rámáyańa, the Mahábhárata, and the Vṙihatkathá, by whom delightful eloquence blazes forth divided like the river with three streams." [F. E. Hall in the Preface to his edition of the Vásavadattá, p. 22.]

of Bhoja himself, and if the date of that reign has been ascertained with any correctness, the prince and his minister must have been characters familiar to the recollection of the author; that they were so, and consequently not yet objects of traditionary fiction, may be inferred from no notice being taken of them in any of the fables contained in the collection. At all events, if there had been a Vararuchi in Bhoja's court, it is not likely that at so recent a period he should have been confounded with the ancient grammarian Káṭyáyana: nor would Somadeva, or any of the old fablers, have asserted, what all their contemporaries could contradict, that Bhoja's Vararuchi lived prior to the birth of Sátaváhana or Śáliváhana, the founder of the Śáka era, an antiquity which is assigned to him in one of the early chapters of the Vṛihat Kathá. Whatever therefore we may think of Vararuchi and Kátyáyana being identified, it is very clear that a writer of the former name did precede the Vararuchi, who appears to have flourished in the reign of Bhoja, and the earlier of the two is most probably intended by the tradition which makes him the contemporary of Vikrama and Amara Sinha.*

I have thus shewn that the supposed coincidence

* [Lassen, Ind. Alt., II, 1156; IV, 805; Müller's Ancient Sanskrit Lit., 239 ff.; Cowell's edition of the Prákṛita Prakáśa, Preface; Goldstücker's 'Pâṇini'. London: 1861, p. 81 ff.; Weber's 'Indische Studien', V, 93 ff.; James d'Alwis, 'Introduction to Kachcháyana's grammar of the Pali language'. Colombo: 1863, p. XXXVI ff.]

of the persons in the verse which assigns the '*nine gems*' to Vikrama, and those enumerated in the Bhoja Prabandha, has no satisfactory existence, and that, except in the two doubtful cases I have specified, it has no existence at all: as far therefore as depends upon the Bhoja Prabandha, we have no reason to consider its hero as the same prince with the Vikrama of the verse, nor that Amara Sinha lived at so comparatively recent a period as his reign. That the latter was not the case, however, we have other and more probable testimony.

An inscription found by Mr. Wilkins at Buddha Gayá, of which he published a translation in the Asiatic Researches,* and which was written to commemorate the foundation of a temple of Buddha by Amara Sinha, bears the date 1005 of the era of Vikramáditya, answering to the Christian year 949: the authenticity of this inscription we have no reason to question, as it professes no object to which suspicion of fraud or interest can be attached, and it is perfectly consistent with the character and traditions of the place in which it was found: the identity of the person is also indisputable, as all ancient authorities concur in representing Amara as a worshipper of Buddha, and he is designated in the inscription in the usual manner as one of the nine gems of Vikramáditya's court.

Admitting therefore the testimony of this record, it follows that Amara Sinha was a person of some ce-

---

* Asiatic Researches, I, 284.

lebrity prior to the date given in it, or A.D. 949, and it is not likely therefore that he should be contemporary with Bhoja, who had scarcely commenced his reign according to Major Wilford's theory, or who did not ascend the throne till 30 years subsequent, according to Mr. Bentley's view of the subject. In fact however the tenor of the inscription renders either equally impossible, since that absolutely authorises our placing Amara long anterior to the period of its composition.

The author states his having derived his knowledge of Amara's being the founder of the temple from its records, or as it is translated "from the authority of the place", an authority which no doubt existed, as most celebrated shrines are furnished with a legend, a lying one it may be granted, which professes to give their history: and it matters not here, of what description was the record of the temple of Buddha, as, if in the middle of the tenth century it had converted Amara Sinha into the hero of a holy fable, it at least proves his prior and remote existence.

To return to the inscription: the writer states that "Amara was the favourite and minister of Vikramáditya, who was certainly a king renowned in the world", and whom he intends by Vikramáditya, can scarcely be doubted, as he dates from that prince's era: it is therefore perfectly clear that at so distant a period as A.D. 949, if the inscription is to be trusted, the same traditionary account of Amara's date prevailed, which is still received, and however accurate or incorrect this tradition may have been, its existence is fatal to the supposition that the subject of it was alive at the period when such a belief was current, and still more so to the opinion we have noticed of his flourishing at some subsequent date.

That the inscription is worthy of credit,* I see nö reason to doubt, and it is assuredly an authority of more weight than the notions of nameless Paṅḋits,† the sole impugners of the belief it sanctions.

The certainty that Amara Sinha lived before the time of Bhoja, and the inference fairly deducible from the only positive record we possess of his living *long before* that period, leave us still in doubt as to the precise time at which he flourished.

Tradition, uniform and consistent, and as we see by the inscription, and as we know from other testimonies, of unvarying tenor for seven or eight centuries, places him in the court of Vikramáditya, in the origin of the Samvat era, or 56 years before Christ; an antiquity far from unreasonable or improbable, although deemed by modern scepticism too remote. The only grounds on which this belief could ever have rested, the authority of the Bhoja Prabandha, I have shewn to be untenable, and I cannot therefore conceive the argument by which it can further be supported. The dispute, to use the words of *Harris* on a similar topic,

* [Comp. also Col. A. Cunningham's Report in As. J. of Bengal, Vol. XXXII, No. 13 ff.]

† Asiatic Researches, VIII, 243.

appears to arise from the 'disputants running into the opposite vice of incredulity, in order to avoid being thought credulous': for even in his day there was occasion to notice a defect, which is outrageously conspicuous in the writers of the present, when ancient India is their theme, "and whose opposition to the many claims of the Hindus is not so much founded in greater learning or superior talents, as in strong prejudices in favour of their own countries, and in high conceit of their own abilities."

The real date of Vikramáditya's reign is however still a desideratum in Indian History,* and in spite of the learned labours of that profound and patient investigator Major Wilford† we have yet to ascertain whether the voice of tradition be that of truth. The circumstances of Amara's being contemporary with him depends upon no positive proof, and there is some inconsistency in making the Buddha philologist the favourite and minister of a monarch, who is always described in the legends recorded of him as a pious worshipper of the orthodox divinities‡ and the liberal

* [Lassen, Ind. Alt., II, 800 ff. Weber, Ind. Stud., II, 416. Ind. Literaturgeschichte, p. 188. Bombay Asiatic Soc. Journal, VI, 27 ff.]

† Asiatic Researches, IX. Essay on Vikramáditya and Sálivábana. [See Prinsep's Essays, ed. 2. Thomas, II, 249.]

‡ The Jains, I am informed, consider Vikramáditya to have been of their persuasion; in the Vŕihatkathá, Sinhásana Dwátrinśati, and Vetála Panchavinśati, he always appears as the worshipper of Durgá or Deví especially.

patron of the regular priesthood. The age of the Amara Kosha can scarcely be fixed within any narrow limits, and we can only feel satisfied of its composition at some period long anterior to the tenth century,* an opinion further warranted by the grammarian Vopadeva, who is generally assigned to the twelfth century,† and who enumerates Amara amongst the eight *old* grammarians,‡ an epithet he would no more have attached to a writer but two or three centuries anterior to himself than any grammarian of the present day would think of giving to Bhaṫṫojí Díkshita, who compiled the Kaumudí about 200 years ago. Amara Sinha may therefore be left agreeably to tradition to the beginning of the Christian era, or, as connected with other traditionary notices of names and events which I shall proceed to describe, he may be brought down to a later date, and placed about the middle or end of the fifth century after Christ.

In the verse which specifies the names of the *nine gems*, and which I have inserted above, we find the name of the astronomer Varáha Mihira who, according to this authority, is therefore contemporary with

---

* [Lassen, Ind. Alt., IV, 633 f., now places Amarasinha before Varáhamihira, about 200 years later than he had done before, II, 1155. See also Goldstücker's Sanskrit Dictionary s. v. Amarasinha.]

† Asiatic Researches, VIII, 467; [to the second half of the thirteenth. See Burnouf, Bhág. Pur., I, CI, and Lassen, Ind. Alt., IV, 599.]

‡ Preface to Colebrooke's Sanskrit Grammar. [Misc. Ess., II, 39.]

Amara Sinha; this astronomer, upon grounds similar to those on which Mr. Bentley reduced the antiquity of Amara, has accordingly been placed by him* in the twelfth century, an opinion contrary to the general belief, and one which there is every reason to conclude is far from correct.

From astronomical data derived from the work of *Varáha Mihira,*† the Vŕihat Sanhitá, it appears that an antiquity must be assigned to this author of either 1216 or 1440 years, reckoning from A.D. 1800; the mean of this is assumed by Mr. Colebrooke, or A.D. 472, as being the probable era of his existence, and as agreeing sufficiently with the date usually given him, or A.D. 499, and not far from that contained in a list of astronomical writers prepared at Oujein, or A.D. 505-6. According to the same authority‡ he is

---

* Asiatic Researches, VIII, 243.

† Colebrooke on the age of Varáha Mihira, introduction to Indian Algebra &c. [Miscell. Essays, II, 466 ff. Lassen, Ind. Alt., IV, 841 ff.]

‡ See also introduction to Colebrooke's edition of the Hitopadeśa, p. II. The notice occurs in the first Tantra or chapter [v. 238] in the same story but somewhat differently told, which is in the Hitopadeśa, (Sir William Jones's works, Vol. XIII, 177) of a Vaka killed by a crab. The astronomer is thus introduced: the Vaka tells the crab that by the position of the planets a twelve years' drought may be expected, as it is said by Varáha Mihira "when the son of Súrya (Saturn) divides the car of Rohiṅí, then in the world Mádhava will shed no rain upon the earth for twelve years."

उक्तञ्च वराहमिहिरेण।

also named in the Pancha Tantra, the original of the Hitopadeśa, and which was translated into Persian in the reign of Núshirván, in the latter part of the sixth and beginning of the seventh century, and this early notice is a decisive confirmation of the accuracy of the above date. It seems therefore to be ascertained, with as much precision as the subject admits, that an astronomical writer denominated Varáha Mihira did flourish at Oujein in the course of the fifth century of our era: and it is farther possible that he was cotemporary with a prince named Vikramáditya, and the subject of our Researches.

Major Wilford, in his elaborate Essay on Vikramáditya* and Śáliváhana, has succeeded in disentangling from the perplexity occasioned by the repetition of names, and the confusion of dates, *three* princes of great power and celebrity, who were all known under the former appellation: the first of these is the sovereign from whom the era in use is denominated, and whose claims to be the patron of the *nine gems* we are contented to leave undetermined; the second Vikrama† is the same with Śrí Karńa Deva, called also Śúdraka and Śúraka and Áditya;‡ he began his reign A.D. 191, and this date agrees with the age of an elder Varáha Mihira, placed by the astronomers of Oujein in the

---

यदा भिंत्ते सूर्य्यपुत्रो रोहिण्याः शकटमिह लोके ।
द्वादशवर्षाणि तदा न हि वर्षति माधवो भूमौ ॥
[See on this quotation Benfey's "Pantschatantra", II, 392 f.]

* Asiatic Researches, IX. † Ibid. 146. ‡ Ibid. 139.

year of Christ 200;* his capital is called Charchitá or Charchita Nagara,† the city of investigation, as the struggle between the original Hindu system, and the innovation of the Bauddhas and others is supposed to have commenced there and at this time. As Śrí Karńa Deva, however, was the sovereign of Magadha or Behar, and resided at a place now called Jangira,‡ half way between Mongir and Bhágalpore, it is impossible that Charchita Nagara could be the same as Ujjayiní or Oujein, in which city alone we are to look for the patron of the *nine gems*, and this prince consequently cannot be the Vikramáditya in question. The third Vikramáditya has better claims;§ he is not designated by any other name or title; his capital was Oujein, and his reign began in 441; a date that accords with the existence of Amara, as the cotemporary of Varáha Mihira in the fifth century, and with his being implicated in the changes which the temporary ascendancy of the Brahmans apparently began about that time to effect in Hindustan.

The persecution of the followers of Buddha by the Brahmanical order is a subject on which both sects are agreed; one of the earliest and most harmless effects of it, it is generally believed, was the anathematising of the Bauddha works, and amongst

---

* Colebrooke's Indian Algebra, introduction, dissertation E. [Misc. Essays, II, 467. Lassen, Ind. Alt., II, 1133.]

† Asiatic Researches, X, 91.

‡ Asiatic Researches, IX, 108. § Ibid. 139. [E. Thomas' edition of Prinsep's Useful Tables, p. 249 f. Lassen, l. l., II, 759.]

them, of the compositions of Amara, all which consequently perished, with the exception of his Vocabulary.* As the persecution is thus restricted to Amara's literary existence, we may infer his personal exemption from its fury by his existence prior to that event, and by ascertaining therefore the time of its commencement we may be able to add another conjecture to those we have formed of our author's age. Celebrated as is the persecution and temporary suppression of the Bauddha heresy, it is an occurrence of which the date is as uncertain as of any other event in Hindu history: its institution is generally attributed to *Śankara Áchárya*,† and with his age therefore must originate our enquiry.

The birth of Śankara presents the same discordance of opinion as every other remarkable incident amongst the Hindus.

The Kadálí Brahmans, who form an establishment following and teaching his system, assert his appearance about 2000 years† since; some accounts place him about the beginning of the Christian era,‡ others in the third or fourth century § after; a manuscript history of the kings of Konga, in Colonel Makenzie's collection,‖ makes him cotemporary with Tiru Vikrama Deva Chakravartí, sovereign of Skandapura in the

* Asiatic Researches, VII, 214.

† Buchanan's Mysore, III, 301.

‡ Wilks's History of Mysore, I, Appendix No. V.

§ Buchanan's Mysore, II, 74.

‖ [Madras Lit. Soc. Journal, Vol. XIV, pp. 6 and 65.]

Dekhan, A.D. 178; at Śringagiri, on the edge of the Western Ghauts, and now in the Mysore territory, at which place he is said to have founded a College that still exists, and assumes the supreme control of the Smártal Brahmans of the Peninsula, an antiquity of 1600 years is attributed to him, and common tradition makes him about 1200 years old. The Bhoja Prabandha enumerates Śankara amongst its worthies, and as contemporary with that prince; his antiquity will then be between eight and nine centuries. The followers of Madhwáchárya in Tuĺuva seem to have attempted to reconcile these contradictory accounts by supposing him to have been born three times; first at Sivuli in Tuĺuva about 1500 years ago, again in Malabar some centuries later, and finally at Pádukachaytra in Tuĺuva* no more than 600 years since; the latter assertion being intended evidently to do honour to their own founder, whose date that was, by enabling him to triumph over Śankara in a supposititious controversy. The Vaishńava Brahmans of Madura say that Śankara appeared in the ninth century of Sáliváhana or tenth of our era;† Dr. Taylor thinks that, if we allow him about 900 years, we shall not be far from the truth,‡ and Mr. Colebrooke is inclined to give him an antiquity of about 1000 years.§ This last is the age which my friend Rammohun Roy, a diligent

---

* Buchanan's Mysore, III, 91. † Ibid. I, 143.

‡ Dedication to the translation of the Prabodha Chandrodaya.

§ Preface to the translation of the Dáya Bhága, [p. XI].

student of Śankara's works, and philosophical teacher of his doctrines, is disposed to concur in, and he infers that, "from a calculation of the spiritual generations of the followers of Śankara Swámí from his time up to this date, he seems to have lived between the seventh and eighth centuries of the Christian era,"— a distance of time agreeing with the statements made to Dr. Buchanan in his journey through Śankara's native country, Malabar,* and in union with the assertion of the Keraĺa Utpatti, a work giving an historical and statistical account of the same province, and which, according to Mr. Duncan's citation of it, mentions the regulations of the castes of Malabar by this philosopher to have been effected about 1000 years before 1798.† At the same time it must be observed that a manuscript translation of this same work, in Colonel Makenzie's possession, states Śankara Áchárya to have been born about the middle of the fifth century, or between thirteen and fourteen hundred years ago, differing in this respect from Mr. Duncan's statement,‡—a difference of the less importance, as

* Buchanan's Mysore, II, 424.

† Asiatic Researches, V, 5.

‡ [See Mackenzie, Collection, II, p. 73 ff.] The manuscript agrees however with Mr. Dnncan's statement in one important particnlar; the admission of Śankara's living in the time of the Malabar prince Cheruman Perumal, a prince who, from his connection with the Malabar Christian Church, has been long an object of attention to the scholars of the West. [Lassen, l. l., IV, 254 f.] According to Scaliger (De emendatione temporum, 525)

the manuscript in question, either from defects in the original or translation, presents many palpable errors, and cannot consequently be depended upon. The weight of authority therefore is altogether in favour of an antiquity of about ten centuries, and I am disposed to adopt this estimate of Śankara's date, and to place him in the end of the eighth and beginning of the ninth century of the Christian era.*

Although the popular belief attributes the origin of the Bauddha persecution to Śankara Áchárya, yet in this case we have some reason to distrust its accuracy. Opposed to it we have the mild character of the reformer, who is described as uniformly gentle and tolerant, and speaking from my own limited reading in Vedánta works, and the more satisfactory testimony of Rámmohun Roy, which he permits me to adduce, it does not appear that any traces of his being instrumental to any persecution are to be found in his own writings, all which are extant, and the object of which is by no means the correction of the Bauddha or any

---

Calicut was founded in 907, and this event is ascribed to that prince by Assemannus (Bibl. Orient., Tom. 3, Part 2nd, 341 et seq.), but who observes that, according to Vischerus, it took place much earlier, or in 825. Cheruman Perumal is said to have granted many privileges to the Christians, inscribed on plates of copper, of which Du Perron procured copies, (Zend Avesta, Dis. Prel. clxxviii, and note) and which according to him corroborate the account of this transaction derived from Assemannus. This date will therefore nearly confirm the above view of Śankara's age and give us about ten centuries for his antiquity.

* [Lassen, Ind. Alt., IV, 618 ff.; 838 ff.]

other schism, but the refutation of all other doctrines besides his own, and the reformation or re-establishment of the fourth religious order. It is therefore probable that the Brahmans enjoyed the ascendancy in his times, and that the violent suppression of any powerful sect had considerably preceded the appearance of his peaceable system of worldly privation and abstract devotion.

Many works in celebration of this distinguished character, and in commemoration of his triumph over the errors of all other systems of theology, have been composed, entitled *Śankara-vijaya*,* or *Śankara-jaya*: they profess to narrate the most remarkable incidents of the reformer's life, and the different disputes held by him with his principal opponents. One of these I have examined: it is the work of Mádhava, a commentator on the Vedas agreeably to the Vedánta notions, and a writer of great celebrity. He is known to have lived about the year 1300,† by his making mention of Sangama, the father of Bukka Ráya and Harihara,‡ the founders of Vijayanagara. According to his

* [See on the Śankaradigvijaya and other accounts of Śankara's life 'Hindu Sects', new edition, p. 197 ff.]

† [1350.]

‡ Asiatic Researches, IX, 414; in addition to the instances there specified it may be observed, that *Sáyaṅa*, the author of the Mádhavíya-dhátu-vṛitti, calls himself the uterine brother of Mádhava and the son of Máyaṅa (?), the prime minister of Sangama, the son of Kampa, monarch of the eastern, southern, and western seas, or in fact of the Peninsula of India. इति पूर्वदक्षिणपश्चिमसमुद्राधीश्वरकम्पराजसुतसङ्गमराजमहामन्त्रिणा मायणपुत्रेण मा-

own statement, his work is but the substance of a much older performance, प्राचीनशङ्करजये सारसंगृह्यते स्फुटम् ॥ and he speaks of Śankara as being celebrated by all the ancient writers, स्तुतो ऽपि सम्यक्कविभिः पुराणैः। confirming therefore at the least the antiquity I have above assigned to that theologian.

As far as the Śankara-vijaya of Mádhava can be admitted as an authority, and it is much too poetical and legendary to be so acknowledged without very great limitation, we may draw the same conclusion that is to be inferred from Śankara's own compositions, that it is a popular error to ascribe to him the work of persecution: he does not appear at all occupied in that odious task, nor is he engaged in particular controversy with any of the Bauddhas: the more prominent objects of his opposition are the Mímánsakas as represented by Mandana Miśra, with whom he holds a long and rather acrimonious discussion, and the Naiyáyikas and Sánkhyas, and the vulgar sects of Vaishńavas and Śaivas are alike the object of his opposition; he is especially hostile to the latter, and particularly to the Kápálikas,* a class of Śiva's worshippers, who again are his most active enemies, and on one occasion assail his existence.

He comes in personal contact with the Bauddhas,

धवसहोदरेण सायणाचार्य्येण विरचिता माधवीया धातुवृत्तिः ॥ [See Westergaard, Rad. Sanscr., pref. p. II; A. Weber, 'Die Sanskrit-Handschriften', No. 789; Th. Aufrecht, Catal. Codd. Sanskr., I, 167.]

* [Hindu Sects, p. 21; 264. Lassen, Ind. Alt., III, 881; IV, 629.]

indeed, according to our authority, in but two instances: the first is a short conference with an Árhata, who advocates the Mádhyamika* doctrines, or those of a Bauddha sect, and which is held in the Bahlika country, a region identified by name and geographical position with the modern Balkh,† and the second happens in Kashmir, where amongst the many sects who oppose Śankara's access to the temple of Saraswatí, a short time before his death, the Bauddhas make their appearance. Besides the positive conclusion presented by these circumstances that Śankara was not engaged actively in any personal conflict with the followers of the Bauddha schism, we derive from them a very probable conjecture as to the situation of the Bauddhas in the time at which Mádhava flourished, and as he places them no nearer than in Kashmir and Khorasan, it appears likely that some period prior to his date was the epoch at which Bauddha faith was compelled to retire from its native seats towards those northern regions in which it still prevails.

The persecution of the Bauddhas is ascribed by Mádhava to another reformer, *Kumárila Bhatta,* the predecessor of Śankara. According to our author Kumárila Bhatta was an incarnation of Kártikeya, the object of whose descent was the extirpation of the Saugatas, and in consequence of whose miraculous victory over

---

* [See H. H. Wilson's Essays and Lectures, Vol. II, 363. Colebrooke's Essays, p. 251. Lassen, Ind. Alt., II, 460.]

† [Lassen, l. l., IV, 731 f.]

his heretical antagonists, the prince Sudhanwá issued the fatal orders to that effect:

आसेतोरातुषाराद्रेर्बौद्धानां वृद्धबालकान् ।
न हन्ति यः स हन्तव्यो भृत्यानित्यन्वशान्नृपः ॥

"The king thus commanded his attendants, 'let those who slay not be slain, the old man amongst the Bauddhas and the babe, from the bridge of Ráma to the snowy mountains'."

The priority of the Bauddha persecution by Kumárila Bhat́t́a to the age of Śankara is further corroborated by the manuscript account of Malabar, the Keraĺa Utpatti, which I have already adverted to. According to this authority, the establishment of this teacher in Malabar, local testimonies of which it is said existed when the work was written, took place about a century before the birth of Śankara, and occasioned the entire expulsion of the Bauddhanmár or Bauddhas from that kingdom; and we find on that side of India other accounts confirming this fact, and that the Brahmans of Tuĺuva who were originally followers of Bhat́t́a Áchárya, the same with Kumárila Bhat́t́a, assert his having had great success against the heretical sects some time before Śankara, who is represented as having disputed with, and converted the followers of Bhat́t́a's particular doctrine.*

As the Bauddha sect, according to Mádhava, was annihilated by Kumárila Bhat́t́a, it would have been a

* Buchanan's Mysore, III, 91. [Lassen, I. I., IV, 708. Wilson's Essays and Lectures, II, 366.]

work of supererogation to commit the same task to Śankara, and we have therefore further reason to doubt his ever having engaged in it at all, much more his having been the author and chief agent of the persecution. As, indeed, his reform is rather addressed to the admitted systems of theology, than to those considered heterodox, we must conclude that these latter had really suffered some temporary or partial discomfiture, so long prior to the age of Śankara Áchárya, as to have left time for the introduction and diffusion of various attempts towards the reformation of the orthodox faith, in the same manner as the innovations of Wickliffe and Huss preceded by a considerable interval the more successful efforts of Luther and Calvin.

According to the authority of Mádhava and that of tradition, Kumárila Bhaṫṫa committed himself to the flames in the presence of Śankara Áchárya: they would consequently be regarded as contemporary. We need not however lay much stress on these accounts, especially as Vyása and Jaimini, nay even Agastya, are all manifest personally to our reformer, if we are to give credit to our guide, and as, according to other authorities, Kumárila Bhaṫṫa was the pupil of Jaimini, the founder of the Mímánsá school of philosophy,* who there is reason to suppose is much more ancient. We can only therefore conclude generally that the triumph

* Dr. Taylor's Prabodha Chandrodaya, 119. [Brockhaus' edition, p. 110. Lassen, Ind. Alt., I, 836. Goldstücker, Páṅini, p. 150; p. 8 ff.]

of Kumárila Bhaťťa and the persecution of the Bauddhas took place at some period anterior to the age of Śankara and before the eighth century; and, agreeably to the inference above deduced, at some period considerably antecedent, in which case the occurrence may be approximated to the date we have thought it probable to be that of Amara, or at least to the time, when his works might have required such celebrity, as to become obnoxious to a hostile and intolerant sect.

We have already had occasion to notice, upon the authority of Major Wilford, that the capital of Śúdraka, whose reign began in 191,* was named Charchita Nagara, with reference to its being the seat of the earliest disputes between the orthodox and dissentient classes of the Hindus. The assertion rests upon the authority of the Kumáriká Khańđa, which in the prophetic style of the Puráńas declares, that 'In the year 3291 of the Kali-yuga (or 191 after Christ) king Śúdraka will reign in the town of Charchita Nagara, and destroy the workers of iniquity;' and this, Major Wilford observes, points out a persecution in religious matters at a very early period. At the same time, we know that the utter extermination of the Bauddha sect in India did not take place till some time between the twelfth and fifteenth centuries, and we must conclude, consequently, that the contending parties were for a long period too equally matched for any permanent and vigorous

* Asiatic Researches, X, 91. [Wilson's Introd. to the Mŕichchhakaťi.]

persecution of either by the other to have taken place, and especially for some time after the beginning of the conflict. If therefore the contest began in the third century, and the temporary ascendancy of the Brahmans was established some time before the eighth, we may conjecture, with every appearance of conjecturing happily, that the fifth and sixth centuries form the season, in which the Bauddhas were most actively and triumphantly assailed by the interested professors of the orthodox creed.*

The time thus made out for the height of the Bauddha persecution agrees in a very remarkable manner with the date of events recorded in the countries where the faith of Buddha now predominates, and was entirely connected with the condition of his Indian votaries in their native realms. It was early in the sixth century (A.D. 519),† that China received from India the prophet Dharma, who gave a new impulse to the worship of Buddha, then languishing in that country, and fixed it as the national faith.. In 530 the religion of Buddha was introduced into Corea;‡ in 540-50 into

* [Lassen, Ind. Alt., IV, 709.]

† Kæmpfer's Japan, B. 2, Chap. 4. The first introduction of the Bauddha faith into China took place much earlier; according to De Guignes, A.D. 65; but he adds, "on n'eut alors qu'une idée confuse de la religion de Fo, et ce n'est que dans la suite, qu'elle a été plus en voque." He also notices 'la protection singulière' which the dynasty of the Liang that reigned from 549 [502] to 557, gave to the Religion of Fo. [Lassen, l. l., IV, 741 ff.; II, Beilage II, p. IX; Köppen, die Rel. Buddha's, I, 587; II, 34.]

‡ [According to Klaproth, 372 in Kao-li, and 384 in Pe-tsi. See Lassen, p. 746 f.]

Japan, and the year 572 was remarkable for the arrival in that kingdom of an immense number of Priests and Idols, who came from countries beyond the sea. We may conclude this branch of our enquiry by citing the opinion of the able historian of Java, Sir Thomas Raffles, that the Bauddha religion was introduced into that island during the sixth and seventh centuries, and that the same period was remarkable for the arrival of numerous Hindu emigrants on Java and the eastern islands.*

The examination I have thus instituted into the age of Amara Sinha has extended itself to limits, no doubt disproportioned to the importance of the enquiry: I had however to correct error, and to controvert prejudice, as well as to contend with the natural difficulties of the subject, and to support my averments by the best authorities within my reach. As to the result of the research, I shall willingly, if convinced by worthy testimony of having erred in my conclusions, submit to correction. Those conclusions, indeed, are only positive within certain limits, and as the sum of the investigation, I have only satisfied myself with the choice of one or two alternatives: either assent to the tradition which places Amara Sinha in the time of the primitive Vikramáditya, 56 years before the *Christian* era, or to the inference deduced from the contiguous position of a number of persons and things connected more or less directly with our author's supposed his-

* History of Java, II, 86. [Lassen, IV, 467 ff.]

tory, which designate the early part of the fifth century as the time at which Amara flourished.

Those notions which attribute an extravagant antiquity to the Hindus are fully as absurd as those which deny them any antiquity at all: as I have combated one set of opinions, therefore, it would have been just to expose the other, as epitomised in Fra Bartolomeo's account of Amara Sinha. To do this, however, it will be sufficient to cite his expressions, pausing only to observe that these absurdities are the composition of a man, who lavished every term of abuse upon the Angli Calcuttenses, then engaged under the auspices of Warren Hastings and Sir William Jones in instituting the legitimate enquiries which alone have displayed to European knowledge the true extent and character of Indian learning, and which he arrogantly and abruptly denounced as vain speculations and idle dreams. After most gratuitously and ridiculously converting Amara Sinha into Amara Chhihna and explaining that to signify librum cœli signa continentem, he proceeds: ita certe hujus vocabuli etymologiam et analysim mihi tradidit linguæ Samscrdamicæ peritissimus vir, Ciangra Aashan, atque hallucinatos fuisse puto Calcuttenses Anglos, qui Amarasinha philosophum et Vikramaditya regis Indici a consiliis virum fuisse adstruunt, ipsique hunc librum nullo prorsus fundamento innixi adscribunt, cum tamen evidens esse videatur, *librum istum unâ cum Idolatria Indica compositum fuisse, ac non solum totius mythologiæ et liturgiæ basim, sed primum librum precatorium esse, quo Brahmanes in ipso suæ* *idolatriæ exordio usi sunt;** elevating in this extraordinary manner a common vocabulary to the distinction of a Ritual and *Liturgy* co-existent with the origin of the Hindu Idolatry, and the basis of the *Brahmanical* superstitions! A blunder of another character, although of an equally absurd description, connected with the Amara Kosha, has been committed by Anquetil Du Perron, and has been adduced by Mr. Mill,† with his usual want of knowledge and judgment, as '*a remarkable instance of the disposition of Brahmans to accommodate by falsification even their sacred records to the ideas of Europeans.*' Du Perron says: si je n'avois pas sçu que le commencement de l'Amarkosh contenait la description du Lingam, peut-être m'eut il été impossible de découvrir, que mes Brahmes, qui ne vouloient pas dévoiler le fond de leurs mystères, paraphrasoient et pallioient plutôt qu'ils ne traduisoient: a description of the Lingam in the introduction to the Amara Kosha! Du Perron's Brahmans must have been much astonished at the discovery, and at the perverse spirit and gross ignorance which converted Amara's account of the contents of his vocabulary, comprising the genders (linga) of nouns, into the mystical mention of an object with which his preamble

* Systema Brahmanicum, 194. [If P. Paul. a S. Bartholomæo ever entertained the notions so severely criticised in the text, he had certainly given them up when he wrote the preface to his "Amarasinha. Sectio prima." Rome: 1798, especially p. XI f. See also his "Vyácarana". Rome: 1804, p. XVII and 329.].

† History of India, Vol. I, 410.

has no kind of connection, except the indispensable employment of a grammatical term, that happens also to have the same meaning, but which occurring where and how it does, the merest novice in Sanskrit literature could not possibly misunderstand. We have had too much of mere pretenders to knowledge in oriental literature, and it is high time to weigh accurately the real merit of all authorities on matters of Asiatic learning and history if we wish to gain any real acquaintance with such subjects, or if we retain the slightest veneration for truth.

The vocabulary of Amara Sinha, though perhaps the oldest extant, is not considered as the first work of the kind; the author himself in his introductory lines mentions generally his having consulted other works, and his commentators particularise the Trikáńd́a and Utpaliní Kosha and the works of Vyád́i, Rabhasa, Kátyáyana, and Vararuchi, as the authorities to which he alludes. The text of the work has been some time known in Europe, though imperfectly,* and it is now placed within the reach of every scholar by the excellent edition of it with a marginal translation,

---

* Du Perron carried two copies to Europe, it was also noticed in the first volume of the *Asiatic Researches* (354): we have seen what Bartolomeo says of the work, and he took home a copy of it. Several copies more or less perfect were presented by Lady Jones to the Royal Society, and Frederick Schlegel in his work 'Ueber die Sprache und Weisheit der Indier', notices a manuscript of it in the Royal Library at Paris with a Latin interpretation [not mentioned by M. L. Deslongchamps in the preface to his edition of the Amarakosha.]

published by Mr. Colebrooke, and printed at Serampore, in 1808: it is to this edition that my references apply. They will be found very numerous, and I am happy to acknowledge it as the guide and basis of my labours, and to bear testimony to its uniform and unrivalled correctness.

The different commentaries on the text of the Amara Kosha, to which I have also made frequent reference, are the same as those employed by its learned translator. I was indebted indeed to his kindness for the copies which were prepared for his use, and which were the best procurable, and I have little or nothing to add to the notices which he has given of their authors.

The commentary which takes precedence of the rest by the earlier date of its composition, is that of *Kshíra Swámí:* it is a work of merit, but concise; and the interpretations frequently differ from those given by the other commentators. The age of the author is not known; but he is one of the authorities cited by Mallinátha, the commentator on several of the most celebrated poems, and who probably wrote in the twelfth or thirteenth century.*

The next in the order of antiquity is the work of *Mukuta* or *Ráya Mukuta Mańi*, compiled according to the author's own account from sixteen older commentaries to which he frequently refers: they seem however to be in many cases original compositions,

* [according to Prof. Aufrecht, (Catal. codd. MSS. Sanscr., I, 113) not before the 14th.]

and not merely glosses on the text of Amara. The list includes the work of *Kshíra Swámí*, *Subhúti*, *Haďďa Chandra*, *Kalinga*, *Konkaťa*, *Sarvadhara*, *Rájadeva*, *Govardhana*, *Dráviďa* and *Bhoja Rája*, and the *Vyákhyámŕita*, *Ťíkásarvasva*, *Mádhaví*, *Madhu Mádhaví*, *Sarvánanda*, and *Abhinanda*. Mukuťa also cites the names of the principal grammatical writers, and quotes many Koshas of which the titles are of frequent and familiar occurrence, amongst which some, as the Viśva and Mediní, are still in existence. The commentary of Ráya Mukuťa is full and satisfactory—it is erroneous sometimes in the etymological analysis of grammatical derivatives, but it is in general accurate, and in most of the schools is of high authority. The date of the composition is inferred from dates mentioned by the author, 1352 Śáka or A.D. 1430.*

The *Vyákhyá Śudhá*† is the ablest commentary on the Amara Kosha, that has yet appeared: the interpretations are full and distinct, and the etymological analysis founded on the most thorough acquaintance with the system of Páńini: the commentator is also a very industrious corrector of the mistakes of his brethren, and rectifies especially the grammatical errors of his predecessor Mukuťa. In compliance with the usual practice I have referred to this writer under

* Asiatic Researches, VII, 216; and Preface to the Amara Kosha. [Misc. Essays, II, 18 ff.; 54 ff.]

† [On this and the two preceding comp. Aufrecht, l.l., p. 182 f.]

the appellation of Rámáśrama; but, as is mentioned by Mr. Colebrooke, the name of the author is variously written in different copies and is sometimes the same with that which I have used, and is sometimes termed Bhánu Díkshita. In the copy I have used I find an apparent solution of this difficulty, and Rámáśrama, or more correctly Bhadra Rámáśrama, is a title implying the author's belonging to a particular class of devotees, whilst his real name is Bhánu Díkshita, and he is the son, as he informs us, of Bhaṫṫoji Díkshita, the celebrated grammarian. I must add, however, that this is denied by the Paṅḋits, who insist that the two persons are distinct, and that Bhánu Díkshita, the son of Bhaṫṫoji, was after his father's death the disciple of the ascetic Rámáśrama, who is the author of other works. The work was written, according to the passage which specifies the author's name, at the desire of Kírttisinha, ruler of Mahídhara, a prince of the Bandhaila* family, and the termination Sinha, we may observe, is attached to the Búndela and Ajmere princes† who make their appearance in the reigns of Shah Jehán and Aurungzebe, in the course of which, or the seventeenth century, a son or pupil of Bhaṫṫoji Díkshita must have written.

---

* [*Baghela* in the Benares edition of the Amarakosha. See Sir H. Elliot's Glossary s. v. The Díkshitas were a subdivision of the Kánaujiya Brahmans; ib. p. 125.]

† Hidjar Singh, Rájá of Búndelkhaṅḋ, Dow III, 126. Judger Singh, Rájá of Búndela, ibid. 154.

The *Vyákhyá Pradípa* is a commentary by Achyuta Upádhyáya: it is a work of little merit, being an unacknowledged abridgment of Mukuťa's work. I have not been able to meet with any account of the author, but he is probably modern.

The preceding commentaries agree in giving the derivation of words conformably to the Sútras of Páńini: those which follow have adopted other systems.

In the original compilation of the Dictionary, prepared as that was under the superintendence and by the labours of natives of Bengal, the grammatical system used was that of Vopadeva: as this is however of modern origin and limited application, it was considered advisable to discard it for the more generally cultivated method of Páńini, and the entire transposition of all the etymologies has been consequently included in my task. In effecting this object, particularly for all the words contained in the Amara Kosha, the preceding commentators were my chief guides, and Rámáśrama's commentary especially has in these cases been consulted. The etymological analysis of many of the remaining vocables depends upon the authority of the Siddhánta Kaumudí, and that of the rest has been supplied by my Pańďits or myself, in conformity, as exact as our acquaintance with the subject permitted, to the system laid down in the Sútras of Páńini.

The commentary of *Bharata Malla* is the favourite authority of the Bengal school, and of all others in which the grammar of Vopadeva is received: it is an able performance, and is particularly full on the subject of various readings. The author has also compiled a Kosha on this topic, or a vocabulary of words which vary in their orthoepy, styled by the Hindus a Dwirúpa Kosha, a compilation rendered very necessary by the fluctuations in the forms of words, which arise from the arbitrary application of those letters that are considered interchangeable, and from the varieties introduced by different modes of pronunciation in different provinces, and caused, in many cases no doubt, by the blunders of copyists, the multiplication and repetition of which have given to different modes of spelling currency and sanction.* Bharata Malla is considered to have flourished in the middle of the last century, and has written commentaries on many celebrated compositions.†

The *Sára Sundarí* is a commentary which has been occasionally consulted: the author is Mathuréśa, who has himself compiled a vocabulary, the Śabdaratnávalí, in speaking of which we shall advert to the few circumstances that are known of him. The commentary is a useful one: it follows the grammar of Padmanábha Datta, the Supadma, a work studied in some parts of Bengal.‡

The *Padártha Kaumudí*, by Náráyańa Chakravarttí, has been referred to, though not frequently: the Kalápa, a grammar of celebrity in the *Bengal* schools,

* [Aufrecht, Catal. Codd. MSS., I, p. 194.]

† [Bharata Malla, or Bharata Mallika, commented e. g. on the Bhaťťi Kávya.]

‡ [Aufrecht, Catal. l. l., I, Nos. 439. 40, and pp. 176 and 192.]

has been followed by this commentator in the analytical part of his work.

The *Trikáńda Viveka*, by Rámanátha Vidyá Váchaspati, a work of considerable merit, and particularly full of orthoepical varieties, will be found frequently cited, and this with two other commentaries, one by Nílakańt́ha and the other by Ráma Tarka Vágíśa, which are sometimes referred to, complete the number of authorities accessory to the text of Amara, which were employed by Mr. Colebrooke in his publication, and have again been made use of in the following pages.*

Authorities of higher rank, though often of less value, than the commentators on the Amara Kosha, and constituting together with that work and its appendages the bulk of the present compilation, are the vocabularies of different authors. Of these the most valuable are easily and generally procurable, and many others it is asserted exist, though rarely to be found. Those which I have been able to obtain I shall now proceed to enumerate, following as correctly as inference and conjecture will admit the order of their antiquity, and furnishing such slender information respecting their authors as the state of everything like biography in India is capable of affording. The comparative age of various compositions is in many cases ascertainable by the references which the writers make to their predecessors, and the absence of the notice of a celebrated work, where mention of it is likely to be

* [Miscell. Essays, II, pp. 54-57.]

found, is a very strong presumption of its not being in existence. The application of this test is very extensive, and conjoined with the information afforded by inscriptions, and that which may be conjectured from the legends of the Puráńas, presents the only chance of our ever being able to extricate the ancient history of India from the labyrinth in which it is at present lost.

The first Kosha after that of Amara, in the copious list of authorities cited by the author of the *Medini*, which has been consulted in the following work, is the *Abhidhánaratnamálá* of Haláyudha Bhatta. It is a vocabulary of limited extent, divided into five books; the first relating to Heaven and the Deities, and the second to Earth; the third to Hell, Water, &c.; the fourth to miscellaneous objects, and the last contains words of various signification. The author cites as his authorities the Amaradatta and the Koshas of Vararuchi, Bháguri, Vopálita, and others. We may conjecture that his work should be of some antiquity, as he is quoted by Mallinátha, who is certainly prior to Medinikara. His omission of the Amara Kosha from his list of authorities can scarcely lead us to infer the priority of his own work, but it is possible that the reputation of that vocabulary was not fully established in his time, and that it is therefore included in the appendix *Ádi*, or etcetera, added to his enumeration. Haláyudha Bhatta* has also written on Prosody, and

* Asiatic Researches, VII, 233, and X, 391. [Miscell. Essays, III.

there is a celebrated writer of the same name, on the religious ceremonies of the Hindus: in both instances honourable mention has been made by Mr. Colebrooke of these works. He is said to be a Konkańa Brahman and the pupil of the Mímánsá writer Bhaťťa Bháskara. If this last account is correct, he may be placed about the seventh century, as his preceptor is uniformly said to have preceded Śankara Áchárya.

Ajaya, or *Ajayapála*, is the next in the list of the Medini, whose vocabulary has been consulted in the following pages. This is a work of small extent, but of considerable authority: it is confined to the Nánártha, or words of various meanings, and they are arranged according to the initial letters. The author does not specify his authorities, nor does he furnish us with any clue to his age or history. From his introductory stanza he appears to be a sectary, probably a Jaina.*

II, 20; 132. Prof. Aufrecht's preface to his edition of the Abhidhánaratnamálá. London: 1861.]

* In a paper in the Transactions of the Literary Society of Bombay [I, 183] by Lieutenant Macmurdo, which I shall again have occasion to notice, an Ajee Pál occurs, who seems to have taken an active part in the introduction of the Jaina Religion into Guzerat, towards the end of the twelfth century, and who may have been the compiler of the vocabulary, or the patron of its author, who consequently ascribes it to him; a practice frequent in the literary flattery of Hindu writers. [That just the opposite was the case, that Ajaya Pála, the nephew and successor of Kumára Pála, was a fierce persecutor of the Jainas, and can have no possible claim to the authorship of the Nánárthasangraha, is evident from the account of him in the Rásmálá (1, p. 205 ff.).

The work is often cited by the commentators on the Amara Kosha.*

The next in the list of the Mediní is the *Dharańi Kosha* or vocabulary of Dharańi Dása, an author of whom we know nothing further, except that he is considered as a Brahman of Kanouj, and the author of a poetical work, denominated the Káśi Vírndávalí. The vocabulary is of some extent, although it is limited to the words of various meanings, arranged according to their final letters and number of syllables. The author specifies no authorities, and states only generally, that his vocabulary is compiled from older writers. He is himself of some antiquity, as besides the place he holds in the Mediní's list, he is often cited by Mallinátha.

The *Trikáńda Śesha* is a vocabulary, in three chapters, composed purposely as a supplement to the Vocabulary of Amara, and thence sometimes termed the Amara Śesha; it follows a similar arrangement, and adds a number of words of comparatively rare occurrence. The author was a Jaina, named Purushottama Deva, and he is the author also of several other philological compilations, as an Ekákshara Kosha,† or Vocabulary of monosyllabic words, which I have occasionally referred to, and the Varńa-viplava-náśa, or a collection of various readings. His most celebrated

See Lassen, III, 568, and As. Res., XVI, 321 ff. Thomas' edition of Prinsep's Essays, II, 256.]

* [Aufrecht, Catal. Codd. MSS., I, pp. 182. 187. 195 f.]

† [Aufrecht, l. l., I, No. 431. 32.]

14*

work, however, after the Trikáńda, is the following, which indeed takes precedence of it in the list of the Medinı́.

The *Háraváli* is a collection almost exclusively of uncommon words. It is divided into two parts, the one containing synonymous words, and the other words of various meanings. The first part is again divided into three portions, according to the extent of the synonymes, and their recapitulation through a whole stanza, or a half, or a quarter. The work is of very limited extent, but it is the produce, according to the author's own averment, of twelve years' reading. He states also, that it was compiled at the suggestion and with the aid of his spiritual preceptor, Śrí Dhŕiti Sinha, an Atithi, or religious ascetic known in the spoken dialects by the appellation Atít, and he mentions Janamejaya, a Pańdit, as having contributed to the compilation. The authorities he alludes to are mostly of a general and miscellaneous description, but amongst them he enumerates, as the Koshas consulted, and consequently prior to his time, the Śabdárnáva, Utpalinı́, Sansárávarta, and those of Váchaspati, Vyádi, and Vikramáditya.* The age of Purushottama, according to the order of the Medinı́, should be earlier than that of the Viśva,† and he may probably have written in the tenth or eleventh century. He is not however quoted by the commentator Mallinátha, who cites the Viśva Kosha.

* [vv. 273-77.] † [Aufrecht, l. l., I, No. 428.]

After the Trikáńda Śesha, we have in the Mediní's list a work entitled the *Ratna Málá.** I have employed a Kosha of this name, but I am not quite confident of its being the same, the Ratna Málá of Írugapa, entitled Dańdádhinátha, said to imply, as it may signify, a military officer of high rank, and probably the patron rather than the author of the work. It is a compilation of considerable authority, especially in the South of India, and its age may be ascertained with tolerable precision; for it is said to have been undertaken at the desire of Harihara, a prince who conjointly with Bukka Ráya,† his brother, founded the city of Vidyánagara or Bijnagar, about 1340, and reigned there till 1350. The name of its supposed author Írugapa‡ occurs also in an inscription in the Mackenzie collection, as a granter of the Village of Bellagola to a *Jaina* Deity, which grant is dated in the *Śaka* year 1284 or A.D. 1362. The vocabulary I have referred to may be possibly the authority alluded to by Medinikara, though it dates rather near to what we may suppose to have been the latter writer's own era, as the title of a vocabulary Ratna

---

* [Aufrecht, l. l., I, Nos. 441-3.]

† Asiatic Researches, IX, 416.

‡ [He is probably identical with Irugadańdeśa, mentioned in an Inscription from Vijayanagara, in As. Res., XX, 21 and 36. See also Lassen, IV, 171. In the printed edition of this work (Madras: 1857) the name of the author is in four places written *I*rugapadańd*ádhi*nátha, in one place I. dańdádinátha, and in another I. dańdeśa. The correctness of the first form is attested by the third.]

Málá (a garland of jewels) is very common. I have already noticed the Ratna Málá of Haláyudha, and I shall have occasion to mention a third vocabulary similarly denominated, but confined to medical terms. The work of Daṅḍádhinátha is a vocabulary of words of various meanings, arranged according to their syllabic length and final letters. The compiler does not specify his authorities.

The next work mentioned, and of the original compilation of which the Mediní is an improvement, appears in the enumeration of this latter; with the epithet *Bahudosham*, or *very* faulty, attached to it. This is the *Viśva Prakáśa Kosha*, a vocabulary of words of various meanings, of considerable extent and merit; and notwithstanding the reproach of Medinikara, a reproach not wholly undeserved, of great authority in the schools of *Benares* and *Western India*. The words are arranged according to their final letters, their initials, and their number of syllables, but beyond these three points of agreement there is no classification, and the work is therefore consulted with some difficulty. Besides the usual contents of a Kosha, the Viśva Prakáśa includes some useful sections on the occurrence of the interchangeable letters, and on varieties in orthoepy, and the whole is frequently referred to in the following pages.

The Viśva Prakáśa is of great value in the enquiry into the comparative dates of the various lexicons, which I have attempted to institute, being one of the very few compilations which allow us to conjecture the present age of their composition, and furnish us with a fixed point, from which we can take with something like confidence a retrospective view. The vocabularies enumerated above contain no dates, and can only be placed at undefined intervals between the Amara Kosha and the Viśva Prakáśa, upon the authority of the Medini, confirmed as that is in most instances by the enumeration of authorities which occurs in those works, and in which the name of the Viśva never appears: most of them are therefore in all probability prior to the year of Śáka 1033, or A.D. 1111, which the author of the Viśva Prakáśa has given as the date of his compilation.

The author of the Viśva Kosha, Maheśwara, is the most communicative of all the Sanskrit Lexicographers, and we are much indebted to the venial vanity which has induced him to expatiate on his personal history.

He informs us, that he is descended from Śrí Kŕishńa, physician to Sáhasánka, sovereign of Gádhipur, a name from which the modern Ghazipur might be supposed to be derived, but which is enumerated by the vocabularies as a synonyme of *Kanyákubja* or Canouj: Sáhasánka also is a synonyme of Vikramáditya, but neither time nor place allow of the persons being identified in this instance,* and some historical notices

* As a mere etymological speculation I suggest the possibility of Sáhasánka being a title of Śri Chandra Deva, who, according to an inscription published by Mr. Colebrooke (As. Res., vol. IX, 441) [or Misc. Essays, II, 286. See also As. Res. XV, 443. Dr. F. E. Hall's preface to his edition of the Vásavadattá, Calcutta:

of the former might possibly be derived from another composition, which Maheśwara informs us he had written, the history of this prince, or the Sáhasánka Charitra. The period in which the *Viśva Kosha* was compiled was one very likely to have been a season of literary patronage at *Canouj*, as the Muselman princes of the houses of Ghizni and Ghor were for some time, both before and afterwards, fully occupied with those dissensions, which gave the Indian sceptre to the latter, and consequently left the Hindu princes in the undisturbed enjoyment of their patrimonial sway, and tranquil exercise of their commendable privileges. The author of the Viśva cites most of the authorities considered ancient, and which are no longer procurable, but amongst those described in the preceding pages the work of Amara is the only one which he has noticed. The correctness of the date of the Viśva is tolerably well confirmed by its successive citation in the works of Mallinátha, the Mediní, and the commentary of Ráya Mukuta, the last of which we have seen is little more than three centuries later.*

1859, p. 18], founded the ruling dynasty of Kanouj, about the end of the eleventh century, which "*realm he acquired by his own strength*". The inscription is unfortunately in *England*, or an examination of the passage in italics in the original might be found connected with the name given to the Prince by Maheśwara or Sáhasánka, compounded as that is of *Sáhasa*, strength or violence, and *Anka*, mark or distinction. [See the references ap. Lassen, III, 810 f.]

* [Aufrecht, l. l., I, No. 428. A. Weber, Verzeichniss der Sanskrit-Handschriften, Nos. 802-4.]

The inference to which I have been led of Amara's having lived in the fifth century, and the position of Maheśwara in the commencement of the twelfth, leave us about six centuries and a half for the appearance of the different vocabularies above specified, and others that have been less fortunate in escaping the ravages of time. The length of this interval appears to be far from disproportionate to the number of similar works published during its continuance, as far as we can judge from analogy; for from the date of the Viśva to that of Ráya Mukuta's commentary in 1430, or three hundred and nineteen years, we have but four vocabularies to enumerate, of which one only can be assigned to that interval with any certainty, and the other three may possibly appertain to the division of our subject which comprehends the works anterior to the Viśva Prakáśa, or the beginning of the twelfth century.

In the period that elapsed between the ages of Maheśwara and Ráya Mukuta, we fix with certainty the author of the *Medinì Kosha*, as he cites the one and is quoted by the other. The work of this writer is an excellent Dictionary of homonymous words arranged according to their final letters and their syllabic lengths, and then further disposed with alphabetical precision: it is a compilation of great accuracy and high authority, and constitutes after the Amara Kosha the basis and bulk of my labours.

The closing section of the Medinì recapitulates the authorities employed in its composition, and comprises amongst others the fullest list of Koshas to be met with: on this account and as they appear to be enumerated according to their supposed comparative antiquity, I shall here transcribe the catalogue, accompanying it with such information as to their present existence as I am able to offer from my own knowledge or from oral accounts of the Pańḋits.

1. The *Utpalini* is one of the supposed authorities of the Amara Kosha; it is certainly of considerable antiquity, and is often quoted by the older writers. It is still procurable,* though not common.

2. The *Śabdárńava* is often quoted by the commentators on Amara; it is also occasionally procurable, but usually in an imperfect state.

3. The *Sansárávartta*, a vocabulary often quoted in works of an early date, but supposed to be now lost.

4. The *Náma Málá*, though rare, is yet obtainable: as it is said to be a work of considerable extent, in that case it differs from the short work of Dhananjaya of the same title which I have consulted.†

5. *Bháguri* is the author of a vocabulary, forming

* My remarks on the possibility of meeting with these works apply to Calcutta and Benares particularly, and may be extended perhaps to the tract of India immediately along the Ganges as far as Haridwár: the state of manuscripts in the Dekhan is probably more complete, and it may be expected that the late accessions to the British Indian Empire both to the west and north will be productive of many valuable additions to Sanskrit bibliography.

† One of them was probably the Nám Málá of Du Perron, which he terms Dictionnaire Samskretain à l'usage des Sciouras. [? सूरि. See Hindu Sects, new edition, p. 337.]

according to the commentators one of Amara's authorities. The work is not to be met with.

6. *Vararuchi* is also considered as one of Amara's originals, although as one of the nine gems he should be contemporary with him. His vocabulary is not procurable.

7. The *Śáśwata* is often cited, and is said to be procurable in a mutilated state.*

8. *Vopálita* is the author of a Kosha to be met with in scattered portions.

9. *Rantideva* is the compiler of a vocabulary no longer to be found in a complete state.

10. *Hara* is another lexicographer, whose work no longer exists, and who is rarely quoted.

Of the above vocabularies most are cited by the commentators on the *Amara Kosha* and are specified in several of the works about to be enumerated, as the authorities which they consulted. Haláyudha, Purushottama, and Maheśwara make mention of most of them also, corroborating therefore the order of priority in which they are placed by the author of the Medini.

11. *Amara,* the first author of the list, whose work is everywhere obtainable.

12. *Subhanka,* the compiler of a vocabulary rarely to be found.

13. *Haláyudha,* whose work, the Ratna Málá, has been described.

14. *Govarddhana,* author of the Sapta Śatí, or

* [Aufrecht, l. l., I, No. 414.]

seven hundred miscellaneous stanzas, from which the idea of the Sat Sai, a similar collection in Hindi, may have been derived in the sixteenth century by Bihárílál, is the author of a vocabulary said to be still procurable in some parts of India.* As he mentions the Vṙihatkathá, of which the antiquity is supposed to be about 700 years, and is thus noticed by Medinikara, he probably flourished in the twelfth or thirteenth century.

15. *Rabhasa*, or *Rabhasála*, is the author of a vocabulary often cited, but rarely to be found.

16. *Rudra*, an author of whose work the same may be observed.

17. *Amaradatta*, the name of a writer or a vocabulary, often cited, but not known to exist.

18. *Ajaya*, or *Ajaya Pála*, noticed above.

19. *Gangádhara*, an author of whom nothing further is known.

20. The *Dharańi Kosha*, which, as well as the following, has been already the object of our attention.

21. The *Háráвali*.

22. The *Trikáńda Śesha*.

23. The *Ratna Málá*.

24. The *Viśva Prakáśa*, forming with the *Medini* twenty-five vocabularies, all prior to the fifteenth century, and of which my original and myself, aided as we were by Mr. Colebrooke's valuable collection of

* [Weber, Handschriften, No. 1381. Colebrooke, Misc. Essays, II, 23. 88.]

manuscripts, have been able to procure no more than nine or ten. They are not however the whole number of works extant in the time of Mediní Kara, and his predecessors, which were either vocabularies themselves, or treated of the forms, inflexions, genders, and meaning of words in a manner that sanctioned their being included in the same class. Thus the author of the Viśva Kosha specifies Sáhasánka, the patron of his family, as the author, the nominal one, it may be imagined, of a vocabulary, and works of a similar character are attributed to the Princes Vikramáditya and Bhoja; the former occurs amongst the remaining authorities of the Mediní, along with works assigned to Bágbhaťťa, Mádhava, Váchaspati, Dharma, Vyáďi, Tárapála, Kátyáyana, Chandra, Soma, and Páńini. There are also other Koshas quoted by Mallinátha and other early commentators, as the *Keśava*, *Yádava*, and *Vaijayantí*, the two latter of which are still found, though not common.

The author of the Mediní gives no account of himself beyond his being the son of Práńakara;* his own name Medinikara appears to be merely an epithet derived from the title of his vocabulary, but the same final syllable *Kara* is in *Bengal* the denomination of a family of the Káyastha race† and would indicate therefore his being a native of that province; it is also

* [In a MS. of this work, in the R. Asiatic Society's possession, the author's father is called Pátúńakara.]

† Asiatic Researches, V, 66.

an appellation common amongst the Mahratta Brahmans, and our author is generally regarded as of that nation. If the Mádhava and Ratna Málá, he cites, are the same with those mentioned above, he could not have flourished earlier than the end of the fourteenth century.

Besides the authorities anterior to the Medini, I have employed many which are of more recent date; before describing them, however, I shall here pause to advert to some of a doubtful character, and whose comparative age it is difficult to ascertain.

The most important of these guides, and after the Amara and Medini the best work I have had access to, is the *Abhidhána Chintámańi* of *Hemachandra*, a Jaina writer of deserved celebrity, and the author also of a series of Jaina hymns* and of a Prákrit grammar: as usually met with, and as printed at the Sanskrit press of Calcutta, this vocabulary is divided into two considerable portions, one appropriated to synonymous, the other to homonymous words. The first part is subdivided into six books, according to a peculiar arrangement, and the first book is of great value as a detailed and faithful account of the superior deities or deified hierarchy of the *Jaina* sect. The second part is classed according to the syllabic extent of the vocables it contains, and they are then arranged according to their

* [The Jaina Mahákávya *Trishashtiśalákápurushacharita*, a copy of which is in the possession of the R. A. S., is also ascribed to him. See Hindu Sects, new edition, p. 283.]

final initial letters. There is some reason to doubt however, whether Hemachandra's original work is not properly limited to the first six books, and whether the Nánártha part has not been added by some later writer.

The introductory lines of this author's vocabulary explain the principles of his arrangement and are confined to the first six sections, taking no notice of that on words of various meanings. Again, this Kosha has been commented on, and the commentary is equally limited to the first six books; and finally, with the exception of the arrangement which is peculiar to it, the second division of the Abhidhána Chintámańi is precisely the same* as the Viśva Kosha, following that in every word and interpretation, and repeating its obscurities and its mistakes. One of these works must therefore be a transcript of the other, and as there is every reason to believe the originality of Maheśwara's work, it follows that the Nánártha part of Hemachandra's vocabulary is borrowed from the Viśva.

If the Nánártha chapters be the work of Hemachandra himself, their being borrowed from the Viśva establishes the priority of the latter work; on the other hand, as Hemachandra is quoted by Mallinátha,

* [That this is not the case, is the well-founded opinion of Prof. Goldstücker; see his Sanskrit Dictionary s. v. *abhidhánachintámańi*. On Hemachandra comp. Lassen, Ind. Alt., III, 567. 1195; IV, 803 f. Colebrooke's Misc. Essays, II, 206 ff. According to the Râs Mâlâ (I, 189-204) Hemachandra died in 1174 A.D., eighty-four years old.]

and as the Commentary on his hymns is dated in the year 1292, it is likely that he lived at a period not long subsequent to Maheśwara, or in the course of the twelfth century; the accuracy of which inference is confirmed by works current in Guzerat, that ascribe the conversion of the sovereign of that country to the Jaina faith to the influence of our author in the Samvat year 1230 or A.D. 1174:* and it is further corroborated by the time falling within those limits, during which the sect of which Hemachandra was so distinguished a member flourished in many parts of Hindustan.

The concurring traditions of the Brahmanical, Bauddha, and Jaina sects report a two-fold persecution of the second, by each of the others severally, although they are not agreed about the order of their occurrence. If I have conjectured rightly, the priority seems due to that instigated by the members of the orthodox

* "About 2500 years from the first promulgation of the Parisnath (Párśwanátha) worship, Heema chaarge Juttee (Hemácharya Yati), a follower of Parsow, much respected by the Shrawuks (Śrávakas or Jainas) for his learning, and who had great authority in all matters concerning religion, resided in Puran Puttur, a celebrated city in the district of Neherwalla, which was at that time governed by a Rajepoot Rája, named Goonmar Pall, who lived about the year of Vikrimajut (Vikrámáditya) 1230, or A.D. 1174, Heema Chaarge succeeded in converting the Raja to the Shrawuk religion." Account of the *Parisnath Gowricha*, worshipped in the Desert of Parhar, by Lieutenant Macmurdo, Transactions of the Bombay Literary Society. It is only necessary to add that Hemachandra is generally called by the Jainas Hemácharya, or, as it is pronounced in several of the dialects, Hemácharj.

faith, and they effected a partial suppression of the Bauddha heresy about the fifth and sixth centuries; they were far from extirpating the schism, however, as the Bauddhas are noticed on the Coromandel Coast by the Arabian travellers in the eighth and ninth centuries,* in Guzerat by Al-Edrisi in the twelfth century:† and we have a family of princes who appear to have followed the doctrines of Buddha, ruling in

* Asiatic Researches, I, 166. It might be questioned whether this really proves what it has been supposed to establish, the *Bod* of Renaudot being possibly nothing more than the *But* (بت) of the *Persians,* [which is the Sanskrit भूत] or an idol in general: on the other hand, although the Persian term has that meaning, the word is not an Arabic one, and its occurrence in the work of an Arabic writer renders it likely to be the representation of some particular Hindu deity. The turn of the sentence also, if rightly translated, is in favour of its being a proper name. "Il y a dans les Indes des femmes publiqnes appellées femmes de l'Idole. L'origine de cette coutume est telle: Lorsqu'une femme a fait un vœu pour avoir des enfans, si elle met au monde une belle fille, elle l'apporte au *Bod,* c'est ainsi qu'ils appellent l'idole qn'ils adorent, auprès du quel elle le laisse, &c."

† .... نهرواره فملكها ملك عظيم يسمي بلهرا وله جيوش وفيله وعبادته صنم البد 'Rex autem Nahroaræ maximus est, et vocatur Balahara, possidetque exercitus et elephantos, colitque idolum Bodda.' [Jaubert's French translation. Paris: 1836, Vol. I, p. 176.] The Nubian geography of Al Sharíf al Edrisi, where this passage occnrs, was translated by the *Maronites* and published at Paris in 1619; the text of the original was printed at Rome in 1592. According to his translators, Al Edrisi wrote about the middle of the twelfth centnry or 1152. Consequently the *Bauddha* faith preceded that of Jina in Gnzerat, and was subverted there by the latter, soon after Al Edrisi wrote; a course of events very consistent with the view I have taken in the text.

Bengal about the same time.* This seems to be their limit.

I have already observed that Mádhava, a writer of the fourteenth century, places them no nearer than in *Kashmir*, and Abúlfazl,† writing in the sixteenth century, under the reign of a highly tolerant prince, and assisted in his enquiries by Akbar's curiosity as well as power, declares that he had never met with a follower of Buddha in Hindustan and had only encountered some old men of that faith in his third visit to *Kashmir*. Later periods are out of the question; for in the present day I never heard of a person who had met with natives of India proper of this faith, and it does appear that an utter extirpation of the Bauddha religion in India was effected between the twelfth and sixteenth centuries.‡ By whom then was this important revolution brought about? I cannot answer this question with confidence, but think it highly probable that the Jainas performed an important part in the event, especially as there is reason to suppose that the period assigned for the overthrow of the Bauddhas was that in which the Jainas had attained in many parts of India their highest pitch of power and prosperity.

An enquiry into the origin and history of the *Jaina*

---

* Asiatic Researches, V, 131, and IX, 437. [Misc. Essays, II, 282.]

† Gladwin's Áyeen Akbary, vol. III, 151, Calcutta edition.

‡ [Lassen, l. l., IV, 709 f. Râs Mâlâ, I, 12 ff. Mackenzie Collection, I, lxv.]

sect, of whose number and consequence so many vestiges still remain, would be inconsistent with the object of the present disquisition, and would in the actual state of our materials be but imperfectly and unsatisfactorily prosecuted. Something has been done towards illustrating the subject by Mr. Colebrooke, and Colonel Mackenzie; and it is to the latter gentleman we must look for its further prosecution with any hope of success, as he possesses amongst his invaluable collection of inscriptions and manuscripts many documents calculated to throw light upon the investigation.* My own conclusions are at present in opposition to those views which assign a remote era to the commencement of the Jaina schism, and I am inclined to regard it as a scion of the Bauddha heresy, which sprang into existence during the early centuries of the Christian era. But whatever may be thought of this opinion, it may be confidently asserted, that the entire downfall of the Bauddhas was preceded by several ages of *Jaina* ascendancy, and it may consequently be conjectured that the relative position of the two sects was not without its influence upon the final result.

The *Jainas* appear to have been in possession of the consciences and patronage of the Ballála Rájás† from the eighth up to the middle of the eleventh century when Vishńu Vardhana was converted it is said to the faith of Vishńu by Rámánuja.‡ The petty Rájás

* [Mackenzie Coll., I, lxvi ff.; 144 ff. Lassen, l. l., IV, 755 ff.]

† Buchanan's Mysore, vol. III, 110.

‡ Wilks (vol. I, 511) says in 1133; but this would make Rá-

of Tuĺuva, or part of the sovereignty of Vishńu Vardhana, however still continued attached to the Jaina faith, and many temples, statues, and inscriptions in the twelfth, thirteenth, and fourteenth centuries were met with in that province by Dr. Buchanan. In a list of Colonel Mackenzie's inscriptions, which the liberality of the proprietor has enabled me to consult, I find also the eleventh and succeeding centuries particularly rich in grants, made to *Jaina* establishments in the peninsula; I have already adverted to a grant made by Írugapa, an officer of rank in the Vijayanagara court in the fourteenth century, to the Bellagola establishment, and we are satisfied, that the sect professed considerable influence in that court, by another document which has been published, an edict promulgated by Bukka Ráya, dated Śáka 1290 (A.D. 1367),* the object of which is to effect a reconciliation between the contending parties of the *Vaishńavas* and *Jainas*, and in which it is declared that there is no distinction nor contradiction between the two religions.

The Literature of the *Jainas*† has yet been too little investigated, for us to be able to form any conjectures as to the period at which it especially flourished. But the few data we are in possession of tend to corrobo-

---

mánuja rather ancient, if, as there is reason to believe, that reformer was born about 1008. See Asiatic Researches, IX, 270. [Lassen, IV, 126 ff. Hindu Sects. New edition, p. 35.]

* Asiatic Researches, IX, 271.

† [A. Weber, Ueber das Śatrunjaya Máhátmya. Leipzig, 1858, p. 6 ff. Lassen, IV, 758 ff.]

rate the idea, that from the tenth to the fourteenth century was the season of the Jaina prosperity.

It is said generally of Púјya Páda, a celebrated grammarian of the sect, that he flourished about 1000 years ago, Amita Gati, a Jaina astronomical writer, dates his work in 1050.* Hemachandra writes his grammar, vocabulary and hymns in the twelfth century. A commentary on those hymns is dated in the thirteenth, and there is great reason to suspect that the Kalpa Sútra, the great authority of the sect in the north of India, was composed in that century also.† We may therefore conclude that the patronage of these periods produced their due fruit, and was accompanied by the appearance and succession of many of the most celebrated writers amongst the Jainas. The modern and present condition of the Jaina sect appear to be additional confirmations both of its late origin and recent prosperity. In the sixteenth century, according to Abúlfazl, they were numerous and powerful, and the open and confident enemics of the Brahmans and their system. In the seventeenth a Jaina monument was erected at Bhagalpur,‡ the construction

* Colebrooke's Algebra of the Hindus, Preliminary Dissertation. [Misc. Essays, II, 462 f.]

† Besides other reasons for this conjecture, there is one that appears conclusive: amongst the subjects of Mahávíra's juvenile studies the Líláratí is mentioned, a work that was not composed earlier than the middle of the twelfth century. [But compare Lassen, l. l., IV, 769, and Weber, l. l., p. 12.]

‡ The Páduká of Vásupújya; repeated copies of this inscrip-

of which is attributed to the Rájá of Jayapur; and in the last century the Jainas could boast of such opulent and powerful members as the Seṫs of Múrshídábád.* In the south of India several corporate bodies of their priesthood still exist,† and in many places in the north and west of India they are yet numerous and respectable; their actual condition therefore, although a fallen one, is not so far declined as to indicate a long period of persecution, and, as contrasted with the utter annihilation of the Bauddhas in India proper, argues the more recent possession of influence and power, and renders it probable that those advantages were exerted to the detriment of their fellow dissentient sectaries, and contributed to their final expulsion from the plains of Hindustan.

To return from this digression however to the immediate subject of our enquiries, the information that is obtainable of Hemachandra's history; we find that little or nothing is known of him beyond his writings.

---

tion have established the date of the monument Samvat 1693 or A.D. 1637.

* Of whose immense wealth the author of the Seir Mutaqerín characteristically remarks that, when Mír Habíb with a party of Mahratta horse surprised Múrshídábád, and carried off from Jagat Seṫ's house two crore of Arcot rupees, this prodigious sum did not affect the two brothers more than if it had been two trusses of straw.

† As at Śravaṅa Bellagola in Mysore (Asiatic Researches, IX, 256) and at Biddery in Canara (Buchanan's Mysore, III, 75). I understand from Colonel Mackenzie that there is also an establishment of Jaina priests at Chittamoor [Hindu Sects, p. 333 ff.]

If we may trust a work entitled the Samaya Bhúshańa, he was originally an inhabitant of Páťaliputra or Patna, and according to the passage we have already cited from the Transactions of the Bombay Society, he appears to have finally settled in Gujerat, and to have performed an important part in the religious revolutions of that country.

Another of my authorities which appears to be prior to the Mediní, though not therein enumerated, is the *Śabda Málá* of Rámeśwara Śarmańa.* The chief reason for my inferring its priority to the Mediní is its citation by Mallinátha, who is himself apparently anterior to the latter by his no where making mention of it, an omission of which so careful and excellent a commentator as Mallinátha unquestionably is could scarcely have been guilty, had so well qualified a guide as the Mediní been within his reach at the time he wrote. The Śabda Málá is a work of limited extent and value, and is little better than a supplement to the Amara Kosha, the order of which it follows, and to which it adds a few words of uncommon occurrence. The *Náma Málá* is another of my authorities of which the age is uncertain. The title occurs in an early part of the Mediní's list, as I have already observed; but the work I have referred to under the name of its author Dhananjaya appears scarcely worthy of a place in that enumeration, as it is a very limited collection of synonymes strung together without any order or

* [Aufrecht, l. l., I, No. 437. 38.]

arrangement. The want of order however is perhaps an argument in favour of its antiquity. The vocabularies that remain to be noticed are all of a date subsequent to that of the Medini, and may be considered as posterior to the fourteenth century. The character I have assigned to the Śabda Málá of a supplement to the Amara Kosha applies still more forcibly to them, as they follow the arrangement of that work, repeat the whole or nearly the whole of its contents, and merely add to them a few new synonymes, varieties of reading, or terms of uncommon occurrence. The *Nánártha* chapters present the chief difference, as they are very scanty in the compilation of Amara, and as the Viśva and Medini afford great facilities to subsequent Koshakáras. As original and independent compositions they are consequently of little comparative value, and of inferior authority to the standard compositions which precede the fourteenth century. The principal of these modern works, and to which reference will be found in the subsequent pages, are the *Bhúri Prayoga*, *Śabda Raṭnávalí* and *Jaṭádhara Kosha*.

The author of the *Bhúri Prayoga* is Padmanábha Datta, the son of Dámodara Datta, apparently the same as the author of the Supadma, a grammar on an original plan, and the basis of a particular school in some parts of Bengal. He professes to render his work a supplement to the Amara Kosha, and accordingly divides it into three similar sections. He has furnished a few additional vocables, but none of much importance. As he enumerates the Mediní amongst the vocabularies consulted by him, he is subsequent to the author of that work.*

The *Śabda Ratnávalí* is the compilation of Mathureśa, one of the commentators on the Amara Kosha, and follows that work in arrangement, and contents. It is chiefly useful for its introduction of various readings amongst the synonymes, but has made very little addition of any other kind. This work was composed according to the date in Śáka 1588 or A. D. 1666, and under the patronage of a Musselman chief whose name, as written in the manuscripts, appears to be Múrchhán Khán.. It should be more probably Músá Khán, a name common amongst the Musselman chiefs of the seventeenth century.†

The vocabulary of *Jaṫádhara* is for the most part a mere transcript of the Amara Kosha, and it is an impudent transcript, for the author acknowledges no authority. He probably thought the remoteness of his position screened him from detection. As he informs us, he was an inhabitant of Chaṫu-gráma or Chittagong. He has added a few terms occasionally to those extracted from Amara, and for these his work has been referred to. The date of the compilation is not specified, but it is no doubt comparatively modern.‡

* [Aufrecht, l. l., I, No. 435.]

† [Aufrecht, l. l., I, No. 439. 40.]

‡ [Aufrecht, l. l., I, p. 191, proves that it was composed before the time of Ráya Mukuṫa.]

Some compilations have been made of late years, chiefly at the suggestion, and for the use of European patrons. Of these the Śabda Sandarbha Sindhu, containing the words of the Amara Kosha, Hemachandra, Viśva, and Medinî, was compiled by Káśinátha Śarmańa for Sir William Jones. A compilation from those and other authorities, but left incomplete, was latterly prepared for Mr. Colebrooke by different hands, one of whom, Vidyákara Miśra, was for some period one of my assistants; and a very voluminous work, the Śabdártha Kalpataru, has been recently compiled for the use of the Madras College.* The first of these is readily obtainable and was purchased by me in Calcutta. Mr. Colebrooke transferred the second to me, and for the third I was indebted to the kind politeness of the late Mr. Ellis, and of Mr. Campbell. The first will be found referred to, though but very rarely, as it offered no additional matter. From the second I have taken some meanings of monosyllabic words, which were quoted from the Ekákshara Koshas, and of which the originals were not in my possession; and from the third I have extracted a number of vocables for which I could find no other authority. This work would have been as valuable as it is copious, had there not been reason to question its accuracy; but the greater part of its references are wholly fanciful, and the Amara Kosha is given as authority for very many terms, which it does not contain. None of these com-

* [ib., No. 455.]

pilations have yet any weight or authority with native scholars.*

The works I have thus enumerated are not the only vocabularies I have consulted, though forming the whole number of those of which the contents and application are of a general nature. Besides these I have employed several medical vocabularies, which comprise also copious lists of plants and drugs, and include a small number of general terms. Those which have been referred to in the following publication, are the *Ratna Málá*, *Rája Nighańtu*, *Bháva Prakáśa*, and *Śabda Chandriká.*

The only copy of the *Ratna Málá* I have been able

---

* A compilation of a superior character to any of these modern works, and indeed to any of the more ancient works, is now in progress in Calcutta: it is entitled the *Śabda Kalpa Druma*, and is a Sanskrit Dictionary alphabetically arranged, with references to the anthorities, and with copious explanations in the Sanskrit language. It is printed in the Bengali character. It is the work of a yonng native gentleman of fortune and family, Rádhákánta Deb, with the assistance of the best Pańdits, and is printing at his own expense, and is an occupation which singularly contrasts with the low luxury, in which Hindus of his age and rank ordinarily expend their time and money. The politeness of the author has favoured me with the first sheets of the work; but, I regret, it was not sufficiently advanced for me to benefit by its contents. He has also obliged me with many critical remarks on the earlier part of my own Dictionary, of which, where practicable, I have availed myself. The Śabda Kalpa Druma must take some considerable time before it is completed. [The seventh volnme, completing the original work, was published in the year 1851; and six years after a supplementary volume appeared under the title '*Śabdakalpadrumapariśishṭaḥ*'.]

to procure contains no specification of its date or author, although from the invocation we may conjecture that the latter was a Bauddha or Jaina sectary. It is a useful list of the names of drugs, both vegetable and mineral, with the common Hindu denomination appended, and is regarded as a work of some antiquity and authority.

The *Rája Nighańtu* is the work of Narahari Pańḋita, who states himself to be descended from a family of Kashmirian Brahmans. From the frequent occurrence of Dakhińí terms in explanation of his Sanskrit text it is inferred, however, that he was an inhabitant of the south of India. Besides the medical works which he refers to he comprises amongst his authorities Amara, Haláyudha, and the Viśva Prakáśa, and by his stopping at the latter it appears probable that he wrote during the interval between the appearance of that work and the Mediní, or some time in the twelfth or thirteenth century. The compilation is almost wholly limited to the Materia Medica of Hindu physicians, or the synonymes and properties of various vegetable and mineral products considered to possess medicinal virtue.

The *Bháva Prakáśa* is a compilation of a more general character, and includes the anatomy, pathology, and therapeutics of the Hindus. It is a very useful work, but not particularly full in the nomenclature of those subjects which come within the scope of the present publication, and is therefore not frequently adverted to. It is the work of Bháva Miśra, the son of Latakana Miśra, and is about two centuries old. The copy I have used, and which belongs to the Library of the Asiatic Society, is dated in the year Samvat 1725, or 150 years ago.

The *Śabda Chandriká* is a vocabulary of vegetable and mineral substances, with a tolerably copious list of animals, and a chapter on compounds, both in medicine and diet. It is accompanied by an interpretation in Bengali and is a useful work. The author is Chakra Páńi Datta, and the compilation is comparatively modern.*

The list of vocabularies which constitute my authorities is not yet completed, and I have to add to their number the *Dwirúpa Kosha* of Bharata Malla, and *Uńádi Kosha* of Ráma Śarmańa. The first of these is a collection of various readings, pointing out the different orthoepy of the same word, and is a compilation of a writer whom we have noticed amongst the commentators on Amara. It is not very frequently referred to in the following work, as similar varieties are abundantly furnished by the author's commentary on the Amara Kosha, which afforded a more ready reference, and most of the examples are also met with in the Śabda Ratnávalí, whence they have been likewise extracted.

The *Uńádi Kosha* is an explanation of the irregular derivatives formed with the affixes Uń and others, or Uńádi, the construction and import of which being

* [Aufrecht, l. l., No. 453.]

reducible to no positive system, they have been formed into a class by themselves. The vocabulary I now speak of has the advantage of being elucidated by a comment written by the author, and I have therefore found it sometimes usefully consulted; but as the comment is constructed according to Vopadeva's system of grammar, I have preferred in all cases where I had a choice the five Uńádi chapters of the Siddhánta Kaumudí, the entire contents of which, constituting a very full series of these derivatives, will be found embodied in the subsequent sheets.*

Of the above works the whole were employed in the original compilation, with the following exceptions: most of the commentators on Amara, the Náma Málá, the Rája Nighańtu, Bháva Prakáśa, the Uńádi chapters of the Kaumudí, and the compilations I have particularised as absolutely modern. In the other instances my only task has been collation, and whether the object of this collation was reconciling different readings in manuscript copies of the same work, comparing the differences of separate vocabularies, or correcting the inaccuracies of my original, it was a task of which the labour can scarcely be computed, except by those who have engaged in similar undertakings. It can be a subject of little interest to the reader to accompany me through any detailed exposition of this part of my labours, or to follow the slow and painful steps, by which I have worked my way through a path

* [Ujjvaladatta's commentary on the Uńádi-Sútras, ed. T. Aufrecht. London, 1859, preface p. xxi.]

so intricate and irksome, often terminating in utter perplexity, and I have no doubt, in spite of all my care, frequently ending in mistake. To the Sanskrit student, however, it may not be unserviceable to convey some idea of the condition in which Hindu manuscripts, and indeed all oriental manuscripts, are found: and I may be perhaps indulged for dwelling with some complacency on a part of my labours, of the character and extent of which so little can be known to any one else. I shall therefore proceed to offer one or two examples of the different descriptions of difficulty, by which this province of my labours has been harassed and obstructed.

Of variations in different manuscripts of the same work abundant specimens might be presented; but it will be sufficient to confine them to the Viśva, of which I had four different copies. One of these, under the term चरर, explains it by छेदन, another by छादन. Three copies assign to चेग्रट as one sense of it ग्रोपण, and a fourth ग्रोषक, whilst there is reason to think that they are all wrong, and that the correct reading should be पोषण. Under the word क्षमा, one copy has वार्षिक, another वालुका, and a third क्षिक्षिका, and in many instances the four copies present as many different readings, and every one erroneous. This is the case with the manuscripts of all the Koshas, and it is to be regretted that the printed editions of those which have been published, are very far from correct, with the single exception of the Serampore edition of the Amara Kosha. Printed copies however, as editions multiply, are likely to become more accurate, whilst from the carelessness and ignorance of transcribers in general the multiplication of manuscript copies is only the propagation and augmentation of inaccuracy.

The varieties of reading presented by different works are still more numerous and embarrassing, than those I have noticed. Thus under the word भित्ति, one of the interpretations occurs in the Medini and Viśva प्रदेश, in the Nánártha Ratna Málá प्रवेश,* and in Ajaya प्रद्योष. Under the term महार्घ, we have in the Medini नारक, in the Viśva and Hemachandra नावक; Jaṭádhara writes a passage उत्सिक्रमुन्नते, the Bhúri Prajoga उत्सि-क्रमुद्धते. One meaning of रूप, as given by my original, is written नालक, Hemachandra has it नाणक, the Viśva नागक, the Medini नालोक, the Dharaṅi कणिक, the Śabda Ratnávali नामक, and the Trikáńḍa मागक, Ajaya Pála has बालक, the Śabda Sandarbha Sindhu तारक, and the Nánártha Ratna Málá* has माणिक, offering ten varieties in as many works on a word of three syllables, not one of which is satisfactory. Differences to a like and even greater extent are numerous, and there are some instances in which I have had occasion to notice not fewer than thirteen equally puzzling varieties on one short word. †

---

* [The confusion becomes still greater by the varieties of reading met with in different copies of one and the same work as mentioned above. Thus in the printed edition of the Nánártha-ratnamálá we find *prakáśa* instead of *praveśa* (I, 154), and *náṭaka* instead of *máńika* (I, 251).]

† As a specimen of my attempts at unravelling some of these

There is great confusion also in the gender of nouns; thus कच्छ in one passage of the Amara Kosha is termed

---

intricacies, which may be amusing to those readers who take an interest in philological riddles, I here subjoin the interpretation of the word वञ्जुर, accompanied by the note which, for my own satisfaction and for the better understanding of the subject, it has been my uniform practice in all such cases to prepare and preserve.

वञ्जुर n. (-रं) 1. An arbour, a bower, &c. 2. An uncultivated field. 3. A sand, a desert. 4. A field. 5. A componnd pedicle. Hem. Ná. 6. A solitude, a wild. 7. A thicket, a wood. Dhar. vide in loco.

Note: great confusion prevails regarding this and the next word वञ्जूर, and the original has increased it by adding a third word वञ्जर, misquoting the Dharañi for it, in which the reading is correctly वञ्जूर. The authorities differ considerably, and there is reason to presume that not one of them is uniformly accurate in the interpretations of these two words. The following are the passages:

वञ्जुरं शाद्वलचये गहनौषधयोरपि ॥ Med. [212.]
वञ्जुरं कुञ्जमञ्जर्योः क्षेत्रे ऽनम्भसि शाद्वले ।
वञ्जूरस्तु वनक्षेत्रे वाहनोषरयोरपि ॥ Hem. [Nân. 598.]
वञ्जुरं तु निर्ज्जनस्थाने विन्दुसरे च वञ्जुरम् ।
वञ्जुरं गहने कुञ्जे ॥ Dhar.
वञ्जुरः पुंसि गहनवरक्षेत्रोषरेष्वपि च ॥ Śabd. R.
वञ्जूरं शाद्वनक्षेत्रे वाहनोषरयोरपि ॥ Viś.
शाद्वसरे वनचये वञ्जूरं गहने ऽपि च ॥ Tri. [III, 370.]

The first inference to be drawn from these readings is that besides the meanings peculiar to वञ्जूर it has those of वञ्जुर also; and the next is that, though वञ्जुर may sometimes occur as a nonn mascnline, yet properly it is neuter, all the authorities agreeing in making it so except the Śabda Ratnávalí. As for the interpretations, the Medini is wrong in शाद्वलचये, which should be either शाद्वले and क्षेत्रे, or शाद्वलक्षेत्रे; also in औषध, which should be ऊषर, from the concnrrence of the Hem., Viś., and Śabda Ratnávali, and the analogy of the other senses. Hemachandra masculine, and in another is a noun, of three genders, whilst again Mukuta asserts that it is never feminine, and Mathureśa, that it is an error ever to make it neuter.* As to the various readings arising from confounding the different nasals and sibilants, and above all from the perpetual interchange of the letters B and V (ब and व) they are innumerable, and of almost impracticable adjustment. The difficulty of separating them indeed seems to have been long ago insurmountable and to have given rise to the following convenient rule, which renders their distinction a matter of perfect indifference:

रलयोर्डलयोस्तद्वज्जययोर्बवयोरपि ।
शसयोर्मनयोश्चान्ते सविसर्गाविसर्गयोः ।
सबिन्दुकाबिन्दुकयोः स्याद्भेदे न कल्पनम् ॥

"The letters R and L, D and L, J and Y, B and V, Ś and S, M and N, a final Visarga or its omission, and

---

seems the most accurate, except that वाहन is put for गहन; the विन्दुसरे of Dharańi is what? and its निर्ज्जनस्थान, though admissible, is more probably निर्ज्जलस्थान; the मरवेष of the Śabda Ratnávalí is evidently a mistake for वनवेष. The Viśva has वाहन also where the rest have गहन, being as usual the same essentially with Hemachandra. The Trikáńda has उसरे for उषरे, and वनवचे for वनवेचे. The Śabdártha Kalpataru has under this word वहने and चीवधे for गहने and उषरे; and the Śabda Sandarbha Sindhu, misquoting its originals, writes वासन for the वाहन of Viśva and Hemachandra. [A MS. copy of the Medini, in the R. A. S.'s possession, reads वसरं स्यादनवेचे महनीवरयोरपि, and in the Śabdakalpadruma s. v. we find the remark विश्वधरणिग्रन्थरत्नावलिषु वसरमिति पाठः]

* [Bhánudíkshita ad Amar. K. II, 1, 10. He does not mention or comment upon the śloka III, 4, 31.]

a final nasal mark or its omission, are always optional, there being no difference between them."* Notwithstanding the latitude which this doctrine permits, the adjustment of these letters, and of ब and व especially, has occasioned me infinite trouble. I may here observe that the classification of words beginning with a B or V, which I have adopted, rests chiefly on the authority of the commentators on Amara, and the chapter of the Viśva on the subject, extended by analogy to those cases to which their specifications do not apply.

To censure the faults of the original compilation with any undue asperity, would ill become one who is conscious of being liable to a similar accusation. Bayle says, it is well in works of this kind, if there are not more than seven errors in a page, and perfection in a Dictionary, according to Dr. Johnson, is the dream of a poet doomed at last to wake a Lexicographer. Both these illustrious men have likewise pointed out the difficulties arising from the mere extent of an undertaking, as well as the impossibility of bestowing the same attention upon many objects, that might be devoted to a few: and the former has justly remarked that, although the first writers of Dictionaries have committed many faults, yet they have done great services, and deserve a glory of which they ought not to be deprived by their successors. That

* [See the Sáraswatí Prakriyá. Súrat: 1829, I, Sútra 15, where the śloka reads thus:

रलयोर्डलयोश्चैव शसयोर्बवयोस्तथा ।
वदन्त्येषां च सावर्ण्यमलंकारविदो जनाः ॥]

errors would therefore occur in the original compilation, might have been expected, and they might also have been visited with a lenient spirit; they exceed however all reasonable limits, and it is in justice to the encouragers and conductors of the work, as well as to myself, that I am induced to notice them. I have corrected at the least several thousand mistakes, and I am confident that, had I engaged to prepare an original compilation, and not to collate and rectify that of the guide I adopted, I should have finished my task in less time, and with less trouble, in a more complete manner, and with more satisfaction to myself. The errors were of every description: words were inserted as original terms, which proved to be merely misspellings of others, and many were assigned to authorities in which they did not occur; the etymologies were mostly fanciful, often erroneous, and not seldom invented to support a word of the compiler's coinage; the interpretations were frequently most grossly inaccurate, and the passages quoted from the different authorities constantly referred to those, to which they did not belong. There were also many faults of omission, and a number of words, even in the Amara Kosha, left out of the compilation: in short the book was put together with an utter indifference to literary reputation, and a dishonest disregard of the duty, which the Pańd́its employed undertook to discharge.

Besides the words extracted from the vocabularies I have specified, and to which an appropriate reference is annexed, a number will be met with without such an appendage: these are additions of my own, consisting chiefly of useful grammatical derivatives, taken from the *Siddhánta Kaumudi*, and a few law terms, from *Manu*, and the *Mitákshará*; in the latter pages of the work, I have also inserted many words which occurred incidentally in the course of such miscellaneous reading as my very restricted leisure has permitted me to indulge in. As improvements and additions of minor importance, I may here mention that I have attached to the nouns the initial letters denoting the gender, as well as the termination of the nominative case singular: and I have referred by appropriate syllables to the several authorities consulted. To those of my originals which have been printed, as the *Hemachandra*, the *Trikáńďa*, and *Háravali*, I have subjoined the numerals, expressing the chapter, section and verse, in which the word is to be found, agreeably to the mode in which those Koshas are divided. To the printed *Medini*, and the second portion of *Hemachandra*, and to the Serampore edition of *Amara*, such a particular reference was unnecessary, the two first following a partially alphabetical arrangement, as I have already observed, and the last being provided with an alphabetical index, by which its contents can readily be consulted. For the manuscript authorities I have contented myself with the indication of the name, as indeed a more precise reference would neither be serviceable nor practicable.

I have now accounted for all the nouns and particles contained in the following work, and the only classes of words admitted into the original vocabularies of the Sanskrit tongue. To the European student of Sanskrit, however, a Dictionary would be of little value, that should not offer any intepretation of the verbs, and particularly when they are identified, as they are in Sanskrit, with the roots of the whole language. I have therefore embodied the *Dhátupátha*, or catalogues of roots, with the other divisions of the general work.

The Sanskrit root, or *Dhátu,* appears to differ from the primitives of other languages in its fulfilling no other office, and being incapable of entering into any form of speech: to fit it for this purpose, it must undergo many preparatory modifications, and it is then evolved with the aid of additional particles into a noun or verb at pleasure. At the same time, as a matter of convenience, the Hindu grammarians have connected it more directly with verbal than nominal inflection, and in the classification adopted in their lists it wears a more determinate shape, and may then be regarded as the crude verb. The import of the Sanskrit root is as undefined as its character, and it is in fact only the general sign of all the possible varieties of action or being that are referable to a common nature. It is usually explained by a noun, and the noun most frequently is in the seventh or locative case: thus (भू) *Bhú* is explained by (सत्तायाम्) *Sattáyám,* in being; (ह्लाद्) *Hlád* by (अव्यक्तशब्दे) *Avyaktaśabde,* in inarticulate sound, &c.* Many roots also have a

* [i. e. in the sense of being, in the sense of inarticulate sound.]

great variety of meanings, thus (अव्) *Av* has nineteen acceptations, (कल्) *Kal*, generally signifying numeration or counting, is susceptible of any meaning a writer may chuse to employ it in, and this indeed so far applies to every other radical, that in derivatives of which the form is clearly traceable to a root of a very different signification the difficulty is immediately solved, by the general law धातोरनेकार्थत्वात्, that roots are capable of various interpretations. These varieties of sense, however, are either rendered perfectly intelligible in books from the context, or they are explained in the commentaries, and most of the verbal inflections are of an application sufficiently precise. As to the individually exact import of the root, it is of very little consequence, as, although it may be a question whether each should be interpreted by an abstract or infinitive noun, this uncertainty is removed at once in practice by the conversion of the root into one or other form: its conversion into the crude verb is the method I have preferred, and it appears in the following pages translated by the English verb in the infinitive mood, with which, however, it must not be confounded, as the Sanskrit root takes an indeclinable infinitive form, which corresponds in power with our infinitive, as designated by the particle *to*.

The Sanskrit roots, as identified with crude verbs, are arranged in ten *Gańas*, or classes, differing in conjugation through a part of their inflection, and consequently discriminated in grammatical works: the arrangement of the *Dhátupátha* is however alphabetical. The number of the roots can scarcely be estimated with precision; for, as crude verbs, they may be inflected in several of the conjugations, and they are usually considered as then forming distinct roots. There are also many roots called *Sautra*, from being noticed in *Sútras*, or rules, of etymological analysis, constructed for the occasion by authors of reputation, and there are many peculiar to the Vedas, which, as well as the preceding, are not always included in the enumeration of the *Dhátupáthas.* In general the number of radicals in the ordinary lists is about 1700, as repeated in different classes they exceed 2000. In the following pages the number is something more than nineteen hundred, and they occur as nearly as possible in the following proportions:

Class the first,	1020
— — second,	73
— — third,	23
— — fourth,	128
— — fifth,	29
— — sixth,	154
— — seventh,	25
— — eighth,	10
— — ninth,	59
— — tenth,	411.

I do not mean to assert that these numbers are faultlessly accurate, but they are sufficiently so to convey a correct notion of the proportion of which the various classes consist: of the whole number, a very considerable proportion also are of rare occurrence.

Although the Sanskrit root is with a few doubtful exceptions* monosyllabic, yet as the crude verb it often appears to consist of several syllables, by the annexation of certain supernumerary letters, which are rejected from every inflection, and serve only to denote the class to which the verb belongs, or the necessity of some peculiar modifications in it or its derivatives. These *Anubandhas* or adjuncts, or indicatory letters, I have in general thought it unnecessary to retain; as, on the one hand, the class is specifically mentioned, and its characteristic formation shewn, by the insertion of the third person singular of the present tense; and, on the other, the appropriate evolutions of the most useful derivative form occur under the respective derivatives. I have however retained some of them, as the letter ङ for instance, as not only accounting for some singularity in the construction of the present tense, but as sometimes furnishing a useful distinction between two roots of otherwise similar form, and yet of very different meaning and classification.

For the roots contained in the following pages I am indebted chiefly to the labours of Mr. Colebrooke. Those of the first and most numerous class are published in the first volume of his Sanskrit grammar, but the other classes existed only in manuscript, which he had the kindness to complete for my use. The accuracy of his compilation and excellence of his authorities have left me little to do but to transcribe, and al-

* [See Benfey's "Vollständige Grammatik der Sanskritsprache." Leipzig: 1852, p. 71 f.]

though I have consulted the lists in the Grammars of Mr. Wilkins and Dr. Carey, and in Mr. Forster's Essay, as well as occasionally adverted to the works of Mádhava and Vopadeva and the roots given in the Mugdhabodha and Kaumudí, I have found occasion to make but few additions to the copious and satisfactory catalogue Mr. Colebrooke had prepared. I have added to some of the roots, however, a variety of modifications of meaning, depending upon the addition of inseparable prefixes or prepositions, the application and effect of which in Sanskrit compositions are of a very various and puzzling character. It would be almost impossible indeed to collect all the shades of import occasioned by the use of these particles, the application of which seems frequently to depend upon the caprice of the writer. They are often also accumulated to eke out measure without regard to meaning, and leave the radical unaffected, a circumstance that forms one of the great objects of the commentaries by which all Sanskrit works of merit are accompanied, and without which, for some time at least, they will scarcely be perusable with any satisfaction or certainty. The examples I have given are taken chiefly from the Mágha, Bhagavad Gítá, and Megha Dúta; they are comparatively but few however, and I soon found it vain prosecuting the collection, as far as poetical license, or the निरङ्कुशाः कवयः, the uncontrolled poets of Sanskrit Grammarians, were likely to lead me.

The whole extent of the Dictionary from these various sources is but indifferently proportioned to a language, which it may be safely said has no limit, and the extent will be thought still less, when it is found that it for a great part consists of the language of Botany and Mythology. For so great a portion being thus appropriated it would be sufficient for me to say, that it is the case with my originals; but there is a still better reason, and incidental reference to a Deity by some of his many titles, and fanciful allusions to a flower or plant, constitute half, or more than half, of the poetry of the Hindus. Their mythology is the main structure, their botany the chief decoration, of their poetical compositions, and I have no fear of being found by the student unnecessarily copious on these two themes. As far as affects my translation of the names of plants and objects of science, I do not mean to be responsible for its accuracy: Mr. Colebrooke's Amara Kosha has been my chief guide, and in other cases I have made use of the Bengalí and Uriya vocabularies published at the College, and of Dr. Roxburgh's Catalogue of the Botanical Gardens, as published by Dr. Carey, with the Bengalí and Hindí names of a large portion of its contents.

Although the number of vocables contained in the Dictionary is comparatively scanty, yet its application may, with a little attention to the genius and grammar of the language, be almost indefinitely extended. Compound words not found in it may be easily resolved into their component parts, and those parts, if not occurring, may be traced to their radicals, and their import thus be ascertained. The obvious meanings of words as derivable from their etymology, though frequently not assigned to them by any authority, and therefore only not inserted, may of course be always admitted, and they may also be extended as epithets to other senses not expressed, to which their analysis makes them applicable. Names of properties and virtues will often be met with used attributively, when their application will be easily understood; and the conversion of simple nouns into a variety of possessive and attributive shapes by the use of regular affixes will easily be conceived by adverting to some of the analogous formations the work itself contains. As to the effect of negative and privative prefixes, and the addition of the abstractive terminations, there can be no difficulty in these respects, as the modified meaning is too palpable to be misconceived, and by attention to these points, and by a knowledge of the elements of the language, without which all attempts at study must be abortive, I trust the Dictionary now offered to the Public will afford every desirable aid to the student of the Sanskrit Language.

XIV.

NOTICE

OF

EUROPEAN GRAMMARS AND LEXICONS

OF THE

SANSKRIT LANGUAGE.

From the Transactions of the Philological Society, Vol. I (1843), p. 13-36.

It has been thought to contribute to the fulfilment of an object which was suggested at the General Meeting in May last for the Society's earliest consideration, namely, the ascertainment of the actual condition of philological inquiry, to offer a short notice of those publications which within the last half century have been designed to promote, amongst Europeans, an elementary knowledge of the Sanskrit language. It appeared to me that the suggestion to which I had adverted, and for which the Society was indebted to a highly valued colleague, whose opinions must ever be entitled to attention, could be followed out successfully only by a division of labour. A comprehensive whole, consisting of many parts, appears to demand for its investigation the acquirements of different members of the Society, of whom, while there are many who might feel themselves equal to undertake some one subdivision, there are probably few who would not distrust their ability to grapple with so vast an undertaking as a universal survey of the present state of philological research. Under the impression, therefore, that an object, which was indisputably of no small importance in the outset of the Society's career—the determination of a fixed point from whence to start—the knowledge of what has been done as a necessary preliminary to what remains to be done—could be most readily attained by separate exertion, he had been induced to enter upon a department which he thought might reasonably be assigned to him, and as prefatory to other branches of an investigation into the existing state of Sanskrit philology, he purposed to submit a brief account of those means of acquiring an acquaintance with the language, which we owed to the talents and industry of European scholars. He might take a future opportunity of offering some notice of the grammatical works of native authorities, and of the labours of European writers, in the elucidation of the affinities which connect the Sanskrit with other cultivated forms of speech.

For a considerable period a notion prevailed that the learned amongst the natives of India were obstinately averse to the communication of instruction in their sacred language to foreigners, and that this was the reason why so many years elapsed before an attempt to acquire it was made by those Europeans, who from one motive or other had sojourned in India. The notion was not altogether unfounded, although the reluctance which no doubt was encountered was less insuperable than was imagined, and originated in a misconception from which the most enlightened native scholars were free. There is nothing in the laws or institutes of the Hindus which authorizes a monopoly of a knowledge of the Sanskrit language by any one caste or order of the people. The only monopoly insisted upon by the Brahmans was that of tuition. They allowed no other caste to teach—they enjoined the military and agricultural castes to learn, even the holy books, the Vedas. They prohibited the Śúdra or servile caste from hearing the sacred books, but they permitted even the mixed castes to read and hear the great historical and mythological poems, and consequently never thought of excluding them from a knowledge of the language in which those books are composed. Their monopoly of tuition, which they most rigorously guarded against aggression, was so far disinterested that it brought with it no pecuniary profit. Even to the present day it is considered derogatory to the purity of the Brahmanical character to give instruction for hire, and although in the service of Europeans the scruple is surmounted, teaching Sanskrit to native pupils is very generally gratuitous. The Brahmans had no doubt a design in thus reserving to themselves the seemingly unrequited duties of instruction, but it is not necessary on the present occasion to inquire what their objects were. It is sufficient to have shown that there was no law to prevent them from expounding the mysteries of their sacred tongue to ears profane, and that Europeans, although no doubt regarded as amongst the lowest of castes, might have become familiar with them at an earlier period had they entertained the wish and adopted the means of obtaining instruction.

It might appear somewhat unaccountable that the Mohammedans of India should have been blended with the Hindus for centuries, and should have paid no attention to the literature of their fellow-subjects, did we not know the disdainful intolerance with which they regard the languages and literature of all nations that profess a different religious faith. The first sovereigns of Delhi would have incurred the imputation of being infidels had they shown any favour to the Pańḍits; and in truth they were not in much danger of undergoing such a censure, as they were of a rude race, more addicted to arms than to letters, and commonly dependent upon the former for their thrones and their existence. Their conduct and example were ill calculated to win the confidence of the Hindus, and they were no doubt as backward to impart, as the Mohammedans were careless to seek for, information. The reign of Akbar, in the latter half of the sixteenth century, first wrought a change in this state of public feeling. A friendly intercourse was then first established between both classes of the people, and in imitation of the patronage bestowed by the monarch upon Hindu literary men, the nobles of his court condescended to express curiosity concerning the national literature, and became the scholars of the Brahmans. The rapidity with which the scruples and reluctance of the latter yielded to the sunshine of imperial favour, must have appeared so marvellous to the Mohammedans, that a fable was invented to account for the alteration. It was said that by the command of the king, Sheikh Feizí, the younger* brother of Akbar's able minister Abúlfazl, had been palmed in early life upon the Brahmans as an orphan youth of their own caste, and that he was initiated by them unwittingly into their learning and doctrines. The tale, though still current, is not very probable. Feizí is the reputed and, in part no doubt, real author of various translations from Sanskrit into Persian: other translations were made under his superintendence.† His competency to the task, and the assistance which he commanded, may easily be accounted for without having recourse to fiction. The enlightened encouragement and royal munificence of Akbar were the keys that unlocked the treasures of Hindu lore. The taste which he introduced survived his reign, and in Dárá Shekoh, the unfortunate son of Sháh Jehán, he found a worthy successor. The speculative and supplementary portion of the Vedas, the Upanishads, were translated by his order into Persian.‡ With the accession of Aurangzib the age of Mohammedan bigotry revived, and the

* [According to the Táríkh-i-Badaúní, the elder brother.]

† [See Sir H. Elliot's Bibliogr. Index to the Historians of Muhammedan India. Calc., 1849, I, 221. 259 ff.]

‡ From the Persian a translation into Latin was made by Anquetil du Perron, who published it under the title of Oupnekhát, seu Theologia Indica. Paris, 1801. 2 vols. 4to. [Prof. Goldstücker's 'Pánini', p. 141 f.]

Hindus fell back into their defensive attitude of silence and suspicion.

The first European settlers in India were merchants and soldiers, who troubled themselves little about the intellectual products of the country. The missionaries, however, who followed on their track, speedily perceived the necessity of making themselves familiar with the native languages and writings, and diligently applied themselves to the study. Their purposes were not literary, and they did not deem it incumbent upon them to impart any of their discoveries to the European public, although it is not unlikely that the archives of the Propaganda Society at Rome may contain specimens of the early labours of the missionaries of the Roman church. At any rate, it has been recently evidenced by the voluminous compositions in Sanskrit verse upon Christian subjects by members of the Jesuit mission at Madura, discovered at Pondicheri not many years ago, and of which an account* was published in the Researches of the Asiatic Society of Bengal, that some of the members of this mission attained an extraordinary command over the language, and composed in it with an accuracy and an elegance unsurpassed by any later Europeans, and even by modern native scholars. The same proficiency was attained by them in Sanskrit, which they acquired in the vernacular tongues, and which has placed Robert de

* Account of a Discovery of a modern Imitation of the Vedas, by F. Ellis. Asiatic Researches, XIV, p. 1.

Nobili and Father Beschi amongst the classics of Tamil literature in the estimation of the natives of the south of India. Indications of this successful study however were few and faint in the west, although they were at length manifested in such meagre compilations as the 'Alphabetum Brahmanicum', and 'Alphabetum Grandonico-Malabaricum', published at Rome in 1771 and 1772 by the Propaganda Society.

The first systematic attempt to impart a more extended acquaintance with Sanskrit to European students, was the publication by Paulinus a S. Bartholomeo, a German missionary* of the name of Wesdin, of a short and imperfect grammar of the language, to which he gave the title of 'Siddharubam, seu Grammatica Samscrdamica', Rome 1790. This was followed by a number of works on the Indian languages, and the mythology and history of the Hindus, in which the information given, although tinted by colouring of local origin, and blended with fictions peculiar to the Peninsula of India, where Paulinus spent fourteen years, is in the main correct, and might have been useful had it not been overwhelmed by an accompanying mass of crude conjecture and misapplied erudition. A more copious and correct grammar was published by Paulinus in 1804, entitled, 'Vyácaranam, seu locupletissima Samscrdamicæ Linguæ Institutio'. The original of this was a native grammar, a copy of

* See a biographical notice of Paulinus in the Nouveaux Mélanges Asiatiques, par M. Abel Remusat, vol. II, p. 305.

which had been translated in India by a Danish missionary of the name of Hanxleden, who seems to have been a much better scholar than Paulinus. His papers having come into the possession of the latter, were either published by him as in the present instance, or employed by him for other works, as in the case of the first book of the Lexicon of Amara Sinha, also published by Paulinus with a Latin translation, which he was enabled to execute, it appears, chiefly by the aid of a manuscript Lexicon, Latin and Sanskrit, compiled by Hanxleden, and appended to the Vyácaranam.

This first grammar of the Sanskrit language, being a translation of an original work, is accurate, although not comprehensive. It is printed with Roman letters in all except the first section, in which the Sanskrit words are expressed in the characters of the Tamil alphabet, of very indifferent typographic execution. The Roman representation of the words in accordance with the original Tamil, is disfigured by corruptions derived from the peculiar pronunciation of the natives of that part of the Peninsula of which Tamil is the vernacular idiom, by whom soft labials are substituted for hard, and soft dentals or semivowels for hard dentals, in certain situations. Thus *Somabá* is written for *Somapá*, and *bhavadi* for *bhavati*, and *vrikshál* for *vríkshát*. With respect also to the Roman orthography, a most barbarous-looking equivalent is not unfrequently given for the original, depending partly upon German and partly upon Italian pronunciation, and which it often requires some consideration to identify;

kashṫáśrita is not at once recognisable in *kaszdaschrida*. The grammar is followed by two vocabularies, one Latin and Sanskrit, arranged according to the analogous senses of the words; the other, Sanskrit and Latin, arranged alphabetically. It is not stated by whom they were compiled, but it is probable that both were the work of Hanxleden. The 'Vyácarana' is not without merit,* and opened the way to the study of Sanskrit by the scholars of the continent; and Paulinus by its publication established a claim to grateful commemoration, although he cannot be considered to have done more than rendered the labours of a brother missionary accessible to the European public.†

Although not yet known in Europe, the labours of our own countrymen in the East, for the dissemination of an accurate knowledge of the Sanskrit language, had preceded the publication of the Vyácarana. The encouragement given to oriental studies by Warren Hastings, the institution of the Asiatic Society by Sir William Jones, and the foundation of the College of Fort William by the Marquis Wellesley, had communicated a powerful impulse and a right direction to the exertions of European scholars in India. Philology could not fail to receive the attention it deserved, and the Asiatic Researches were at an early period enriched

* [For less lenient opinions on the 'Vyácarana' compare Sir H. Elliot, l. l., p. 265, Note †.]

† Schlegel questions his fully understanding the writings of Hanxleden: "der Pater Paulinus theilte mit was er nur sehr unvollkommen verstand." Indische Bibliothek, I. l. 9.

by the observations of Sir William Jones and Mr. Colebrooke on various points regarding the structure and nature of the Sanskrit language. The compilation of elementary works expressly for the use of English students was necessarily one of the first objects of the institution of the College, and it was for the benefit of the junior civil servants of the East India Company attached to the College, that the two first published English grammars of the Sanskrit language, those of Dr. Carey and Mr. Colebrooke, were compiled and printed in Serampore and Calcutta.

Dr. William Carey was a member of the Baptist mission in Bengal. After a residence of eight years in the country, during which he had studied with unwearied assiduity the Bengali and Sanskrit languages, he was appointed Professor of both in the College of Fort William early in 1801. He immediately set about compiling a grammar,* and the first part of this work was published in 1803.† It was completed in 1806. It forms an immense volume, extending to a thousand quarto pages. This is in great part ascribable to the size of the Sanskrit types employed, which in the first stages of Sanskrit printing in India were of unnecessarily gigantic dimensions. With a due allowance on this account, enough remains to constitute the grammar a singular monument of in-

* Letter to Dr. Ryland, June 15, 1801. Memoir of Dr. Carey, D. D., p. 454.

† A Grammar of the Sungskrit language, by William Carey. Serampore, 1806. Reviewed, Quarterly Review, vol. I.

dustrious application. The work is divided into five books. The first explains the forms and powers of the letters of the alphabet, and then treats of what is termed in original grammars *Sandhi*, or combination; a series of rules providing for the coalescence or modification of letters when they come into junction or juxtaposition, so as to avoid harshness or hiatus in their articulation; a subject more minutely investigated and more systematically regulated in Sanskrit than in the grammar of any other language. The second book is appropriated to what native grammarians designate *Śabda*, literally a sound, or as here understood, an articulate sound, a word; under which head are comprised declinable words, whether substantives, adjectives, or pronouns; and indeclinable words, adverbs, prepositions, and conjunctions. The third book treats of the *Dhátus* or roots, as capable of verbal inflexion; first, as simple verbs in the ten classes or conjugations under which they are arranged in original works; and secondly, as derivative verbs, causals, desideratives, and frequentatives. The fourth book of 'Carey's Grammar' describes the formation of derivative words and of compound nouns, and treats of the genders of nouns. The fifth book comprehends the syntax and a few pages of exercises. To the whole is added, by way of an appendix, an alphabetical list of roots.

The Sanskrit Grammar of Dr. Carey is modelled upon the plan of the native grammars, and for the most part follows a similar order. The native authorities also are those chiefly current in Bengal, and he was assisted in the compilation by Bengali Paṅḋits; he therefore speaks their language and adopts their technical phraseology to an extent that is not a little embarrassing to a mere European scholar. It is also inconveniently troublesome in use to a beginner, especially from the separation which it admits between the rules and the examples, so that many pages invariably intervene before the application of the precept, by which alone its purport is rendered intelligible, occurs. Numerical references from the examples to the rules are inserted, it is true, at the foot of the page in which the former are met with, but the verification imposes extra trouble upon the student, and is likely to be carelessly made: the want of a definite impression in the first aspect of a rule is seldom subsequently supplied. The section which treats of the formation of derivative words is broken up into unnecessarily multiplied subdivisions, which, with an appearance of classification, only render the subject more complicated and reference more uncertain. The exemplifications of the syntax are meagre and uninteresting. On the other hand, the chapters on conjugation are very copious and instructive, affording examples of a number of the most useful verbs in more or less detail. There are some inaccuracies, but they are not of a nature or extent to detract materially from the usefulness of an ample exhibition of conjugational varieties, as the conjugation of the verbs is the only real difficulty in Sanskrit grammar. The list of roots is a very serviceable and important addition. The whole is provided with a comprehensive index. The 'Grammar' is in truth a compilation of very great merit, although, from its adhering so closely to native technicalities, it cannot ever be of much advantage to European students. To scholars more advanced it is calculated to be of frequent service, and to any one who should propose to make himself acquainted with an original grammar of the Bengal School it would prove an invaluable auxiliary.

Shortly prior to the publication of Dr. Carey's complete Grammar appeared the first part of a grammar, compiled by the late Henry Thomas Colebrooke, a member of the Civil Service of Bengal, who throughout a long and active public life in India, in the course of which he ascended to the highest distinctions of the service, cultivated the language and literature of the Hindus with singular ability, untiring diligence, and unrivalled success. Succeeding to the position occupied by Sir William Jones, he proved himself worthy to be his successor, as, if he brought with him to the study an inferior order of scholastic attainments, and a less poetical imagination, he surpassed that distinguished orientalist in the profundity and exactitude with which he accomplished all he attempted, and for which he was indebted to a severer turn of thought and a predilection for scientific and mathematical investigation. At the time at which the College of Fort William was established, Mr. Colebrooke held the important office of one of the Judges of the High Court of Appeal of Bengal, but the interest which he felt in the institution induced him to allow himself to be named as Professor of Hindu Law and the Sanskrit Language, and he acted for some time as Examiner in the Persian, Hindustani, Bengali, and Sanskrit Languages. From his connexion with the College originated the grammar now noticed, which was published in 1805.

Mr. Colebrooke's 'Sanskrit Grammar' forms a small folio volume, extended beyond its due proportion by the same circumstance which magnified the bulk of Dr. Carey's work—the unnecessary size of the Devanagari types. The general arrangement is much the same as that of Dr. Carey, being regulated by the nature of the subjects explained. There are many essential varieties however in the details. The letters, their several powers, and the changes which they undergo in connexion with each other, are first described. Then follows the declension of nouns. Three chapters succeed, of which one treats of the genders of nouns, one of the formation of the feminine gender, and one of indeclinables. The rest of the work is occupied with the general rules of conjugation, exemplified by a rich collection of the Paradigms, in more or less detail, of all the verbs of the first conjugation, as derived from the best standard authorities, whose variations are carefully pointed out in accompanying annotations. No further portion of the grammar was ever published, Mr. Colebrooke considering that, after other entire grammars had been provided, it was not necessary to finish his own work, and his time and interest being engaged in other occupations and inquiries. The only materials which he seems to have collected were the remaining conjugations of the simple verbs, of which he gave the author a manuscript copy. The Paradigms were less fully developed than they would have been if they had been designed for publication. The subjects of derivation, composition and syntax were untouched, much to the regret of all those who are familiar with Mr. Colebrooke's labours in various departments of Hindu literature and science.

The grammar of Mr. Colebrooke, like that of Dr. Carey, is based upon the writings of Hindu grammarians. He has followed however the authorities of a different school, that of which Benares is considered to be the high seat, and which in its origin is more ancient than the school of Bengal. He has consequently adopted their terminology in the technicalities which he employs and the precepts which he enunciates, but he has arranged the rules according to a classification of his own. The technical language of his rules, as of those of Carey's grammar, is startling and perplexing to a European student, and almost incomprehensible without the aid of an interpreter. The difficulty here also is enhanced by the want of contiguous examples, by which the rules may be at once illustrated and rendered intelligible. The examples are in a different and sometimes in a distant part of the volume, and although references are sometimes specified numerically, yet they are not always inserted, and are never of ready applicability from the nature of the divisions into books, chapters and sections. Thus, as an example both of the phraseology and of the separation of rule and illustration, let us take the following—it is one out of some hundreds. Section 7. chapter IV. of Book I. treats of the permutations of finals. Rule I. runs thus: —"A blank (*lopa*) is substituted for *n* final of a crude noun that is denominated *pada*, except the vocative singular, unless in the neuter gender." Now here we have first the theoretical peculiarity that a letter is said not to be elided or expunged, but a blank is said to be substituted for it; and secondly, the use of the term *pada*, by which is meant the crude noun before all inflexional terminations beginning with a consonant, exclusive of those of the nominative case in the three numbers, and of the accusative singular and dual, and also before affixes forming derivatives, and before other nouns forming compounds. The first application of this rule occurs after an interval of forty pages, under the declension of nouns ending in *n*, as *rájan*, a king, which loses its final *n*, agreeably to the precept, before the inflexional terminations beginning with consonants, as *rájabhis*, by kings; *rájasu*, in or amongst kings; but keeps it in the vocative, as *rájan*, oh king. The other applications do not occur in the volume at all, as the work does not comprehend the construction of derivatives and compounds, in which the final of *rájan* is equally lost, as *rájya rájatva*, royalty; *rája-dharma*, the duty of a king. Had these exemplifications been attached to the rule, the obscurity would have been dissipated, and a definite and permanent impression of a very extensively useful precept would have been effected. Where, however, familiarity with the arrangement and with the phraseology is acquired, Mr. Colebrooke's grammar becomes of inestimable value from its extreme precision and remarkable comprehensiveness. The rules provide most accurately, and in the shortest possible space, for every contingency of inflexion, whether of nouns or verbs.

Although not exactly in the order of publication, yet it will be convenient, whilst yet in the regions of the East, to notice two other productions of the Calcutta press upon the subject of Sanskrit grammar. The first of these was as early in point of compilation as either of its predecessors, having been prepared in 1804. The author, Mr. Forster, declares however, that subsequently to the appearance of the grammars of Carey and Colebrooke, he was so sensible of the inferiority of his own that he had allowed it to slumber longer in the press than was necessary, with a view to its eventual suppression. Mr. Forster was also a member of the Civil Service of Bengal, and was a distinguished Bengali scholar. He was a man of a vigorous and active mind, but without Mr. Colebrooke's scholarship and perspicacity, and of a more mechanical than even methodical turn. His work is entitled, 'An Essay on the Principles of Sanskrit Grammar',* and is

* 1 vol. 4to, Calcutta, 1810. Reviewed by Bopp in the 'Heidelberger Jahrbücher, 1818', No. XXX.

illustrative of the author's peculiarities, displaying great labour and considerable ingenuity. It is, to a great extent, an attempt to give a tabular form to Sanskrit grammar, the exemplifications of the rules for the permutation of letters, the inflexions of declension and conjugation, and the development of derivative verbs and nouns, being collected in tables to which the rules refer. The construction of these tables, the relations that some of them bear to others, and the connexion between them and the rules they exemplify, are not always happily contrived, and the complex and troublesome system of the references from the rules to the tables, and from one table to another, renders the work wholly unavailable for elementary study. It contains however a vast number of useful specifications, and may be occasionally consulted with benefit by riper students. The work, as far as printed, comprises the usual divisions of the grammar; but it was the intention of the author to have given a second volume, in which he was to have inserted a translation of the 'Mugdhabodha', the native grammar, which is the standard authority in Bengal, and which is ascribed to Vopadeva, a grammarian of the twelfth century.*

The other Sanskrit grammar published in Calcutta is of comparatively recent date. It is the work of Mr.

* There is, in the library of Trinity College, Cambridge, a neatly written copy of Mr. Forster's essay, including, it is believed, the materials of the second portion of his work.

Yates, a member of the Baptist mission, a body which for its number has furnished a greater proportion of first-rate Sanskrit and Bengali scholars than any other class of persons in Bengal. Mr. Yates's grammar is constructed upon the plan of popular European grammars, with a view to the simplification of the system and abridgement of time and labour in the acquirement. He has not altogether failed in his object, although it may be doubted if the principles of popular vernacular grammar be applicable to so copious and complicated a language as Sanskrit.* Mr. Yates's grammar forms a moderately sized octavo volume, and may be consulted with facility. It does not seem to have made much way in Europe, its necessity having been superseded by similar productions in this part of the world. At no time however, not even at the present, do any of the publications of the Anglo-Indian press penetrate through what may be termed, to use an Indian illustration, the bound-hedge of English literature.

When the Asiatic Society of Calcutta was first instituted, and for a few years following, the inquiries of our countrymen into the languages and literature of India seem to have excited some attention and interest. Much of this was owing to the European reputation of Sir William Jones, acquired in an English university, and maintained by his correspondence on

---

* Indische Bib., vol. II, p. 11.

oriental subjects with the most eminent of the continental orientalists. The novelty of the objects investigated, and the attractive though erroneous tendency of some of the Society's fancied verifications of ancient mythology and scriptural history, contributed also to awaken and to keep interest alive. The public mind was also then at leisure to receive new impressions, as little of novelty or importance in literature was offered for its amusement or instruction about the period when the first volume of the 'Asiatic Researches' appeared, or in 1788. In a very brief time, however, came the all-absorbing interest of the momentous events springing from the revolution in France, and when literature revived it assumed a more inviting form than archæological conjecture or philological speculation, busying themselves with a distant people and remote antiquity. It is not surprising therefore that no note was taken of the grammatical labours of Englishmen residing in the East, and that they found their way slowly and with difficulty even to the few who stood in need of their aid and longed for their appearance. A striking instance of this occurs in the case of the late Professor Chézy, who until 1810 had not heard of the existence of Carey's 'Sanskrit Grammar'. In the preface to his excellent edition and translation of 'Sakuntala' he has described, in an animated and interesting tone, the wretched means and the unremitting application by which he acquired his first knowledge of Sanskrit, and the delight with which he welcomed the bulky volume of Carey, and the more elegant and available grammar of Wilkins, which had been published in London at the end of 1808.*

The publication of the grammar of the late Sir Charles Wilkins constitutes an important era in the annals of Sanskrit philology. Its European origin and complexion, its distinct and elegant typography, and the higher merits of method and perspicuity, recommended its contents to the notice of continental scholars, and tempted as well as enabled them to embark in a study from which they had previously been repelled by the uncouth form and inadequate structure of the vessels provided for their conveyance. From the appearance of the grammar of Wilkins may be dated the impulse given to the cultivation of Sanskrit, and, as an obvious consequence, of comparative philology both in France and Germany, and the somewhat tardy, though it is to be hoped not unpromising, emulation which the labours of the philologists of the continent have at length aroused amongst ourselves.

Sir Charles Wilkins, like Colebrooke and Forster, reflects lustre upon the civil service of Bengal. Stimulated and encouraged by the example of Mr. Halhed, also a Bengal civilian, the first Englishman who directed his attention to Sanskrit, although better known by his

* "La bibliothèque du roi possédait bien à la vérité un essai informe du grammaire, un manuscrit composé, à ce que je crois, par quelque Missionnaire Portugais, mais ne renfermant que le paradigme du verbe substantif, le tableau de déclinaisons, une partie du vocabulaire d'Amera et une liste des dhatous; le tout fourmillant d'erreurs les plus grossières."

grammar of the Bengali language, Mr. Wilkins engaged about the year 1778 with ardour in the study, and, in despite of the absence of all elementary assistance, soon became profoundly acquainted with the structure of the language, and with its standard literature. An undeniable proof of the success which had rewarded his diligence was manifested in 1784 by the publication of his translation of the philosophical episode from the 'Mahábhárata', the 'Bhagavad Gítá', which was printed in London under the patronage of the Court of Directors, at the recommendation of the most illustrious governor-general that British India ever obeyed, Warren Hastings. The difficulty of acquiring the knowledge of a difficult language, such as Sanskrit, without any other appliances and means than grammars and lexicons in the language itself, and preceptors ignorant of English, and unfamiliar with our notions of elementary tuition, can be conceived by none but those who have been placed in similar circumstances. Fortunately the author's experience of the difficulty was brief, for had not the grammar of Sir C. Wilkins come to his rescue, whilst guessing at the obscurities of the 'Mugdhabodha' through the equally puzzling interpretation of a Paṅḋit, he would probably have relinquished the task in despair. Such as it was, the experiment qualified him to do justice to the perseverance and industry by which his precursors in the path have enabled others to follow their route. Upon the return of Mr. Wilkins to England, he brought with him translations of three popular native grammars, and from these, and other original authorities, he compiled a grammar, of which the first pages were printed in 1795. The types of the 'Devanágarí' letters employed were cut and cast under his personal direction; and for the more accurate execution of the work he set up a printing press in his own house. When his preparations were complete, and, as stated, the first pages of the grammar were printed, the house was set on fire; the manuscript books, matrices and punches were saved, but the types and press were destroyed, and the prosecution of the work was stopped. So many causes of delay retarded its resumption, that Mr. Wilkins at last had determined to abandon his design, when the establishment of the East India College at Haileybury supplied him with a sufficient inducement to renew and complete his labours. The grammar was accordingly finished, and was published towards the close of 1808.

The general plan of Wilkins's grammar is, like that of his predecessors, suggested by the arrangement of native grammarians. To the alphabet and laws of Sandhi succeed the declension of nouns in the order of their final letters, and then the declension of pronouns. The conjugation of verbs, simple and derivative, follows, and then the formation of participles and analogous nouns. The remaining chapters treat of the formation of miscellaneous derivative nouns, of indeclinable words, of the construction of compounds, and of the genders of nouns, and the work ends with the syntax.

The main objects, which Mr. Wilkins professes to have had in view in the classification of his grammar and the enunciation of its precepts, are perspicuity and correctness, and it must be admitted that, with some few exceptions of comparatively trivial importance, he has accomplished both. The principal defects of the grammar are an insufficient provision of general principles, and in some respects an inconvenient classification. The examples are numerous, and for the most part well selected, but the rules which they exemplify do not adequately define existing analogies of construction, a knowledge of which is essential to reduce, connect and simplify what in its present state appears as a somewhat unwieldy and unretainable mass of incoherent details. An unnecessary multiplication of declensions is one consequence of this want of a connecting principle. In the conjugation of the verbs the separation of the four tenses, to which the analogy of conjugational modification is restricted, from the other six tenses, which according to the author are common to all conjugations, scatters the component members of an individual body over a number of pages, so as to render it a matter of extreme difficulty, and to a beginner almost an impossibility, to trace and reunite them so as to form an entire verb. It is to be remarked, as a consequence of this plan, that the whole grammar does not furnish a solitary example of an entire verb inflected throughout in its various moods, tenses, and persons, an omission that is particularly embarassing to a beginner. In regard to the indefinite preterite tense, one of the most perplexing parts of conjugation, an attempt has been made to reduce its multiform construction to a fixed number of modes, but not with much success, as no general principle has been laid down, whilst it is very evident that all the essential modifications are resolvable into no more than two, or that this tense comprehends the præter-pluperfect and the aorist past—the inflexions of each of which are diversified upon principles not difficult to be detected. The chapters on the derivation of words are totally devoid of method, and it might be objected to them that the examples are needlessly copious, but that, as no printed dictionary of the language existed when the grammar was published, this copiousness of words was of infinite value, as in some degree supplying the deficiency. Finally, is may be objected to the chapter on syntax, that it is not so ample as could be wished, nor are the illustrations in general interesting or striking; notwithstanding these exceptions, however, the justice of which may possibly be with reason called in question, the grammar of Sir C. Wilkins is undeniably a work of great merit and utility, and must ever be regarded as of standard authority.*

---

* Schlegel thus speaks of it: "Finally, Wilkins has with uncommon clearness and ingenuity reduced, if I may use the expression, the Algebra of Sanskrit grammar to familiar arithmetic. It is true that we miss many things in his book, the absence of which, considering the large scale on which the work is planned, cannot well be excused. His terminology also is not always hap-

The facilities now afforded by the grammatical works on Sanskrit published in the English language were immediately and zealously applied by men of the highest literary character upon the continent to the acquirement of a knowledge of the language and literature of the Hindus. The success that attended their diligence was speedily displayed in the publication of various interesting disquisitions, either upon subjects of a general nature, or the structure and affinities of the language, especially by those accomplished scholars, Frederick and Augustus Schlegel, by Professors Chézy of Paris, Bopp of Berlin, and Frank of Munich. Some time, however, elapsed before a complete Sanskrit grammar was attempted.

The first Sanskrit grammar published on the continent, after the publication of Wilkins's grammar in England, and the arrival in Europe of the grammars published in Calcutta, was the work of the late Professor Othmar Frank,* then attached to the University

---

pily chosen; but nevertheless, as a beginning, the grammar is exceedingly convenient and serviceable."—*Ind. Bib.* [I, p. 10]. Burnouf observes: "Parmi ces ouvrages (the different Anglo-Sanskrit grammars) c'est encore celui de Wilkins qu'on peut consulter avec le plus de fruit, et quelques reproches que l'on soit en droite de lui adresser il reste encore comme un beau monument du savoir de la patience de l'auteur."—*Journ. As.* Mai 1825. He quotes also Chézy's opinions, as expressed in the 'Moniteur', 1810, No. 30, and says, "qu'il n'a pas trop dit quand il parle de l'étonnante perfection qui règne dans ce travail, et quand il ajoute que malgré quelques fautes il n'est pas moins digne de l'admiration et de la reconnaissance des savants."

* "Grammatica Sanskrita: edidit Othmarus Frank."

of Wurtzburgh, a scholar of the most extensive erudition, and a critic of the most candid and amiable temperament, but whose judgment was sometimes carried away by that turn for metaphysical speculation which is not uncommon amongst his countrymen. From the cultivation of Persian literature and philosophy he passed with avidity to Sanskrit philology and metaphysics, and in the former department took the lead in the compilation of a grammar for German students. It was written in Latin, and published at Wurtzburgh in 1823. The want of a fount of moveable types compelled the author to have recourse to lithography to represent the Devanágarí letters; and as they were not written in the best style, nor always accurately, they are very injurious to the appearance of the volume and inconvenient in use. Professor Frank acknowledged his obligations to the works of Colebrooke and Wilkins, but he had also consulted the original grammars printed in Calcutta, which by this time had reached Europe—the 'Sútras' of Páńini, and the 'Siddhánta Kaumudí'. He has however chiefly followed the arrangement of Wilkins, modifying, it may be doubted if judiciously, the order of the declensions, and abridging, but not always improving, the chapters on conjugation and derivation. He is equally deficient in the enunciation of general principles, and his rules are assertions of the bare fact that words assume certain forms, without any attempt to explain how or why. His principal additions consist of tables exhibiting the inflexional changes of nouns and verbs in a convenient and readily consulted manner. The table of conjugations however limits the paradigms of nine out of the ten classes of verbs to the persons of the present tense of the indicative mood, and is of proportionably restricted usefulness. This part of the grammar is open to the objection made to that of Wilkins, that the tenses are distributed in various places, accordingly as they are formed with what Prof. Frank denominates primary or secondary inflexions,* and that no example is given in the whole grammar of an entire verb. Prof. Frank has taken some pains to explain the meaning of the principal grammatical terms used by native grammarians, derived chiefly from Carey. He has also attempted to build upon the doctrines of the original authorities a theory of the language generally, and of the analogous construction and offices of the different parts of speech, but he has not developed his views in sufficient detail, or with sufficient distinctness, to admit of their being fully comprehended; and it may be doubted, as he has not specified his authorities, whether the original grammarians have anywhere suggested, what he imagines he discovers in them, a typical genius of the language, or its relation to the distinctions of matter and spirit. Speculations of this nature were favourite themes with Prof. Frank, and have sometimes perhaps impaired the beneficial results of his unquestionable abilities, industry, and learning.

* "Flexus primi," "F. secundarii."

The grammar by which German scholars have been chiefly introduced to the acquirement of Sanskrit in their several universities, is that of Prof. Bopp of Berlin. This, which was originally written in German,* was published in parts at the several dates of 1824, 1825, and 1827. The Professor's own Latin version† of the more considerable portion was published in 1829, and the remainder, with some emendations and improvements, in 1832. The grammar was again published in an abridged and amended form in 1834. This last edition is, like the first, in German.

The first German edition, and the first part of the Latin version, were founded, the author states, upon the grammars of Wilkins and Forster; and he expresses his opinion that the structure of the language may be more fully developed from the materials which they furnish than from any advantage or assistance derivable from the study of the native Sanskrit grammarians. This avowed depreciation of the authorities on which the works that served Prof. Bopp as guides were declaredly based,‡ contrasted with the title he

* "Ausführliches Lehrgebäude der Sanskrit Sprache".

† "Grammatica Critica Linguæ Sanskritæ".

‡ "Cum grammaticam hanc conscribere instituerem, magnaque viderem Wilkinsii et Forsteri de lingua Sanscrita merita, facile intellexi, has litteras non tam accuratiori et copiosiori Grammaticorum indigenarum studio augeri et adjuvari posse, quam libera adhibita critica arte, quæ rationem et leges, quibus lingua in formationibus suis sit usa, examinare et explicare studeat." [See Lassen's criticism in the "Indische Bibliothek", III, p. 22 ff.]

had given to his own work of 'A Critical Grammar', has exposed him to some rather severe animadversion on the part of his countrymen; one good effect of which, however, was to induce Prof. Bopp to direct his attention to the original grammar of Páńini at least, and to enrich the second portion of his Latin version, and the second German edition of his work, with many important observations derived from that source. It may be doubted, however, if the prejudice which he seems to have early contracted against native grammarians has not been injurious to the comprehensiveness of his views and the perspicuity of his arrangement.

Although entitled an abridgement, the last German edition of Prof. Bopp's 'Grammar' can scarcely be regarded as an abbreviation, except typographically. It is printed in a smaller type and more compact shape, but it contains much additional matter, and the differences which it exhibits are rather alterations than omissions or curtailments. The grammar has, in fact, been remodelled in many important respects, and so materially improved, that it may be considered to have superseded the earlier editions; as it also presents the author's latest conclusions upon the subject, it will be sufficient to confine our attention to a brief notice of this particular publication.*

The general arrangement of Bopp's 'Grammar' conforms to that of Wilkins's, but differs in some of the

* [The second edition appeared in 1845, and the third in 1863.]

details. To the account of the alphabet succeed the rules of literal combination, or *Sandhi*, or as they are termed of Euphony. Under this head, however, Bopp has included changes not simply euphonic, nor properly comprised within the limits of combination as proposed by the original grammarians. The terms *Sandhi* or *Sanhitá*, which are applied to this portion of grammar, both denote a holding together, a coalescence or combination, which can, of course, alone take place between two or more letters when they are in contact or contiguity. The object proposed by such laws of combination is, to avoid any harshness or hiatus occasioned by the actual or proximate concurrence of incongruous sounds. Prof. Bopp has extended his rules to changes which occur in single letters in the middle of words, having no regard whatever to the sounds by which they are preceded or followed, but dependent upon inflexional provisions, upon laws affecting declension and conjugation. How far these are to be treated as merely euphonic changes may admit of question, but most assuredly they are not changes resulting from the contact or contiguity of incongruous letters, and are so far inconsistently included under the denomination *Sandhi*. It may be convenient to bring these literal changes together under one head, and anticipate in some degree the laws of inflexion; but on the other hand, it confounds things essentially different, and is a departure from the precision and simplicity of the original system.

Some remarks on the character of Sanskrit roots,

and the prepositions with which they combine to form compound verbs, precede the chapters on declension. In the earlier editions, Prof. Bopp, after specifying the general principles upon which nouns were inflected, classed them under six declensions, but in the last edition he has reduced these to one, to which he has subjoined a long series of what he designates as irregular nouns, classing them in the order of the declensions of Wilkins according to their final letters. The reduction of all nouns to one declension is perfectly consistent with the doctrines of the native grammarians and with their scheme of terminations, which is more or less applicable to every case of nominal inflexion. It may be doubted, however, if the irregular nouns of Bopp can be always regarded as deviations from rule, and their being given separately prevents their analogy of construction, mutually or universally, from being so evident as it might be. There are two principal sources of varieties in inflexion, changes of those letters or syllables which are subjoined to the inflective word or base to express cases or persons, and changes of the inflective word or base itself. The former constitute the essence of declension, and there is little irregularity in them. The changes of the base are peculiar either to individuals or to classes of nouns, but in the latter are founded on common principles, and these can scarcely be denominated irregularities. Prof. Bopp has not thought it necessary to advert to this distinction, attaching little or no importance to the scheme of terminations given in original grammars;

he has looked to the inflected noun, not in its elements, but as a whole, and has considered any special modifications which it may undergo as deviations from general rules. This method is, no doubt, more conformable to European notions, but it appears to be less simple and less easy of recollection than that of the original authorities.

The declensions of adjectives, numerals and pronouns follow those of substantive nouns, and useful tables are inserted in all the editions exhibiting the forms of various nouns in their several cases, in a convenient and serviceable manner.

The subject of conjugation is next treated of. More importance is here attached to the technical inflexional terminations of the original system than was assigned to those of declension. It may be questioned however if even in this instance the terminations are sufficiently prominent. There is also a departure from the technical scheme even as represented by Wilkins, in omitting without remark the indicatory letters of the terminations, that is, certain letters added to the actual termination which are not used to construct the inflexions, but which denote certain invariable modifications of the base to which the inflexional terminations are attached. Thus the terminations of the three persons singular of the present tense are called by Bopp *mi*, *si*, *ti*; in original works they are *mip*, *sip*, *tip*. The *p* is indicatory, signifying that, for the radical vowel of the base, a Guńa letter or diphthong is to be substituted, which substitution does not take place before the terminations of the dual *vas*, *thas*, *tas*, or of the plural *mas*, *tha*, *anti*. Is is true that this is an instance of what Schlegel calls the Algebra of Sanskrit grammar, and the use of such indicatory letters is purely technical and arbitrary. But what else than technical and arbitrary are significant words when they are employed in a specific and conventional acceptation? Instead of the Sanskrit sign *p*, the presence of which requires a definite change, and the absence of which prohibits that change, Prof. Bopp is obliged to propose different words for the two contingencies, and to give to those words significations which they do not naturally bear, in order to apply them to the object in view, and which senses are in this application of the words merely conventional. Those personal terminations before which the vowel of the base may be changed he calls light—*leichte*—*leves*; those before which it is unchanged he terms heavy—*schwere*—*graves*. It is obvious that these terms can convey, *à priori*, a no more precise notion of the influence exercised by the terminations upon the base than any given letter or syllable. Until explained their purport is unintelligible, and they have this disadvantage, that when explained their fitness is liable to be disputed. What is the meaning of a light or heavy syllable? Why is *mi* lighter than *mas*, *ti* than *tha*? The single indicatory letter, the algebraic sign, has its conventional significancy and no other, and its intention being once defined, it cannot be mistaken or misapplied. However unphilosophical therefore it may be thought, the short-hand of the Sanskrit grammarians has in these respects a decided advantage over the proposed designations. It has its own office and no other.

In the classification he first adopted, Prof. Bopp distributed the verbs amongst four conjugations. In his last work he reduces the number to two, which is an improvement. He follows however, in regard to the tenses, the same course as Wilkins, dividing the four conjugationals, which he calls special, from the other six, which he terms general. The rules which he prescribes for the structure of the former under their several classes or conjugations, are illustrated by comparatively few examples, but he has added useful tables of the personal terminations of both orders of tenses, so that the construction of a complete verb may be effected with comparative facility. It is however in this part of Sanskrit grammar that the only serious difficulty lies. The peculiarities in the modifications of verbal bases, not of the terminations, are so numerous and anomalous, that when they are scattered over a wide space, and are to be picked up piece-meal, they are very apt to elude the search, and slip from the recollection of the student. It seems preferable therefore to adopt the arrangement observed by Mr. Colebrooke with regard to the first class of verbs, and give examples of all those most frequently recurring, in paradigms, more or less copious, according to the circumstances of each verb. The peculiarities of every verb are thus brought together under their common original, and that may be readily remembered as a whole which can scarcely be acquired by the separate contemplation of its *disjecta membra.* Prof. Bopp seems to have felt this difficulty, and in order to enable the student of his Grammar to advert more promptly to an anomalous construction in various instances, he has added to the conjugations an alphabetical list of what he terms irregular verbs, with numerical references to the paragraph in which the irregularity is described. The cases may be thus more easily referred to, no doubt, but such reference implies previous knowledge of the irregularity. The reader must know, for instance, that the verb *Anja* does offer an anomaly, before he attempts to find what that anomaly may be. In fact, he must have already learnt, although he may have forgotten it, and the index is therefore only a supplement to the recollection. Upon the whole, although it cannot be denied that Prof. Bopp's treatment of this branch of his subject is much more satisfactory than that of his predecessors, Mr. Colebrooke excepted, it leaves much to be desired.

As a specimen of Prof. Bopp's mode of dealing with the conjugation of Sanskrit verbs, the following view which he takes of the personal inflexions may be cited.

1. "The characteristic signs of the persons are the following:—The first person has in the singular and plural *m*, and in the dual *v*, the connexion of which, with the essential elements of the first personal pronoun, or *m* in different cases of the singular, and *v* in the nominatives of the dual and plural numbers, as

explained in a preceding passage, is very obvious. In the imperative singular of the active voice the first person substitutes *n* for *m*, and the deponent voice drops the consonant in all the persons of the singular number, so that *me* becomes *e*; *ma* becomes *a*; *mi* becomes *i*, and *ai* is substituted for *mai* or *nai*. The syllable *as* in the plural ending *mas* is, I doubt not, identical with the termination of the plural nominative of *as*, since the personal endings of the verb correspond as to their purport to the nominatives of nouns. The termination *mas* is therefore to be resolved into *m* and *as*, and the latter appears also in the terminations of the first person dual *vas*, as *ad-vas*, we two eat.*

"The dual termination of the nominatives of nouns, or *au*, is derived from *as*, of which it is merely an emphatic amplification. (Comp. Gr. § 206.) The abbreviated terminations *ma*, *va*, in the subordinate tenses, are dependent upon the unabridged terminations *mas*, *vas*, as neuters on masculines and feminines. (Ibid. § 231.) As neuter, and in fact dualistic, the dual endings of the middle voice *áthe*, *áte*, are in my opinion to be considered as agreeing with the nominative dual of regular neuter nouns, the primitive of which ends in *a*. So *te* from *áte* is identical with

* [It is needless to state that some of the views quoted above have been considerably modified in the two later editions of the Sanskrit grammar, and in the second German edition of the Comparative Grammar.]

the isolated pronoun *te*, they or those two, formed from *ta* with the affix *i*. Also *te* and *the* agree with the masculine nominatives plural of the pronouns through the analogies comprehended in rule 243-4.

2. "The second person has, through all varieties of number and tense, these characteristic elements, *t*, *th*, *dhv*, *dh*, *h*, *sv*, *s*, of which the last is the widest deviation from the pronominal primitives *tva*, *tve*, subordinate from *te* (in like manner as *συ* is formed out of *τυ*, and *σι* third person out of *τι*); the closest analogy to the pronoun being *dhve*, *dhvam*, of the Átmanepada, the *v* of which, again, in the second person of the imperative singular is connected with *s*, as *sva*. *S* in truth predominates in the singular, as *tudasi*, thou tormentest; *atudas*, thou hast tormented, &c. *Th* and *dh* are common substitutions for *t*, as *prathama* for *pra-tama*, the first; *adh-ara* for *a-tara*, lower; and *adhama* for *a-tama*, lowest: as further exemplifications of these in the second person take the following. From *tud*, active voice, second preterite, second person singular, *tutoditha*; present, second person dual, *tudathas*; plural, *tudatha*; middle voice, present, second person plural, *tudadhve*; imperfect, second person singular, *tudasva*. *Ad* in the second person singular imperative makes *ad-dhi*. The transition of *as* into the dual ending *thas*, and *as* in the third person into *tas*, depends upon the same principle as the formation of *mas* and *vas* in the first person of the plural and dual numbers, that is, it is the annexation of the plural termination of the nominative case of nouns to the

especial sign of the third personal pronoun, as they were of the same termination to the signs of the first and second personal pronouns *m* and *v*.

3. "The third person has, in the three numbers in both voices where the terminations undergo no contraction, the letter *t* for its characteristic element, the conformity of which with the pronominal *t* is as open as day. The development of *ám* in the dual of the potential, &c., we elucidate through the principle of *ávám*, we two; *yu-vám*, ye two; as also in the second and third persons of the Atmanepada, the endings *áthám* and *átám*."

The chapters on conjugation in Prof. Bopp's grammar contain some interesting analogies between the Sanskrit and Greek inflexions of the verb, but these belong to the subject of comparative philology. There is also some bold and ingenious theory upon the construction of some of the general tenses, such as the two futures and the conditional, which he regards as compounded, not simple tenses; also of the complete development of the substantive verb *as*, esse, to be; which is always considered elsewhere as defective. Some of Prof. Bopp's views are rather startling at first, but they are not therefore to be hastily rejected, and may upon further investigation prove to be well-founded.

Consideration is also due to Bopp's theory of the formation of the infinitive mood, which Sanskrit grammarians always treat as a verbal derivative indeclinable noun; also to his views of the formation of the indeclinable past participle ending in *twá* and *ya*, and the adverbial participle ending in *am*. All these are regarded by Bopp as the objective or instrumental cases of nouns, of which the other cases are defective or obsolete, although traceable possibly in the ancient Sanskrit of the Vedas, of which he has given some proofs; others may be perhaps discovered when our acquaintance with the texts of the Vedas is more extensive.

After disposing of those derivatives, which are commonly held by us to be parts of a verb, the Grammar proceeds to describe other verbal derivatives, to which, as well as to the preceding, Bopp gives the name of Primitives. To them succeed derivative words formed from nouns, as patronymics, possessives, and the like. In both classes he has adopted an arrangement equally simple and convenient—an alphabetical list of the suffixes employed by native grammarians to construct derivative upon primitive words, illustrated by examples of the words formed upon this principle. In doing this, however, Prof. Bopp has omitted what might by some be considered as the most useful part of the classification. These suffixes, as well as those used in forming the inflexions of declension and conjugation, are composed of two elements, the letter or letters which are really added to or substitnted for the original ending of the base, and a letter or letters which are merely indicatory of certain changes in the body of the base: the latter Prof. Bopp omits. Thus, in the first part of his Taddhita, or nominal derivatives, he gives the letter *a* as forming patronymics, abstracts, collectives and adjectives from primitive nouns, as *vásishtha*, son of Vasishtha; *sauhrida*, friendship, from *suhrid*, a friend; *kápota*, a flock of pigeons, from *kapota*, a pigeon; *rájata*, silver or silvery, from *rajata*, the metal, silver. In these examples it will be noticed the original short vowel of the base is transmuted to a long vowel or diphthong; it is exchanged, in technical language, for its vríddhi, or augmented substitute. The rule that says such change takes place has to provide for each separate case separately, but in the notation of the original scheme it is a general rule that an indicatory nasal of the cerebral class in any suffix whatever denotes the increase or vríddhi of the vowel of the base. Accordingly, the affix is here said to be not *a*, but *ań*, the *ń* being the indicatory, the *a* the essential element; consequently, *ań* being applied to the words particularized, *a* is either added to or substituted for the proper termination of the primitive, the radical vowel of which also undergoes a definite modification. There is another important considera-tion to recommend the preservation of the indicatory letter. The essential letter of a suffix may be the same, but the effect upon the base may be different; in one instance its addition may require, in another prohibit, any change of the radical vowel; two opposite results proceeding from the same adjunct, as it stands in Bopp's scheme. The cause of the difference is at once seen when the indicatory letter is inserted and its influence is known. Derivatives formed with *a* alone may or mày not change the vowel of the base, but those formed with *aṅ* do require the change; those formed with *aṅ*, or *a*, and the nasal of the guttural class of consonants, never admit it. *Śiva* with *aṅ* must make *śaiva*; *chiti* with *aṅ* makes *chintá*. It would therefore have been of benefit to the student, as furnishing him with a key to similarity and dissimilarity of derivation, if the indicatory had been added to the essential elements in the alphabetical lists of the suffixes.

The chapters on derivation are followed by those on compound nouns and indeclinables; no chapter on syntax is included in either of the editions. The author in the first edition announced his purpose of delaying it until after the publication of the glossary to his edition of Nalus. It has not yet however appeared, and no notice is taken of the omission in the last edition. The subject could not fail to derive interesting and important elucidation from Prof. Bopp, although, as he justly observes, Sanskrit syntax may be disposed of in a very moderate compass, as the principles of construction are for the most part conformable to those of general grammar or the grammars of kindred languages, and rarely deviate from the limits prescribed by the nature of its own copious and perfect system of grammatical forms.*

---

* "Syntaxin nondum absolvere potui, ne tamen extensum hac de re opus expectent lectores; Sanskrita enim lingua apud antiquiores inprimis auctores locupletissimæ et perfectissimæ suæ

From this brief and necessarily imperfect sketch of the Sanskrit grammar of Prof. Bopp, it will no doubt be evident that he has treated the subject with profound attention, and has given to Sanskrit students a most valuable and instructive work. The last edition is in particular to be recommended as a compendious and comprehensive guide to the study of Sanskrit grammar, and it fully merits the character which was given to the first edition of it by another distinguished German scholar and critic, Prof Lassen, when adverting to the authorities which Prof. Bopp professed to have followed; he described it as more systematic than the grammar of Wilkins, more perspicuous than that of Forster, and more concise than either.

But one other grammar remained to be mentioned, concerning which the author could say little, as it was his own. It was published in 1841.* Its especial object is to render the acquirement of Sanskrit easy to beginners. How far this is effected remains to be determined. From the remarks which had been hazarded upon some portions of Prof. Bopp's Grammar, it would be readily inferred that the author had made more use than Prof. Bopp had done of the methods of native

grammaticæ raro transgreditur fines a natura constitutos, ita, ut qui ea repetere noluerit quæ ad generalis grammaticæ pertinent principia, et eodem jure in cujusvis alius ex eadem familia linguæ compendio locum habeant, 'paucis capitibus absolvat syntaxin Sanskritam."

* [Second edition 1847.]

grammarians, and he had only to hope that he might not thereby have merited the sentence which was pronounced upon Mr. Colebrooke's Grammar, that "whilst it is of value as an introduction to the study of native grammars, it is insufficient and excessively obscure as a grammar of the language."

Several works connected with the objects of the grammars which have been adverted to, and which are in an especial degree subservient to the acquirement of the Sanskrit language, have been compiled and published by European authors regarding the Sanskrit radicals. Lists of these are attached to Carey's 'Sanskrit Grammar', and to his 'Bengali Dictionary', and as identical with verbs they are particularized by Wilkins and Forster. The former also published a separate work, in which the roots are arranged in alphabetical order, with the meaning as expressed in original lists, the translation of the original term, a short sentence illustrative of its use, and the indicatory letters denoting peculiarities of conjugation. The chief defects of this publication are occasional inaccuracies and general poverty of exemplification.

A work of a similar purport, but superior execution, was subsequently published by the late Dr. Rosen, and was characterized by that ability, judgement, and learning which he displayed still more conspicuously in his edition and version of the first part of the 'Rigveda', and which have ensured to his too brief career the admiration and regret of all Sanskrit scholars. In this compilation the roots are arranged alphabetically by their final and then their initial letters. Their Sanskrit equivalents, as given by two standard native writers, Káśináthа and Vopadeva, are inserted and translated by the Latin infinitive. The classes in which they are conjugated are specified, and short paradigms of the principal tenses are supplied. The most novel and useful feature of the work is the exemplification of the senses of the radicals as they occur in their inflected forms in short but well-chosen passages extracted from the different books which had been printed at the period when the work of Dr. Rosen was compiled. The same plan of illustration is then adapted to another and important novelty, the most useful of the compound verbs, or those in which the inseparable prepositions are prefixed to the radicals, constituting the great body of the verbs that occur in Sanskrit compositions. The examples are referred to the originals whence they are extracted, and are translated into Latin with fidelity and elegance.

A still more elaborate description of Sanskrit radicals has been subsequently published. It was printed at Bonn in 1841, and is the work of Mr. Westergaard, a young but distinguished scholar, whose ardour in the cause of Sanskrit has induced him to repair to India in order to prosecute his studies to still higher proficiency. He has deservedly received for this purpose the patronage of the Danish government. The materials of his list of roots were derived from this country. Mr. Westergaard laboured for some time with most extraordinary diligence in the Library of the East India

Company, and drew his information and examples chiefly from the manuscript volumes of the Company's collection. The roots are arranged alphabetically according to their final and initial letters. The class and voice in which each is conjugated are specified, and a paradigm more or less complete, according as authorities warrant the forms, is available. The meanings are then stated and exemplified by citations from published and unpublished texts, and the structure and use of the derivative verbs are also shown and exemplified. To them succeeds the series of compound verbs according to the order of their prefixes, with passages illustrating their application. Reference to the authorities whence the forms and examples are derived is constant and careful. As the examples are very numerous, and as no facilities exist in Sanskrit manuscripts, such as verbal indices, or any similar auxiliars, the labour and research by which they were collected must have been very great and persevering. They are for the most part judiciously selected, but they are not translated, and this is a serious drawback from the value of the compilation; for passages detached from the context of a work not familiarly known and not easily accessible do not always admit of ready and confident interpretation. It would no doubt have materially augmented Mr. Westergaard's trouble to have given translations of all the passages he has quoted, but it would have proportionably enhanced the usefulness and interest of the compilation if he had followed Dr. Rosen's example in this respect. A translation by himself is also necessary to support his rendering of the purport of a simple or compound verb, and secure its being acquiesced in by others. It is of infinite importance in the early stages of Sanskrit study, that in all books of an elementary character radical words should be rendered by unquestionable and unexceptionable European equivalents. When the native grammarians give the sense of a radical by a word of obvious import, then the European interpreter is tolerably safe, although even here he may be unlucky in his translation, and fail to make use of the most appropriate expression. When, however, he has to deduce the sense of a radical from his own understanding of some of its inflexions as they occur in composition, and where usage, licence, or metaphor may have given their own colouring to the primitive signification, it is very possible that the translator may mistake or may be misled as to the sense, and confound a lax or general with a literal and particular meaning. It is true that Mr. Westergaard defines the sense which he ascribes to the verb that he inserts as he understands its use in the example quoted, but then comes the question whether he has understood the passage rightly; the answer to which, although no doubt in most instances affirmative, may sometimes be given with doubt and hesitation.

Of subordinate contributions to the elucidation of Sanskrit grammar, independently of the attempts made to illustrate such original works as have been printed in Europe, or to develope the affinities of the language, the author could offer but a brief and passing intimation. They are scattered through a variety of continental publications on Oriental or general literature, many of which are little known in this country, and of various merits and character, from the Transactions of the Imperial Academy of St. Petersburgh to the 'Mercure de France' of Paris. Amongst the richest in articles on Sanskrit philology, not comparative, may be especially noticed a periodical conducted by the illustrious William Augustus von Schlegel, the 'Indische Bibliothek', a work which has been discontinued for some years. Its place in Germany has been latterly taken by a periodical of a more comprehensive character, the 'Zeitschrift für die Kunde des Morgenlandes', embracing the literature of the East, not of India alone, and conducted by an association of the most eminent German oriental scholars. In the former of these collections may be especially particularized, 1. the observations of Prof. Schlegel himself upon the actual state of Sanskrit philology in 1820;* and 2. a general view of the state of Sanskrit literature in 1824;† 3. a remarkable and most elaborate dissertation on the verbal derivatives formed with the suffixes *Ya* and *Twá*, intended to establish their analogy to the gerunds of the Latin verb by Baron William von Humboldt;‡ and 4. a review of Prof. Bopp's Grammar by Prof. Lassen.§ In the 'Zeitschrift' we have a theory of the

* Vol. I, p. 1. † Vol. II, p. 1. ‡ Vol. I, part 4, and Vol. II, part 1. § [Vol. III, p. 1.]

formation of compound nouns with the interrogative pronoun by Dr. Nesselmann, and a paper on the substitution of the cerebral for the dental nasal under certain circumstances, by Dr. Boehtlingk. There are no doubt communications of like tendency and value in other collections with which I am unacquainted. The 'Journal Asiatique' of the Asiatic Society of Paris is less rich in contributions to Sanskrit philology than to other branches of Asiatic literature.

Less has been attempted in the collateral branch of lexicography than in grammar. The character of native lexicons will be more particularly adverted to on some other occasion. It would be sufficient at present to state that they correspond in their arrangement to vocabularies as we employ the term, rather than to dictionaries, the words being classed in them according to analogy of meaning without regard to alphabetical order. They omit also many words of popular currency, as being too familiar to need explanation, and withhold consequently much that is most wanted by a European student. The best work of the class was selected at an early period for publication and translation by Mr. Colebrooke. The 'Amara Kosha', or lexicon of Amara Sinha, was printed at Serampore in 1808, accompanied by a marginal translation into English, by illustrations and additions derived from the numerous commentaries on the original text, and by a most useful alphabetical index. A reprint of the text with a French translation at the foot of the page has recently been published at Paris; the work of a young and highly promising Sanskrit scholar, also prematurely lost to the cultivation of Hindu literature, M. Loiseleur des Longchamps.

At the same time that the vocabulary of Amara Sinha was published, a dictionary on a more extended scale, and alphabetically arranged, was compiled, under the instructions of Mr. Colebrooke and the immediate supervision of one of the most celebrated native scholars in Bengal, by a number of Paṅḋits. The main object of this compilation was to bring together the contents of as many of the original Koshas, or vocabularies as were procurable, to arrange them in alphabetical order, and add their etymology, according to grammatical authorities. Soon after its completion the author obtained a copy of this work, and having carefully collated all the words with the authorities whence they were taken, incorporated with them the whole of the radicals as well as other words omitted in the compilation, and transferred the etymologies from the Bengali to the Benares terminology. He made a translation of the work, and with the encouragement of the Bengal government published it in 1819. The plan of the original compilation necessarily left many deficiencies. Shortly before he left India, however, he had an opportunity of making more extensive additions, which remedied in some degree the imperfections of the first edition, although no doubt still leaving many accessions to be made. This second edition was published in 1832. Such as it is, this dictionary is the only one yet published; and although no person could be more sensible than the author how far it falls short of such a lexicon as the study of Sanskrit demands, yet he had the satisfaction of knowing that it had materially contributed to the extension of a knowledge of Sanskrit in Europe. Although no other dictionary has been published, its place has in a great measure been supplied by useful glossaries attached to some of the books edited by European scholars, particularly by Prof. Bopp in the glossary to his edition of 'Nalus', and Prof. Johnson of the East India College in his editions recently published of the first book of the 'Hitopadeśa', 'Selections from the Maháblárata', and 'Megha Dúta'. Prof. Bopp is also engaged upon a glossary on a large scale, of which the first part only is published. When glossaries of this kind, and when verbal indices to standard works shall have been sufficiently multiplied, it will then be comparatively easy to compile a Sanskrit dictionary that shall place its compiler on a level with Facciolati or Stephens.

The author had thus endeavoured to bring before the Society a general view of the advance that had been made in the rudimental cultivation of Sanskrit philology; and it would probably be admitted, even from this brief and imperfect notice, that, considering the period within which the study of Sanskrit had been prosecuted by Europeans, the progress had been creditable, and that no lack of intelligence or activity had been displayed in clearing away the impediments by which the first steps of the acquirement were beset. The facilities provided were no doubt far from sufficient; the approach might still be embarrassed by perplexing labyrinths, dark passages and cumbrous obstructions; the first labours of the pioneer must be necessarily rough and incomplete; but the path had been laid open, and it remained for succeeding exertions to smooth, to level, and to embellish it.

XV.

REVIEW

OF

PROFESSOR MAX MÜLLER'S "HISTORY

OF

ANCIENT SANSKRIT LITERATURE".

Second Edition, London: 1860.

From the Edinburgh Review, Oct. 1860, p. 361-85.

TOWARDS the close of the last century great interest was excited, among the scholars of Europe, by the information that the Hindus are in possession of a sacred literature which is the most ancient and authentic in the world, and which exhibits a view of the creation and government of the universe wholly subversive of the records on which Christianity was founded. This literature is embodied in a work, or series of works, collectively termed the 'Veda', written in an old dialect of Sanskrit known to only a few of the most learned of the Brahmans—a class who at that time regarded Europeans with mixed feelings of terror and contempt, and whom no inducement whatever could prevail upon to communicate to strangers and outcasts any knowledge of their venerated scriptures.

The curiosity thus excited was naturally further stimulated by the difficulty of its gratification, and repeated efforts were made to break through the barrier, but without success; in the genuine native spirit evasion was grafted upon direct refusal, and fraud was had recourse to to appease the eagerness of the European inquirer, who was ill qualified to detect imposition. Thus Mr. Holwell,* in his 'Interesting Historical Events', published in 1766, gives a long account of what he terms the contents of the 'Chartah Bhade' and 'Aughtorrah Bhade', intending thereby the 'Chatwára Veda', or four Vedas, and 'Aṭhárah Veda', eighteen Vedas; the latter being no Vedas at all, but the eighteen Puráńas, from which the particulars he details are evidently derived through a very inaccurate medium in Persian or Hindustani. He also affirms that a translation of the Vedas existed by Baldæus, a chaplain in the service of the Dutch East-India Company, in Ceylon, in 1760: this is equally inaccurate—no such translation was ever published: in the description of Malabar and Ceylon, published by the learned chaplain, in 1762, he has a chapter on the 'Afgoderey der Oost Indische Heydener'; but this, like Holwell's own account, represents the mythology of the Hindus agreeably to the Puráńas, modified by popular superstitions and practices. Again, Colonel Dow, in the preface to his History of Hindustan, published in 1768, prints as specimens of the Vedas a few verses which are in reality taken from a work on rhetoric. Mr. Walker, in the preface to his translation of 'The Code of Gentoo Laws', shows himself more accurately informed than his predecessors, but his information is still imperfect. 'The

* [Compare K. J. H. Windischmann, "Die Philosophie im Fortgange der Weltgeschichte". Bonn: 1832, p. 585-634.]

'Pańdits,' he says, 'who compiled the code were to a 'man resolute in rejecting all solicitations for instruction in Sanskrit; and even the persuasions and influence of the Governor-General, Warren Hastings, 'were exerted in vain.'

The Brahmans, who supplied Dow with surreptitious passages from the Vedas, were not the sole manufacturers of such pious frauds, and very extensive compositions in Sanskrit were put forth in the south of India, under that designation, by the missionaries of the Propaganda, showing a wonderful amount of industry and extraordinary command of the language, but written in the style of the Puráńas—not of the Vedas. They were discovered by Mr. Ellis, of the Madras Civil Service, at Pondicheri, and are described by him in the 14th volume of the 'Asiatic Researches': amongst them was the original of a work of which a translation had been printed in Europe, in 1778, at Yverdon 'L'Ezour Vedam traduit du Sanscretan par 'un Brame.' The original had been brought from Pondicheri, and presented to Voltaire, who, transferring it to the Royal Library, expressed his belief that it was four centuries older than Alexander, and that it was the most precious gift for which the West had been ever indebted to the East;—how little he knew of the matter is evident from the work, which is an attempted refutation of Hinduism by a Christian author.

The unsatisfactory nature of these attempts augmented the desire of European scholars to procure authentic copies of the originals, and the failure to do so suggested a doubt whether they were any longer in existence: this suspicion was dissipated by Colonel Polier, who at last procured a copy from Jaypur, through Don Pedro de Silva, the Portuguese physician of the Raja. Colonel Polier brought it to England in 1789, and presented it to Sir Joseph Bankes, by whom it was transferred to the British Museum, where it is preserved. It is a handsome M.S., but is limited to the text, which without the scholia is of comparatively little use. Subsequent research, in which Sir Robert Chambers, one of the Judges of the Supreme Court of Calcutta, was pre-eminently successful, multiplied copies of portions, at least, of the Vedas, which, with other MSS. collected by him, were sold many years after his decease to the King of Prussia, and are now at Berlin. A catalogue by Professor Weber was published in 1853. As Sir Robert was not a Sanskrit scholar, he contributed no further to our knowledge of the originals: even Sir William Jones was but little acquainted with the original text.

In the meantime Mr. Colebrooke, a member of the Bengal Civil Service, who had been diligently raising himself to that pre-eminence as a Sanskrit scholar which was eventually undisputed, engaged, amongst other pursuits, in the study of the Vedas, for which his position as a civilian at Benares and the relaxing scruples of the Brahmans offered him favourable opportunities. In 1805 appeared the first authentic analysis of the Vedas from his pen, in his essay on the Vedas, published in the eighth volume of the Asiatic

Researches, conveying as copious a description of their contents as the scope and extent of his dissertation permitted, and characterised by that care and precision by which all Mr. Colebrooke's contributions to Hindu literature are distinguished. The notice was avowedly of a general nature, and the materials were in some instances admitted to be imperfect, but the result was a distinct appreciation of the character of the four works known as the Vedas,—the Ŕich, Yajush, Sáman, and Atharvan, with specimen translations of a portion of their contents of a curious and interesting purport; the first precise information of some of their chief supplements or Bráhmańas, and of their principal commentaries; arguments in proof of their authenticity, and a speculation as to the probability of their dating as early at least as the 14th century B.C. Here our knowledge was suspended, and Mr. Colebrooke's essay continued for thirty years our only authority on the subject of the Hindu Vedas. Notwithstanding the fulness and accuracy of Mr. Colebrooke's essay, it was always felt that an actual translation of the Vedas, or of their principal portions, was still wanting as the only guide upon which reliance could be placed for a comprehensive and correct appreciation of their contents; and at last, upon the institution of the Oriental Translation Fund, the late Dr. Rosen was encouraged and assisted to translate the Rig-Veda, the most important of the four. Of the eight books in which this work is arranged Dr. Rosen translated the first only into Latin; it was published in 1838 with the text in both Nágarí and Roman characters. Unfortunately his premature death put a stop to the erudite and conscientious execution of his task.

The next step towards the illustration of the Vedas was made by the Oriental Text Committee, in co-operation with that of the Translation Fund, by the publication, in 1842, of the text and translation of the Sáma-Veda, by the late Rev. Mr. Stevenson, of Bombay, who had previously published at that Presidency an English version of the two first sections of the first Ashṫaka or eighth of the Ŕig-Veda. The Sáma-Veda is short, and is a repetition or recast, for the greater part, of the Ŕig-Veda. It has been since reprinted, with a German translation, a copious glossary, and most laborious illustrations by Professor Benfey, of Göttingen.

For the study of the Hindu Scriptures had now been taken up in France and Germany with that intense zeal and indefatigable assiduity which characterise continental literary erudition. In 1842 M. Nève, of Louvain, a pupil of Burnouf, published his 'Études sur le Ŕig-Véda'. Professor Roth, of Tubingen, another pupil of Burnouf, who, in various communications addressed to the Oriental Society of Germany, had afforded novel and interesting information respecting Vedic literature, published in 1846 his three dissertations 'Zur Literatur und Geschichte des Weda'; a publication of no great extent, but entirely new, and of the highest interest and value, and which has evidently given an electric impulse to the study of the Vedas upon the Continent, extending, although with much less intensity, to this country.

The next publication was also by Professor Roth, the text and partial explanation of the Nirukta by Yáska, an ancient commentator on passages of the Veda, and an author of a short glossary of Vedic terms. M. Nève, of Louvain, next published his 'Essai sur le Mythe des Ŕibhavas', 1847, and detached hymns were published, with translations by Professor Lassen, of Bonn, and the late Eugène Burnouf, of Paris. More important works are the original texts. That of the Sáma-Veda has been alluded to. Professor Weber, of Berlin, has just completed, in three large quarto volumes, the texts of the Yajur-Veda, (that portion called the White Yajush,) of the Śatapatha Bráhmańa, and of the Sútras, or Precepts of Kátyáyana, both of which are illustrative of the Yajur-Veda. The text of the Atharva-Veda has been printed by Professors Roth and Whitney: the latter an American Sanskritist; and the most voluminous and important, the Ŕig-Veda, with an elaborate commentary by Sáyańa Ácharya, who flourished in the 14th century of our era, is in course of publication by Professor Max Müller, of Oxford, under the authority and at the cost of the Home Government of India. Three volumes have been published;* it will be completed in two, or at most in three more, and is an extraordinary specimen of diligence, acumen, and scholarship which does infinite credit both to the editor and his patrons, who have thus preserved

* [Vol. IV, 1863.]

from the risk of decay a most venerable memorial of human belief. A French translation of the whole work from manuscript has been published by the late M. Langlois, and an English version, by Professor Wilson, proceeds *pari passu* with Professor Müller's text. Three volumes containing half the Ŕig-Veda, or four out of its eight Ashtakas, have been published.

Speaking of the Vedas, it is usually assumed that a collective or homogeneous work is intended; but, as above intimated, the works to which the designation is applied, are four in number,—the Ŕig-Veda, the Yajur-Veda, the Sáma-Veda, the Atharva-Veda, each of which is a Sanhitá or collection complete in itself, of detached hymns and prayers, mixed up in the Yajush with ritual directions. But these four works, constituting the mere utterance of the Vedic religion, form but a small portion of the religious literature even of the Vedic period. In addition to the Sanhitás, we have Bráhmańas, Súktas, Upanishads, Prátiśákhyas, Vedángas, and scholia of the most minute and profound description, all professing to spring from, and illustrate and carry into effect, the worship taught by the Vedas, a more or less extensive acquaintance with which is essential to a thorough understanding of the Veda, although it is rarely, if ever, now mastered by the Brahmans, and is manifestly beyond the reach of the European Sanskritist. Such acquirement is fortunately not indispensable to the determination of the great outline of the primitive system of religious belief inferable from the texts which are now before us, but it is no doubt of great importance to an accurate estimate of their purpose and their history. A sense of their value in these respects has induced Professor Müller to bring his immense reading and unequalled research to bear upon the subject, and has given to the public the subject of our present notice, 'A History of Ancient Sanskrit Literature, as far as it illustrates the primitive religion of the Bráhmańas'.

Referring to the light which the cultivation of Sanskrit in its philological bearings has reflected upon the history of mankind, identifying, through the incontestable testimony of language, races long separated by half the globe, and diametrically opposed in complexion, constitution, laws, and religion, and pointing out the necessity of beginning with the beginning, Professor Müller observes:—

'It is wilh lhe Veda, therefore, lhal Indian philology ought to begin if it is to follow a ualural and historical course. So great an influence has the Vedic age (the historical period to which we are juslified in referring the formalion of the sacred texts) exercised upon all succeeding periods of Indian history, so closely is every branch of literature connecled with Vedic tradilions, so deeply have the religious and moral ideas of lhat primitive era taken root in lhe mind of the Indian nalion, so minutely has almost every privale and public act of Indian life been regnlated by old traditionary precepts, that it is impossible to find the right point of view for jndging of Indian religion, morals, and literalure wilhont a knowledge of lhe literary remains of the Vedic age. No one could fairly say that those men who first began to stndy Sanskrit, now seventy years ago, onght to have begun wilh reading the Veda. The difficnllies connecled with the study of the Veda would have made such a course nllerly impossible and useless. But since the combined labonrs of Sanskrit scholars have now rendered the study of that language of more easy access, since the terminology of Indian grammarians and commentators, which not long ago was considered unintelligible, has become more familiar to us, and manuscripts can be more readily procured at the principal public libraries of Europe, Sanskrit philology has no longer an excuse for ignoring the Vedic age.' (P. 9, 10.)

Consistently with this view of the subject, the *Vedas*, as we have observed, must mean something more than a single work, and in Professor Müller's opinion 'it 'would be much nearer the truth to take Veda as a 'collective name for the sacred literature of the Vedic 'age, which forms, so to speak, the back ground of the 'whole Indian World.' With regard to this literature, although no doubt some has perished, yet a large proportion still remains, and until it shall have been more completely investigated, a work of very many years, it would scarcely be safe to take a comprehensive view of the whole age. Professor Müller modestly observes that what he has to offer are but Prolegomena or treatises on some preliminary questions which may be determinately answered from the materials now available to Sanskrit scholars: his principal object, he adds, is 'to put the antiquity of the Veda in its proper light;' meaning thereby not only the chronological distance of the Vedic age from our own, measured by the revolutions and progress of the heavenly bodies, but also and still more the distance between the intellectual, moral, and religious state of men as represented to us during the Vedic age, compared with that of other periods of history,—a distance which can be measured by the revolutions and the progress of the human mind.

After some interesting observations upon the unity of the Aryan races, and their divergence west and east at a period prior to history, Professor Müller proceeds to trace the development of the religious speculations which have given to the Hindu mind its predominant character, and have rendered them regardless or contemptuous of the ephemeral transactions which constitute political history. Adopting as a starting point the separation of Buddhism from Hinduism in the 6th century B.C., he proceeds from thence through three periods up to that which he regards as the earliest period, describing the different classes of literature bearing upon that point. The copiousness of detail with which he elucidates the various stages is far beyond the limits of a notice like the present; and we must be content to advert briefly to the principal stages through which the Professor traces the upward ascent of the system, distinguishing them into what he terms the Chhandas, Mantra, Bráhmańa, and Sútra periods.

The first or *Sútra* period; a Sútra, literally a thread, is applied to a short and often obscure didactic rule, the peculiarities of which, as Professor Müller observes, it is not easy to explain to one who has not worked his way through the Sútras themselves: they are the groundwork of all the systems of philosophy as well as of grammar, as in the case of the Sútras of Páńini, and are only intelligible by the assistance of commentators who amplify their language and expound its purport. In this place the Sútras intended are those only which are connected with the Vedas, but which do not purposely belong to the Vedic age, being included within the order of Smŕiti works, or those handed down by memory or tradition, and not of the Śruti or the literature of revelation,—the Mantras and Bráhmańas. One great distinction is that the authors of the latter when named are said to be *seers* of the prayers and hymns—not the authors—whilst the Sútras are attributed to human authors, all of whom, according to Professor Müller, are anterior to Buddha.

Under the head of Sútras or Precepts Professor Müller classes the works called *Vedángas* or members, angas, of the Veda, usually enumerated as six, although perhaps on insufficient authority. We are not, however, to look for the Vedángas to those small and barren tracts which are known by this name, and which represent only the last unsuccessful attempts to bring the complicated and unintelligible doctrines of former ages into a popular form. They are Śikshá, pronunciation; Chhandas, metre; Vyákarańa, grammar; Nirukta, explanation of words; Jyotisha, astronomy; and Kalpa, ceremonial. The first two are considered necessary for reading the Veda, the two next for understanding it, and the last two for employing it at sacrifices. Under the first division *Śikshá*, Phonetics, or Pronunciation, comprising rules regarding letters, accents, quantity, organs of enunciation, delivery, and euphonic combinations, Professor Müller has entered into a detailed account of a class of Vedic literature first made known to us by Professor Roth, in his essay on the Literature of the Veda. This consists of works termed *Prátiśákhyas*, being respectively (prati) intended for the use of the branches or Śákhás of the Vedas. Every such Śákhá, it is to be presumed, had its own Prátiśákhya, but at present only four are known to exist, one for each Veda.

That for the Rig-Veda is considered as belonging to the Śakala Śákhá; but, as Professor Müller observes, there is not a single instance of a MS. of the Rig-Veda at present known to which the rules of this Prátiśákhya apply. Probably the same may be said of the other three, for the rules of the Prátiśákhyas were not intended for written literature, they were only to serve as a guide in the instruction of pupils who had to learn the text of the Veda by heart and repeat it as part of their daily devotions. The text of this Prátiśákhya, with a commentary, has been printed by Professor Müller, as far as the sixth book, with a German translation; and the whole has been printed and translated into French in the Journal Asiatique by M. Regnier. The Prátiśákhya of the White Yajush has been edited by Professor Weber, in his Indische Studien.* Such laborious minutiæ and elaborate subtleties relating to the enunciation of human speech are not to be met with in the literature of any other nation.

The standard authority for the *Chhandas* or metre of the Vedas is an author named Pingala, who can

* [Vol. IV, p. 65-160; 177-331. The Atharva-Veda-Prátiśákhya was published, with a translation and notes, by Prof. Whitney in the 7th vol. of the Journal Am. Or. Soc. Compare Prof. Goldstücker's "Páṇini", p. 183-214, and A. Weber, Ind. Studien, V, p. 89-135.]

scarcely however be regarded as belonging to the Sútra period, nor does he confine himself to the metre of the Vedas or even of Sanskrit, giving rules also for Prákrit prosody. A very full account of his system is given by Mr. Colebrooke in the tenth volume of the Asiatic Researches.* As Pingala is the authority for the prosody, so is Páńini for the grammar of the Veda; but, as remarked by Professor Müller, there is an obvious inconsistency in this, for the main body of Páńini's grammar relates to the post-Vedic development of the language, and the Vedic peculiarities are only occasionally specified. There were, however, many grammarians prior to Páńini, as Mr. Colebrooke, in the first and only published volume of his Sanskrit grammar, remarks, and to some of them we might look for a more accurate representation of Vedic grammar if they had not perished.

The next of the Angas is termed *Nirukta*, and, as generally met with, is a short vocabulary of synonymous words found in the Vedas, most of which are now unused or obsolete. The author to whom it is ascribed, Yáska, has added to it two sections, in which he explains various texts of the Veda, and enters largely into the etymology of the language. The text has been published by Professor Roth, with an explanation of particular portions. The Nirukta, together with the Prátiśákhyas, and Páńini's grammar, supply the most interesting and important information on the growth

* [= Miscell. Essays, II, 62 ff.]

of grammatical science in India—a science cultivated by only two nations in antiquity, the Hindus and the Greeks, as here pointed out by Professor Müller, who has also indicated some interesting points of agreement and difference in their treatment of the subject. The following are selected from his remarks as of general interest:—

'There are only two nations in the whole history of the world which have conceived independently, and without any suggestions from others, the two sciences of Logic and Grammar, the Hindus and the Greeks. Although the Arabs and Jews, among the Semitic nations, have elaborated their own system of grammar, in accordance with the peculiar character of their language, they owe to the Greeks the broad ontlines of grammatical science, and they received from Aristotle the primary impnlse to a study of the categories of thought and speech. Our own grammatical terms came to ns from the Greeks; and their history is enrions enough, if we trace them back throngh the clumsy and frequently erroneous translations of the literary statesmen of Rome, to the scholars and critics of Alexandria, and finally to the early philosophers of Greece, the Stoics, Aristotle, Protagoras and Pythagoras. But it is still more instructive to compare this development of the grammatical categories in Greece with the parallel, yet quite independent, history of grammatical science in India. It is only by means of sneh a comparison that we can learn to understand what is organic, and what is merely accidental, in the growth of this science, and appreciate the real difficulties which had to be overcome in the classification of words and the arrangement of grammatical forms. The Greeks and Hindus started from opposite points. The Greeks began with philosophy, and endeavoured to transfer their philosophical terminology to the facts of language. The Hindus began with collecting the facts of language, and their generalisations never went beyond the external forms of speech. Thus the Hindus excel in accuracy, the Greeks in grasp. The grammar of the former has ended in a colossal pedantry; that of the latter still invigorates the mind of every rising generation throughout the civilised world.'

Again:—

'It is in the Sútra literature that we meet with discussions on language of a purely scientific character; and what we do find in the Prátiśákhya, in the Nirukta and Páńini, is quite sufficient to show that at their time the science of language was not of recent origin. I can only touch upon one point. It is well known how long it took before the Greeks arrived at a complete nomenclature for the parts of speech. Plato knew only of Noun (ὄνομα) and Verb (ῥῆμα), as the two component parts of speech, and for philosophical purposes Aristotle too did not go beyond that number. It is only in discussing the rules of rhetoric that he is led to the admission of two more parts of speech, the σύνδεσμοι (conjunctions) and ἄρθρα (articles). The pronoun (ἀντωνυμία) does not come in before Zenodotos, and the preposition (πρόθεσις) occurs first in Aristarchos. In the Prátiśákhya, on the contrary, we meet at once with the following exhaustive classification of the parts of speech (XII, 5).

'The noun (náma), the verb (ákhyáta), the preposition (upasarga), and the particle (nipáta) are called by grammarians the four classes of words. The noun is that by which we mark a being, a verb that by which we mark being; the latter is called a root (dhátu). There are twenty prepositions, and these have a meaning, if joined with nouns or verbs. The rest of the words are called particles. The verb expresses an action; the preposition defines it; the noun marks a being; particles are but expletives.' (Pp. 159-62.)

The *Kalpa Sútras* constitute the next division of the dependent branches of the Veda, and, as extended in their application to all precepts regulating the ceremonial observances of the Hindu which are of Vedic origin, form an extensive series of works which for practical purposes are the most important of the whole. They are distinguished into three classes, as *Śrauta*,

Gŕihya, and *Sámayáchárika Sútras*: the first prescribe the especial Vedic ceremonials or sacrifices, such as those to be celebrated on the days of new and full moon; the second enjoin the household or domestic rites, practised at various stages of the life of the Hindu from conception to death. The third regulate the daily observances of the twice-born; they are comparatively of little note, but the Sútras of the two first orders are of much greater moment. The Śrauta ceremonials are now rarely if ever performed, but the Gŕihya or domestic rites are more or less regularly observed, and the prayers derived from the Vedas are still repeated at their celebration; the Vedic texts are taken from the several Vedas on which the Sútras are considered to be dependent, each Veda having its own Sútras. Professor Müller enumerates as still extant and entire three of the Black Yajush, one of the White, three of the Sáma, two of the Ŕich, and one of the Atharva. Many more are quoted in different compositions, which are no longer procurable. The chief Sútrakáras of the Black Yajush are Ápastamba, Baudháyańa, Satyáshádha Hirańyakeśi, and Manu, whose Sútras exist in fragments only. Kátyáyana is the author of the Sútras of the White Yajush. Maśaka, Látyáyana and Dráhyáyańa are the authors of those of the Sáma, Áśvaláyana and Śáńkháyana of those of the Ŕich, and the Atharva has the Kuśika Sútras. Professor Müller attributes to these Sútras an important part in the development of the Hindu religion.

The Kalpa Sútras, Professor Müller observes, mark

a new period of literature and a new purpose in the literary and religious life of India. They were adopted by different schools, and came in time to supersede the authorities on which they were founded. Professor Müller enumerates nineteen (p. 211) works of this class as either actually existing, or quoted by different scholiasts.

The last of the Angas is the *Jyotisha* of the Vedas; but here also the tract or tracts that pass under this designation are brief and meagre and of little authority. They are not, however, without interest, especially in connexion with indications of a knowledge of astronomical phenomena found both in the Mantras and Bráhmańas. As Professor Müller notices, notwithstanding the modern form of the Jyotisha tracts, the doctrines represent the earliest stage of Hindu astronomy, and show that the lunar mansions and the solar-lunar year were part of their system.*

The next subject to which the work relates is a description of the systematic indices or *Anukramańís* of the Veda. The most perfect of those still extant is that of the Ŕig-veda, attributed to Kátyáyana, which specifies the first words of each hymn, the number of verses, the name and family of the author, the name of the deity to whom it is addressed, and the metre of every verse. Before this there had been separate indices for each of these subjects, and it was from com-

* [A. Weber, Ueber den Vedakalender, Namens Jyotisham. Berlin: 1862.]

prising all of them that the index of Kátyáyana was termed the Sarvánukrama or Universal Index. The separate indices were ascribed to Śaunaka, and some of them exist at least as quotations, or, in one instance, entire. One of his peculiarities and a proof of the minuteness with which the texts were studied, is a specification of the Mańd̤alas, the Anuvákas, and the number of Súktas or hymns in each, giving 1017 of the latter. Another enumeration is that of the Vargas and verses, as 10,417 of the latter; there are other enumerations, showing some, though not a very wide difference, as 10,409, 10,616, 10,622. There is even an enumeration of all the words, reckoning them at 153,826. One advantage of these calculations is their precluding the possibility of any wide deviation from the original text. The other Vedas have also their indices, but the only authors handed down are Śaunaka and his pupil Kátyáyana, who is the author of one of the indices of the Yajush, as well as of the Ŕich.

As with these works we take leave of the Sútra period, in which the authors of the different compositions, although reputed saints, are mortals, and are named, we may pause to inquire how far it may be possible to ascertain the date of their existence, and so far the era of the more modern contributions to the literature of the Vedas. Śaunaka is an important personage in Hindu legend, not only in connexion with the Ŕig-veda, but with the Mahábhárata, being one of the Ŕishis to whom it was related̤. In connexion with the Veda his immediate pupil was Áśvaláyana, whose

Sútras we have, and from whom Kátyáyana derived his knowledge. We have no means of tracing the date of Śaunaka and Áśvaláyana, except as preceding Kátyáyana, of whose period we have some indications, although not perhaps entitled to much reliance. But Kátyáyana is the reputed author of the Várttikas, additions and emendations of the grammatical Sútras of Páńini, and if the same person be intended, which is more than questionable, he is the same as Vararuchi, whom Hindu tradition makes cotemporary with Nanda, the predecessor of Chandragupta, Rájá of Páṫaliputra, —the Sandrocoptus to whom Megasthenes was sent ambassador by Seleucus. If we can trust to the tradition, then we have a final point for the date of Kátyáyana, the second half of the fourth century before the Christian era.*

The identity of the Sandrocottus or Sandrocoptus of the Greeks, with the Chandragupta of the Hindus, first pointed out by Sir Wm. Jones, was subsequently more fully developed by Professor Wilson in his introduction to the drama of the Mudrá Rákshasa, of which he is one of the principal characters. For it is not now called in question and is regarded by Professor Müller as the sheet-anchor of Indian chronology. He has entered into very copious details on the subject, not only from the classical and Hindu authorities, but those of the Jains and Buddhists, to the latter of whom Chandragupta is a person of historical interest,

* [Goldstücker, l. l., p. 89 ff. Weber, Ind. Stud., V, 43 ff.]

as the grandfather of Aśoka, their great patron. There is some discrepancy as to dates between their chronology and that of the Brahmans, but not of very irreconcilable character. The dates of Buddha's Nirváńa vary considerably, but are reducible to two classes. The Chinese, Tibetans, and Mongols place it ten centuries more or less B.C.; the Singhalese, Burmans, Siamese, six centuries; and this latter is most consistent with their records of the progress of the religion. Buddha's death is placed by them 543 B.C., but Professor Müller suggests that the date should rather be 477 B.C., which will explain the difference of something more than sixty years between the Buddhist and Hindu and Greek chronology; but as he observes, whatever change may have to be introduced into the earlier chronology of India, nothing will shake the date of Chandragupta; and consequently, if Kátyáyana flourished about his time, we may consider the fourth century B.C. as the period of his Sútras and Anukramańís. Reckoning upwards from this time through his predecessors Áśvaláyana and Śauńaka, we may reasonably prove them to have lived in the first half or the beginning of the fourth century B.C.; and as there were authors of Sútras prior to Śaunaka, Professor Müller proposes to extend the Sútra period to the sixth or seventh century:—prior to which we have the literature that is considered by the Hindus as constituting the periods of their inspired or scriptural Vedas.

Having assigned to the latter literature of India the

upward limit of six centuries B.C., Professor Müller proceeds to examine another and confessedly more ancient class of Vedic writings, differing in style both from the Sútras which are posterior, and from the Mantras which are anterior to them. These are the *Bráhmańas*, whose currency constitutes a distinct stage in the progress of the religious history of the Hindus.

According to the generally recognised classification of the Vedic literature it comprises two great divisions, the Karma Káńđa and Jnána Káńđa, the practice and speculation, the ceremonial and the philosophical sections, the liturgy and theosophy, or in the language of the commentators, the Mantra and the Bráhmańa; meaning by the first the prayers, hymns, charms, and other formulæ to be cited or chanted at the sacrifice; by the second inquiries into the nature of man and God, and the relations of matter and spirit. The definition of the Bráhmaṇa is, however, very far from definite, and the scholiasts are driven to the conclusion that it is no otherwise to be characterised than that whatever in the Veda is not Mantra is necessarily Bráhmańa,* a very vague and unmeaning distinction, and much too comprehensive to constitute a special characteristic. It would be difficult indeed to assign any specific attribute to the Bráhmańas as we have them, the Aitareya Bráhmańa of the Ŕich, the Śatapatha Bráhmańa of the White Yajush, which has been

* [Goldstücker, l. l., p. 69 ff. Haug, Ait. Br., I, p. 1-7.]

published by Professor Weber, and of which an analysis is given by Professor Müller, and the Gopatha Bráhmańa of the Atharva, also described by our author; in none of these does philosophical speculation take any prominent share; their object is usually to illustrate the ceremonial or the Mantras, by explaining their origin and import, and repeating legends illustrative of both, citing summarily the texts which are used on a particular occasion. These old stories form the most valuable portion of the sacrifice of Śunaḣśepha, for instance, in which his own father offers him as an immolation. As told in the Aitareya Bráhmańa, it is a very remarkable legend; it is translated by Professor Müller, but had been previously published by Professor Wilson in the Journal of the Royal Asiatic Society.* Again, in the Śatapatha, we have the Hindu version of the escape of Manu from the deluge. The original of the story is repeated in the Mahábhárata and the Matsya and other Puráńas,† and was originally translated by Sir William Jones. Many other interesting particulars occur in these Bráhmańas which are of great value to both the political and religious history of the Hindus, but little or nothing to justify

* [Ait. Br. VII, 3. Journal R. A. S., Vol. VIII, p. 96 ff. H. H. Wilson's Essays and Lectures, Vol. II, p. 247-69. See also the references in Muir's Sanskrit Texts, I, 104 ff.]

† [Mahábh., III, 12746 ff.; Matsya Pur. 2; Burnouf, Bhág. Pur., III, p. XXIII ff.; Weber, Ind. Stud., I, 161 ff.; Kellgren, de ovo mundano (1849), p. 45-62; Muir's Original Sanskrit Texts, II, 329 ff.]

their character of Brahma Káńda or theosophy of the Veda.

Where then is this to be found? In works termed *Árańyakas* and *Upanishads*, which may be considered as belonging to the class of Bráhmańas, and which are often found as integral portions of them, or even of the Sanhitá, or collections of the Mantras, although at the same time held to be distinct. The Árańyakas* are so called, according to Sáyańa, because they were to be read in the forest, as if they were the text-books of the anchorites, whose devotions were spiritual. Several of these have been published in the Bibliotheca Indica, especially the Bŕihad-árańyaka and Taittiríya-árańyaka, the former of which is also translated by Dr. Roer. The mystical philosophy of this class of literature may be seen from the translation; it is also evident that the Árańyakas, however sometimes confounded with the Bráhmańas, intimate their prior existence.

A still more numerous class of works, although in some instances of rather equivocal date and authenticity, is the chief repository of Hindu speculation. These are the *Upanishads*, the Mysteries of Theosophy. Of these some fifty were translated into Persian by order of Dárá Shakoh, and from the Persian by Anquetil du Perron, into Latin, under the title of 'Oupnekhat', or 'Theosophia Indica'. The double translation makes wild work of the original, but their number is

* [Goldstücker's "Páńini", p. 129. Weber, Ind. Stud., V, 49.]

by no means complete; and besides other lists there is one by Mr. Elliot, in the Journal of the As. Soc. of Bengal,* which specifies 108 works, which are known as Upanishads to the Brahmans of the south of India. Many, probably most, of them are no doubt of modern date, originating with the tenets of particular sects or individuals; those that are apparently the most ancient and authentic are the Bŕihad-árańyaka, Aitareya, Chhándogya, Taittiríya, Íśa, Kena, Praśna, Kat́ha, Muńd̄aka, and Máńd̄úkya; all which have been printed in the 'Bibliotheca Indica', edited by Dr. Roer, who has also translated the greater number. Translations of several have been made by other hands, especially by the late Rammohun Roy, who hoped that through the Monotheism of the Upanishads he might wean his countrymen from idolatry. Although their general tendency is Monotheistic, or rather perhaps Pantheistic, yet, as Professor Müller observes, there is so much freedom and breadth of thought in them, that it is not difficult to find in them some authority for almost any shade of philosophical opinion. Notwithstanding this vagueness, however, the Upanishads that wear an authentic aspect may be regarded as well as the Árańyakas as the Jnána káńd̄a, or philosophical portion of the Veda; although it may be doubted if they immediately succeeded the Mantra or Karma period. They may even be regarded as subsequent in some respects to the Bráhmańas, not only because they oc-

* [for 1851, p. 607. Weber, Ind. Stud., III, 324 ff.]

casionally repeat or refer to their legends, but because the Bráhmańas are more practical and have a more near relation to ceremonial rites, the practice of which is in all religions prior to speculation. The further history of the Bráhmańas as belonging to various *Charańas*, schools or fraternities, adopting in preference some divisions of the original texts, is given by Professor Müller, and is followed by a list of the *Gotras* or Brahman families and their branches, constituting what the author calls the Brahmanic Peerage of India. Seven chief families are enumerated in one list, of whom there are forty-nine subdivisions; but there are other lists still more numerous, and Brahmans in various parts of India still profess to draw their descent from some of these ramifications. To prove that these lists were not merely arbitrary compositions, Professor Müller shows their practical bearing on two important acts of the ancient Brahmanic Society,—the common consecration of the sacrificial fires and inter-marriage.

After offering some specimens of the contents of the *Bráhmańas*, Professor Müller proceeds to consider their probable era, and manifest and long-continued posteriority to the Mantra of proper Vedic period, every page containing the clearest proof that the spirit of the ancient Vedic poetry, and the purport of the original Vedic sacrifices, were both beyond the comprehension of the authors of the Bráhmańas. There is also clear evidence that the Bráhmańas are not the work of a few individuals—they represent a complete period through which the whole stream of thought poured in one channel, and was directed to the construction and development of what may be regarded as the system of Brahmanical Hinduism, but faintly if at all indicated by the original Vedic verses.

Professor Müller thinks it impossible to assign a shorter interval than two centuries for the origin and accumulation of the mass of Brahmanical literature that must have existed. We confess that we are disposed to look upon this limit as much too brief for the establishment of an elaborate ritual, for the appropriation of all spiritual authority by the Bráhmans, for the distinctions of races or the institutions of caste, and for the mysticism and speculation of the Áraṅyakas or Upanishads: a period of five centuries would not seem to be too protracted for such a complete remodelling of the primitive system and its wide dissemination through all those parts of India where the Brahmans have spread. There seems no reason to question the general accuracy of the lists of teachers preserved by Brahmanical tradition, and which as Professor Müller remarks would extend the limits of this age to a very considerable degree. These traditions are preserved in different supplementary works or Vanśas, also regarded as Bráhmaṅas—several of which are extant. There are several of these in the Śatapatha Bráhmaṅa, which Professor Müller quotes, and he concludes that from their extent it is possible that the limit he suggests will have to be extended. We quite concur in this anticipation, and think there can be little doubt that, instead of two centuries, we may venture to conjecture four or five, and so carry the commencement of the Bráhmańa period to the 10th or 11th century B.C.

We now only come to what is properly the Veda—the *Mantra* period of Professor Müller—the collections of prayers, hymns, formulæ, ritual injunctions, charms—which have been brought together in the Sanhitás or collections of the four Vedas. The Hindus themselves are content to look upon the fourth as of an equivocal character, and usually speak of the Vedas as three.

Setting this aside then, we should have for the scriptural Vedas the remaining three; but here also a very important distinction is to be made, and the Yajush and the Sáman are to be regarded as long subsequent to the Ŕich, originating in a different object and possessing different characteristics connected evidently with the development of the ritual, and approaching, through intervals of greater or less extent, to the period of the Bráhmańas.

The Yajur-veda is two-fold—the Taittiríya or Black Yajush, and the Vájasaneyi or White, originating, no doubt, with a schism of which Yájnavalkya was the probable author. Both these forms indicate their subservience to an established ceremonial; they are liturgies and rubrics interspersing short injunctions of a ritual purport, which are given in prose, with verses to be repeated at the ceremony, many of which are the same that occur in the Ŕig-veda, from which they are in all probability derived.

In the course of time it had become the practice to

accompany part of the sacrifice by songs, and hence arose the third or Sáma-veda, of which the verses are to be chanted: a very large portion of its contents are the same as the hymns of the Ŕich, and perhaps the whole might be identified if we had the whole of the early Śákhás.

It is then to the *Ŕig-veda Sanhitá* that we must look for the most authentic and primitive representation of the Hindu religious belief. We must not, however, lose sight for a moment of the meaning of the term Sanhitá or collections. The Ŕig-veda Sanhitá is not a work of one author or of one purport; it is a mere bringing together of a number of metrical compositions, varying in authorship, intention, and date, generally of a religious character but not always, and although offering occasional intimations of ceremonial and priestly worship, yet possessing nothing of a decidedly liturgical character, or direct applicability to either Śrauta or Gŕihya rites. The verses may be employed and are employed at such rites, and they were also recited at sacrifices in praise of the deities to whom any particular act of sacrifice was addressed, usually by priests, termed the Hotŕi, in a loud and distinct tone, and with due regard to the rules of euphony, any deviation from which vitiated the ceremony. Here, therefore, we have evidence that there was a ceremonial in existence when some at least of the hymns of the Ŕich were composed; and even rites of a somewhat sacred character, as the Darśapúrńamásau, or sacrifices at the new and full moon, and the whole array of priests, sixteen in number, are alluded to. But these allusions are incidental and transitory; they show that some of the hymns must have been preceded by rudiments of a liturgical ceremony, yet many others have not the slightest reference to anything beyond the simple adoration, by the presentation of butter or some juice to the deities, who are the objects of the praise or prayer. The different issues of the Súktas, so often mentioned by themselves as being old or new, will allow for the gradual evolution of liturgical rites emerging evidently into the rubrics of the Yajush and the chaunts of the Sáma. On this subject Professor Müller observes:—

> 'We may, therefore, safely ascribe the collection of the Ṛig-veda, or, as Professor Roth calls it, the historical Veda, to a less practical age than that of the Bráhmańa period; to an age, not entirely free from the trammels of a ceremonial, yet not completely enslaved by a system of mere formalities; to an age no longer creative and impulsive, yet not without some power of upholding the traditions of a past that spoke to a later generation of men through the very poems which they were collecting with so much zeal and accuracy.'

Professor Müller conceives nevertheless that there is some priestly influence distinguishable in the Sanhitá of the Ṛig-veda, as exemplified by its classification into Mańdalas or Circles, of which seven are attributable to as many different Ṛishis and their descendants. There may have been such collections in use by different Gotras; but, to say the least, some of those persons to whom they are ascribed are of a rather equivocal character, and the compiler of the whole Sanhitá may have adopted the distinction as handed down by tradition without caring to be very exact as to detail. The question is not of much moment; the priority and posteriority of the Súktas relatively being unquestioned, they are undoubtedly of very various, possibly of very distant, eras, and we know too little of the chronology of the Ŕishis, their reputed Seers, to base the date of the composition upon that of the author. The Súktas of the Ŕig-veda had run through a long course of years, possibly centuries, before they were brought together in one general collection. The business of collection must have occupied some considerable time,—according to Professor Müller, two centuries; but we know too little of the process of reducing the scattered Mantras into a collective form, to be able to assign any fixed period to it. It is uniformly ascribed to Kŕishńa Dvaipáyana, surnamed Vyása the arranger, assisted by a number of reputed sages, intending possibly a school or series of schools in which the Sanhitás of the Vedas were brought into their present shape during an interval of the duration supposed, or about two centuries, bringing the compilation, agreeably to an amended compendium, to the 12th or 13th century before the Christian era.

In what state did the several hymns circulate when they were first brought together? Had they been current orally alone, or in writing, and, if the former, were they reduced to writing when they were collected? That the Mantras were for a long time, perhaps for ages, current orally, there can be little reason to doubt. The pains taken to secure their accurate ennnciation, and the elliptical style of their composition, are evidences of oral transmission. The question, as stated by Professor Müller, is, was the collection of the ten books of Vedic hymns the work of persons cognisant of the art of writing; were the thousand and seventeen hymns of the Ṛig-veda, after they were gathered into one body, preserved by memory or on paper? Professor Müller answers these questions by an interesting excursus on the probable period when the art of writing was first known to the Hindus, and draws the inference that before the time of Páńini, and before the first spreading of Buddhism in India, writing for literary purposes was not in use. The chief ground for this inference is the absence of any word not only in the hymns, but even in the grammatical lectures of Páńini, which presupposes the existence of writing, whilst in the ancient works of a people like the Jews, to whom writing must have been known from of old, such words as writing, scripture, book, volume, are of constant recurrence. Nothing of this kind occurs in any Sanskrit works older than Manu and the Mahábhárata. At the same time Professor Müller admits that the Hindus were acquainted with the art of writing before the time of Alexander, and the expressions *likhita* and *likhápita*, written, and caused to be written, occur on the inscriptions of Priyadarsi, which are no doubt of the third century B. C., and therefore, as far as is yet known, of Páńini's date, cotemporary with him, or even older; consequently, no argument can be drawn from his omissions or phraseology against a knowledge of the art of writing in his time. The question is not without its difficulties. That the Súktas could be handed down from generation to generation by memory alone we need not hesitate to admit, but if they had not been committed to writing when they were collected and classified into *adhyáyas* and *mańdalas*, the task of compiling and perpetuating would have been but imperfectly accomplished, if some more durable condition had not been impressed upon the collection than that of being entrusted to the memory alone.*

To the Mantra period Professor Müller adds one still earlier, to which he gives the appellation of *Chhandas*,—the metrical or poetical period; understanding thereby the time at which those hymns or mantras were composed, which may be regarded as of most archaic character, emanating from the first religious sentiments of a simple people, and preceding the institution of a ceremonial, or the organisation of a priesthood. It seems scarcely necessary to make this a distinct era;† it is the same as the Mantra period, in which we have seen a wider space is evidently required for the new, intermediate, and ancient hymns which are recognised by the authors of the hymns themselves, especially as Professor Müller thinks it essential to caution against too hasty conclusions as

* [See on this question Prof. Goldstücker's "Pâṇini", p. 13-67, and Weber, Ind. Stud., IV, 89 ff.; V, 18 ff.]

† [Haug, Ait. Br., I, p. 23. Goldstücker, l. l., p. 71.]

to the comparative recent date of many hymns, in which sentiments worthy of the most advanced ceremonial, or the presence of philosophical ideas, are to be found; there being, as he observes, very little to guide us in forming a judgment of what is genuine and primitive in the ancient poetry of so peculiar a race as that of the Aryans in India. In this want therefore of a safe criterion we may be content to look upon the Mantra period as one complete in itself, though extending over a long space of time, and in some instances to a very remote antiquity. At the same time even that is not the most distant term to which we may trace the literature of the Vedas; for, as Professor Müller remarks, ages must have passed before the grammatical texture of the Vedic Sanskrit could have assumed the consistency and regularity which it exhibits. Throughout, every tense, every mood, every number and person, of the verb is fixed, and all the terminations of the cases are formally established.

'From this point of view the Vedic language and poetry may be ascribed to a modern or secondary period in the history of the world, if only it be understood that what preceded that period in India, or in any other part of the Aryan world, is lost to us beyond the hope of recovery, and that, therefore, to us the Veda represents the most ancient chapter in the history of the human intellect. We find no traces in the Veda, or in any Aryan work, of a growing language, growing in the sense in which some of the Turanian languages may be said to be still growing at the present day. The whole grammatical mechanism is finished, the most complicated forms are sanctioned, and the only changes of which the Aryan speech, arrived at the point where we find it in the Veda, admits, are those of gradual decay and recomposition.'

Having come to this conclusion that we have in the hymns of the Ṛig-veda some of the oldest records in the history of man, we may now inquire what was the condition of society which it discloses, and more especially what was the religion of the people? How far it afforded the sanction which the Hindus affirm of it to the religion that has prevailed for at least twenty centuries in Hindustan?

'The Veda', says Professor Müller, 'has a two-fold interest: it belongs to the history of the world and to the history of India. In the history of the world the Veda fills a gap which no literary work in any other language could fill. It carries us back to times of which we have no records anywhere, and gives us the very words of a generation of men, of whom otherwise we could form but the vaguest estimate by means of conjectures and inferences. As long as man continues to take an interest in the history of his race, and as long as we collect in libraries and museums the relics of former ages, the first place in that long row of books which contains the records of the Aryan branch of mankind, will belong for ever to the *Ṛig-veda.*'

It has pleased some of the most enthusiastic cultivators of the literature of the Vedas, amongst whom our author must be distinguished, to imagine a state of Indian society of a pure, simple, and patriarchal description, in which the feeding of flocks and herds was the main occupation of life, and whose chief recreation was the adoration of the deified elements or the composition of those songs in their honour which constitute a large portion of the actual collection.

'There was a time when the poet was the leader, the king, and priest of his family or tribe, when his songs and sayings were listened to in anxious silence and with implicit faith, when his prayers were repeated by crowds who looked up to their kings and priests, their leaders and judges, as men better, nobler, wiser than the rest, as beings nearer to the gods in proportion as they were raised above the common level of mankind. These men themselves living a life of perfect freedom, speaking a language not yet broken by literary usage, and thinking thoughts unfettered as yet by traditional chains, were at once teachers, lawgivers, poets, and priests. There is no very deep wisdom in their teaching, their laws are simple, their poetry shows no very high flights of fancy, and their religion might be told in a few words. But what there is of their language, poetry, and religion has a charm which no other period of Indian literature possesses: it is spontaneous, original, and truthful.'

For all this there seems to us to be but little warrant in any of the hymns, and the general tenor of them leaves no doubt that at the date of their composition society had assumed a more artificial character, and that the people were not encamped on the borders of rivers, or spacious Havanas, but were collected in hamlets and towns, and that their leaders were neither poets nor patriarchs, but princes whose favour and munificence were sought for and bestowed upon priests and poets. No doubt the principalities were of small political power, but they were independent and constantly at variance with one another, although their contests partook more of a predatory than a national hostility. It is also clear that a considerable portion of India was occupied by races not only of a different character and creed, but actively inimical to the practices of the Hindus, with whom the latter were in a normal state of antagonism. The subjugation or the servitude of these races must have been the work of time. Professor Müller has not entered upon this subject, but confines his attention to the religious condition which the Vedas exhibit as existing at the various periods throughout which the hymns may be traced.

The first and most obvious conclusion to be drawn from the hymns of the Veda, whatever may be their relative antiquity, whether twenty or twelve centuries B. C., is that the religion which they inculcate is not that of the Hindus of the present day. The Brahman who, from the time of the code of Manu as we have it, had arrogated to himself the attributes of a god upon earth, is in the Veda only one of seven, or even of sixteen priests, acting as a sort of master of the ceremonies, but not invested with any superior rank or authority. Of the distinction of caste at all the indications are faint and uncertain, with one exception —that of a remarkable hymn in the 10th Mańdala, the tenor and style of which place it indisputably in a comparatively recent stage, and bring it at least to the Brahmanic period, by which time we know that the Brahmanical system had been organised.* There is no mention of temples nor of public worship; the ceremonial is entirely domestic, and so far the formulæ, the language of the Súktas, still constitute the liturgy of the domestic rites of the Hindus. It is very doubtful if images were known, although mention of personal peculiarities, as of the handsome jaws of Indra, might

* [Muir, l. l., I, 6 ff.; 42; II, 210.]

be suggested by a sculptured representation of him. Something else may, however, be meant; but the great feature of difference is the total absence of the divinities, both nomina and numina, who have for ages engaged, and, to a great degree, engrossed, the adoration of the Hindus. We have no indications of a Triad, the creative, preserving, and destroying power; Brahmá does not appear as a deity, and Vishńu, although named, has nothing in common with the Vishńu of the Puráńas; no allusion occurs to his Avatáras. His manifestation as Kŕishńa, the favourite divinity of the lower classes, for some centuries at least, does not appear. As a divinity Śiva is not named, nor is his type the Linga ever adverted to. Durgá and her triumphs, and *Káli*, whom the 'blood of man delights a thousand years', have no place whatever in the hymns of the Vedas. These differences are palpable, and so far from the Vedas being the basis of the existing system, they completely overturn it. It would be an interesting subject of inquiry to discover when, and by what means, the vast mass of the modern mythology of the Hindus sprang into existence and attained its circulation throughout India.

What then was the religion of the Vedic Hindus, as exhibited in the Súktas? Recollecting that these are most probably of widely different dates, and that they were collected and put together without much, if any, regard to system, we cannot expect to find a coherent and systematic form of worship or belief: each Súkta must be taken by itself, expressing its own notions.

By far the greater portion of them are addressed to the personified elements, especially to Agni or Fire, as represented in three phases, in heaven as the sun, in mid-air as lightning and meteoric phenomena, and on earth in the ordinary elementary type. Indra, the atmosphere, is the next in importance, especially as the sender of rain and consequent fertility, and to these two perhaps half the Súktas are addressed. Connected with them are the sun, the two divinities termed Aśvins and the Dawn, and Indra and Varuńa; and the Viśvadevas, or universal deities, may, without much violence, be brought within the same category. These deities are eulogised and magnified, and they are implored for food, cattle, progeny, safety, long life, and all worldly enjoyments. Varuńa especially appears to be the punisher of crime, and his protection against wickedness is frequently implored. Indra is, in an especial degree, the god of battles and giver of victory, but his attributes and the legend relating to him are not unfrequently ascribed to other divinities, as to the Aśvins and to Agni. A prominent and rather unintelligible object of praise and prayer is the Soma plant,* a sort of asclepias, the bruised leaves and stems of which yield a juice, which by standing ferments into an intoxicating liquor, which is supposed to gratify the gods and animate them to extraordinary exploits.

* [Haug's Essays on the Sacred Language of the Parsees. Bombay: 1862, p. 132 f. Aitareya Bráhmańa, ed. Haug, Vol. I, p. 59 ff. F. Windischmann, "Ueber den Somacultus der Arier". München: 1847. F. Spiegel, "Érân". Berlin: 1863, p. 235.]

That this beverage was partaken of by the assistants can alone explain their elevation of it to the rank of a deity, and can have originated only in a stage of semi-barbarism, such as we can imagine might have won the adoration of the American Indians when first acquainted with ardent spirits. In hymns, too, which are apparently of an early date, we have the details of the Scythian sacrifice of the horse; and there are indications of the occasional offering of human victims, although of rare and special occurrence.* As a general rule, however, the offerings are of an innocent description—the Soma juice, clarified butter, and cakes of barley or other grain fried with butter and poured upon the fire. The same is presented to all the gods alike, and in this, as in other respects, there is so much in common that all the Vedic divinities may be resolved into one, as a general type of one universal being.

What indications do we find of a future existence or a system of rewards and punishments? The Vedic Hindus recognised unreservedly the difference between a material and spiritual state of being, and looked to the survival of the soul, and its occupation of an incorruptible body amongst the Pitṛis or Manes. There is no detail as to their condition, nor have we any positive intimation of punishment of sin after death, beyond deprecating its consequences during life, and

* [A. Weber in "Zeitschrift der deutschen morgenl. Gesellschaft", Vol. XVIII, 262-87.]

the designation of Yama as judge of the dead. It was also part of the Vedic creed that holy men, as in the case of the *Ŕibhus*, might attain the condition of gods. These intimations, however, are incidental and vague, and all that we can positively conclude from them is that the Vedas recognised, after the dissolution of the body, the life of the soul which animated it, and its continued existence in some heavenly sphere. There is no very distinct reference to the metempsychosis; none whatever to the fact of transmigration; an omission the more worthy of notice that it is the foundation of all the philosophical systems of the Hindus, and consequently proves their being posterior to the Vedas.

Had the Vedas any knowledge of one almighty and all-wise Creator and Ruler of the universe? They had a belief in such a Being, although evidently not unmingled with uncertainty and doubt. Professor Müller has given us a very remarkable Súkta, in which a state of things before creation is clearly apprehended, the course of creation summarily sketched, and the question stated, Who knows what is the truth? There are several passages of this kind in the Súktas, but to some of which at least very reasonable suspicions of a later age attach, being of the nature of the mysterious, which is manifested in the Upanishads. We are much disposed to look upon several of those cited by Professor Müller as open to this objection, and to think that in his enthusiasm he has been led to give a value to expressions which is more exalted than they deserve. Thus, for instance, in the hymn above alluded to, and which has been gracefully put into metre by a friend, we have the following passage:—

> 'Darkness there was; and all at first was veiled
> In gloom profound—an ocean without light;
> The germ that still lay covered in the husk
> Burst forth, one nature from the fervent heat;
> Then first came Love upon it.'

Now the term 'love' here appears to us to convey a notion too transcendental to have had a place in the conception of the original author. The word is *káma*, which scarcely indicates love in the sense in which it may here be understood, although not absolutely indefensible; but *káma* means desire, wish; and it expresses here the wish, synonymous with the will, of the sole existing Being to create. It is a familiar Vedic phrase in speaking of the time before creation, to say 'THAT, the one Being, was alone. He said,—May I be 'many!—then sprang the world into existence.' It is the wish, or rather the will, therefore, of God that the world should come into existence that the passage is speaking of, and not any such emotion as is ordinarily understood by 'love'. At any rate, this hymn and various others, particularly two in the tenth Maṅḋala, hymns 81, 82, addressed to Viśvakarmá, the Omnificent, establish beyond controversy that the Vedic cosmogony was that of none of the subsequent schools; neither asserting with the Sánkhyas the coeternity of matter and spirit, nor with the Vedántas the existence of spirit alone. However dim the knowledge, however vacillating the opinion, it is evident that the authors of the old hymns of the Veda were disposed to believe in the primary existence of one God when nought else existed, and that the world was created by his fiat, and organised by his wisdom and might.

These are the conclusions to which a careful consideration of the contents of the textual portion of the Vedas, the Sanhitás, reasonably leads; and it is unnecessary to point out how important they are, not only to the history of the Hindu religion, but to that of the religion of the ancient world, at an era prior to any of which we possess a written word, with the exception of the Pentateuch. Students of ancient history and religion will feel greatly indebted to the erudition and laborious research of Professor Müller. It is not possible, in a brief survey like the present, to render justice to a work, every page of which teems with information that no other scholar ever has, or could have, placed before the public; and although many of the details are likely to interest those only who delight to explore the dark paths of antiquity, and to trace the progress of human opinion and belief, yet the work must ever hold a foremost place, not only in the history of India, but in that of the human race.

INDEX.

ADDITIONAL NOTE to Vol. II, p. 16, and Vol. III, p. 185.

We are indebted to Dr. Kern, of Benares, for the following quotations from the text of the Bṛihatsanhitá:

प्राजापत्ये शकटे भिन्ने कृत्वेव पातकं वसुधा ।
केशास्थिशकलशबला कापालमिव व्रतं धत्ते ॥

रोहिणीशकटमर्कनन्दनो यदि भिनत्ति रुधिरोऽथवा शशी ।
किं वदामि यदनिष्टसागरे जगदशेषमुपयाति संक्षयम् ॥
रोहिणीशकटमध्यसंस्थिते चन्द्रमस्यशरणीकृता जनाः ।
क्वापि यान्ति शिशुयाचिताशनाः सूर्यतप्तपिठराम्बुपायिनः ॥

The couplet beginning यदि भिंत्ते is not found in any of the seven MSS. he has consulted. See also Böhtlingk's "Indische Sprüche", Nos. 1886 and 2648 f.

From the printed edition of the Vikramárkacharitra (Madras: 1861) we add the following two stanzas as a supplement to Prof. Benfey's note (Pantschatantra, II, p. 393):

उक्तञ्च वराहमिहिरेण ।
अर्कसुतेन हि भग्ने भौमश्शुक्रस्य रोहिणीशकटे ।
द्वादशचाब्दान्नहि नहि वर्षति वर्षाणि वारिदो नियतम् ॥
रोहिणीशकटमर्कसूनुना भिद्यते रुधिरवाहिनी सरित् ।
किं ब्रवीमि नहि वारिसागरे सर्वलोक उपयाति संक्षयम् ॥
मतान्तरे ।
यदा भिनत्ति मन्दोऽयं रोहिण्याश्शकटं तदा ।
वर्षाणि द्वादशात्यन्तं वारिवाहो न वर्षति ॥

See Böhtlingk, l. l., Nos. 2354 and 2367.

CORRECTIONS.

Vol. I.

Page 68,	line 19 and 22	*read*	Kríshńá
- 77,	- 12	-	Kámákhyá
- 79,	- 5	-	Kámákhyá
- 103,	- 2	-	Goloka
- 112,	- 30	-	Vŕihaspati
- 116,	- 19	-	Rádhá
- 119,	- 19	-	Puráńas
- 123,	- 2	-	Páńdu

Page 127,	line 22	*read*	Viśwámitra
- 127,	- 23	-	Bharadwája
- 129,	- 19	-	Yájnavalkya
- 129,	- 24	-	Taittiríya
- 137,	- 2	-	Nishadha
- 152,	- 25	-	Tretá
- 154,	- 22 and 26	-	Várhishadas
- 154,	- 23, 26, 27	-	Ushmapas, Ájyapas
- 154,	- 25	-	Somapas
- 157,	- 10	-	Śáliváhana
- 158,	- 28	-	Sangráma
- 179,	- 6	-	Badariká
- 179,	- 11	-	Badarikáśrama
- 228,	- 16	-	Páńdu
- 260,	- 15	-	Golden City
- 273,	- 18	-	Viśwámitra
- 274,	- 2	-	Śárira
- 295,	- 9	-	Śŕinjaya
- 297,	- 6	-	Bharadwája
- 307,	- 31	-	Śŕinjaya
- 310,	- 9	-	Brahmá
- 312,	- 23	-	Ajámídha
- 313,	- 27	-	Paráśara
- 348,	- 20	-	Vijayanagara
- 351,	- 20	-	Pushpapura
- 357,	- 10	-	Púrva
- 364,	- 18 and 25	-	Chandravarmá
- 372,	- 22	-	Ďákiní
- 372,	- 26	-	Pachísí
- 377,	- 9	-	Máhishmatí

Vol. II.

Page 26,	line 23	*read*	Rohańáchala
- 47,	- 28	-	from
- 77,	- 8	-	śreshthí
- 120,	- 23	-	Śáliváhana

Page 138,	line 28	*read* chháditaṁ
- 164,	- 11	- Mitragupta
- 208,	- 19	- endeavouring
- 209,	- 22 and 29	- Chandravarmá
- 210,	- 11	- Chandravarmá
- 221,	- 4	- Chandravarmá
- 248,	- 17	- Dhúminí
- 248,	- 18	- Nitambavatí
- 315,	- 8	- Ṙitusanhára
- 354,	- 16, 19 and 24	- Charmańwatí
- 364,	- 24	- Káńwa
- 372,	- 2 and 24	- Airávata
- 394,	- 21	- Śálagrama

Vol. III.

Page 25,	line 28	*read* पिष्कद्रो ऽंग्रहरः
- 96,	- 15, 19 and 24	- Brahmá
- 108,	- 13	- Śankara
- 108,	- 13	- Śrídhara
- 108,	- 14	- Sánkhyas
- 127,	- 24	- Medinikara
- 128,	- 15	- Śrotavya
- 128,	- 16	- Śruta
- 141,	- 23	- adhyátma
- 177,	- 14	- Manoramá
- 189,	- 21	- Śáliváhana
- 213,	- 13	- Vijayanagara
- 240,	- 12	- Prayoga
- 291,	- 11	- Átmanepada

Berlin, printed by Unger Brothers, Printers to the King.

BIBLIOGRAPHICAL PUBLICATIONS

OF

MESSRS. TRÜBNER & CO.

60, PATERNOSTER ROW, LONDON.

IMPORTANT TO

Librarians, Collectors of Books, & Booksellers.

In Two Volumes, 8vo., pp. 1950 of Letter-press, Seven Chromo-Lithographic Plates of Binding-Specimens, Sixteen fac-simile Plates of Papyri and Early Types, numerous Woodcuts, etc. Price £2 : 8s.; Large Paper, £4 : 4s.

MEMOIRS OF LIBRARIES:

INCLUDING

A Practical Handbook of Library Economy.

By EDWARD EDWARDS.

Table of Contents.

PART I.—HISTORY OF LIBRARIES.

(IN FIVE BOOKS.)

EDWARDS'S MEMOIRS OF LIBRARIES—*continued.*

Chap. 2 to 5. History and Contents of the British Museum
„ 6. The Origin and Growth of the Bodleian Library.
§ i. *The Founder: his Enterprise and his Helpers.*
§ ii. *History of the Bodleian, from the time of Selden.*
„ 7. The State and Prospects of the Bodleian Library.
§ i. *Notices of the more conspicuous Bodleian Treasures.*
§ ii. *The Oxford University Commission of* 1854.

Appendix to Chap. 7 :—
(1.) Note on the Acquisition of the Selden Library.
(2.) Hearne's Account of his Dismissal from the Under Librarianship.

„ 8. The Minor University Libraries and the Collegiate Libraries of Oxford.
„ 9. The Public Library of the University of Cambridge.
„ 10. The Minor Libraries of Cambridge.
„ 11. The Public Library of Humphrey Chetham at Manchester:—
§ i. *Life of a Manchester Merchant during the Civil Wars.*
§ ii. *The Merchant's Foundations under Trusteeship.*
§ iii. *Character, Contents, and Defects of the Chetham Library.*
§ iv. *The Chetham Manuscripts.*
„ 12. The Cathedral Libraries of England.
„ 13. The Archiepiscopal Library at Lambeth Palace.
„ 14. The Libraries of the English Inns of Court.
„ 15. The Older Libraries of English Towns, and their Management by Municipal Corporations.
„ 16. The Parochial and Quasi-Parochial Libraries of England.
Chap. 17. The History of the Public Libraries Acts of 1850 and 1855.
„ 18. The Working of the Public Libraries Acts of 1850 and 1855.
„ 19. The Law Libraries of Edinburgh.
„ 20. The University, Town, and Parochial Libraries of Scotland.
„ 21. The Library of Trinity College, Dublin, and the other chief Libraries of Ireland.
„ 22. The Minor Libraries of London.
„ 23. British Private Libraries which have been dispersed.
„ 24. Notices of some existing British Private Libraries.

Book IV.—The Libraries of the United States of America.

Chap. 1. The Collegiate Libraries.
„ 2. The Proprietary Libraries.
„ 3. The Town Libraries.
„ 4. The State and Congressional Libraries.
„ 5. The Smithsonian Institution.
„ 6. Public School and District Libraries.

Book V.—The Modern Libraries of Continental Europe.

Chap. 1. The Imperial Library of France.
„ 2. The Minor Libraries at Paris.
„ 3. The Provincial Libraries of France.
„ 4. The Libraries of Italy.
„ 5. The Royal and National Libraries of the German States.
„ 6. German University Libraries.
„ 7. German Town Libraries.
„ 8. The Libraries of Belgium, Holland, and Switzerland.
„ 9. The Libraries of Sweden, Denmark, and Norway.
„ 10. The Libraries of Poland, Hungary, Russia, and Turkey.
„ 11. The Libraries of Spain and Portugal.
„ 12. Past, Present, and Future.

PART II.—ECONOMY OF LIBRARIES.

(IN FOUR BOOKS.)

Book I.—Book-Collecting.

Chap. 1. Rudiments of Book-Collecting, with more especial reference to Public Libraries.
„ 2. Copy-Tax.
„ 3. Gifts.
„ 4. Public Historiography and Public Printing.
Chap. 5. International Exchanges.
„ 6. Purchases:—
§ i. *Choice of Authors and of Editions.*
§ ii. *Inferences that may be drawn from Library Statistics in the selection of Books for Purchase.*

EDWARDS'S MEMOIRS OF LIBRARIES—*continued.*

OPINIONS OF THE PRESS.

"Of the industry bestowed upon this extensive compilation, and of the marvellous condensation of fact which it supplies, it is difficult to speak in terms of proper commendation; even to the most accomplished bibliographer it cannot fail to be of great service, but how much more to the tyro or ordinary bibliographer."—*Brownson's Review.*

"There is more variety, interest, and even life, in the Memoirs of Libraries, than might be expected. Mr. Edwards has a more comprehensive mind and a more sensible judgment than always characterise the tribe of librarii. His style has not an undue spirit of rhetoric, which throws off anything approaching to the manner of Dryasdust."—*Spectator.*

"Both as a history of libraries and a manual of their economy, this work is valuable: delightful to the scholar in the first respect; in the second, indispensable to the librarian."—*Critic.*

"We now take leave of these volumes, feeling that we have given a very imperfect indication of their contents, and strongly recommend them to the consideration of all persons connected with or interested in libraries, public or private, because they contain a vast quantity of information never before collected, and much that would be sought for in vain elsewhere."—*Bookseller.*

"Mr. Edwards's style is pleasant, and free from the slang and pedantry of many more costly productions in the field of bibliography. If we feel occasionally inclined to differ from the author's views and deductions, we do so at all times with some deference, because throughout the work it is evident that he has been earnest to furnish the fullest and most satisfactory information which it was in his power to do."—*Leader.*

"It is now generally conceded that the civilization of a people may be judged rather by the number and value of its private libraries, than by the extent and magnificence of those provided by the Sovereign. Such being the case, it is incumbent upon us to examine our position in this particular, by comparison with other nations. This we are now enabled to do, for the first time, by the aid afforded in Mr. Edwards's 'Memoirs of Libraries,' which exhibits a mass of evidence such as only the greatest devotion to the subject, perseveringly continued through many years, could have accumulated. So completely is the subject exhausted, that it would be vain and useless for the inquirer to push his researches further in order to obtain a clear view of the libraries of the past and present; for what of interest or value he finds not in these volumes he will scarcely hope to obtain elsewhere."—*Gentleman's Magazine.*

"The various schemes propounded for the classification of knowledge—the extent to which libraries may safely be made available for public use—their internal economy, and the qualifications essential for their management—these are subjects which it would have afforded us both pleasure and profit to have discussed with Mr. Edwards. But it is time to take leave of him with the respect due to a writer whom some diffuseness, occasional want of discrimination, and a few doubtful views, will not debar from a cordial reception wherever industry is appreciated or erudition recognised."—*Press.*

ALLIBONE'S DICTIONARY—*continued.*

"It is thought that this Index will contain between 40,000 and 50,000 names, yet no author is mentioned whose works are not noticed in the first part of the Dictionary.

"It is a Critical as well as a Biographical and Bibliographical Dictionary. Here the author has a great advantage over his predecessors, *without a single exception.* Makers of books approaching to the character of this are in the habit of giving their own opinions, or opinions adopted as their own, which must be based upon very partial knowledge, and one, therefore, of little value; or are apt to be tinctured with prejudice and party bias, and are therefore entitled to little confidence. But Mr. Allibone contents himself with adducing the opinions upon various writers, as they come under his notice, of critics of great and extended reputation, who have earned a claim to be heard with respect, if not in all cases with entire acquiescence. These invaluable specimens of criticism are quoted verbatim, and distinguished by a smaller type, which adds greatly to the beauty of the work."

To the above Summary of the Work the Publishers beg leave to append the following remarks:—

It contains, it is believed, the names of every Author in English Literature and Science, living and dead, that anybody would think of looking for. Their dates are given, and the dates of their several publications. Critical notices by writers of authority are always added, and with such fairness and copiousness as challenge a constant surprise, and afford, besides, a most instructive and entertaining exhibition of the judgments of capable men upon the qualities and characters of the celebrities of literature. The compiler of these authoritative criticisms, however, does not avoid his own responsibilities, but frankly and ably sets down his own opinions, wherever any interest of moral truth or literary justice is involved.

The second division of the work will contain "a copious index of *subjects,*" arranged alphabetically, under such heads as Agriculture, Antiquities, Chemistry, Divinity, Drama, Law, Political Economy, Biography, etc. etc.; so that the inquirer can find at a glance all the authors of any note under the title of the subject upon which he has written. This division, besides being a most interesting presentment of authorship classified—a table of the sciences and of their cultivators—is an invaluable index to the biographies and literary notices, for the use of students in every profession, and of every specific pursuit. Together, the two divisions will be to study what the alphabet of the ledger and the account of stock on hand are to the merchant. Booksellers, school committees, and librarians, will perceive their practical interest in it, as much as merchants, farmers, lawyers, doctors, clergymen, and mechanics, in their several ways require it; and authors, too—for the living labourers in literature are all upon the record—will find themselves, each in his appropriate place, in this great gathering of celebrities. In a word, the book is constructed upon a plan, and the plan executed with such success, that it will serve not only as a directory, but as a guide to study, a catalogue, invoice, and manual to the trade in literature.

MODE AND TERMS OF PUBLICATION.

THE WORK—Volume I., comprising the letters A to J, pp. 1005, is issued. The second Volume, comprising letters K to Z, already stereotyped as far as letter S, will be published, with the Index of Subject-matter, in Autumn, 1859, and exceed 1000 pages.

FORM AND STYLE—2 Volumes, imperial 8vo., containing above 2000 pages, elegantly and closely printed in double column, on the finest paper.

PRICE—£1 : 16*s.* (Thirty-six Shillings) per Copy, to subscribers before publication—18*s.* to be paid upon delivery of each Volume; £2 : 8*s.* to non-subscribers, or 24*s.* each Volume.

*** *A specimen page will be forwarded on application to the Publishers.*

ALLIBONE'S DICTIONARY—*continued.*

CRITICAL OPINIONS.

"Most truly is Mr. Allibone's Dictionary a great work, which cannot fail of being extensively useful, from the comprehensiveness of its plan, and also for the ability, persevering industry, patience of research, impartiality and accuracy, with which it is executed. The introduction of brief critical testimonies to the character and value of the works of eminent authors is a happy thought, and cannot fail to be of great service to future bibliographers and librarians in the selection and purchase of books.

"Mr. Allibone's list of authorities consulted includes (I believe) every work of any value. My own knowledge of American authors has hitherto been derived chiefly from the best edition of 'Allen's American Biography,' and from Mr. Trübner's concise but truly valuable 'Guide to American Literature.' But henceforth Mr. Allibone's researches will leave nothing to be desired."—*Rev. Thomas Hartwell Horne, in a Letter to the Publishers.*

"Mr. Allibone, an American gentleman of wide reading, is engaged on a 'Critical Dictionary of English Literature,' a work very seriously needed. Lowndes is very imperfect. Watt is out of date, is also very imperfect, and is out of print. Mr. Allibone is said, on high American authority, to be well prepared for his task. His method, of which we can judge for ourselves, is novel: his plan being to supply the *facts* about his authors himself, and to quote *opinions* about them from distinguished critical contemporaries and successors. For example, under the title of 'Opinions on Burke,' there are forty brief excerpts from Samuel Johnson, Arthur Murphy, Lord Jeffrey, Professor Smyth, Dugald Stewart, James Prior, the Earl of Chatham, King George III., Charles James Fox, John Roche, M. Cazales, William Wyndham, Gerard Hamilton, Mr. Curwen, Rev. Thomas Campbell, Dr. French Laurence, Edward Gibbon, Richard Cumberland, William Wilberforce, Thomas James Mathias, Lord Thurlow, Rev. Dr. Samuel Parr, Henry Grattan, Oliver Goldsmith, Mr. Richards, the Duke de Levis, Warren Hastings, R. B. Sheridan, F. Schlegel, Robert Hall, George Crabbe, Samuel Warren, T. B. Macaulay, Rev. Dr. C. A Goodrich, Mr. Shackleton, Sir James Mackintosh. Sir Robert Peel, Lord John Russell, Lord Erskine, and Lord Brougham. This gives an idea of the work. By such a plan the reader is presented with a History of Opinion on great writers, as well as a History of their Works. If Mr. Allibone's 'Dictionary' proves to be as able in execution as it is felicitous in conception, it will be welcome to many libraries in England as well as in America."—*Athenæum, Jan. 5th,* 1856.

"That which the entire bookselling trade of London could not effect, a Philadelphian gentleman has been quietly to some extent executing in distant America. Mr. S. Austin Allibone, by great and conscientious labour, extending over a long period of time, has completed the compilation of 'A Critical Dictionary of English Literature, and British and American Authors, Living and Deceased, from the Earliest Accounts to the Middle of the Nineteenth Century.' Some sheets of this work having been shown to us, we are enabled to give some account of its nature and plan. In the first place, it will contain upwards of *thirty thousand* names—a larger number than has ever been collected before in any similar work. Watt's 'Bibliotheca' contains rather less than 23,00 names, and Chalmers's has only 9000. In the next place, each name has a short biographical notice appended; and in many cases critical observations, mostly extracted from well-known and respectable sources, are appended to the list of works. One volume of 1500 closely but clearly printed pages will be the full extent of the work, which will thus be within the reach of those whose means do not permit them to purchase large and expensive works. It would be too much to expect perfection in such a task, executed by a single hand; but, from what we have seen, we have no hesitation in predicting that Mr. Allibone's Dictionary will be a most valuable work."—*Critic, December,* 1855.

"Mr. Allibone's work is warmly commended by Irving, Prescott, Bryant, Everett, Bancroft, Sparks, and other distinguished scholars and men of letters in America. The only book of the kind now in use is 'Watt's Bibliotheca Britannica,' supplemented by the London Catalogues. Watt is in four bulky and expensive quartos, and is now nearly 30 years old. That it has nothing about American books is a sufficient motive for another work being required in the States; but in England, also, a book of bibliographical reference, with critical and biographical notices, is a desideratum, and we are prepared to receive Mr. Allibone's Dictionary with favour." —*Literary Gazette.*

"We have had an opportuniny of inspecting that portion of Mr. Allibone's Bibliographical Dictionary which has already been printed, and are glad to hear that the entire work will be ready for issue in a very short time. We understand that arrangements have

ALLIBONE'S DICTIONARY—*continued.*

been made by Mr. Trübner to publish it in America and in England on the same day."—*Critic, Feb. 15th*, 1856.

"It has been reserved for an American gentleman to produce the first complete Dictionary of the literature and literary men of England and America, which has yet appeared in either country. The work will contain about 31,000 biographies and literary notices, and an examination of the first 464 pages, completing the letters A, B, and C, has convinced us that the author has brought to his task all the requisites of the Encyclopædist—the most patient industry and painstaking love of detail and accuracy. The Rev. T. Hartwell Horne, than whom we know no greater authority upon bibliographical matters, and to whom the work was submitted as far as printed, passes the following high eulogium upon it:—'Most truly is Mr. Allibone's Dictionary a *great work*, which cannot fail of being extensively useful, from the comprehensiveness of its plan, and also for the ability, persevering industry, patience of research, impartiality, and accuracy, with which it is executed,' etc. The work will be published by subscription, and not to be accessible to the book trade for a whole year after publication, and then only at an increased price. Mr. Trübner, the American bookseller, of Paternoster-row, has succeeded in effecting an arrangement by which he will issue subscribers' copies in this country simultaneously with the American publishers."—*Bent's Lit. Advertiser, Feb.* 1856.

Copy of Letter from Cardinal Wiseman to S. Austin Allibone, Esq.

"London, Feb. 18, 1859.

"Dear Sir,—I thank you very sincerely for the first volume of your Dictionary of Authors. I have tested its value in two different ways: first, by looking at the accounts of comparatively unknown or obscure authors, hardly to be found in ordinary biographical works, and then by glancing at the history of celebrated ones, whose lives have occupied volumes. Your work stands both tests admirably. I have found more about the first class of writers than I have ever seen elsewhere, and than I could have anticipated in so comprehensive a work; while the interesting points in the literary lives of those belonging to the second, are brought out in sufficient detail and treated with sufficient accuracy to render further reference or inquiry unnecessary. I congratulate you on the success of your herculean undertaking, and am

"Yours very faithfully,

(signed) "N. Card. Wiseman."

From Lord Macaulay.

"Holly Lodge, Kensington, April 9, 1859.

"Sir,—Since I wrote to you last (Jan. 29, 1859), I have had frequent occasion to consult your Dictionary, and I have scarcely ever failed to find what I sought. I have no hesitation in saying that it is far superior to any other work of the kind in our language. I heartily wish you success proportioned to the labour and cost of your undertaking.

"I have the honour to be, Sir,

"Your faithful servant,

"S. Austin Allibone, Esq., &c. &c. &c."

(signed) "Macaulay.

In one Volume 8vo. of 750 pages, half bound, price 18s.

TRÜBNER'S BIBLIOGRAPHICAL GUIDE TO AMERICAN LITERATURE:

A Classed List of Books published in the United States of America,

FROM 1817 TO 1857.

With Bibliographical Introduction, Notes, & Alphabetical Index.

COMPILED AND EDITED BY NICOLAS TRÜBNER.

CONTENTS.

TRÜBNER'S BIBLIOGRAPHICAL GUIDE—*continued.*

This work, it is believed is the first attempt to marshal the Literature of the United States of America during the last forty years, according to the generally received bibliographical canons. The Librarian will welcome it, no doubt, as a companion volume to Brunet, Lowndes and Ebert, whilst to the bookseller it will be a faithful guide to the American branch of English Literature—a branch which, on account of its rapid increase and rising importance, begins to force itself daily more and more upon his attention. Nor will the work be of less interest to the man of letters, inasmuch as it comprises complete Tables of Contents to all the more prominent Collections of the Americans, to the Journals, Memoirs, Proceedings and Transactions of their learned Societies—and thus furnishes an intelligible key to a department of American scientific activity hitherto but imperfectly known and understood in Europe.

A HANDBOOK OF AFRICAN, AUSTRALIAN, AND POLYNESIAN PHILOLOGY,

As represented in the Library of His Excellency Sir George Grey, K.C.B.

HER MAJESTY'S HIGH COMMISSIONER OF THE CAPE COLONY.

CLASSED, ANNOTATED, AND EDITED BY

SIR GEORGE GREY AND DR. W. H. J. BLEEK.

Vol. I. Part 1.—South Africa, 8vo. pp. 186. 7*s*. 6*d*.

Vol. I. Part 2.—Africa (North of the Tropic of Capricorn), 8vo. pp. 70. 2*s*.

Vol. II. Part 1.—Australia, 8vo. pp. iv., 44. 1*s*. 6*d*.

Vol. II. Part 2.—Papuan Languages of the Loyalty Islands and New Hebrides, comprising those of the Islands of Neugone, Lifu, Aneiteum, Tana, and others, 8vo. pp. 12. 6*d*.

Vol. II. Part 3.—Fiji Islands and Rotuma (with Supplement to Part 2, Papuan Languages, and Part 1, Australia.) 8vo. pp. 34. 1*s*.

Vol. II. Part 4.—New Zealand, the Chatham Islands, and Anckland Islands, 8vo. pp. 76. 3*s*. 6*d*.

Vol. II. Part 4 (*Continuation*).—Polynesia and Borneo, 8vo. pp. 77 to 154. 3*s*. 6*d*.

The above is, without exception, the most important addition yet made to African Philology. The amount of materials brought together by Sir George, with a view to elucidate the subject, is stupendous; and the labour bestowed on them, and the results arrived at, incontestably establish the claim of the Author to be called the father of African and Polynesian Philology.

OPINIONS OF THE PRESS.

"We congratulate the Governor of the Cape on the production of a most important aid to the study of the twin sciences of philology and ethnology, and look forward to the completion of the Catalogue itself as a great and permanent step towards civilization of the barbarous races whose formation, habits, language, religion, and food, are all, more or less, most carefully noted in its pages."—*Leader*.

"It is for these substantial reasons that we deemed it worth a brief notice to call attention to these excellently arranged Catalogues (with important notes), describing the various works in the library of Sir George Grey, and by which this great philanthropist will greatly aid in civilizing the numerous peoples within the limit of the colony of the Cape of Good Hope."—*Brighton Gazette*.

TRÜBNER'S BIBLIOTHECA GLOTTICA.

THE LITERATURE OF AMERICAN ABORIGINAL LANGUAGES.

BY HERMANN E. LUDEWIG.

With Additions and Corrections by PROFESSOR WM. W. TURNER.

EDITED BY NICOLAS TRÜBNER.

8vo.; fly and general Title, 2 leaves; Dr. Ludewig's Preface, pp. v—viii; Editors' Preface, pp. ix—xii; Biographical Memoir of Dr. Ludewig, pp. xiii, xiv; and INTRODUCTORY BIBLIOGRAPHICAL NOTICES, pp. xiv—xxiv, followed by List of Contents. Then follow Dr. Ludewig's Bibliotheca Glottica, alphabetically arranged, with additions by the Editor, pp. 1—209; Professor Turner's additions, with those of the Editor to the same, also alphabetically arranged, pp. 210—246; Index. pp. 247—256; and list of Errata, pp. 257, 258. One volume, handsomely bound in cloth, price 10*s*. 6*d*.

This work is intended to supply a great want, now that the study of Ethnology has proved that exotic languages are not mere curiosities, but essential and interesting parts of the natural history of man, forming one of the most curious links in the great chain of national affinities, defining as they do the reciprocity existing between man and the soil he lives upon. No one can venture to write the history of America without a knowledge of her aboriginal languages; and unimportant as such researches may seem to men engaged in the mere bustling occupations of life, they will at least acknowledge that these records of the past, like the stern-lights of a departing ship, are the last glimmers of savage life, as it becomes absorbed or recedes before the tide of civilization. Dr. Ludewig and Professor Turner have made most diligent use of the public and private collections in America, access to all of which was most liberally granted to them. This has placed at their disposal the labours of the American Missionaries, so little known on this side of the Atlantic that they may be looked upon almost in the light of untrodden ground. But English and Continental libraries have also been ransacked; and Dr. Ludewig kept up a constant and active correspondence with scholars of "the Fatherland," as well as with men of similar tastes and pursuits in France, Spain, and Holland, determined to leave no stone unturned to render his labours as complete as possible. The volume, perfect in itself, is the first of an enlarged edition of Vater's "*Linguarum totius orbis Index.*" The work has been noticed by the press of both Continents, and we may be permitted to refer particularly to the following:

OPINIONS OF THE PRESS.

"This work, mainly the production of the late Herr Ludewig, a German naturalized in America, is devoted to an account of the literature of the aboriginal languages of that country. It gives an alphabetical list of the various tribes of whose languages any record remains, and refers to the works, papers, or manuscripts, in which such information may be found. The work has evidently been a labour of love; and as no pains seems to have been spared by the editors, Prof. Turner and Mr. Trübner, in rendering the work as

TRÜBNER'S BIBLIOTHECA GLOTTICA—*continued.*

accurate and complete as possible, those who are most interested in its contents will be best able to judge of the labour and assiduity bestowed upon it by author, editors, and publisher."—*Athenæum*, 5th April, 1858.

"This is the first instalment of a work which will be of the greatest value to philologists; and is a compendium of the aboriginal languages of the American continents, and a digest of all the known literature bearing upon those languages. Mr. Trübner's hand has been engaged *passim*, and in his preface he lays claim to about one-sixth of the whole; and we have no doubt that the encouragement with which this portion of the work will be received by scholars, will be such as to inspire Mr. Trübner with sufficient confidence to persevere in his arduous and most honourable task"—*The Critic*, 15th Dec. 1857.

"Few would believe that a good octavo volume would be necessary to exhaust the subject; yet so it is, and this handsome, useful, and curious volume, carefully compiled by Mr. Ludewig, assisted by Professor Turner, and edited by the careful hand of Mr. Trübner, the well-known publisher, will be sure to find a place in many libraries."—*Bent's Advertiser*, 6th Nov. 1857.

"The lovers of American linguistics will find in the work of Mr. Trübner scarcely any point omitted calculated to aid the comparative philologer in tracing the various languages of the great Western Continent."—*Galway Mercury*, 30th Jan. 1858.

"Only those deeply versed in philological studies can appreciate this book at its full value. It shows that there are upwards of seven hundred and fifty aboriginal American languages."—*Gentleman's Magazine*, Feb. 1858.

"The work contains an account of no fewer than seven hundred different aboriginal dialects of America, with an introductory chapter of bibliographical information; and under each dialect is an account of any grammars or other works illustrative of it."—*The Bookseller*, Jan. 1858.

"We have here the list of monuments still existing of an almost innumerable series of languages and dialects of the American Continent. The greater part of Indian grammars and vocabularies exist only in MS., and were compiled chiefly by Missionaries of the Christian Church; and to Dr. Ludewig and Mr. Trübner, we are, therefore, the more indebted for the great care with which they have pointed out where such are to be found, as well as for enumerating those which have been printed, either in a separate shape, in collections, or in voyages and travels, and elsewhere."—*Leader*, 11th Sept. 1858.

"I have not time, nor is it my purpose, to go into a review of this admirable work, or to attempt to indicate the extent and value of its contents. It is, perhaps, enough to say, that apart from a concise but clear enumeration and notice of the various general philological works which treat with greater or less fulness of American languages, or which incidentally touch upon their bibliography, it contains not less than 256 closely-printed octavo pages of bibliographical notices of grammars, vocabularies, etc., of the aboriginal languages of America. It is a peculiar and valuable feature of the work that not only the titles of printed or published grammars or vocabularies are given, but also that unpublished or MS. works of these kinds are noticed in all cases where they are known to exist, but which have disappeared among the *débris* of the suppressed convents and religious establishments of Spanish America."—*E. G. Squier, in a paper read before the American Ethnological Society*, 12th Jan. 1858.

"In consequence of the death of the author before he had finished the revisal of the work, it has been carefully examined by competent scholars, who have also made many valuable additions."—*American Publishers' Circular*, 30th Jan. 1858.

"It contains 256 closely-printed pages of titles of printed books and manuscripts, and notices of American aboriginal languages, and embraces references to nearly all that has been written or published respecting them, whether in special works or incidentally in books of travel, periodicals, or proceedings of learned societies."—*New York Herald*, 29th Jan. 1858.

"The manner in which this contribution to the bibliography of American languages has been executed, both by the author, Mr. Ludewig, and the able writers who have edited the work since his death, is spoken of in the highest terms by gentlemen most conversant with the subject."—*American Historical Magazine*, Vol. II., No. 5, May, 1858.

"Je terminerai en anonçant le premier volume d'une publication appelée à rendre de grands services à la philologie comparée et à la linguistique générale. Je veux parler de la Bibliotheca Glottica, ouvrage devant renfermer la liste de tous les dictionnaires et de toutes les grammaires des langues connues, tant imprimés que manuscrits. L'éditeur, de cette précieuse bibliographie est M. Nicolas Trübner, dont le nom est honorablement connu dans le monde oriental. Le

TRÜBNER'S BIBLIOTHECA GLOTTICA—*continued.*

premier volume est consacré aux idiomes Américaines; le second doit traiter des langues de l'Inde. Le travail est fait avec le soin le plus consciencieux, et fera honneur à M. Nicolas Trübner, surtout s'il poursuit son œuvre avec le même ardeur qu'il mise à le commencer."—*L. Léon de Rosny, Revue de l'Orient, Février*, 1858.

"Mr. Trübner's most important work on the bibliography of the aboriginal languages of America is deserving of all praise, as eminently useful to those who study that branch of literature. The value, too, of the book, and of the pains which its compilation must have cost, will not be lessened by the consideration that it is first in this field of linguistic literature."—*Petermann's Geographische Mittheilungen*, p. 79, Feb. 1858.

"Undoubtedly this volume of Trübner's Bibliotheca Glottica ranks amongst the most valuable additions which of late years have enriched our bibliographical literature. To us Germans it is most gratifying that the initiative has been taken by a German bookseller himself, one of the most intelligent and active of our countrymen abroad, to produce a work which has higher aims than mere pecuniary profit, and that he, too, has laboured at its production with his own hands; because daily it is becoming a circumstance of rarer occurrence that, as in this case, it is a bookseller's primary object to serve the cause of literature rather than to enrich himself."—*P. Trömel, Börsenblatt*, 4th Jan. 1858.

"In the compilation of the work the editors have availed themselves not only of the labours of Vater, Barton, Duponceau, Gallatin, De Souza, and others, but also of the MS. sources left by the missionaries, and of many books of which even the library of the British Museum is deficient, and furnish the fullest account of the literature of no less than 525 languages. The value of the work, so necessary to the study of ethnology, is greatly enhanced by the addition of a good Index."—*Berliner National-Zeitung*, 22nd Nov. 1857.

"The name of the author, to all those who are acquainted with his former works, and who know the thoroughness and profound character of his investigations, is a sufficient guarantee that this work will be one of standard authority, and one that will fully answer the demands of the present time."—*Petzholdt's Anzeiger*, Jan. 1858.

"The chief merit of the editor and publisher is to have terminated the work carefully and lucidly in contents and form, and thus to have established a new and largely augmented edition of "*Vater's Linguarum totius orbis Index*," after Professor Jülg's revision of 1847. In order to continue and complete this work the editor requires the assistance of all those who are acquainted with this new branch of science, and we sincerely hope it may be accorded to him."—*Magazin für die Literatur des Auslandes*, No. 38, 1858.

"As the general title of the book indicates, it will be extended to the languages of the other Continents in case it meet with a favourable reception, which we most cordially wish it."—*A. F. Pott., Preussische Jahrbücher*, Vol. II. part 1.

"Cette compilation savante est sans contredit, le travail bibliographique le plus important que notre époque ait vu surgir sur les nations indigènes de l'Amérique."—*Nouvelles Annales des Voyages*. Avril, 1859.

"La Bibliotheca Glottica, dont M. Nicolas Trübner a commencé la publication, est un des livres les plus utiles qui aient jamais été rédigés pour faciliter l'étude de la philologie comparée. Le premier tome de cette grande bibliographie linguistique comprend la liste textuelle de toutes les grammaires, de tous les dictionnaires et des vocabulaires même les moins étendus qui ont été imprimes dans les différents dialectes des deux Amériques; en outre, il fait connaître les ouvrages manuscrits de la même nature renfermés dans les principales bibliothèques publiques et particulières. Ce travail a dû nécessiter de longues et patientes recherches; aussi mérite-t-il d'attirer tout particulièrement l'attention des philologues. Puissent les autres volumes de cette bibliothèque être rédigés avec le même soin et se trouver bientôt entre les mains de tous les savants auxquels ils peuvent rendre des services inappréciables."—*Revue Américaine et Orientale*, No. I., Oct. 1858.

The Editor has also received most kind and encouraging letters respecting the work from Sir George Grey, the Chevalier Bunsen, Dr. Th. Goldstucker, Mr. Watts (of the Museum), Professor A. Fr. Pott (of Halle), Dr. Julius Petzholt (of Dresden), Hofrath Dr. Grasse (of Dresden), M. F. F. de la Figaniere (of Lisbon), E. Edwards (of Manchester), Dr. Max Müller (of Oxford), Dr. Buschmann (of Berlin), Dr. Jülg (of Cracow), and other linguistic scholars.

TRÜBNER'S BIBLIOTHECA-TECHNICA: A SUBJECT-MATTER INDEX TO THE PUBLISHED INVENTIONS OF ALL NATIONS, 1823 TO 1853 INCLUSIVE. In 1 vol. 8vo., pp. viii., 26, xvi. 1050. 24*s.*

The object of this work is to record in the form of a Dictionary the Literature of Technology and its kindred branches, dispersed over the different Journals and Magazines of all Nations.

In the Press,

MAPOTÉCA COLOMBIANA: CATALOGO DE TODOS LOS MAPAS, PLANOS, VISTAS, ETC., RELATIVOS A LA AMERICA-ESPANOLA, BRASIL, E ISLAS ADYACENTES. Por el Dr. EZEQUIEL URICOECHEA, de Bogota, Nueva Granada. 1 vol. 8vo.

A very useful companion to all works relating to the Bibliography of America.

BIBLIOTHEQUE AMERICAINE: OU CATALOGUE RAISONNE D'UNE PRECIEUSE COLLECTION DE LIVRES RELATIFS A L'AMERIQUE QUI ONT PARU DEPUIS SA DECOUVERTE JUSQU'A L'AN 1700. Par PAUL TROEMEL. 8vo.

Amongst the 556 articles of which the Collection consists, at least 100 are not mentioned by any bibliographer. Indeed, only about 150 of them are found in Ternaux and Rich, which of itself is ample testimony of the importance, and must secure to the publication more than ordinary interest in the eyes of bibliographers and literary men.

TRÜBNER'S BIBLIOTHECA JAPONICA: A DESCRIPTIVE LIST OF BOOKS ILLUSTRATIVE OF JAPAN AND THE JAPANESE, FROM 1542 TO THE PRESENT TIME. Edited, with Critical and Historical Notes, by Dr. G. M. ASHER.

The above work cannot fail to prove of great interest now that Japan is thrown open for European enterprise. The best Dutch, German, Portuguese, Spanish, Italian, French, English, Russian, and American Authorities, have been consulted in its production.

TRÜBNER & CO.,

60, PATERNOSTER ROW, LONDON.